A NATURALIST IN WESTERN CHINA

BY E. H. WILSON
INTRODUCTION BY GEOFFREY SMITH

VOLUMES I & II

CADOGAN BOOKS
LONDON

Introduction © Geoffrey Smith 1986
Cover © Sue Grimshaw 1986

First published in Great Britain in 1913
by Methuen & Co. Ltd.

This edition published in 1986 by
Cadogan Books Ltd
16 Lower Marsh, London SE1 7RJ

ISBN 0–946313–49–0

Printed and bound in Great Britain by
Redwood Burn Ltd, Trowbridge, Wiltshire

Also available in the Plant Hunters series
with introductions by Geoffrey Smith:

THE DOLOMITES by Reginald Farrer
THE VALLEY OF FLOWERS by F. S. Smythe
PLANT HUNTING ON THE EDGE OF THE WORLD
by F. Kingdon Ward
THE RAINBOW BRIDGE by Reginald Farrer
THE MYSTERY RIVERS OF TIBET by F. Kingdon Ward

INTRODUCTION TO THIS EDITION

Ernest Henry Wilson exemplifies the assertion that the true liberty of man is to find the right path suited to his talents, or be forced by circumstances to discover a correct course and thereafter to follow it. At an early age Wilson settled on the career which best suited his abilities; then circumstance and opportunity combined in such a way as to enable him to express those inherent gifts in fullest measure.

Born in Chipping Campden in Gloucestershire, Wilson left school when barely in his teens to take up an apprenticeship—or as some accounts have it, a post as general assistant—at a nursery garden in Solihull. At the age of sixteen, Wilson, on recommendation, entered for service in the Birmingham Botanic Gardens. To supplement what must have been a meagre education he attended classes at the Birmingham Technical College. Belated though his education may have been, this did not prevent him gaining the Queen's Prize for Botany, and entry to that admirable training ground for embryo plant hunters, gardeners, and botanists—The Royal Botanic Gardens at Kew, where he enrolled in the Royal College of Science.

Wilson had an ambition at this stage to become a lecturer in botany. Circumstances offered, it might be argued almost forced, a change of route. The famous nursery of Veitch & Sons asked the Directors of Kew to recommend someone with a knowledge of botany, and the ability to judge a plant's potential in gardening terms, combined with the capacity and skill required to undertake the demanding task of plant hunting in Central China. This made a formidable list of necessary qualifications. Wilson was chosen as being the most suitable candidate for the job in hand.

There was a sound reason for sending a qualified plantsman to search out and collect seeds and plants in the region of Ichang and Szenio. It was largely due to the impassioned pleading of a British Customs Officer, Augustine Henry, who worked in the area, that Wilson was sent post-haste to China via Boston in the United States. Henry, alarmed by the wholesale destruction of the forests in the countryside where he was working, believed that unless a systematic, comprehensive collection was made before deforestation, many plant species might disappear altogether. Henry, an accomplished amateur botanist, had proved by material collected in his free time and sent to the Royal Botanic Gardens, Kew, just how rich in garden-worthy plants the region was.

Wilson reached China in 1899 and promptly made his way to Szemoa, Yunnan, and a pre-arranged rendezvous with Augustine Henry. Some time previously Henry had observed a most unusual tree with flowers which, though insignificant in themselves, were enhanced by a large triangular white bract. Both the man who first found and recorded this extraordinary tree and Augustine Henry had been unable to collect seeds to send back to Britain. They wrote in such glowing terms of what the Chinese call 'The Dove Tree'—Europeans, less poetically, 'The Handkerchief Tree', and botanists, commemoratively, *Davidia involucrata*—that Wilson's prime commission, taking precedence over all else, was to find a specimen of 'The Dove Tree' and send home seeds. In addition he was to send back plants, seeds, bulbs, or similar propagative material to Veitch & Sons, and herbarium material for Kew from anything else of interest uncovered during his search for the elusive Davidia.

Wilson is a factual writer, concerned with unembroidered reality, and the book reveals the author's character quite clearly: patience, determination, courage, a desire to reach an understanding with the native Chinese and Tibetan people, combined with a high degree of prefessional integrity—these, then, were the qualities which contributed to his success as a plant hunter.

Nothing seems to disturb his composure. A porter absconds with a considerable sum of money and, as the culprit had nearly a day's start, Wilson decides it best to accept the loss quietly—"as the thief was thoughtful enough to leave us about half the amount contained in the box".

The book is really more than the extended field notes of a plant hunter dealing with matters exclusively botanical. There are sections devoted to sport, food crops, fruit both wild and cultivated, and the sequence of events which precipitated the revolution and overthrow of the Manchu Dynasty.

Above all, this is a record in detail of eleven years spent travelling and plant hunting in China. Amongst the three thousand and more species which Wilson introduced, a thousand proved new to cultivation in Western European gardens. Amongst these are several which have enriched my own gardening experience over the years and have become an essential part of the seasons' pattern.

Lilium regale, whose discovery and introduction nearly cost Wilson his life, would have been enough of an achievement to earn him high honour. Added to this is his *Acer griseum* of the cinnamon exfoliating bark and vivid autumn colour. Popular though the 'Paper Bark Maple' is, it is by no means so widely grown as Wilson's own favourite 'Beauty Bush'—*Kolkwitzia amabalis*—which I see each time my eyes stray from the written page and look out through the study window across the garden. Clematis montana 'Rubens' shares the same border, swathing a moribund apple tree in mounds of fragrant flowers. He also collected Kiwi Fruit (*Actinidia Chinensis*), the lovely *Paeonia veitchii* which I first saw growing in a Northumbrian garden from seed sent by Wilson, and *Meconopsis integrifolia*. Thus Wilson earned a place in the halls of the immortals alongside Farrer, Forrest, Kingdon Ward, and Hooker.

Wilson died with his wife in a car accident before he was forty years old. We can only reflect on what might have been had he lived long enough for his many talents to reach fruitful maturity.

GEOFFREY SMITH
1986

A NATURALIST IN WESTERN CHINA

WITH VASCULUM, CAMERA, AND GUN

BEING SOME ACCOUNT OF ELEVEN YEARS' TRAVEL,
EXPLORATION, AND OBSERVATION IN THE MORE
REMOTE PARTS OF THE FLOWERY KINGDOM

BY

ERNEST HENRY WILSON, V.M.H.

WITH AN INTRODUCTION BY

CHARLES SPRAGUE SARGENT, LL.D.

VOL. I

METHUEN & CO. LTD.
36 ESSEX STREET W.C.
LONDON

TO

MY WIFE

First Published November 6th 1913

PREFACE

IN the following pages I have endeavoured to give a general account of Western China, more especially of its natural history and of the manners and customs of the non-Chinese peoples inhabiting the Chino-Thibetan borderland. The attempt is based as broadly as possible, and it is earnestly hoped that the information will be of interest to many sorts and conditions of people.

My travels in Western China began early in 1899, and had for their object the collecting of botanical specimens and the introducing of new plants into the gardens of Europe and North America. I have made four separate expeditions, covering in all nearly eleven years, and the nature of my work made it necessary for me to eschew the beaten tracks of the Flowery Kingdom.

The opportunity to travel and study the natural history of China I owe to the business enterprise of the house of Veitch, the famous nurserymen of Chelsea, to whom I was recommended by Sir William T. Thiselton-Dyer, then Director of Kew Gardens, at the instigation of Mr. W. Watson, the present Curator of that establishment. My first two expeditions were in the interest of Messrs. Veitch ; the last two in that of the Arnold Arboretum of Harvard University. The results of these four trips are well known in the horticultural and botanical circles of Europe and North America.

In my wanderings in China I have been singularly fortunate. The Chinese treated me always with kindly courtesy and respect. I was in interior China during the Boxer outbreak and the Russo-Japanese War, and visited places shortly before or after anti-foreign riots, but never experienced any incivility meriting the name. I engaged and trained as collectors a number of Chinese peasants, who served me faithfully throughout my journeys, and we parted with genuine regrets. At the commencement of my travels in China, Mr. Augustine Henry, now Professor of Forestry at Dublin, imparted to me much sound advice which I did my utmost to follow. To this gentleman and to the devoted services of my Chinese collectors must be largely attributed the results of my work in China.

It is exceedingly pleasant to recall the kindly acts and hospitality of the many people I have been privileged to meet during my wanderings. Exigencies of space forbid the mention of names but do not affect my sincere appreciation. But for meeting them one's life would have been very much the poorer and lonelier. To my friend, W. J. Tutcher of Hong-Kong, this book in part owes its inception, and to another friend, J. Hutson Edgar, I am indebted for much information concerning the peculiar customs of the Thibetans and other non-Chinese races.

In the preparation of this work, I have received much encouragement from Professor Charles S. Sargent, who has also contributed an introduction of the greatest value. To my friend Herman Spooner I am indebted for invaluable criticisms of the manuscript. To Walter R. Zappey, my associate on the third expedition, I owe much for assistance in details concerning the colours and measurements of the game-birds and mammals.

Two or three of the chapters I first published in the *Gardeners' Chronicle* during 1905-6, and that on insect white-wax in the *Chemist and Druggist*, 1906, but these have been remodelled to suit present requirements, and amended and corrected in accordance with increased knowledge.

With six exceptions, the illustrations are from

PREFACE

photographs taken by myself with a whole plate
Sanderson camera for the Arnold Arboretum, and
permission to use them I owe to Professor Sargent.
The photographs were developed and printed by Mr.
E. J. Wallis of Kew, who obtained from the negatives
the best possible results. For the illustration of
Budorcas tibetanus, I am indebted to Mr. Samuel
Henshaw, Director of the Museum of Comparative
Zoölogy at Harvard College.

It is quite impossible to record the full extent of
one's obligations, since much information is unconsciously absorbed through contact with many
people and extensive reading. I should, however,
be lacking in filial respect did I not record my sense
of indebtedness to the Alma Mater who gave me both
inspiration and opportunity—the Royal Gardens, Kew.

ERNEST H. WILSON

THE ARNOLD ARBORETUM
HARVARD UNIVERSITY
July 1913

CONTENTS

CONTENTS

INTRODUCTION

THE botanical explorations carried on in China in recent years make it possible to compare the forest flora of eastern continental Asia north of about lat. 22° 30′ with that of eastern North America north of the Rio Grande. In these explorations Mr. Wilson has played an important part, and more than any other traveller has shown us the remarkable richness of the flora of western central China and the distribution and value of many of the most important Chinese trees. A comparison of the flora of eastern continental Asia with that of eastern North America made at this time cannot be entirely conclusive, for although much has been done to make known the Chinese flora much is still left undone ; and there are still vast regions of the Celestial Empire into which no botanist has as yet penetrated, and these may be expected to yield new harvests of still unknown plants.

It is not surprising that the forest flora of China is richer in genera than that of eastern North America, for although the area of the two regions under consideration is not very dissimilar there is a great difference in their topography. In eastern North America only a few mountain peaks reach an altitude of 6000 ft., and these are wooded to the summit. In China mountain ranges are more numerous, with peaks which sometimes rise far above the upper limits of vegetation, and on some of these mountain ranges the timber line is at least twice as high as the highest land in eastern America. The connection of the great mass of mountains of south-western China with the Himalayas which must be considered their western prolongation, and the great tropical region which extends uninterrupted by any large body of water southward from south-western China, will account for the presence in the Chinese flora of many Himalayan and tropical forms which have no counterpart in eastern North America. On the other hand, the flora of eastern North America has drawn from the large and arid plateau of Mexico many genera of Cactaceæ, the Agaves, Yuccas, Dasylirion, and other genera which have no representatives in China. While the

INTRODUCTION

larger mountain systems, the greater height of land, and its more prolific neighbours can account for a larger number of genera in eastern
Asia than in eastern North America, it is not possible to find an
explanation for the greater number of species there of widely
distributed genera like Acer, Picea, Prunus, Sorbus, and Berberis,
which are more numerous in China than in any other part of the
world, or for the absence from eastern Asia of larger numbers of
species in genera like Cratægus and Amelanchier.

In eastern continental Asia there is nothing to compare with
the great maritime pine belt which extends from southern Virginia
to eastern Texas, and is one of the remarkable features of the flora
of eastern North America ; and the great forests of *Pinus Strobus* L.,
which once extended from northern New England and eastern
Canada to northern Minnesota, are but poorly replaced in north-
eastern Asia by trees of *Pinus koraiensis* S. and Z., scattered over a
comparatively restricted area in eastern Siberia and Korea. The
Black Oaks, with their lustrous leaves and biennial fructification,
which are so abundant and conspicuous, except in the extreme north,
all over eastern North America, are wanting in eastern Asia ; while
the Bamboos, the most widely distributed and the most generally
useful of all the forest plants of China, are represented in North
America by two small and unimportant species of Arundinaria
confined to the swamps and river bottoms of the southern states.

As a rule, to which, of course, there are a few exceptions, the
trees of eastern North America are larger and more valuable than
related Chinese species ; but of Chinese shrubs it can be said generally that they produce more beautiful flowers than the shrubs of
eastern North America, although to this statement there are also
some exceptions. A more detailed examination of the principal
groups of forest plants in the two regions will show the similarities
and the differences of the forest flora of the two regions.

CYCADACEÆ.—Four species of Cycas are found in southern
China, and in Florida the family appears in two species of Zamia.

CONIFERÆ.—This family is represented in China by fourteen,
and in eastern North America by nine, genera. In eastern North
America there are only two genera which are not also represented
in China, Taxodium, which is replaced there by the nearly related
Glyptostrobus and Chamæcyparis, represented, however, in Japan
by two important trees. Libocedrus, Cupressus, Cunninghamia,
Pseudolarix, Keteleeria, and Fokienia have no eastern American
representative. In Pinus, eastern North America, with fifteen
species, has the advantage of eastern continental Asia, in which

only eight species occur; and in eastern America Pine trees are individually larger, more numerous, and more generally distributed than in China. In Picea, China, with its twenty species, has a decided advantage over eastern America, where only three species occur, and in Abies, China, with its nine species, is richer than eastern North America, where there are only two species, and of these one is found only on the highest peaks of the southern Appalachian Mountains. Of Tsuga there are two species in eastern North America and two species in China, but *Tsuga canadensis* Carr. is a larger tree and much more widely distributed than any of the Chinese species. Larix, on the other hand, is better represented in eastern continental Asia, where it is widely distributed with several species from eastern Siberia to the mountains of Western China, where it sometimes forms large forests, while in eastern America there is a single species confined to the north-eastern part of the continent and is a small tree which southward is found only in swamps. Juniperus is represented in China by six species, and in North America by five species; but none of the Chinese Junipers are as large or as widely distributed as *Juniperus virginiana* L.; and none of them produce so valuable wood as that species and *J. barbadensis* L. Thuya is represented in each region with a single species of about equal importance. In eastern America Taxodium is a large and valuable timber tree widely distributed in the South Atlantic and Gulf regions, while its Asiatic representative, Glyptostrobus, is a small tree confined to the banks of a few streams in south-eastern tropical China.

TAXACEÆ.—In this family the advantage is all with China, with Taxus, Torreya, Cephalotaxus, Ginkgo, and Podocarpus, while in eastern America it appears with only a single species each of Taxus and Torreya, small trees found only in a few small isolated groves in western Florida.

GNETACEÆ. — Represented in continental Asia by Ephedra and Gnetum, this family does not appear in eastern North America.

PANDANACEÆ.—One species of Freycinetia and two species of Pandanus represent this Old World family in southern China.

PALMÆ.—About the same number of species of Palms are reported from the two regions, fourteen species in seven genera in China, and sixteen species in eight genera in eastern North America. The species in the two regions belong to different genera, with the exception of *Cocos nucifera* L., which is found on all the tropical shores. In eastern North America Palms extend farther north than in China, and some of the dwarf species cover in the southern United States great areas of dry sandy land with almost impenetrable thickets, as dwarf Bamboos make travel on some of the mountain slopes of Western China almost impossible.

LILIACEÆ.—Of this family Heterosmilax is found only in eastern Asia, but Smilax occurs in the two regions, in each of which it is about equally represented by a number of species ; Yucca and Dasylirion are American.

ARACEÆ.—Plants of this family are sometimes woody in southern China, where species of Pothos and Rhaphidophora are large climbers, but in eastern North America all the members of this family are herbaceous.

PIPERACEÆ.—Piper, with woody species in southern China, is the only genus of this family in the two regions.

CHLORANTHACEÆ.—Of this small tropical family Chloranthus, in China, is the only representative in the two regions.

SALICACEÆ.—In the number of species of Populus in the two floras there is no great difference. None of the Asiatic species grow to a larger size, perhaps, than the American Cottonwood (*Populus deltoidea* Marsh.), but with this exception the Asiatic species are larger and more valuable trees than the American species, notably the Manchurian *Populus Maximowiczii* A. Henry, and the north China *Populus tomentosa* Carr., which are among the largest and most beautiful Poplar trees of the world. In Salix there is probably no great difference in the number of species in the two regions, although there is still much to be learned of the alpine species of Western China. In eastern North America Willows are mostly shrubby, only three or four species attaining to the dignity of small trees, while in eastern Asia there are probably ten or twelve arborescent species, and some of these are trees of considerable size.

JUGLANDACEÆ.—In this family the advantage is with eastern continental Asia, with four genera against two in eastern North America, where there is no representative of Pterocarya, Engelhardtia, or Platycarya. Juglans is common to the two regions, but Carya is not known in China ; and the presence in eastern North America of this genus in many widely distributed species, valued as timber trees and for the nuts produced by some of the species, economically, at least, makes up for the absence of the three genera which occur in China and not in eastern North America. Juglans, in eastern America with three species, and continental Asia, with four species, is of nearly equal importance in the two regions. None of the Asiatic species, however, compare in size with the American *Juglans nigra* L., but *Juglans regia* L., whose original home is now believed to be on the mountains of northern and Western China, yields the most valuable nuts and the most valuable timber produced by any species of the genus.

LEITNERIACEÆ, a family of a single species of Leitneria, is North American.

MYRICACEÆ.—Comptonia is confined to eastern North America, but Myrica, with a small number of species, occurs in the two regions, with one species, *Myrica Gale* L., common to them both. In North America there is no species which at all resembles *Myrica rubra* Lour. with its edible fruits.

BETULACEÆ.—In eastern North America Carpinus appears as a small widely distributed tree, but in continental Asia seven or eight species of the two sections, into which this genus has been separated (Eucarpinus and Distigocarpus), are common. Ostrya is represented in each region by a single species, the eastern American Ostrya being much more generally distributed and more abundant than the Chinese species, which appears to be confined to the mountain forests of Hupeh and Szechuan. The monotypic Ostryopsis is confined to Mongolia and China. Of Alnus there are five species in eastern North America, four of these being shrubs and one a small tree ; but in eastern continental Asia there are at least six or seven species of this genus, and one of these, *Alnus cremastogyne* Burk., is a large tree sometimes 100 ft. high, shading the banks of many streams in Western China with groves of splendid specimens. Betula forms a considerable part of the forests of eastern Siberia, and is common on many of the mountain ranges of China, especially those in western Szechuan, where it reaches altitudes of 10,000 ft. In eastern Asia, however, there is no species which, like *Betula nigra* L. of eastern North America, can thrive on the banks of streams in the nearly tropical heat of regions like Florida, Louisiana, and Texas, where this tree grows to its largest size. The number of species in the two regions is not very different, and as timber trees the Birches of one region are probably as valuable as those of the other. It is doubtful, however, if any eastern Asiatic Birch tree ever grows to the size sometimes attained by *Betula lutea* Michx., of the forests of north-eastern North America.

FAGACEÆ.—In eastern North America there is a single species of Fagus ranging from eastern Canada to Florida and Texas, and one of the largest and most common trees of all this region. In eastern continental Asia Fagus does not extend into the north, and appears to be confined to the mountain forests of the central western provinces, in which three species are now known ; these are smaller and less important trees than the American Beech.

INTRODUCTION

Castanea is more important in the number of species in eastern continental Asia than in North America, but it is doubtful if any Asiatic species is anywhere as common or forms such a large part of the forest as the American *Castanea dentata* Borkh. forms on some Appalachian slopes ; and in height and girth of trunk this American tree has no Asiatic rival. In eastern North America there are two other species ; of these one is a small tree or shrub and the other a shrub, both bearing a single nut in the involucre. In Western China there are also two species with similar fruit, but one of these, *Castanea Vilmoriniana* Dode, is a noble tree and the largest of the eastern Asiatic Chestnuts ; the other is a small shrub, to be compared with the American *Castanea nana* Muhl. The Japanese *Castanea crenata* S. and Z. reaches Korea, and *Castanea mollissima* Blume, another small tree, ranges from the neighbourhood of Peking to the mountains on the Thibetan border. Castanopsis, which is related closely to Castanea, has its headquarters in south-eastern Asia, with several species in southern China, and one in California, but no representative in eastern North America. It is possible that the number of species of Quercus is greater in eastern continental Asia than in eastern North America. Oak trees, however, are much less widely distributed in the former region and are not numerous at the north, the Chinese Oaks being chiefly confined to the southern provinces and usually evergreen. Some of these evergreen Oaks should be referred to Pasania, distinguished from the true Oaks by the arrangement of their flowers in bisexual aments, the pistillate in several-flowered clusters below the staminate, like the flowers of Castanea and Castanopsis. As has been already stated, there are no Black Oaks in China, and no species which are counterparts of the eastern American Chestnut Oaks. .The northern White Oaks are inferior in size to several of the White Oaks of eastern North America, and it is doubtful if any of the southern evergreen species equal in size *Quercus virginiana* Mill., the Live Oak of the southern United States.

ULMACEÆ.—No Elm tree of eastern Asia equals the so-called American Elm (*Ulmus americana* L.) in size and beauty, but it is probable that the genus Ulmus has a larger representation of species in western continental Asia than it has in eastern North America, although it is still impossible to speak with much knowledge of Chinese Elm trees, which are very imperfectly understood. It is interesting that the section of the genus (Microptelea), which flowers in the autumn, has representatives in the two regions, two in eastern America and one in China, the only other species of this group growing on the Himalayas. The monotypic Planera occurs only in eastern North America, and Pteroceltis and Zelkowa have no American representatives. Celtis is common to the two regions, but the trees of this genus are larger and appear to be more generally distributed in eastern North America than in eastern continental Asia. The tropical genus Trema is represented in both regions.

MORACEÆ.—Of this family the monotypic Maclura is American, and Broussonetia, Cudrania, and Artocarpus, which occur in China, have no American representatives. There are two species of Morus in each of the two regions, but neither of the two American Mulberries compare in value with the Chinese *Morus alba* L., for the leaves of this tree and its numerous varieties furnish the best and chief food of the silkworm in all countries where silk is made. In Ficus the advantage is with China, both in the number of species and in the size of individuals, only two species having secured a foothold in tropical Florida, where they are comparatively small trees. Its nearness to tropical south-eastern Asia, which is one of the great centres of distribution of this genus, will account for the presence of some forty species of Ficus in southern China, where some of the species grow to a very large size.

PROTEACEÆ.—Helicia, in south-eastern China, is the only genus represented in the floras of the two regions.

LORANTHACEÆ.—In this family Phorodendron is North American; Arceuthobium is North American and Japanese, and Loranthus and Viscum are found in China and not in eastern North America.

SANTALACEÆ.—Pyrularia and the monotypic Darbya have not been found in China. Henslowia is eastern Asiatic, and Buckleya has a representative in the floras of the two regions.

OPILIACEÆ.—One species of the tropical genus Cansjera, in south-eastern China, is the only woody member of this family in our two regions.

OLACACEÆ.—Of this tropical family Schœpfia and Ximenia have reached southern Florida from the West Indies, each with a single species ; in China it appears only in Schœpfia.

ARISTOLOCHIACEÆ.—This family is represented in the floras of the two regions by the genus Aristolochia, with more numerous woody species in China than in eastern North America.

POLYGONACEÆ.—No arborescent or shrubby species of this family is reported in China, but in tropical Florida two species of Coccolobis occur, and a species of Brunnichia is widely scattered through the southern United States.

INTRODUCTION

NYCTAGINACEÆ.—*Pisonia aculeata* L., an inhabitant of tropical shores in many parts of the world, probably reaches south-eastern China, as it occurs in Formosa ; with other species of this genus it is common in tropical Florida.

TROCHODENDRACEÆ.—This family is not represented in the flora of eastern North America but appears in China in Euptelea.

CERCIDIPHYLLACEÆ and EUCOMMIACEÆ, too, have no American representatives, but appear in Western China each with a monotypic genus, Cercidiphyllum and Eucommia.

RANUNCULACEÆ.—In this family Pæonia occurs in China but not in eastern North America, and the monotypic Xanthorrhiza is Appalachian. Clematis is common to both regions, with a much larger number of species in eastern Asia than in eastern North America, where the genus is poorly developed.

LARDIZABALACEÆ is an Asiatic and Chilian family, with Decaisnea, Stauntonia, Holbœllia, Akebia, Sinofranchetia, and Sargentodoxa in China.

BERBERIDACEÆ.—The woody plants of this family are much more numerous in China than in eastern North America. Mahonia and the monotypic Nandina do not occur in the latter region, where there is only one species of Berberis, while in eastern continental Asia, which must be considered the headquarters of the genus, some forty species are now recognized.

MENISPERMACEÆ.—The woody members of this family are represented in eastern North America by Menispermum and Cocculus. These occur also in western continental Asia, where Sinomenium, Diploclisia, Stephania, Cyclea, Tinospora, Limacia, and the monotypic Pericampylus are also interesting members of this family.

MAGNOLIACEÆ.—Magnolia is represented in the two floras by about the same number of species. In China, however, species occur in two groups, one of which produces its flowers before the appearance of the leaves, and in the other the leaves are nearly fully grown before the flowers open. To the latter group all of the American species belong. Some of the American Magnolias are larger trees than the Chinese species, and no Asiatic Magnolia compares in beauty with *Magnolia grandiflora* L. of the southern United States or equals *Magnolia macrophylla* Michx. in the size of leaves and flowers. Liriodendron appears in each region with a single species, but the American representative of this genus is a larger and much more widely distributed tree. Illicium and Schisandra appear in the two regions, the former with three species in China and one in the south-eastern United States, and the latter with one American and eight Chinese species. Michelia, Kadsura, and the monotypic Manglietia and Tetracentron are Chinese, the latter being one of the largest and most interesting of the Chinese trees.

CALYCANTHACEÆ.—Calycanthus, with several species, is eastern North American only, and Meratia (Chimonanthus), with two species, is Chinese and does not appear in eastern North America.

ANONACEÆ.—This tropical family reaches eastern North America with several species of Asimina, its most northern representative, and with Anona in tropical Florida. Uvaria, Artabotrys, Unona, Polyalthia, and Melodorum represent it in south-eastern tropical Asia.

LAURACEÆ.—In eastern North America this great, mostly tropical, family appears only in Persea, Ocotea, Sassafras, Litsea, Lindera, and Misanteca, but in eastern Asia there are eight genera of Lauraceæ, Cryptocarya, Beilschmiedia, Cinnamomum, Machilus, Sassafras, Litsea, Lindera, and Cassytha. Of Sassafras there is a species in each region, but the American species is a much more widely and generally distributed tree, the Chinese Sassafras being confined to the mountain slopes of western Hupeh and Szechuan. Litsea, which appears in eastern North America in one small shrub, in China is represented by at least a dozen species, among them several small trees. Lindera, too, is more important in eastern continental Asia than in eastern North America, where there are only two shrubby species, while China can boast of nearly ten times as many species ; some of these are large trees. The greater wealth of China in plants of this family appears, too, in the important genus Cinnamomum, including the species which yields the camphor of commerce, and in Machilus, of which several species are large and valuable timber trees.

CAPPARIDACEÆ.—This family appears in the tropics of the two regions with Capparis and Cratæva. Capparis is common to both, but Cratæva of south-eastern China has no American representative.

NEPENTHACEÆ.—One species of Nepenthes represents, in southern China, this Old-World family of a single genus.

SAXIFRAGACEÆ.—This family occurs in each of the two regions, with Philadelphus, Hydrangea, Decumaria, Itea, and Ribes. Deutzia (with one species in Mexico), Cardiandra, Schizophragma, Pileostegia, and Dichroa occur in China but not in eastern North America, which has no woody genus of the family not found also in eastern continental Asia.

INTRODUCTION

PITTOSPORACEÆ.—Pittosporum, which reaches southern and Western China with a few species, is the only genus of this family in the two regions.

HAMAMELIDACEÆ.—This family is more important in the number of genera in eastern continental Asia than in eastern North America, where there is one endemic genus, Fothergilla. Hamamelis and Liquidambar occur in the two regions, and in China the family is represented also by Distylium, Corylopsis, Fortunearia, Sinowilsonia, Loropetalum, Sycopsis, Eustigma, Rhodoleia, and Altingia. In each region the Liquidambar is a large, widely distributed, and valuable timber tree. The Chinese Hamamelis, like one of the American species and the species from Japan, flowers in the winter.

PLATANACEÆ.—Platanus, the only genus of the family, which is represented in eastern North America by a large, common, and widely distributed tree, has not reached eastern Asia.

ROSACEÆ.—Of the thirty-four genera of the woody plants of this family found in the two regions, Neillia, Stephanandra, Sorbaria, Sibiræa, Exochorda, Cotoneaster, Osteomeles, Chænomeles, Docynia, Pyrus, Eriolobus, Pyracantha, Rhaphiolepis, Eriobotrya, Photinia, Stranvæsia, Rhodotypos, Kerria, Prinsepia, Pygæum, and Maddenia occur in China only. Three genera, Aronia, the monotypic Neviusia, and Chrysobalanus are American and not Chinese ; and ten genera are common in the two regions, Physocarpus, Spiræa, Rosa, Malus, Sorbus, Amelanchier, Cratægus, Rubus, Potentilla, and Prunus. Of the genera common to the two regions, Physocarpus, with one species in eastern Siberia, is better represented in eastern North America, where the genus is widely distributed with several species. On the other hand, the closely related Spiræa has a few small eastern American species, but abounds in China, which is the centre of greatest distribution of this genus. Eastern continental Asia, too, is greatly superior to eastern North America in species of Rosa, and in their variety and horticultural value, for China is the home of *Rosa lævigata* Michx., *Rosa bracteata* Wendl., *Rosa Banksiæ* R. Br., *Rosa multiflora* Thunb., *Rosa indica* L., the origin of the Tea Roses of gardens, and of *Rosa rugosa* Thunb. The number of species of Malus is probably about the same in the two regions, but it is interesting that those of eastern North America all belong to a group (Coronariæ) which is not represented in eastern Asia, where the small-fruited species with a deciduous calyx predominate. Sorbus in eastern North America is represented by two species of the Aucuparia section, while in eastern Asia there are nearly thirty species in this group and at least ten species of Aria which does not appear at all in the flora of eastern North America. Amelanchier, which is very widely distributed through eastern North America, with a number of species, of which two are small trees, has but one shrubby Chinese species. In Cratægus the difference between the floras of the two regions is even more remarkable. In all of eastern continental Asia only twelve species have been found ; in eastern North America are more forms of Cratægus than of any other genus of plants, and probably a thousand species. In Rubus the difference in the number of species in the two regions is probably not great ; several of the American species, however, produce more valuable fruit than any of the Asiatic species. *Potentilla fruticosa* L. appears in the two regions with two other related species in eastern Asia and one in eastern North America. The composition of Prunus is unlike in the two regions. Of the true Plums (Prunophora) there is only a single species in eastern continental Asia (*Prunus salicina* Lindl.), confined to southern and Western China, no plum tree being found anywhere in the north ; in eastern North America plum trees have a wide distribution from the valley of the St. Lawrence River to Florida and Texas, a larger number of species occurring in the Arkansas-Texas region than in any other part of the world. Padus, on the contrary, is represented in eastern North America by only four species, while in eastern continental Asia about seventeen species are recognized. None of these, however, equal the American *P. serotina* Ehrh. in size or in value as a timber tree. Laurocerasus appears in eastern North America in two species and in eastern China in three species. Cerasus has but three eastern North American representatives and a much larger number in eastern continental Asia ; and Amygdalus, Persica, and Armeniaca occur in eastern Asia and not in eastern North America.

CONNARACEÆ.—Rourea in southern China is the only representative of this family in the two regions.

LEGUMINOSÆ.—Of the genera of woody plants of this family the following occur in eastern North America but not in eastern continental Asia : Lysiloma, Prosopis, Parkinsonia, Cercidium, Amorpha, Eysenhardtia, Robinia, Coursetia, and Ichthyomethia ; and the following in eastern continental Asia and not in eastern North America : Fordia, Ormosia, Millettia, Maackia, Caragana, Clitoria, Pueraria, Rhynchosia, Dalbergia, Euchresta, Mezoneurum, Cæsalpinia, Pterolobium, Entada, and Albizzia. The following genera have representatives in the two regions : Pithecolobium, Acacia, Leucæna (probably naturalized in southern China), Mimosa,

INTRODUCTION

Cercis, Cassia, Gleditsia, Gymnocladus, Sophora, Cladrastis, Wisteria, Erythrina, Desmodium, Lespedeza, Dalbergia, and Sesbania.

RUTACEÆ.—In eastern Asia representatives of this family are certainly more important than those found in eastern North America, for they include Citrus, Limonia, Atalantia, two genera of interesting trees, Phellodendron and Evodia, besides Toddalia, Acronychia, Murraya, Clausena, Orixa, and Skimmia, while in eastern North America this family is represented only by Helietta, Ptelea, Amyris, and by Zanthoxylum which occurs also in the other region which contains the larger number of species.

ZYGOPHYLLACEÆ is represented in eastern North America by Guaicum and Porlieria, and in eastern continental Asia by Zygophyllum.

COCHLOSPERMACEÆ.—A species of Amoreuxia in southern Texas is the only member of this family in the two regions.

SIMARUBACEÆ appear in tropical Florida in a species of Simaruba and in Picrasma, and in Texas in Castela, while of this family China has given to the world one of its valuable trees in Ailanthus, and is also represented by Picrasma, Brucea, and Harrisonia.

BURSERACEÆ.—One species of Bursera is eastern North American, and the species of Canarium in China represent this family in the two regions.

MELIACEÆ.—Of the woody plants of this family in the two regions Swietenia is certainly the most valuable, although it is the only eastern American representative of the family; while in China, representatives of this family are Aglaia, Amoora, Turræa, Cedrela, and Melia, one species of the last being widely and generally naturalized in the southern United States.

MALPIGHIACEÆ.—This family reaches tropical Florida with a species of Byrsonima and southern Texas with a species of Malpighia : its only genus in China is Hiptage.

POLYGALACEÆ.—Of this family only a few Chinese species of Polygala are frutescent, the species of this genus in eastern North America being herbaceous.

DICHAPETALACEÆ.—This small family is represented in the two regions by a single species of Dichapetalum in south-eastern China.

EUPHORBIACEÆ.—Woody plants of this family are more numerous in China than in eastern North America, where the following genera only appear : Andrachne, Drypetes, Croton, Ditaxis, Ricinella, Bernardia, Gymnanthes, Sebastiana, Stillingia, Hippomane, and Mozinna. These eastern North American representatives of the family are all small shrubs with the exception of Drypetes,

Gymnanthes, and Hippomane, which are small trees of tropical Florida. In eastern continental Asia woody plants of this family occur in Bridelia, Andrachne, Sauropus, Phyllanthus, Glochidion, Securinega, Breynia, Bischofia, Aporosa, Daphniphyllum, Antidesma, Microdesmis, Aleurites, Croton, Blachia, Claoxylum, Acalypha, Alchornea, Mallotus, Macaranga, Homonoia, Endospermum, Gelonium, Homolanthus, Erismanthus, Sapium, Sebastiana, and Excœcaria. Nearly all of these are tropical genera which, coming from the south, have obtained a foothold in south-eastern China. Only Andrachne, Croton, and Sebastiana have representatives in the two regions. Aleurites, a genus of trees which produce the wood-oil of commerce, is probably the most valuable genus of the family in the two regions.

BUXACEÆ.—One species of Pachysandra occurs in each of the two regions; the other genera of this family in the two regions, Buxus and Sarcococca, are Chinese.

CORIARIACEÆ, a family of a single genus, Coriaria, has a representative in China but not in America.

EMPETRACEÆ.—Empetrum occurs in north-eastern North America and in north-eastern continental Asia, and the other genera of this family, Corema and Ceratiola, are eastern North American, and have no Asiatic representatives.

ANACARDIACEÆ.—In this family, Pistacia, Rhus, and Cotinus are represented in the flora of the two regions. Metopium is American, and Spondias, Mangifera, and Dracontomelum are Chinese. In China, *Pistacia chinensis* Bunge is a large, widely distributed, and valuable tree, but in the United States *Pistacia mexicana* H.B.K. has secured only a precarious foothold on the northern bank of the Rio Grande in Texas. Of the members of this family in the two regions *Rhus verniciflua* Stokes, the Chinese Lacquer tree, is no doubt the most valuable.

CYRILLACEÆ.—This exclusively American family is represented in eastern North America by Cliftonia and Cyrilla.

AQUIFOLIACEÆ.—Of this family, Ilex is widely distributed in the two regions, and the monotypic Nemopanthus is east North American. Ilex usually grows to a larger size in China than in eastern North America, but is less northern in its range in the former region where most of the species are evergreen.

CELASTRACEÆ.—In this family, Celastrus and Evonymus are common to the two regions. Tripterygium, Perrottetia, Microtropis, and Elæodendron are eastern Asiatic and not American, and Pachystima, Maytenus, Crossopetalum, Gyminda, Schæfferia, and Mortonia are American. Only one species of Celastrus and three species of Evonymus occur in eastern North America, but in eastern continental Asia the species of these genera are much more numerous, and the species of Evonymus are usually larger and more beautiful plants.

HIPPOCRATEACEÆ.—Of this small tropical family there is a species of Hippocratea in tropical Florida and two or three in southern China.

STAPHYLEACEÆ.—Represented in China by Staphylea, Turpinia, Euscaphis, and Tapiscia, this family is much more important in eastern continental Asia than in eastern North America, where there is a single species only of Staphylea.

ICACINACEÆ.—Without an eastern North American genus this family appears in China in Iodes, Mappia, and the monotypic Hosiea.

ACERACEÆ.—Eastern continental Asia with its sixty-four species is far richer in Acer than eastern North America, where only ten species occur. The American Maples, however, are more widely distributed, and are larger and more valuable timber trees; Dipteronia and Dodonæa of this family are Chinese.

HIPPOCASTANACEÆ.—Of this family, Æsculus appears in two arborescent species in China, one in the north and one on the mountains of the west, but in eastern North America, where more species are segregated than in any other part of the world, four arborescent and four shrubby species occur in the southern United States. The monotypic Bretschneidera is Chinese.

SAPINDACEÆ.—Of the woody plants of this family found in our two regions, Urvillea, Serjania, Exothea, Hypelate, Cupania, and the monotypic Ungnadia are American, and the monotypic genera Xanthoceras and Delavaya, with Nephelium, Schmidelia, Kœlreuteria, and Pancovia, are Chinese; Sapindus is common to the two regions.

SABIACEÆ.—Without representatives in eastern North America, this family appears in China in Sabia and Meliosma.

RHAMNACEÆ.—Of this family, several genera reach tropical Florida from the West Indies and the dry region of Texas from Mexico, and the number is larger in eastern North America than in eastern continental Asia. The exclusively American genera are Rhamnidium, Reynosia, Ceanothus, Condalia, Karwinskia, Colubrina, and Gouania; and the Asiatic genera are Ventilago, Paliurus, and the monotypic Hovenia. Sageretia, Zizyphus, Berchemia, and Rhamnus have representatives in the two floras. Species of

Rhamnus, however, are more numerous in eastern continental Asia than in eastern North America, and *Rhamnus davuricus* Pall., and other Chinese species, from which a green dye is made, are more valuable than any of the American species.

VITACEÆ.—Of the Grape family, three genera, Tetrastigma, Cayratia, and Leea, occur in China and not in eastern America ; and Ampelopsis, Parthenocissus, and Vitis are common to the two regions ; Cissus reaches tropical Florida but has not been reported from southern China. Species of Vitis are less numerous in eastern North America than in eastern continental Asia ; and in North America there is no species which corresponds with the spiny-stemmed Grape vines of China (Spinovitis).

ELÆOCARPACEÆ.—The forest flora of the two regions is only represented by the Asiatic Elæocarpus and Sloanea (Echinocarpus) of this family.

TILIACEÆ.—Tilia is widely distributed in the two regions with rather more species in the Asiatic region. In size and in value as ornamental trees there is not much difference between the American and Asiatic Lindens. The Asiatic genera Grewia, Corchoropsis, and Triumfetta do not appear in eastern North America.

MALVACEÆ.—In eastern North America there are woody species in Pavonia, Hibiscus, and Thespesia, and in western continental Asia only in Urena, Hibiscus, and Abutilon.

BOMBACEÆ.—Only the Asiatic Bombax represents this family in the woody plants of the two regions.

STERCULIACEÆ.—The large genus Sterculia has several Chinese representatives, including *Sterculia platanifolia* L. f., now naturalized in several of the southern United States. Of this family these genera also appear in China : Heritiera, Reevesia, Kleinhovia, Helicteres, Pterospermum, Abroma, and Buettneria, among which are several large trees, while in eastern North America are only Hermannia, Melochis, and Nephropetalum, all small shrubs of arid Texas.

DILLENIACEÆ.—Unrepresented in eastern North America, the family appears in China in Tetracera, Actinidia, and Clemato-clethra.

THEACEÆ.—Much more important in eastern continental Asia than in eastern North America where only Gordonia and Stewartia occur, this family has several woody plants in China, including Thea, Gordonia, Stewartia, Schima, Ternstrœmia, Eurya, Hartia, Tutcheria, and Adinandra. One of the species of Thea, from the leaves of which tea is made, is the most important member of the family ;

and in another (Camellia) are found some of the most valued and generally cultivated ornamental trees and shrubs.

GUTTIFERÆ.—Of this family only Ascyrum, Hypericum, and Clusia appear in eastern North America, but in eastern continental Asia, Ascyrum, Hypericum, Cratoxylon, Garcinia, and Calophyllum represent this family.

TAMARICACEÆ.—With Tamarix and Myricaria in eastern continental Asia this family has no representative in eastern North America, although one species of Tamarix is occasionally naturalized in the southern United States.

CISTACEÆ.—Hudsonia of the Atlantic coast region is the woody representative of this family in the two regions.

COCHLOSPERMACEÆ and KŒBERLINIANÆ.—A shrubby species of Amoreuxia of the former, and a species of Kœberlinia of the latter, both in Texas, are the only members of these families in the two regions.

CANELLACEÆ.—A West Indian species of Canella which has reached tropical Florida is the only member of this family in the flora of the two regions.

FLACOURTIACEÆ.—Without a representative in eastern North America this family contributes some of its most interesting trees to the Chinese flora in Xylosma, the monotypic Carrieria, Itoa, and Idesia, and in Poliothyrsis.

STACHYURACEÆ, of which Stachyurus is the only genus, is Asiatic.

TURNERACEÆ.—A shrubby species of Turnera from southern Texas is the representative of this family in the two regions.

PASSIFLORÆ.—Although Passiflora appears in several herbaceous species in the southern states, *Passiflora ligulifolia* Mast. of southern China is the only woody species of the family in our two regions.

CARICACEÆ.—*Carica Papaya* L., now naturalized in many of the warm countries of the world, is possibly a native of southern Florida.

DAPHNACEÆ.—In this family the advantage is with eastern continental Asia, as Dirca is its only American representative, while in China there are species of Daphne, Edgeworthia, Wickstrœmia, and Aquilaria.

ELÆAGNACEÆ.—In this family Shepherdia is American, Hippophaë Chinese, and Elæagnus is found in the two regions.

LYTHRACEÆ.—The monotypic Decodon is the only woody plant of this family in eastern North America, while in China appear species of Lagerstrœmia and Woodfordia, and the monotypic Lawsonia.

RHIZOPHORACEÆ.—Rhizophora is common on the shores of tropical Florida, but the family is more largely represented in tropical China by Kandalia, Bruguiera, and Carallia.

COMBRETACEÆ.—Represented in tropical Florida by Bucida, Conocarpus, and Laguncularia, this family appears in China in Combretum, Quisqualis, and Illigera.

MYRTACEÆ.—Rhodomyrtus, Eugenia, Psidium, and Bæckea of the Myrtle family have reached south-eastern China, while in tropical Florida occur Eugenia, Anamomis, Chytraculia, and Syzygium.

MELASTOMACEÆ.—Of this family woody species of Barthea, Allomorphia, Blastus, Bredia, Anplectrum, and Memecylon occur in China, but a species of Tetrazygia is the only woody member of the family in eastern North America.

ARALIACEÆ.—An arborescent species of Aralia and a species of Echinopanax are the only tree and shrub of this family in eastern North America; in eastern continental Asia the family is more largely represented by Aralia, Acanthopanax, Fatsia, Nothopanax, Heptapleurum, Dendropanax, Heteropanax, and Hedera.

CORNACEÆ.—Of this family Garrya occurs in eastern North America but not in China, where are found the monotypic Camptotheca, a large tree, Davidia, Alangium, Helwingia, Torricellia, Marlea, and Aucuba. Nyssa and Cornus are common to the two regions. Nyssa in America is widely and generally distributed from New England to Florida and Texas, with several species, of which two are large trees, but in China only a small tree is now known, confined to the central provinces. On the other hand, Cornus is more numerous in species in China than in eastern North America, six of the species at least being arborescent and one a tree occasionally 100 ft. high.

CLETHRACEÆ.—Of this family there are three species of Clethra in each of our two regions.

ERICACEÆ.—In the number of genera of this family eastern North America has the advantage of the Asiatic region, with twenty-three genera in the former and only seventeen in the latter. Such genera as Bejaria, Leiophyllum, Menziesia, Kalmia, Zenobia, the monotypic Oxydendrum, Gaylussacia, and Arctostaphylos have no eastern Asiatic representatives. Enkianthus, Craibiodendron, and Diplycosia are Chinese, without American representatives, and the following genera are common to the two regions : Vaccinium, Gaultheria, Chamædaphne, Loiseleuria, Phyllodoce, Andromeda, Arctous, and Rhododendron. No single genus except Cratægus so well illustrates, perhaps, the differences in the floras of the two regions as Rhododendron. In eastern North America there are only six species of true Rhododendron, all confined to the extreme eastern part of the continent, and, with one exception, of restricted range, but some one hundred and sixty species have already been distinguished in eastern continental Asia, where the genus is widely distributed and where, on the mountains of the western and south-western provinces, is the greatest segregation of these plants in the world. On the other hand, only three species of Azalea have been found in China, while in eastern North America, which is the region of their greatest development, ten or twelve species are recognized.

THEOPHRASTACEÆ.—The only member of this family in the floras of the two regions is a single species of Jacquinia in tropical Florida.

MYRSINACEÆ.—This family has a much larger representation in eastern continental Asia than in eastern North America, only one species each of Ardisia and Rapanea having reached tropical Florida, while in southern China there are several species of Ardisia, Rapanea, and Myrsine, and where also Mæsa, Embelia, and Ægiceras occur.

PLUMBAGINACEÆ.—With Plumbago in the two regions the family is also represented in China by Ceratostigma.

SAPOTACEÆ.—In this family eastern North America has the advantage with six genera, while only three genera reach southern China. Of these only Sarcosperma is not represented in the American flora. The other genera which are found in China, Sideroxylon and Chrysophyllum, occur in tropical Florida, which has been reached also by Dipholis and Mimusops, while Bumelia, which is an American genus, is widely distributed through the southern United States with several species.

EBENACEÆ.—Of this family only one genus, Diospyros, is represented with two species in eastern North America, and eight or nine species in China. As a fruit tree one of the Chinese species is much more valuable than the North American species.

STYRACEÆ.—Of this family Styrax occurs in the two regions. Halesia, with three species, is eastern North American ; and the monotypic Alniphyllum and Pterostyrax are Chinese.

SYMPLOCACEÆ.—Symplocos, the only genus of the family, appears with one species in the southern United States, and is largely represented in China, where twenty species are distinguished.

OLEACEÆ.—In this family also the advantage is with eastern continental Asia, with eight genera, while only four are eastern North American. Fraxinus, Chionanthus, and Osmanthus are common to the two regions, Adelia is American only, and Fontanesia, Forsythia, Syringa, Ligustrum, and Jasminum are Chinese and not American. Fraxinus is widely distributed in each of the two regions, with probably about the same number of species in each, but the American species are usually larger and more valuable timber trees. As an ornamental plant the American Chionanthus is superior to the Chinese representative of the genus, but China's contributions to gardens from this family in Forsythia, Syringa, Ligustrum, and Jasminum more than make up for the beauty of the American Chionanthus.

LOGANACEÆ.—Gelsemium, with one species, and Buddleia, with a species of southern Texas, are the only woody representatives of this family in eastern North America. These genera occur in China with Strychnos, Gærtnera, and Gardneria.

APOCYNACEÆ.—Vallesia, Thevetia, and Trachelospermum are woody plants of this family in eastern North America. It has a larger representation in southern China in Plumeria, Melodinus, Rauwolfia, Alyxia, Alstonia, Parsonsia, Pottsia, Wrightia, Ecdysanthera, Anodendron, Trachelospermum, and Scindechites.

ASCLEPIADACEÆ.—Roulinia, with a species of southern Texas, is the only woody plant of this family in eastern North America, but in eastern continental Asia occur woody species of Pentaneura, Cryptolepis, Periploca, Taxocarpus, Calotropis, Holostemma, Graphistemma, Metaplexis, Henrya, Gymnema, Marsdenia, Stephanotis, Pergularia, Dregea, and Hoya.

CONVOLVULACEÆ.—Ipomœa and Argyreia are Chinese representatives of this family, and a woody species of Ipomœa has reached Florida from the tropics.

BORRAGINACEÆ.—Cordia, Bourreria, and Ehretia are the North American genera of this family, with woody species. Cordia and Ehretia appear in China in a larger number of species than in eastern North America, and Tournefortia is Asiatic and not American.

VERBENACEÆ.—Aloysia, Lantana, Citharexylon, Duranta, Callicarpa, and Avicennia, represent this family in the southern United States. In China, Callicarpa, with several species, Premna, Gmelina, Vitex, Clerodendron, Caryopteris, Sphenodesma, and Avicennia make a larger representation of the family, only Callicarpa, with one American species, and Avicennia occurring in the two regions.

INTRODUCTION

LABIATÆ.—A few small shrubs of Salvia in Texas, and the genus Elsholtzia, with several species in eastern continental Asia, represent the woody plants of this family in our two regions.

SOLANACEÆ.—Species of Lycium and Solanum, which occur in each of the two regions, are the only woody plants of this family.

SCROPHULARIACEÆ.—Of this family Leucophyllum, a small shrub of western Texas, is the only woody plant in eastern North America, but in eastern continental Asia it is represented by the important genus Paulownia, of several species of large trees, and by Brandisia.

BIGNONIACEÆ.—In this family Campsis and Catalpa are common to the two regions. The monotypic Chilopsis, and Aniso-stichus and Crescentia occur only in the southern United States. Oroxylum, Dolichandrone, Stereospermum, and Radermachera are Chinese and not American.

GESNERACEÆ.—Æschynanthus and Lysinotus, with woody species in China, are the representatives of this family in the two regions.

MYOPORACEÆ.—A species of Myoporum of southern China is the representative of this small family in the two regions.

RUBIACEÆ.—Of this family the American woody representatives are Cephalanthus, the monotypic Pinckneya, Exostemma, Genipa, Randia, Catesbæa, Hamelia, Guettarda, Erithalis, Chiococca, Strumpfia, Psychotria, Morinda, and Ernodea. Of these Cephal-anthus, Randia, Guettarda, Psychotria, and Morinda occur also in China, where also are woody representatives of Adina, Luculia, Wendlandia, Hedyotis, Mussænda, Adenosacme, Myrioneuron, Webera, Gardenia, Diplospora, Antirrhœa, Conthium, Ixora, Damnacanthus, Lasianthus, Pæderia, Hamiltonia, Leptodermis, Serissa, Emmenopterys, Dunnia, Pavetta, and Uncaria.

CAPRIFOLIACEÆ.—Of the ten genera of woody plants of this family found in the two regions, Dipelta, Leycesteria, Kolkwitzia, and Abelia (with a species in Mexico) occur only in China. Of the other genera, Sambucus, Viburnum, Symphoricarpos, Linnæa, Lonicera, and Diervilla are common to the two regions. Symphori-carpos is chiefly American, with a single Chinese species, and Vibur-num, with some seventy species, is richer in China than in eastern continental America, although the American species grow to a larger size and are more ornamental. Lonicera is poorly represented in eastern North America with twelve species, while in eastern continental Asia more than one hundred species are recognized, the region of their greatest segregation being on the mountains of the central and western provinces.

GOODENIACEÆ.—A Chinese species of Scævola is the only woody plant of this family in the two regions.

COMPOSITÆ.—Iva and Baccharis, of the Atlantic coast region, are the American shrubby representatives of this family, which occurs in China in several species of Blumea and in Pertya.

It appears, therefore, that 129 natural families are represented in the two regions under consideration ; that of these 92 are common to the two regions, that 12 occur in eastern North America, but not in eastern continental Asia, and that 25 occur in eastern continental Asia and not in eastern North America. Of the 692 genera in the two regions 155 are common to both, while 158 are found in eastern North America and not in eastern continental Asia, and 379 are found in eastern continental Asia and not in eastern North America. Of the tropical genera 76 have reached southern Florida and 89 south-eastern China.

From Mexico the flora of the United States has derived 42 genera of the woody plants of Texas.

It is impossible to form an accurate estimate of the comparative number of species of woody plants in the two regions .. this time, but including Cratægus it is probable that the number is as great in eastern North America as in eastern continental Asia.

C. S. SARGENT

ARNOLD ARBORETUM
July 1913

A NATURALIST IN WESTERN CHINA

CHAPTER I

WESTERN CHINA

MOUNTAIN RANGES AND RIVER SYSTEMS

WESTERN China is separated from Thibet proper by a series of parallel mountain ranges running almost due north and south, and divided by narrow valleys. On some maps the name Yun-ling is applied to the whole system, with sections marked Hsueh shan, Hung shan, Taliang shan, and so on. A great many local names, the majority of them unpronounceable when converted into English, are also applied to this system, but outside certain maps no one general name for it exists. Later we shall have much to say about this region, for the time being it suffices to note the general trend of the ranges and a few of their important features.

Made up largely of razor-backed ridges, following one another in quick succession, these ranges are separated by narrow valleys, or rather ravines. The higher peaks are well above the snow-line, and for height, savage grandeur, and wondrous scenery are comparable only to the Himalayan alps of India. The whole region is practically uncharted and unsurveyed, and it is the author's firm conviction that some of the peaks rival in altitude the greatest of the Himalayan giants.

About lat. 33° N., in the neighbourhood of Sungpan Ting, a mighty spur is thrown out from these ranges of perpetual snow, and extends, with a slight southerly dip, due east for some 10° of longitude, terminating in low hills near Anluh

Hsien, in north-eastern Hupeh. This spur appears on maps under the general name of Kiu-tiao shan (nine mountain ridges), Ta-pa ling, or Ta-pa shan. The two latter names have direct reference only to important peaks of the spur, and the first is the most appropriate, since it denotes a series of parallel chains closely packed together. The Kiu-tiao shan forms the boundary between Szechuan and the northern provinces of Kansu and Shensi, and is the watershed between the middle Yangtsze and the Han River systems. Attaining its greatest altitude in the neighbourhood of Chengkou Ting, long. 108° 30′, lat. 32° 15′ N. (approx.), it radiates from this climax buttress-like spurs in all directions. Those on the south form the boundary between Szechuan and Hupeh and extend downwards beyond the Yangtsze River. Subsidiary spurs and others thrust out from more easterly points of the range, make the whole of north-western Hupeh exceedingly wild and rugged. In the middle of the province the Yangtsze River has forced itself through these spurs, which run at right angles to its course, and formed the famous Yangtsze Gorges.

Another spur, or rather series of spurs, not so clearly defined as the preceding, and of less altitude, is thrown out in the neighbourhood of Tali Fu, long. 100° E., lat. 25° 42′ N. (approx.), in western Yunnan. It extends across northern Yunnan, southern Kweichou, and northern Kwangsi, and forms the boundary between Hunan and Kiangsi on the north and Kwangtung on the south. In eastern Kiangsi it is deflected north and north-north-east, finally reaching the sea in the neighbourhood of Ningpo, long. 121° 35′ E., lat. 29° 50′ N. (approx.). This mountain system extends across some 21 parallels of longitude, and forms the watershed between the Yangtsze River on the north and numberless rivers on the south. Of these the Red River, reaching the sea in the Gulf of Tongking, and the West River, which enters the sea near Macao and Hongkong, are the chief.

Innumerable lateral spurs are given off by this system, and the country is extremely broken, especially in the western parts, with which we are concerned. The province of Kwei-chou is one mass of mountains, and the same is true of southern Hupeh and southern Szechuan. In these three areas there are subsidiary ranges of considerable altitude dipping in various directions and connected up with spurs to form a heterogeneous and complex mountain system. The outstanding feature of the whole region west of 112th parallel of longitude is the entire absence of plain or plateau, or anything in the nature of flat, level country, with the solitary exception of the area forming the Chengtu Plain. Of this we shall speak in due course. East of the 112th parallel the Yangtsze River flows through a flat, alluvial plain in which isolated, or more or less connected, mountain ranges and spurs occur, but with this region we are not in this work concerned.

The most important region comprised within the mountain systems above described and west of the 112th parallel is that termed by Richthofen the " Red Basin of Szechuan." This region includes the whole of Szechuan east of the Min (Fu) River to near the Hupeh boundary. It is a region of vast agricultural wealth, with a magnificent river system, teeming with large cities, towns, and villages, and supporting an enormous population. With the solitary exception of cotton, which is imported from the coast, it is self-contained, with a surplus of produce to spare for export. Salt is produced in unlimited quantities in very many districts ; coal, iron, and other minerals of economic importance abound. In short, the " Red Basin " is one of the richest and fairest regions in the Chinese Empire.

The whole of Western China, with which this work is concerned, lies within the Yangtsze River basin. According to the geographical information at present available, the Yangtsze has its source almost due north of Calcutta, in latitude about 35° N., on the south-east edge of the Central Asian steppes. Its exact length is unknown, but it is estimated to exceed 3000 miles. From its source it pursues a tortuous course, nearly due south, through wild and partially unknown country for 1000 miles. Then suddenly turning eastward it flows right through the heart of China for some 2000 miles, finally reaching the sea immediately to the north of Shanghai.

From its mouth to Ichang, 1000 miles, it is navigable for steamers at all seasons of the year, though in winter difficulties in the way of shoals and sand-bars are encountered. The greatest difficulty is experienced between Hankow and Ichang, and this section is operated by a small fleet of shallow draught steamers specially built for the trade. The regular steamer-fleet plying between Shanghai and Hankow is also specially designed for the service and is luxuriously fitted. Ocean-going steamers of deep draught can ascend as far up as Hankow, except in low-water season. In summer the river overflows and invades much of the low-lying country contiguous to its course, and the chief difficulty in navigation at such times is to keep to the channel. The difference between summer and winter level is very considerable and varies to a large extent, according to the width of the river and the nature of its banks. At Ichang the river is 1100 yards from bank to bank, and the average difference between summer and winter levels is about 40 feet ; in the gorges which commence some 5 miles west of Ichang, the river is narrowed to a third of its usual breadth and the difference exceeds 100 feet. Above Ichang the river is obstructed by rapids, rocks, and other impedimenta, and is navigated by specially built native boats that range up to 80 tons displacement. The difficulties of navigation are more especially confined to the stretch of the river between Ichang and Wan Hsien, a distance of about 200 miles. From Wan Hsien to Pingshan Hsien, some 500 miles farther west, the navigation becomes easier.

Much has been written on the possibility of opening the Yangtsze River to merchant steamer traffic from Ichang westwards. So long ago as April 1900, two British river gunboats of shallow draught, small in beam and length, and of a special design, ascended as far as Chungking, the commercial capital of Western China, distant above Ichang some 400 miles. Later these boats ascended as far west as Pingshan Hsien and one of them succeeded in reaching Mei Chou, a city on the Min (Fu) River, about 140 miles above its junction with the Yangtsze at Sui Fu. Since this exploit two larger and more powerful British gunboats have been built for this work and are now stationed at Chungking, which has been made a naval base. France and Germany, following the British lead, have also gunboats stationed at Chungking. During suitable seasons these craft move up and down the river, and regularly every year one or more visit Pingshan Hsien and Kiating Fu, the latter city being about 100 miles north of Sui Fu on the Min River.

The advent of the gunboats had been anticipated early in 1898 by a small launch called the *Leechuan*, commanded by Captain C. Plant and owned by the late Mr. Archibald Little, the pioneer foreign merchant of these regions. The experimental test made by this launch took practical shape in 1900 when a commercial steamer named the *Pioneer*, captained by Plant and operated by a British syndicate, in which Mr. Little figured, was placed on this service. She made a trip prior to the Boxer outbreak, after which she was chartered by the British Government and was finally purchased for naval purposes.

On 27th December 1900, a German merchant ship, the *Suihsiang*, specially designed and built for the purpose, left Ichang for Chungking, but was wrecked and totally lost below the Tungling Rapid only some 40 miles above Ichang.

Early in 1910 the task was again taken in hand; this time a powerfully constructed tug named the *Shutung*, towing alongside a flat for passengers and cargo, was employed. This outfit, owned by a Chinese syndicate, was commanded by the same Captain C. Plant. The venture proved successful, and fourteen round trips were made during the year. It is fitting that the man who pioneered the whole business should succeed in demonstrating the practicability of merchant steam navigation on the Upper Yangtsze. The work, however, is dangerous, exceedingly difficult, and, moreover, costly, and unless some improvements are made in the river-bed, it will be some time before any considerable fleet of steamers ply on these waters.

Above Pingshan Hsien navigation is only practicable for small native craft in certain short interrupted sections. The river flows for the most part through gorges or between steep mountains, and its course is frequently broken by dangerous rapids and cataracts that produce a seething, foaming swirl in which nothing can live. In the autumn of 1911 an adventurous French naval officer made an extraordinary journey down the Upper Yangtsze to Sui Fu in native boats specially built for the purpose. An account of this journey should prove exciting reading.

It has been mentioned that the most difficult stretch of the Middle Yangtsze was that between Ichang and Wan Hsien. This is the region of the world-famous Yangtsze Gorges. Five in number, these gorges extend from the immediate west of Ichang to Kuichou Fu, a distance of about 150 miles. Throughout this stretch the river flows between perpendicular walls of rock, is narrowed to a third or less of its usual width, and becomes in consequence very deep. Soundings taken by the British gunboats in their ascent in 1900 gave 63½ fathoms of water in two places, and this when the water at Ichang was rather less than 6 feet above zero mark ! The cliffs, composed largely of hard limestone, are 500 to 2000 feet or more high, and commonly 500 to 1000 feet or more sheer. The scenery hereabouts is savagely grand and awe-inspiring.

Foreign maps without exception give the name of Yangtsze Kiang (variously spelt) to this magnificent river. So far I have never met a Chinese to whom this name is intelligible. I have read that the name denotes " Son of the Ocean," and is applied to the section between Wuhu and the sea. This may be so, I have no knowledge on the point. Many local names are given to stretches of this river, but from Sui Fu, in western Szechuan, to its mouth it is universally spoken of by Chinese as the Ta Kiang (Great River), occasionally it is rendered Chang Kiang (Long River), or simply Kiang, meaning *The* River. West of Sui Fu it is called the Kinsha Ho (River of Golden Sands); the Chinese do not consider this the main stream, but regard the Min (Fu) River as the principal. They recognize that the Kinsha has the larger volume, but it is navigable only for some 40 miles and then loses itself in wild and barbarous regions. The Min, on the other hand, is navigable to Chengtu, some 200 miles above Sui Fu, and is therefore to the utilitarian mind of the Chinese of much greater importance. From near Batang northward the Kinsha Ho is known by the Thibetan name of Drechu, and finally near its source it goes under the Tangut name of Murussu.

In ascending the Yangtsze from Ichang to Chungking the observant traveller is struck by the insignificant character of the tributary streams. Apparently the only one of importance joins the main stream at Fu Chou on the right bank. This stream, the Kien Kiang, rises in western Kweichou and flows through the heart of this province. It is navigable from its mouth to Szenan Fu, and beyond, for specially constructed native boats. Apart from this river there is no tributary of seeming importance until Chungking is reached, yet nearly every town and village of note stands at the junction of some small stream with the Yangtsze. Here and there men will be found hauling small, stout-bottomed boats over the stones at the mouths of these small rivers. That the main stream is joined by many tributary streams a glance at the map proves. In western Hupeh the country is wildly mountainous, and the streams are torrents, pure and simple. In eastern Szechuan the country is much less wild and the streams of a different character, and why they appear unnavigable is, on the surface, not obvious.

In 1910 I journeyed overland by a little-known route from Ichang to Chengtu. Entering Szechuan a little to the north of Taning Hsien, I travelled due west to Paoning Fu, and from thence south-west by the main road. On this journey I crossed all the principal streams which join the Yangtsze on its left bank east of the Min River. The surprising thing observed was the fact that they were one and all navigable for boats of varying sizes for long distances. On inquiry, I found that navigation ceased on most of them some 2 to 5 miles before their union with the Yangtsze. The Kuichou Fu, Yunyang, and Kai Hsien Rivers may be cited as examples, affording evidence of this state of things.

Near the embouchure of tributary streams the Yangtsze is generally narrowed and the water gorged by boulders and detritus choking the mouths of these lateral waterways; rapids and races frequently occur at these points. The accepted view is that enormous quantities of debris are brought down by these tributaries and deposited at their mouths. This theory is all very well when applied to mountain torrents, but most of the streams under discussion pursue a comparatively placid course with easy currents for some 50 miles or more before reaching the Yangtsze. Their volume and force of current is insufficient even in summer floods to carry down the enormous quantities of detritus which choke up their mouths. My personal observations put the responsibility on the main stream itself. During the summer floods the Yangtsze brings down vast quantities of mud and detritus, which it deposits wherever opportunity offers. Flowing as the Yangtsze does, more or less between steep banks, the mouths of tributary streams afford the most favourable places for the deposition of this debris. The volume of the main stream is enormously greater, and its current so much stronger, than that of the tributaries that it simply thrusts them back and silts up their mouths. The small quantity of debris brought down by the tributary streams would also be deposited hereabouts owing to the slacking of the flow consequent upon the damming of their debouchure.

At Chungking the Yangtsze is joined on its left bank by the Kialing or so-called " Little River."   A glance at a map shows that this river is made up of three streams which unite near Ho Chou.   The Kialing River and its tributaries drain a fan-shaped area, in extent more than half of the entire Red Basin situated north of the Yangtsze.   Their importance is due to their being navigable for such extreme distances.   The most easterly branch is navigable, for small craft, to some 40 miles north of Tunghsiang Hsien ; the next branch is navigable to Tungchiang Hsien ; and the next to north of Pa Chou.   The central (Paoning) river is navigable for fairly large boats to Kuangyuan Hsien, and skiffs laden with medicines and other native products descend to this town from Pikou, in the province of Kansu.   The most westerly branch is navigable to Pai-shih-pu, a few miles north of Chungpa, and one of its western tributaries taps the north-east corner of the Chengtu Plain.

The Kialing River system is thus the greatest collecting and distributing waterway in Szechuan, and its commercial importance, probably greater than that of the Yangtsze itself and its tributaries west of Chungking, is not generally understood. The To kiang, which joins the Yangtsze at Lu Chou, though a natural stream, owes very much of its volume and importance to water artificially lead from Kuan Hsien across the northern part of the Chengtu Plain via Sintu Hsien, and a secondary branch via Han Chou, which meet together at the great market town of Chao-chia-to.   In summer it is possible to descend in boats from Han Chou and Sintu Hsien to Lu Chou.

The Min (Fu) River proper, save at lowest water, is navigable from Kuan Hsien and Chengtu downwards. The Chengtu branch is artificially formed by canals led across the plain from Kuan Hsien, and unites with the Kuan Hsien stream and its tributaries at Chiangkou. A tributary of the Min, which joins at Hsinhsin Hsien, is navigable in high water for small boats to Kiung Chou, a city situated at the extreme south-west corner of the Chengtu Plain.

The Min (Fu) River rises some 35 miles north of the Sungpan Ting, near the boundary of north-west Szechuan and the Amdo region in lat. 33° N. (approx.). Immediately to the south of Sungpan city it plunges into wild, mountainous country, flowing through a gorge from which it emerges only a few miles north of Kuan Hsien, where it becomes navigable for rafts only.

At Kuan Hsien a famous and gigantic irrigation system is in operation, but of this we shall deal in due place.

The Min is really only a tributary of the Tung River, which it joins at Kiating Fu, but since it admits of navigation it is of more practical importance, and for this cause the Chinese give it pre-eminence. The Tung River is only navigable for a few miles above Kiating, though rafts descend from a much higher point west. Its tributary the Ya, which joins it immediately west of Kiating, is of greater commercial importance, and a very considerable raft traffic ascends and descends this stream from Yachou, which is the centre of the brick-tea industry of western Szechuan.

The Tung River is really one of the longest rivers in Szechuan, having its source in the north-eastern corner of Thibet, about lat. 33° 40′ N. It flows through the western frontier of the tribes country, where it is known as the Tachin Ho (Great Gold River), and ultimately strikes the highway from Chengtu to Lhassa at Wassu-kou, a hamlet 18 miles east of Tachienlu. From this point to its union with the Min at Kiating it is called the Tung Ho, though around Fulin it goes by the name of Tatu Ho. Owing to its unnavigability its commercial importance is small, but this does not excuse the geographer's scant appreciation of it in the past, even if it explains the Chinese view.

Considerably west of Pingshan Hsien the Yangtsze is

joined by the Yalung River, an artery almost equal in volume to the main stream itself. This river rises in the north-eastern limits of the Thibetan highlands in the same general country as the Yangtsze, but to the south-east. It flows more or less due south throughout the whole course, but the region it traverses is, if anything, less known than that through which the Yangtsze flows. In its upper parts it is called the Niachu, since it flows through the country of the Niarung tribes, and its map cognomen, " Yalung," is probably a transliteration of the name Niarung.

On its right (south) bank the Yangtsze receives many streams rising in northern Yunnan and Kweichou, but none equalling in importance those uniting on the left bank. However, all are significant factors in the distribution of merchandise in these parts, even though geographically they are of comparatively small moment. The important thing to be remembered in connection with the river-system here mentioned is this—the Yangtsze River is the main artery of China in general and Western China in particular, but Szechuan owes its agricultural wealth and general prosperity principally to the Kialing and Min Rivers with their network of navigable contributary streams and canals. The rivers west of Sui Fu flow through wild, mountainous, sparsely populated regions, and their course is so much obstructed that virtually no boats ply on their waters and even ferries are scarce.

CHAPTER II

WESTERN HUPEH

General Topography and Geology

THE country comprising western Hupeh, with which
we are concerned, lies west of the 112th parallel of
longitude. The city of Ichang, situated on the
Yangtsze River, just west of this parallel and about 1000
geographical miles from the mouth of the river, is a convenient
starting-point for exploring this region. This important town
is a treaty port, opened to foreign trade in 1877. The population is roughly estimated at 30,000. There is also a small
foreign community consisting of a British Consul, Imperial
Maritime Customs' staff, a few business men, and missionaries
of Roman Catholic and various Protestant denominations.
There is very little local trade, but Ichang being practically the
head of steam navigation on the river, is a most important
transhipping port. Six steamers regularly trade between
Ichang and Hankow, and the thousands of native craft lined
up in tiers attest its importance as an entrepôt of trade. In
the near future it is destined to be a most important junction
on the Hankow-Szechuan railway and already important work
on this enterprise has been commenced there. Ichang is well
known, and every year foreigners visit it in increasing numbers
intent on seeing the famous gorges which lie immediately
beyond. It is easily reached from Shanghai and from Peking.
From Shanghai palatially fitted and specially designed steamers
leave every night for Hankow, 600 miles up the Yangtsze.
From Peking and Hankow a good express train runs to and
fro weekly. Between Hankow and Ichang a regular fleet of
steamers keep up constant communication. Ascending the
river by steamer from Hankow the hilly country commences

about 40 miles below Ichang. At first low, the hills gradually
increase in height, and by the time Ichang is reached one is
fairly among the mountains. In the vicinity of the town the
hills are pyramidal in outline, with prominent cliffs near by ;
north, south, and west of the town the country is much cut up,
forming an archipelago of peaks 2000 to 4000 feet high,
the peaks themselves being offsets from spurs attaining altitudes of 7000 to 9000 feet, situated some days' distance beyond.
These pyramidal hills around Ichang are very interesting and
never fail to attract the attention of travellers. They are
made up of a substratum of pebbly conglomerate, on which are
reared thin, horizontally deposed strata of marine limestone,
red shale and sandstone, over-capped with sandy clays. The
strata are piled with great regularity, and when erosion is
equal on all sides the characteristic pyramidal shape is produced and maintained. This formation is general from the
edge of the great plain to Ichang, and occasionally it contains
thin beds of coal. It is of comparatively recent age, dating
back to Permo-Mesozoic times. The dominant fossils it
contains are Cycads, and the youngest rocks probably belong
to the Oölitic series. The cliffs and bold peaks to the north,
south, and west of Ichang are made up principally of Paleozoic
limestones, with a little shale and sandstone, the latter of the
Mesozoic period. The strata are folded in apparent conformity
and are without notable metamorphism. In eastern Szechuan
these rocks extend beneath the Red Basin. The Yangtsze
has forced itself right through them and formed a series of
mighty chasms in which the structure of the various forma-
tions is beautifully exhibited.

In the neighbourhood of Hwangling Miao (30 miles west of
Ichang), and westwards for 10 miles to the Tungling Rapid,
granitic gneiss is exposed. These are the oldest rocks in this
region and the only Pre-Cambrian formation known *in situ* in
the Middle Yangtsze. This section of the river is called the
Ta-shih Ho (River of Dregs and Boulders), and well does it
deserve this appellation.

The next oldest rocks of importance are those forming the
cliffs opposite Nanto, in the Niukan Gorge and in the eastern
half of the Wushan Gorge. This is a massive formation 4000 to

5000 feet thick, in the major part composed of dark grey or liver-coloured limestone free from chert and containing both Cambrian and Ordovician fossils. It is, in fact, a great marine limestone in all its phases. It weathers into wonderful escarpments, often sheer for 1000 to 2000 feet, with slightly projecting summits, and is frequently many miles in extent. The cliffs on the right bank of the river opposite Nanto, which extend nearly to Hwangling Miao, are typical examples. At one of the major rapids during the low-water season, known as the Hsintan, some 45 miles west of Ichang, a bed of shale is beautifully exposed. This bed is some 1800 feet thick, and composed principally of olive-green argillite, with local black shale and quartzite. It is of the Middle Palaeozoic age.

Resting apparently conformably on this series of shale is a vast deposit of Upper Carboniferous limestone 4000 or more feet thick. This is the characteristic formation throughout the Ichang and Mitan Gorges ; it occurs also throughout the western end of the Wushan Gorge and in the Kui Fu (Wind-box) Gorge beyond. The prevailing rock is dark grey or blackish limestone, full of marine fossils and with occasional thin layers of anthracite coal. This also weathers into wonderful escarpments, but commonly they are boldly rounded with less linear dimensions. This formation is the most general throughout western Hupeh, on both sides of the river, though greater on the north than on the south, where the Cambrian-Ordovician formation preponderates. Next in succession come the Permo-Mesozoic beds of red shale and sandstone, with thin layers of marine limestone and coal, which were described in reference to Ichang. These beds are characteristic of the country west of the Mitan Gorge, as far as the entrance to the Wushan Gorge, principally on the left bank. Coal occurs in this stretch in many places, more especially around Patung Hsien. Glacial deposits and signs of glacial action are in evidence in many parts of western Hupeh, though nowhere on a large scale. The most accessible of these is on the Yangtsze itself, opposite Nanto, a hamlet situated on the extreme western end of the Ichang Gorge and some 20 miles above Ichang city. At this point can be seen a glacial deposit about 120 feet thick, overlaid by marine limestone of the Cambrian-Ordovician age referred to above. All the evidences of ice action are well disclosed, and the whole deposit is most instructively exhibited. Since the deposition of these various systems great regional disturbances have taken place and the strata has commonly been bent up from a great depth. The summits of the very highest peaks in western Hupeh are usually comprised of Silurian (? Devonian) shales.

None of the useful or precious minerals occurs in quantity in western Hupeh. Coal is scattered through the entire region, but is nowhere found in abundance and the quality is indifferent. Iron ore is worked in places and in one or two localities the quality is good, but usually it is poor. Copper occurs in two districts (Chienshih and Hsingshan) but is not worked to any great extent. Salt, so abundant throughout the Red Basin of Szechuan, does not occur. The sandy clays and marls are used in brick and tile making, and lime is burnt in several places and used for building purposes. Both the clays and the limestone here mentioned belong to the Permo-Mesozoic beds. The carboniferous limestones are quarried and used for various construction works.

In the Gorges the main stream is joined by numerous lateral branches which flow through glens of wondrous beauty. These streams, winding their way through, usually fill nearly the entire bed of the glen and are bounded by walls of cliff 300 to 1000 feet sheer. Waterfalls are numerous and wherever it is possible vegetation is rampant. The tops of the cliffs are worn into curious and grotesque shapes. Caves abound and in these stalactites and stalagmites occur. Subterranean springs are common and many of the small rivers originate from such sources. They issue forth from some cave, or from the face of a cliff, or well up through level rocks. The Hsingshan River is an example of this mode of origin. The Chinese attach much legendary lore to all these caves and subterranean springs, and frequently associate fine temples with such spots.

In the vicinity of the Yangtsze the more commanding peaks and crags are crowned by temples, usually belonging to the Taouist cult. Commonly these temples cap seemingly inaccessible points, and one marvels how the material used in erecting them was transported thither. Whenever possible a few trees, usually *Xylosma racemosum*, var. *pubescens* (Wintergreen), Gleditsia, Cypress, Ginkgo, and Pine are planted near the temples and add much to the beauty of the scene. Such temples are well built, but unfortunately, since the interior is usually dark, filthy, and uninviting, a close inspection robs them of most of their charm. From the distance they look most picturesque, the style of architecture being in harmony with the surroundings, and one admires very much the taste and culture which called them into existence. The preservation of the " Good Luck " of towns, villages, and communities by the warding off of evil influences is a matter of great moment in China, and with this good work the temples are associated. The pagodas, found all over China, have been erected solely with this end in view. Geomancy enters very largely into Taouism and holds a most important place in Chinese thought, and, in fact, governs many of their actions. As illustrating this we will take an example at Ichang. Facing the town, on the right bank of the river opposite, is a pyramidal hill nearly 600 feet high, called by foreigners the " Pyramid." This hill was supposed to exert a baneful influence over the town, and was held responsible for the town's poverty in local *literati*. Not until a temple was built on an eminence behind the town, sufficiently high to enable it to overlook the Pyramid, was this evil influence counteracted, and the Goddess of Good Luck induced to smile on the town. The very year this temple was completed a student passed the provincial examinations with high honours. Was not this the beneficial result of the building ? The temple, called Tungshantzu, is richly endowed and forms a strikingly conspicuous object from all points of approach. The logic of " Fung Shui," as this cult is called, is beyond the grasp of the average Occidental brain, but of its effect on the Chinese mind one is constantly made familiar.

Too wild and savage for extensive agricultural development, and with a marked absence of useful mineral deposits, western Hupeh is one of the poorest, most sparsely populated, and least known parts of China. For these same reasons it is of particular interest to the botanist, since the vegetation there has been less molested than is usually found to be the case in China generally. Even here, it is hardly necessary to say, every available bit of land either is, or has been, under cultivation, but much of the country is of such a nature as to preclude agricultural development, even under Chinese patience and ingenuity.

Up to 3000 or 4000 feet, wherever it is possible, the mountain-slopes, hill-tops, and valleys are cultivated, but the country is made up so much of sheer cliff and crag, and is generally of such a rocky character, that even where cultivation is possible the crop won from the soil is poor and scarcely recompenses for the outlay of labour involved in its production. Above 6000 feet the higher slopes and mountains defy even Chinese skill and patience, and it is here that patches of virgin forest and much woodland remain. The higher mountains are rich in various Chinese medicines, and men eke out a livelihood in gathering them. Considerable areas in this higher country were formerly cleared and crops of the Irish potato raised. But some twenty odd years ago the potato disease attacked and devastated the crops, and ruined the peasants, who were forced to migrate to lower and more congenial altitudes. Ruined houses and numerous graves, overgrown with coarse herbs, brambles, and shrubs, tell of former habitation ; but to-day, in the higher parts of this region, it is possible to walk from morning till night without seeing an inhabited dwelling or a living person. Wherever the valleys admit of sufficient cultivation to support them, small riverine villages occur. Tiny hamlets, farmhouses, and peasants' huts are frequent up to 4500 feet altitude. Above this little agriculture is attempted and the population is exceedingly sparse.

I have travelled pretty extensively in the back-blocks of China during my eleven years' acquaintance with the country, and consider north-western Hupeh the most difficult part of China to explore, the Chino-Thibetan borderland not excepted. The absence of food-supplies and accommodation for coolies, the lack of roads, and the difficult nature of the country in general, render travel in this region exceedingly arduous.

As an Appendix to this chapter, it may be of interest to give an account of the flora obtaining in the vicinity of Ichang, which, from the amount of collecting that has been done in its neighbourhood, holds a classic place in the annals of botanical exploration work in China.

APPENDIX

The Flora of Ichang

The Flora of Ichang and the neighbourhood up to 2000 feet altitude, as included in this note, is essentially of a warm temperate character, and includes not a few sub-tropical forms. Nevertheless, we find also a number of cool temperate plants, and what really obtains is a fusion of these three floras, with the warm temperate element in the ascendancy. The following characteristic plants will serve to illustrate the point : *Aleurites Fordii, Liquidambar formosana, Ligustrum lucidum, Cæsalpinia sepiaria, Toddalia asiatica, Wisteria sinensis, Rhododendron indicum, Pyracantha crenulata, Primula sinensis, Anemone japonica, Aspidistra punctata, Reinwardtia trigyna,* and *Woodwardia radicans.* The low hills around Ichang are very barren-looking, being mostly clad with " spear grass " (*Heteropogon contortus*), with a few shrubs and herbs here and there, and relieved by small woods of *Pinus Massoniana* and *Cupressus funebris*, with occasional groves of the common Bamboo, *Phyllostachys pubescens.*

However, it is not to these low hills that we look for the floral wealth of Ichang, but to the limestone cliffs of the glens and gorges. Here the variety is astonishing, a striking feature being the quantity of well-known flowering shrubs.

The two first shrubs to flower in the early spring are *Daphne genkwa* and *Coriaria nepalensis.* It is a thousand pities we cannot succeed with the Daphne in England, since it is such a lovely plant—by far the finest species of the genus. Here, at Ichang, it grows everywhere, on the bare exposed hills, amongst conglomerate rock and limestone boulders, on graves, and amongst the stones which are piled around the tiny cultivated plats in the gorge, sometimes in partial shade, but more usually fully exposed to the scorching sun. The plants are, on the average, about 2 feet in height, and are but seldom branched. Imagine the annual suckers from a Plum tree, and you have the appearance of these Daphne plants.

For two-thirds of their height they are so densely clad with flowers that they look like one large thyrse. The colour is lilac, often very dark ; but a white form is not uncommon. Its outward resemblance to Lilac leads to its being so called by the foreign residents at Ichang.

The Coriaria is not so well known and is not nearly so attractive. Its flowers are polygamous, and the plant when in fruit is rather showy. The Chinese consider its foliage and stem poisonous to cattle.

Wisteria sinensis is abundant, often scaling high trees, but the semi-bush form is the more common. Its flowers are borne in great abundance, and vary much in shade of colour, the white form being, however, rather rare.

Another well-known shrub which abounds here is *Loropetalum chinense*. On the tops of the cliffs, amongst loose conglomerate and limestone boulders, it forms a well-nigh impenetrable scrub. The bushes are seldom more than 3 feet in height, very much branched, and when in full flower look like patches of snow at a distance. Messrs. Veitch grow the plant very well, but there is an enormous gulf between the best grown pot plants and the plants in a state of nature. In Devon and Cornwall, if planted in a rockery, it ought to thrive.

Rose bushes abound everywhere, and in April perhaps afford the greatest show of any one kind of flower. *Rosa lævigata* and *R. microcarpa* are more common in fully exposed places. *Rosa multiflora*, *R. moschata*, and *R. Banksiæ* are particularly abundant on the cliffs and crags of the glens and gorges, though by no means confined thereto. The Musk and Banksian Roses often scale tall trees, and a tree thus festooned with their branches laden with flowers is a sight to be remembered. To walk through a glen in the early morning or after a slight shower, when the air is laden with the soft delicious perfume from myriads of Rose flowers, is truly a walk through an earthly paradise.

In March and April *Sophora viciifolia* is very fine in the glens and gorges when it is covered with masses of bluish white flowers. This plant has a very wide distribution. It is common in Yunnan, and in the warm valleys of rivers bordering Thibet. The Ichang plant is much less spiny than that of Yunnan and western Szechuan. Possibly the latter is really the Indian *S. Moorcroftianum*.

Two very common plants on the cliffs in the glens are *Eriobotrya japonica* (Loquat) and *Meratia præcox*. Both flower about Christmas. These are two out of many plants which formerly were erroneously supposed to be natives of Japan.

Among conglomerate boulders *Caryopteris incana* is common, but is not nearly so fine as it is farther west. *Pyracantha crenulata* and *Vitex Negundo* are exceedingly common, and so also is *Cæsalpinia sepiaria*. This thorny shrub is semi-scandent in habit, and very like the better known *C. japonica*. Its handsome foliage and erect thyrsoid racemes of bright yellow flowers make it a very conspicuous object.

Symplocos cratægoides, with its pretty white flowers and bright blue fruits, is abundant. This is a useful and charming shrub, and deserves to be better known. *Deutzia Schneideriana, Lagerstrœmia indica, Rhododendron indicum, Jasminum floridum, Nandina domestica, Ilex cornuta, Viburnum utile*, and *Buddleia officinalis* are all extremely common shrubs. Of other well or lesser known shrubs which are common, I may mention—

Abelia chinensis, A. parvifolia, Rhus Cotinus, Buddleia asiatica, Ilex pedunculata, I. corallina, Deutzia discolor, Desmodium floribundum, Elæagnus pungens, E. glabra, Spiræa chinensis, Eurya japonica, Hypericum chinense, Hydrangea strigosa, Berchemia lineata, Evonymus alata, Polygala Mariesii, Viburnum brachyboiryum, V. propinquum, Thea cuspidata, Rubus parvifolius, and many other species. *Chaenomeles sinensis* with red, and *C. cathayensis* with white or blush-white flowers, are commonly cultivated. Lengthy as is the list, I am not justified in omitting *Itea ilicifolia*. This Holly-like shrub, with long, pendent racemes of white flowers, is one of the handsomest of all the Ichang shrubs. Of fluviatile shrubs, the commonest are *Distylium chinense, Salix variegata, Ficus impressa, Rhamnus davuricus, Adina globiflora, Myricaria germanica*, and a curious Box (*Buxus stenophylla*). Climbers are very much in evidence, and include such beautiful plants as *Lonicera japonica, Trachelospermum jasminoides, Pucraria Thunbergiana, Clematis Henryi, C. Benthamiana, C. Armandi, C. uncinata, Vitis flexuosa, Parthenocissus Henryana, P. Thomsonii*, and *Mucuna sempervirens*

This last is a rather remarkable plant. Two miles above
Ichang, on the right bank, is an enormous specimen, called by
foreigners the "Big Creeper." It covers several hundred
square feet of ground, climbing over several Pine trees and
many Bamboos. The base of the main trunk is almost as thick
as a man's body ; the flowers are dark chocolate coloured, and
are borne in racemes on the old wood ; the legumes are 2 to 2½
feet in length, and contain many large black bean-like seeds.
It flowers in May.

Ichang does not possess a great number of trees, but the
variety is really astonishing. *Paulownia Duclouxii* and *Melia
Azedarach*, with their enormous panicles of flowers, are very
striking in the spring. In the autumn, *Sapium sebiferum*, with
its wonderful autumnal tints, stands alone. In winter the evergreen *Ligustrum lucidum*, and *Xylosma racemosum*, var. *pubescens*, are very conspicuous. The latter nearly always shelters
some wayside shrine. Perhaps the commonest trees are—

*Gleditsia sinensis, Rhus javanica, Platycarya strobilacea,
Quercus serrata, Cedrela sinensis*, and *Pterocarya stenoptera*.
The Mistletoe occurs on the last-named tree. Other less common
trees are *Sterculia platanifolia, Populus Silvestrii, Cratægus
hupehensis, Celtis sinensis, Dalbergia hupeana, Acer oblongum,
Cunninghamia lanceolata, Ailanthus glandulosa, Broussonetia
papyrifera, Ulmus parvifolia, Hovenia dulcis, Sapindus mukorossi, Salix babylonica*, and *Sophora japonica*. Of this latter a
curious form occurs in which the leaves and young shoots are
clothed with a dense white velvety indumentum.

As with flowering shrubs, so with herbs, though in a less
degree, Ichang is the home of many favourite garden plants.
One of the commonest and best known is *Primula obconica*.
This charming herb abounds everywhere, but more especially
in moist, grassy places on the banks of the Yangtsze and in the
glens. Occasionally, under very favourable conditions, in
height, size of flower, and luxuriance of foliage, it approaches
the cultivated form, but more usually it is a dwarf and
almost insignificant weed.

Again, Ichang is the home of the Chinese Primrose, and
the type of the cultivated Chrysanthemum occurs there also.
Other favourites which are common are—

Corydalis thalictrifolia, Anemone japonica, Sedum sarmentosum, Saxifraga sarmentosa, Iris japonica, Reinwardtia trigyna, Lycoris aurea, L. radiata, Rehmannia angulata, Hemerocallis fulva, and *H. flava*. Other characteristic herbs are : *Adenophora polymorpha, Bletia hyacinthina, Asarum maximum, Ophiorrhiza cantonensis, Viola Patrinii, Delphinium chinense, Lysimachia Henryi, L. clethroides, Potentilla chinensis, P. discolor, Fragaria indica, Thalictrum minus, Mazus pulchellus, Verbena officinalis, Platycodon grandiflorum*, and many *Compositæ, Leguminosæ*, and *Umbelliferæ*.

Perhaps Ichang is best known to horticulturalists generally as the home of the lovely *Lilium Henryi*. This acknowledged favourite occurs on the limestone and conglomerate rocks, but is now by no means common. *Lilium Brownii* and its varieties, *chloraster* and *leucanthum*, are fairly common ; *L. concolor* occurs, but is rare.

Ferns are not rich in species, but *Woodwardia radicans, Osmunda regalis, Pteris longifolia, P. serrulata, Nephrodium molle, Cheilanthes patula*, and *Gleichenia linearis* are very abundant. A variety of *Adiantum Capillus-Veneris* is very common on stalagmitic limestone in the glen. Pieces of these rocks covered with Ferns are detached and find their way all over China, being popularly known as " Ichang Fern-stones."

A hasty reference to the common floating plants of the ponds and ditches around Ichang must bring this note to a close. *Euryale ferox*, with its handsome foliage, is very common ; *Nelumbium speciosum* is, of course, cultivated. Other common aquatics are—*Limnanthemum nymphoides, Jussiæa repens, Salvinia natans, Trapa natans, Azolla filiculoides, Marsilea quadrifolia, Monochoria vaginalis, Eriocaulon Buergerianum*, and several species of Potamogeton and Utricularia. In late autumn, when the Azolla changes to a rich crimson tint, the ponds look very fine. In some rice fields near Ichang Dr. Henry found a very anomalous plant. It was made the type of a new genus—*Trapella sinensis*, and doubtfully referred to the natural order *Pedalineæ*.

CHAPTER III

METHODS OF TRAVEL

Roads and Accommodation

THE advent of steam navigation on the upper-middle Yangtsze has brought Chungking, the commercial metropolis of Western China, three weeks nearer the coast and occidental civilization. This is a very considerable gain to the would-be traveller in these regions, yet it only postpones for a little time longer the inevitable. Sooner or later the traveller must dispense with the comforts and luxuries of modern occidental methods of travel and adapt himself to those more primitive and decidedly less comfortable of the Oriental. In the regions with which we deal there is nothing in the nature of wheeled vehicular traffic save only the rude wheel-barrows in use on the Chengtu Plain. There are no mule caravans, and scarcely a riding pony is to be found. For overland travel there is the native sedan-chair and one's own legs; for river-travel the native boat. Patience, tact, and abundance of time are necessary, and the would-be traveller lacking any of these essentials should seek lands where less primitive methods obtain. Endowed with the virtues mentioned, and having unlimited time at his disposal, he may travel anywhere and everywhere in China in safety, with considerable pleasure and abundant profit in knowledge. With her industrious toiling millions, her old, old civilization, her enormous natural wealth and wondrous scenery, China alternately charms and fascinates, irritates and plunges into despair, all who sojourn long within her borders. No country, outside Europe and North America, is of such perennial interest to the world at large as China. Ever-changing yet ever the same, she is the link which connects the twentieth century with the dawn of civilization, epochs before the Christian era. To travel leisurely through this vast country is an education which leaves an indelible impress on all fortunate enough to have had the experience. The Chinese do not see time from the Westerner's view-point, and for the traveller in the interior parts of China the first, last, and most important thing of all is to ever bear this in mind.

The majority of travellers still ascend the river above Ichang in native boats, and it will probably be a long time before a regular fleet of steamers ply these dangerous waters and render the native boat obsolete. The journey from Ichang to Chungking and beyond has been described so often that the subject is threadbare, and I have no intention of describing it over again. Volumes have been written on this subject, and some day perhaps a writer will arise and do full justice to the theme.

I have made the journey up and down many times, and on each occasion have been more and more impressed with the sublime beauty of the Gorges. The scenery in these savage chasms is all and more than any writer has described it as being. It must be seen to be fully understood and appreciated. The more often one travels up and down this stretch of the river the deeper grows one's awe and respect for the many rapids, swift currents, and innumerable difficulties which impede navigation.

The native boats are perfectly fitted for the navigation of these difficult waters ; they are the outcome of generations of experience, and the balance-rudder and turret-build have been used in these craft long before their adoption by Western nations. The men, too, who earn their livelihood in navigating these boats, understand their business thoroughly. Much has been written by hasty travellers on the shortcomings and incompetence of these men, that is as unwarrantable as it is undeserved. These Chinese boatmen are careful, absolutely competent and thorough masters of their craft, and the more one sees of them and their work the more one's admiration grows. Oriental methods are not occidental methods, but they succeed just the same ! When on the boat the Westerner will do well to adapt himself to Eastern methods ; any attempt to

enforce those of the West generally ends in disaster. Many
accidents on the Yangtsze have been caused through the
foreigner, ignorant of local conditions, difficulties and dangers,
forcing the captain of the boat to proceed against his better
judgment. The traveller is advised when engaging a boat to
do so through a responsible Chinese business house, to have an
agreement drawn up setting forth the arrangements desired,
and then to leave the boat-master to carry out his engagement
in his own way. This is the only way to ensure safety, and on
paper no one would attempt to gainsay it, yet in practice this
is commonly done, but always to the jeopardy of the trans-
gressor.

Since we shall have much to say on the subject of overland travel a word or two anent roads seems fitting and
desirable. To the uninitiated this subject may seem trivial,
but to the experienced it is otherwise. Chinese roads make a
lasting impression on all who travel over them, and the vocabu-
lary of the average traveller is not rich enough to thoroughly
relieve the mind in this matter. The roads are of two kinds,
paved and unpaved. I have yet to meet the traveller whose
mind is thoroughly made up as to which of these is worse and
the more difficult to negotiate. A clever writer once wrote :
" An Imperial highway in China is not one which is kept in
order *by* the Emperor, but rather one which may have to be
put in order *for* the Emperor." [1] When any important official
takes up duties in a distant part of the empire the local officials
put the roads over which he has to travel in some semblance of
repair. Such work is always hastily done by labour forced and
grudgingly given, and in mountainous districts the first severe
rainstorm destroys considerable portions of it.

It is nobody's real business to look after the roads, and
nobody does. The land devoted to roadways is commandeered, and in agricultural districts the farmer takes
good care to keep these roads down to a minimum width. It
usually happens that the roadways get narrower and narrower
every year, until the advent of some important official forces
the local authorities into having them repaired and restored
to their original width. Roads in China owe their origin to

[1] Arthur H. Smith, *Village Life in China*, p. 35.

the same causes that obtain elsewhere in the world, namely, military conquest and commercial interchange between distant localities.

Throughout the length and breadth of China run imperial highways, few in number, it is true, but of vast importance, since they connect the imperial capital with the capitals of the provinces. These were made for military purposes in early times, when the Emperors were busy conquering the country and extending their territories. They are all of great strategical importance, and were originally paved throughout with huge blocks of stone. Often, indeed, they were actually blasted and excavated from solid rock. They vary in width according to the configuration of the country and the nature of the traffic they have to carry. In the northern parts overland travel is commonly done by cart, and the roads are adapted to such traffic. In the parts with which we are concerned the country is too wild and rugged for wheels, and the only recognized mode of travelling is by means of sedan-chair. The imperial roads were originally made sufficiently wide to enable two chairs to pass one another freely. Ten to twelve feet is a broad highway in these parts, and it must be conceded that roads of such width amply serve their purpose. Unfortunately this width is rarely maintained for any considerable distance. The grading of these ancient highways was well done, and the whole work speaks volumes for the ability and energy of those old-time engineers. Like much else in China these roads were once magnificent, but to-day they are far from this. In general they are sadly neglected. Floods have destroyed them here and there, often the paving blocks have been stolen for house-building and other purposes, and gaps of unpaved, muddy stretches, almost impassable in rainy weather, occur all too frequently. Sufficient of the original road remains to stir admiration for the skill and foresight of the engineers, long since dead, and to set the traveller longing for those halcyon days of old.

In the prosperous parts of China, highways connect all the principal cities, town, and villages. These are usually 8 to 10 feet wide, and though originally paved throughout, are now in a state of more or less disrepair. Nearly all the towns and villages in Western China are situated on the banks of streams for the simple reason that the valleys offered lines of least resistance. Even when the streams are not navigable they afford easier means of access to the interior than the mountains and forest-clad country. In a general way all the older roads in China follow the courses of streams as closely as possible, leaving them only when the nature of the country necessitates the departure, and watersheds intervene.

Bypaths and narrow tracks permeate the country in every direction, and abound even in the most sparsely populated mountainous regions. Some one has very wisely made out that the exchange of salt was the first commerce engaged in by mankind at large. Salt is, and long has been, a Government monopoly in China, consequently the practice of salt-smuggling has gone on from time immemorial, and the majority of the mountain-paths were very probably first struck out by smugglers of salt. Indeed, many important trade-routes to-day, in China, presumably originated in this way. The province of Szechuan is abundantly rich in salt and also in mountain-paths. From a lengthy study I have come to regard this network of bypaths as the result of salt traffic, and more especially illicit traffic. There are to-day many such paths throughout the Hupeh-Szechuan boundary, used for practically no other traffic than that of salt, and by these paths salt still reaches certain districts in defiance of the law. Very useful, if difficult, the traveller finds these bypaths, for without them it would be impossible to traverse some of the wildest and most interesting parts of central and Western China.

When travelling overland in China it is not possible to use tents, and one has perforce to make use of such accommodation as the country affords. The Chinese do not understand tents, and it is unwise to try innovations in a land where the people are unduly inquisitive. The traveller gets along best when he avoids publicity as much as possible. On all the main roads there are inns of sorts, usually very filthy, and in season abounding in mosquitoes, creeping things, and stinks, the latter, in fact, being always in evidence. On the byways, and more especially in the mountains, accommodation is hard to find and is of the meanest description. However, one is usually tired, and any shelter suffices for a night's halt. In wet weather, or when held up through flooded torrents or what not, the absence of proper accommodation is acutely felt. In the wilds of China one hungers for the dâk bungalows of India and Ceylon, or accommodation on similar lines.

A traveller in China should have with him an outfit, comprising bed, bedding, victuals, cooking paraphernalia, and *insect-powder*. It sounds rather forbidding on paper, but labour is cheap, and a little experience enables one to keep the size of outfit within reasonable limits. The necessary coolies should always be obtained through a respectable agency and an agreement made in writing, stating all necessary details. A head-man, called a " Fu-tou," should be given charge of the coolies.

In parts of China where foreigners are well known, it is possible to dispense with the luxury of a sedan-chair, but it must be remembered that a sedan-chair is an outward and visible sign of respectability. It is the recognized medium of travel, and, quite apart from its real use, it is a necessity, since its presence ensures respect. In the out-of-the-way parts of China, even though it is carried piecemeal, a chair is of greater service and value to the traveller than a passport. According to treaty, all foreigners travelling in China must furnish themselves with a passport, which must be shown on request. This is a matter of considerable importance, and should never be omitted.

One thing more is necessary ere the caravan is fully equipped, and that is a good cook. Unless the traveller speaks Chinese he must have a servant able to speak broken English. A good travelling servant is hard to find, but the last thing the average traveller should dream of doing is to engage an interpreter. A good domestic servant will fill this function in so far as it is necessary.

CHAPTER IV

IN QUEST OF FLOWERS

A Journey in North-Western Hupeh

ON 4th June 1910 I left Ichang for Chengtu, via a new route through the wilds of north-west Hupeh. With 600 miles of overland travel ahead the caravan had been fitted up with all the skill at my command, and with enthusiasm to spur us on I felt that the difficulties would not prove insurmountable. Nearly all the men had been associated with me on former journeys of a similar nature.

We took the lesser road by way of San-yu-tung glen for Hsingshan Hsien, in consequence of the main road being congested by coolies engaged in blazing a trail for the Hankow-Szechuan Railway. The caravan consisted of twenty carrying-coolies, several men for collecting and general work *en route*, a chair for the Boy, and another for myself. My own start was not propitious. I was riding in my chair and had scarcely cleared the precincts of the foreign settlement when one of the poles snapped. This occasioned an hour's delay, but happening where it did new poles were secured without difficulty. It is never easy to make an early start the first day, and it is always advisable to count on a short stage. It was one o'clock when we reached the mouth of the San-yu-tung glen, 5 miles above Ichang, and overtook the main caravan. The weather was hot, and we only did another 15 li[1] to Sha-lao-che, making 35 li in all. This little hamlet consists of a few scattered houses, and we availed ourselves of the largest, which happened to be a wine-distillery, and the smell of stale brewing was very strong.

The journey up the San-yu-tung glen was very interesting,

---

[1] Ten li=three English miles.

much of the scenery being rugged and grand. The cliffs of hard limestone are usually 500 feet or more sheer, and are the home of Goral and other animals, and also of many cliff-loving plants. In the crevices and niches the Chinese Primrose (*Primula sinensis*) finds its home, but the flowers were past and the flower-stems all bent towards the cliffs to ensure the seeds being deposited in the rock crevices. This plant is the parent of our greenhouse Primulas, and in February and early March the cliffs present a wonderful picture, being covered with colonies of plants, one mass of warm mauve-pink flowers. Wherever the cliffs are not absolutely sheer, vegetation is rampant. Pine trees (*Pinus Massoniana*) fringe the summits and *Rosa microcarpa* was in full flower, otherwise there was very little blossom to be seen. Most of the shrubs being spring-flowering were in young fruit.

There was considerable delay in starting the next morning. One or two of the coolies gave up, and others had to be found. The road was vile all day, and it took us 10½ hours to cover 45 li. For the first 10 li the road continues to ascend the glen, which narrows and presents even finer scenery than that of yesterday. We passed a lovely natural grotto full of stalagmites inside, and with the dripping external rocks one mass of Maiden-hair Fern. These rocks are known throughout the Lower Yangtsze Valley as " Ichang Fern-stones," and command a ready sale.

In the glen *Parthenocissus Henryana* is abundant ; in the juvenile stage the leaves of this plant have prominent white veins, and are very attractive, but in the adult stage this variegation is lost, and they become very ordinary by comparison.

The glen soon became impassable, and we climbed the cliffs and ultimately overlooked the country generally. Terraced fields are much in evidence, and every available inch of country is under cultivation. Wheat, barley, and peas, all ripe, were the principal crops, and their yellow culms enlivened the landscape. We saw a small patch or two of the Opium Poppy hidden away under trees and of very poor quality. Pear and Plum trees are commonly cultivated hereabouts, Bamboo groves and Cypress trees abound. Here and there we caught an occasional glimpse of the white-tailed Paradise Fly-catcher (*Tchitrea incei*).   Pheasants were calling, and likewise the English Cuckoo.

Around Niu Ping (Cow-flat), which was our destination for the day, much rice is cultivated, and the farmers were busy transplanting the tiny rice-plants.   The whole country is finely terraced and is backed by limestone cliffs of Cambrian-Ordovician Age.   Near our destination we passed a fine Ginkgo tree showing curious root-like protuberances on the branches. In rocky places by the wayside, and especially in the walls of the terraced fields, *Rehmannia angulata* abounds.   Plants $1\frac{1}{2}$ to 2 feet high carry six to a dozen large, rosy-pink, foxglove-like flowers.   The local name is " Fêng-tang Hwa " (Honey-bee Flower).

" Cow-flat " is a tiny place of about a dozen houses.   Our quarters were cramped but comfortable, and the people very nice.   There is a road from this hamlet to Nanto, distant 30 li.   When I first visited this place in 1901 I was an object of great curiosity from the moment of my arrival to the time of departure.   I have been here several times since and am now treated as an old-time acquaintance.

It was quite cool during the night, and a blanket was required.   At Ichang the very thought of a blanket was enough to bring forth perspiration !   We left about 6 a.m., and after ascending and descending a series of lateral spurs finally reached the small river which enters the Yangtsze at Nanto. After ascending this river for a few miles we commenced a steep ascent.   Now by an easy and then by a heavy grade the road winds in and out among the mountains, and we did not reach our halting-place for the night until 6.30 p.m.   The last coolie arrived an hour later.   The length of the whole journey is supposed to be only 60 li, but we all agreed that it is a good 70. Whatever the distance, it is certainly a hard day's travel.

The mountain sides are very steep, with razor-like ridges. Terraced cultivation is everywhere carried out, rice is cultivated in the bottom-lands and maize on the slopes, with occasional patches of Irish potato.   Where it is too steep, or for other reasons unsuitable for cultivation, the mountain-sides are covered with shrubs and trees, chiefly scrub Oak and the common Pine. Small trees of *Cornus Wilsoniana* in full flower were common here and there. Odd trees of *C. kousa*, also, in full flower, were conspicuous in the outskirts of the woods and copses. This small tree is exceedingly floriferous. In habit it is flat-topped with horizontally-spreading branches, and the flowers borne erect, well above the foliage. The white bracts, which are so conspicuous, frequently exceed 5 inches in diameter ; with age they become tinged with pink. The fruit is large, orange-red, and edible. This Chinese form will probably prove a better plant under cultivation than the Japanese form with which gardeners are familiar. The plant loves a sunny, well-drained situation. But the display of the day was made by the wild Roses. By the side of streams the Rambler Rose (*Rosa multiflora*), with both white and pink flowers, was abundant. In the woods higher up the Musk Rose (*R. moschata*) filled the air with its soft fragrance. Here and there occurred *Actinidia chinensis*, scaling tall trees and wreathing them with white and buff-yellow fragrant flowers. In the forenoon noted *Rehmannia angulata*, especially common on steep stony places in full sun.

Our halting-place, Lao-mu-chia, is about 3500 feet altitude, and consists of about six houses and a tile-factory. Hereabouts much charcoal is burnt for export to Nanto and down river. During the day's journey we met several men laden with bales of Pear and Crab-apple leaves. These leaves are commonly used as a substitute for tea, and there is a considerable export from these parts to Shasi.

On leaving Lao-mu-chia we immediately commenced the steep ascent of the Hsan-lung shan, and a climb of 1000 feet brought us to the summit, where there is a small temple in a ruinous condition. After a precipitous descent of a few hundred feet the road meanders over and among the tops of hills, composed of granitic-gneiss, which is rapidly disintegrating, and ultimately descends to the bed of a torrent and joins the main road from Ichang to Hsingshan Hsien.

Near the summit of Hsan-lung shan, which is composed of Cambrian-Ordovician limestones, the Chinese Tulip tree (*Liriodendron chinense*) is common in the woods, and so is *Viburnum tomentosum* with its sprays of snow-white flowers.

Styrax Hemsleyanum and *Amelanchier asiatica*, var. *sinica*, the
June berry, are other trees with white flowers remarkable for
their beauty and abundance of blossom. On the more open
slopes *Symplocos cratægoides*, *Lonicera Maackii*, var. *podocarpa*,
Diervilla japonica, and *Cratægus cuneata* made a fine display.
Thin woods of *Pinus Massoniana* and Sweet Chestnut (*Castanea*)
also occur ; the Pine trunks are gashed for the ultimate purpose
of producing kindling wood. In open places *Rubus corchorifolius* abounds, and its red, raspberry-like fruits with their
delicious vinous flavour were good eating. In the descent
Dipteronia sinensis, a small bushy tree with erect trusses of
small white flowers, occurs, and *Actinidia chinensis* is common.
The hermaphrodite and male forms of this climber have large
white flowers quickly changing to buff-yellow, and the fragrance
is very pleasing. A form with purely female flowers is unknown.
At the foot of the descent we joined the main road from Ichang
to Hsingshan Hsien, and following this route we reached
Shui-yueh-tsze, a village of 100 houses, situated in a tiny rice
flat, at five o'clock. The people were very inquisitive, and I
held an impromptu reception until bedtime.

On joining the main road, we saw evidences of the survey
for the Hankow-Szechuan Railway. The proposed route was
marked by bamboo poles, and on the rocks with Arabic
numerals and initials in Roman letters.. The route descends
a stream, just before reaching Shui-yueh-tsze, to Liang-ho-
kou, and then continues down the Hsingshan River to the
Yangtsze, which it connects with at Hsiang-che. Its construction even in this region promises to be a difficult task,
and will call for great ability on the part of the engineers.
Much tunnelling and blasting will be necessary, yet from
Hankow to this point the task is simple compared with that
which lies beyond. The cost will be enormous even in a
land of cheap labour. It is highly improbable that the gentry,
who are so violently opposed to the employment of foreign
capital in this venture, realize the magnitude of the task and
its ultimate cost.

The next day's journey proved interesting but arduous.
By an undulating path we reached the top of the ridge, which is
known as T'an-shu-ya (Lime tree Pass), from a gigantic Linden

which occurs there. This tree (*Tilia Henryana*) is about 80 feet tall and 27 feet in girth, and though hollow appears to be in good health. The young leaves are silvery, and the tree, from its size, is a conspicuous object for miles around.

Descending through a cultivated area we entered a glen which we followed for 20 li : the scenery in the lower end is magnificent. Cliffs of hard limestone rear themselves almost perpendicularly some 2000 feet and more. In the upper part of the glen *Pterocarya hupehensis* is common alongside the burn. An odd tree or two of the rare *Pteroceltis Tatarinowii* also occurs here. Throughout the glen Lady Banks's rose (*Rosa Banksiæ*) is especially abundant. Bushes 10 to 20 feet high and more through them were one mass of fragrant white flowers. It occurs in thousands and is particularly happy, growing on rocks and over boulders by the side of streams. *Cæsalpinia sepiaria*, with erect thyrsoid panicles of fragrant yellow flowers, is also abundant hereabouts. Growing on the cliffs, *Illicium Henryi*, with its dull crimson flowers, is also worthy of note. On issuing from the glen we struck a shallow, rock-strewn stream of considerable width, and after ascending it for a short distance made a very precipitous ascent of a couple of thousand feet. Crossing over a ridge and a flat area, a descending road led to Shih-tsao-che, which we reached as night was closing in. This hamlet consists of about a dozen houses scattered through a narrow valley.

During the day I collected specimens of thirty different kinds of woody plants. The striking plants of the afternoon's journey were the Amelanchier and *Dipelta floribunda*, both masses of flower. Walnut (*Juglans regia*) and Varnish trees are abundant above 3000 feet ; the sides and tops of the mountains are clothed with woods of Oak and Pine, particularly the former. We also saw many fine Willow and Ailanthus trees. *Primula obconica*, *Lysimachia crispidens*, and a blue-flowered Salvia are abundant up to 2000 feet. Near the inn a few trees of *Catalpa Fargesii* occur, but were not yet in flower. Hereabouts *Daphne genkwa* is abundant, but it was scarcely in flower at this altitude.

It rained a little in the early morning and showers fell at intervals during the day, nevertheless, the weather was good for travelling, since it was not too hot. Most of the journey was downhill. Soon after starting in the morning we crossed one or two low ridges, intercepted by narrow plateaux, and about noon commenced the descent to Hsingshan Hsien. The descent is precipitous in parts, but the mountain-sides are mostly under cultivation. About half-way down coal is mined, but the quality appears to be indifferent. Lime is burnt in small quantities and paper-mills occur near Hsing-shan.

Hsingshan, the only district city in these wilds, may claim to be one of the smallest and poorest Hsiens (*i.e.* cities of the fourth class) in the whole of China. It is situated on the left bank of a stream and contains scarcely a hundred houses, most of which are in a ruinous state. The wall facing the river varies from 4 to 12 feet in height. A road, apparently the main road, runs along the top of this wall. The east gate is closed by sewage ; the north gate is so low that one has to bend the head when passing through ! The whole town is dull and lifeless, as far as business is concerned, but children are plentiful, as they are everywhere else in China. The town is backed by a steep mountain, up two sides of which a wall is carried : most of the mountain-side enclosed within the wall is given over to terraced fields. The river is broad, with a shingly bottom, and the water clear and limpid. Thick-bottomed boats ply between Hsiang-t'an and Hsiang-che, a village at the head of the Mitan Gorge, on the Yangtsze. No one stays in Hsingshan, and we journeyed on to Hsiang-t'an. This name signifies " fragrant rapid " : the waters may perhaps be sweet, but the village is foul and stinking. We had some little difficulty in securing lodgings, poor as they were, and an objectionable coolie had to be evicted before we could settle down for the night.

Flowers were not common during the day. We passed a magnificent tree of *Keteleeria Davidiana*, 80 feet tall and 16 feet in girth. This tree shelters some graves, and was probably planted long ago. In the descent we passed through orchards of *Cratægus hupehensis*, all in full flower. This Hawthorn is one of several kinds cultivated in China for their edible fruit. The interesting *Torricellia angulata* occurs sparingly, and here and there large plants of *Mucuna sempervirens* cover large trees. *Catalpa ovata* is common on the plateaux and an interesting small-leaved Poplar occurs around farmhouses, but is rare.

Hsiang-t'an being in water communication with the Yang-tsze boasts quite a considerable trade. Medicines are the principal export. Rifle-stocks, roughly shaped out of Walnut wood, are exported from this neighbourhood to Hangyang in increasing quantities annually. They are worth locally 300 cash (about 6d.) each. The village is situated on the left bank of the river, and possesses an Opium Likin and a Viceroy's Bank. Pigs seem more in evidence than human beings, as judged from the four visits I have paid the place in different years. Being only 300 feet above Ichang, Hsiang-t'an enjoys a hot, dry climate.

Leaving Hsiang-t'an we immediately crossed the river by ferry and ascended a narrow valley, which soon becomes a ravine and finally a wild, entrancing gorge. At the head of this gorge we took a small mountain-path which entailed a severe climb from the river-bed to the tops of the surrounding mountains. In this ascent the Musk Rose was a wonderful sight, and *Loropetalum chinense* abundant but out of flower. Once on top of the mountains an undulating path leads to Peh-yang-tsai, where we found lodgings in a new and fairly clean farmhouse.

In the gorge I gathered *Rehmannia Henryi*, a herb less than 1 foot tall, with large, white, foxglove-like flowers. Here-abouts the root-bark of Lady Banks's rose is collected, and after being dried is pressed into bales for export to Shasi. This bark is used for dyeing and strengthening fish-nets, and it is claimed that it renders the net invisible to fish. In the valley *Kœlreuteria bipinnata* occurs, but is rare ; the flora of the ravine generally is similar to that of the San-yu-tung glen.

The mountains are clad with Oak (largely scrub), *Pinus Massoniana*, and Cypress. A few Keteleeria trees occur and also *Liquidambar formosana*. *Populus Silvestrii*, with its light grey bark, is a very common tree hereabouts. Wood Oil trees were a wonderful sight and most abundant. In the ravine they were in full leaf, and the fruits were swelling, but from 1500 feet to 3000 feet they were leafless and covered with flowers.

By the side of streams at low altitudes the Rambler Rose
(*Rosa multiflora*) was a pretty sight with its white and pink
blossoms, but the Musk Rose (*R. moschata*) was the flower of the
day—bushes 6 to 20 feet tall and more in diameter, nothing
but clusters of white fragrant flowers. Growing on some old
graves I found a sulphur-yellow flowered form of *Rosa Banksiæ*; this, I think, must have been planted. Rose bushes are a
special feature in this region and numerically are the commonest of shrubs. Around our lodgings the Hardy Rubber tree
(*Eucommia ulmoides*) is cultivated for its bark, which is
valued as a tonic medicine.

Peh-yang-tsai is a scattered hamlet, situated in a narrow
valley, some 2500 feet altitude. Facing our lodgings is a
massive peak called Wan-tiao shan, its face a sheer precipice
of hard limestone, the summit and farther slopes apparently
well forested. The people of this hamlet, like the country
people everywhere in these parts, were extremely nice and
obliging, and it was a real pleasure to be amongst them.

Wan-tiao shan looked too tempting to be passed by without
investigation, so we spent a day, and a very hard day too,
in making its ascent and descent. Leaving our lodgings at
8 a.m., several hours were occupied in rounding the spurs and
surmounting the cultivated and scrub-clad land which subtend
the mountain proper. At 6000 feet we reached Bamboo
scrub, and a path through this led to an area where medicinal
Rhubarb was cultivated, and where the drug " Tang-shên "
was extraordinarily abundant. At 6500 feet we entered the
timber. At the margin of the woods, to the left of the road,
are extensive plantations of the drug " Huang-lien." This
interesting plant (*Coptis chinensis*) is grown under a framework of brushwood reared some 3 to 4 feet above the ground.
The drug is used as a tonic and blood-purifier.

As the path winds the trees are at first small, with plenty
of Bamboo scrub, but this belt is very narrow and speedily
gives place to large trees which extend to within 500 feet of the
summit, where Bamboo scrub again becomes troublesome.
Everywhere above 5000 feet, where the woods are thin and
sunlight penetrates freely, Bamboo scrub is found, rendering
travel excessively arduous and, unless a path is cut, im-

possible. In the dense shade of the forest the Bamboo does not thrive.

The forest, though full of splendid timber, is not rich in variety. The Chinese Beech (*Fagus sinenis*) is the commonest tree. This species always has many trunks, and trees 60 to 70 feet high, with stems 3 to 6 feet in girth, abound. The interesting *Tetracentron sinense* is very abundant ; trees 60 to 70 feet by 8 to 10 feet girth are plentiful. The leafage of this tree is very thin and characteristic. Large trees of White Birch and of several species of Maple occur scattered through the forest. The smooth-leaved Davidia (*D. involucrata*, var. *Vilmoriniana*) occurs sparingly, and good-sized trees of various Cherries, Bird Cherries, Mountain Ash, and Wild Pear are common. Rambling over the tops of the largest trees is *Berchemia Giraldiana*. Several species of Rhododendron occur ; one species (*R. sutchuenense*) forms a tree 30 feet and more tall and 5 feet in girth. Shrubs in variety abound ; in the glades *Viburnum tomentosum* was wreathed in snow-white flowers. In more open places the Musk Rose is rampant, and near the summit *Rosa sericea* is abundant.

The summit forms a sloping, undulating flat, about an acre in extent, covered with grass and a few shrubs. On the apex stands a small temple now partly in ruins. A sharp, rocky ridge extends from the summit, linking the mountain up with the ranges to the northward. The face on two sides is a vertical precipice, 2000 feet and more sheer. From the summit (alt. 7850 feet) we got an extensive view of the surrounding country. Nothing but mountains on every side ; to the north and north-west these are heaped one beyond another in quick succession and are separated by narrow defiles down which torrents rush and roar. Very difficult looked the country in front of us, but the call of the unknown was strong. We descended by the same devious path, indeed, there is no other, and reached our lodgings as darkness overtook us. Specimens of some forty odd different plants rewarded the day's labour, several of them new and uncommonly interesting. On the extreme summit Box is a common shrub, and growing with it I discovered a new species of Lilac (*Syringa verrucosa*).

The following day we continued our journey northwards.

Just beyond Peh-yang-tsai we passed through copses of small Oak (*Quercus variabilis*), where the Jew's ear Fungus is cultivated. The culture is as follows : Oak saplings, about 6 inches thick, are cut down, trimmed of their branches, and cut into staves 8 to 10 feet long. These are allowed to lie on the ground for several months, where they become infested with the mycelium of the fungus. They are then stacked slantingly in scores or thereabouts, and the fructifications of the fungus develop. These are ear-shaped and gelatinous and are by the Chinese esteemed a delicacy. I tried them, but did not find them very palatable, and the experiment resulted in a bad stomach-ache !

On leaving these plantations the road descends to a ravine along which it meanders for a mile or two. Many shrubs were in flower in the ravine, and I gathered amongst other things specimens of a new genus, allied to Holbœllia, with fragrant yellow flowers. (I subsequently secured seeds of this plant, since named *Sargentodoxa cuneata*, and succeeded in introducing it into cultivation.) At the head of this ravine a steep ascent through woods of Oak and Birch leads to a cultivated area where there are two or three scattered houses and many Tea bushes. Near one house the Chinese Coffee tree (*Gymnocladus chinensis*) occurs ; the pods of this tree are saponaceous and are esteemed for laundry purposes.

From the Tea plantations the road leads through Pine woods, now by an easy, now by a heavy grade, but always ascending, and we were all glad when our destination (Hsintientsze) was reached. Near this place are some fine old woods, rich in a variety of deciduous trees and shrubs. I noted a Horse Chestnut (*Æsculus Wilsonii*), two kinds of Beech, *Styrax Hemsleyanum, Meliosma Veitchiorum*, the Davidia, and many different kinds of Maple and Oak—all of them large trees. In the margins of the woods *Viburnum ichangense* was particularly fine, and many Cherry trees, with both pink and white flowers, common. In moist shady places in the woods a blue Primrose (*P. ovalifolia*) carpets the ground for miles. The yellow-flowered *Stylophorum japonicum*, an Epimedium, and various species of Corydalis are abundant in and near the woods.

The hamlet of Hsin-tientsze, alt. 5600 feet, consists of one rather large house. It is built on a slope a few hundred feet below the summit of the ridge, and from the front of the house a wonderful view of the surrounding country is afforded. Nothing but mountains as far as the eye can range, and not 20 square yards of level ground in sight! Our quarters, though cramped, were, all things considered, fairly comfortable, and were as good as could be expected in these wilds.

The next morning we made an early start in order to cover the 60 li between Hsin-tientsze and Mao-fu-lien. Immediately on leaving we traversed an old wood especially rich in species of Maple. Davidia and Beech are also common, whilst the interesting *Cornus sinensis* occurs sparingly as a thin tree 60 feet tall. *Pinus Armandi* is present, but Conifers generally are very scarce in this particular locality.

We meandered around the mountain-sides, by a tortuous ascending path, until we reached a gap in the ridge and crossing over made a breakneck descent of a couple of thousand feet. A new kind of Poplar, having the young foliage bronzy-red, was common on all sides, and in the descent I gathered *Primula violodora*, *Rhododendron Augustinii*, *Acer griseum*, and a pink-flowered Staphylea, the last two both small trees. The most interesting find, however, was a new Hydrangea (*H. Sargentiana*), a shrub 5 to 6 feet tall, with stems densely felted with short bristly hairs and large, dark green leaves with a velvety lustre—in foliage alone this species is strikingly handsome.

At the foot of the descent we came upon small woods of *Pinus Henryi*, a tree averaging 60 feet in height, more or less pyramidal in shape, with bark usually rough and black, but sometimes red in the upper parts. The cones vary considerably in size and are retained on the tree for several years. In the valley near the Pine woods there is considerable cultivation. Walnut trees are common and Cunninghamia abounds.

Leaving this valley, a long but fairly easy ascent led to the top of another ridge, and a precipitous descent brought us to another narrow valley. These ascents and descents were most fatiguing and occurred with exasperating frequency every day, and several times a day at that. Another climb of over 2000 feet and we reached our destination for the day, finding accommodation in an inn which is also a large medicine depot, and is owned by a wealthy man from the province of Kiangsi. This inn is a large, rambling two-storied structure with several outhouses and a large courtyard. There is not sufficient level space to accommodate the whole place, and the front part is supported on posts. It serves as general store for the whole country-side, and in addition is a veritable museum. Dirt in every shape and form draped everything, and the stink from adjacent piggeries was tempered with the odour of various aromatic herbs. The business instinct of the house is strong, as I found to my cost when changing some silver and buying a goat. The rites of ancestor-worship were strictly carried out every morning and evening, and everything done to ensure continued and increasing prosperity. The burning of incense and candles and the performance of mystical genuflexions may assist business, but a little more attention to cleanliness and sanitation would make a stronger appeal to the foreigner. At least, such were my conclusions after a thirty-six hours' stay in the place.

It rained a good part of the next day, but as we had decided upon a day's rest it did not inconvenience us. In the forenoon I went out for a few hours to investigate the woods around Mao-fu-lien. Some very large trees of Sassafras (*S. tzumu*) occur here—the largest specimen is nearly 100 feet tall and 12 feet girth. The Chinese Sassafras has no medicinal value, and the wood is used for box-making and fuel only. Oak and Sweet Chestnut are plentiful and form small woods. The Chestnut (*Castanea Vilmoriniana*) is a singular species, with a single ovoid nut inside the spiny fruit ; the flowers have a peculiarly unpleasant smell. Around the inn are cultivated many trees of the Hardy Rubber and also *Magnolia officinalis*. Walnut and Varnish trees are abundant, and behind the house is a fine flat-leaved Spruce (*Picea pachyclada*). The mountain-tops are clothed with Grass, Brambles, scrub Oak, bushes of the pink-flowered *Rhododendron Mariesii*, and the scarlet *R. indicum.*

The view from the inn is one of steep ridges and high mountains, separated by deep, narrow chasms as far as the eye can range. It is indeed a fascinating country, but exhausting to travel over.

A fine morning followed yesterday's rain, the country looked refreshed, and the air was laden with fragrance from the myriad flowers on every side. The coolies grumbled loudly over the extortionate charges at the inn, and several hours elapsed before they recovered their cheerfulness. The day's journey commenced in a steady ascent to the top of a ridge followed by the usual precipitous descent. Hereabouts *Staphylea holocarpa*, a small, very floriferous tree, with both white and pink flowers, is very common and most strikingly beautiful. Another interesting plant is *Salix Fargesii*, a dwarf-growing Willow, having large very dark green leaves. A small torrent marks the foot of the descent, and from this point on we occupied several hours in an exhausting climb to the summit of another ridge, finally crossing over at 7300 feet altitude. In the ascent a new Spruce, having short square leaves and small cones, was discovered, and many small trees of Hemlock Spruce were noted. Near the head of the ridge, on cliffs, Box (*Buxus microphylla*) is very common, and a rosy-red flowered Primrose is abundant in grassy places. A dwarf Bamboo forms dense thickets on the top of the wind-swept ridge.

The descent quickly leads into copses of Birch, and later into fine woods composed of mixed deciduous trees and shrubs and a few conifers. In these woods we spent a profitable time, collecting in all specimens of some fifty different kinds of woody plants. We saw one or two large trees of Davidia and many of Tetracentron. Cherries in variety are plentiful, and were a wonderful sight—nothing but masses of pink and white. Three kinds of Rhododendron were collected, and six in all noted. Maples in variety are very common, but one large tree of *Acer griseum*, with its chestnut-red bark, exfoliating like that of the River Birch, was the gem of all. Various *Pomaceæ* and one or two species of *Lauraceæ* make up a fair percentage of the small trees. Viburnums in variety, Honeysuckles, Diervillas, Deutzias, Philadelphus, and *Neillia sinensis* are everywhere abundant. In rocky, more open places *Viburnum rhytidophyllum* with its long, thick wrinkled leaves looked particularly happy, and in places exposed to the sun a Crab Apple (*Malus* sp.) with pink flowers was a sight for the gods. On wet, humus-clad rocks *Pleione Henryi* luxuriates, and herbs in endless variety crowd every available spot. A fine torrent collects up the waters of countless smaller streams, and falls down the narrow ravine, often in a series of waterfalls hundreds of feet high, the noise of the falling water alone breaking the silence of the forest depths.

With some difficulty, owing to the timidity of the people, we obtained lodgings in a peasant's hut at Wên-tsao, alt. 6150 feet. This tiny hamlet consists of four small houses, scattered and pitched on the steep mountain-slope. It is surrounded on all sides by precipitous mountains covered with forests. Around the houses small patches have been cleared, and wheat, a little maize, and a few peas and vegetables are cultivated.

The forests of this region are particularly rich, and in order to better appreciate them I propose to interpolate here extracts from my journal of another date :—

" *May* 30.—Wên-tsao. On a precipitous slope facing our lodgings a score or more Davidia trees occur ; they are one mass of white, and are most conspicuous as the shades of night close in. Two large trees of *Pterostyrax hispidus* are growing amongst these Davidias, and are laden with pendulous chains of creamy-white flowers."

" *May* 31.—Go over and investigate the Davidia trees and the forests generally. Crossing a narrow neck a woodcutter's circuitous path leads us down to a narrow defile through a fine shady wood. Ascending a precipice with difficulty, we soon reach the Davidia trees. There are over a score of them growing on a steep, rocky declivity ; they vary from 35 to 60 feet in height, and the largest is 6 feet in girth. Being in a dense wood they are bare of branches for half their height, but their presence is readily detected by the numerous white bracts which have fallen and lie strewn over the ground. The tree starts up from below when felled ; indeed, it naturally throws up small stems after it gets old. The bark is dark and scales off in small, irregular flakes. By climbing a large Tetracentron tree growing on the edge of a cliff, and chopping off some branches to make a clear space, I manage to take some snapshots of the upper part of the Davidia tree in full flower. A difficult task and highly dangerous. Three of us

climb the tree to different heights and haul up axe and camera
from one to another by means of a rope.   The wood of Tetracentron is brittle, and the knowledge of this does not add to one's
peace of mind when sitting astride a branch about 4 inches
thick with a sheer drop of a couple of hundred feet beneath.
However, all went well, and we drank in the beauties of this
extraordinary tree.   The distinctive beauty of Davidia is in
the two snow-white connate bracts which subtend the flower
proper.   These are always unequal in size, the larger usually
6 inches long by 3 inches broad, and the smaller $3\frac{1}{2}$ inches
by $2\frac{1}{2}$ inches ; they range up to 8 inches by 4 inches and
5 inches by 3 inches.   At first greenish, they become pure white
as the flowers mature and change to brown with age.   The
flowers and their attendant bracts are pendulous on fairly
long stalks, and when stirred by the slightest breeze they
resemble huge Butterflies hovering amongst the trees.   The
bracts are somewhat boat-shaped and flimsy in texture, and the
leaves often hide them considerably, but so freely are they
borne that the tree looks, from a short distance, as if flecked
with snow.   On dull days and in the early morning and
evening the bracts are most conspicuous.   The fruit super-
ficially resembles a small walnut, but the inner shell is absolutely unbreakable.   To my mind *Davidia involucrata* is at
once the most interesting and beautiful of all trees of the
north-temperate flora.

" With the Davidia is a good-sized tree of the Horse
Chestnut (50 feet in height by 4 feet in girth).   Higher up
Hornbeam and Tetracentron are common, and Birch, white,
red, and black, luxuriate.

" Maples are a feature of these woods ; all are tall trees, but
of no great thickness.   Unfortunately very few are flowering,
and indeed this is true of the forest trees generally this year.

" Perhaps the commonest tree in these forests is the Beech ;
parts being formed entirely of these trees.   So light-demanding
are they that they suffer no competitors or even undergrowth.
For the first time it is possible for me to say definitely that
two distinct species of Beech exist in this region.   One forms
a tree with a single trunk, the other always has several trunks.
The former species has glabrous, shining green leaves, a large,

dense, much-branched head ; it makes a tree 40 to 50 feet
high with a trunk 5 to 10 feet in girth, and, save for its smaller
stature, very strongly resembles the European Beech. The
second species, which is the recognized Chinese Beech, grows
much taller, but never attains the girth of the other. It
generally has six to twelve trunks, averaging 2 to 5 feet in girth,
arising closely together and slanting away from one another
as they grow. The bark is light grey and the leaves sub-
glaucous and hairy below ; branches somewhat ascending
but with the young branchlets slender and pendulous. A
local name for the Beech is ' Peh Litzu.' Small plants are
common, but no flowers are to be discovered.[1]

" In the shade of trees, *Ribes longeracemosum*, var. *Wilsonii*,
a remarkable black currant, with racemes 1 to 1½ feet long, is
common, whilst *Rodgersia æsculifolia*, with large, erect, thyrsoid
panicles of white flowers, is rampant.

" Five species of Oak—three deciduous and two evergreen
occur. *Meliosma Veitchiorum* and many species of *Pomaceæ*
and Cherries are common, whilst the Varnish tree is everywhere abundant. In dense shade various evergreen Barberries
occur, and in open country *Neillia sinensis* forms dense thickets.

" Of Conifers, *Pinus Armandi* and *P. Henryi* are scattered
over the cliffs ; *Picea Wilsonii* and a flat-leaved Spruce (*P.
pachyclada*) are rare, whilst the Hemlock Spruce[2] is fairly
common on the cliffs—neat, dense trees of no great size with
their young leaves just unfolding and old cones abundant.
The White Pine (*P. Armandi*) is more common higher up on
the mountains ; with its long needles, graceful port, and light
grey bark this tree is strikingly handsome ; the cones are
pendulous, borne at the ends of the glabrous branches. The
very resinous wood is used locally for torches, burning with a
clear, bright flame, and gives a good light."

[1] In 1910 I succeeded in introducing young plants of both species into
the Arnold Arboretum from this region.

[2] *Tsuga chinensis*.

CHAPTER V

FOREST AND CRAG

ON leaving Wên-tsao a sharp descent for a couple of hours brought us to the upper waters of the Hsingshan River, which we left several days ago. Crossing this stream by a covered bridge we reached the hamlet of Li-erh-kou. Around this hamlet trees of the Hardy Rubber (*Eucommia*) and *Magnolia officinalis* (Hou-p'o) are cultivated for their bark. A steady ascent from Li-erh-kou through occasional woods of Oak and Birch, interrupted by areas where people were busy ploughing the fields and sowing maize, brought us to the hamlet of Chintien-po, where we lunched. Near this place is a fine new Meliosma (*M. Beaniana*), a tree 60 feet high. It was leafless, but one mass of creamy-white flowers borne in pendulous panicles. Near by this tree I discovered one small specimen of the " Judas tree " (*Cercis racemosa*). Prior to this discovery I knew of only two trees some fifteen days' journey south-west of Ichang. This new tree was about 25 feet high, with a stem half decayed through at the base, and a mop-like head. In spite of its partial decay the tree appeared in vigorous health, and was one mass of silvery-rose coloured flowers, borne in short racemes. The leaves of this species are hairy below. Varnish and Walnut trees occur in abundance, and we met several coolies laden with cakes of fat, expressed from the fruits of the Varnish tree (*Rhus verniciflua*). The double-flowered form of *Spiræa prunifolia* is commonly planted on graves, and the bushes were wreathed in flowers.

Soon after leaving Chin-tien-po we commenced a precipitous ascent, and after climbing for several miles reached the neck of a ridge where *Viburnum rhytidophyllum* luxuriates. From this neck the ascent is more gradual, and but few crops are grown, as it is nearing the limits of cultivation in these regions. Near some limestone cliffs are two magnificent trees of Maackia, each 60 feet tall and 7 feet in girth. The bark of this tree is smooth, of a light grey colour, and the unfolding leaves are silvery grey. Here, too, are many small trees of the Bladder tree (*Staphylea holocarpa*) and Peach bushes. These were in full flower, and flitting amongst the flowers and drinking in the honey were many beautiful little sun-birds (*Æthopyga dabryi*). *Rhododendron indicum* was left behind at 5500 feet altitude.

A few hundred yards beyond the limestone cliffs we crossed over at 7000 feet altitude, into Fang Hsien, and traversed a narrow moorland valley clothed with grass and bounded by rounded hills covered with thickets. In this moorland are acres of *Astilbe Davidii* and *A. grandis*, with several Senecios and other ornamental herbs. The thickets are composed chiefly of Birch and Willow, with a few Poplar and Silver Fir, and an occasional flat-leaved Spruce. The vegetation was scarcely in leaf, and it was evident from the appearance of the ground that snow had only just melted away. We flushed a Solitary Snipe and secured a cock pheasant for the larder, but very little life of any sort was visible in these uplands. At the head of this moorland valley we entered a narrow defile and, after skirting the side of a mountain through thickets in which various Maples and Currants were prominent, reached Hung-shih-kou. This is a miserable hut of wood in a half-ruinous condition, kept by a family clothed in rags. It is situated at an altitude of 6300 feet, by the side of a considerable torrent, and is walled in by precipitous, well-wooded mountains.

At night some of the coolies slept in a loft above the room I occupied, and every movement they made caused dust and dirt to fall over my bed. On waking in the morning I found myself covered with this filth, and nearly choked with the dust into the bargain. The owner of this hovel is a hunter, and he has shot the Serow of this region, which is known as " Ming-tsen Yang." He had a couple of pairs of horns and a flat skin which we secured, and, judging from this fragmentary material, the beast must be larger than any known species of Serow. (In 1907 my associate, Mr. Zappey, made several trips after this animal, but to no purpose, though he secured a tantalizing glimpse of just one specimen.)

The name Hung-shih-kou signifies " Red stone mouth," and has reference to the outcropping of red sandstone which occurs here and extends to Hsao-lung-tang, 20 li distant, which we made our halting-place for the next day. Though we had only 20 li to cover we started early, glad to escape from the miserable lodgings into the woods again. Ascending a stream, through brushwood thickets composed of Willow, Birch, Spiræa, and Roses, we twice crossed the stream by rotten bridges of roughly hewn tree-logs before reaching our destination. On the way we passed several fine trees of *Picea Wilsonii*, beneath which old graves nestle. The largest trees are about 70 feet tall and 6 feet in girth ; the leaves bright green, and the habit distinctly stately ; the cones are borne in large clusters, and many still remained on the trees. Here also are small trees of the White Pine (*Pinus Armandi*) with cones 9 inches long. A new Poplar was discovered in flower, and Veitch's Viburnum and Spiræa were common with their young leaves just unfolding.

The handsomest tree in these parts is, however, the Chinese form of *Betula utilis*, a Birch with orange-red bark, which on exfoliating exposes the glaucous waxy bloom of the layer below. Trees 40 feet high are still pyramidal in habit, much branched, with slender, ascending branches on which the lenticels are very prominent. The older trees, as seen on the tops of the mountains, are mop-headed, 60 to 80 feet tall, with a clean trunk for 40 feet more, and are still strikingly handsome though blown and battered by the wind.

The hamlet of Hsao-lung-tang (Small Dragon-pool), alt. 7400 feet, consists of two dilapidated wooden huts pitched on opposite sides of a lovely burn, which flows through a narrow sloping valley lying almost due east and west. This valley is flanked by steep ridges clad only with grass and scrub. Odd patches of Birch and Silver Fir attest to forests which have all been destroyed by fire. From the numerous old graves and abandoned fields it is evident that formerly more people dwelt in this valley than do so to-day. Tiny patches of cabbage and Irish potato occur around the huts ; and also plantations of Tang-kuei (*Angelica polymorpha*, var. *sinensis*), a valued

Chinese medicine.   The people declare the valley too cold for wheat or barley !

On the occasion of my first visit to this place in 1901, I had to retrace my steps owing to dearth of supplies. Since that date no white man had visited this region.   In the direction in which we were bound these are the last inhabited houses for over a hundred li.

I took a photograph of the hostel on my arrival, but what I should have liked to photograph was the interior. This was impossible, since, even at midday, a light was necessary to see into the farthest corners.   Dirt and filth in many forms abounded, and although plenty of timber is to be had for the felling, the house, through the idleness of its keeper, has been allowed to fall into a most ruinous state.   Of one low story, the house is bisected into four compartments, and is provided with no outlet for the smoke or for the ingress of light, save through the doorway and holes in the roof ; the floor, of course, is mother earth. Pigs were quartered in one section, into which our arrival also forced the owners. Cows and goats occupied a hovel 6 feet from the door, the floor of which was fully a foot deep in filth. Luckily, the weather continued gloriously fine, and the miserable surroundings were less evident in consequence. (In passing, I might record the fact that this was the only occasion on which I enjoyed fine weather in this place. Twice previously I had been marooned here for days, and either stayed in bed or shivered by the doorway watching the rain.)

Bee-keeping is one of the principal industries of the peasants in these wilds, and around this hostel are scores of beehives. The hives are hollowed-out logs of Silver Fir, about 3 feet 6 inches long by 1 foot wide, two pieces of wood are fixed crosswise in the centre, and opposite these three or four holes are bored to allow the bees ingress and egress. Rude boxes often take the place of these logs. The beeswax is not separated from the honey, the honeycomb being eaten as removed from the hives. Though the climate is rigorous, the bees are healthy and strong, and disease is unknown among them.

The morning following our arrival we ascended the Shamu-jen range behind our lodgings. The first 500 feet was steep going, but afterwards the climb was easy. At about

8000 feet woods of Silver Fir occur. The trees at first are of no great size, but their dimensions increased as we ascended. Most of the larger trees have been felled and converted into coffins ; the remains of thousands of them are scattered everywhere around. On the decayed trunks of many of these trees large bushes of Rhododendron are growing, thereby proving that the trees have lain there these many years past. Some of the prostrate trunks measured over 150 feet in length and 6 feet in diameter. None of this size is now standing, but plenty that are over 100 feet tall occur. The upper part of the ridge is a cliff some 200 feet high, under the lee of which Birch and Maple are common and wild Rhubarb is also found. We discovered a more or less easy path up the cliff, and crossed over at 9700 feet altitude. The highest peak in this range is probably a couple of hundred feet higher. The summit is of hard limestone with rare outcroppings of red sandstone. Stunted wind-swept Silver Fir and various kinds of Currant extend to the summit. Rhododendron and a dwarf Juniper (*J. squamata*) are also common. The descent was through woods of Birch and Bamboo to an open, grassy, scrub-clad, sloping moorland, through which a considerable torrent flows. The Bamboo, so common hereabouts, is very beautiful, forming clumps 3 to 10 feet through. The culms are 5 to 12 feet tall, golden yellow, with dark, feathery foliage ; the young culms have broad sheathing bracts protecting the branchlets. Taken all in all, this is the handsomest Bamboo I have seen.[1]

In the vicinity of the stream shrubs in great variety abound ; of these the Willows, Roses, Spiræas, Philadelphus, Hydrangeas, odd bushes of *Rhododendron Fargesii*, and clumps of *Aralia chinensis* are the principal features. The Rhododendron referred to is one of the most beautiful, with compact trusses of white or, more commonly, rosy-red (occasionally deep red) flowers ; the leaves are small, displaying the trusses of flowers to great advantage. This species is usually a bush 5 to 8 feet tall, and of about the same dimensions through the head ; more rarely it is 15 to 20 feet tall. The steep grassy slopes are almost devoid of trees ; the fine pasture land and the typical moorland character of this narrow valley

[1] In 1910 I successfully introduced it into cultivation.

constitute a region that is very different from others in central China.

In the afternoon we visited Ta-lung-tang (Large Dragon-pool), a deep, silent pond about a stone's throw across, nearly circular in outline with reedy margins, walled in by steep grassy mountain slopes. In short, in situation and appearance the very kind of pool that in any country legends would be wrapped around, and so in this case many curious stories concerning elfs and demons are centred round this silent pool. The day was gloriously fine and sunny, but the wind, which swept through the valley in considerable force, was very cold. Whether it be due to local conditions or to the altitude I could not determine, but the tree flora is comparatively poor and of little interest, and very unlike the belts that occur between 4000 and 6500 feet. The altitude, however, favours coarse herbs, and these are rampant. Many interesting shrubs also occur, but with the exception of Silver Fir, Birch and Poplar trees are rare.

With a prospect of 60 li of unknown road before us we planned a daylight start, but this scheme did not mature, as the men had to prepare and cook their morning meal before starting. The entire absence of food supplies makes travelling hereabouts extraordinarily difficult. Yesterday four of the men journeyed back 45 li in order to buy food-stuffs, and returned only after dark ; several of them were up most of the night grinding maize and preparing cakes for the march.

On leaving Hsao-lung-tang we ascended the lesser branch of a stream through a narrow valley flanked by bare grassy mountains having here and there small patches of Silver Fir and Birch forest. The road is one steady climb, never steep but often difficult owing to the Bamboo scrub. The decaying stumps and stark tree trunks speak eloquently of the magnificent forests which must have formerly existed here until destroyed by axe and fire. To the botanist and lover of Nature this vandalism is painful, but presumably it was necessary for economic reasons. The unwitting cause of it all has been the Irish potato. But Nature took her revenge when, twenty-three years ago, the Potato disease devastated the crop and ruined the country-side, causing a general exodus of all the people. Nature is fast reclaiming the whole region, but re-afforestation is a slow process.

Nearing the head of the pass we entered large timber— a fragment of the virgin forest, composed exclusively of Silver Fir and Birch with a dense undergrowth of Rhododendron. The last named comprise four species—*R. Fargesii, R. maculiferum, R. sutchuenense,* and *R. adenopodum,* most of them bushes 10 to 20 feet tall, their flowers making one blaze of colour. The Silver Fir and Birch trees are of huge dimensions, but none was fruiting. On emerging from this patch of forest we entered a rolling moorland covered with Bamboo scrub which merges gradually into areas clad with the dwarf Juniper, coarse grasses, and herbs, amongst which a species of Onion was abundant. This moorland extends across the rounded saddle of the range and for several miles down the other side. The crest of the saddle I made 9500 feet altitude, and from this point we obtained a fine view of the series of bare, savagely jagged peaks from which the range (Sheng-nêng-chia) takes its name. The highest peaks probably exceed 11,000 feet altitude, and the lower slopes are forested, but the country is not attractive. Animal life is remarkable for its absence, and hardly a bird was to be seen. The solitude which reigned in this remote, inaccessible region was broken only by the noise of rushing waters and the low whining of the wind amongst the tree-tops. In shady places blocks of ice still remained, and about the head of the pass the grass was only just beginning to show green. Save for an alpine Primula and a Dandelion no flowers of any sort were to be seen.

On crossing the pass we again entered Hsingshan Hsien, and after wandering across moorland for a few miles a short steep ascent led us across a lateral spur into Patung Hsien. From this point a precipitous descent of 2000 feet brought us to a ruined and deserted hut at a place called Wapêng, the only accommodation the country-side affords. In the descent we passed hundreds of curious rock-stacks—bare blocks of shale standing erect, with acute edges, like gaunt sentinels guarding the neighbourhood. The mountain-side was formerly under cultivation, but is now abandoned and covered with grass and coarse herbs. Around the hut a little Medicinal Rhubarb and much Tang-shên was growing, telling of former plantations of these and other medicines. The country on all sides is very steep and much cut up, but stark decaying tree trunks, the sole remnants of former forests, mar the beauty of the landscape on all sides.

We reached Wapêng (alt. 8400 feet) fairly early in the afternoon, and the men were busy till nightfall collecting fuel and rigging up a bamboo shelter beneath which to pass the night. The day had been gloriously fine and the night proved equally so, with a distinctly frosty nip after sundown. A roaring fire made things look cheerful, and everybody was in the best of health and spirits. The sides of the hut were airy and the wind played about one all night. The roof was partially wanting and afforded a good view of the starry heavens above. It was a lonely place, yet one felt peculiarly happy and glad to be privileged to visit a region so remote from the world in general.

There was no difficulty in getting the men up next morning, and we were off just as the sun's rays broke over the landscape. Dark mists obscured the view for an hour or so, but as the sun rose these disappeared and we enjoyed another gloriously fine day. A steep and precipitous, nay breakneck, descent of a 1000 feet brought us to a narrow well-wooded valley, walled in by forest-clad mountains. The Silver Fir does not descend more than 500 feet from Wapêng, below which its place is taken by Hemlock Spruce. This Spruce is not plentiful, but giants 100 feet tall by 12 feet in girth occur. The forests as we descended quickly become of mixed character, and finally conifers completely disappear. The variety of trees and shrubs was astonishing, and nearly all the more interesting trees of western Hupeh were to be found and in quantity. Maples are particularly abundant, and I gathered specimens of a dozen species in flower. Four species of Rhododendron occur scattered, but not in quantity. On rocks in places an interesting orchid (*Pleione Henryi*) abounds and was one mass of flowers. The Davidia is fairly common, and the curious *Euptelea Franchetii* and *Tetracentron sinense* are the commonest of trees. A feature in these woods was *Staphylea holocarpa*, a small tree covered with pendulous trusses of white and rosy-pink flowers. A Horse Chestnut (*Æsculus Wilsonii*), the Chinese Yellow-wood (*Cladrastis sinensis*), Hemsley's Styrax and *Pterostyrax hispidus*, all of them large trees, were fairly common; Cherries, Bird Cherries and many *Pomaceæ* abound. Birch is one of the commonest constituents of these forests; in the more open areas Bamboo scrub forms dense thickets, and high up in the woods *Rhododendron maculiferum* forms trees 25 feet tall with a trunk 1 foot in diameter.

Here and there clearings have been made for the cultivation of the medicine "Huang-lien" (*Coptis chinensis*). In one abandoned clearing were hundreds of *Lilium tigrinum* luxuriating amongst the grass and tall herbs. In dark shady places the noble *Lilium mirabile* is common. This lily has tubular snow-white flowers spotted with red within, and glossy green, cordate leaves. An occasional Spruce or Pine tree occurs, and at the edge of the forests Cunninghamia appears. Many of the cliffs are clothed with Hemlock Spruce. Birch is fairly common, but, with the exception of one or two evergreen species, Oak is very scarce. Hornbeam is not plentiful, and Magnolias are decidedly rare trees; Ash is general, and the Linden, represented by three or four species, abundant. The Laurel family is represented by four species, all of them deciduous, including a handsome kind with young foliage of a bronze-red. Honeysuckles are rare, save for the climbing species *Lonicera tragophylla*, which has golden-yellow flowers. Clematis in variety are common, especially *C. montana* (white and rosy-red forms) and *C. pogonandra* with its top-shaped yellow flowers. Many species of Schisandria, all of them a wealth of flowers, *Holbœllia Fargesii*, and the botanically interesting *Sinofranchetia sinensis* are the principal climbers.

The road follows the course of a torrent which rises near Wapêng and quickly becomes a considerable stream. The path is narrow, very rocky and difficult to follow, and how our chairs got through was a puzzle. Both torrent and path ultimately plunge into a narrow ravine shut in by lofty cliffs, unclimbable and bare. In places the rocks are of limestone, but from 5000 feet downwards slate and mud-shales predominate.

At 4500 feet altitude we reached the edge of the forest and entered a cultivated area, where there are a few inhabited houses—the first we had seen for two days. Barley and Irish potato are the crops. Near the edge of the forest the torrent flows underground for about a mile. On rocks here *Lonicera pileata* abounds as a fluviatile shrub ; the curious climber *Hosiea sinensis* is common, covering rocks fully exposed to the sun. In the open country I noted in full flower a fine specimen of the Chinese Tulip tree (*Liriodendron chinense*), 70 feet tall and 5 feet in girth.

A precipitous descent, through fields margined with Tea-bushes, led to the tiny hamlet of Sha-kou-ping, where the torrent we had followed joins with a very considerable stream flowing down from the north-east. The united waters plunge at once into a ravine and finally enter the Yangtsze a few miles above the city of Patung. Sha-kou-ping is only 2600 feet above sea-level, and is hemmed in on all sides by lofty cliffs. The flora is that common to the glens and gorges around Ichang, and the wealth of flowers was extraordinary. The Banksian rose is one of the commonest shrubs hereabouts, and was laden with masses of fragrant white flowers. Opium Poppy was abundant and the whole country-side was gay with the colour of flowers. *Styrax Veitchiorum* occurs here, and trees 12 to 40 feet tall were masses of ivory-white.

From Sha-kou-ping we toiled slowly up the rocky ravine down which the main stream rushes. A paper-mill or two are located here, but houses are few and far between. The rocks are of slaty shales, often very rotten, and the torrent is a succession of rapids and cataracts. In spite of the turbulent nature of its waters it is full of fish, some of them of good size.

The hamlet of Ma-hsien-ping, our intended destination, proved to be a miserable place of some half a dozen hovels all filled with people engaged in collecting tea. We therefore journeyed on for another 10 li to some farmhouses at Shui-ting-liangtsze, and arrived just as the sun was setting behind the range. We found accommodation in a large farm-house, alt. 3900 feet. The day's journey proved very arduous, but there was much by way of compensation. The scenery was sublime and the flora wonderfully rich and varied. In all I gathered specimens of upwards of fifty new kinds of woody plants, many of them previously unknown. This region is one of the richest I have visited, and I subsequently secured a fine haul of seeds, the great majority of the plants raised from them being now found growing and thriving in many gardens of Europe and America. (Later I again traversed this same region, and owing to heavy rains was over a week in crossing the country between Hsao-lung-tang and Shui-ting-liangtsze, a flooded torrent holding us up for three consecutive days.)

It was nearly midnight when all was quiet last night, the men being loud in their grumbling against taking the road to Taning Hsien instead of that to Wushan Hsien. The reports we had heard indicated a bad time ahead for all of us and for the men in particular, owing to the extreme poverty of the country-side. I heard them as I lay in bed, but fortunately no complaints were brought to me.

It was later than usual when we got away in the morning. After a steep ascent we meandered along the mountain-side, and ultimately crossed over into Fang Hsien again by a low pass, alt. 5600 feet. This is the real watershed of the Han and Yangtsze River systems. The Sheng-nêng-chia is a gigantic spur thrust out from the backbone of the chain, and the streams which take their rise from three sides of this spur flow down to the Yangtsze. From the watershed we had a good view of the Sheng-nêng-chia peaks bearing E.S.E., and of some equally lofty mountains to the east, evidently in the vicinity of the Yangtsze itself. On both sides of the watershed is a rather broad cultivated valley bounded by razor-backed hills clothed with woods of Oak and Pine. Varnish trees abound on the edges of the fields and Walnut trees are also common. Farmhouses are scattered over the country-side, and the crow of the Pheasant, the coo of the Wood Pigeon and the notes of the Cuckoo were heard on all sides. By the wayside are many fine trees of Sweet Chestnut and Magnolia, and one very fine specimen of *Corylus chinensis*, 120 feet tall

and 12 feet in girth.   Many medicines are cultivated hereabouts,
more especially Rhubarb and Tang-shên.   *Populus lasiocarpa*, with huge handsome foliage, is one of the commonest
trees.

After a few miles the cultivated valley ends and we entered
a narrow defile flanked by steep, well-wooded mountains.
Hereabouts the interesting *Sinowilsonia Henryi* is common,
forming a small, bushy tree with handsome foliage and long,
pendulous racemes of inconspicuous flowers.   The most ornamental tree, however, is a fine Crab Apple, which was laden
with umbels of pure white fragrant flowers borne on long slender
stalks.   Issuing from this defile we entered a small cultivated
flat and found lodgings at the hamlet of Pien-chin, alt. 5200 feet.

The vegetation during the day's journey was not very
remarkable, though I added sixteen kinds of plants to the
collection.   Noteworthy on the rocks and cliffs was *Viburnum
rhytidophyllum*, with its large flat corymbs of dirty white
flowers, which are not very pleasing to the nostril.   In the
defile the mountain-side is rich in shrubs; amongst which various
Rhododendrons were prominent ; *Rhododendron indicum* was
common and *Rosa sericea* was just opening its flowers.   All day
Oak woods were common; but these never contain much that is
of more than passing interest.   In abandoned cultivated areas
a small Poppy, resembling the common Iceland Poppy, with
deep yellow (occasionally orange) flowers was very abundant
and attractive.   In shady places the large yellow flowers of
Chelidonium lasiocarpum made a fine show, and common on
bare limestone cliffs are *Corydalis Wilsonii* and *C. tomentosa*,
both species with yellow flowers and glaucous foliage.   Around
our lodgings there was much cultivation, maize, barley, pulse,
and the Irish potato being the principal crops.   Several paper-
mills occur by the side of the stream, bamboo pulp being the
raw material from which the paper is made.

On leaving Pien-chin we followed a river to a point where it
is joined by a tributary stream which we crossed and then
ascended the road which skirts its banks.   This stream is gentle
for a Hupeh torrent, and for 10 li the road is of the easiest.   The
mountain-sides are covered with shrubs and trees; among which
Cercidiphyllum was conspicuous.   Occasional houses and small

patches of cultivation occur, but the country generally is very sparsely peopled. *Populus lasiocarpa* is abundant, and large branches are commonly driven in the ground to make fences ; these branches take root and form groves. A magnificent tree of *Ailanthus Vilmoriniana*, 150 feet tall and 20 feet in girth, was passed, and I was astounded at the huge size of this specimen. Tangled masses of *Actinidia chinensis* and various kinds of wild roses were everywhere abundant, filling the air with soft fragrance. Leaving this delightful mountain stream we made a steep ascent of 900 feet and then, to our great surprise, entered a broad level valley. This valley was evidently in earlier times a mountain lake—to-day the margins are cultivated and the centre is a marsh. The whole district is known as Chu-ku-ping or Ta-chu-hu,—the latter name having reference to its former condition as a lake. A flat area of this character is unique in these regions, as far as my knowledge goes. Several roads cross this flat and we took the one for Taning Hsien. By the wayside strawberries, white and red, luxuriate and were very good eating. Quite a number of horses and cattle were grazing in this valley, and the country could support many more.

After meandering some 15 li over the easiest of roads we made a very steep and fatiguing ascent to alt. 7300 feet, and crossed over into the province of Szechuan. From the neck of the divide, looking away E.S.E., we obtained a good view of the Sheng-nêng-chia and the main and subsidiary ranges and peaks—nothing but mountains on every side save the tiny valley at our feet which we had just crossed. In the ascent we passed many shrubs in full flower ; particularly striking were the various kinds of Viburnum, Deutzia, Abelia, and Cornus. A precipitous descent through a ravine and we reached the hostel at Hwa-kuo-ling, alt. 6350 feet, where plantations of Rhubarb were common and several other medicinal plants cultivated.

The road we were following is called the " Great salt road," but we only met four men carrying salt in the day's march. Indeed, on the whole journey we encountered practically no traffic. This wild mountainous country supports only a very sparse population and foreign trade has no chance hereabouts. Our great difficulty was in securing enough food for the men.

At Chu-ku-ping we managed to get one good meal from the local head-man and bought portions of a wild pig recently killed. At the hostel nothing was obtainable and the men had to eke out on the small rations they had with them. Goitre is common in these regions and nearly every one is affected. It would seem to be hereditary, since I noticed children in arms showing unmistakable swellings in the throat.

Boisterous winds and heavy clouds alternating with bright sunshine marked our first day's journey in eastern Szechuan. We were again amongst cliffs of hard limestone and the scenery strikingly resembles that of the Yangtsze Gorges and contiguous country. The whole region is too steep for cultivation, and habitations are few and far between and most dilapidated in character. The soil is stiff, clayey loam and the few crops we saw were wheat, Rye (*Secale fragile*), Irish potato, maize, and pulse. The cliffs are for the most part well timbered, and the common trees and shrubs of Hupeh are represented. *Pinus Armandi* is very abundant and *P. Henryi* is also common. Odd trees of Spruce and Hemlock also occur. A fine specimen of *Acer griseum*, 60 feet tall, 7 feet in girth, with curious cinnamon-red papery bark was the feature of the day's march ; unfortunately, it was badly situated for photographing. Beech, Yellow-wood and *Dipteronia sinensis* were common trees *en route*.

The road is one long succession of ascents and descents and most fatiguing. In the afternoon, after a particularly trying ascent, we wandered for an hour or so through woods of Oak (chiefly *Quercus variabilis* and *Q. aliena*) and Sweet Chestnut, the latter laden with its white, evil-smelling flowers. Walnut and Varnish trees are everywhere abundant and *Campanula punctata* is a common weed of cultivation. No foreigner had ever before traversed this region and the people were very timid, locking up their houses and hiding themselves from view at our approach. The cliffs in this neighbourhood are full of caves and many of these are bricked up to form places of refuge in troublous times. We found lodgings for the night at Peh-kuo-yüen, alt. 3750 feet, in the house of the head-man of the hamlet. Food-stuffs were scarce and there was great difficulty in persuading the people to part. What little we did eventually obtain was at famine prices and the grumbling was loud on all sides.

The following morning we descended by a moderately easy path to a torrent and then commenced a heart-breaking ascent of some 2600 feet. It was excessively hot and I do not remember perspiring so much before. A rugged, precipitous, sparsely populated country is this, and I never wish to see it again. Limestone regions are magnificent from the scenic point of view, but for travelling over they are fierce and arduous beyond words! Our destination was Hsao-pingtsze and no one knew the distance. Inquiries made as often as possible always elicited the same reply : " Seven or 8 li from Peh-kuo-yüen, 7 or 8 li to Hsao-pingtsze." Late in the afternoon the distance to go increased to 30 li and did not shorten until we suddenly sighted the two huts which form the hamlet of Hsao-pingtsze !

The ascent was largely under cultivation, but the final stage was through jungle. *Lonicera tragophylla* is common and was in full flower, but we saw no good plants. A bush of *Schizophragma integrifolium*, one mass of the purest white, on the cliffs, was conspicuous from afar. But the flora generally is very ordinary, with *Rhododendron discolor* and *R. Mariesii* common here and there. On reaching the top of the cliffs we entered a cultivated slope where Walnut and Varnish trees abound. The district is called Ta-ping-shan and consists of several scattered farmhouses surrounded by fields of maize, pulse, barley, and Irish potato. At one of these farmhouses my followers managed to secure a good meal and high spirits prevailed in consequence.

On leaving this place we continued to ascend by an easy path skirting rolling downs. A few scattered houses occur for a couple of miles but were mostly deserted, and we soon left all signs of cultivation and habitation behind us. The downs are treeless and clad mostly with grass with scattered bushes of Willow, Barberry and Spiræa. The depressions between the hills were masses of blue Forget-me-not. The whole region would make excellent grazing ground for cattle. Crossing over at 7950 feet altitude, we descended by an easy road for a mile or so and passed a couple of huts surrounded by extensive plantations of Medicinal Rhubarb. Many fine herbs luxuriate hereabouts, and among them *Iris Wilsonii* with its yellow flowers was conspicuous, covering large areas. Eventually we reached the edge of a precipice, down which the road fairly tumbles for 5 li to Hsao-pingtsze. This hamlet, as the name indicates, is situated on a tiny flat (probably caused by a landslide) and boasts two miserable, dilapidated houses. We took up lodgings in the smaller and presumably less squalid of the two, but there were little to choose between them in all conscience. On three sides the hamlet is walled in by steep cliffs and the fourth is the edge of a precipice itself. It was only some 30 yards from our hut to the edge of this precipice, and the view from this point is one of the most extraordinary and wonderful my eyes have ever beheld. Below me (some 4000 feet the morrow proved) at an acute angle lay a small village with a considerable river flowing past it. Beyond this was range upon range of bare, treeless, sharp-edged ridges, averaging 5000 to 6000 feet in height, with outstanding higher peaks and grander ranges in the beyond. The rocks are mainly of limestone, white, grey and reddish, giving a bizarre appearance to the whole scene. Never have I looked upon a wilder, more savage and less inviting region. A storm was brewing and the light rapidly failing, making it impossible to take a photograph, though no photograph could have produced a picture that would give an adequate idea of the savage grandeur of the whole scene. It was indeed sufficient to awe and terrorize one. Such scenes sink deep into the memory and the impressive stillness produces an effect which is felt for long years afterwards. Soon the angry rain-clouds darkened and blotted out the whole scene and the next moment a thunderstorm burst over us. This storm lasted through the night and, the roof of our hovel being like a sieve, the rain soon converted the mud floor of the hut into a quagmire. We huddled together and did what we could to keep dry and warm, but the night proved long and cheerless.

Soon after daybreak next morning we made our escape from these wretched quarters, but rain was still falling, and of the wonderful scene of the preceding evening nothing was visible from the gap but an ocean of clouds. The descent is most precipitous and for the first 2000 feet we fairly tumbled down. Afterwards it became more gradual and led over a steep cultivated slope of red clayey soil, making walking difficult. Nowhere is this descent easy, and very glad were we all that our route was down instead of up this mountain-side. At the foot of the descent the road leads through a rocky defile to emerge on the banks of a clear-water river some 60 yards broad. Across this we were ferried to Tan-chia-tien, the village we saw from near our lodgings last night. This village consists of some fifty houses which are huddled together and overhang the river in front and cling to the cliff behind in an extra-ordinary manner. From this village a kind of long street with houses scattered here and there along its length extends for 2 miles to the village of Chikou, situated at the junction of this river with another of almost equal size. A mile or so from Chikou up the secondary stream are the salt wells of Taning-ching.

The road we struck at Tan-chia-tien is a highway leading northwards to Shensi and southwards to Kuichou Fu on the Yangtsze River. Hereabouts and down to Taning Hsien, 12 miles distant, and northwards I know not how far, the cliffs are sheer to the water's edge. The road is well graded and a good 6 feet broad, and has been excavated or blasted from the solid rock.

From Chikou to Taning Hsien is said to be 30 li with not a house or hovel between. To cover this we with difficulty engaged boats, long, narrow, lightly built affairs (Sin-po-tzu), turned up at prow and stern, with no oars and steered by long sweeps projected fore and aft. The current was strong and rapids numerous ; aided by a freshet we covered the whole distance in half an hour. The brief journey was through one grand chasm, the walls of rock being sheer to the water's edge with no space even for a shingle-bank to lodge. These cliffs are treeless and mostly bare with here and there grassy patches and clumps of delicate, graceful Bamboo (*Arundinaria nitida*). The road zigzags around the cliffs on the right bank well above high-water mark, and every inch of it has been blasted from the hard wall of rock. Stone gates and barriers occur at intervals, but there are no houses. This road is of such a nature that time and neglect can affect it but little, but it is now scarcely used except by occasional pedestrians and salt-carriers when the river is impracticable. I tried hard to discover when and by whom the road was built but found no one who could tell me. It is evidently one of the ancient arteries of China, and probably dates back to the discovery of the salt-wells. It struck me as being an old military road and may probably have been built centuries ago when Kuichou Fu was a place of infinitely greater importance than it is to-day.

The river I have mentioned, known locally as the Taning Ho, rises near the borders of Shensi, Hupeh, and Szechuan, and after flowing nearly due south enters the Yangtsze at Wushan Hsien. From Chikou boats descend to its mouth, 200 li distant.

Taning Hsien, alt. 750 feet, the most easterly inland town in Szechuan, is situated on the right bank of the river, here about 100 yards broad, and sweeping from the gorge in a fine curve. The town is wedged in on the side of a mountain-slope up which the city wall ascends for several hundred feet. The river-front is bounded on one side by the city wall, and the shops, houses and yâmens are crowded together near the river. The upper slopes enclosed within the city wall are given over to agriculture. The town, comprising about 400 houses, is the residence of a district magistrate, and boasts a trade in salt and odds and ends. Formerly it was the centre of a large opium traffic.

At Taning Hsien the Chinese Banyan (*Ficus infectoria*), so abundant and characteristic of the central parts of Szechuan, puts in an appearance. Near a temple, a few hundred yards from the north gate of the town, I observed from the boat what appeared to be a Mantzu cave built in the face of lime-stone rock. On inquiring I was told of four or five similar caves in this neighbourhood. Later I may have something to say about these caves, but it is interesting to be able to register their presence at the extreme eastern edge of the province, since heretofore they have been considered a feature of the more western parts. Physically and geologically speaking, the country east of the Taning River belongs to western Hupeh. Almost immediately west of it the characteristic red sandstone of Szechuan commences.

For twenty-two consecutive days my followers and I had struggled through the wild, lonely mountain fastnesses of north-western Hupeh, suffering much from bad roads, worse accommodation and scarcity of food supplies. For the first time on record the journey had been accomplished by a foreigner, and one and all of my followers were happy in the thought of the comparative luxury and plenty of the country which was now before us.

CHAPTER VI

THE RED BASIN OF SZECHUAN

Geology, Mineral, and Agricultural Wealth

THROUGHOUT the eastern and central parts of the province of Szechuan, from near the Hupeh boundary to the valley of the Min River, the predominant rocks are red clayey sandstones, probably of Jurassic age. These rocks are of immense thickness and impart a characteristic red colour to the surface, and for this reason the late Baron Richthofen gave the term " Red Basin " to the whole region. This basin is nearly triangular in shape, the city of Kuichou Fu marking the " apex." Imaginary lines connecting Kuichou Fu with Lungan Fu in the north-west, and Kuichou Fu with Pingshan Hsien keeping a little to the south of the Yangtsze River, respectively mark the northern and southern "sides." Another line from Lungan Fu and thence skirting the valley of the Min River to Pingshan Hsien marks the " base " of the triangle. The entire basin is nearly 100,000 square miles in area, and is surrounded on all sides by lofty mountain ranges, those on the west rising above the snow-line. In the east the boundary ranges are composed principally of Upper Carboniferous limestone, as described in Chapter II. The western boundary ranges are largely made up of shales. The Yangtsze River traverses the basin from west to east, following a course nearly parallel with the southern limits of the basin itself. Within this triangle there is abundant life, industry, prosperity, wealth, and intercommunication by water. Outside of it on all sides the contiguous country is sparsely inhabited, little productive and no river is navigable save the Yangtsze, where it leaves the basin.

In ancient geological times this region was doubtless a vast inland lake with a fairly even floor. Since the draining off of the waters the Yangtsze River and its network of tributary streams have eroded channels 1500 to 2500 feet deep through these soft sedimentary rocks, and converted the whole basin into a thoroughly hilly country. To-day practically the only level area is the Plain of Chengtu, some 80 miles long and 65 miles wide, with an average altitude of 1800 to 2000 feet above sea-level. The rest of the basin is broken up into a network of low, rolling or flat-topped mountains averaging about 3000 feet above sea-level, and nowhere exceeding 4000 feet altitude. The whole of this region is under agriculture, the highest development of which obtains on the Chengtu Plain, perhaps the richest area in the whole of China. Anent this particular part we shall have something to say later.

How great a period of time has elapsed since the disappearance of the waters from this basin is purely conjectural. But that this triangle has long constituted a well-marked boundary is evidenced by the fact that remarkably few of the plants found in the mountains bordering the eastern limits at 2000 feet altitude and upwards are common to the mountains bordering the western limits. The genera are of course the same, but the species are usually distinct. The difference between the floras of the eastern and western border-ranges is too great for a mere 500 miles of longitude to account for solely. The same is true of the fauna in so far as the game birds and animals are concerned, as Chapters XI and XIII, Vol. II, dealing with these will confirm.

From evidence presented by the flora to-day it appears doubtful if ever the Red Basin was covered with great forests. Rather would I suppose that subsequent to the disappearance of the waters the region bore some resemblance to the " bad lands " of certain parts of the United States of America. All this is admittedly pure conjecture. Everywhere to-day, trees, shrubs, and herbs are common, but the flora, in contra-distinction to that of the contiguous regions, is relatively poor, and the species largely common to the entire basin. Further, the majority of these species are widely spread throughout the warmer low-level legions in China, some indeed ranging to the extreme eastern limits of the country. A theory is apt to become fascinating, and may easily be carried too far.   The facts above recorded are best left until the geology of China generally is more accurately known.

Coming down to historical times we learn that the region previous to the advent of the Chinese was peopled by an aboriginal population divided into the kingdom of Pa in the east and the kingdom of Shu in the west.   This aboriginal population has entirely disappeared, but records in the shape of well-constructed caves having square entrances are found scattered all over the Red Basin.   These caves are especially abundant around Kiating Fu.   A little investigation of these interesting places has been attempted, and fragments of pottery and odds and ends discovered.   The entrances to these caves could only be closed from the outside, and from this fact, and other details, it is probable that they served as the burial-places of the chiefs and more wealthy among this extinct people, rather than as dwelling-places or harbours of refuge.   Doubtless they have been subsequently used for these latter purposes, but that they were designed for tombs seems to best explain their origin.   From Chinese history we learn that as early as 600 B.C. the kingdom of Pa had relations with the Chinese kingdoms of Ts'u, which occupied the regions north of the barrier ranges.   Later, Pa princesses married Ts'u kings. Ts'u was in time conquered by Ts'in (another Chinese kingdom), which gradually absorbed Pa, and finally conquered Shu about 315 B.C.   A military road was commenced from the neighbourhood of modern Hanchung Fu, designed to connect with the region around modern Chengtu, by Ts'in-shih Hwang about 220 B.C.   This road, which enters Szechuan from across the barrier ranges near Kuangyuan Hsien, is still in existence as the great highway connecting Chengtu with Hanchung Fu, Sian Fu, and, ultimately, Peking itself.   For the next fifteen centuries the history of this region is full of war, rebellion, and internecine strife.   Usurpers established petty dominion over the country from time to time, only to disappear amongst awful slaughter and bloodshed.   There is scarcely a square mile of the whole region but what recalls scenes of valour, treachery, and carnage.   In the latter half of the thirteenth century the famous Tartar, Kublai Khan, carried his arms victoriously over nearly the whole of modern China, and formed an Empire which the succeeding Ming and Manchu dynasties maintained more or less intact.

Since the time of Kublai Khan many rebellions have swept over Szechuan, decimating the population and paralysing industry. The present population is mainly derived from immigrants (voluntary and otherwise) who settled there during the early half of the eighteenth century. A census taken in A.D. 1710 returned only 144,154 souls for the whole province. To-day the population is estimated at 45,000,000! In spite of all the long-sustained wars and bloody rebellions, agriculture has managed to subsist, and the whole of the Red Basin is a lasting monument to Chinese genius and industry in matters agricultural. An abundant water-supply and constant tillage are necessary to obtain a full crop from these sandy clays and marls. Fortunately, the whole region is one vast network of streams, all of which drain into the mighty Yangtsze. The Chinese have taken full advantage of this intricate river system, and devised manifold methods of irrigation. These devices, combined with the untiring patient industry of the people, have converted an incipient " bad land " into a rich and fertile region of terraced fields. In no part of China that I have visited are the people entitled to greater praise for meritorious agricultural accomplishment than throughout this Red Basin.

In many parts of this region the river valleys are so steeply eroded that very little cultivatable bottom-land is formed. Consequently the rice belt is relegated to slopes and summits of the low, flattened hills. In limestone regions the bottom-lands constitute the main rice belt; but in the sandstone regions the opposite obtains. The climate of the whole region is mild and genial, and during both winter and summer the land is cropped. Rice is the great summer crop with maize, millet, sweet potato, sugar-cane, tobacco, pulse, and various other crops. The principal winter crops are wheat, rape, peas, broad beans, cabbage, Irish potato, etc. Formerly opium was cultivated in enormous quantities as a winter-crop, but this has lately been almost entirely suppressed. Cotton does not thrive in the Red Basin; though its culture is attempted in many districts, notably Yilung Hsien and in Tungchuan Fu. Cotton is the one commodity that this region has to import, and nearly all its surplus products go to meet this deficiency. But, if cotton is very little grown, many kinds of hemp are produced in quantity; though very little is used for textile purposes. Silk production is everywhere an industry of importance; and in many districts the staple. Only the very poorest are without some silk garment; though such is only habitually worn by the more wealthy. Tea is grown in many districts both for local consumption and for export. In the more westerly parts tea for the Thibetan market is a staple product. Wood Oil and many other valuable economic trees are also largely cultivated. Fruit is generally grown, including peaches, apricots, plums; apples, pears, and oranges in variety. Oranges thrive remarkably well in this red sandstone; and the extensive orchards are a wonderful sight during the month of December. Tangerine varieties are most generally cultivated; and the fruit in season can be purchased at the rate of twelve hundred or more for two shillings ! The tight-skinned varieties are less frequently grown, and are more expensive. Around Lu Chou are plantations of Litchi trees. When they came from their original homes the settlers evidently brought with them their favourite trees and grains and planted them around their new homesteads. These introductions; and the favourable climate, explain the presence of such a vast variety of cultivated plants, which is probably greater than that found in any other province in China.

The steeper and rougher country is covered with small woods of Oak, Pine; and Cypress, elsewhere trees are confined to the vicinity of streams, houses, temple-grounds, wayside shrines; and tombs.

The streams are navigable for extreme distances, and a perfect network of roads traverse the basin in every direction. These roads are, on the whole, well built for Chinese roads, but are not kept in thorough repair any more than those elsewhere in the land. The streams, however, are well supplied with ferries; and well-built bridges, substantially constructed of stone, and kept in good repair, are a feature throughout the entire region. Large cities, market villages, hamlets, and farmhouses dot the land, which everywhere appears prosperous and its inhabitants contented. Drought occasionally brings famine, but, on the whole, the Red Basin suffers much less from this dread calamity than do other and less favoured parts of the eighteen provinces of China.

The mineral wealth of the Red Basin is not varied, but enormous brine deposits occur scattered over the whole area, and are worked at depths varying from almost surface level to 3000 feet. In the eastern parts, Kuichou Fu, Wên-tang-ching, for example, the rivers have scoured the rocks until the brine-deposits are practically exposed. In the west, however, as at Wu-ting-chiao, situated on the left bank of the Min River a few miles below Kiating Fu, the brine is found at about 500 feet down. At Tzu-liu-ching, on the left bank of the To River, where the richest deposits occur, the brine is found at depths from 1000 to 3000 feet.

Salt is worked in some thirty-nine districts in the Red Basin. It is everywhere a Government monopoly, and its production and subsequent distribution are rigorously controlled. The annual output is estimated at about 300,000 tons. At Tzu-liu-ching most of the brine is evaporated by inflammable gas; in all other places the brine is evaporated by coal heat. In boring the deep wells, it is uncertain whether brine or gas will be struck, but both are equally valuable. The occurrence of this inflammable gas indicates the presence of petroleum beds at still greater depth.

Coal is found in greater or lesser quantities scattered all over the Red Basin, and is always found not very far removed from brine pits. This coal varies from lignite to anthracite. The average quality is poor, but one or two good seams have been found, notably at Lung-wang-tung, a few miles north of Chungking.

Our early description of the Red Basin needs some amplification to explain the presence of coal and other minerals. Although the sedimentary sandstones are in a state of undisturbed stratification over a great part of this area, yet there is dissecting this Red Basin a number of linear elevations, in which the underlying limestone is bent up from a great depth. This limestone forms in every case an axial core, lined on either side by highly inclined strata, among which there is ordinarily noticeable, next to the axis, a double belt of coal-formation, followed on either side by strata of red sandstone standing on edge. Baron Richthofen estimates that " the area of the coal-bearing ground in Szechuan probably exceeds in size the total area of every other province of China." But probably throughout nine-tenths of this area the coal-measures are buried deep beneath the superincumbent strata, and with trifling exceptions can never become available for mining. In the linear elevations, above referred to, the belts of coal-formations, though narrow, are of great length. They are most readily accessible in those places where rivers have cut through and exposed the ends of the seams. Mining is done by means of horizontal adits working from an exposed surface inwards. Coal is very generally obtainable throughout the Red Basin; and is the ordinary fuel of the entire region.

Iron-ores occur scattered throughout the entire region, but though in the aggregate the iron-smelting industry is a considerable one, in no one place is iron made on a large scale.

Sulphate of iron (copperas) is found in combination with coal in one or two districts, notably in Kiangan Hsien. Lime is common to all the linear elevations mentioned above, occurring in juxtaposition with coal, and is burnt in kilns in the usual way.

Gypsum is found and worked in one or two places, notably Mei Chou and Pengshan Hsien, both districts on the Min River, between Kiating and Chengtu.

Mineral oil in small quantity occurs in the district of Pengch'i Hsien, where a native company has made some attempts to develop the industry, but with unsatisfactory results.

Other less important minerals occur in small quantities. The precious metals, gold and silver, are not found in the Red Basin proper but in the mountainous country to the west of this region, where copper, lead, and zinc ores also occur.

In reference to gold it should, however, be mentioned that rude placer mining is carried on during the winter months, throughout the numerous shingle banks exposed in the beds of the Yangtsze, Kialing, and Min Rivers. On the Yangtsze this precarious industry is first to be noted some 50 miles below

Ichang, but it is not general until the region west of the Gorges is reached. The industry is carried on by the unemployed peasantry, and the returns are most insignificant. This gold is in all probability brought down by the Yangtsze and its larger tributaries during the summer floods. There is no record of any gold-bearing quartz having been found *in situ* in the Red Basin proper. In the mountains bordering its western and north-western limits, gold quartz is found in greater or less quantities, and all the principal rivers of this region either take their rise in, or flow through, these ranges. This fact explains the presence of small quantities of gold far removed from the gold-bearing strata.

CHAPTER VII

EASTERN SZECHUAN

NARRATIVE OF A JOURNEY FROM TANING HSIEN TO TUNGHSIANG HSIEN

THE region described in this chapter was traversed by Lieut.-Colonel C. C. Manifold and Captain E. W. S. Mahon when surveying for a possible route for the proposed Hankow-Szechuan Railway in 1903 or 1904, I am not sure which. There is no record of any other traveller having crossed this part of eastern Szechuan, though it is very possible that missionaries may have done so. I do not know the conclusions arrived at by these surveyors, but the construction of a railway along the route I traversed would be a difficult and costly undertaking.

The following narrative is compiled from my diary, and may, perhaps, convey a brief idea of the nature of the country and the flora found in the more easterly parts of the Red Basin. As will be gathered, I took ten days to cover the distance, but I travelled leisurely, and the journey could be accomplished in six days.

June 28.—Yesterday we spent the day at Taning Hsien, refitting and preparing for our journey westwards to Chengtu Fu. Money exchange proved an involved and difficult business. Ten-cash pieces, both Hupeh and Szechuan currency, are accepted here at 20 per cent. discount. This means that the purchasing power of a thousand such cash is only equal to 800 string-cash. Farther west, Hupeh 10-cash pieces are not current, and the Szechuan 10-cash piece is only accepted for two days' journey west of this town. We had therefore to burden ourselves with string-cash, which added considerably to the weight of our loads. A thousand cash in 10-cash pieces weighs less than 2 lb.; in string-cash the same equivalent weighs over 8 lb.! If there is one reform more badly needed than another in China it most certainly is in the matter of currency.

Leaving Taning Hsien by way of the west gate we made a slight ascent and entered a narrow, highly cultivated valley, flanked on our right by fairly high and on the left by lower mountains, nearly treeless and sparsely cultivated. The town of Taning lies in a depression, and the morning mists obscured the general view. It is a very small place, with much of the land enclosed within its walls given over to cultivation. An outer gate, wall, and block-house guards the west gate proper.

Ascending the valley by an easy road which more or less skirts a fairly large tributary stream of the Taning Ho, we reached the village of Che-tou-pa before noon. Rice was abundantly cultivated everywhere, irrigation being effected by means of large " Persian " wheels. Much cotton is cultivated following wheat, the winter crop. Maize was 5 feet tall and in full flower. *Paliurus orientalis*, a thin tree 30 to 50 feet tall, is very common, and was laden with white, circular, odd-looking fruits. Weeping Willows, Cypress, and fine specimens of a hairy-leaved, small-fruited Hog Plum (*Spondias*) were noteworthy, with Bamboo groves in abundance.

On leaving Che-tou-pa we deserted the main tributary stream and ascended a small branch. The valley narrows, and the hills are more wooded, chiefly with Cypress. The road is easy, though here and there sadly in need of repair. We journeyed slowly, and eventually crossed over a ridge of low hills to the hamlet of Lao-shih-che, which we reached at 5 p.m. This tiny place, alt. 1950 feet, and 55 li from Taning Hsien, consists of half a dozen houses, scattered through a narrow valley with rice fields on all sides. The people were very nice, but inquisitive.

We were on the edge of the Red Basin and much of the soil had the characteristic red colour. Wood Oil trees are commonly cultivated, but cotton was not in evidence during the afternoon. In a grove I noted some magnificent trees of *Pistacia chinensis* and *Sapindus mukorossi*. The young shoots of the former are cooked and eaten, but the round fruits of the Sapindus are used as soap. Celtis trees are common, their smooth, pale-grey bark rendering them conspicuous. On a ridge we noted many trees of the interesting " Button tree " (*Adina racemosa*). These trees were 30 to 60 feet tall, 2 to 4 feet in girth, and the finest specimens of their kind I have met with. The Chinese Pine (*Pinus Massoniana*) is general, but by far the commonest tree of the day was the Cypress (*Cupressus funebris*).

The road proved a pleasant change ; instead of wild and savage scenery, low rounded hills backed by steeper mountains, all rather treeless, and for the most part cultivated, were the order of the day. Here and there were a few outstanding cliffs of limestone with an occasional temple crowning odd crags. At Taning Hsien we secured a number of new coolies, and these men described the country passed through in the afternoon as Laolin (wilderness). This immensely amused my Ichang men, who recommended these newcomers to try the Sheng-nêng-chia before speaking of " Laolin " !

The day was grilling hot, and all were fairly exhausted on arrival at Lao-shih-che. Whether it was the heat or the after effects of a day's holiday I could not determine, but I was called upon to play " Doctor " to nearly half my followers. The majority were suffering from stomach troubles, several from filthy sores. Epsom salts, permanganate of potash, and iodoform dressings soon improved the majority.

The next day was gloriously fine, but scarcely so hot as the previous day, or perhaps the slightly increased altitude made it more bearable. The whole day we travelled nearly due west through a narrow valley bounded by moderately high parallel ranges. The road continues easy with occasional ascents and descents. We were still on the fringe of the Red Basin, but in the afternoon grey sandy soils were most in evidence. Rice is cultivated wherever sufficient water is obtainable, and was scarcely ever out of our view. Maize is the other principal crop, with various kinds of pulse and the Irish potato. The sweet potato is cultivated here and there, and Wood Oil trees are even more abundant than before. Much oil is evidently produced in this region, and we noted many oil-presses during the day. The parallel ranges are from 500 to 1000 feet above the valley, sparsely cultivated, and for the most part well timbered with Cypress (*Cupressus funebris*), Pine (*Pinus Massoniana*), and Oak (*Quercus serrata*). Poplar is a common tree, and by the sides of streams Weeping Willows abound. Shrubs in variety occur the most noteworthy being *Itea ilicifolia* and *Torricellia angulata*. Nowhere else have I seen this latter shrub so plentiful; it favours the sides of streams, ditches, and rocky gullies, forming a densely leafy bush 8 to 12 feet tall. The fruit when ripe is black, and is borne in large pendulous cymes. The Itea occurs in rocky places, and its pendulous tails of greenish-white flowers are often 18 inches long. The leaves very closely resemble those of the common Holly, and when not in flower it might easily be mistaken for that plant.

Houses are scattered along the route, but the population is sparse. We met a few mule trains, but there was really very little traffic on the road. We found accommodation for the night at Hsia-kou, a prettily situated hamlet, alt. 2800 feet, 65 li from Lao-shih-che. Our lodgings were spacious, but the occupants of the house looked unprepossessing opium sots.

At To-chia-pa, a small hamlet passed a few miles before reaching Hsia-kou, a road branches off to the northward and leads to Chêngkou Ting. It was said to be a hard road to travel over.

On leaving Hsia-kou we immediately plunged into a ravine with steep limestone cliffs 300 to 500 feet high; the road follows the dry bed of a torrent. At the head of this ravine we made a slight ascent, and wandered across low mountain-tops for a few miles, then descended and crossed a branch of the Kuichou Fu River by a covered bridge. Up to this point Pine and the Chinese Fir (*Cunninghamia lanceolata*) are common. At the bridge I photographed the largest tree of *Platycarya strobilacea* I have seen. This specimen was fully 75 feet tall, with a girth of 6 feet. I had no idea it could attain such dimensions. A few miles beyond this point we forded the main branch of the Kuichou Fu River, a broad, shallow, clear-water stream, and about noon reached the village of Chiao-yang-tung. Soon afterwards we were overtaken by a furious thunderstorm, which arose with amazing suddenness. The fury of the storm spent itself in a torrential downpour of short duration, but rain fell steadily during the rest of the day.   The rain did not improve the mud road, and our progress was slow and difficult in consequence.   During the whole afternoon we made a steady ascent, skirting the mountain-sides through woods of Pine and Oak.   Eventually the road enters a narrow sloping valley, at the head of which we found lodgings for the night in two houses which constitute the hamlet of Shan-chia-kou, having travelled 65 li.   Around this place the flora is varied and essentially cool-temperate in character. Bushes of Mock Orange (*Philadelphus*) were conspicuous on all sides with their wealth of pure white flowers.   The Hautboy strawberry is abundant, and around our hostel I gathered in a few minutes enough of these luscious fine-flavoured white berries to stew for dinner.   The Torricellia was again common. It ascends up to 3500 feet altitude, and often forms a small inelegant tree.

We saw very little rice during the day, maize and Irish potato being the chief crops.   There is practically no traffic on this road ; the mule-trains seen yesterday evidently came down the road from Chêngkou Ting.   Population is sparse, and what there is looked strongly addicted to the opium habit. So far, however, we had not seen any signs of poppy.

A magnificent day ushered in the new month.   The morning was bearably hot, but the afternoon scorchingly so.   A hundred yards beyond our lodgings we reached the head of a ridge, and an abrupt descent of a couple of thousand feet or so led to a narrow valley where much rice, maize, Irish potato, and a little Hemp (*Cannabis*) are cultivated.   The parallel ranges flanking this valley are of limestone with outstanding bare rocks and cliffs, very little cultivated but with good woods of the common Pine.   Here and there in the valley we passed fine trees of Sassafras, Sweet Chestnut, Sweet Gum (*Liquidambar*), Chinese Fir, and Poplar.   At the head of the valley we made a slight ascent to the top of a ridge.   Below us, some 2500 feet, flowed a considerable river walled in by lofty limestone precipices.   It was 10.30 a.m. when we reached the top of this ridge, and the rest of the day's march was a more or less precipitous descent to the river, which we reached at Sha-to-tzu about 3 p.m. In its early stages the descent is as difficult as it well could be—over loose Rowley-raglike debris, down and up steep steps, and over slopes of greasy clay. We crossed one or two cultivated slopes, but most of the time the road skirts around the sides of cliffs. At the edge of one precipice, 500 to 1000 feet sheer, the road is carried through a narrow tunnel some 50 yards long and 3½ feet broad at the exit. This tunnel is partly natural and partly made by blasting the hard limestone. It was quite dark within the tunnel save for a faint glimmer of light at the exit. Both chairs and loads were with difficulty carried through this tunnel. This roadway is of recent date, and is unique in my experience of Chinese roads. Rough as it is it saves about 10 li and a very steep ascent and descent.

From the tunnel-way the road skirts the tops of the cliffs with many exasperating and wearying ascents and descents. Finally we descended to a small tributary of the main stream and, crossing over, reach Sha-to-tzu, a busy market village and, for the nature of the country, of considerable size. Up the tributary stream some 10 li, iron is mined and smelted, the quality being described as good. Around Sha-to-tzu, coal is worked and lime burnt.

The river we had with so much fatiguing travel reached enters the Yangtsze at Yunyang Hsien, distant 150 li. It is a clear-water stream of considerable volume, and is navigable for small boats from just below Sha-to-tzu to within 15 li of its mouth. Salt and a little peddling traffic was noticeable on the road; also odd loads of medicines, including Tu-chung, the bark of *Eucommia ulmoides*. The salt is a product of Yunyang Hsien, and is not allowed to enter Taning Hsien. The quality is said to be superior to that found within the latter district.

The flora of the day's journey was not particularly interesting, being very much the same as that found in the glens and gorges around Ichang. A new Stachyurus and *Abelia Engleriana* were collected. The Heavenly Bamboo (*Nandina domestica*) was particularly abundant in rocky places, its elegant foliage and large erect trusses of white flowers with conspicuous yellow anthers making it very attractive. In autumn and winter the masses of scarlet fruit render it extremely beautiful. Wood Oil trees were general in rocky places, and *Hypericum chinense*, a wealth of rich golden yellow, was strikingly handsome, nestling on the cliffs everywhere. Quite a little Ramie (*Bœhmeria nivea*) is cultivated, and the people were busy stripping the fibre-containing bark from the stems. The leaves, like those of several other plants, are used for feeding pigs. The stripping and cleaning is all done by hand labour.

The day's march was full of interest, but the intense heat and hard road made the 60 li very trying, and all were glad when the end of the stage was reached. The scenery was magnificent, and forcibly reminded us of the glens and ravines around Ichang. The railway surveyors must have been filled with despair when they encountered this steep limestone country !

Sha-to-tzu is only about 700 feet altitude, and, in spite of the swift-flowing stream which passes its " front door," was suffocatingly hot. We managed to find a good inn with quarters removed from the street and remarkably private in character. We had no difficulty in changing silver here, but 10-cash pieces are no longer negotiable. String-cash was the only kind the people would accept.

Just below Sha-to-tzu we crossed the river by a ferry which is assisted by a convenient rapid, and commenced a steep ascent. A few hundred feet up we were afforded a good view of the village we had just left. It contains about a hundred houses, crowded together on a narrow, fan-shaped slope. A few temples shaded by large Banyan trees were conspicuous, and the whole made a decidedly pretty scene. The ascent is through cultivated fields, groves of Wood Oil trees, and finally Pine woods. At 3100 feet altitude we crossed a gap, and 200 feet more led to the top of the range. The rest of the day we followed an undulating, easy road which meanders through rocky, Pine and Cypress clad mountain-tops, and finally descends to Chê-kou-tzu, which was our destination for the day.

The country is very pretty ; farmhouses are scattered along the route, and where possible the land is under cultivation. Rice was of course *the* crop where water is obtainable, maize and Irish potato elsewhere. Tobacco is grown ; a little of this crop has been noted every day since leaving Taning Hsien. Limekilns were common all day. In one place we saw a number of men out with guns after Muntjac. They fired several times, but did not succeed in killing the animal during the time we watched the sport.

A few li before reaching Chê-kou-tzu we passed an unusually large house of much architectural beauty. It was erected by a rich man named T'ao, who held the purchased rank of " Hsien." He died some twenty years ago, and the family has fallen on evil times, thanks to idleness and opium.

The flora was not very interesting. Some fine trees of Cypress and odd ones of *Catalpa Duclouxii* were noteworthy. Pine abounds, and I saw several examples of " clustered cones." These cones, a hundred and more crowded together, were all small, and appeared to have displaced the male flowers. Chê-kou-tzu, alt. 2050 feet, consists of some forty houses situate above the mouth of a stony stream and backed by low mountains, on the top of which is an ancient fort.

On leaving Chê-kou-tzu we immediately entered a pretty valley, highly cultivated with rice and bounded by low, rolling hills. A large number of farmhouses and a small hamlet occur in this small but prosperous valley. Throughout the whole forenoon we traversed a number of such depressions separated one from another by low ridges, always ascending slightly with the valleys narrowing until finally they become mere basins surrounded by rocky limestone mountaintops. Crossing a final ridge we entered Kai Hsien at a place called Shih-ya-tzu, 35 li from Chê-kou-tzu. Up to this point the scenery is very pretty, the rocky mountain-tops being clothed with woods of Pine and Cypress. Oak is common, and in more open places and around habitations we passed fine trees of Spondias, Pistacia, Paulownia, Tapiscia, and *Hovenia dulcis* ; the last covered with masses of white flowers.

The afternoon's journey was all downhill, ending in a very precipitous descent to Wên-tang-ching. The road led through maize plats, odd rice fields, and bare, treeless hilltops, with no flora of interest. Nearing our halting-place for the day it was fearfully hot, and the absence of shade was severely felt.

Here and there the hilltops are crowned by old forts built of dressed stone. These relics (Chaitzu) of turbulent times abound all over the salt districts and more wealthy regions of eastern Szechuan. Limekilns, small clay-covered affairs, were common *en route*, and many of the rice fields had been dressed with slaked lime.

Wên-tang-ching is a town of considerable size, by far the largest place we had met with since leaving Ichang. It is built on steep slopes bounding the two sides of a clear-water stream, and backed by high limestone cliffs. On the south-west side these cliffs are stark and sun-baked. Large quantities of salt are produced here. The brine pits are situated on the foreshore and immediate neighbourhood of the stream. The supply depends on the state of the river, the lower the water the more brine is obtainable. During summer floods the industry is suspended. The salt is white, powdery, of moderate quality, valued at twenty-six cash per 16-ounce catty. It is distributed throughout the north and west of the Hsien, but cannot enter the city of Kai Hsien itself. Dust-coal is mined in the neighbourhood and used for evaporating the brine.

The town consists of about a thousand houses and boasts several temples and large guild-halls, that belonging to the Shensi guild being very prominent on account of its large size and ornate architecture. Two small pagodas protect the luck of the place, and many Chaitzu crown the surrounding hills. The inhabitants are not prepossessing, being unusually dirty and over-curious. Some were not over-civil, and there was a slight scuffle between my men and some rowdies. Our inn was dark, suffocatingly hot, and most undesirable in every way. It was the best we could find, and served its purpose, uncomfortable as it was. Behind the inn is a huge cave with vast stalactites and a cool breeze blowing through it. This is the curiosity of the town, and was pointed out with a great show of pride.

All along the route from Taning Hsien there has been much argument over the price of food-stuffs. The natives constantly putting up the price on my men, this led to heated words, but generally ended in the men getting a fair price. Many of them had travelled too far not to know " the ropes."

Wên-tang-ching is only 750 feet altitude, and with the

heat from stark surrounding cliffs and hundreds of furnaces is a regular inferno. Prosperous it may be, but it failed to appeal to us, and one and all were glad to quit it.

A steep ascent of a few hundred feet and we cleared the town. After passing through a large graveyard we descended to an alluvial valley where much sugar-cane, maize, tobacco, and a little cotton is cultivated. The road is broad, paved with blocks of hard stone, and traverses the valley to its head at Ma-chia-kou, 12 li from Wên-tang-ching. Ma-chia-kou is the coal port for the salt-wells. Coal is carried overland some 30 li, and at this point put into small boats and conveyed to the brine-pits. This coal is valued at three cash per catty, the carriers receiving one cash per catty for carrying it down. The boats are small, steered by sweeps fore and aft, and can descend this stream to Kai Hsien, 60 li below Wên-tang-ching, and from thence to Hsiao Ch'ang on the Yangtsze, 110 li distant. At Ma-chia-kou the road leaves the main stream, which flows down from the northward, and after crossing a neck descends to a broad stony torrent, which it ascends through uninteresting country, eventually leading through a limestone ravine. The coal supply is of primary importance to the salt-wells, consequently the road is kept in good repair. During the forenoon we met hundreds of coolies and many women laden with coal. Iron is found in this neighbourhood, and pigs of this metal were being carried down to the boats.

On leaving the above-mentioned ravine we traversed a valley of rice fields and reached Yi-chiao-tsao about noon. Five li above this hamlet we crossed over, and during the rest of the day's march descended a narrow valley flanked by steep Cypress-clad slopes. Sweet potato is abundantly cultivated, also rice and maize. Houses are frequent, and the people appear fairly well-to-do.

We found lodgings for the night at Wang-tung-tsao, alt. 1350 feet, having covered our usual 60 li. The day was terribly hot, making the journey very fatiguing. The inn is beautifully situated in a grove of Bamboo and Cypress, but is poor and abominably stinking. Really, it is a pity that such a vile house should defile such a charming spot.

The next day was also grilling hot, with no signs of a storm to cool the air.   Descending a few li we struck a rather broad stream with many red-sandstone boulders in its bed.   The road ascends this stream to its source, and steep ascents and descents were all too frequent.   We lunched at the village of Kao-chiao, and a more hot, fly-infested, stinking hole, with people more inquisitive, I have not experienced.   Savage, snarling, yelping dogs abounded, and these, with the other discomforts, did not add relish to the meal.   My followers seemed to share my views of this village, and grumbling and malediction were loud on all sides.   Our meal did not occupy long, and we all felt better when clear of this filthy, pestiferous place.

The whole day was spent among sandstone, grey and red, and we were seldom out of sight of rice fields.   Pine abounds, but the Cypress does not appear to be at home here, and occurs very sparingly as compared with previous days.   Wood Oil trees are common, but the flora generally is not interesting. Elæagnus bushes are common and were in ripe fruit.   The stems of this shrub (Shan-yeh-wangtzu, or Yang-ming-nitzu) are commonly used for making the long stems of tobacco pipes so frequently seen in this region.   The Burdock (*Arctium major*) is common in stony places and often cultivated, being used as medicine under the name of " Yu-pangtzu."

Three li before reaching our lodgings we crossed a ridge, and passing through a stone gateway, entered the district of Tunghsiang Hsien.   We found an inn at P'ao-tsze, a small scattered hamlet, alt. 2650 feet, 65 li from Wang-tung-tsao. The inn is clean and prettily situated in a little valley bounded by low red-stone hills all under cultivation.   The host is evidently a man of substance, and amongst other things owns a reclining chair of novel workmanship, of which he is evidently very proud.

There was no breeze last night, and I slept badly, partly owing to the heat and partly to the occupants of the inn talking in high argumentative tones till past midnight.   This is a common habit of the Chinese and very exasperating to any one trying to get to sleep.

With only 50 li to do to Nan-pa ch'ang the men were in high spirits and set out in style.   The road proved easy—by one o'clock we had covered the distance, and had a couple of long rests into the bargain. On leaving P'ao-tsze we made a short, steep ascent, and then descended by an easy road leading over and among sandstone bluffs. Twenty-five li on we reached the bed of a small stream and followed it to its union with a large, clear-water stream flowing down from the northward. This stream flows past Nan-pa ch'ang and is navigable for small boats down to Tunghsiang Hsien and up-stream some 290 li to Tu-li-kou. Near our destination we passed many coolies carrying down bright anthracite coal. This comes from Fu-che-kou, some 50 li away, and the men receive 200 cash per picul (100 catties) for carrying it down. We also noted iron in flat slabs, which comes from Tung-che-kou, 25 li distant.

Pine was again the common tree, but Cypress also was fairly common. The sandstone is evidently more favourable to the Pine than to the Cypress. We saw two or three trees of the rare " Hung-tou-shu " (*Ormosia Hosiei*). The wood of this tree is highly valued and so heavy that it sinks in water. Wood Oil trees continued abundant, and around Nan-pa ch'ang plantations of Mulberry were being made. Evidently sericulture is about to be attempted in this district.

Nan-pa ch'ang, alt. 1550 feet, is a village of considerable size, and is built on a flat bordering the stream. Formerly it was one of the most important centres of the opium trade in Szechuan, and its product was of very superior quality. The opium trade is now completely stopped, and this place has suffered tremendously in consequence. It also boasts a trade in general merchandise, supplying a large area of country to the northward. But opium was its real source of wealth, and with the disappearance of the opium traffic all trade has declined. To the northward a lot of tea is grown and the leading people of Nan-pa ch'ang are endeavouring to divert this trade from its present headquarters, Taiping Hsien, to their own village.

Around Nan-pa ch'ang there are a few Mantzu caves. Everything was very quiet in the village and we attracted little or no attention. We saw a couple of uniformed police, odd street lamps, and other signs of modern ideas. Leaving this village the next morning at 7 a.m., in four small boats, we dropped down the beautiful clear-water stream, and reached

Tunghsiang Hsien at 3 o'clock.   The distance is 140 li by water, 90 li by land.   Numerous rapids obstruct the stream, but since the volume of water is comparatively small they are not dangerous.   The river is bounded by sandstone cliffs, often steep and covered with Pine, Cypress, and mixed shrubby vegetation.   Chaitzu are common, and here and there we passed villages.   Cultivation is general, and the crops were beginning to show signs of suffering from drought.   Pulse in variety is abundantly cultivated, together with rice and other favourite articles of food.   Ordinarily the whole region is one of plenty and prosperity.

It was a pleasant change dropping swiftly down this beautiful river, and we all enjoyed the journey.   On reaching Tunghsiang Hsien a thunderstorm broke and the rain cooled the air delightfully.

We entered the city of Tunghsiang, alt. 1400 feet, through the east gate, and found accommodation in a quiet and moderately clean inn.   The city, though not large, seemed a busy place.   Formerly it boasted a large traffic in opium, and its general trade was then very considerable.   It nestles among low hills on the right bank of the river, and is faced on the opposite bank by steeper and higher mountains.   Sandstone cliffs and bluffs abound, and in some respects the whole scene reminded me of the country around Kiating Fu.

Our inquiries into the matter of currency disclosed the fact that Szechuan dollars are accepted here, but 10-cash pieces were still useless.   The Roman Catholic and China Inland Mission have established outstations here.   An Irish missionary belonging to the latter was staying here at the time of my visit, and I enjoyed for an hour or so the pleasure of his company. It was pleasant to hear my own tongue spoken again.   Not since leaving Ichang, 35 days before, had I encountered a single foreigner.

CHAPTER VIII

THE ANCIENT KINGDOM OF PA

Narrative of a Journey from Tunghsiang Hsien to Paoning Fu

FROM Tunghsiang Hsien the recognized route to Chengtu or Paoning Fu descends the river via Suiting Fu to Ch'u Hsien, then strikes westward to Chengtu, north-west to Paoning Fu. I had no fancy for the main route, since, by going due west from Tunghsiang Hsien to Paoning Fu, we should explore new ground. My map (War Office, Province of Ssu-ch'uan, Eastern Sheet) gave no route, but indicated villages, and it was evident, therefore, that these villages were connected by a road of some sort. Chiangkou seemed a good place to start for, so my men were instructed to find a cross-country road to this town. At first the innkeepers, chair hongs, and local officials denied all knowledge of any such road, and indeed of such a place. But any one who has travelled in China values such denials at their proper worth and is not discouraged. The men who had charge of these inquiries were trusted followers of ten years' standing, and though entirely ignorant of the geography of the region could be relied upon to ferret out a route if such existed. After about six hours' investigation, from the magistrate's Yamên downwards, I was informed that a small mountain road did exist, but was over hard and difficult country, affording the poorest of accommodation. This was sufficient; they were told to get an itinerary of this route and engage a few local men as extra carriers. I went to bed about 10.30 p.m., satisfied that by 6 o'clock next morning everything would be ready for our cross-country jaunt. In my travels about China I have been singularly fortunate in never having any trouble with the Chinese. In the spring of 1900

I engaged about a dozen peasants from near Ichang. These men remained with me and rendered faithful service during the whole of my peregrinations. After a few months' training they understood my habits thoroughly and never involved me in any trouble or difficulty. Once they grasped what was wanted they could be relied upon to do their part, thereby adding much to the pleasure and profit of my many journeys. When we finally parted in February 1911, it was with genuine regret on both sides. Faithful, intelligent, reliable, cheerful under adverse circumstances, and always willing to give their best, no men could have rendered better service.

This cross-country journey from Tunghsiang Hsien to Paoning Fu, via Chiangkou, promised to be of more than ordinary interest. There was a novelty about it also, since there was no record of any foreigner having attempted it before. The route lay across the old kingdom of Pa (see Chapter VI, p. 66), and I hoped to find some evidences of this ancient race. Chinese history is dry, difficult reading, and it is hard to dig out solid facts. Wars, rebellions, and massacres deluge everything in blood ; the arts of peace are seldom given any prominence. The Chinese historians have always treated the aboriginal races with arrogant contumely, rendering it almost impossible to discover at this late date anything about the arts and life of these lost peoples. That the modern province of Szechuan boasted kingdoms and dynasties of its own before the advent of the early Chinese is historical fact. The first Emperor of the Ts'in dynasty, Tsin-shih Hwang or Shih Hwang-ti (221–209 B.C.), incorporated part of the kingdom of Pa with the rest of his dominions and nominally also that of Shu, whose capital was near modern Chengtu Fu. The succeeding Han dynasty (206 B.C. to A.D. 25) made the conquest complete. Since this time no aboriginal chief has ruled the Red Basin of Szechuan, though it has been conquered and re-conquered time and again by usurping Chinese and alien races. During the period A.D. 221–265, the Chinese Empire was divided into three kingdoms, one of which, under the Emperor Liu-pei, had its capital at Chengtu. Liu-pei and three of his generals and statesmen are handed down as popular idols, and everywhere in Szechuan stories are told of the doughty deeds accomplished by these heroes of old. With this brief introduction I again take up my narrative :—

My principal men once more proved equal to the occasion, and on 8th July everything was arranged for our cross-country journey. An itinerary had been made out, and the Hsien provided us with a couple of uniformed soldiers. (He sent six, but I managed to get them reduced to two.) Heretofore on this journey we had managed to avoid taking official escort, although it is the custom to do so in Szechuan. No ordinary traveller desires this honour, but it is thrust upon him and cannot easily be avoided. The presence of this escort renders the officials responsible for the traveller's safety in accordance with treaty arrangements. It is necessary to pay these men a few cash, but often they prove useful in odd ways. Cash is cheap, and an extra hundred per day for each soldier does not amount to any considerable sum. The difficulty is in keeping the escort down to two men. Four and six are common numbers, and if one did not protest continuously an almost unlimited number of authorized and unauthorized ragamuffins would attach themselves to one's caravan. If there is cash to be made the legitimate escort is often not above farming in a few extra " hands," thus securing more money. The escort is provided with a letter from the official supplying it wherein the number of men dispatched and their destination is given, so by examining this it is possible to check any attempt at fraud. On dismissing these men at their journey's end it is necessary to give them a card to carry back to their superior. Their letter is stamped by the official who provides the new escort, and the card signifies that their duty has been satisfactorily carried out. If they return without a card for any reason or other they are liable to be punished.

Leaving Tunghsiang Hsien by the west gate we followed the main road to Suiting Fu for a few li, then branched off to the right. The road is well paved, and we met plenty of traffic. For the first 20 li the road is practically level, winding in and out among low hills. It then makes a steep ascent to the top of some bluffs, where Mien-yueh ch'ang is situated, 30 li from the city of Tunghsiang. Throughout the rest of the day the road was easy, leading through and among low hilltops and shallow valleys intercepted by hills 300 to 500 feet high. Cypress and Pine are abundant, so also are Pistacia and *Albizzia lebbek*, both making large umbrageous trees. *Vitex Negundo* is the commonest shrub, sometimes attaining to the dignity of a small tree : it was everywhere covered with masses of lavender-purple flowers.

The country is highly cultivated. Rice predominates, with various kinds of beans (especially Lutou, *i.e.* green beans) next in importance—both crops evidently follow after wheat. We passed odd patches of cotton and very many Plum trees. The region is well populated, bypaths abound, and it was no easy matter for us to keep to the right road. At one point the road bifurcates, one branch leading to Shuang-ho ch'ang, the other to Shuang-miao ch'ang, our proposed halting-place for the night. The names of these two villages, when spoken rapidly, sound much alike, even to Chinese ears. My men got somewhat confused, and for a time there was danger of the caravan following two divergent routes.

We passed through the market village of Wang-chia ch'ang (ch'ang signifies market village), a curious little place, dominated by a temple in the middle, the roofs of the houses uniting to form a central covered way, beneath which the road passes through the village.

Shuang-miao ch'ang was our intended destination for the day, but being market day the village was filled to overflowing. A hundred or more people followed us into an inn, and in a little while there was hardly room to breathe. Many were obviously under the influence of wine. It was too hot to tolerate such overcrowding curiosity, so we pushed on a further 5 li, where we happened on a decent farmhouse, which we commandeered. The owner being away, his wife was at first sorely afraid, but in a couple of hours her confidence was gained and all was well. The men had difficulty in obtaining food and lodging. The majority went back to the village, but none complained : they all realized the impossibility of my remaining the night in such a crowded place.

Our quarters were new and shaded by a grove of Bamboo and Cypress, but mosquitoes were multitudinous, rendering life miserable. The place is called Hsin-chia-pa, alt. 1950 feet. We had covered 80 li, through a rich and interesting country. Lady Banks's rose was particularly abundant, with stems 2 feet round, festooning trees 40 to 50 feet tall. Mantzu caves occur sparingly. In several places we passed cultivated patches of *Panicum crus-galli*, var. *frumentaceum*.

We parted excellent friends with our hostess at Hsin-chia-pa, a trifling present and 400 cash made her extremely happy ; her thanks were both genuine and profuse. Soon after starting we made a precipitous ascent of 1000 feet and crossed what is probably the water-shed of the Suiting and Sanhuei Rivers. A descent led to the head-waters of a small river, where is situated the tiny market village of San-che-miao. Market was in full swing, the one short street with its few hovels being crowded with people. We passed through without stopping to satisfy the curiosity of the crowd. At this village several roads converge, the one we followed continuing to descend the stream, and leading through a rocky jungle-clad defile. The cliffs are of red and grey sandstone, steep, rugged, and crowned with Pine and Cypress. As fluviatile shrubs *Distylium chinense*, various Privets (*Ligustrum*) and *Cornus paucinervis* abound. The last-named is a low-growing shrub with spreading branches, and laden with small flat corymbs of white flowers it formed a most attractive bush by the water's edge. In the jungle-clad slopes through which the road winds Tea bushes 15 feet and more tall are common. They looked uncommonly like spontaneous specimens, but were possibly planted long ago, though some of them have been undoubtedly naturalized. Occasional trees of the Red Bean (" Hung-tou "), *Ormosia Hosiei*, occur ; at one time this was probably a very common tree in this region. Its timber is most valuable, and the tree has been ruthlessly felled. There is practically no cultivation in this defile, or room for any, and not a house for 20 li.

After traversing this wild and interesting ravine for several hours we made a steep ascent to the top of the cliffs, and on the way up discovered spontaneous plants of the Tea Rose (*Rosa indica*) in fruit. These were the first really wild specimens I had met with. Once on top of the cliffs we found that the country all around is under cultivation, chiefly rice, with houses at frequent intervals. After a few li the road descends to the river again, and crossing by stone steps we reached the market village of Peh-pai-ho, where we found accommodation in a large house. This village, alt. 1600 feet, also known as Peh-pai ch'ang, is a small place with unprepossessing residents. Our quarters were dark, fairly filthy, and loafers crowded around until bedtime.

The day's journey of 60 li was through a sparsely populated country, which, considering the low altitude, was unusually wild and jungle-clad. The flora had points of interest, the finding of Tea bushes and bushes of the Tea Rose in the rocky defile being particularly noteworthy. On bare sandstone cliffs large white trumpet-flowered Lilies were common, with their stems thrust out at nearly right angles to the cliffs. We met very few people on the road, and most of the women we saw had natural feet. In the early morning we passed quite a lot of *Panicum crus-galli*, var. *frumentaceum*, cultivated.

The itinerary my men secured at Tunghsiang Hsien did not err on the side of accuracy. Constant inquiries were necessary, but the results were confusing. The river which flows past Peh-pai ch'ang was said to unite with the Chiangkou stream at Chiang-ling-che, 70 li distant.

A heavy thunderstorm occurred in the night, accompanied by a downpour of rain which lasted intermittently into the early forenoon of the next day. The country needed rain badly, and the air was cool and fresh in the morning. Peh-pai ch'ang is a regular warren of dilapidated houses, filthy and stinking, with a loafing and unduly curious population. A loin-cloth belonging to one of my chair-bearers was stolen during the night, and my followers had little that was complimentary to say about the village or its inhabitants.

Following the river down-stream for 5 li, we reached Lei-kang-k'êng of the maps. This hamlet (pronounced Lei-kang-t'an, from a fine waterfall on a small river which, flowing from the north, joins the main stream at this point) consists of a deserted temple, a few scattered houses, and an old fort high up on the cliffs. It and Ta-chên-chai, another old fortress, are the only places marked on the map—both are to-day of no importance. The market villages, the real places of importance, are not shown. Maybe these villages have sprung up comparatively recently, and the forts, from long-continued peace, lost their importance. This is the only feasible explanation which occurs to me. This section of the country is only known from Chinese maps, and these were probably compiled during military times long ago.

From Lei-kang-k'êng a steady ascent for 30 li leads to the top of a ridge where is situated the important market village of Peh-shan. This place boasts a fine temple and about a hundred houses. Like all such villages in these parts it consists of one central street, practically closed over by the nearly uniting eaves of the houses. These market villages are a striking feature of this part of Szechuan. They are situated approximately 30 li apart, and nine markets are held monthly in each. These are arranged in such manner that the three villages lying nearest to one another hold market on different days, thus between them practically covering the month. On market days the country-folk assemble from all sides to buy and sell. Pedlars and itinerant merchants constantly journey from market village to market village. Such markets are of the highest importance in a sparsely populated country, but the denizens of these villages suffer from too much spare time. Market days are what they exist for, and on : the other days are mainly spent in gambling and sloth. This system of market villages dates away back to the very dawn of Chinese civilization, and in the region we are concerned with here, is very little changed from what it was in the earliest times.

Five li before reaching Peh-shan ch'ang we struck a road which comes from Suiting Fu, 120 li distant. The country hereabouts is split up in low mountain ranges, averaging 3000 feet altitude, composed of grey and red sandstones. The river-valleys are mere ravines clothed with dense jungle, Pines, and Cypress, with no bottom lands nor cultivation of any sort. Some 500 feet up the cultivated area begins and extends to the summit. Terraced rice fields abound, tier upon tier, intercepted by low bluffs, the tops of all of which are cultivated. The whole country is very pretty, and in

many respects peculiar, as far as my experience goes.   Most of
the women have natural feet, and many were busy weeding
and firming the rice plants.

On leaving Peh-shan ch'ang the road makes a steep descent
to a stream and a correspondingly steep ascent to the top of
the bluffs again, winding round to the crest of a ridge where
is situated the market village of Yuen-fang.   This place,
alt. 3100 feet, which was our destination for the day, having covered the allotted 60 li, is prettily situated.   We found
lodgings in a new and clean house boasting a veranda overlooking a grove of Pine and Cypress trees.   The crowd which
collected was small and though inquisitive kept at a respectful
distance.

The flora proved identical with that of the previous day's
journey.   I again met with sub-spontaneous Tea bushes in
the jungle and also saw a number of the Red Bean trees.
Perhaps the most interesting objects noted during the day
were the tombstones.   These are very different from any I
have seen elsewhere.   They are of freestone, often highly
sculptured, the workmanship being superior and the effect
both artistic and dignified.   One or two old stone mausoleums
were magnificently sculptured.   The aboriginal population
of this region were accomplished workers in stone, and their
work may have served as patterns for the Chinese to copy
from.   In conception the designs are evidently not pure
Chinese, and I strongly suspect " Mantzu " influence, to use
the Chinese term for the aboriginal population.

At Fu-erh-tang there is a particularly fine family temple,
and near by a Mantzu cave in an isolated piece of rock.
Around many of the mausoleums and family temples ancient
stone pillars (wei-tzu, *i.e.* masts) occur.   Wayside shrines and
small temples, dedicated to Kwanyin (Goddess of Mercy) and
to the tutelary genii are common, the images being carved in
stone and mostly coloured blue and white.   The day's journey
was more than usually interesting ; somehow one felt instinc-
tively that one was traversing a region closely associated with
man from very ancient times.

Leaving Yuen-fang ch'ang soon after 6 a.m., we traversed
country similar to that of the day before, and reached Pai-

(pronounced P'an)-miao ch'ang at 10 o'clock. Here, contrary to what my map indicated, I found no river. Replies to inquiries gave it as 30 li farther on, and so it proved. The map for this region is hopelessly inaccurate, and it was quite useless attempting to be guided by it. Pai-miao ch'ang is a small village built on the top of a ridge and surrounded in part by woods of Cypress and Pine. Crossing an undulating area we descended by an easy path, finally reaching the T'ungchiang River, 10 li above Chiangkou. This river is fully 100 yards broad, with red-coloured water and a sluggish current. Boats were easily secured and we dropped down-stream to Chiangkou, which we reached at 3 o'clock, just before a heavy thunderstorm broke. The day's journey was said to be 70 li, the road was easy, with flora and scenery identical with that of the preceding days.

Chiangkou (alt. 1600 feet) is the second town in size and importance in the department of Pa Chou. It consists of about 500 houses, built on the fringe of a promontory between two rivers, backed by low, steep, well-wooded hills. The rivers unite at this point and are navigable downwards to Chungking. The more easterly stream descends from T'ung-chiang Hsien, the westerly stream from Pa Chou, each town distant from Chiangkou 180 li. Both streams are navigable for small boats up-stream to these towns.

A Fêng Chou (official next below a Chou in rank) resides at Chiangkou. From a distance the town looks well-built and prosperous, but it does not improve on closer inspection. The position is admirable and undoubtedly the town is of considerable commercial importance, yet we had great difficulty in exchanging twenty taels of silver. Like other towns we had passed through, Chiangkou was feeling the suppression of the opium traffic severely, and until new industries arise to take the place of the opium trade the resources of all these places will be crippled.

We found accommodation in a poor but quiet inn, and, thanks to the thunderstorm, no curious crowd gathered to annoy us. My principal men spent several hours in finding out a cross-country road to Yilung Hsien, and eventually succeeded.

On leaving Chiangkou we ferried across the Pa Chou River and then made a steep ascent of a few hundred feet. The rest of the day we meandered along the crest of a range of low mountains, following an undulating path. In parts the road was good, in others ankle deep in slippery mud. Thundershowers fell at intervals and it was fairly cool.

The country generally is similar to that traversed during previous days. Tobacco is a rather common crop hereabouts and we saw a little cotton. Maize is very rare, but rice is abundantly cultivated. Shrines and small temples continued common and in good repair. Kwanyin and Tuti are the common deities, the latter representing an old man and his wife, constituting the tutelary genii. Dignified, ornately carved tombstones and mausoleums were everywhere in evidence.

Our intended destination for the day was Chên-lung ch'ang, 60 li from Chiangkou, but on reaching there we found market in full swing, and, to avoid the crowd, we journeyed on another 6 li. On market days these villages are impossible, from the foreigner's point of view. I rode through this village in my chair, and the crowd which gathered at the upper end of the place mustered several hundreds. Wine appears to flow freely on market days and many were under its exciting influence. Prudence as well as comfort therefore demands that one avoid all crowds as much as possible when travelling in the interior regions of China. Women attend these markets in force and appear to be a power in this part of the Celestial Empire. Their bearing and manners generally are very free for Chinese women ; natural, unbound feet are the rule.

Chên-lung ch'ang is clustered on the narrow neck of a sandstone ridge, and in common with all such villages boasts a fine village temple. We lodged for the night in a poor wayside inn at Hei-tou-k'an, alt. 3100 feet.

The next day was cool, with showers at odd times, but of no consequence. With the exception of one steep descent and an ascent in the late afternoon, the road was more or less level all day, traversing the tops of the low mountains. These sandstone mountains are dissected by innumerable deep, narrow ravines, clothed with Pine, Cypress, and a dense jungle of miscellaneous shrubs. Unlike limestone country no bottom-lands are formed, and cultivation is relegated to the higher parts of the ranges. Farmhouses are scattered here, there, and everywhere, but the villages are all situated on the tops of the mountains, most frequently on the divide of a ridge.

Fourteen li from Hei-tou-k'an we passed through the village of Tai-lu ch'ang, where market was in progress and many pigs on sale. Thirty li from this place we passed Ting-shan ch'ang, a village of considerable size, charmingly situated on the neck of a ridge, backed by a Chaitzu and a fine cypress grove. Chaitzu, of which frequent mention has been made, are a feature of these parts. They are old forts, said to have been mostly constructed during the great sectarian rebellion of A.D. 1796–1803. A small official (Hsao-shoa-tang) resides at Ting-shan ch'ang. In spite of its fine situation this village was unusually filthy and was dominated with the strong odours of a wine distillery. The usual crowd of loafers followed us for some distance on quitting this village.

In the late afternoon we arrived at Lung-peh ch'ang, alt. 3000 feet, after travelling 74 li. We lodged in a rambling, dilapidated inn, fairly clean, with rooms removed some little distance from the street—the village sewer. Market not being in progress the crowd of inquisitive idlers was relatively small.

The flora was not particularly interesting, but we passed a number of fine Camphor trees (*Cinnamomum Camphora*). The crops, however, were rich and varied. Rice and sweet potato preponderate, odd patches of cotton were noted and also others of Indigo (*Strobilanthes flaccidifolius*). In the afternoon coolies laden with salt passed us. This salt is pure white and granular and comes from Nanpu Hsien. From our lodging Ting-shan ch'ang was visible, 30 li distant and nearly due east. The map shows a river flowing past this village, but the only one we could get tidings of was 50 li from that place.

After a comfortable night's rest we continued our journey through country similar to that of foregoing days, but less well-wooded and more inclined to be arid, with broader valleys more under cultivation. Our route followed the boundary between Pa Chou and Yilung Hsien. We passed through two market villages and stayed for the night in a farmhouse 1 li before reaching Fu-ling ch'ang, alt. 2800 feet. We purposely stopped at this place in order to escape market day at the village, but did not avoid a constant crowd until after dark, when the doors were closed. We found all these crowds quiet and orderly enough, but a continuous mass of faces, with wooden expression, blocking the doorway, obstructing light and air, is very trying. Immensely useful as these markets are to the country-side, they have decided drawbacks from a traveller's point of view. A good police force is really more necessary in these villages than in the cities. The more lawless element fears a Hsien (Magistrate), but has little respect for a Ti-pao (Village Head-man). Local produce is mostly in evidence in these markets ; a few needles, aniline dyes, trumpery odds and ends, chiefly of Japanese origin, are about the only foreign goods met with.

We saw more cotton during the day than we had elsewhere observed on this journey, and the crop looked flourishing. Kao-liang (*Sorghum vulgare*) was a common crop, but rice and sweet potato again preponderated. The sorghum and rice were bursting into ear. Wood Oil trees occur, but are not plentiful, and commercially this crop is unimportant hereabouts. Mixed with the cotton were odd plants of the oil-seed yielding *Sesamum indicum* (" Hsiang-yu ").

In the late afternoon we traversed country which somewhat resembled that around Tunghsiang Hsien—on all sides, as far as the eye could see, nothing but ridge upon ridge of low sandstone mountains. These ranges average about 3000 feet in altitude, those to the east and north being higher than those to the west and south. The map is all wrong for the region, so I could not definitely place our route. The river Sheng-to, so boldly indicated, escaped us, though we should have crossed it had the map been correct. The market villages passed were smaller than heretofore, very filthy and stinking, yet most charmingly situated on the neck of low ridges, and well shaded with trees. Camphor trees are very common, and " Pride of India " trees (*Melia Azedarach*) particularly abundant. The stage said to be 70 li proved very easy, the weather being dull and cool.

Our stay over at the farmhouse was hardly a success; we had a full crowd until bedtime, and in spite of fair promises four of my men who remained in the house with me had neither dinner nor bedding. As a punishment I paid only half our usual rate, much to the householder's chagrin. Fuling ch'ang was quite deserted when we passed through in the early morning. It occupies the narrow neck of a sandstone ridge, after the usual manner of these villages. The same is true of Shih-ya ch'ang, 30 li farther on. Ten li beyond this latter village we passed a nine-storied pagoda and sighted the town of Yilung Hsien, to the northwards, about a mile distant as the crow flies and at equal altitude (2500 feet). Yilung is a very small town, situated on the mountain-top, backed by a steep bluff and surrounded by a wall of dressed sandstone. Two-thirds of the land enclosed within the city wall is given over to cultivation. We passed to the south-west of the town by a road which makes a steep descent and ascent and then meanders along the tops of the mountains until Tu-mên-pu is reached. The mountains are lower, more flat, the valleys wider, and the whole country more treeless. Cotton is abundantly cultivated throughout this region, and it is evident that the district of Yilung produces a very considerable quantity. Rice and sweet potato are the common crops, the latter thriving on the hot almost soilless rocks. The earth is drawn into ridges, often leaving bare rock between, and cuttings are inserted. These cuttings, leafy shoots about 6 inches long, quickly take root and form plants that produce an abundant crop. Sorghum is fairly common in places, but maize is very scarce. Stone monuments were less in evidence, but we passed a fine O-mi-to Fu stone surmounted by a hideous T'eng-kou. Six old hats protected this stone from the rain and sun ; in front was a huge mass of ashes and the remains of many Joss sticks. We were informed that the tutelary genius of this spot is renowned for his benevolence, and that it was hoped shortly to erect a shrine over the spot.

We had been unfortunate in the matter of market days all along, and found another in progress at Tu-mên-pu. Seemingly having gained nothing by staying the night a little beyond or before reaching these villages, we experimented and stayed at one. It was not a success. A mob rushed our inn and bedlam reigned for a couple of hours. Eventually it thinned down, but many of the more insistent and curious remained until bedtime. There was much noise, but the crowd was friendly enough; nevertheless, I was glad it proved to be the last market village of its kind we encountered before reaching Chengtu.

Tu-mên-pu or ch'ang, alt. 1950 feet, 70 li from Fu-ling ch'ang, is a large and prosperous village boasting much trade on market-days. Something of everything in the way of native produce was on sale, and the narrow street was thronged to overflowing. Five li before reaching this place our road converged with one leading to Pa Chou city by way of Yilung Hsien.

I had a poor night's sleep in consequence of loud talking being carried on far into the early hours, a woman (as usual) being the principal offender. This was an emphatic reminder of the hubbub of the crowd which besieged us on arrival, and I was really glad to quit Tu-mên-pu. A few li beyond this village we branched off from the main road, which goes to Nanpu Hsien. Much salt comes from this township, and during the last two or three days we had met many carriers laden with this commodity.

Forty li beyond Tu-mên-pu we passed the poor village of Shui-kuan-ying, protected by dilapidated gates which denote its former military character. In years gone by it was a barrier of some considerable importance. Twenty li farther on we reached the village of Chin-ya ch'ang, alt. 2150 feet, which differs from all we had met with heretofore in having a broad main street fully exposed to the heavens. To our great joy market was not in progress. We found lodgings in a new and quiet inn, which proved a welcome change ; the people, too, were courteous and much less inquisitive. The day was exceptionally hot, and all were glad to reach the end of the allotted stage of 60 li. Twelve li before reaching Chin-ya ch'ang we struck a main road leading from Nanpu Hsien, and following it entered the village through an isolated ornate gateway. Beyond the village is a bluff of grey sandstone studded with square-mouthed caves. These caves are crude imitations of Mantzu caves, and are of recent origin, and purely Chinese.

The day's journey was through less interesting country than usual. The broad valleys and nearly treeless mountains are all under cultivation. Cotton was again common in the forenoon, but much less so afterwards. This crop looked as flourishing as Chinese cotton usually does. Tobacco is sparingly cultivated. The tobacco leaves are merely sun-dried before using, and the quality is therefore poor. Sweet potato was more plentiful than ever ; the arid sandstone rocks evidently suit this crop. Rice was, of course, everywhere abundant, sorghum common, but maize was very scarce and suffering from drought. The Irish potato is very little cultivated in these parts. Around Tu-mên-pu white-wax is produced in small quantities on the Privet (*Ligustrum lucidum*), but the cultivation is slovenly carried out, the trees being dwarf and ill-cared for. A few Cypress trees were noted, but Paulownia is a common tree, and Wood Oil trees rather plentiful. A little silk is raised, but the industry is unimportant hereabouts. Odd trees of the Banyan (*Ficus infectoria*) occur near houses and shrines. We passed a few fine tombs, but the average headstone is less ornate than those formerly met with.

We experienced a brief but terrific thunderstorm during the early hours of the morning, and rain continued to fall slightly when we set out from Chin-ya ch'ang. For 20 li we followed an abominable road of mud. This was very greasy, and caused many of us to come " croppers." Ultimately, we reached a paved road, and, 6 li farther, a tributary stream of the Kialing River. This tributary is broad, broken by cataracts and rapids, and quite unnavigable at this point. It unites with the Kialing River, locally known as the " Paoning Ho," at Ho-che kuan. This is a small riverine port boasting a remarkably fine shop where coal, lime, and especially Chinese wine (sam-shu), were on sale. On the paved road we met several men carrying Bombay cotton yarn—the first example of foreign goods we had encountered on the whole journey !

At Ho-che kuan the Kialing River is smooth and placid, and when in flood is fully 400 yards broad. We ferried across the river to the right bank, and then traversed an alluvial flat of considerable size, highly cultivated with rice and sorghum, with here and there a little abutilon hemp. At the head of this flat, some 10 li from the river, we crossed over some levelled hillocks into a basin—evidently an old lake bed—surrounded by bare mountains 200 to 500 feet high. This depression was a lake of luxuriant padi (rice), with houses here and there, nestling in clumps of trees. From this basin we passed through a low, narrow gap between the hills, and came abruptly to the Paoning River a little below the city itself. We were ferried across and found lodgings in a large and fairly comfortable inn. The flora of the day's journey was without special interest, Cypress being the only kind of tree really common. But shading some graves, opposite Ho-che kuan, occurs the largest specimen of the " Pride of India " (*Melia Azedarach*) I have met with. This tree is 70 feet tall, and 10 feet in girth.

Paoning Fu is a city of past rather than of present greatness. It is still a most important administrative centre, but its real interest lies in its great historic past. From the early days of Chinese conquest it has been a strategical point of vast importance. During the Ming dynasty (A.D. 1368–1644) a generalissimo of forces had a palace here. The terrible rebel, Chang Hien-tsung (A.D. 1630–46 *circa*), ravaged the country roundabout, but spared the city itself. The result is that many of the official residences and temples date back to ancient times.

Formerly Paoning was the centre of a lucrative and thriving silk industry, but this has steadily declined during the last twenty years, and to-day it is a mere figment in comparison. Attempts are now being made by the officials to rejuvenate and foster this industry, which apparently failed more through lack of business ability and tenacity than anything else. On the neighbouring hills I was told " wild silk " is produced, the " worms " feeding on the leaves of a scrub Oak, " Ching-kang " (*Quercus serrata*).

The city occupies an extensive alluvial flat on the left bank of the river within an amphitheatre of low, bare, often pyramidal, hills, 300 to 600 feet high. Viewed from the opposite bank there are no outstanding architectural features visible, save a pavilion, which is practically the only building breaking the monotony of level roofs. The area within the city walls is largely occupied by yamêns, temples, and residences of the more wealthy. Business is mostly carried on outside the city proper, and is confined mainly to one street. Umbrellas were the most noticeable articles on sale, but the city is famous for its superior vinegar, great jars of which were on view.

Hedges of the thorny shrub, *Citrus trifoliata*, are a prominent feature of this city and its suburbs, giving to the quieter streets a country-lane-like appearance. The water supply of the city is from wells, which are often very deep. This water is said to be good, but that supplied to our inn had a very "earthy" flavour. From what I saw of the city during a day's stay there, I received the impression of its being clean, its people very orderly and courteous, and the decline in its prosperity most marked. The Paoning Ho is a shallow river, and opposite the city about 500 yards broad when in flood. It is navigable for boats of considerable size downwards to Chungking. Up-stream small boats ascend to Kuangyuan Hsien. A certain amount of merchandise descends in small boats from Pikou, in Kansu, to Chaohua Hsien. These rivers are most important to Paoning Fu, for, in addition to export trade, the coal and wood used in the city itself are conveyed over these waterways. On the right bank facing the city is a ledge of cliff, on which nestle several temples and pavilions, sheltered by groves of Cypress. In a gap in this cliff is situated the busy little village of Nan-ching kuan. Timber is very scarce around Paoning. Cypress wood is commonly used in house-building; Alder wood (*Alnus cremastogyne*) occasionally being employed for window frames, etc., but its chief use is as fuel. Pine occurs, but, save as fuel, is worthless. Cunninghamia, that most useful of Chinese conifers, does not occur in this neighbourhood. The wood of the Hung-tou tree (*Ormosia Hosiei*), so highly esteemed for carpentry, was formerly fairly common and cheap. To-day, however, it has to be brought from a distance, and, in consequence, is expensive. Oak and "Huang-lien" (*Pistacia chinensis*) are the only other timber trees of note. Paoning is an important missionary centre, and the seat of a Protestant bishopric. During my brief visit I had the pleasure of spending a few hours with the kindly and energetic Bishop Cassels and certain of his coadjutors, who did all they could to render my stay pleasant.

Leaving Paoning Fu and following the main road via Tungchuan Fu, by easy stages I entered the city of Chengtu Fu nine days later, having occupied fifty-four days on the journey from Ichang.

The journey from Tunghsiang Hsien to Paoning Fu fully bore out my expectations. The crowds on market-days were a decided drawback, but not once was I insulted or called (in my hearing) uncomplimentary names. The avaricious greed and cunning of the inhabitants were most marked. They were constantly putting up the prices of food-stuffs on my followers, which led to much argument and high words, and several times I was called upon to settle such disputes. The greed of the Szechuanese peasant and small shopkeeper is a byword among the Chinese of other provinces. The term " Szechuan Lao-ssu " (" Szechuan Rat ") is applied derisively to the whole population by the Chinese from other provinces. Niggardly and avaricious they undoubtedly are, but they are great agriculturists, and the question of the " mote and beam " may well be left open. As mentioned before, the province is largely peopled by descendants of immigrants, and these folk almost invariably style themselves men of the provinces their ancestors came from !

The outstanding features of this ancient part of Szechuan are :—

1. The elaborate system of market villages situated at equal distances of 30 li apart, each with its nine market-days per month, and alternating with the markets of neighbouring villages. Each village is situated on the mountain-top and usually on the neck of a divide, with one central more or less covered street.

2. The rice belt is confined to the mountain slopes and summits, the valleys being ravines, jungle-clad as a rule, with little or no cultivatable bottom-lands. The highly cultivated nature of the region and the presence of cotton in quantity around Yilung Hsien.

3. The numerous fine mausoleums with remarkably good

sculpturing ; the peculiar, dignified style of headstones and mural monuments generally.   The number of wayside shrines and deities all in excellent repair.

4. The independent bearing and buxom appearance of the women, and their evident influence in general market business. Throughout the whole region natural, unbound feet are the rule.

5. The region is far from being thickly populated, and cannot be termed wealthy, but apparently it is largely self-contained and self-sufficient.

6. The intense curiosity of the people due to the fact that few had ever seen a foreigner before.

CHAPTER IX

THE CHENGTU PLAIN

" THE GARDEN OF WESTERN CHINA "

THE plain of Chengtu is the only large expanse of level ground in the great province of Szechuan ; it is also one of the richest, most fertile, and thickly populated areas in the whole of China. Its extreme length from Chiang-kou in the south to Hsao-shui Ho beyond Mienchu Hsien in the north, is about 80 miles as the crow flies ; its extreme width from Chao-chia-tu in the east to Kuan Hsien in the west, about 65 miles, in a straight line. From Kiung Chou in the extreme south-west to its north-east limits beyond Teyang Hsien is about 80 miles. The circumferential boundaries are very irregular, the total area being under 3500 square miles. Chengtu Fu, the provincial capital, and seventeen other walled cities, are situated on this plain, together with very many un-walled towns of large size. Farmhouses dot the plain in every direction ; the total population probably exceeds 6,000,000.

This plain is really part basin part sloping alluvial delta, having an elevation ranging from about 1500 feet above sea-level in the south and east to 2300 feet in the north-west and west. It is bounded to the west and north-west by the steep descent of a high mountainous region, which at very little distance from it reaches above the snowline. In the extreme north-west the snowclad Chiuting shan actually overlooks the plain. On its other boundaries the sandstone hills of the Red Basin rise sharply in bluffs 1000 to 1500 feet above the level of the plain. The high barrier ranges protect the plain from the cold northerly and westerly winds, but to these must be ascribed the rapid changes in temperature, the fogs, raw atmosphere, and the overcast skies so characteristic of Chengtu Fu.

The plain owes its abundant fertility to a complete and marvellous system of irrigation, inaugurated some 2100 years ago by a Chinese official named Li-ping and his son. The headquarters of this irrigation system is Kuan Hsien, a city situated on the extreme western edge of the plain, where the Min River debouches from the mountains. The principle on which the system is based is simple in conception, but very intricate in detail. An obstructing hill called Li-tiu shan was first cut through for the purpose of leading the waters through and distributing them over the plain. The passage having been excavated, the waters of the Min River were divided, by means of an inverted V-shaped dyke, a little distance above the canal into two main streams, the " South " and " North " Rivers, as they are called. The waters of the " North " stream are carried through the Li-tiu shan cut, and after passing through the city of Kuan Hsien are divided into three principal streams. The most southerly of the three, called " The Walking Horse," flows directly east, and irrigates the districts of Pi Hsien and Chengtu. The central stream, called the " Cedar Stem River," flows north-east, and is utilized to irrigate the western and northern parts of the above-named districts. Branches of these two streams flow past the south and north walls of Chengtu, uniting near the east gate of the city. The third, or northern branch, known as the " South Rush River," flows north towards the city of Pêng Hsien, and then south-eastwards past Han Chou. All the subdivisions of this branch and its anastomosing canals and ditches unite near Chao-chia-tu to form the head-waters of the To River, which flows due south past the famous salt-wells of Tzu-liu-ching, and finally enters the Yangtsze at Lu Chou. This " South Rush River " is fed by numerous torrents which descend from the ranges bounding the north-west edge of the plain. These streams—broad, stony, irresponsible things with no defined banks—exist only during rains or the melting of the snow in spring. In crossing the northern parts of the plain the traveller can form some estimate of what the whole was like before the irrigation canals were dug and dikes erected. But to return to the system at Kuan Hsien. The "South" River, which occupies the original bed of the Min River, is divided into four principal streams almost immediately opposite the Li-tiu Hill. The most easterly branch, named the "Peaceful River," irrigates the districts of Kuan Hsien, Pi Hsien, and Shuangliu Hsien. The next branch, called the "Sheep Horse River," irrigates other parts of the above-named districts, uniting with the "Peaceful River," at Hsinhsin Hsien. The third stream, called "Black Stone River," irrigates the department of Chungching Chou, and unites with the other streams at Hsinhsin Hsien. The fourth stream, called "Sand Ditch," flows south-west through Tayi Hsien and Kiung Chou, joining the other streams at Hsinhsin Hsien. All the streams which intersect the Chengtu Plain, save those forming the upper waters of the To River, unite at Chiangkou, a village at the extreme south-eastern edge of the plain, some 45 English miles south of Chengtu city.

This system of anastomosing canals, ditches, artificial and natural streams, forms a complex yet perfect network. The current in all is steady and swift, the bunding secure, and floods unknown. Not only are all these streams and canals available for irrigation, but they are also utilized to generate power required in various industries. Flour-mills abound, driven by vertical or horizontally fixed water-wheels. Similar mills are used for crushing Chinese rape-seed, preparatory to pressing for the extraction of the oil.

It must not be supposed that Li-ping and his son completed the system which obtains to-day. They were the originators, and the lines they laid down have been followed and enlarged upon by succeeding generations. These famous irrigation works are perhaps the only public works in all China that are kept in constant and thorough repair. Every year the bunding is repaired and all silt removed from the bed of the channels. An official styled Shui-li Fu—"Prefect of Water-Ways"—residing at Chengtu, has charge of the system. In late winter the water is diverted at Kuan Hsien from the "North" River to admit of the removing of silt, etc. In the early spring, conducted with much pomp, there is an annual ceremony of turning on the waters. The motto of Li-ping, "Shen tao t'an, ti tso yen '' (Dig the bed deep, keep the banks low), has become an established law in these parts, and is rigorously carried into effect. Amidst so much that is decaying and corrupt in China it is refreshing to find an old institution maintaining its standard of excellence and usefulness through century after century. The originators of this work have been deified, and two magnificent temples overlooking their work at Kuan Hsien bear witness to the gratitude of the millions who have enjoyed, and continue to enjoy, prosperity from the labours of the famous Li-ping and his son. The " hero-worship " here exemplified would do credit to the people of any land.

The larger of the two temples merits some description. It is by far the finest example I have seen in my travels, and is probably not excelled by any temple in all China. It nestles midst a grove of fine trees, facing the river on the side of a hill, with broad flights of steps leading from terrace to terrace. The buildings are of wood, finely carved and lacquered. The court-yards of stone are broad and spacious, with ornaments in bronze and iron of old and unique workmanship. There are figures representing Li-ping, his wife and son, also many finely gilded and inscribed votive boards, gifts of a long line of succeeding emperors, viceroys, gentry, and guilds. Not a weed is allowed to grow, the whole place being kept scrupulously clean by the Taouist priests in charge. In the courtyards are many interesting trees and shrubs, trained in Chinese manner with consummate skill. Two magnificent specimens of the Crêpe Myrtle (*Lagerstrœmia indica*), trained into the shape of a fan some 25 feet high by 12 feet wide, and said to be over 200 years old, are finer than anything of the kind I have seen elsewhere.

The whole of the plain is subdivided into small fields, every field or series of fields having its own level, differing (sometimes only by one or two inches) from that of its neighbours. This arrangement necessitates a complicated code of regulations, which, sanctioned by custom and usage, determines the pro-portions in which the water of any one canal is distributed into its branches, and the order of succession in which proprietors of different fields are allowed to make use of it. The system has been so far perfected that each rice field receives, exactly at the right time, a sufficient supply of running water. So complete is the whole arrangement that scarcity, much less famine, is practically unknown on the Chengtu Plain.

There are no extremes of climate in this region. In summer the temperature seldom reaches 100° F., in the shade ; in winter it seldom falls below 35° F. It is humid at all times and essentially cloudy, more especially in winter, when the sun is rarely seen, owing to banks of mists. The land is always under cultivation, yielding two main crops that ripen in April or May, and August or September respectively. Catch crops are obtained between these two main harvests. Rice is the chief summer crop, but certain districts produce millet, sugar, pulse, Indigo (*Strobilanthes flaccidifolius*), and tobacco in quantity, Pi Hsien being noted in particular for the latter crop. Wheat and Chinese rape are the chief winter crops with Broadbeans (*Vicia Faba*), peas, barley, and Hemp (*Cannabis sativa*), common in certain districts. Wên-chiang Hsien is famous for its hemp, which is grown in quantity as a winter crop and exported largely to other parts of Szechuan and down river. This product, known colloquially as " Huo-ma," has been wrongly identified by many travellers. As summer crops, Ramie or " Hsien-ma " (*Bœhmeria nivea*) and Abutilon hemp or " Tuen-ma " (*Abutilon Avicennæ*) are both cultivated more or less in quantity. The only Jute or " Huang-ma " (*Corchorus capsularis*) I ever saw was in July 1910, growing near Yao-chia-tu. In the northern parts of the plain, Mienchu and Teyang Hsiens, a little cotton is raised, but commercially the crop is unimportant. Opium was never cultivated in quantity on the plain.

All the Chinese vegetables and culinary oil-producing plants are cultivated in quantity in the Chengtu Plain, and their general excellence is not excelled elsewhere. To enumerate them it would be necessary to give a complete list of such plants cultivated in all but the coldest parts of China. This enumeration is reserved for a subsequent chapter.

A striking feature of the plain is the enormous number of large houses and farmsteads dotted here, there, and everywhere, and shaded by groves of Bamboo, Nanmu, and Cypress. The frequency of these houses, with their enveloping groves, gives a well-wooded appearance to the entire region, and the general view is broken up in such a manner that from no point can many miles of the plain be seen at one time.

The variety of trees is very great ; fully fifty species could easily be enumerated. Alongside the streams and ditches, Alder, " Ching-mu " (*Alnus cremastogyne*) abounds, and forms one of the principal sources of fuel. In the more northern parts of the plain the curious *Camptotheca acuminata*, with clean trunk, grey bark, and globose heads of small white flowers, displaces the Alder. Around the houses Bamboo, Oak, "Pride of India," Soap trees (*Gleditsia*), Cypress, and Nanmu are the commonest trees. The Nanmu is a special feature around temples. Several species of the genus *Machilus* are called Nanmu, all agreeing in being stately, tall, umbrageous evergreens. The wood they yield is highly valued, and the trees are particularly handsome. The Banyan tree, so abundant a little farther south, is very rare here, and neither Pine nor Chinese Fir (*Cunninghamia*) are common. Occasionally trees of the Red Bean (*Ormosia Hosiei*) occur, always, however, in temple-yards or shading wayside shrines. The great industry of Chengtu Fu is sericulture, consequently Mulberry trees abound, and *Cudrania tricuspidata* (Tsa shu), the leaves of which are also used for feeding silkworms, is likewise fairly common.

In such a highly cultivated area the natural flora has, of course, been destroyed. The few indigenous shrubs and herbs that remain are relegated to the sides of streams and grave-yards. In places the Chinese Pampas Grass (*Miscanthus sinensis* and *M. latifolius*) is common ; in autumn the fawn-coloured plumes are most attractive. Occasionally thorny shrubs like Barberry, Christ's thorn, colloquially " Teh-li-pê kuo-tzu " (*Paliurus ramosissimus*), and "San-chia pi" (*Acanthopanax aculeatum*) are used as hedge plants. The commonest fence, however, is made by bending down and interlacing the bamboo-culms.

Since the plain is strewn with cities, villages, and farm-steads, a network of roadways necessarily obtains. A main artery extends north-north-east, through the plain and beyond to Shensi province, and ultimately reaches far-distant Peking. This road was commenced from the Shensi end by the great

Shih Hwang-ti (he who commenced building the Great Wall) about 220 B.C. It extends from Chengtu in a south-westerly direction to Kiung Chou, and thence to remote Lhassa. Other highways connect the provincial capital with Chungking, the great mart on the Yangtsze River to the south-east; Kuan Hsien in the west, and the Marches of the Mantzu beyond. Roads of secondary importance link these highways with other roads and connect the capital with all the principal cities of the plain and regions beyond. Most of the roads were originally paved with one or two slabs of stone laid lengthwise down the middle, with bare earth on either side. The constant wheel-barrow traffic, a feature of the entire region, has worn deep grooves into these slabs. All too frequently the slabs have disappeared altogether, leaving unpaved long stretches of roadway. In dry weather these roads are dusty, but easy to travel; in wet weather they are from ankle to knee-deep in sheer mud. Often they are practically impassable, and travelling over them in ordinary rainy weather is an experience beyond words to describe. They illustrate admirably the contrariety of things which obtain in China generally. Here in the wealthiest region of the west, if not of the whole of China, the average road is of the meanest width, and in an abominable state of repair. There is much talk of the need of railways in China,—true, they are needed badly, but good highways, *roads*, are an infinitely greater want. The highways and byways on the Chengtu Plain are a disgrace to the entire population of this fertile, wealthy region. "What is every-body's business is nobody's business" is a saying that is as applicable in China as in Western lands. The roads exist for the good and welfare of all, but it is nobody's real business to protect them; they are, in consequence, neglected by all—peasants, farmers, officials, and gentry alike.

Mean as these roadways are, they are spanned by hundreds of large honorary portals and memorial arches, mostly con-structed of red, or more rarely grey, sandstone, or occasionally of wood. In the vicinity of the more wealthy cities (Han Chou, for example) these portals and arches are extraordinarily abundant. Many are masterpieces of Chinese architecture. All are well built and covered with sculptures in relief, re-

presenting scenes of mythical or everyday life. The ends of
the ridge pole and the gable eaves are usually long drawn out
and revolutely upturned, adding additional lightness and
beauty to the whole. These long, exaggerated, upturned
eaves are a characteristic feature of the houses, temples, and
shrines met with all over this region.

The innumerable ditches, canals, and streams are all well
bridged. The bridges are kept in good repair, and reflect the
highest credit on the engineers who constructed them. They
are built of red or grey sandstone, more rarely of wood, as near
Han Chou. The stone bridges vary from one to a dozen or
more arches, sometimes hog-backed, but more usually the
" Roman Arch " is employed ; others are of causeway or
trestle design, with or without balustrades, ranging from a
single slab laid across a narrow ditch to many such laid on
a series of piers built in the bed of the streams. Near Sintu
Hsien there is an example of one of these trestle or pier-
bridges 120 yards long. Outside the east gate of Chengtu is a
red-sandstone bridge of nine arches, which is generally regarded
as the bridge mentioned by Marco Polo. A similar bridge
exists near Yao-chia-tu, but this has some twenty arches. Immediately outside Han Chou there is a covered wooden bridge,
120 yards long, 6 yards broad, resting on eight stone piers.
This bridge, known as the Chin-ying chiao (Bridge of the Golden
Goose), is the handsomest, most ornate wooden structure of
its kind I have met with in my travels.

In reference to the bunding of the streams and canals it
should be mentioned that cobble-stones enclosed within long
sausage-shaped, bamboo-latticed crates are universally employed for this purpose. This system is said to date back
to the later times of the Ming dynasty only. Previous to that
period the principal abutments and revetments were of iron,
fashioned into the shape of gigantic oxen, turtles, pillars, etc.
At the places where canals unite or divide, or where the water
cascades to a lower level, the earthworks are protected by walls
of stones firmly cemented together.

Another item, and one which astonishes every traveller,
is the enormous size of the blocks of stone used in the bridges,
more especially those erected on piers. I have no -exact

measurements by me, but these slabs would average at least 12 yards long by 20 inches square at the ends. Commonly the blocks are of hard limestone, occasionally of conglomerate. The slabs of sandstone when used are shorter. At Chao-chia-tu sandstone slabs are used as fencing.

Any attempt to describe the cities on the Chengtu Plain would necessitate more space than is at my disposal. They differ, with the exception of the provincial capital, in no marked particular from other cities of Szechuan. In size they vary considerably, some of the large unwalled towns being commercially more important than the walled cities. Most of the cities and surrounding districts are noted for certain things; for example, Mienchu Hsien for its wheaten flour and paper, P'i Hsien for tobacco, Wên-chiang Hsien for hemp, P'êng Hsien for indigo, Shuangliu Hsien for straw-braid, and so on. The majority of these cities are very ancient; all contain fine temples, as becomes such centres of wealth. Chengtu (long. 104° 2' E., lat. 30° 38' N.) was described by Marco Polo, who visited it during the thirteenth century, as a " rich and noble city." Modern travellers, and their name is well-nigh legion, have all agreed with the great Venetian's dictum. In many respects Chengtu, with its population of 350,000 people, is probably the finest city in the whole of China. It is built on a totally different plan from that of Peking, or even Canton, so that comparisons are difficult. The present city of Chengtu is comparatively modern, but occupies much the same site as the capital of the aboriginal kingdom of Shu. This kingdom was conquered by Shih Hwang-ti (the " First Emperor ") some time between 221–209 B.C., who nominally added it to his dominions. The succeeding dynasty of Han (206 B.C. to A.D. 25) incorporated it as an integral part of China. During the epoch of the Three Kingdoms the site (or thereabouts) of the city was occupied as the capital of the kingdom under Liu-pei. Succeeding dynasties have always made it a most important seat of administration, and princes of the imperial clan or viceroys have resided there. It is still the seat of a Viceroy who governs the province of Szechuan and nominally controls all Thibetan affairs.

Great Britain, France, and Germany have each established

a Consulate-General there, but on the plea that the city is not an "open port," the Chinese have successfully resisted the purchase of land on which to erect suitable houses and offices for the staffs representing these Powers. The result is that these officers are housed in dilapidated Chinese quarters, insanitary, dangerous to health, and unbecoming the dignity of the Powers they represent. It is nothing short of a scandal to thrust men into such abominable quarters. Chengtu Fu is far removed from London, Paris, and Berlin, also from Peking, but is it fitting to make backwoodsmen of these representatives? Missionaries of every denomination are firmly entrenched at Chengtu, and can acquire all the property their funds admit of either for residences, hospitals, schools, or churches.

The city is surrounded by a magnificent wall, some 9 miles in circumference, with eight bastions, pierced by four fine gates. This wall is 66 feet broad at base, 35 feet high, and 40 feet broad at top, along which runs a crenulated balustrade. It is faced and paved with hard brick (the walls of all the other cities on the plain are of sandstone), and is kept in thorough repair. During Manchu times a Tartar garrison was stationed here, a large area on the south-west side of the city being walled off to form a Manchu city. Within the city walls are many fine residences, private and official, temples, a large parade ground, etc. The city is clean and orderly, with an efficient police. To wander through the streets noting the varied industries carried on is a liberal education in Chinese ways of doing things. The wares on sale are of infinite variety, and are themselves indicative of the wealth which is everywhere apparent. The shop-signs, lacquered and gilded, hang vertically downwards, and proclaim in their large artistic characters the titles of the shops and the wares on sale. The city is full of officials, both in and out of office, who move about the streets in sedan-chairs carried at a great speed. The chairs are peculiar in having the long poles curved, with the body of the chair resting on top of the curve. When carried, such a chair is well above the heads of the crowd. The streets are always crowded with pedestrians, chairs, and wheel-barrows. Different trades occupy their own particular quarter. Certain streets are devoted to carpentry in all its branches, boot-shops, shops devoted to hornware, skins and furs, embroideries, second-hand clothes shops, silk goods, foreign goods, and so forth. Silk-weaving is the great industry in Chengtu, hundreds of looms being in use.

Evidences of Occidental influence abound. A provincial university and many schools for imparting Western learning exist. Two agricultural experimental farms, an arsenal, mint, bazaar, and many buildings of semi-foreign design. The arsenal and farms are outside the city. An electric lighting plant was operating at the time of my last visit (1910), and the installation of a telephone service was in progress. The Imperial Post is strongly established here under control of Europeans, and this is the only Western innovation really accomplishing good work. The others (and I have not covered them all) are experiments pure and simple. These are controlled by officials among whom jealousy is rife and peculation not un-known. The good intentions of honest officials are easily nullified by jealous-minded sycophants and ultra-conserva-tives. The city exhibits numerous examples of blighted experiments, some of them mere follies, but the majority calculated to be beneficial if properly controlled and carried through. The city-fathers and officials have exhibited mad haste to acquire such Western knowledge as they deem useful. They have no real idea of what they want, and there is little co-ordination in any matter. The students rule the colleges ; their fathers, the gentry, rule the province. " China for the Chinese," and "away with all foreigners and foreign influence" is their slogan. This cry is perfectly legitimate, but they should move slowly. They think they are fully fledged men, whereas they are mere babes in the knowledge of the things they covet so much. The unfortunate Rebellion which has spread with such rapidity and brought about so much disaster to the nation, originated with the hot-heads of Chengtu. Primarily it was aimed not so much against the dynasty as against foreign capital. The Central Government had agreed to a foreign loan, which, amongst other things, had for its object the construction of a railway from Hankow to Chungking. It was this loan that was the fat in the fire which produced the conflagration—the last straw, if you will, but the primary cause of the Rebellion. The dynasty has been dethroned (it was effete, anyway, and should have passed fifty years ago), a dictatorship under the guise of a republic cleverly formed by the only man who can save China from anarchy if not disruption—Yuan-shih-kai. But foreign loans have become more absolutely necessary than ever before. The present system of government can only be transient, another dynasty must arise. I mentioned above that the province was under a viceroy, and that the gentry ruled the province. This is the keynote to the whole difficulty. The Viceroy had to carry out the instructions of the Imperial Government at Peking ; he had also to please the gentry. The wishes of the two powers became diametrically opposed, and not all the tact of the cleverest diplomats could save the situation. The Viceroy (Chao Êrh-hsün) was removed to Manchuria, and his brother (Chao Êrh-fêng), recalled from the Thibetan Marches (where China's new toy, in the shape of an army modelled on quasi-Western lines, had been indulging in an altogether uncalled-for war of aggression), appointed to the post. The new Viceroy arrived too late to check the revolt, and was ultimately murdered. The gentry have declared that no foreign capital, and the necessary foreign supervision of such capital, shall enter into the construction of a railway in Szechuan. With Chinese money and Chinese engineers the scheme shall be accomplished, say these autocrats. The Central Government thought otherwise and made other arrangements. Then came the revolt, fulminated by the gentry of the Chengtu Plain, which speedily got beyond their control, and where it will really end is beyond prophecy. The Manchu dynasty, when it ascended the Dragon throne in A.D. 1644, immediately set to work and rescued Szechuan from the bloody grip of the rebel and arch-destroyer, Chang Hien-tsung, and brought peace to the land. Two hundred and sixty-seven years later this dynasty has been dethroned by rebellion initiated by the gentry of the Chengtu Plain. Dynasties and republics may come and go, but in the future, as in the past, industry, combined with agricultural skill, will continue to win sustenance, derive wealth, influence, and power from this fertile and beautiful region—the Garden of Western China.

CHAPTER X

NORTH-WESTERN SZECHUAN

Narrative of a Cross-Mountain Journey to Sungpan Ting

A FEW days after our arrival at Chengtu in 1910 I determined upon a journey to the border-town of Sungpan Ting, for the express purpose of securing seeds and herbarium specimens of certain new coniferous trees previously discovered by me in that region. During 1903 and again in 1904 I had visited this interesting town. On the first occasion I travelled by the ordinary main road, via Kuan Hsien and the Min Valley. The next year I followed the great north road across the Plain of Chengtu to Mien Chou, then travelled via Chungpa and Lungan Fu, by another recognized highway. On these journeys I gleaned tidings of a by-road leading from Shihch'uan Hsien across the mountains, finally connecting with both the above routes. This route promised to be interesting as well as novel. Only Roman Catholic missionaries had previously traversed it, so far as I could learn. An Hsien was selected as the real starting-point for this trip.

With this object in view we passed through the north gate of Chengtu city early on the morning of 8th August. Following the north road as far as the city of Han Chou, then branching off and travelling via Shihfang Hsien and Mienchu Hsien, we reached the city of An Hsien, some 300 li from Chengtu, after three and a half days. The road led us right through the luxuriant Chengtu Plain to its extreme north-western limits near Hsao-shui Ho. Afterwards we crossed some low foot-hills to a small stream leading to An Hsien. The journey was very easy, though fatiguing owing to the extreme heat of the season. The city of An Hsien is small, of little importance, prettily situated on the left bank of a stream backed by bare mountains which rear themselves some 2000 feet above the level of the river. Two streams uniting here form a river navigable during high-water season to Mien Chou, a city on the Fou Ho—the western branch of the Kialing River system. An Hsien is a little beyond the north-western limits of the Chengtu Plain, and its river gives it direct communication with Chungking, during the summer at least.

Leaving by the north gate, we took a road that ascends the main branch of the river which is kept from flooding the city by a well-made low bund of stone slabs, firmly cemented together. After traversing a small cultivated valley we plunged into a rocky defile and crossed the river by an iron suspension bridge, 110 yards long. This bridge is old and in poor repair, and it swayed considerably as we walked singly across. A few miles farther on we recrossed the stream by a similar bridge, and reached Lei-ku-ping, our destination for the day, at 6 p.m. A certain amount of rice is cultivated hereabouts, but maize is the staple crop. As an under-crop to maize, *Amorphophallus konjac* ("Mo-yu") is commonly cultivated, the tubers being used as food after their acrid properties have been removed by washing in water. We met considerable traffic, mostly coolies laden with sheep-skins and medicines from Sungpan, which they put on boats at An Hsien for conveyance to Chungking; much potash (lye) in small tubs, and oil-cakes consisting of the residue of Chinese rape-seed after the oil is expressed. Coal of very poor quality, mostly dust, is obtained in the surrounding mountains, and we met scores of mules, ponies, and coolies engaged in transporting it.

Lei-ku-ping, alt. 2750 feet, is a large market village, possessing one principal street with gates at each end, which are closed after sunset. The centre of a large and important industry in tea, Lei-ku-ping largely supplies Sungpan Ting and the country beyond. The tea is grown in the surrounding districts and brought to the village for sale. Later we shall have more to say concerning this industry.

It rained heavily during the early hours of the morning, and though it was fair when we set out, showers fell the whole forenoon. On leaving Lei-ku-ping we ascended a few hundred feet to the head of a low divide, and then descended to the village of Che-shan, situated on the right bank of a considerable stream. This village shares in the tea industry for the Sung-pan market, but is of less importance than Lei-ku-ping.

From Che-shan to Shihch'uan Hsien the road ascends the right bank of the river, which flows between steep precipitous mountains. The path is usually several hundred feet above the stream, broad and fairly easy for the most part, but constantly ascending and descending. The mountain-sides are steep but, where not absolutely vertical, are all under cultivation, Maize being the staple crop. There is very little limestone, the rocks being chiefly loose sandstone and mud shales. These shales weather rapidly, and the steepest cultivated slopes are usually composed of these rocks.

The river is broad, and could easily be made navigable for boats during the high-water season. Even in its present condition rafts could be floated down, but we saw no traffic whatsoever on its waters. The water was dirty, and much driftwood was strewn along the shores. This is collected, dried, and stacked, forming apparently the principal source of fuel. Trees are very scarce, but around houses occur Sophora, Pistacia, Pteroceltis, *Sterculia platanifolia* (Wu-tung), *Kœlreuteria bipinnata*, and Alder. The Kœlreuteria was just coming into flower ; the flowers are golden yellow produced in large, much-branched, erect panicles ; the leaves are very large and much divided. Shrubs are not plentiful but, much to my surprise, the Tea Rose (*Rosa indica*) is quite common, and evidently spontaneous, by the wayside, on the cliffs, and by the side of the stream.

A few li below the city of Shihch'uan Hsien the river is spanned by a bamboo suspension bridge, about 80 yards long, supported on cables made of split, bamboo culms plaited together. These cables, eight in number, are nearly 1 foot in diameter, and are fastened to stanchions fixed on either side of the river. Two similar cables on either side of the bridge are carried across at higher levels, and have attachments of bamboo rope supporting those which form the base of the structure. A capstan arrangement is used for making the cables taut, and the lower ones are covered with stout wicker-work to form a footway.   Like all such structures, this bridge is heavy, sags very much in the middle, and is very unsteady to walk across.   The life of these bridges is only a few years, and strong winds often make them very unsafe.

Shihch'uan Hsien is a small city charmingly situated at an altitude of 2800 feet, on the left bank immediately below the junction of two rivers.   It is surrounded on all sides by steep, more or less cultivated mountains.   Inside the city are many trees, which add considerably to the effect.   A pavilion and a small pagoda crown two prominent hills, and assure the " luck " of the place.   A narrow suburb runs ribbon-like between the river and the city wall.   This wall is broken down in places, and the gates are low and small.   We found accommodation in a large, curiously constructed inn remarkable for the strength of its stinks and the abundance of vermin and mosquitoes it sheltered.   The day's journey was given as 65 li, but the li were long, consequently the coolies with their loads arrived late. Cash was needed, but on opening a box to obtain some silver for exchange we found that some one had stolen from it about 30 taels and 5 dollars.   The load belonged to a coolie we had engaged at Taning Hsien, and retained because he had given unusual satisfaction ! The previous day he had engaged a local coolie to carry his load, on the ground that he was feeling sick.   He was last seen near Che-shan, still unable to carry his load.   Evidently he was the culprit, but he was thoughtful enough to leave us about half the amount contained in the box. Since he had about three-quarters of a day's start I concluded it was best to quietly cut the loss, my first and last in China. The delays incident upon lodging a complaint with the official would have involved me in further expense and trouble, with but small chance of recovering the money lost.

The main road to Sungpan continues to ascend the right bank of the river to its source, then crosses over a range and enters the upper Min Valley at Mao Chou.   I had been over most of this route in 1908 when crossing the Chiuting range from near Mienchu Hsien to Tu-mên, thence to Mao Chou.   The route we had in view leads to the north-west from Shihch'uan Hsien.   From Chengtu to this point we had travelled without escort, but with the difficulties of an unknown route before us

I thought it best to secure such at this city. Sending my card to the Hsien's yamên, in the ordinary way, I informed this official of my project, and asked for the customary escort. Half an hour afterwards my card was returned with the information that there was trouble at Sungpan and no escort would be supplied ! The refusal was as curt as it was insolent, but whether the Hsien was actually responsible I never found out. In the whole of my eleven years' travel in China this was the first and last experience of official discourtesy. Thus two annoying experiences, both unique in their way, yet, happily, trivial and unimportant, marked my visit to Shihch'uan Hsien, a town which, from the commencement of my travels in the western Szechuan, I always had a keen desire to visit.

The next day we left Shihch'uan Hsien at sunrise, glad to escape from the malodorous, vermin-infested inn. No one put in an appearance from the yamên, and no attempt to prevent our taking the route proposed was made. I had rather feared this might happen, but my fears were fortunately groundless. On leaving the city by the north gate we struck a stream nearly equal in volume to the main river. The road ascends the left bank, and almost immediately plunges into a narrow, wild ravine, through which we continued the whole day. Like all such roads it skirts the mountain-side, being usually several hundred feet above the river, but is constantly descending to the water's edge, only to ascend again a few hundred yards farther on. It is in good repair, although the rocks are of soft mud shales, and signs of landslips were frequent. Wherever possible maize is cultivated, but houses are few and far between. The country strongly reminded me of that around Wênch'uan Hsien in the upper Min Valley farther west. Trees are very scarce, the Wu-tung (*Sterculia*) being perhaps the most common. The shrubs denote a dry (xerophytic) climate, nearly all having small leaves, either thick or covered with a felt of hairs. Of these shrubs, *Abelia parvifolia*, *Lonicera pileata*, *Ligustrum strongylophyllum*, and various kinds of Spiræa, are common. Bushes of the wild Tea Rose are not infrequent. Five li before reaching Kai-ping-tsen, our destination for the day, we crossed a clear-water tributary by a remarkably well-built stone-arch bridge. During the day we passed several " rope " bridges, made of a single thick cable of plaited bamboo culms—sure signs of difficult borderland country. Near Shihch'uan Hsien we passed a bamboo suspension bridge, similar to the one already described; at Kai-ping-tsen there is another such bridge. There was a fair amount of traffic on the road. Potash salts (lye), shingles, and oil-cake were the principal loads encountered, all being carried on men's backs, the first-named being the most common.

Kai-ping-tsen, alt. 3200 feet, is a small village of about fifty houses, situated on the left bank of a stream some 50 li north of Shihch'uan Hsien. A new, empty house afforded us comfortable lodgings; the people were courteous, and made our brief stay with them very pleasant. A remarkably fine headstone, recently erected over the tomb of a much-respected widow, was the chief thing of interest in the village.

On leaving Kai-ping-tsen we continued to ascend the left bank of the stream through country similar to that of the previous day, for 30 li to the market village of Hsao-pa-ti. This village, all things considered, is of considerable size (about one hundred houses), with many farmhouses scattered around. The mountains are less rugged and steep, and are given over to the cultivation of maize. The houses are low, built of mud shales and roofed with slabs of slate. Market was in progress; food-stuffs, fuel, and potash salts being the principal goods on sale. A bamboo suspension bridge spans the river and a road leads across country, ultimately joining with the main road between Shihch'uan Hsien and Mao Chou. On leaving Hsao-pa-ti the road deserts the river and ascends through maize fields over a rather low ridge. It then descends to a small tributary, after crossing which a steep climb of 1000 feet leads to the summit of another ridge. From this point we sighted the main stream again, flowing through a smiling valley, at the head of which nestles the village of Pien-kou, which was our destination for the day. This village proved a good 20 li from the ridge, though it looked close at hand. The road led through fields of maize to the valley, and finally across the river by an old, very shaky bamboo suspension bridge, which swayed tremendously and was really unsafe.

Pien-kou (Yüan-kou of the maps), alt. 3800 feet, is a market village of some importance, but a fire had recently destroyed half the houses. We had some difficulty in obtaining lodgings, the only decent place being full and the occupants unwilling to move. After a little time persuasive insistence won, and we settled down comfortably, if crowded. One of the occupants was down with fever. I dosed him with quinine, and supplied him with enough to last several days, much to his appreciation. This act got noised abroad, with the result that applications for medicine quickly became too numerous. Quinine is a drug much appreciated by Chinese, being about the only foreign medicine they have real confidence in.

The day's journey was said to be 70 li. It was long and uninteresting. The flora is miserably poor ; Alder being the only really common tree.

The road we were following ultimately joined the Mao Chou-Sungpan main road near Chên-ping kuan, about 160 li below the town of Sungpan. We could get no tidings of a road crossing to the Lungan-Sungpan highway, but all the same we felt sure of finding one. Thus far the route indicated on my map was all wrong, and we were left very much in the dark as to our actual whereabouts. However, I was long since accustomed to this state of affairs.

Leaving Pien-kou, a journey of 40 li brought us to Peh-yang ch'ang, a village of a dozen scattered, dilapidated houses. The road was distinctly bad in places owing to landslips. The rocks are mainly mud shales standing on edge. We followed the right bank of the river we had pursued from Shihch'uan Hsien for the first 22 li, then crossed over to the left bank by means of a shaky improvised bridge of two tree logs, the bamboo suspension bridge which formerly crossed the stream hereabouts having broken down. At this cross-over point resides a Chinese official, locally styled a Tu-ssu. This official was most courteous, helping us with advice and guidance to cross the stream.

The journey generally was a repetition of the two former days, through a rocky but uninteresting gorge. Wherever possible, maize is cultivated, and we noted two odd patches of rice. Houses are few and far between, and we met only a few coolies laden with potash salts, charcoal, and shingles.

The flora was not interesting, Alder, Pterocarya, and *Cornus controversa* are the only common trees. *Buddleia Davidii* is abundant by the stream side, and was in full flower. The Tea Rose also is fairly common. A Lily without bulbils, otherwise very like *Lilium Sargentiæ*, is plentiful in places. At Peh-yang ch'ang, alt. 4100 feet, we found a road leading off to the right, and connecting with the Lungan-Sungpan highway at Shui-ching-pu ; this we decided to follow.

Above our lodgings at Peh-yang ch'ang the river bifurcates, one branch, a clear-water stream, being locally adjudged the larger. It is up this stream the road connecting with the Mao Chou-Sungpan highway ascends. The people told us that this road was similar in character to the one we had followed thus far, but more difficult, especially since the proper bridges had nearly all been recently destroyed by floods. The cross-over to the Min Valley is near a place called Hwa-tszeling, where fine forests of Silver Fir and Spruce occur. Pien-kou is a considerable wine market, much of the product finding its way to Sungpan over this rough cross-country road.

A fatiguing march marked our first day's journey towards the Lungan-Sungpan highway. We made two long ascents and descents, and commenced a third ascent, putting up for the night at Hsao-kou, after covering 55 li. The second ascent was fully 2000 feet, and very steep, through maize fields, culminating in abandoned herb-clad areas. The descent was mainly through coppice and brush. Houses occur scattered here and there, wherever cultivation is practicable, maize being the staple crop ; the Irish potato and peas are also grown. The road proved difficult, but I had traversed worse.

The forests have been destroyed, brushwood now covering the uncultivated areas. Topping the loftier crags, and in inaccessible places generally, a sprinkling of conifer trees still exist, but we did not get near them. The vegetation generally is that common to the 5000 to 6000 feet belt in west Szechuan, but is less varied than in many parts I have visited. In the valleys Alder was common, and on the slopes the Varnish tree (*Rhus verniciflua*) and Walnut (*Juglans regia*) occur in quantity. In coppices the Davidia, both the hairy and glabrous varieties, is plentiful, but no large trees were noted. Throughout the bottom-lands and abandoned cultivated areas "Summer Lilac" (*Buddleia Davidii*) was a wonderful sight—thousands of bushes, each one with masses of violet-purple flowers, delighting the eye on all sides, the variety *magnifica*, with its reflexed petals and intense coloured flowers, being most in evidence. I gathered also an *albino* form, one small solitary bush, the only one I have ever met with. Forming a much-branched bush 4 to 8 feet tall, with rose-purple flowers, *Hydrangea villosa* was, next to the Buddleia, the most strikingly ornamental shrub. On moist rocky slopes plants of *Rodgersia æsculifolia* occur in millions. It was in the fruiting stage, but when in flower the acres of snow-white panicles must have presented a bewitching sight. Nowhere else have I seen this plant so abundant or luxuriant. The slender arching plumes of white flowers, produced by *Spiræa Aruncus*, covered acres of ground ; an apetalous Astilbe (*A. rivularis*) was also abundant, and worthy of note.

The hamlet of Hsao-kou, alt. 5900 feet, consists of three scattered houses, surrounded by maize plats, with remains of other ruined houses near by. It is encompassed on all sides by steep mountains, some of them culminating in lofty limestone crags and rugged razor-like ridges with pinnacled peaks—all of them inaccessible. At the back of the inn are a few Larch trees, and near by several large trees of a flat-leaved Spruce. The Hou-p'o (*Magnolia officinalis*) is cultivated hereabouts, and also around all of the houses we passed during the day. The innkeeper likewise cultivates a medicinal Aconite (*Aconitum Wilsonii*), which is valued as a drug in Chinese pharmacy.

We encountered only three men carrying goods during the whole day ; two were laden with potash salts, the third with the bark of a Linden (*Tilia*), used locally for making sandles. Evidences of forest fires were all too frequent during the day's march.

The next day rain ruined what otherwise would have been a more than ordinarily interesting march. From 7 a.m. until 2 p.m. we struggled up some 4000 odd feet to the summit of the pass leading across the Tu-ti-liang shan ; then descended another 4000 feet to the hamlet of Hsueh-po, where we secured lodgings in a large and good house. Rain commenced shortly before 11 a.m., and continued the rest of the day. Our perspective was limited to a few hundred feet ; now and again a strong gust of wind would scatter the mists, admitting momentary glimpses of cliffs and inaccessible peaks clothed with jungle and with occasional Conifer trees, but such views were rare.

The hamlet of Hsao-kou is very scattered, and we passed two or three more houses soon after leaving our lodgings. But after about 3 li houses and cultivation vanished, as did also the Buddleia and Hydrangea previously so abundant. The ascent, at first gradual, soon becomes precipitous, through a jungle growth of shrubs and coarse herbs. The latter with the thin brushwood is cut periodically and burnt. The ashes so obtained are placed in wooden vats fitted with sieve bottoms, boiling water is poured over them, and the liquid drains into tubs, where it is evaporated and salts of potash (lye) left as a residue. This product is packed in flasks and carried to market towns for sale. We passed several rude huts where men were engaged in this occupation. The road ascends a small torrent and is nowhere easy. By throwing logs across the stream and boggy places, lumber-men have succeeded in making some sort of a path. But crossing these wet, slippery logs was difficult. At one such crossing I slipped, but by jumping into the rock-strewn torrent somehow managed to avoid a nasty accident. Near the summit, and for some distance down the Lungan side of the pass, are split pieces of wood, arranged to form a long flight of shallow steps that assist the roadway materially. The descent after a few hundred feet becomes gradual, leading through open, park-like slopes, quite unlike anything I have encountered elsewhere in China. Now largely denuded of trees these glades are covered with grass, and horses, goats, and pigs are raised here in some quantity.

Formerly this range of mountains must have been covered with conifers, but the lumber-man's hands have been heavily laid on these forests. We passed none but small, decrepit specimens of no value. Hemlock, Spruce, and Silver Fir are all represented. The outstanding feature of the march was

the abundance of Cercidiphyllum trees.   Throughout the moist
slopes and park-like areas on both sides of the range this tree
is common.   Stumps of decaying giants abound, one of these,
which I photographed, measured 55 feet in girth !   This
specimen had been broken off some 30 feet above the ground,
and was a mere hollow shell, but still supported many twiggy,
leafy branches.   These stumps are relics of the largest broad-
leaved trees I have seen anywhere in China.   Growing interspersed with these remains were many specimens of the same
tree, 60 to 80 feet tall, 8 to 10 feet in girth, perfect in
outline, with myriads of neat, nearly round, bright green
leaves.   One of these was in young fruit, and for the first
time in my travels I secured specimens of the fruit of this
beautiful and interesting tree.   (Later I collected ripe seeds,
and this tree is now growing in the Arnold Arboretum, where
it promises to be quite hardy.   It proved to be a variety
distinct from the Japanese species.)

This tree (*Cercidiphyllum japonicum*, var. *sinense*) attains
to greater size than any other broad-leaved tree known from
the temperate zone of eastern Asia.   In size it is only
approached by its close ally, Tetracentron, which is also
common in the woods on the Tu-ti-liang shan.   A local
name for the Cercidiphyllum is " Peh-k'o," a name strictly
applied all over China to the Maidenhair tree (*Ginkgo biloba*).

The summit of the range is composed of mud shales, which
seem favourable to the growth of vegetation generally.   Between 8000 feet altitude and the summit *Rhododendron
calophytum* is extraordinarily abundant, trees 40 to 50 feet tall
and 5 to 7 feet in girth, with handsome cinnamon-brown bark,
cover many acres.   *Euptelea pleiosperma* and *Pterocarya hupehensis* are other interesting trees plentiful hereabouts.   The
bark of the last-mentioned tree is used locally for roofing
purposes.   Willows in many species are common ;   the bark
of certain of these and also that of Linden trees is used by
the peasants for making sandals.   *Viburnum erubescens*, var.
Prattii, with pendulous panicles of white fragrant flowers,
followed by fruit which is at first scarlet and then changes
to black, is perhaps the commonest shrub.   Various Araliads,
Sorbus, etc., grow epiphytically on all the larger trees that

have a rough humus collecting bark. Maples in variety, Micromeles laden with fruit, and many other interesting trees were striking constituents of these woods. Tall growing herbs made a grand display, especially the apetalous *Astilbe rivularis*, *Spiræa Aruncus*, *Anemone vitifolia* with white and pink flowers like the Japanese Anemone, *Artemisia lactiflora* with large panicles of milk-white, fragrant flowers, Balsams (*Impatiens*) with yellow, pink, and purple flowers; mixed with them also were Meadow Rue (*Thalictrum*), Aconites, many Senecios, and *Meconopsis chelidonifolia* growing about 3 feet tall with clear yellow flowers, saucer-shaped and $2\frac{1}{2}$ inches across. Acres of the country-side are covered by these various herbs.

There was indeed plenty to interest one ; the flora of this region is undoubtedly rich, and it was most unfortunate that the rain prevented an exhaustive investigation.

Hsueh-po, alt. 6000 feet, consists of a few houses surrounded by high mountains with a good-sized torrent, which rises near the head of the pass, and flows through the narrow valley. Maize is cultivated as the staple crop. The Hydrangea and Buddleia previously noted ascend to this altitude, and were a wealth of blossoms. Alder also extends to this point ; Poplar likewise. This latter tree has a very graceful port and the leaves have red petioles and veins when young.

Our lodgings were good and weather-proof, which was fortunate, since it rained heavily the night through, and until eleven o'clock in the forenoon of the next day. Afterwards it was fair, but threatening, heavy clouds and mists obscured the country-side from our view. Around the inn are several trees of a handsome, flat-leaved Spruce (*Picea ascendens*) with pendulous branchlets. This tree, known locally as " Mê-tiao sha or sung," is the most esteemed timber tree in these parts. The trees are felled, hewn into planks about 25 feet long, 5 inches thick, and 12 inches broad, and carried on men's backs to a point on the river whence it is possible to float down rafts. Lumbering is a very considerable industry in these mountains, the timber finding its way to Chungpa. This fine Spruce was fruiting freely. (Later I secured plenty of seed, and successfully introduced it into Western gardens.)

On leaving Hsueh-po, we crossed the torrent and descended

the left bank.   At K'ung chiao the torrent is joined by another of equal size, the united waters forming a fine clear-water stream.   From this point downwards rice is cultivated.   The stream continues to receive affluents, a very considerable one joining it at Tu-tien-tsze.   At Peh-mu chiao, 10 li above Tu-tien-tsze, the timber logged in the surrounding mountains is made into rafts and floated down.   Just below Shui-ching-pu the stream unites with the main branch of the Lungan River (the Fou Ho), and the rafts are floated down past the city of Lungan to Chungpa, a large village of vast commercial importance, in direct water communication with distant Chung-king, it being within the Kialing River system.

Tu-tien-tsze is a small market village and a Roman Catholic Mission centre.   This Church has a strong following throughout the region we had traversed from An Hsien.   The country folk everywhere in this part were most courteous and civil. This, I think, is probably due to the influence wielded by the self-sacrificing priests of the Roman Faith.   But whatever the cause, I shall always retain pleasant memories of the people encountered everywhere in this little-known region.

The road proved easy all day, usually skirting the mountains well above the stream.   At Tu-tien-tsze a cross-country road leads to Lungan Fu, some 130 li distant.   Ten li below Tu-tien-tsze we crossed to the left bank of the stream by a covered bridge.   Descending a few miles and crossing a promontory we reached the main river (Fou Ho) opposite Shui-ching-pu.   Ferrying across to this village, we found lodgings in a large house owned by a Shensi man of the Mohammedan persuasion.

Shui-ching-pu, alt. 4200 feet, is a market village of about 200 houses, situated on an alluvial flat, surrounded by mountains largely under cultivation.   A river of considerable size, which brings down an unusual quantity of detritus, joins the main stream on the left bank immediately below the village.   A road ascends this stream, leading to Wên Hsien in Kansu province.   It was said to be difficult, traversing a mountainous region peopled with Sifan.   Iron is a local product of some importance hereabouts.   Gold is also mined in the neighbourhood.   The quartz, after it has been broken into small pieces, is pounded into dust in mills like those commonly used for hulling rice. The dust is washed and the gold separated by means of quicksilver. Placer mining is carried out all along this Lungan River by unemployed peasants, but the yield is small. In 1904, when I first journeyed to Sungpan by way of Mien Chou, Chungpa, and Lungan, the officials were endeavouring to put a stop to placer mining. Placards were posted forbidding the people to wash for gold, on the ground that landslips were caused through the removal of the rocks, etc., on the foreshore.

From Hsueh-po to Shui-ching-pu is said to be 60 li. The valley which we traversed is all under cultivation ; farmsteads are general after Peh-mu chiao is reached. Alder, Walnut, and Poplar are the common trees, with Pear, Plum, and Peach trees around houses. In a garden I saw one magnificent specimen of the Crêpe Myrtle (*Lagerstrœmia indica*), 25 feet tall, 2½ feet girth, just one luxuriant mass of carmine-red flowers. Here and there the moist rocks are beautifully carpeted with ferns, *Woodwardia radicans*, *Blechnum eburneum*, and Maidenhair being particularly rampant. The Buddleia and Hydrangea, previously mentioned, are abundantly present, and were a wealth of pleasing flowers.

At Shui-ching-pu we joined the highway between Lungan Fu and Sungpan. The intrepid Captain W. J. Gill,[1] in June 1877, was the first Occidental to traverse this route. Since that date several travellers and missionaries have been over this road, but the total is small.

My first journey over this highway was, as mentioned above, in 1904. At that time I had no camera, and the recollection of the wonderful scenery had much to do with my second journey to these parts in 1910. I saw the country through the eyes of a botanist, and for this reason I hope a continuance of this narrative will prove justifiable.

Leaving Shui-ching-pu about 7 a.m., we saunteringly covered the 50 li to Hsao-ho-ying by 4 p.m. The road ascends the left bank of the stream for some 20 odd li to a point just above the small village of Yeh-tang. At this place the river is joined by another of nearly equal size on its right bank. A by-road ascends this tributary and leads across the mountains

[1] *River of Golden Sand.*

through country sparsely peopled with Sifans, and connects with the Mao Chou—Sungpan highway a few miles below Sungpan Ting. The road we followed crosses the left affluent of the Fou River by means of an iron suspension bridge 24 yards long, erected immediately above the union of the two streams. A few li beyond this place the road plunges into a wild gorge. The scenery is wonderful. Limestone cliffs clad with vegetation rear themselves 1000 to 2000 feet above the torrent which hereabouts rushes headlong over huge rocks. Wherever possible, maize is cultivated on the slopes and rice in the bottomlands. We crossed to the right bank by a covered wooden bridge just below a place where landslips have produced a series of cataracts. About 3 li below Hsao-ho-ying the gorge suddenly opens out, leaving room for a small circular valley, in the middle of which the walled village above named is situated. Viewed from this point where there is an old gateway, the village presents a charming picture of peace and plenty locked in by precipitous mountains. On entering the village, however, one is quickly disillusioned. Abject poverty is only too apparent. The one main street is broad, flanked by more or less ruined houses, with much of the land within the walls given over to maize plats. The people are in keeping with their dilapidated surroundings.

Hsao-ho-ying, alt. 5300 feet, signifies " Camp on the Small River." It is an ancient garrison village. Eighty years ago some 700 soldiers were quartered here. This number was speedily reduced as the surrounding country was conquered. To-day the garrison is put down at 40 men, but it is doubtful if even this number remains. Three yamêns belonging to military officials of low rank are the only respectable buildings in the place.

At Shui-ching-pu we were assured we could exchange silver at Hsao-ho-ying. This proved a fable and landed us in an awkward dilemma. However, " Mo-li-to " (*Fata viam invenient*), as the locals have it !

The flora of the day's journey was not particularly rich, though we passed many plants of interest. Around Hsao-ho-ying, the Walnut (*Juglans regia*), Varnish (*Rhus verniciflua*), Poplar, Apple, Pear, Plum, Peach, and Tu-chung (*Eucommia*

ulmoides) are commonly cultivated. By the side of the torrent
the Buddleia was again a wonderful sight. In a temple yard
near Yeh-tang is a magnificent tree of *Meliosma Beaniana*,
about 60 feet tall and 12 feet in girth, the head being fully 80
feet in diameter. The pinnate leaves produce abundant shade.
This tree was covered with small pea-like purple fruits which
later afforded me a supply of ripe seeds. (The pinnate-leaved
members of this small family are all handsome trees, and none
was in cultivation previous to my explorations. I have
succeeded in introducing three species, all of them promising
to thrive under cultivation. One, *M. Veitchiorum*, is now
flourishing just within the main entrance to Kew Gardens.)

From Hsao-ho-ying to Shuh-chia-pu, 30 li, the road ascends
a narrow valley which is without special interest, the bottom
lands and lower slopes being cultivated with maize and buckwheat. Houses occur at intervals. Just above Shuh-chia-pu,
a poverty-stricken hamlet of about a score of houses, the
river bifurcates. The road ascends the left and larger branch,
plunging immediately into a narrow gorge. The track, all
things considered, is good, though there is room for improvement.
The scenery in this gorge, for magnificent, savage grandeur,
would be hard to surpass. The cliffs, chiefly limestone, are
mostly sheer, and 2000 to 3000 feet high. Wherever vegetation
can find a foothold it is rampant, and a luxuriant jungle of
shrubs clothes all but the most vertical walls of rock. By the
side of the torrent coarse herbs, shrubs, and small trees abound.
The mountain crests and ridges are covered with Spruce and
Pine. Now and again glimpses of vicious-looking, desolate
peaks, towering above the tree-line, were obtainable. The waters
of the torrent roar and dash themselves into foam in their
passionate endeavour to escape to more open country. In more
peaceful stretches the river describes a series of S-curves with
shingly areas covered with *Myricaria germanica* and *Hippophaë
salicifolia* (Sallowthorn), jutting out into the current. In one
place the cliffs recede somewhat, leaving room for a narrow
valley, where three or four peasants' huts are pitched. Around
these cabins forlorn patches of maize, buckwheat, cabbage,
Rhubarb (*Rheum palmatum*, var. *tanguticum*), and Tang-kuei
(*Angelica polymorpha*, var. *sinensis*) are cultivated. The

abandoned clearings are covered with coarse herbs, among which
Senecio clivorum, growing 4 to 5 feet tall, with its golden yellow
flowers, was prominent. *Astilbe Davidii* also abounds ; likewise the Buddleia. A sub-shrubby Elder, growing 3 to 5 feet
tall, with masses of salmon-red fruits, was a pretty sight in
all the more open moist places. (The species proved to be
new and has been named *Sambucus Schweriniana*, Rehder, in
Plantæ Wilsonianæ, Part II. p. 306 (1912).) The vegetation
indeed is rich and varied, and a large harvest of specimens
rewarded the day's labours. After scrambling some 30 li
along this gorge we reached the hostel of Lao-tang-fang just
as night was closing in. We encountered considerable traffic
on the road. Coming from Sungpan were coolies laden with
medicines, sheep-skins, and wool. Journeying thither the coolies
were laden chiefly with wine in specially constructed tubs,
preserved pork and rice. Lao-tang-fang, alt. 7600 feet, consists
of one large new hostel, not quite completed at the time of our
visit ; a long row of "bunks" are built along one side, with
benches for the accommodation of loads on the other. The
whole structure is of wood, the roofing being of shingles badly
laid. The mud floors were very damp, and vegetation was
springing up in the corners and under the bunks. Skins of
Serow and Budorcas served as mattress on the bunks, or
settees, and no two of these skins exhibited the same coloration.
Both animals are said to be common in the neighbourhood,
more especially the Serow. The Parti-coloured Bear, or Giant
Panda, also occurs here in the Bamboo jungles.

The hostel was full to overflowing and undoubtedly supplies
a much-needed want. For the sake of future travellers, if for
no other reason, I heartily hope success attends the landlord's
venture. Formerly a most miserable structure occupied this
site, and I have unpleasant memories of a night spent there in
1904. Except for a tiny cabbage-patch there was no sign
of cultivation around the hostel, but clearings were being
made for the purpose of cultivating Tang-kuei and other
medicines. The view from this spot is savage and grand
beyond power of words. On all sides are precipitous mountains, towering 3000 feet and more above the torrent, all more
or less densely forested. Almost facing the river is a limestone

cliff with upturned strata on edge, sheer and bare of vegetation. Behind this is another nearly vertical slope covered with stark, dead Conifer trees. In the distance, looking back on the road we had followed, bare, vicious-looking peaks, probably 14,000 to 16,000 feet high, were visible. All around the hostel the lesser slopes are covered with impenetrable forest of broad-leaved deciduous trees. The higher parts and the crags are clothed with Conifers, tall, slightly branched trees of no great size—altogether a wonderful scene of natural beauty, at present undefiled by the hand of man.

It was cold during the night ; the wind played freely through the unfinished structure, and the thickest of clothing was needed in order to keep warm.

The next day we made a later start than usual, and travelling most leisurely covered the 40 li to San-tsze-yeh before 5 p.m. The journey was one long scramble through a continuation of the savage ravine. The chairs had to be carried piecemeal, and all of us reached our destination very much fatigued. We enjoyed a gloriously fine, sunny day, the narrow streak of sky visible from the bed of the ravine being of the purest Thibetan-blue. The camera was kept busy and I secured a fine set of views, but so steep is the country and so dense the jungle that it was impossible to photograph trees.

The rock-strewn torrent, with its thundering, seething waters, occupies practically the entire bed of the ravine, leaving scant room for the road which winds along its banks. We crossed this torrent many times, either by fording it or by means of half-rotten log bridges. Luckily the waters were low and caused us no trouble. In 1904 I ascended this ravine shortly after heavy rains, and have the liveliest recollections of the difficulties encountered. Much of the road and many of the bridges had been washed away, making it necessary to hew a pathway through the jungle and improvise bridges by felling trees in several places.

No words of mine can adequately depict the savage, awe-inspiring scenery of this wild ravine. Stupendous limestone cliffs, 3000 to 4000 feet high, often too steep for the scantiest vegetation to find a foothold, but more generally sparsely or plentifully forested, wall in the torrent and its accompanying roadway. Waterfalls abound, but lateral torrents are few. The flora is very rich, but largely inaccessible. Practically all the trees, shrubs, and herbs common to the 7000 to 9000 feet belt occur here. Conifers are the principal trees. Silver Fir, Spruce, Hemlock, Larch, White Pine, Juniper, and Yew are all represented. The Pine (*P. Armandi*) is the commonest tree up to 8500 feet, clinging to the sheer cliffs in a remarkable manner. With its stunted branches and short leaves it was hardly recognizable, suggesting a green Maypole rather than a Pine tree ! Many of the Spruce and Silver Fir were fruiting freely, the erect, violet-coloured symmetrical cones of the latter being very handsome. Larch (*L. Potaninii*) abounds, overtopping all the other Conifers, but the trees are small. All the Conifers are hereabouts designated " Sung-shu " (literally Pine trees), but the timber of the Larch, flat-leaved Spruce, and White Pine, valued in the order given, are most prized for building purposes generally. Of the broad-leaved deciduous trees, Maple (*Acer*), Linden (*Tilia*), and Birch (*Betula*) are the most common. A few Poplar occur, but Oak is exceedingly rare, the few noted being scrubby evergreens of no great beauty. The variety of shrubs is very great, all the more woodland genera being rich in species. Sorbaria, with its large panicles of white flowers, was one of the most attractive. Spiræa, Viburnum Lonicera, Rubus, Philadelphus, Sorbus, and many other families, made a fine display either with their flowers or fruit. Strong-growing herbs, like the various species of Senecio, Astilbe, Aconitum, and Anemone, cover miles of the roadside. In shady places the handsome Maidenhair fern, *Adiantum pedatum*, was a charming picture ; in sunny spots the lovely *Gentiana purpurata*, with intense carmine-red flowers, was a sight never to be forgotten.

About 10 li below San-tsze-yeh the ravine widens out into a narrow valley, with the mountain-slopes on the left bank of the torrent less precipitous and grass-clad. We passed the ruins of some old forts, and shortly afterwards a Sifan hamlet consisting of three or four farmsteads, with numerous prayer-flags fixed on the roofs. In the tiny valley wheat, barley, buckwheat, oats, peas, and broadbeans are cultivated, and the crops were ready for harvesting.

San-tsze-yeh, alt. 9200 feet, consists of ruinous hovels built on a level with the infant stream which at this point breaks up into three equal branches, all of which have their source in the near neighbourhood. Looking back on the route we had traversed we saw that all the higher peaks are barren and desolate, the highest of all being flecked with snow. The whole plexus is made up of the spurs and buttresses of the mighty snow-clad Hsueh-po-ting. To the north-east from San-tsze-yeh are other tremendous peaks, bare, barren, and uninviting in appearance. The aspect of the country around this hamlet is purely Thibetan. The scant crops and abject poverty of the inhabitants speak plainly of a country where altitude and climate set agricultural skill and industry at defiance. Such regions the Chinese abhor and cannot colonize. The pastoral Sifan, with their herds of cattle and sheep, remain masters of the soil though politically subject to Chinese authority. The conquest of this wild region must have been a most difficult task and speaks volumes for the military genius which accomplished it.

During the night at San-tsze-yeh I had a violent attack of ague, probably caused by a chill, which culminated in a fit of vomiting. This seizure and the howling of many dogs were against a good night's sleep. In consequence we took things very gently the next day, and I used my chair much more than usual.

Twenty-five li above San-tsze-yeh, to the right of the stream which descends the narrow valley, there is a most interesting place. A torrent heavily surcharged with lime descends from the eternal snows of the Hsueh-po-ting, depositing along its course thick lime encrustations of creamy white. The place is considered holy by the Sifan, to whom any natural phenomenon strongly appeals. A temple has been erected here and a series of some fifty tarns constructed by leading the waters from the stream and making small semicircular dams. All are at slightly different levels, and the waters as they flow from one to another continue to build up the dams by leaving deposits of lime behind. The bed of each tarn is creamy white, but owing to the light being reflected in different colours, according to the varying depth of each, an attractive scene of many-coloured waters is presented. Some are clear azure blue, others creamy white, pink, green, purple, and so on. The temple is called " Wang Lung-ssu " (Temple of the Dragon Prince), and it is fitting that the Sifan, children of nature as they are, consider the place holy. Near the temple the waters have built up a wonderful series of waterfalls, and every fallen tree and bush obstructing the waters is speedily encrusted with lime. Above the temple the stream is fully 80 yards wide, and the bed is creamy white with soft encrustations of lime, the ripple marks being beautifully defined. These lime-deposits extend for a mile or two and present a most striking scene.

From the bed of this stream, a short distance above the temple, a fine view of the snow-clad Hsueh-po-ting is obtainable. The face visible carries but little snow, and immediately below the glaciers are wonderful cliffs of red-coloured rock. In contrast the colour-effects are most remarkable. There was said to be another temple some few li higher up towards the snows, but I was too fatigued to visit it.

All around Wang Lung-ssu are fine forests of Spruce, Silver Fir, Birch, with miscellaneous trees and shrubs. In the vicinity of the lime-deposits the trees look very unhealthy, many are bleached and dead, others yellow and dying. From the vegetation it is evident that these lime-deposits are recent and spreading rapidly. A few Rhododendrons occur on the margins of the stream and in the woods, but are not happy. Right by the water's edge I gathered *Arctous alpinus*, var. *ruber*, a tiny alpine shrub with red fruit closely allied to the Blueberries, and found also near the glaciers in British Columbia ! This pretty little plant, only some 4 to 6 inches high, is quite common hereabouts, but had not before been recorded from China. Near the tarns *Cypripedium luteum*, a yellow-flowered counterpart of the North American Moccasin flower (*C. spectabile*), is very abundant. (Later I succeeded in introducing live roots of this species to the Arnold Arboretum, where plants are now growing.)

The forests of this immediate neighbourhood are rich in fine Spruce trees, 80 to 150 feet tall and 6 to 10 feet in girth, with short branches producing a spire-like effect, are characteristic of the region. The Silver Fir are less noteworthy, but, like the Spruce, were fruiting freely. (Both were subsequently introduced to cultivation.) Larch overtops all other trees, reaching its limits at about 12,000 feet altitude. The vegetation of the ranges flanking the narrow valley, up which the main road ascends, presents a remarkable contrast. The range to the left of the stream, above 10,000 feet altitude, is covered only with scrub and grass ; whereas the range on the right bank is heavily forested up to altitude 12,000 feet. Early in the afternoon, after covering 40 li, we reached the lonely hostel of San-chia-tsze, alt. 12,800 feet, situate some 600 feet below the head of the pass. During the first 25 li of the day's march we passed several large farmhouses, but nearly all are deserted and falling into ruins. Around these houses a few plats of wheat, barley, flax, and Irish potato are cultivated ; also cabbage, garlic, and other vegetables in minute quantities. Tobacco (*Nicotiana rustica*), in small quantities for household use, is grown around San-tsze-yeh, and the crop looked very happy. These sporadic attempts at cultivation represent the vain and futile efforts of the Chinese settlers to eke out an existence from the inhospitable soil. This side of the pass is evidently much colder than the Sungpan side, since there, at greater elevations, good crops of wheat, barley, and peas can be raised.

Apart from the forests already mentioned, herbs dominate the flora. A great variety were still in flower, the various species of Senecio and Gentiana being most striking. *Gentiana detonsa*, a slender plant a foot and more tall, with numerous large deep blue flowers, looked particularly happy, flaunting its blossoms in the sun. On rocky screes the yellow-flowered *Clematis tangutica* is abundant and was covered with its top-shaped blossoms. The hedges bordering the fields are composed chiefly of Wild Gooseberry and *Sorbaria arborea* : the latter was in full flower. In copses by the stream, up to 11,500 feet, Hornbeam, Cherry, Red Birch, Willow, Maple, and Hazel-nut are common. The Hazel-nut is mainly *Corylus ferox*, var. *thibetica*, a variety having a spiny fruit closely resembling that of the Sweet Chestnut (*Castanea*).

The hostel of San-chia-tsze is maintained for the accommodation of travellers, and a posse of soldiers is stationed here to keep down banditti. The hostel is a roomy but miserable cabin, built of shales and roofed with shingles held down by stones. The floor is of mud and very uneven; there is no outlet for smoke, save the doorway, and no windows. At midday a candle was necessary to avoid falling over things when moving about indoors. During different visits I have suffered many days and nights in this lonely spot, on one occasion being snowed in for three consecutive days. The cabin is situated on a narrow sloping valley running nearly east and west, a mile or so above the tree-limit, flanked on the northern side by a ridge of stark, crumbling rocks. To the south the range culminates in bare peaks and eternal snows of the Hsueh-po-ting. The moorland country all around is typical of Eastern Thibet, so perhaps a few details are permissible. The treeless spurs and valleys are covered with extensive heaths of scrub, made up of several species of Spiræa (including *S. mollifolia*, *S. alpina*, and *S. myrtilloides*), *Sibiræa lævigata*, *Lonicera hispida*, *L. chætocarpa*, *L. prostrata*, *L. thibetica*, and others, several Barberries, Currants, shrubby Potentillas, Astragalus, Sallowthorn, small-leaved, twiggy Rhododendrons, and Juniper. As the altitude increases, one by one these shrubs give out until only the Juniper is left. This ceases about 15,000 feet; alpine herbs ascend another 1000 feet, and the limit of vegetation is roughly 16,000 feet. The Juniper scrub is from 1 to 2½ feet tall, very dense and difficult to traverse, but furnishes excellent fuel. Mixed with this scrub are herbs in great variety, the Poppyworts (*Meconopsis*) being particularly abundant. Possibly the commonest herb between 12,500 feet and 14,000 feet is *Meconopsis punicea*, a lovely species having large, dark-scarlet nodding flowers. (It was from near this vicinity that I succeeded in introducing this plant in 1903.) The violet-blue flowered *M. Henrici* is common between 13,000 feet to 14,000 feet, but much less so than around Tachienlu. The prickly *M. racemosa*, with blue flowers, is plentiful in rocky places between 13,000 feet to 14,500 feet. From 11,500 feet to 13,000 feet the gorgeous *M. integrifolia*, growing 3 feet tall, with its peony-like, clear yellow flowers 8 to 11 inches across, occurs, but is not plentiful. The intense colours among alpine flowers everywhere is well known, and this region is no exception. The yellow is mostly supplied by

Senecio, Saussurea and other *Compositæ*, slender growing Saxifraga, etc.   The blue and purple by various Aconites, Larkspurs, and Gentians ; among the latter *Gentiana Veitchiorum*, with large erect flowers, covers large areas.   The Lousewort (*Pedicularis*) and Fumewort (*Corydalis*) are represented by many species, having flowers embracing all the cardinal colours. Primulas occur, but not in many species.   Androsace, Sedum, Cyananthus, and other alpine genera abound.

Large flocks of sheep are pastured on these uplands, but yak are not kept in quantity hereabouts.   There is not much variety of game.   Blue sheep are common, Budorcas are found near the timber line ; on the higher crags occasional flocks of Goa, or Thibetan gazelle, occur.   Snow-partridge, Thibetan Hazel-hen, Snow-cock and allied game-birds, together with Thibetan Hares, are fairly numerous.   The Wolf is the only carnivorous animal really common.

The Hseuh-po-ting snows are visible on clear days from the wall of Chengtu city, and are accounted the " Luck of the Plain."   The Chinese claim that so long as snow covers this peak the prosperity of Chengtu and its surrounding plain is assured.   It was a perfect moonlight night on the occasion of my last sojourn at San-chia-tsze, and late in the evening I beheld the " Luck of Chengtu," with its crown of eternal snow lit by the radiant moonlight.   The loneliness of the region, the intense stillness on all sides, and the wonderful peak with its snowy mantle, made a most impressive scene.

A glorious morning followed a perfect night.   From the head of the pass (alt. 13,400 feet) I obtained further good views of the Hsueh-po-ting, bearing west-south-west and secured some photographs.   The peak is probably 22,000 feet high, in shape an irregular tetrahedron, the south-west slopes carrying enormous snow-fields.   The north-east face is very steep and carries but little snow.   The surrounding peaks are bare and desolate looking ;   no vestige of life was discernible, and the whole scene was lonely, most forbidding, even awesome, though bathed in brilliant sunshine.

Below San-chia-tsze are the stone ruins of an old fort and stockade, relics of ancient warring times, but now covered with various herbs, especially Saxifrages, which were masses

of yellow, and other coloured flowers.   The head of the pass
is marked by a ruined tower and fort, from the summit of which
Thibetan prayer-flags waved.   That robbers still haunt these
regions was brought home to us by the sight of a partially
covered coffin near the head of the pass.   A few weeks before,
a poor coolie, bound towards Lungan Fu to purchase rice, was
attacked here, robbed, and killed.   The bandits got clear away.
The coolie's " pai-tzu " (a framework for carrying loads on)
and various appurtenances lay on top of the coffin and remain
to tell the story of the crime.   All around are grassy areas,
covered at the season of our visit with blue and yellow alpine
flowers.

At the head of the pass small boulders of sandstone, marble,
granite, and other rocks lay scattered around.   Just below are
beds, which resemble coal-ashes, probably of volcanic origin.

From the pass we dropped down into a valley which quickly
led to fields of golden wheat and barley.   The crops were
ripening, and here and there the reapers were busy.   Passing
a ruined fort, several Sifan farmsteads, and a lamasery, the
road led to the summit of a grassy ridge.   Descending a few
hundred feet we sighted the city of Sungpan nestling in a
narrow, smiling valley, surrounded on all sides by fields of
golden grain, with the infant Min, a clear, limpid stream, winding its way through in a series of graceful curves.   In the
fields the harvesters were busy, men, women, and children,
mostly tribesfolk, in quaint costume, all pictures of rude
health, laughing and singing at their work.   Under a clear
Thibetan-blue sky, the whole country bathed in warm sunlight, this busy scene of agricultural prosperity gladdened the
hearts of all of us, fatigued and exhausted as we were from the
hardships of our journey through savage mountains with their
sublime scenery and wonderful flora.

CHAPTER XI

SUNGPAN TING

THE LAND OF THE SIFAN

THE city of Sungpan is situated on the extreme north-west corner of Szechuan, about long. 103° 21′ E., lat. 32° 41′ N., at an altitude of 9200 feet, and is the farther-most outpost of Chinese civilization in this direction. The surrounding country, more especially to south-west, west, and north-west, is inhabited by Sifan, a people concerning which very little is known. Originally established as a military post after the conquest of the neighbouring regions by the Emperor Kienlung about A.D. 1775, Sungpan has developed into a most important trade entrepôt. It is a city of the second class (styled " Ting "), but the head civil official has the local rank of prefect, his full title being " Fu-I-Li Min-Fu," which signifies " the Barbarian-cherishing, Chinese-governing Prefect." This fanciful title has reference to the official's control over the neighbouring Sifan tribes—a control which is purely nominal. The military importance of this stronghold is still fully recognized, and its strategic value is beyond question. A Chinese general (Chen-tai), in command of ten regiments, has his headquarters here, with jurisdiction extending south to Kuan Hsien, east to Lungan Fu, and north-east to Nanping in Kansu province.

The town is most picturesquely situated, occupying considerable space in a narrow, highly cultivated valley flanked by steep mountain-slopes 1000 to 1500 feet high. The Min (Fu) River, which takes its rise some 35 miles to the north, winds a circuitous course down the valley and flows through the town in an S-curve, entering and leaving through the city walls at unfordable points. On the western side the town is backed by a steep slope, up two sides of which a wall is carried.

The west gate of the city is situated at the top of this slope, and is exactly 1000 feet above the river. Save for a yamên and a temple or two the whole of the mountain-slope within the walls is given over to terraced cultivation, the city proper being clustered in the valley alongside the river. The wall surrounding three sides of the city is very substantially built of brick, being fully 20 feet thick and more high, but that which ascends the mountain-sides is in places only 2 feet thick and 4 feet high ; a steep ravine, however, immediately outside this wall, affords additional protection. Since the Chinese first established themselves here the town has undergone many vicissitudes. Time and again the Sifan have swept down upon it, captured it, and massacred all who fell into their hands. So frequent have been these attacks, and so great is the Chinese dread of treachery on the part of the Sifan, that it is only within the last few years that any of these people have been allowed to remain overnight within the city walls.

In 1910 Sungpan had a resident civil population of about 3000 people, and a floating population equalling, if not exceeding, this number. The houses are nearly all of wood, generally well built, with rather curiously-carved porticoes ; the timber employed for building is mostly Juniper, which is floated down the Min River from a point some 15 miles to the north-north-east. In October 1901 the city was two-thirds destroyed by fire, but on the occasion of my last visit in 1910 the devastated area had been practically rebuilt. The streets are badly paved, ill-kept, and the city possesses no buildings of architectural beauty. Near the south gate the military section of the town is situated, and a considerable amount of market-gardening is carried on there. The people are very fond of flowers, nearly every house boasting some in pots, on the walls, or in borders. Stately Hollyhocks, with multi-coloured flowers, are a feature. With these are generally planted Tiger Lilies, Chinese Asters, and small-flowered Poppies, the whole making a bright and pleasing effect. The Chinese Aster (*Callistephus hortensis*) is wild in the neighbourhood ; the Poppy is a species closely allied to *Papaver alpinum*. The population is mainly Mohammedan Chinese, who carry on a remunerative barter-trade with the surrounding tribes. Tea is the all-important medium employed, this commodity and a few odd sundries being taken in exchange by the tribesmen for their medicines, skins, wool, musk, etc. During the month of July a fair is held annually for trade purposes. The people from far and near attend this fair, a vast amount of business being transacted. Trading caravans also make long journeys into the country north-west to the borders of the Kokonor regions. Wool, sheep-skins, and various medicines in great quantity are exported from Sungpan to different parts of China.

The trade passing through Sungpan is, I am convinced, not only greater than has been estimated, but is increasing annually. In 1903, on the occasion of my first visit to this town, I enjoyed the companionship of W. C. Haines-Watson, Esq., then Commissioner of the Imperial Maritime Customs at Chungking. This gentleman investigated the trade of this region, estimating the exports to Thibet at Tls. 801,000, and those into China at Tls. 512,000 ("Journey to Sungp'an," *Jour. China Branch Roy. Asiat. Soc.*, 1905, xxxvi). Our visit occurred before the city had recovered from the disastrous fire of 1901, and trade was suffering in consequence. In 1910 trade was evidently booming. I have no figures to guide me, but comparing the two visits I would put the trade with China alone at a million taels. This trade has three outlets : one, east, via Lungan Fu to Chungpa ; another, south-east, via Mao Chou, Shihch'uan Hsien to An Hsien ; the third through Kuan Hsien to Chengtu. The first two routes afford water communication from Chungpa and An Hsien respectively, with Chungking on the Yangtsze River. By these routes most of the goods intended for Chungking and beyond are conveyed. The trade via Kuan Hsien is mainly with Chengtu and other cities on the plain. This latter trade route has been looked upon as the most important, whereas it is really less so than either of the other two outlets.

The late Captain W. J. Gill in 1877 was the first Occidental to visit Sungpan. Since that date several foreigners have paid visits, and missionaries of Protestant denominations have made abortive attempts to establish stations there. I have visited this place three times, and on each occasion enjoyed the stay and departed with regret.   Did the Fates ordain that I should live in Western China I would ask for nothing better than to be domiciled in Sungpan.   Though the altitude is considerable the climate is perfect, mild at all times, with, as a general rule, clear skies of Thibetan-blue.   During the summer one can always sleep under a blanket, in winter a fire and extra clothing are all that is necessary.   Excellent beef, mutton, milk, and butter are always obtainable at very cheap rates. The wheaten flour makes very fair bread, and in season there is a variety of game.   Good vegetables are produced, such as Irish potatoes, peas, cabbages, turnips, and carrots, and such fruits as peaches, pears, plums, apricots, apples, and Wild Raspberries (*Rubus xanthocarpus*).   Nowhere else in interior China can an Occidental fare better than at Sungpan Ting. With good riding and shooting, an interesting, bizarre people to study, to say nothing of the flora, this town possesses attractions in advance of all the other towns of Western China.

The valley, which varies from $\frac{1}{4}$ to $\frac{1}{2}$ mile in width, and the mountain-slopes, rising from 1000 to 1500 feet above, are given over to wheat and barley cultivation, with occasional fields of peas and flax, the latter being valued for its seeds, which yield an oil used as an illuminant.   In the latter half of August the whole country-side is one vast sheet of golden grain bending to the wind.   This grain is reaped, leaving a generous stubble, which is immediately ploughed under.   The ploughs are simple, consisting of an iron-shod shear, a straight handle of wood, and a long shaft, to which is harnessed a couple of oxen or half-bred yak.

In harvesting the grain, tribesfolk (chiefly Po-lau-tzu), who come from the upper reaches of the Tachin Ho, many days' journey to the west-south-west, play an all-important part.   Every year these people visit this region for the express purpose of this work, and are, in fact, indispensable.   As the crop is reaped it is tied into little sheaves and stacked ears downwards on high hurdle-like frameworks (Kai-kos) to await threshing.   The threshing is done by wooden flails, both men and women taking part in the work.   The corn is ground in mills driven by water-power.

The name " Sungpan " has reference to forests of Spruce

and Fir and the circuitous course of the river Min (Fu). The river still pursues its winding course, but the forests have long since disappeared. It is only in temple grounds and among tombs that any trees remain. The mountains are absolutely treeless, where not under cultivation they are covered with scrub and long grass. The outer crust of the mountains consists of a rich flaky loam, probably of glacial origin, rather heavy, but specially adapted for cereal cultivation. In the grass and scrub Pheasants are very plentiful in the neighbourhood of cultivation, so also is a long-eared, light-grey-coloured Hare. Musk Deer, Wapiti, and White Deer occur in the neighbour' hood. On the moorlands a Marmot, called " Hsueh-chu- ' (Snow-pig), burrows in large colonies.

North-west of Sungpan is the Amdo country, a region of grasslands. The Chinese designate it " Tsaoti," which may be interpreted " Prairie." This region is made up of rolling country above 11,000 feet altitude, where vast herds of cattle, sheep, and many ponies are reared. A great part of this region is peopled with pastoral Sifan, but the more remote parts are in the hands of nomads belonging to Ngo-lok and Nga-ba tribes, of evil reputation as robbers and bandits, dreaded alike by Chinese and the more peaceably inclined Sifan. These robber tribes are of Tangut origin, having their headquarters around the Kokonor region. Being of nomadic habit they wander far afield, and rob caravans and kill the settlers weaker in numbers than themselves. When I arrived in Sungpan in 1910 I found there some 200 soldiers from Chengtu bent on a punitive expedition against these banditti. About a year previously a Chinese official had been murdered in the Amdo country, not many days' journey from Sungpan, and no redress had been obtained. Nine persons were held guilty for this crime, but in spite of demands on the part of the Chinese the clan would not give up these people. The affair ended in the Chinese killing as many members of this robber clan as the small army sent on the expedition could capture. It is from the Amdo region that Sungpan derives most of its wool, skins, and medicines, consequently the trade depends very largely upon peace obtaining there.

The Sifan (Western people) are unquestionably of Thibetan

origin. They are not nomads, but essentially a pastoral and agricultural people. In dress, speech, and facial characteristics they agree closely with the inhabitants of anterior Thibet. Their houses are similarly constructed, and Lamaism dominates their lives. As a people the Sifan are divided into several tribal clans : those around Sungpan style themselves Murookai ; those a little to the south-west of this town Lappă. Immediately around Sungpan the Chinese language is generally understood, but away from the town colloquial Thibetan only is spoken, each hamlet having an interpreter to conduct all affairs with the Chinese. These people are ruled by head-men who are held directly responsible for the proper maintenance of law and order. The Chinese policy is one of non-interference in so far as it is consistent with the status of China as the paramount power.

The Sifan men as seen in the streets of Sungpan and the immediate neighbourhood are swarthy in appearance and average 5 feet 6 inches in height or rather more ; in walking they have a clumsy gait and are generally awkward and sullen when approached. Their dress is a sort of " cover-all " made of grey or claret-coloured serge, confined around the waist by a girdle ; the right shoulder is generally uncovered. This garment is often edged with fur ; sometimes it is made entirely of sheep-skins, with the wool worn inside. Short trousers and high felt boots cover the legs and feet, though in the streets they frequently go barefooted. The head-gear is either a low, stone-coloured, soft felt hat, with turned-up brim bordered with black, or a high, cone-shaped, light grey felt hat edged with white sheep-skin. Occasionally those living near Chinese settlements affect a dirty turban. The hair is worn long and gathered up inside the hat. The Lamas have their heads close-cropped or shaven, and when seen in the streets are usually hatless. In ceremonial dress they wear a sort of cocked hat made of grey serge covered with a mass of fluffy yellowish woollen stuff. Muleteers and men generally, when travelling, go armed with swords, knives, and long guns, the latter fitted with a fuse and a fork to rest the barrel on when taking aim. All wear charm-boxes on their chests, and carry a flint-box and tinder suspended from their girdle ; somewhere about their person a wooden, often silver-lined, eating bowl is also carried. The wealthy prize a leopard skin garment most highly.

The young girls are occasionally passing fair to look upon, but from hard work and exposure lose all charm of youth very early. The women are generally flat-faced, very dirty, and far from prepossessing. They have, however, considerable character and an important voice in household and all business matters. Toward foreigners they are timid, but amongst themselves their manners are playful, free and easy, and they laugh and sing at their work. Their outer dress consists of one shapeless piece of serge, which envelops them down to their ankles. Sometimes this is grey, more usually it is blue in colour, with a fancy bordering of dark red or yellow in front and around the bottom. High boots of untanned leather encase their feet and lower legs. Their hair is long and black, worn parted in the middle and collected into one large plait behind ; around the forehead it is worn in a series of tiny plaits ornamented with coral-beads, amber-coloured stones, and small shells. The large plait is usually wound around the head, together with a piece of cloth to form a kind of padded turban, the whole being decorated with shells and beads. Occasionally saucer-shaped felt hats are worn. In holiday attire, silver rings and gaudy red and yellow tassels are added to their coiffure. They are very fond of silver rings, bracelets, and large ear-rings ornamented with beads of turquoise and coral. In gala costume the dress is decidedly picturesque.

The men assist in tilling the soil, and in sowing and harvesting the crops, but the women do the bulk of the work around the homestead, the men being away herding the flocks or on journeys. Though they lead hard lives they seem a happy and contented people in spite of the fact that they are almost without exception afflicted with goitre. Their houses are built of wood and shale-rocks, being either one-storied, flat-roofed, with or without a raised part behind, or, as is more usual, two-storied and similarly roofed. They count their wealth in head of cattle, horses, and sheep. Wheat, barley, and peas are the staple crops. Meat, butter, and milk enter very largely into their diet. Buttered tea is generally drunk, but they are very partial to a kind of small beer which they brew from barley ; they are also fond of Chinese wine.

Monogamy is the rule, but polygamy is common, it being merely a question of wealth. Polyandry is not practised, but the morals are lax, as is the case everywhere else under Lamaism. Marriage is by consent on the part of the girl, presents of oxen and sheep being made on behalf of the bridegroom to the girl's parents ; children are appreciated, but the Sifan are not a prolific people. The second son generally enters a lamasery, as is customary throughout Thibet. Widows are permitted to remarry. The dead are disposed of by burial or by being thrown into the rivers.

Abundant signs of Lamaism are everywhere apparent. Prayer-flags flutter from the housetops, mountain-peaks, across streams, and surmount cairns of rocks. Mani-stones are heaped by the wayside ; praying-wheels, turned either by hand, by the wind, or by the currents of streams, occur on all sides. From the people at their work, either in low crooning tones or in loud chorus, the mystic hymn, " Om mani padmi hom," is continually ascending to heaven. The chant of the Sifan is decidedly musical, rising and falling in soft rhythmic cadence. I have often listened to them with much pleasure, though from a distance, since if one tried to approach closely they ran helter-skelter away. They are naturally very superstitious, being fond of charms, afraid of evil spirits, and reverence unusual natural phenomena. Though my associations with the Sifan were brief I always received the utmost courtesy at their hands, and found much that was pleasing and interesting among these happy, unsophisticated children of Nature.

CHAPTER XII

THE CHINO-THIBETAN BORDERLAND

" The Marches of the Mantzu "

IT is impossible to define, with any approach to accuracy, the political boundary between Szechuan and Thibet. Indeed, no actual frontier has ever been agreed upon, consequently it does not exist, except at one point, on the highway leading from Tachienlu, via Batang, to Lhassa. There, on the Ningching shan, three and a half days' journey west of Batang, stands a four-sided stone pillar, some 3 feet high, having been erected in A.D. 1728. The guide-book to Thibet says : " All to the east is under Peking ; the territory to the west is governed by Lhassa." As to the regions north and south of this stone, nothing is said.

For all practical purposes the Min River, from Sungpan Ting in the north-west to Kuan Hsien, may be regarded as the frontier thereabouts. From Kuan Hsien southwards an imaginary line drawn through Kiung Chou, Yachou, Fulin to Ningyuan Fu, and thence to the Yangtsze River, may be accepted as completing the frontier line. This constitutes a well-defined ecclesiastical boundary between the peoples. Also it corresponds very closely with the western limits of the Red Basin, which constitutes an unmistakable physiographical frontier. It is true that at certain points, such as Lifan Ting, Monkong Ting, Tientsuan Chou, and Tachienlu, the Chinese have succeeded in establishing trading-centres and military depots. But in all these places the population is mixed and the centres themselves surrounded on two or more sides by non-Chinese people. West of the boundary here indicated the Chinese occupy a very limited aggregate area, being confined to the high roads and to a few valleys suitable for rice and maize cultivation.   The largest of these areas is the region known as the Chiench'ang Valley, of which the city of Ningyuan Fu is the capital.   This narrow strip extends down to the Upper Yangtsze River, being bounded on the east by the independent kingdom of Lolo, which occupies the higher slopes of the Taliang shan and has never been conquered by the Chinese.   Immediately to the west of the valley the country is peopled by semi-independent tribes akin to the Thibetans.   Indeed, the Min River, with such land to the immediate west suited to rice-culture, may well be regarded as the real boundary of western Szechuan from Sui Fu on the Yangtsze River to Sungpan Ting, in the extreme north-west corner of the province.   An arc-line, commencing at Sungpan Ting and connecting with the boundary stone west of Batang, thence southwards, skirting the right bank of the Drechu (Upper Yangtsze), would form roughly the boundary of Thibet proper.   Nominally the whole of this region is considered by the Chinese part of Szechuan province.   In certain books and maps parts of this region are referred to as Eastern Thibet, and much confusion has arisen from this misnomer.

The country included within the boundaries here given constitutes the hinterland between Szechuan and Thibet, and failing a more lucid term it may be designated the "Chino-Thibetan borderland," a title which, if clumsy, has the merit of being both descriptive and accurate.   Several trade routes traverse this borderland, but with one exception these have been little travelled by foreigners—the exception being the great highway between Chengtu Fu and Lhassa De, which crosses this region from Yachou, via Tachienlu and Batang to the boundary, and is closely controlled by Chinese.   Apart from this highway and the country in its immediate vicinity as far west as Tachienlu, the whole borderland is very much a *terra incognita*.   It is made up of a series of stupendous mountain ranges, separated by narrow valleys, well forested in the lower parts with all the higher peaks extending above the snow-line.   These ranges are comparable only with the Himalayas, of which, indeed, they constitute a north-east extension. This rugged region is populated by many independent or quasi-independent tribes, more or less Thibetan in origin, with the exception of the Lolo.

It is a region where altitude and climate, rather than longitude and latitude, define the frontiers.   In the north-west the highlands of Central Asia abut more closely on the Red Basin than they do in the south-west, and form uplands suitable as grazing-grounds for herds of yak, cattle, horses, and sheep. These areas are peopled by nomadic Thibetans, with whom agriculture is relatively unimportant.   The broken country, made up of mountain-crag and valley, which forms the greater part of this hinterland, is occupied by various tribes, with whom agriculture is the paramount industry, and wheat, barley, and buckwheat the staple food-stuffs.   The forests of this region contain much game, of which these people are skilled hunters.   Lastly, in the more fertile valleys, where rice and maize can be successfully grown, Chinese settlers are found, but, as mentioned earlier, away from trading-centres and the great highway between Chengtu and Tachienlu, they are not much in evidence

In the first chapter brief reference to the mountain chains and rivers of this region has been made, but perhaps a few of the more striking features may be given in detail here.   Unlike the mountains bordering the eastern limits of the Red Basin, which are mainly of hard Carboniferous and Ordovician limestones, those of the west are principally of mudshales and granitic rocks.   Here and there, for example Mount Omei and its sister mountains Wa and Wa-wu, hard limestones have been forced up through the older rocks and form bold peaks and stupendous precipices.   There is indeed plenty of limestone throughout the hinterland, but Pre-Cambrian rocks preponderate enormously.   These and the shales (probably Silurian) disintegrate very readily in their exposed parts and erosion is rapid. In the deforested parts landslides are general.   The region is fairly rich in gold, silver, copper, lead, iron, and other minerals, but very little mining is carried on.   Coal is very rare, except in a few localities where limestone predominates, as near Mount Omei and the surrounding region.   Salt is known from one locality only (Pai-yen-ching in the Chiench'ang Valley).   Around Tachienlu hot springs of calcareous and chalybeate waters, more or less rich in sulphur, are common.   These springs are usually found in close proximity to torrents, very often occur-

ring in the actual bed of such streams. In many the waters
are actually boiling, and I have several times cooked eggs in
them. These hot springs are much resorted to by the people
of the surrounding regions for bathing purposes, the waters
being esteemed as a cure for rheumatism, skin affections, and
other complaints.

Three large rivers, Tung, Yalung, and Dre, flow through
this borderland, mainly from north to south, as necessitated by
the direction of the mountain axes. These rivers have tributaries in abundance, and the majority of them, draining from
eternal snows, carry down enormous quantities of water and
detritus. None of these rivers is navigable save for rafts,
specially constructed boats, or skin coracles, over very short
and interrupted stretches. Bridges and ferries are few, nevertheless the highways and by-ways of this region skirt the banks
of these rivers and their main tributaries.

The valleys of all these streams, and for the purpose of
what follows the Min above Kuan Hsien may be included, are
deeply eroded, the waters flowing between steep slopes or precipices. These valleys are all very similar, being narrow, shut
in by lofty treeless mountains, and all enjoy a much hotter,
drier climate than their altitude warrants. Long stretches
are very barren and desert-like, more especially when the outcropping rocks are solely granitic. Owing to this dry, hot
climate, interesting anomalies obtain in these valleys. At
Hokou, on the Yalung, maize can be cultivated up to nearly
9500 feet altitude, whereas at Tachienlu, in the same latitude
and 1000 feet less altitude, it is impossible to bring this cereal
to maturity. Green parrots (*Palæornis derbyana salvadori*)
occur as summer migrants in the valleys of the Yalung and
Drechu up to 10,000 feet altitude. Rock pigeons occur in
multitudes throughout all these valleys above 4000 feet altitude.
Monkeys also are common. The flora generally is specially
adapted to withstand drought, and is more closely allied to
that of the Yunnan plateaux than to the contiguous country.
Doubtless at one time the mountain-slopes flanking these
valleys were wooded, though it is improbable that the lower
slopes were ever heavily forested; but such timber as grew
there has long since disappeared, and to-day these slopes are

clothed only with coarse grass and scrub. Landslides are a feature of these regions, especially during the melting of the snows or after heavy rains in the surrounding high mountains. At such times travelling hereabouts is highly dangerous, as nearly every traveller can testify from ocular proof. I have witnessed several disastrous landslides, involving loss of life and much destruction of property. In 1910, when descending the Min Valley, I unfortunately got involved in a minor one, and sustained a compound fracture of the right leg just above the ankle. In many places rockslides are constantly occurring, and warning notices to travellers not to tarry are frequently displayed throughout the Upper Min Valley and elsewhere.

Small villages and farmsteads are scattered through these valleys where, goaded by stern necessity, the inhabitants maintain a grim struggle to win a sustenance from the inhospitable soil. Where rice and maize can be cultivated Chinese settlers are found, but above the altitudes admitting of this the tribes are in full possession and cultivate crops of wheat, barley, buckwheat, peas, and linseed—the latter for its oil, which is used as an illuminant. Exceptionally good Chilli peppers (*Capsicum*) are grown in these valleys, and certain regions, for example Mao Chou, in the Min Valley, are renowned for this produce. Around habitations a few trees, chiefly Poplar, Alder, and Willow, are always present, affording a welcome shade. *Cupressus torulosa*, a handsome timber tree, often 80 to 100 feet tall, is very much at home in these valleys and probably at one time covered quite considerable areas hereabouts. This tree is well worth the attention of those engaged in reafforestation work in dry, warm-temperate regions. Other trees partial to these same conditions are *Sophora japonica, Diospyros Lotus, Pistacia chinensis, Erythrina indica, Kœlreuteria apiculata, Ailanthus Vilmoriniana,* Celtis spp., and the Soap trees (*Sapindus mukorossi, Gleditsia spp.*). Many fruit trees occur, including the Pear, Apple, Peach, Apricot, and Walnut ; the latter (*Juglans regia*) is the commonest tree up to 8000 feet. The natives hack the lower trunk to make the tree fruitful, so they claim, showing that the old adage—"beating the Walnut tree"—is known outside of Europe. Mulberry trees, the *Cudrania tricuspidata*, and tall-growing Bamboos are common up to 4500 feet altitude.

Many of the shrubs found growing in these valleys are spinescent and nearly all are adapted to withstand drought. In the majority the leaves are very small or covered with a dense felt of hairs. These shrubs are usually scrubby in appearance yet many produce ornamental flowers or fruit. The " Southernwood " (*Artemisia* spp.), with silver-grey, elegantly dissected foliage and yellow flowers, are perhaps the commonest shrubs met with hereabouts. Barberries are another special feature, and when laden with masses of red fruit and autumn-tinted foliage present a most attractive picture. This same remark applies to various species of Cotoneaster, all having ornamental fruit. Many kinds of Rose occur, but often the species are local. Common to all these valleys, though most abundant in that of the Yalung, is *Rosa Soulieana*, with fragrant flowers, opening sulphur-yellow and changing to white. So also is Miss Willmott's charming rose (*R. Willmottiæ*), with its abundant straw-yellow prickles, neat glaucescent leaves, rosy-pink flowers, and orange-red fruit. The beautiful *R. Hugonis* is confined to a narrow stretch of the Min Valley between 3000 to 5000 feet. This is the only rose with yellow flowers I have met with in China. The fruit is black and falls very early. *R. multibracteata*, an odd-looking species having pretty pink flowers, is very common in the upper reaches of the Min Valley and less so in that of the Tung. Forms of the Musk Rose (*R. moschata*) and of *R. sericea* occur but are local. With the exception of the " Southernwood," all these shrubs confine themselves closely to water-courses. In more arid places *Caryopteris incana* and other species, with intense blue flowers opening in late July, are very abundant, so also are different species of Indigofera, with pink to red-purple flowers. Several species of Buddleia and two varieties of the lovely *Clematis glauca*, with glaucous foliage and top-shaped, yellow, passing to bronze-coloured flowers, ought not to be overlooked. The shingly and sandy foreshores are covered with Willow, Sallowthorn, and False Tamarisk (*Myricaria germanica*). In the Tung Valley, between

4000 and 5000 feet altitude, a " Prickly Pear " (*Opuntia Dillenii*) has become naturalized. This American colonist has made itself very much at home, covering many miles of barren rocky slopes. It grows 6 to 10 feet tall, and when covered with its yellow or pale orange flowers is very ornamental. The edible nature of the fruit is well known to the natives but is little esteemed. An extract obtained by boiling the fleshy stems is locally employed as a supposed cure for hæmorrhoids.

Amongst the coarse grass and scrub, the dominant features of these regions, a variety of showy herbs occur, nearly all having bulbous or thickened rootstocks in some form or other. To garden lovers everywhere these valleys are of special interest, inasmuch as they are the home of many beautiful Lilies. Each of these valleys has species or varieties peculiarly its own, which range up to about 8000 feet altitude, yet whilst very local these Lilies are numerically extraordinarily abundant. In late June and July it is possible to walk for days through a veritable wild garden dominated by these beautiful flowers. In the Min Valley the charming *Lilium regale* luxuriates in rocky crevices, sun-baked throughout the greater part of the year. It grows 3 to 5 feet tall, and has slender leaves crowded on stems bearing several large funnel-shaped flowers, red-purple without, ivory-white suffused with canary-yellow within, often with the red-purple reflected through, and is deliciously fragrant. In the Tung Valley, Mrs. Sargent's Lily (*L. Sargentiæ*), a taller growing species than the foregoing, with broader leaves, having bulbils in the axils, equally handsome flowers of similar shape, but varying from green to red-purple without and from pure white to yellow within, is very abundant in rocky places among grass and scrub. The flowers of this species are collected, boiled, and dried in the sun, then minced, fried with salt and oil, and eaten in the same way as preserved cabbage. The bulbs of the Tiger Lily (*L. tigrinum*) and its elegant ally, *L. Thayeræ*, which are white, are cooked and eaten. Several other Lilies abound in these valleys, including the lovely *L. Bakerianum* and other species not yet named.

A herb very common in the Tung Valley is *Thalictrum*

dipterocarpum. This Meadow-rue grows 6 to 8 feet tall, has elegant, much-divided foliage, and multitudinous, large, lavender-purple flowers—by common consent the handsomest member of its family. In the Min and Tung Valleys, but very local, *Incarvillea Wilsonii*, which grows nearly 6 feet tall and has handsome flowers very like those of *I. Delavayi*, occurs. This plant is monocarpic and has not yet flowered in cultivation, although I introduced it into the Veitchian nurseries as long ago as 1903. *Salvia Przcwalskii*, with large purple flowers, is another striking herb common in the valleys above 8000 feet altitude. This list of ornamental herbs could easily be extended if any useful service would be served thereby. On bare rocks various species of Selaginella abound ; the Mullein (*Verbascum Thapsus*), Deadly Nightshade (*Hyoscyamus niger*), and Thornapple (*Datura Stramonium*) are common weeds by the wayside. The poisonous properties of the two last named are well known to the natives. From this brief sketch it will be seen that these narrow, dry, almost desert-like valleys, with their abnormally warm climate, possess a flora which, if limited in number of species, contains many plants of more than passing interest and horticultural value.

As mentioned earlier (p. 149), this hinterland is peopled by various independent and semi-independent tribes about which little is known. The whole region is analagous with that separating India and Thibet, and this statement of fact will perhaps convey a more intelligible idea than the most voluminous details. These tribes are divisible into four distinct groups, in accordance with their official status and form of government.

1. States independent, non-tributary, hostile to both Chinese and Lama authority, as the Lolo kingdom. I have no intimate acquaintance with the Lolo—a people once spread over much of Yunnan, but now relegated to the region of the Taliang shan, where they have never been conquered by the Chinese. This race possesses a written language peculiar to itself and is probably indigenous.

2. States really independent and even hostile toward China, directly controlled by the Dalai Lama and Council, whose policy is supposed to be modified by High Commissioners appointed

by China, as, for example, Chantui, Derge, and Sanai.   The territory occupied by these tribes is west of the Yalung River and contiguous to that of Thibet proper ; the people are indistinguishable from those inhabiting anterior Thibet generally. These more western regions have been styled the " Thibetan Marches."   Some four years ago, an acting viceroy of Szechuan, one Chao Êrh-fêng, was appointed Warden of these Marches. With an army of Chinese soldiers he indulged in a most aggressive policy and speedily subjected the whole region to Chinese control.   He broke the Lama power, destroyed the principal lamaseries, and beheaded the abbots and other dignitaries. His task was rendered fairly easy owing to affairs in Lhassa, consequent upon the British expedition to that city, and the flight of the Dalai Lama, the whole making impossible any concerted action by Lhassa De in support of their adherents in the Marches.   (In 1911 Chao Êrh-fêng was appointed Viceroy of Szechuan and was subsequently murdered in Chengtu city by Chinese revolutionists.)

3. States tributary-controlled, governed by hereditary native princes and subject to the Viceroy of Szechuan in temporal affairs, but more or less strongly influenced by the Dalai Lama, owing to Lamaism being the accepted religion. Of these the kingdom of Chiala, the Horba states, and the Chiarung tribes are the chief.   They occupy most of the territory between the Min and Yalung Rivers north of a line connecting Yachou with Tachienlu and Hokou.   The Chiala kingdom I shall deal with separately when describing Tachienlu, the capital city.   The Chiarung are dealt with in the next chapter.

4. A number of very small states, governed by quasi-independent chiefs, indirectly controlled by Chinese officials appointed for that purpose and by the surrounding tributary kingdoms.   They are, in fact, tiny buffer areas very useful to the Chinese in maintaining the balance of power among the larger, more independent kingdoms.   Many of these principalities are made up of people who may reasonably be looked upon as remains of the aboriginal population of parts of Szechuan and this hinterland.   These petty states are scattered through the more easterly parts of this hinterland

from Mao Chou in the north through the Chiench'ang Valley to borders of Yunnan province.   The power exercised by the chiefs varies according to their proximity to thickly populated Chinese districts or otherwise.   In the former it is almost nominal, whereas in the latter case it is very considerable.

In addition to the above are certain feudal states whose overlord owes his office directly to Chinese influence, and who is bound, if called upon, to render military service to China. These feudal chieftainships are hereditary and were originally bestowed as rewards for assistance rendered to the Chinese in breaking up the Chiarung confederacy during the reign of the Emperor Kienlung.   Many of these, for example the Tsa-ka-lao chief, have very considerable power and influence in the temporal affairs of the surrounding tributary-controlled kingdoms.   The people are mainly of the same stock as the Chiarung tribes.   All the chiefs of these feudatory states and tributary kingdoms are closely related by inter-marriage.

The Chinese designate the inhabitants of this borderland " Mantzu," a contemptuous term signifying " Barbarian " and of no ethnological value whatever.   But the policy they have pursued in dealing with these people has been shrewdly wise if unscrupulous.   With arms and money the Chinese have displayed their power and obtained what practically amounts to a suzerainty over the whole borderland.   A former emperor said : " Wardens of the Marches should seek to checkmate the native tribes by becoming intimately acquainted with them and their customs and thus able to prevent any united action.   In this way the tribes will remain weak and easy to manage.   They should be encouraged to appeal to Chinese authorities for advice and protection in their disputes with one another. These authorities will, of course, be in no hurry to settle their cases.   If the tribes are taught to fear the Chinese, and the officials act with energy, all trouble will be avoided."   This crafty advice has long been acted upon by the Chinese, with much success from their own view-point.

From this brief and very incomplete general account it may be gathered that this hinterland is a fascinating region, presenting ethnological and other problems of great interest, the solution of which is worthy of the attention of Western scientists. It is hoped that a properly equipped expedition will at no very distant date be organized and dispatched to survey and investigate fully this little-known Chino-Thibetan borderland.

CHAPTER XIII

THE CHIARUNG TRIBES

Their History, Manners, and Customs

WITHIN the limits of the Chino-Thibetan borderland, as defined in Chapter XII, from Sungpan Ting southwards to Yachou Fu, and west to the valley of the Upper Tung or Tachin (Great Gold) River, the territory is divided amongst numerous cognate tribes collectively spoken of by Chinese as "Chiarung." These people are essentially agriculturists, making their homes in the upland valleys. They are all, though tributary to China, ruled by their own hereditary chiefs; each tribe occupies a properly defined area, with its own capital town, the political centre of the entire region being Monkong Ting. These tribes are non-Chinese and are not indigenous to this region. They are also distinct from the people found in anterior Thibet. They speak a difficult and at first sound unpronounceable jargon, which, if it be the mother of Thibetan dialects, is widely different from that spoken in Thibet to-day. But Thibetan letters have, without difficulty, been applied to it, and scholars, priests, officials, and merchants both read and speak the Lhassa-Thibetan language with greater or less fluency.

The origin of these people is obscure, yet there is good reason to believe they come originally from the region around the head-waters of the Tsang-po (Upper Brahmaputra River), and probably have common origin with the people of Nepal and Bhutan. Personally, I am of the opinion that they came over with Genghis Khan, or his son Ok-Ko-Dai, at the commencement of the thirteenth century, and assisted in the conquest of western Szechuan. As a reward for military services rendered they were given the territory they occupy to-day. During the course of time they waxed powerful, menacing the territory to the east of the Min River, and even taking possession of certain parts. In Ming times the Chinese made war with them on many occasions. They were a source of trouble to the Manchu dynasty until the famous Emperor Kienlung determined upon crushing their power. After a very fierce struggle this was accomplished by a Chinese general named A-kuei. First he subjugated the region of the Hsaochin Ho (Little Gold River), then, after much difficulty, he captured Lo-wu-wei (modern Hsuching), the capital of the Tachin Ho (Great Gold River), took the king prisoner, and made a map of the entire region. The king, named Solomuh, was sent to Peking, where, after a grand court ceremony, he was sliced to pieces. The conquest was completed early in A.D. 1775. Military colonies were then established by the Chinese in strategic places, the more fertile regions were confiscated, and Chinese settlers induced to take possession. In crushing this confederacy the Chinese were assisted by the tribes, being to some extent divided amongst themselves. Some of them fought on the Chinese side, and as a reward certain areas situated at strategic points were fiefed out and established as feudal states for the benefit of these allies, an overlord with hereditary control being appointed to each. The Chinese handled this campaign with consummate skill, and the administrative system established has remained unchanged down to the present day. The power of the tribes was completely broken ; and the feudal states and the military colonies have safeguarded the Chinese from any concerted action on the part of these people ever since. It will, however, be readily understood that the tribes farthest removed from regions fully occupied by Chinese enjoy to-day greater independence than those in close contiguity.

Originally these " Chiarung " had one common language, but time, isolation, and the dividing up into clans has produced many very dissimilar dialects. These people are now split up into eighteen tribes, occupying very unequal areas of territory, and though all are interrelated by marriage they are by no means at peace with one another. Feuds are constant, and fighting among themselves is very much the rule. Since this keeps them weak in power the Chinese policy is to intervene as seldom as possible. On the map are indicated as accurately as our knowledge admits the positions occupied by some of these tribes and feudal states. It is almost impossible to render into English the guttural sounds denoting the names of many of these tribes. But, fortunately, the more important, namely, Mupin, Wassu, Somo, Damba, Bati-Bawang, Wokje, are the least difficult to pronounce. The whole territory occupied by these people is about 250 miles from north to south, and 200 miles east to west at broadest point. The population is about half a million.

Two main roads, one from Kuan Hsien, the other from Lifan Ting, cross this region and unite near Monkong Ting. In addition, a network of cross-country by-ways connects the various villages and states.

The Chiarung are essentially agriculturists, cultivating with much skill crops of wheat, barley, peas, buckwheat, maize, Irish potato, and miscellaneous vegetables. Sheep, cattle, ponies, and goats are kept by the more wealthy, often in quantity. The horses are sold to Chinese traders, but the wool is woven into cloth for their own use. Milk, butter, and meat enter largely into their diet. They are also skilled gun- and swordsmiths, more especially the Somo people, who manufacture most of these weapons in use among the tribes themselves and the people of eastern Thibet generally. Many are also highly skilled masons, builders, and well-sinkers, and as such have a reputation even amongst the Chinese. During August many visit the upper reaches of the Min River every year to take part in harvesting the crops ; indeed, for this purpose they supply most of the labour in that region. Often they are in request in Chengtu and other cities for sinking wells and such-like work.

The Chiarung live in settlements of from several to a hundred families or even more, always in positions admirably suited for defence. These settlements usually crown some bluff or eminence ; very often they are perched like an eagle's aerie high up on the steep mountain-side. The architecture which obtains throughout is characteristic and peculiar. Each settlement is dominated by one or more tall, chimney-like towers, either square, hexagonal, or octagonal in shape, 60 to 80 feet high, and resembling from a distance the stack of some large factory in Western lands. The exact significance of these towers it is difficult to fathom, but it is evident that they can serve as storehouses, watch-towers, and harbours of refuge in times of stress and war. They have also some obscure connexion with religious matters, possibly in this they have some remote affinity with the pagodas of China and Burmah. The houses are more or less square, flat roofed, solidly built of shale-rock and mud. Those belonging to the chiefs and men of property are three or four stories high. The walls are thick, pierced with loopholes and several narrow latticed windows. At all four corners of the roof turrets 3 to 4 feet high are built, sometimes there are more in different patterns. From these prayer-flags are displayed, often with the green branches of Juniper. On the roof also is fixed an incinerator for the sacrificial burning of fragrant juniper branches as incense. Part of the roof is frequently occupied by a hurdle-like framework called " Kai-kos," 10 to 15 feet high, which is employed for drying grain upon. The rest of the roof is used for religious exercise, eating, sleeping, and recreation; in harvest-time it serves as a threshing-floor. The ground story is made up of a courtyard surrounded by sheep and cattle-pens, the kitchen, and usually a guest-room.

The turrets, upper rim of the walls, edges of the window-spaces, base and base angles of the walls, are washed white, commonly white lines stretch diagonally up the walls, and the swastika cross, with other devices and symbols, are displayed in white on these walls. Crowning the edges of the roof, or arranged on separate structures, symbols denoting a globe, upturned crescent, and the swastika are commonly displayed. The lamaseries are similarly constructed, only larger, and usually with more stories. The houses of the peasants also are on the same plan, but of one or two stories only. All these structures are closely packed together with one to several towers reared above the whole assemblage. The different emblems and symbols of Nature worship may occur in the structure of Thibetan houses and lamaseries, but the tall tower is peculiar to the Chiarung.

Another interesting feature of these regions is the bridges. All these structures are of designs differing from those found throughout China proper, but agreeing closely with those in use throughout Sikhim, Bhutan, and Nepal, thus furnishing additional evidence of the affinity of these peoples. All the smaller streams and torrents are bridged by logs arranged on a semi-cantilever principle, and call for no special remark. But the larger streams are crossed by suspension bridges constructed of split and plaited bamboo cables. These bridges are very similar to the cane bridges of Sikhim and Bhutan. They are found throughout the territory occupied by these tribes and the narrow strip of territory wedged in between the Min Valley and the western limits of the Red Basin. This latter strip was formerly occupied by these tribes, and is to-day largely peopled by their descendants or half-caste Chinese. As mentioned in Chapter X, pp. 117, 130, iron suspension bridges occur in one or two places in the north-west corner of Szechuan. This style of bridge is common from the valley of the Ya River, and the Tung at Luting chiao, southward to the frontier of Burmah, and is probably of Shan origin. Similar bridges of iron rods and chains are met with in Bhutan, where they are considered to be of Chinese origin (White, *Sikhim and Bhutan*, p. 191). Throughout the Chino-Thibetan Borderland iron and bamboo are equally common, yet it is a singular fact that their use in bridge-building is restricted to definite areas.

Cable or rope bridges are abundant throughout the entire region, and extend much farther west and south than the Chiarung territory. These simple but extremely useful structures consist of a bamboo hawser stretched across the stream usually from a higher to a lower point ; if the stream is moderately narrow the question of incline is of less importance. The hawser may be anything from 8 inches to 1 foot thick, and being heavy sags considerably in the middle, unless the stream is very narrow, as around Tachienlu, where a rather different method of crossing than that about to be explained is in vogue. To cross one of these cable bridges a person is supplied with a length of strong hempen rope hanging free from a saddle-shaped runner of oak or some other tough wood. The runner clips the cable, and the hempen rope is fastened under and around the legs and waist to form a " cradle." When all is properly secured the person throws one arm over the top of the runner, gives a slight spring, and glides down the inclined cable at increasing speed. The impetus obtained in the downward rush carries the passenger over the central dip and more or less up the lesser incline on the opposite side. If the momentum is insufficient to land the person, the remaining distance has to be traversed by taking hold of the hawser and hauling hand over hand. Crossing these bridges is fearsome work until one is accustomed to it. It is speedily accomplished, and there is practically no danger so long as one keeps a cool head and the ropes do not break. It is a common sight to see men with loads and women with children on their backs cross these bridges. But heavy loads are usually fixed to the runners and hauled across by a rope attached to them.

None of the rivers traversing Chiarung territory is navigable in the ordinary sense of the term, but skin coracles, broadly oval in shape, descend certain stretches of the Upper Tung River. These frail boats serve also to ferry over goods and passengers at certain necessary places. They are made of cattle hide stretched over ribs of tough, light wood. The whole coracle is very easily carried by one man, and closely resembles pictures of the boats used by ancient Britons prior to the Roman invasion. They are steered by a man seated in the stern operating a paddle, and accommodate about two passengers. A passage down or across stream in one of these coracles consists very largely in describing, more or less rapidly, a series of wide circles and half circles. As a novelty, productive of excitement, not unmixed with danger, these coracles and cable bridges can with confidence be recommended to " World's Fair " promoters and showmen generally. The skin coracle is in general use at ferries throughout Eastern Thibet and the Marches, and is not strictly a Chiarung specialty.

In height the tribesmen average about 5 feet 7 inches or rather more ; the face is usually oval, with rather pointed chin, straight nose, sometimes inclining towards aquiline. They dress ordinarily in undyed serge cloth of local make, worn in the same manner as that of the Sifan. The legs are swathed in felt putties ; the head-gear is either a turban or black pudding-basin-shaped felt hat.   Those living near Chinese settlements and the highways have their head in part shaven, and wear their hair in a queue Chinese fashion.   On holiday occasions their garments are brightened with red bordering, and high felt boots are worn.   The women are short in stature (about 5 feet), sturdy and buxom, somewhat gipsylike, with dark olive complexions, and when young are often good looking.   Their ordinary outer dress is a garment of grey native serge of no definite shape, reaching to just below the knee and bound around the waist with a scarf. The legs and feet are bare or encased in top-boots.   Commonly they go bare-headed with their long black hair parted down the middle and hanging down the back in one large plait. They are fond of large bangles, ear-rings, etc., made of silver inlaid   with   turquoise   and   coral.   On   festive   occasions garments edged with red and very often made of blue cloth are worn.   The more wealthy dames decorate themselves very lavishly with silver ornaments, and wear covering their heads a piece of cloth held down by means of their large plait of hair, which is wound around and decorated with silver and beads of coral and turquoise ; the lower part of the piece of cloth hangs free over the back of the neck and shoulders.   These dames are women of character, and have a ruling voice in household and family matters generally ; also, from what I saw of them, they appear to conduct most of the business. These women lead a strenuous life ; they cultivate the fields, tend the flocks, take the farm produce to market, hew wood, and carry water.   The domestic duties of cooking, making and mending clothes and general household work devolve upon the men.   Yet the women are not unkindly treated, and are far from being down-trodden.   Being of cheerful disposition, they seem well suited to the free outdoor life they lead, and laugh and sing as they ply their task.   Among themselves these people are frank and easy in manner, and the women enjoy a freedom of position unknown amongst the Chinese.   A party of dames and men were fellow-travellers with me once for a couple of days.   When the time came to separate they made merry over cups of wine ; the women officiated, and cordially invited me to join them.   With their laughter and song they made cheery companions, and I was sorry to part from them.

The families are small, but the children are usually strong and healthy. Girls marry between the ages of seventeen and twenty, polygamy is common, but polyandry is unknown except, perhaps, in the upland regions bordering Thibet proper. Temporary marriages, so general in Thibet, are also unknown amongst the Chiarung. Nevertheless, the standard of morals in vogue among these people is a very low one. In certain states hetairism precedes maternity. In Badi-Bawang the unmarried girls and childless women wear only two sporran-like fringes of woollen threads or pieces of fur, suspended from a girdle passed around the body above the hips. The legs are exposed, but the upper parts of the body are usually covered by a coarse serge garment. Only after their first child is born may they wear skirts, since the gods have then purified them. A pregnant damsel selects from among her lovers a husband, who thus becomes the accepted father of her child, her word in this matter being final. Maternity alone ratifies marriage, and indeed saves women from promiscuity. The defloration of virgins is the prerogative of chiefs and head-men, but is not always exacted. In many ways these people are apparently shameless, according to Chinese and Occidental ideas alike. It is no uncommon sight to see women of all ages, quite nude, bathing in streams by the wayside. This same custom is also common at Tachienlu, where the hot springs are favourite bathing-places for both sexes. But after maternity the women are said to remain constant ; divorce or legal separation after ratified marriage are not practised.

The explanation of the above and other curious customs of these interesting people is found in their religious beliefs. Although orthodox Lamaism is more or less paramount the mysterious Bönpa religion, with its marked tendency toward phallic worship, lurks throughout the lonely valleys of the Chiarung tribes. In Badi-Bawang it is the recognized state religion. It should also be remembered that these regions constituted the famous matriarchal kingdoms of Chinese historians. Indeed, even to-day, certain states have queens holding nominal or actual authority, and in these in some capacity a woman must always rule. Occasionally the difficulty is overcome by styling the ruling head a " Queen " quite irrespective of sex !

Lamaism appears in three forms, the Yellow, Red, and Black, the latter representing the Bönpa cult. The religious centre is Tsong-hua on the Tachin River, about 60 miles west of Monking Ting. But lamaseries are scattered over the land, occurring separately by themselves or in association with the residences of the hereditary chiefs. The Yellow or orthodox sect is first in importance and numbers, and is controlled directly from Lhassa. The ritual differs in no way from that practised throughout the hierarchy of Lamaism. The same remark applies to the unorthodox Red sect, which is of much less importance, and whose priests are allowed to marry.

The Black or Bönpa sect has a ritual bearing an outward resemblance to orthodox Lamaism, but apart from this there is little else in common. In many things the Bönpa are the avowed enemies of the orthodox. They turn their praying wheels from left to right instead of from right to left ; they pass sacred objects on the right instead of on the left ; also they refuse to repeat the mystic Mantra, " Om mani padmi hom," replacing it with one peculiarly their own. As to the origin of this Bönpa it is difficult to say. My friend, Mr. J. Hutson Edgar of the China Inland Mission, who has travelled among and studied these Chiarung tribes more closely than any one else living, inclines to regard it as the remains of the old Nature worship of Thibet, which probably underlies all the religious systems of Eastern Asia.

In the state of Wassu are several temples belonging to this Bönpa sect. Through the courtesy of the chieftain I was allowed to inspect some of these temples, and succeeded in obtaining fair photographs of the idols. These latter, made of stone, wood, straw, and plaster, represent giants and demons with their female energies ; the walls are decorated with paintings depicting erotomania. Hideous and disgustingly obscene are the contents of these temples, where phallic worship holds unblushing sway. The Wassu chief informed me that the Mantra used by these Bönpa priests is " Hom ma-te ma-tsi ma-yöor tsa-lien doo." He kindly gave me a copy of this hymn, but I have not yet succeeded in getting it translated into intelligible English. The principal symbol in use is the Fylfot or swastika, which they call " Yungdrung." A mystical bird, " Chyong " or " Garuda," is also regarded with great favour as an emblem of fruitfulness. In the Bönpa temples at Tung-ling shan, near the residence of the Wassu chief, I also recognized the image of Kwanyin (Goddess of Mercy), the God of Wealth, and many demons similar in appearance to those found in ordinary Buddhist temples throughout China proper. It would thus appear from the catholic nature of the contents of their temples that these people accept a measure of Buddhism, and Lamaism both orthodox and unorthodox, and the Bönpa in its entirety. An atmosphere of secrecy and mystery enshrouds the Bönpa temples, which are frequently built in places difficult of access. The cult has been subjected to much persecution at the hands of Lamaists, yet, notwithstanding, it retains a firmer hold on the people of most of the Chiarung states than any other form of religion. In their hearts children of nature, their daily life one constant struggle against an inhospitable soil and climate to win a crop necessary for their sustenance, these people very naturally incline most toward the gods of Increase and Fecundity.

CHAPTER XIV

ACROSS THE CHINO-THIBETAN BORDERLAND

KUAN HSIEN TO ROMI CHANGO ; THE FLORA OF THE PAN-LAN SHAN

URING the summer of 1908, when in Chengtu, I determined upon a journey to Tachienlu. Previously, in 1903 and again in 1904, I had visited this town by three different routes. This time I decided upon following the road leading from Kuan Hsien via Monkong Ting and Romi Chango. The only published account of this route that I have knowledge of is in a Report by Mr. (now Sir) Alexander Hosie,[1] erstwhile H.B.M.'s Consul-General at Chengtu, who returned from Tachienlu over this road in October 1904. What is written in this Report about the forests of that region created a desire within me which nothing short of actual experience could satisfy. Again, this route promised further acquaintance with the tribesfolk inhabiting the hinterland. Sir Alexander's description of the road portrayed a difficult journey, but I felt sure that by taking time and but lightly burdening my men I could get through all right. This confidence was fully justified, as events proved, and what I saw of the forests and mountain scenery, together with the quantity and variety of plants discovered and collected, abundantly repaid me for the hardships experienced. The journey is estimated at 1326 li, approximately 330 English miles, but, whilst mere mileage is of little moment in mountainous countries, I should consider 250 miles a more accurate figure.

With Tachienlu as my goal I left the city of Chengtu on the morning of 15th June, and at noon the next day reached

[1] *Journey to the Eastern Frontier of Thibet*, presented to both Houses of Parliament, August 1905.

the city of Kuan Hsien. An afternoon sufficed to complete my arrangements. The caravan consisted of eighteen carrying coolies and one head coolie, two chairs, two handy men, an escort of two soldiers, my Boy, and self, making a party of thirty all told. The journey occupied twenty-three days from Kuan Hsien.

What follows is compiled from my diary :—

The famous bamboo bridge, known as the An-lan chiao, over which the road to Monkong Ting passes, was having its annual overhauling; in consequence, on leaving Kuan Hsien we had to journey down stream some 5 li to a point where it was possible to cross the various arms of the Min River by improvised bridges and ferry. In so doing we had an opportunity of realizing, somewhat hazily be it confessed, what this area must have been like before Li-ping's wonderful irrigation works came into existence. Without counting the streams flowing Chengtu-wards we crossed five distinct arms of the Min River proper scattered over an area a mile wide, covered with sand, shingle, and coarse grass (*Miscanthus sinensis*). The detour involved 15 li, and it was not until 9 o'clock that we were opposite the An-lan chiao. This most remarkable structure is about 250 yards long, 9 feet wide, built entirely of bamboo cables resting on seven supports fixed equidistant in the bed of the stream, the central one only being of stone. The floor of the bridge rests across ten bamboo cables, each 21 inches in circumference, made of bamboo culms, split and twisted together. Five similar cables on each side form the " rails." The cables are all fastened to huge capstans, embedded in masonry, which are revolved by means of spars and keep the cables taut. The floor of the bridge is of planking held down by a bamboo rope on either side. Lateral strands of bamboo keep the various cables in place, and wooden pegs driven through poles of hard wood assist in keeping the floor of the bridge in position. Not a single nail or piece of iron is used in the whole structure. Every year the cables supporting the floor of the bridge are replaced by new ones, they themselves replacing the " rails." This bridge is very picturesque in appearance, and a most ingenious engineering feat.

From the An-lan chiao the road ascends the right bank

of the Min River, and is broad, in good repair, but with many awkward gradients. We found lodgings for the night at Hsuan-kou, alt. 2640 feet, a market village of some 300 houses, situated on a tributary immediately above its union with the main stream, which describes a very sharp turn on leaving a narrow gorge. The Min River from the An-lan chiao to this point is full of minor rapids, and the current is very swift. Near Hsuan-kou timber is made into rafts and floated down to Kuan Hsien, thence to Chengtu and elsewhere.

During the day's march we passed some good-sized trees of Black Birch, Nanmu (*Machilus* spp.), Hog-plum (*Spondias axillaris*), and small trees of *Cryptomeria japonica*, the latter obviously planted. A large trumpet-flowered Lily was abundant in rocky places by the wayside. Rice occurred sporadically, but the principal crop was maize. Around the inn Tea-bushes are abundantly planted.

On leaving Hsuan-kou we crossed the tributary by a small bamboo suspension bridge, and ascended the left bank by an easy road for 30 li to Shui-mo-kou. Throughout this stretch Cryptomeria is common. All the trees are small and obviously planted, yet I cannot rid myself of the idea that it must be indigenous somewhere in this vicinity. It occurs scattered over a large area, always near habitations, yet it is scarcely feasible to suppose that this tree has been brought from Japan for the purpose of planting it hereabouts.

Shui-mo-kou is an ordinary Chinese market village of some 350 houses lining either side of the main street. It is interesting, however, as being the last purely Chinese village in this direction, also the last place wherein supplies can be purchased or silver exchanged until Monkong Ting is reached. I hired an extra man, and all my followers laid in a stock of rice and food-stuffs generally. At Kuan Hsien, appreciating fully the difficult road before us, I had reduced all loads to two-thirds the normal weight. In spite of this the carriers were heavily laden with extra supplies, and could hardly stagger along on leaving Shui-mo-kou.

A short distance beyond the above village there is a steep ascent, but after a few li the road becomes easy and winds around the mountain-side. Scrub Oak and unhappy-looking

trees of Cunninghamia are abundant, but the flora generally
is poor. Wild Strawberries cover the more grassy slopes, and
were laden with white and red luscious fruit. We passed a few
houses, and finally reached the top of the ridge, alt. 5600 feet,
which is known as the Yao-tsze shan. Crossing over we entered
the territory under the jurisdiction of the Wassu chieftain,
who resides at Tung-ling shan, near Wênch'uan Hsien in the
Min Valley.

Descending by a path, which at first easy soon becomes
very precipitous and difficult owing to the abundance of loose
rocks, we reached Hei-shih ch'ang, our destination for the day,
at 6 p.m. In this descent, near the head of the pass, the
" Yang-tao " (*Actinidia chinensis*) is abundant, and was laden
with a wealth of large, white, fragrant flowers. By the wayside,
Rosa microphylla is very plentiful, and bushes 2 to 4 feet tall
were covered with large pink blossoms. One small tree of
Carrieria calycina, laden with curiously-shaped, waxy-white
flowers borne in erect panicles, was also worthy of note. But
the flora generally has been destroyed to make way for crops
of maize, oats, and pulse.

Hei-shih ch'ang, alt. 4000 feet, is considered to be 60 li
from Hsuan-kou, and consists of three or four houses, situated
in a ravine alongside a torrent, with wild mountains on every
side. Our lodgings were roomy, and the people both courteous
and attentive.

Rain fell heavily next morning when we started out, but
ceased about 9 a.m. ; the weather remained dull the rest of the
day until 4 p.m., when rain recommenced to fall and continued far into the following night. Crossing the torrent by
means of a covered wood bridge the road immediately ascends
a steep mountain called Che shan from the abundance of
Varnish trees growing thereon. The ascent, though very steep,
is short, and afterwards for the next 30 li the road skirts the
mountain-sides until the summit of the Chiu-lung shan is
reached. Descending this ridge it ultimately enters a narrow
grassy valley. Here we found lodgings for the night in the
solitary hostel of Hoa-tzu-ping, alt. 6100 feet, having covered
50 li during the day.

Until reaching the valley the country generally was either

under maize or covered with a dense jungle.   The flora was of
passing interest only, being similar in character to that found
everywhere in western Szechuan between 4000 and 6000 feet
altitude.   The more interesting shrubs collected were a yellow-
flowered Schisandra, a white-flowered Clematoclethra, and the
Yunnan Holly (*Ilex yunnanensis*) with small, neat leaves,
clusters of purplish, fragrant flowers, and hairy shoots.
Actinidia Kolomikta, a large climber with white, fragrant
flowers and added beauty in the shape of a multitude of white
leaves, is excessively common.   Nearly all the species of
Actinidia and the allied genus Clematoclethra, other than those
clothed with rufous hairs, have these white leaves, which
usually become pinkish as the season advances.   All the species
are handsome climbers, and the majority bear very palatable
juicy edible fruit.

The trees of this region, though not numerous or of any
great size, include such remarkable subjects as Davidia, Pterostyrax, Tapiscia, Tetracentron, Beech, and Horse Chestnut.
Occasional trees of *Cornus kousa* occur, and were a wealth
of white flower-heads enlivening the country-side.   Walnut
trees are common around houses and wild strawberries by
the wayside.   In the grassy valley the beautiful *Ilex Pernyi*
occurs with *Rodgersia æsculifolia* and *Lilium giganteum* in
quantity.   Around Hao-tzu-ping odd patches of maize are
cultivated, but where clearings have been made the ground
is mostly covered with grass and coarse herbs.

During the day we met many men laden with huge logs
of Teih-sha (*Tsuga*, Hemlock Spruce) and Hung-sha (*Larix*,
Larch) timber.   These logs were dressed, and carried on a
wooden framework.   I measured one with a tape ; it was
18 feet 6 inches long, 7 inches thick, and 9 inches broad.   It is
astounding how such loads are carried over vile mountain
roads.   As fellow-travellers during the day we had some
tribesmen in charge of a small mule caravan of tea, bound
for the state of Wokje.

After leaving Hoa-tzu-ping we soon reached the head of
the valley which merges into a narrow jungle-clad ravine.
After a precipitous climb of 30 li we reached the summit of
the Niu-tou shan, alt. 10,000 feet, where dense mists blotted

out the landscape. A similarly precipitous descent of 20 li brought us to Chuan-ching-lou, where we put up for the night.

The flora was very interesting, but owing to a thick pall of mist I was able to observe only the plants immediately alongside the pathway. Perhaps the commonest shrub of the day was *Salix magnifica*, which is abundant everywhere, but more especially near the watercourses. This extraordinary Willow has leaves up to 8 inches long and 5 inches wide, with catkins 1 foot or more long. It forms a straggling bush 5 to 20 feet tall and, except when in flower or fruit, would scarcely be taken even by the closest observer for a Willow. (I first discovered this plant in 1903, and in 1908 succeeded in introducing living plants into cultivation.) Many other kinds of Salix, varying from prostrate shrubs to small trees, occur on the Niu-tou shan ; indeed, this mountain is remarkable for its wealth in Willows (subsequently I succeeded in introducing into cultivation about a dozen species from this locality). The Actinidia and Clematoclethra previously noted again very abundant. *Clematis montana*, var. *grandiflora*, with large white flowers, was a pleasing sight ; so also was a Deutzia (*D. rubens*) with pretty rose-tinted flowers. I saw no deciduous broad-leaved trees of any size, but herbs were luxuriant everywhere, especially the Rodgersia, which covers acres of the mountain-side. The Conifers were the most interesting plants of the day. In the ascent, save for odd trees of Silver Fir and Yew, I saw nothing but Hemlock Spruce. This tree delights in rocky country, clinging to the cliffs in a most remarkable manner. In the descent, however, Silver Fir, Spruce, Larch, Hemlock, and White Pine all occur, but the trees are being rapidly felled, and no large specimens were to be seen. From this place come the logs of timber noted yesterday. The Larch (*L. Mastersiana*) is first met with below T'ang-fang, alt. 9400 feet, where it is common more especially to the right of the road, and descends to 7200 feet altitude.

Chuan-ching-lou, alt. 7000 feet, 50 li from Hoa-tzu-ping, consists of one large, dirty hostel, and three other houses, situated in a narrow ravine, walled in by lofty mountains. A noisy torrent which descends from the Niu-tou shan flows past the inn, and vegetation is rampant on all sides. The road over the Niu-tou shan is difficult, and in many places dangerous. Here and there steps have been cut in the hard rock to assist the traveller, but in the main the road is strewn with loose stones and boulders—vile to walk on or over.

We were unfortunate in the matter of weather, for it again rained as we continued our journey. Following the torrent through a narrow ravine for 5 li we reached Êrh-tao chiao, where the torrent connects with a very considerable stream which flows from the Pan-lan shan. The united waters form a river which, after traversing very wild country, joins with the Min near the foot of the Niangtsze-ling on the Wênch'uan Hsien side of the pass. Turning sharply to the left at Êrh-tao chiao we ascended the stream, which is called Pi-tao Ho, and soon crossed over by a wooden semi-cantilever bridge to the left bank. From this point the next 25 li to Wu-lung-kuan is easy, going through a narrow valley where occasional houses occur and a certain amount of cultivation obtains. Above Wu-lung-kuan the road becomes increasingly difficult, and in many places is execrable. The river is joined by numerous lateral torrents, some of large size, and as the valley narrows into a ravine becomes an untamable, roaring torrent. The scenery, such as the mists permitted of our seeing, is savage and grand. Here and there perpendicular cliffs of limestone cropped out through the mists, their summits covered with Pine trees. We crossed and re-crossed the torrent many times, and after covering 65 li reached Ta-ngai-tung, which was our destination for the day. This hamlet, alt. 7600 feet, consists of one large hostel, which was in moderately good repair, and is completely surrounded by steep mountains heavily clad with mixed shrubs and small trees, the upper parts being covered with forests of Conifers. The flora generally is very similar to that of the Niu-tou shan, though scarcely as rich. All the Conifers except Silver Fir are present, though Larch only puts in its first appearance near the hostel. At Êrh-tao chiao I photographed a magnificent Juniper tree, 75 feet tall, 22 feet in girth, with graceful pendent branches, and a Black Pine which retains its cones over many years. (It proved to be a new species, and has been named *Pinus Wilsonii*). This Pine is common on the cliffs, but White Pine (*P. Armandi*) is rare, although we passed the largest specimens of this tree I have ever met with. *Deutzia longifolia* with lovely rosy-lilac-coloured flowers, *Spiræa Henryi* with yard long, flat sprays of pure white, and *Neillia longeracemosa* with rose-coloured flowers were perhaps the commonest shrubs in blossom. Poplar is the only large deciduous tree hereabouts. Maple is not uncommon, and near Ta-ngai-tung I gathered specimens of a Black Birch having short, stout erect catkins.

Early next morning we continued our journey, spending the whole day toiling up the ravine through wild and savage, yet wondrous, scenery, with a profusion of vegetation on all sides. Coniferous trees preponderate, the species being the same as those previously mentioned, with a couple of new Spruces added. Yew is less abundant, but Larch much more so, though large trees are very scarce. To my astonishment the Larch cones were ripe, and I collected a quantity of seed. A Poplar with large leaves, silver-grey on the under side, is very common, and we passed some very large specimens. A Rose with large bright red flowers made a fine display, so also did the pink-flowered Deutzia mentioned above. Two Lady-slipper orchids (*Cypripedium Franchetii* and *C. luteum*), with rosy-purple and yellow flowers respectively, occur, but are rare. In the bed of the torrent *Hippophaë salicifolia* (Sallow-thorn) is common, and varies from dwarf spiny bushes to trees 25 feet tall, the long slender foliage silvery-grey below forming a pleasing contrast to the brighter greens of surrounding trees and shrubs. Many kinds of Maple (*Acer*), Linden (*Tilia*), and Mountain Ash (*Sorbus*) are plentiful, and *Tetracentron sinense*, an interesting tree exceeding in size all other deciduous trees of this particular region, occurs sparingly. Hydrangeas, Spiræas, Honeysuckles, Mock-orange, Brambles, Roses, Actinidia, Clematoclethra, Viburnum, and other ornamental shrubs struggle for possession of every available spot. The variety and wealth of bloom was truly astonishing, and I know of no region in Western China richer in woody plants than that traversed during the day's march.

The weather continued exasperatingly showery, but luckily no great quantity of rain fell, otherwise the route would have been impassable. Heavy mists limited our view, but whenever the clouds lifted we saw nothing but steep mountain-sides, beetling crags or cliffs, bare here and there but mostly clothed with mixed vegetation, giving place ultimately to forests of Conifers. The road is vile beyond the power of language to describe. In several places poles have been fixed horizontally into holes made in the face of the cliffs and half-rotten planks laid on these to form a roadway. Such bridges as exist are of logs, often rotten, and were always difficult to cross. The river is simply a roaring torrent, cascading over huge boulders and madly endeavouring to escape to less savage regions. At one point it receives a torrent, which, judging from the colour and temperature of the waters, evidently comes down from eternal snows.

During the day we passed a few miserable hovels, but there is no room for cultivation, and the people are wretchedly poor. We stayed for the night at Yü-yü-tien, alt. 8800 feet, 42 li from Ta-ngai-tung, where there are two poor hostels. These useful if squalid structures are all alike on this route, being one-storied, constructed of wood, and roofed with shingles held down by stones. A portion is sectioned off as private quarters for the family in charge, and near by the kitchen is located. A series of bunks is built around all sides of the place, the central part being occupied by benches for the accommodation of loads. Travellers furnish their own food-supplies, since nothing is obtainable at the hostel except, perhaps, some green vegetables in minute quantities. Shelter for the night and a fire to cook food and dry clothing are all these places afford. But the foreign traveller enjoys a welcome quietude and freedom from curious crowds. A sound night's sleep rewards the labours of the day, and he awakens refreshed, perfectly fit, and all eager to drink in more of the wondrous scenery, the charm of woodland, crag, and stream.

At Têng-shêng-t'ang, 8 li beyond Yü-yü-tien, the ravine widens out into a shallow valley, and the road boldly ascends the grassy, scrub-clad mountains to the left of the stream. Hereabouts Barberries in great variety luxuriate. After a severe ascent we crossed over a shoulder, and for the rest of the day skirted the side of a grassy ridge carpeted with brilliantly coloured alpine flowers.

The main stream takes its rise in some snowclad peaks, of which we obtained a glimpse and a photograph, but a considerable tributary flows down from the Pan-lan shan Pass. The mountains to the right of this affluent, and also to the right of the main stream, are forested up to 11,500 feet altitude with Spruce, Silver Fir, and Larch. The bed of the valley is covered with bushes of Willow, Hippophæ, and Barberries. Up to 10,000 feet altitude *Cypripedium luteum* is not uncommon on humus-clad boulders and in the margins of woods.

The flora of the grassy ridge leading up to the Pan-lan shan Pass is strictly alpine in character, and the wealth of herbs was truly amazing. Most of the more vigorous growing had yellow flowers, and this colour predominated in consequence. Above 11,500 feet altitude, the gorgeous *Meconopsis integrifolia*, which has huge, globular, incurved, clear yellow flowers, covers miles of the mountain-side. Growing on plants from 2 to 2½ feet tall the myriads of flowers of this wonderful Poppy-wort presented a magnificent spectacle. Nowhere else have I beheld this plant in such luxuriant profusion. The Sikhim cow-slip (*Primula sikkimensis*), with deliciously fragrant pale yellow flowers, is rampant in moist places. Various kinds of Senecio, Trollius, Caltha, Pedicularis, and Corydalis added to the over-whelming display of yellow flowers. On boulders covered with grass and in moderately dry loamy places, *Primula Veitchii* was a pleasing sight with its bright rosy-pink flowers. All the moorland areas are covered so thickly with the Thibetan Lady-slipper Orchid (*Cypripedium tibeticum*) that it was impossible to step without treading on the huge dark red flowers reared on stems only a few inches tall. Yet the most fascinating herb of all was, perhaps, the extraordinary *Primula vincæflora*, with large, solitary, violet flowers, in shape strikingly resembling those of the common Periwinkle (*Vinca major*), produced on stalks 5 to 6 inches tall. This most unprimrose-like Primula is very abundant in grassy places. The variety of herbs is indeed legion, and the whole country-side was a feast of colour. Silence reigns in these lonely alpine regions, a silence so oppressive as to be almost felt and only broken on rare occasions by the song of some lark soaring skywards. We flushed an occasional Snow-partridge and saw one or two flocks of Snow-pigeons, but bird-life generally was extremely sparse. Save a few voles and mice we saw no animals, but Bharal and Wolves were said to occur here, the former in quantity.

After travelling 38 li we reached the hostel at Hsiang-yang-ping, alt. 11,650 feet, and remained there for the night. This place is part temple, part inn, and is kept by a priest, to whose clothing and person water was evidently a stranger. The medicine Pei-mu (*Fritillaria Roylei* and other species) is common in this region, and as fellow-guests for the night we had a number of people engaged in digging up the tiny white corms of this plant. Some Chinese traders also were there buying up this medicine at 60 cash per ounce. In Chengtu it is worth, wholesale, 400 cash per ounce, so their profit is a handsome one. Among the medicine-gatherers were several Wokje tribesfolk, about 5 feet 8 inches tall, sturdily built, with straight noses and fearless expression. Two of their women were with them, and had they been clean and decently dressed they would have been decidedly handsome and attractive. We enjoyed during the day a certain amount of sunshine, interrupted by occasional showers, but soon after our arrival at Hsiang-yang-ping it commenced raining in torrents, and continued to do so far into the night.

It ceased raining before daylight, to our great joy. Making an early start we toiled slowly over the dreaded Pan-lan shan, crossing the pass in a dense, driving, bitterly cold mist. The ascent is nowhere difficult, and none of us suffered seriously from the effects of the rarefied atmosphere, in spite of the evil reputation this pass has for mountain-sickness. The ridge is narrow, razor-backed, the summit being composed of sandstone, with marble embedded, piled up at an acute angle and devoid of vegetation. Snow, unmelted from the winter, lay in odd patches immediately below the pass, and on all sides there was much fresh snow. The dense mists prevented any extended view, but what little of the region was visible was bare and desolate. Two or three of the lovely Snowbird, *Grandala cœlicolor*, were flitting around the snowy patches, their intense blue plumage contrasting remarkably with the white carpet around. I made the pass, 14,250 feet altitude, and the tree-limit about 11,800 feet.

The flora above 12,000 feet altitude is purely alpine and similar in character to that of the region around Sungpan and elsewhere throughout the Chino-Thibetan Borderland at the same altitude. *Meconopsis integrifolia* occurs in countless thousands ; also, to my pleasant surprise, the dark scarlet-flowered *M. punicea*. Although by no means so plentiful as around Sungpan, there were many thousands of this beautiful herb scattered around. Primroses are most abundant ; *Primula vincæflora* ascends to 13,000 feet, where its place is taken by the lovely *P. nivalis* and another closely allied species.

On crossing over I photographed the pass and then descended with all possible speed to the miserable hostel of Wan-jên-fên, alt. 13,700 feet, where our lunch awaited us. A little below this hostel a few bushes of Willow, small-leaved Rhododendrons, and Caragana spp. first appeared and became abundant as we descended. Soon Larch and occasional Spruce appear, and at 11,300 feet altitude trees are fairly numerous. A shrubby, evergreen Prickly Oak is characteristic of these wind-swept mountain-sides, the golden-brown undersurface of its leaves rendering it most conspicuous. (This Oak is almost as beautiful as the Golden Chestnut of California (*Castanopsis chrysophylla*), and I am very pleased to report its successful introduction to cultivation.)

In addition to the shrubs mentioned above, dwarf Juniper, Spiræa, and Sallowthorn also abound. This moorland country is very interesting and shows unmistakable signs of a drier climate than that enjoyed by the regions on the opposite side of the pass.

A torrent which rises near the head of the pass is soon augmented by tributaries and quickly becomes a roaring unfordable stream. The mountain-slopes close in, and at the tiny hamlet of Kao-tien-tzu the road plunges into a ravine. The sides of this ravine are wooded, Larch and Spruce being abundant, with miscellaneous shrubby vegetation. The elegant *Syringa tomentella*, a Lilac with branching panicles of fragrant flowers, is very common. On issuing from this ravine we crossed a tributary torrent, more turbulent in character than even the main stream, and found in front of us open country largely under cultivation.

Our caravan was to have stopped for the night at the hamlet of Kao-tien-tzu, but with greater zeal than knowledge pushed on 20 li farther to Reh-lung-kuan. This blunder upset my plans and put all things awry. The collecting work had to be curtailed; it was 10 p.m. before I got any supper, and much of our work had to remain over until the morrow.

The Pan-lan shan is the boundary between two Chiarung states. On crossing over we quitted the state of Wassu and entered that of Wokje. The Wassu territory is wildly mountainous, well forested, and but little suited to agriculture. In consequence it is sparsely populated, and we encountered very few of the inhabitants *en route*. The hostels and houses on the main road are in the hands of Chinese or half-castes. The men of Wassu are tall (5 feet 8 inches or thereabouts), with large, muscular frames, frank, open countenances, and are noted hunters of the beasts of forest and crag. The women are sturdy, buxom, and engagingly frank. Both men and women are darker complexioned than the Chinese, and, I am sorry to say, infinitely less cleanly in appearance. They are very fond of jewellery, both sexes wearing bangles of silver and copper, and silver rings studded with coral and turquoise. The women also wear large silver ear-rings, usually having insets of coral and turquoise. The men are addicted to opium-smoking, though possibly this is strictly true only of those engaged near the main roads as porters and muleteers who have come in close contact with the Chinese.

Reh-lung-kuan, alt. 10,900 feet, is a Wokje village consisting of about a score of houses, a small lamasery, and a tall square tower. We found here a spacious and very fair inn, and the people were courteous and obliging. Our carrying coolies were able to purchase opium and a certain amount of food-stuffs. This explained their anxiety to cover 75 li, instead of stopping 20 li short at Kao-tien-tzu.

On leaving Reh-lung-kuan we descended the right bank of the river, which rises near the Pan-lan shan pass, for 33 li to the hamlet of Kuan-chin-pa, a short day's march being necessary in order to accomplish the work left over. The day was fine and warm, with a strong, cool breeze.   Looking back on our route the snows of the Pan-lan shan were visible the whole day.   The road was in good repair, and skirts the mountain-sides well above the stream.   In ancient times this valley was filled with glacial detritus, through which the strong torrent has cut a deep, narrow bed.   This stream, known locally as the Nei chu, is really the principal branch of the Hsaochin Ho (Little Gold River).   Formerly gold in considerable quantities was mined in this valley, and we passed many old workings during the march.

The country generally reminded me forcibly of the Upper Min Valley, near Sungpan, above 8000 feet altitude.   On the left bank of the stream the mountain-sides are very steep and largely covered with woods composed of Spruce, Silver Fir, and a few Pine trees.   On the right bank the mountains are more sloping and mainly under cultivation.   Wheat is the staple crop and ripens in early August ; buckwheat ranks next in importance, followed at a respectable distance by peas, beans, and Irish potato.   The Wokje people are evidently skilled agriculturists and in their own way fairly well-to-do. The prosperous condition of this state was evidenced by the plenitude of large houses, lamaseries, and by the relatively dense population.   The hostels, however, are all in the hands of half-breeds, descended from early Chinese colonists.   The larger houses and lamaseries are usually perched on some bluff composed of glacial mud, grits, and boulders.   They are more or less square, two-storied, with flat mud roofs, having small turrets at each corner, from which prayer-flags flutter ; a branch of. some kind of Conifer is usually in evidence near these flags.   Chortens and other Lamaist monuments occur here and there, while inscribed Mani-stones are common. The peasants' houses are low, one-storied, built of sandstone shales, the roof either flat or with very slight slope.

That the climate of this valley is relatively dry and warm is clearly shown by the flora, which is markedly xerophytic. Two species of Cotoneaster, several Clematis, the Sallowthorn, Prickly Oak, Barberries, and Roses are the chief constituents. A curious Bush Honeysuckle, with small leaves and tubular, white, fragrant flowers borne in pairs, is locally abundant.

(This proved to be a new species and has been named *Lonicera tubuliflora*.) Another common plant is the shrubby *Clematis fruticosa*, with simple oblong leaves and golden yellow, nodding flowers. A Lilac (*Syringa Potaninii*), with erect panicles of rose-purple flowers, is another interesting shrub, plentiful in this valley. Poplar, a Hard Pine (*Pinus prominens*), with almost prickly cones, and a White Birch, the bark of which is used for lining straw hats, are the more common trees by the wayside. I also gathered a few late flowers of *Incarvillea Wilsonii*. In a general way this Incarvillea resembles Delavay's species, but averages 4 to 6 feet in height. Another new plant collected was a Primrose akin to *Primula sibirica*, but with taller scapes and longer pedicels.

Kuan-chin-pa, alt. 9500 feet, consists of two small and rather poor inns, with the ruins of a large square tower near-by.

Twelve li below Kuan-chin-pa, and also on the right bank of the river, is the village of Ta-wei, a considerable place for this region, boasting a large lamasery. This place has an evil reputation, but no ill-will was displayed toward me. Many Lamas clad in claret-coloured serge crowded around and watched me as I photographed the village, and displayed much interest in my camera, dog, and gun. Nevertheless, the reputation of this village is well founded, and I would advise travellers to avoid staying overnight there. From Ta-wei a road leads across the river and over the mountains to Mupin.

On continuing our journey we followed the right bank of the stream for a further 27 li to Mo-ya-ch'a, where, owing to an old landslide, it was necessary to cross over to the left bank. This was accomplished by means of a wooden semi-cantilever bridge. Such bridges have been fairly common *en route*, but this was the first our road had led over. From this bridge the road descends the left bank, keeping high up above the river to Kuan-chai, which was our destination for the day. The whole valley is very arid, though a considerable area was under wheat. A few Poplar and Willow trees occur near the river, otherwise only high up on the mountain-sides were any trees discernible. The flora is similar to that of all the principal river-valleys of this hinterland, as described in Chapter XII. *Rosa Soulieana* is very abundant. I gathered several new plants, but the country is too arid to be of much interest botanically.

Situated at an altitude of 8500 feet, Kuan-chai is a small village and the residence of the Wokje chieftain. The chief's house is very large, the upper structure, all of wood, is well built, and the whole is dominated by several tall towers, and fine Walnut trees occur scattered around. The prosperous condition of this little state was further evidenced during the day's march. Large houses are frequent, many being perched high up on the steep mountain-sides. Wheat is the principal crop grown, and at Kuan-chai was just bursting into ear. Maize and the Irish potato are likewise commonly cultivated. A little flax and Hemp (*Cannabis*) also occur, the oil expressed from the seeds of these plants being in general use as an illuminant. We passed odd fields of opium poppy, the plants being only a few inches tall. On the fan-shaped slope, at the head of which the village of Kuan-chai is situated, all the crops were remarkably luxuriant.

At Ma-lun-chia a considerable torrent joins the Nei chu on the right bank. A by-road ascends this tributary, leading to Fupien and thence to Lifan Ting. Our road was for the greater part good and we easily covered the 67 li, enjoying bright sunshine the whole day.

Immediately beyond the chief's residence the road mounts over a steep bluff, where is situated the hamlet of Hsao-kuan-chai. This place is reputed to have offered a stern resistance to the Chinese in their conquest of this valley a hundred odd years ago, and was only captured after a long siege. The remains of the sangars and old forts are still to be seen. From this point the road continues to wind along the left bank of the river for 40 li to the town of Monkong Ting. Both sides of the valley are very arid, and the flora poor and uninteresting. Very few houses occur in the valley, but high up on the mountain-sides we saw many scattered about and surrounded by wheat fields. At Laoyang the river is joined on the right bank by another of almost equal volume. The main road from Lifan Ting, via Fupien, descends this tributary stream and joins at this point the road we were following. From what little we could see of the valley of this Fupien stream it appeared to be as arid and barren as the one we had descended from Reh-lung-kuan. Continuing our journey and on rounding a bend in the river, we suddenly sighted, perched on a rocky promontory, the town of Monkong Ting. After passing through a gateway we noticed a separate township, rather prosperous looking, situated in a lateral valley a little to the left of the main road. This is the official town of Monkong Ting, where reside the principal officials, civil and military. Crossing a torrent by a wooden bridge we entered the place first sighted from the bend in the river. This proved to be an old military camp of poverty-stricken, dilapidated houses, scattered alongside a street about 100 yards long. Two hundred yards beyond this camp we reached the thriving business town known as Hsin-kai-tsze. Monkong Ting, therefore, consists of three distinct towns or villages: (1) the official town, (2) an old military camp, (3) the business town. All three are unwalled, though a gateway has to be passed on entering each. The situation is most picturesque and strategically very strong. Monkong Ting is the political capital of this region and a place of very considerable importance. The two Chiarung states of Wokje and Mupin have their boundaries at this point, and the rest of the valley to Romi Chango is divided into feudal states.

The streets of Hsin-kai-tsze were thronged with people, chiefly tribesfolk, selling medicines and buying various articles for their own use. They made a very picturesque crowd, the women being especially noticeable by reason of their display of silver dress-ornaments, bangles, and ear-rings. The inns were all crowded, but the head official obligingly secured a couple of rooms for us and treated us with much courtesy and goodwill. The people were naturally curious and grouped themselves around us, but their manners were deferential.

Hsin-kai-tsze, alt. 8200 feet, is a most important medicine mart, being famous for its " Pei-mu " (*Fritillaria* spp.), " Rhubarb," " Ch'ung-tsao " (a caterpillar infested with the fungus *Cordyceps sinensis*), and "Chung-hoa" (an Umbelliferous plant, possibly *Ligusticum Thomsonii*). All of these are collected and brought in for sale by the tribesfolk. Musk and deer-horns also figure in the trade.

Several roads radiate from this centre ; one of these leads from the official town to Mupin, over the pass of Chia-chin shan, which was said to be higher than that of the Pan-lan shan and surrounded by snow-clad peaks.

The Wokje state preserved its prosperous appearance to the end, and is evidently a thriving, happy little country. The people strongly resemble the Wassu folk, though possibly they are scarcely as tall and have slightly sharper features. The Chinese language is understood and in common use along the main road, where the people imitate the Chinese in shaving their heads and wearing a queue. Lamaism evidently has a strong hold on these people, judging by the number of lamaseries we saw.

I had intended remaining a day at Monkong Ting, but owing to the crowded condition of the town decided to defer this holiday until we reached Romi Chango. The inn in which rooms were provided for us was crowded with persons who were noisy over their cups and business dealings far into the night, rendering sleep well-nigh an impossibility.

Just outside Hsin-kai-tsze the road crosses over by a log bridge to the right bank of the stream. This bridge was being repaired, and only two very uneven logs were in position. A thin rope was stretched across to serve as a hand-rail on the left side. Crossing was really dangerous, the waters below being deep and turbulent. The official kindly provided local experts to carry our gear over, and the way these men accomplished the task filled me with admiration. I rewarded them with 1000 cash, to their astonished delight. My dog was lashed firmly to a flat board and carried across on a man's back. He struggled violently, and the man only just managed to get him over before he got half loose. I walked over behind the dog and was relieved when the 30 yards across the yawning gulf were safely passed. Everything came over all right, but my followers clung to the local men like grim death, the majority shaking in their nervous fright. Such dangerous experiences are not desirable, and I heartily hoped that we had no more such bridges to cross. From this bridge we descended 60 li to the hamlet of Shêng-ko-chung, alt. 7600 feet, through arid country and over a bad road. The river is here a broad and turbulent stream, flowing between steep banks composed of loose rocks. A few Poplar, an occasional Cypress (*C. torulosa*), and the Kœlreuteria (the latter was covered with masses of small yellow flowers) are the only trees of note. The region is very sparsely populated, but high up, on the left bank more especially, are a few houses of the same architecture as those of Wokje.

As travelling companions during the day we had a party of tribesfolk, chiefly women in holiday attire. They were very cheerful, laughing and singing most of the time. On parting company at Shêng-ko-chung they made merry over cups of Chinese wine, the dames officiating as to the manner born.

It rained heavily during the night, and it was cool and delightfully fresh in the morning when we recommenced our journey down the valley of the Hsaochin Ho. Thirty li below Shêng-ko-chung we passed the large lamasery of Gi-lung, coloured white and picturesquely situated on the right bank of the river. Over a hundred Lamas reside here and exercise considerable authority over the neighbourhood. About 10 li beyond this lamasery the river suddenly develops into a series of boiling, roaring cataracts. The fury of the waters was most fearsome to behold, and a wilder stretch of river is scarcely imaginable. Earlier in the day we had crossed to the left bank, and just below the very worst bit of this savage waterway we recrossed to the right bank over a rotten and most unsafe wooden bridge. Some 7 li below this point we reached the hamlet of Pan-ku chiao, alt. 7100 feet, where we found accommodation for the night, having covered 70 li. Just above the hamlet a torrent joins the river on its left bank, and up this lateral valley mountains clad with snow were plainly visible. Bridges are scarce and the few that exist look as if they had not been renewed since this region was conquered, well over a hundred years ago. One thing is certain, they cannot possibly last much longer : the two we crossed during the day were all askew and decidedly dangerous.

The district is rather less arid than that around Monkong Ting, yet the flora is very poor. Poplar is a common tree, so also is the Kœlreuteria, which was a fine sight, with a wealth of flowers, and it evidently enjoys a dry, hot situation. The sub-shrubby *Incarvillea variabilis* and *Amphicome arguta*, both with large, tubular, pink flowers, are very abundant by the roadside. Other common shrubs are Bauhinia, *Sophora viciifolia*, Ceratostigma, with lovely blue flowers, Ligustrum and *Rosa Soulieana*. On the cliffs *Cupressus torulosa* is dotted about. Maize is the principal crop, occupying in season almost every inch of available land. Houses are fairly numerous, but most of them are relegated to the higher slopes well above the valley. The scenery in places is rugged and grand. In front of the inn at Pan-ku chiao limestone cliffs rear themselves some 2000 feet, abutting on a cultivated slope where Walnut trees are scattered around. Crowning a bluff is a tall tower, and near-by another in ruins, telling of glories now departed.

On leaving Pan-ku chiao we descended the right bank of the Hsaochin Ho, some 42 li to the point where it joins the Tachin Ho or Upper Tung River. This final stretch is little else but one long succession of cataracts and strong rapids, the turbulent waters being thick with brown mud. High bare cliffs predominate, but here and there occur more or less flat fan-shaped areas under cultivation, with houses shaded by Poplar, Willow, and Walnut trees. *Diospyros Lotus, Hovenia dulcis*, and the large-leaved *Ligustrum lucidum* are other trees common hereabouts. Maize is evidently the chief summer crop in these regions, but wheat is grown, a red, beardless variety, with stout ears, and harvesting was in progress. Rock-pigeons are very abundant, and were busily engaged in exacting their toll of the ripening grain.

After passing the hamlet of Yo-tsa we sighted on the opposite (left) bank a large lamasery sequestered midst a fine grove of trees. A little beyond this is the village of Tsung-lu, a curious-looking place, boasting of a score or more tall towers. Skin coracles are employed to ferry over to these places.

The Hsaochin Ho is prevented from joining the Tachin Ho at right angles by a rocky spit which at times is evidently flooded over. Marble and granite are common rocks hereabouts, the latter being full of mica flakes which glistened in the sun. Ascending the left bank of the Tachin Ho for a couple of li, then crossing over a bamboo suspension bridge 90 yards long, we soon reached the small town of Romi Chango. The whole day's journey was only 45 li, but owing to the heat and rough road we all arrived very much fatigued and in sore need of a day's rest.

From all I could learn it would appear that the region in the vicinity of the river from Monkong Ting to Romi Chango, after its conquest by the Chinese about A.D. 1775, was divided into feudal states, and certain chieftains installed in possession as rewards for services rendered during the struggle. The chiefs, styled Shao-pês, hold hereditary office and are directly responsible to Chinese authority for the good behaviour of the people under their rule, also, if necessity arises, they are bound to supply armed men to assist the Chinese cause. Lamas alone are exempt from such military duties ; ordinarily the people of these feudal states are agriculturists.   These Shao-pês are subordinate to the Chinese military commander stationed at Monkong Ting.   The two chief Shao-pês reside, one at Monkong Ting, the other at Che-lung, a village in the mountains, 20 li removed from the left bank of the Hsaochin Ho and 60 li below Monkong Ting.   Another Shao-pê resides at Ta-ching, 120 li to the north-east of Monkong Ting ;   a fourth at A'n-niu, a place in the mountains to the south-west of the region controlled by the Che-lung Shao-pê.   Beyond the original grant of territory these feudal chiefs receive no rewards, monetary or otherwise, from the Chinese.   The system has much to recommend it and evidently works very well.   It keeps the Chinese authority supreme, while it allows the native people to be governed by their own recognized chiefs.   The difference between the chieftain of a semi-independent Chiarung state and a Shao-pê appears to be that, whereas the former is an absolute ruler over a territory long hereditary to his tribe, the latter is more in the nature of an alien ruling over a tract of country fiefed to his forbears by the Chinese, after they conquered this region and broke up the Chiarung confederacy. The territory occupied by these feudal states formerly belonged to the Chiarung tribes, and the people are principally derived from that stock.   Chinese settlers have intermarried with the natives, and in the vicinity of the main road the population is mixed.   The people living in the lower stretches of the Hsaochin Ho are an inferior race, of poor physique, and most abominably filthy.

CHAPTER XV

ACROSS THE CHINO-THIBETAN BORDERLAND

Romi Chango to Tachienlu; the Forests of the Ta-p'ao Shan

ROMI CHANGO, or Chango, as it is commonly called, is a poor, unwalled, straggling town of about 130 houses. It is without rank, but a magistrate, subordinate to the Tachienlu Fu, and a military official, controlled from Monkong Ting, reside there. The town is really a Chinese settlement, situated in the extreme north-east corner of the state of Chiala. It is built on the right bank of the Tachin Ho, at a point where the river, making a right-angled turn from the northward, is joined by a very considerable torrent from the west. The Tachin, a river 100 yards broad, with a steady current and muddy water, sweeps round majestically. High cliffs on the left bank, steep mountain-slopes on the right, lofty mountains to the east and west wall in the town, at the western entrance to which a massive square tower stands sentinel. Chango is a very poverty-stricken place, with a small trade in medicines and sundries. It draws its supplies of rice, paper, and Chinese commodities generally from Kuan Hsien, and everything is phenomenally dear. This is only natural when the distance and difficulties of the journey are duly considered.

A small road descends the right bank of the Tachin Ho, by means of which Luting chiao may, with great difficulty, be reached. A road ascends the right bank of the Tachin Ho and leads to the interesting Chiarung states of Badi and Bawang, where the Bönpa religion holds full sway. Badi, the capital of these now united principalities, is only 60 li from Romi Chango. The chieftain is dead, but his widow, assisted by a steward, acts as regent for her infant son. Badi-Bawang is one of the ancient matriarchal kingdoms of Chinese historians, and at all times a woman holds an important place in its government. Badi, the larger of the two states, is very rich in gold, which, though unworked during recent years, is jealously guarded. Chinese visitors, rich or poor, are cross-questioned as to their business and closely watched during their sojourn in this state. The Badi-Bawang folk often visit Chango on business, and during our stay there we saw several. Most of them were peasant girls and women, dressed so scantily as to scarcely hide their nakedness. They were short in stature, and apparently unwashed from birth! However, since these were " hewers of wood and drawers of water " of the poorest class, it would be unfair to judge the whole race by them.

In Chango we lodged at a comfortable inn, having a clean room, well removed from the street and overlooking the river. We spent a quiet day resting and refitting for the final stage of our journey to Tachienlu. The people were not over-inquisitive and those in charge of the inn were exceedingly obliging. Soon after our arrival the magistrate sent me word that he was suffering from pains in the stomach and vomiting, and would be grateful for some medicine to relieve his suffering. I sent him some Epsom-salt and an opiate. The next day word came that he was much better, only too tired to leave his room. A traveller gets many such requests for medicine, and I have generally found quinine, Epsom-salt, and opium pills most useful cures, for which the people were always grateful.

On leaving this lonely town of Chango, which I made 6700 feet altitude, the road to Tachienlu ascends the right bank of the tributary torrent. We were warned that the road was very difficult, leading through forests and over high mountains. It was not long before these statements were verified. The torrent quickly develops into an angry, irresponsible stream ; the road in many places had been washed away and much wading was necessary. Our carriers had great difficulty in getting along, and had the waters of the torrent been a few feet higher the road would have been quite impassable. All the bridges were rotten and most insecure. High up on the mountain-sides we saw several large hamlets, but there are very

few houses in the valley—quite sufficient, however, for whenever the road led past a house we had to traverse an open
sewer, often a foot deep in dung and refuse. Such filthy
surroundings are characteristic of Thibetan houses. The
Chinese would collect all this sewage for their fields, but the
Thibetans, who are but poor agriculturists at best, have not
yet learned the value of manure. At such places I usually
climbed over the fences and walked through the crops, but my
men waded through the filth and gave vent to their wrath in
loud, angry imprecations. The people of Chiala are typical
Thibetans and use the lower stories of their flat-roofed houses
as pens for horses and cattle. A few li above Chango the flora
begins to lose its purely xerophytic character, and becomes
more and more luxuriant as the ascent proceeds. The higher
slopes are well forested with mixed trees, but near-by the road
trees are scarce. The mountain-sides flanking the stream
are very steep, being often sheer cliffs. Such places are
dotted with Cypress (*Cupressus torulosa*) and prickly leaved
Evergreen Oak.

After journeying 60 li we reached the village of Tung-ku,
alt. 7800 feet, where there are several large Thibetan houses,
decorated with prayer-flags, but only two or three hostels, and
these very poor in character. The owner of the one we stayed
in is a noted hunter, and many pelts of the Budorcas, Serow,
and Black Bear were in use as bed-mattresses. His family
told us the hunter was away after Musk-deer; they also
informed us that both the Thibetan-eared and Lady Amherst
Pheasants are common hereabouts. Around the village
Walnut trees are most abundant. Wheat is a common crop
and was just ripening. Maize too was plentiful and is evidently
the staple summer crop everywhere in these regions.

The next day we covered another 60 li, putting up for the
night at the poor hamlet of T'ung-lu-fang. We crossed the
river four times by wooden bridges, each more rotten than the
other. The river was in partial flood, and a goodly portion of
the road was either washed away, obliterated by landslides,
or under water. Often we had to make a path for ourselves
up the mountain-side. The under-water portions of the road
I traversed on the back of one of the soldiers we had with us

from Chango, until he stumbled and gave me a ducking.   After
this I waded.   There was no traffic on the road so called, and
I marvelled how my coolies managed to get their loads along.
Our chairs were carried piecemeal and even then with difficulty
over the worst places.   The river was a roaring torrent throughout the whole day's journey, in places really awesome to behold, dashing itself headlong over enormous boulders, or boiling
as if forced up by some malignant spirit.   In many places our
path actually overhung this torrent, and one false step meant
death.

About 10 li above Tung-ku the river makes a right-angled
turn and is joined at this point by another stream of almost
equal volume from the westward.   From this place the road
skirts   the   river   through   a   narrow,   savage,   magnificently
wooded   ravine.   Maple, Ash, Hornbeam, Birch, Poplar,
Hemlock Spruce, and Prickly Oak are the chief constituents
of these woods, followed by Evodia, Rhus, Cypress, Willow,
Elm, Sallowthorn, Bamboo, and miscellaneous shrubs.   The
Maples (*Acer Davidii* and *A. pictum*, var. *parviflorum*) are
larger trees than I have seen elsewhere.   The Ash and Hornbeam are all fine trees, and the Hemlock Spruce in many cases
over 100 feet tall, with a girth of 12 to 15 feet.

On leaving this magnificent fragment of virgin forest the
country became less interesting.   Where the cliffs are not sheer
and bare the mountain-slopes have been cleared to a very
large extent.   The ravine widens into a narrow valley which is
covered with scrub.   The cliffs and mountain-slopes high up
are sparsely clad with Cypress, White and Hard Pine, Spruce,
Silver Fir, and Hemlock.   The scenery is sublime.

We passed very few houses and these of the meanest
description.   Very little land is under cultivation ;   maize
is the chief crop, with patches of wheat and oats here and
there.   The country is not suited to cultivation, and one marvels how the few people living there manage to find even the
most miserable subsistence.   Yesterday we noticed herds of a
small breed of cattle.   The people are shorter in stature than the
average, and perfectly proportioned dwarfs are fairly common.
Since leaving Monkong Ting, goitre has been manifest among
the inhabitants, and in this river-valley it is very prevalent.

T'ung-lu-fang, alt. 8800 feet, consists of about half a dozen scattered houses. The one we stayed in is of Thibetan architecture, fairly clean, and owned by a Chinese settler. None of these houses affords any bedding for the coolies, and of course nothing is purchasable—all food-stuffs have to be carried by the travellers themselves.

The people at T'ung-lu-fang informed us that we should not be able to reach Mao-niu, as the road had been badly washed away in several places, and under the lee of some cliffs was flooded to a depth of 4 feet or more. This gratuitous and discouraging information proved, luckily for us, to be scarcely accurate, since, after a struggle, we managed to get through. My head coolie declared it was the very worst road we had ever traversed, and I was inclined to agree with him. Worse it could not have been and constitute a roadway at all! For fully half the distance the track was under water or washed completely away, and we were forced to wade or make a new path over the mountain-side. Just how we got over the 30 li I cannot describe, but we all came through with nothing worse than a severe wetting.

Mao-niu is a fair-sized village for the country, and is mainly perched on a flat 200 feet above the torrent, and surrounded by a considerable area under wheat—a veritable oasis, in fact, surrounded by high mountains. Formerly it was the principal village of a petty state to which it gave its name. It now belongs to the state of Chiala. As far as Mao-niu the scenery and flora is similar to that around Tung-ku and calls for no special remark. The outstanding feature is the woods of Hard Pine (*Pinus prominens*). The steeper the country the happier this Pine appeared to be. The bark of the trunk is deeply furrowed, often red in the upper parts of the tree ; the cones are quite prickly, and are retained for many years. The wood is very resinous, and is evidently much esteemed for building purposes. The Hemlock Spruce is common, and all the trees are of great size.

At Mao-niu the main stream leads off in a westerly direction to Th'ai-ling, a large village of over 100 houses and several lamaseries. It is also the centre of a considerable gold-mining industry, and has the reputation of being a lawless district.

We were informed that the road thither was in a dreadful state of disrepair, and that most of the bridges had been washed away by recent floods.

On clearing the cultivated area around Mao-niu we plunged immediately into a narrow, heavily forested ravine, down which a considerable torrent thundered. Conifers preponderate in these forests, Spruce being particularly abundant. We noticed some huge trees, but the average was about 80 to 100 feet tall. White and Red Birch are common, and I was fortunate enough to secure seeds of the latter. The Sallowthorn (*Hippophaë salicifolia*) is exceedingly common, forming trees 30 to 50 feet tall with a girth of 4 to 10 feet. The size of these trees very much surprised me. Willows, Cherries, and different species of Pyrus are also plentiful. Deutzia, Hydrangea, Philadelphus, Rosa, and Clematis are the principal shrubs, and many were in flower. *Primula Cockburniana*, which has orange-scarlet flowers, is the most noteworthy herb hereabouts.

After wandering several miles through the forests we reached the hamlet of Kuei-yung, alt. 10,100 feet, and 60 li from T'ung-lu-fang. This place consists of half a dozen houses, purely Thibetan in character, built on a slope and surrounded by a considerable area under wheat, barley, and oats. The mountains all around are heavily forested with coniferous trees, and in the far distance a snow-capped peak glittered on the horizon.

The house we lodged in is three-storied with the usual flat mud roof. The walls built of shale-rock are most substantial. Entering through a low doorway we had first to traverse a yard filled with cattle dung, then a piggery where a steep ladder led upwards to a couple of dark empty rooms in which we installed ourselves. A ladder from these rooms led to the roof, where I should have preferred to sleep had it not been raining. The house boasts neither table, stool, nor chair, and we had to improvise as best we could. The Thibetans squat on the floor for their meals, and therefore have no use for tables or chairs. The housewife, a most cheery if dirty person, had a very musical laugh. Things generally appeared a joke to her, and incited her to frequent laughter, which it was pleasant to hear. My followers were oddly amused at the strangeness of things, and appeared to enjoy the novelty.

Yet it was not out of love for our quarters that I stayed over a day at Kuei-yung, but to photograph various trees and investigate the Conifers. Photography in the forests is no mere pastime. It took over an hour on three occasions clearing away brushwood and branches so as to admit of a clear view of the trunk of the subject. I secured a dozen photographs, which entailed a hard day's work. The trees of Larch and other Conifers, Birch, and Poplar are very fine. The Larch (*L. Potaninii*), though not plentiful, is of great size, and trees 100 feet by 12 feet in girth occur. But the most astonishing feature of these forests is the large trees of Sallowthorn (*Hippophaë salicifolia*). I had never imagined it could attain to the size of specimens I saw during the day. I photographed two old trees 50 feet tall, 12 and 15 feet in girth respectively. I saw others taller but less in girth. Another interesting tree hereabouts is a Cherry (*Prunus serrula*, var. *tibetica*), which has a short, very thick trunk, and wide-spreading head. The leaves are willow-like, 3 to 4 inches long; the fruit is red, ovoid, on pendulous stalks. The tree averages about 30 feet in height, the head being 60 feet and more through.

The next morning we bade farewell to our cheery hostess at Kuei-yung, and continued our journey. The road immediately plunges into the forest, and winds through and among magnificent timber. The forests are very fine, and coniferous trees 100 to 150 feet tall, with a girth of 12 to 18 feet, are quite common. The latter consist of four species of Spruce, three of Silver Fir and one of Larch. The handsomest of the Silver Firs is *Abies squamata*, which has purplish-brown bark, exfoliating like the bark of the River Birch. The Larch becomes general in the ascent, and ultimately overtops all other trees and extends to the tree-limit. White and Red Birch, Poplar and Sallowthorn are the only broad-leaved deciduous trees really common. An Evergreen Oak (*Quercus Ilex*, var. *rufescens*), with prickly leaves like a Holly, is abundant. In the shelter of the forests this Oak makes a good-sized tree, but in the more exposed places it is reduced to a small shrub. The wood is very hard and makes the finest of charcoal. Shrubs are not rich in variety, but Bush Honeysuckles, Barberries, Spiræas, and Clematis are plentiful. Herbs, especially the Sikhim cowslip (*Primula sikkimensis*), *P. involucrata*, Anemone, Caltha, Trollius, and various *Compositæ* luxuriate on all sides, and the glades and marshy places were nothing but masses of colour. The men who were in front of me saw several troupes of monkeys and some Eared-pheasants, but I saw no animals and very few birds.

We camped near the tree-limit, at about 12,000 feet altitude, and erected a small hut of spruce boughs under a large Silver Fir tree. My Boy preferred to pass the night in his chair, and the men arranged themselves around a log fire. The neighbourhood has an evil reputation for highway robbers, but we felt sure there was small possibility of any attack on us being made. It rained a little during the day, and a sharp shower fell in the early evening, but the night proved fine. The altitude, however, affected our sleep ; it was also very cold, and we were all glad when morning broke. My dog suffered as much as any of us ; he refused to eat his supper, and I never saw him so utterly miserable. The coolies looked a most woebegone crowd, shivering with cold and generally wretched. They seemed to have no idea of making themselves comfortable ; it would have been a simple matter for them to have rigged up a shelter of spruce boughs, but they were too indifferent to do this or even to collect firewood. We brought with us from Kuei-yung, as guide, a Thibetan, and it was he who got together all the wood required for a fire.

There was a slight frost and a heavy dew, but the sun, which rose like a ball of fire, soon warmed us and dispersed the dew. The road is of the easiest, winding through timber and brush alongside a small stream, up to within 1000 yards of the head of the Ta-p'ao shan Pass, where the ascent becomes steeper. It is, however, only the last 500 feet that make any pretence of being difficult. Above the place where we camped the Conifer trees rapidly decrease in size, Larch becomes more and more abundant, and ultimately forms pure woods. It overtops every other kind of tree, and extends up to 13,500 feet altitude. Just below the limits of the Larch a dwarf Juniper appears and ascends to near the head of the pass. The scaly-barked Silver Fir (*Abies squamata*) ascends to 12,500 feet and two species of Spruce to 13,000 feet. This side of the pass enjoys a moist climate, and the tree-line (13,500 feet approximately) is remarkably high. Above the tree-line the mountain-sides, to within a few hundred feet of the pass, are covered with scrub composed, as usual in these regions, of Willow, Berberis, small-leaved species of Rhododendron, Spiræa, Juniper, *Potentilla Veitchii*, *P. fruticosa*, and *Rhododendron Przewalskii*, the latter being the most alpine of all the large-leaved members of its family. Herbs, of course, made a wonderful display of colour. In addition to those previously mentioned, other species of Primula, the yellow and violet-blue Poppyworts (*Meconopsis integrifolia* and *M. Henrici*), various Stone-crops (*Sedum* spp.), and Saxi-frages are abundant. But the most striking of all the herbs is a Rhubarb (*Rheum Alexandræ*), an extraordinary plant, with a pyramidal inflorescence 3 to 4 feet tall, arising from a mass of relatively small, ovate, shining, sorrel-like leaves, and composed of broad, rounded, decurved, pale yellow bracts overlapping one another like tiles on a house-roof. The local name of this plant is " Ma Huang " (Horse Rhubarb) ; it prefers rich boggy ground where verdure is luxuriant and yak delight to feed. Such places were studded with its most conspicuous tower-like spikes of flowers. The Rhubarb and yellow Poppywort (*Meconopsis integrifolia*) are always most rampant around places where yak have been herded.

Unmelted snow of the preceding winter was lying in patches just below the summit of the pass, a bare, narrow ridge crowned by a cairn of stones surmounted with many prayer-flags, and 14,600 feet above sea-level. This narrow neck is composed of slate and sandstone, with a certain amount of marble rock scattered about, and connects two massive ranges clad with eternal snows. The day was gloriously sunny, and we had a rare opportunity of enjoying and appreciating the delights of this alpine region. Except for a feeling of giddi-ness when stooping, and a general shortness of breath, I suffered no inconvenience from the altitude. In spite of their loads only two or three of my men were seriously affected ; the gradual ascent was, I think, responsible for our good fortune in this matter. From past experience I had rather dreaded the effects this pass might have on my followers, and was pleasantly surprised at the ease with which they negotiated it.

With the weather conditions so favourable the view from the summit of the pass far surpassed my wildest dreams. It greatly exceeded anything of its kind that I have seen, and would require a far abler pen than mine to describe it adequately. Straight before us, but a little to the right of our viewpoint, was an enormous mass of dazzling eternal snow, supposed to be, and I can well believe it, over 22,000 feet high. Beneath the snow and attendant glaciers was a sinister-looking mass of boulders and screes. In the far distance were visible the enormous masses of perpetual snow around Tachienlu. In the near distance, to the west-north-west of the pass, another block of eternal snow reared itself. Looking back on the route we had traversed we saw that the narrow valley is flanked by steep ranges, the highest peaks clad with snow, but in the main, though bare and savage-looking, they scarcely attain to the snowline. On all sides the scenery is wild, rugged, and severely alpine. A cold wind blew in strong gusts across the pass, and we were glad when our photographic work was finished, and we could hurry down. Several fine Eagles and Lammergeiers were soaring aloft, but we saw no animals, though Wild sheep and Thibetan gazelle were said to frequent this region.

Descending by a precipitous, break-neck path, over loose slate, sandstone shales and greasy clayey-marls for 15 li, we reached the head of a broad valley. The pass on this side offers a far more severe climb than the side we had ascended. On reaching the valley the track we followed connects with the main road to Th'ai-ling, Chantui, and Chamdo. Commercially speaking this is the highway into Thibet from Tachienlu. It leads through grasslands, affording good pasturage for animals, and though the mean elevation is very considerable the passes are less steep than those on the political highway via Litang and Batang. This Ta-p'ao shan region is notorious for its highway robberies. We met five tribesmen who told us that in the previous night their camp had been rushed by an armed band and everything they possessed carried off. Every Thibetan is by nature a robber, and behaves as such when he fancies he can do so with impunity. They rob one another freely, but the tribesmen are their favourite victims.

From the head of the valley to Hsin-tientsze, the first habitation, is reckoned as 30 li. The road is broad but uneven, winding through a valley, and keeping close to a torrent which descends from the Ta-p'ao shan snows. The mountains on either side of the valley in all their higher parts range above the snowline; their lower slopes are covered with grass, small Conifer trees, and brushwood. In the valley itself shrubs of large size, chiefly Willows, Honeysuckles, Barberries, and Sallowthorn abound. Odd trees of Larch and Spruce occur, all of small size. Flocks of Snow-pigeons were plentiful, and I shot several of these birds for our larder.

From Kuei-yung, 120 li, there is no house of any description save Hsin-tientsze, alt. 10,800 feet, a filthy and miserable hostel. Near Kuei-yung we passed a charcoal-burning camp where a few men were engaged, otherwise we did not meet a living soul, until we had crossed the pass. It is indeed a most lonely region, but of great interest to a Nature lover. I count myself particularly fortunate in being favoured by perfect weather for crossing the pass, more especially as it was the first day without any sign of rain since leaving Kuan Hsien.

The thermometer registered 36° F. when we turned out next morning, and our ears and fingers tingled with cold, even though it was 8th July. The smoke inside the inn was too much for my eyes, so I breakfasted out in the middle of the roadway. I think everybody was glad to quit Hsin-tientsze with its vermin and stinks. There was an odd patch of wheat around the hostel, but it looked miserable; the season is too short and the climate too severe for cultivation hereabouts at this altitude.

We followed a broad, uneven road, which had suffered much from animal traffic, for 60 li to Jê-shui-t'ang (Hot-water pond), alt. 9800 feet. The descent is gradual, and the day's journey proved a delightful loiter through a shrub-clad valley. We met several hundreds of yak and ponies, all laden with brick tea encased in raw hides and bound for interior Thibet. The Thibetans in charge were an unkempt, wild-looking lot of men, with long guns, swords, and conspicuous charm-boxes. Many of them wore their hair in a long plait with a sort of black yarn braided in, the whole being wrapt around their heads to form a turban ; a few wore felt hats with high conical crowns. One or two women were with these caravans tending the animals exactly in the same way as the men. Ability to whistle and heave rocks with sure aim seemed to be the essential parts of a yak-muleteer's profession. Yak are slow, phlegmatic animals, and on sighting any unusual object they stand stock-still for a little time, and then make a mad rush forward. They appeared to be docile enough, but their long horns looked dangerously ugly, and we got out of their way as much as was possible. Each caravan was accompanied by one or more large dogs. These animals trot alongside the caravan and take no notice of any one, but when tethered and on guard in camp will allow no stranger to approach. They are massively-built dogs, and their savage appearance is heightened by a huge red-coloured collar of woollen fringe, with which they are commonly decorated.

The flora was merely a repetition of that of the previous afternoon's journey. The valley and contiguous hill-sides are covered with scrub, except for clearings here and there which serve as yak-camps. In addition to the shrubs mentioned as occurring around Hsin-tientsze, Prickly Oak, Juniper, several kinds of Rose, and the Thibetan Honeysuckle (*Lonicera thibetica*) are common ; Barberries in variety are a special feature. Conifers are scarce and all of small size ; all the larger timber has been felled and removed long ago At the hamlet of Lung-pu, reckoned 40 li from Hsin-tientsze, crops of wheat, barley, oats, and peas put in an appearance, and became more general as we descended the valley. Around Jê-shui-t'ang the cereals were just coming into ear.

During the day, which was beautifully fine, we had grand views of the snowclad peaks around Tachienlu and the steep ranges with pinnacled peaks to the east-south-east of that town. Around Jê-shui-t'ang there are several hot springs, in some of which the water was actually boiling. These springs are rich in iron, but in those I examined no sulphur was evident.

Our quarters at Jê-shui-t'ang were a considerable improvement on those of Hsin-tientsze, but we were, nevertheless, glad to leave very soon after day dawned. It is considered to be 90 li from this place to Tachienlu, but I should say 60 li is a nearer estimate. We enjoyed another sunny day. The road is easy and leads through a continuation of the valley that we entered on descending from the Ta-p'ao shan Pass. The valley and mountain-sides for some 300 to 500 feet above it become more and more under cultivation. Cereals, peas, and Irish potato are the principal crops. The potatoes were being harvested, and I noticed that red ones predominated. The region generally has been denuded of its trees, and where not under crops is covered with scrub and coarse herbs. In rocky places small trees of White and Hard Pine (*Pinus Armandi, P. prominens*) occur, also a few comparatively large trees of a very distinct-looking Peach having narrow, lance-shaped, long pointed leaves, rather small fruits, downy on the outside.[1]

Around habitations tall trees of Poplar are common, and an occasional Spruce and White Birch occur. The Spruce (*Picea aurantiaca*) is a particularly handsome species, with square, dark green needles on spreading branches and red-brown pendulous cones clustered near the top of the tree. The Apple, Apricot, Peach, Plum, and a few Walnut trees are cultivated. The fields are fenced with hedges of Wild Gooseberry (*Ribes alpestre*, var. *giganteum*) and the handsome *Sorbaria arborea*, which has large erect masses of snow-white flowers. Over these and other shrubs various species of Clematis trail, the most common being *C. nutans*, var. *thyrsoidea*, which was laden with a multitude of creamy-yellow nodding flowers. The most beautiful shrub, however, was a Lilac growing 12 to 15 feet tall, and covered with huge panicles of pink or white fragrant flowers. (It proved a new species, and has been named *Syringa Wilsonii*.)

[1] At the time I paid no further attention to this Peach, but in 1910 I secured ripe fruit, and found to my astonishment that the stones were perfectly smooth, free, and relatively very small—characters denoting a distinct species of Peach. It proved to be new, and has since been named *Prunus mira*. I regard this as among the most remarkable of the discoveries I have been privileged to make. This new Peach is now in cultivation, and by crossbreeding with the old varieties of the garden Peach (*P. Persica*) may result in the production of entirely new and improved races of this favourite fruit.

We crossed the stream by a wooden cantilever bridge and, on rounding a bend, the goal of our long journey came into view. We were all well-nigh dead beat, and it was with thankful and joyous hearts that we greeted the cluster of closely packed houses, which, nestling in a narrow valley, constitute the important border town of Tachienlu.

CHAPTER XVI

TACHIENLU, THE GATE OF THIBET

The Kingdom of Chiala, its People, their Manners and Customs

THE town of Tachienlu is situated in long. 102° 13′ E., lat. 30° 3′ N. *circa*, at an altitude of about 8400 feet. By the most direct route it is twelve days' journey from Chengtu Fu, the provincial capital, on the great highway which extends westwards to Lhassa. It is the Ultima Thule of China and Thibet, where a large and thriving trade is done in the wares of both countries. It is also the residence of the King of Chiala, who governs a very considerable tract of country and exercises a strong influence over conterminous states peopled with Thibetans. The first Occidental other than Roman Catholic priests to visit Tachienlu was the late Mr. T. T. Cooper in 1868. Since that date it has been visited by many scores of travellers, and has become fairly well known to the outside world. It is a more than ordinarily interesting place, and though much has been written concerning it the subject is far from being exhausted.

The present town is built in the narrowest of valleys at the head of a gorge, down which the river Lu cascades, falling some 4000 feet before it joins the river Tung, 18 miles distant. A branch of the Lu River bisects the town, being crossed by means of three wooden bridges, and is joined immediately below the north gate by another stream, which flows from the Ta-p'ao shan snows. The town is hemmed in on all sides by steep, treeless mountains whose grassy slopes and bare cliffs lead up to peaks culminating in eternal snow. On the whole, the situation is about the last in the world in which one would expect to find a thriving trade entrepôt. Formerly, Tachienlu occupied a site about half a mile above the present town, but about 100 years ago it was totally destroyed by a landslip, due to a moving glacier. Some day a similar fate will doubtless overtake the existing town.

Notwithstanding its great political and commercial importance Tachienlu is a meanly built and filthy city. It is without a surrounding wall, save for a fragment which runs across near the south gate, and it has no west gate. The narrow, uneven streets are paved with stone in which pure marble largely figures, though this is only evident after some heavy downpour has washed away the usual covering of mud and filth. The houses are low, built of wood resting on foundations of shale rocks. The principal shops are by no means of imposing appearance, and, indeed, the only places noteworthy are two Chinese temples and the palace of the local king. The latter consists of several lofty semi-Chinese buildings of wood with sloping roofs and curved eaves surmounted by gilded pinnacles, the whole structure being situated in a large compound and surrounded by a high stone wall. The residences of the Chinese officials are poor, ramshackle places, and the same is true of the various inns. In the latter most of the business is transacted. Some inns that I visited contained valuable collections of porcelain and bronze-ware, and an extraordinary number of old French clocks. Very few of the clocks were in working order, but many were of large size, and how they all reached this remote place is a mystery to me.

The population of Tachienlu consists of about 700 Thibetan and 400 Chinese families and, with its floating members, is reckoned at 9000 people. In and near the town are eight lamaseries boasting 800 lamas and acolytes. The population is very mixed, consisting of pure Thibetans, pure Chinese, and half-breeds. Very few purely Chinese women are to be found in Tachienlu.

As seen in and around Tachienlu the Thibetans are a picturesque people. Of medium height and lithely but muscularly built, they have an easy carriage and independent mien. The young women are usually sprightly in manner, always cheery, with dark-brown eyes and finely cut features. Both sexes are fond of jewellery ornamented with turquoise and coral, but they are strangers to soap and water, and personal cleanliness is neither appreciated nor practised.   Meat, milk, butter, barley-meal, and tea constitute the favourite food of these people ; they are also fond of Chinese wine.   Everybody carries on his or her person a private eating-bowl, and the average Thibetan disseminates an odour strongly suggestive of a keg of rancid butter !   The everyday dress of these people is a loose, shapeless garment of dull red or grey woollen serge, sometimes sheep-skins are substituted in part.   Top-boots of soft hide with the hair inside usually encase the feet and lower legs of both sexes.   The men wear their hair in a queue wound round the head and ornamented with beads and rings of silver, coral, and glass.   A large silver ear-ring with a long silver and coral pendant usually decorates the left ear.   The women wear their hair parted down the middle and made up into a number of small plaits, which are gathered into a queue, bound at the end by a bright red cord, and wound around the head.   Silver and coral are lavishly used in their coiffure and about their persons generally.   When in holiday attire these people are more gaily dressed, red-coloured trimmings to their garments being then much in evidence, whilst the wealthy affect silk and fur robes.   Ornaments of silver and gold, inset with coral and turquoise, are most profusely worn.   The lamas shave their heads and wear a raiment of coarse serge of a dull red or brownish colour.   This has no shape, being simply a large piece of cloth thrown over the left shoulder, leaving the right bare.   A similar piece of cloth is wound two or three times round the waist and reaches down to the ankle, forming a kind of pleated skirt.   They are usually bareheaded and bare-footed, and each lama carries in his hand a rosary and a small praying-cylinder.   They swagger through the streets with an insolent mien, and lack the good manners so delightful in the ordinary unsophisticated Thibetan.   The lamaseries are usually very richly endowed with land, and most charmingly situated midst groves of Poplar and other trees.   Nearly all Thibetan families of affluence maintain a lama on the premises to perform by proxy their religious duties.   Many other lamas find employment as temporary chaplains to less wealthy families on occasion of marriage, illness, or death.

Commercially, Tachienlu is a most important centre,

enjoying a monopoly of the trade between this part of China and Thibet. The value of the trade is estimated at about one and three-quarter million taels. The Thibetans bring in musk, wool, deer horns, skins, gold-dust, and various medicines, and take in exchange brick tea and miscellaneous sundries. The trade is largely one of barter, but much less so than that of Sungpan Ting. Sycee and Indian rupees were formerly the only coinage current, but the Chinese during the last few years have been minting in Chengtu a rupee of their own for the special purposes of this trade-centre. Its use has been insisted upon, and, in consequence, the Indian coin has been ousted from the field. Most of the " bigger " trade is in the hands of the lamaseries on the one hand, and Chinese from the province of Shensi on the other. About 30 li to the north-east of Tachienlu gold is found at an altitude of about 11,000 feet, and placer-mining is carried on there. The gold-washing is done in exactly the same way as elsewhere in Western China, but the method of paying the miners is peculiar,—the arrangement being six baskets for the owner of the mine and a seventh for the miners. Silver also occurs at this same place. The Thibetans hold the view that gold and other precious metals grow, and that their death may result if too much is removed at any one time. How far they actually believe in this superstition is a moot point, but at times it serves as an unanswerable argument. Nine years ago a difference of opinion in the matter of assessing the profits arose between the Chief of Chiala, owner of the mine, and the head Chinese official at Tachienlu, who was apparently over-avaricious in the matter. The Chief very quietly advanced the above theory, and closed down the mines for an indefinite period ! Gold in great quantity occurs in the state of Litang, west of Tachienlu ; much also is mined around Th'ai-ling to the north of this town.

Being on the great highway from Peking via Chengtu to Lhassa, officials are constantly passing through Tachienlu, and the political importance of the town is very great. Although only a city of the second class the head Chinese official has the local rank of Prefect (Chiung-Liang Fu), and holds the post of commissary for the Chinese troops stationed in Thibet. Although Batang, 18 days' journey westwards, is more accurately

the frontier town, Tachienlu is actually the " Gate of Thibet."
The country around and beyond is physically purely Thibetan
in character, and is ruled by native chieftains. Garrisons of
soldiers and a few resident Chinese officials protect the interests
of the Celestial empire and keep a sharp eye on the actions of
the local rulers.

It was stated at the commencement of this chapter that the
King of Chiala resides at Tachienlu, and perhaps a few details
concerning this kingdom and its people may be of interest.
According to the Guide Book of Thibet this State came under
Chinese influence during the Ming Dynasty, about A.D. 1403,
and its Chief was given the rank of a second-class native official,
with control over the tribes west of the river Tung and southwards to Ningyuan Fu. " The Manchu Dynasty, in consideration of the above, made the then Chief a third-class native
official, with power over three trading companies. New chiefs,
chiliarchs, and centurions to the extent of fifty-six were created.
This illustrious Chief now controls six subsidiary chiefs, one
chiliarch, and forty-eight centurions." Since the date of this
appointment the Chinese have increased their grip over these
regions, to the curtailment of the Chief's power and authority.
Nevertheless, the Thibetans of this region acknowledge this
Chief as their supreme ruler, and in domestic affairs his authority
is absolute. His native title is " Chiala Djie-po " (King of
Chiala) ; his Chinese title, " Ming-ching Ssu," which may be
translated " Bright-ruling official." The King and Chinese
Prefect (Fu) are supposed to be colleagues, but in reality the
King is subordinate, and when paying official visits must make
obeisance before the Fu. In what little dealings I had with
them I found both to be courteous and obliging, but suspicious
and jealous of one another.

The present King is a slimly built, intelligent man, about
forty odd years of age. He took considerable interest in our
collecting work around Tachienlu, and with his brother, who is a
hunter of much renown, paid us many unofficial visits. He was
never tired of watching my companion, Mr. Zappey, fixing up
his birds' skins. My own work amongst flowers interested him
but little. As a parting gift Mr. Zappey stuffed and mounted
a Hoopoe for the King, who evinced almost childlike pleasure

on receiving it. In return, he made Mr. Zappey and myself several presents, and urged us to visit his country on a future occasion. We found that these Thibetans possessed keen and accurate knowledge of the birds and animals of their country, which made them enthusiastic hunting companions. During the reign of the former king, his brother, the present Ruler, was banished, and suffered dire hardships during his exile, and often wanted for food. The missionaries stationed in this neighbourhood on more than one occasion assisted him, and I understood from them that he had not forgotten their kindly help. The history of the family is a tragic one. The present King's brother was supposed to have been poisoned, and two sisters died early deaths, the result, it is said, of immoral associations with lamas.

The state of Chiala is of considerable size, comprising practically the whole of the territory lying between the Tung River, Chiench'iang Valley, and the Yalung River from lat. 28° to 32° N. The five Horba states in a measure also come under the influence of the King of Chiala. From all I can learn this region has the best right to be considered the kingdom of Menia, or "Miniak," of European maps. The whereabouts of "Miniak" has considerably puzzled geographers, but the evidence seems to point to the kingdom of Chiala as representing it in the greater part. North-east of Chiala is the large and prosperous state of Derge, famed for its copper, silver, and swordsmiths. Monsieur Bons d'Anty, French Consul-General at Chengtu, visited Derge in the autumn of 1910, and on his return gave me a most interesting account of this region. He informed me that Derge is a region of much cultivation, surrounded on three sides by snowclad ranges. The various industries for which the state is famous are not carried on in towns, but by the peasants individually in their homes, and from thence carried to towns for sale. In the valley of the Upper Yalung, abutting on the north-west frontier of Chiala and the south-east frontier of Derge, is a wedge of country known as Chantui, peopled by a race of Ishmaels, whose hands are ever turned in conflict against their neighbours. A similar people occupy a wedge of country in the Drechu valley north of Batang, where they are known as

the Sanai tribe.   Monsieur Bons d'Anty considers that these
people are of Shan origin, and remnants of an aboriginal population of this region.   This authority has spent many years
in studying the ethnological problems of this borderland, and
is most competent to express an opinion.   It is well known that
the Shans formerly ruled in western Yunnan, and there is
no reason why they should not, in the distant past, have
ascended the valleys of the Yalung and Drechu and established
themselves there.   But whatever the origin of these people
of Chantui and Sanai, they are dreaded by their neighbours,
who regard them all as robbers and murderers (Ja-ba) quite
beyond the pale.

The religion of the people of Chiala is Lamaism, both the
orthodox " yellow " and unorthodox " red " sects being represented, but the former are the more numerous and powerful.
Some one has described Lamaism as " mechanical," a most
descriptive term, since the religion consists in the main of
turning praying-wheels by hand, water, or wind, counting
beads, and the continual muttering or chanting of the mystic
hymn, " Om mani padmi hum."   Lamaism draws its inspiration from Lhassa, where all the priests repair for study, the
head of the sect being the Dalai Lama.   Aided and abetted by
Chinese authority, the King of Chiala has never submitted
to the Dalai Lama in temporal affairs ; he has maintained his
freedom and right to govern his own people untrammelled by
Lhassa interference, in spite of the dire threats and treachery
on the part of lamaseries within his jurisdiction.   In 1903 the
Dalai Lama issued an ultimatum to the King of Chiala threatening to take from him and the Chinese by conquest all the
territory west of the Tung Valley.   The British Expedition
prevented the carrying out of this threat.   The Dalai Lama
undoubtedly had designs of territorial expansion at the expense
of China's vassal states.   The Chinese knew this, and it was
fortunate for them that Great Britain stepped in and broke
the power of Lhassa De.   I was in Tachienlu during 1903 and
1904, and from what I saw and heard there it was plain that
the British were unwittingly pulling China's " chestnuts from
the fire."   The Chinese were not slow to perceive the advantageous position they were in after the power of the Dalai

Lama was dissipated. Almost immediately a " Wardenship of the Thibetan Marches " was established, and a war of conquest engaged upon against certain wealthy lamaseries in Litang and other states, who owned direct allegiance to Lhassa, and heretofore had boasted their independence of China. This war was relentlessly and victoriously pursued under the leadership of Chao Êrh-fêng, and resulted in the extension of Chinese authority over a very considerable tract of country. Indirectly the King of Chiala's position has been very much weakened as the outcome of these conquests.

The state of Chiala is made up of mountain, dale, and plateau, being essentially a highland country affording good pasturage for yak, sheep, and horses. A chain of snowclad peaks traverses it near its eastern boundaries. It is a region where altitude regulates the mode òf life, the wealth, and marriage customs of its people. The inhabitants are less nomadic than the people to the north and west, but, in common with all other Thibetans, their wealth is represented by herds of yak, horses, and cattle, and flocks of sheep and goats. They are great hunters of Musk-deer, Wapiti, Bear, and other animals, the commercial products of which they trade to the Chinese. The same is true of the medicinal roots and herbs, which grow abundantly in these uplands. Where altitudes admit, agriculture is practised, but is supplementary to grazing and relatively unimportant. Wheat, barley, oats, buckwheat, peas, and Irish potato are the chief crops. During the winter months these Thibetans live in well-built houses situated in the valleys, and in the spring they migrate to the uplands. The nomads do not move about aimlessly, but have clearly defined regions and are subject to responsible head-men. Where agriculture is carried on the womenfolk mostly remain to look after the crops and to do other work pertaining to the farmstead.

Wealth and convenience decide which form the matrimonial alliance shall assume among these people, and polygamy, monogamy, and polyandry obtain. Above 12,000 feet altitude polyandry is the rule, and in many places women so united wear distinguishing and honorary badges. Such women are usually the business and ruling heads of their

establishments. This custom of polyandry is characteristic
of Thibet, and the following note on the subject, written by a
friend who has spent many years of his life among these people,
is worthy of much thoughtful study :—

"So many able men have written about polyandry that
what follows will be without interest to those who have studied
the system ; but to the great mass who are comparatively
unacquainted with Thibet and her customs these notes may be
of some value. The writer has spent several years among
Thibetans and cognate tribes, and has lived for months alone
on the wild steppes as well as in the more civilized and well-
cultivated valleys.

"The term ' polyandry ' is here applied (*a*) to women living
permanently, and cohabiting legally, with more than one man ;
(*b*) to those who have been, or are, married temporarily to more
than one man or companies of men.

"The former, true polyandry, is confined to the pastoral
nomads of the grassy plateaux ; the latter, quasi-polyandry,
is rampant in all the commercial and political centres on the
border and throughout Thibet. In both cases a low conception of the relation of the sexes has made it possible ; and
climate and political conditions have made it desirable.

"The past hints, and the present proves, that indifference
to female virtue connotes the people known as Thibetans
and tribes of common origin, and I understand it to be
the indirect cause of polyandry. From time immemorial the
Thibetan has been taught that the female is a kind of Pan-
dora's box, in which are all the evils that have cursed mankind.
All down the ages woman seems to have been the slave of man :
dangerous because of latent evil, but also valuable on account
of her ability to render him service. In the old barbaric days,
when prowess was the prime virtue and a thoroughgoing
communism the rule, woman was only a tribal asset, like the
animals she tended. Then came religion, a deification of all
that rude minds could not explain. It was probably the
mysterious Bönpa of to-day which lingers in the lonely valleys
where nations meet, and which could have been no friend of
virtue if the accounts of orgies in its temples before indecent
idols are true, and the unseemly dress of young women and

barren wives either demanded or sanctioned by it.   Explain it
as we may, the fact remains that Thibetan women are to-day,
as they seem to have been in the time of Marco Polo, the most
immodest of their sex, and the Thibetan men strangely indifferent about matters which other races demand as essentials.

" All outside work is done by the women, who represent the
coarser element of Thibetan society, and their language is often
filthy in the extreme.   The domestic arrangements make no
provision for privacy.   Men and women must eat, live, and sleep
perforce in the same apartment, and there is no effort on the
part of the male to shield the female from conditions which are
inimical to virtue.

" The morality of the Thibetans has made such a system
possible.   This will not be denied by any one who knows them
even slightly ; but it will sound strange to many when I say
that the climatic and political conditions are such that the
reformer is puzzled to think of anything to offer as a substitute !   To the untutored Thibetan mind it must seem
absolutely necessary.   Undoubtedly the high altitudes are
unfavourable to women.   The Thibetan views woman very
much as he does an animal, *i.e.* she can do so much work.
Living and working at 12,000 feet altitude and upwards requires
the strongest material.   Woman very imperfectly fulfils these
requirements, and maternity and nursing, apart from unfitting
her for work, would be well-nigh useless, since infant mortality
would be abnormally high.   On the relatively thinly populated
plateaux the conditions obtaining are emphatically against
woman being wanted in numbers.   Here robbing and escaping
from robbers is the normal condition.   It will be evident
at once that family duties are not only inconvenient, but
interfere with the woman's efficiency personally, and at the
same time misdirect the energies of the male portion of the
community.

" The nomad is a herdsman, continually moving to and fro
with his flocks and belongings.   The woman, and the centre
she forms, would impair the necessary freedom of movement ;
it would also follow that she and her belongings would often be
unprotected for long periods.   Polyandry, by not encouraging
permanent settlements and at the same time being the best

security against marauding bands, must seem eminently rational to the nomad.

" Polyandry also entails the family property. This is very important, as division of the flocks or grazing-grounds would soon ruin every one. Whatever the ideal system for these Thibetans may be, the one which provides one wife, one family, and one flock for all the male members of the family is the most convenient. Anything else would be suicidal. Both polygamy and monogamy presuppose racial increase and the formation of new and independent centres, but polyandry promises the great desideratum of the Thibetan—an almost stationary community and an intact patrimony.

" In a land of polyandry, priestly celibacy, and nondescript roving, the number of unmarried women must be large. This class, with the Chinese, Lamas, and Thibetan merchants, is responsible for the quasi-polyandry of the plain, which only differs from prostitution inasmuch as it has the sanction of the country and carries with it no odium. The priest is a celibate, as a rule, by profession, but an inveterate roué in practice. Quite a large number of women are required wherever lamaseries exist. In Lhassa, where thousands of students from all parts of the country study for years, the number of women married temporarily, openly, or in secret, to individuals or small communities is very great. The wandering Thibetan merchants form another class who demand a supply of temporary wives for longer or shorter periods. These may often be men who have formed polyandrous unions in the mountains, but the exigencies of circumstances demand their presence on the plain. In other words, there is no reason why a man may not be a polyandrian legally, and in practice a polygamist.

" But the most interesting phase of this system arises from peculiarities of Chinese domination. Chinese soldiers, officials, and merchants residing temporarily in Thibet form a very large body. These victims of circumstances leave their wives in far-away China. There is a legend that the Lamas have put an embargo on the dainty Chinese woman : but, more probably, her lord and owner has neither the mind nor the money to introduce her to the dangers and hardships of a Thibetan journey. But he rarely, if ever, pines for the wife of his youth. Polyandry and polygamy meet, and temporary marriages, for one month to three years, are the rule. The highest official and the meanest soldier take advantage of the system. With the former it is temporary monogamy or polygamy, but with the latter, owing to pecuniary limitations, one woman often becomes, *pro tempore*, the wife of a small community of soldiers. These wives or their children, for obvious reasons, are seldom, if ever, brought out from Thibet ; the former make new alliances and the children are claimed by the Lamas.

" The question of Thibetan morality is a very complex one, and it is almost impossible to disentangle the cause from the effect. True polyandry is owing, indirectly, to a low moral perception ; but it might be correct to blame it, in a measure, for the more degenerate quasi-polyandry. Whatever we may think of the former, from the standpoint of absolute morality, it is relatively a moral system and solves many problems. To change it without changing the conditions would be tantamount to driving the brave nomad women into the towns to become the temporary wives of Chinese rabble, priestly roués, and peripatetic Thibetans. Perhaps my hinting that polyandry as a system is in many ways well suited to the plateaux will evoke much unfavourable comment, but there are good men, Roman Catholic and Protestant, priest and layman, who have noticed the same difficulty.

" The effect of the system on the women is another question about which we cannot afford to be dogmatic. When young the Thibetan women are often very pretty, but they age quickly and become as weirdly ugly as the mediaeval witches. To say that polyandry is alone responsible for this change would be sentiment unsupported by facts ; but undoubtedly this system, combined with hard work, loathsome uncleanliness, and often grotesque head-dress tends to give a great many women an inhumanly vile expression.

" The families on the plateaux are very small and many women are barren. This is a blessing in disguise, owing to the impossibility of the nomad country supporting more than a very limited population, and the small amount of arable land capable of relieving the congested centres. Polyandry is both

directly and indirectly the cause of this limitation of offspring.
A glance at the system will show how these uncultured Mal-
thusians obtain their end : Three men, for instance, centre
their affections on one woman, who in her lifetime rears two
or three children. As monogamists each of these men would
have had his own wife and probably a total of fifteen
children. But another factor has to be taken into consideration : polyandry not only limits a woman's natural
fecundity, but in a great number of cases is the direct cause
of barrenness.

" About the domestic arrangements I cannot speak
authoritatively, but I have never heard internal discord used
as an argument against polyandry. It must often happen
that one or two husbands are away tending flocks, worshipping
at holy mountains, or robbing travellers. But this is an
accident ; the domestic equilibrium is rarely disturbed by
petty jealousies. The defloration of the bride or brides—
for there is no reason why two or more sisters should not
come into the community—is the right of the elder brother,
and the first child is, by courtesy, assigned to him ; but the
child or children of the union are, in reality, a joint possession.
The girls in the community either follow their mother's
example, or go into the towns and become the temporary
wives of Chinese, Lamas, or wandering merchants. In the
former case a dowry is given to the parents, but in the latter
the ' fair one ' makes the most of her time and the simplicity
of her husband or husbands.

" Polyandry in one form or other is probably practised
whenever Thibetan communities are found. Its existence
may be denied emphatically, but closer investigation will
only prove the wide distribution of the ' Münchausen '
family. However, an exception may be allowed in the deep,
populous valleys of Eastern Thibet. Here individualism is
the rule, and new centres are formed and thrive without the
shadow of a grim Frankenstein disturbing them. So completely has the old dread of offspring been effaced that
marriage is always preceded by a tentative period, and
maternity alone establishes a girl's right to be admitted
into her husband's family. Here the quondam upholder of

polyandry, realizing that the fruitful earth and the fruitful woman bring wealth and strength respectively, becomes a confirmed polygamist. To the student of ethnology this metamorphosis suggests the permanency of the valley Thibetan and the gradual absorption or total extinction of his mountain brother."

CHAPTER XVII

SACRED OMEI SHAN

Its Temples and its Flora

THE lofty and sacred eminence known as Mount Omei, or Omei shan, is situated about long. 103° 41′ E., lat. 29°32′ N., one day's journey from the city of Kiating. A gigantic upthrust of hard limestone, it rises sheer from the plain (alt. 1300 feet) to a height of nearly 11,000 above sea-level. From the city of Kiating a fine view of this remarkable mountain is obtainable during clear weather, the mirage of the plain seemingly lending it additional height. Viewed from a distance it has been aptly likened to a couchant lion decapitated close to the shoulders, the fore-feet remaining in position. The down-cleft surface forms a fearful, well-nigh vertical precipice, considerably over a mile in height ! It is one of the five ultra-sacred mountains of China, but the origin of its holy character is lost in antiquity. We are told that in a monastery here the patriarch P'u (an historical personage) served Buddha during the Western Ts'in Dynasty (A.D. 265–317). P'u-hsien Pu'ssa (Samantabhadra Bodhisattva), Mount Omei's patron saint, descended upon the mountain from the back of a gigantic elephant possessed of six tusks. In one of the temples (Wan-nien-ssu) there is a life-sized elephant cast in bronze of splendid workmanship which commemorates this manifestation. Upwards of seventy Buddhist temples or monasteries (either word is applicable, since the buildings are really a combination of both) are to be found on this mountain. On the main road to the summit there is a temple every 5 li, and they become even more numerous as the ascent finally nears the end. These temples are controlled by abbots and contain upwards of 2000 priests and acolytes. The whole of the mountain is, or rather was, church property, much of the land on the lower slopes suitable for cultivation having from time to time been sold away from the church. Voluntary subscriptions are now the chief sources of revenue of the religious houses, though many of the temples have money as well as land endowments.

Many thousands of pilgrims, coming from all parts of the Chinese Empire, visit this mountain annually. At the time of my visit there were several pilgrims who had walked all the way from Shanghai, some 2000 miles distant, for the express purpose of doing homage before the shrines of Mount Omei. Thibetans and even Nepalese make pilgrimages here. The images and sacred objects are numberless, many of them being of pure bronze or copper. Three mummified holy men, lacquered, gilded, and deified, the elephant above mentioned, and a tooth of Buddha are among the more interesting objects. The tooth is about a foot long and weighs 18 English lb., and is in all probability a fossil-elephant's molar. On the extreme summit of the mountain, the Golden Summit, as it is called, are the ruins of an ancient temple which was built of pure bronze. It is said to have been erected by the Emperor Wan-li (A.D. 1573–1620), and was destroyed by lightning in 1819. Since this catastrophe nine or ten abbots have come and gone, but none has been able to collect enough money to rebuild it. The mass of metal at present heaped around, consisting of pillars, beams, panels, and tiles, is all of bronze. The panels are particularly fine pieces of work. I measured one panel which had dimensions as follows : 76 inches high, 20 inches wide, 1½ inches thick ; some of the panels are slightly smaller than this. All are ornamented with figures representing seated Buddhas, flowers, and scroll-work, and on the reverse with hexagonal arabesques. Many of the panels have been incorporated in one of the two small temples which now stand on the crest of the precipice. Wan-li's tablet, which was contained in the ancient bronze temple, is to-day accommodated in an outhouse along with fuel. The crown-piece is detached and lies outside. This tablet is of bronze, but is hollow. With crown-piece and pedestal it measures 90 inches high, 32 inches wide, and 7 inches thick. Another grand relic left to the tender mercies of the elements is a huge bell which stands 54 inches high and is 120 inches round the middle. On the edge of the cliff are two bronze pagodas, each about 12 feet high, and the remains of a third, which formed part of the ancient temple. It is a saddening sight to gaze around on these most interesting relics so ignominiously neglected.

From the summit of Mount Omei, when the sky is clear and clouds of mist float in the abyss below, a natural phenomenon similar to that of the Spectre of the Brocken is observable. I have never seen it myself, since rain fell almost continuously during the week I spent on the summit, but it has been described as a " golden ball surrounded by a rainbow floating on the surface of the mists." This phenomenon is known as the " Fo-kuang " (=" Glory of Buddha "). Devotees assert that it is an emanation from the aureole of Buddha and an outward and visible sign of the holiness of Mount Omei. The edge of the precipice is guarded by chains and wooden posts, but pilgrims in a state of religious fervour have 'been known to throw themselves over on beholding the Fo-kuang. From this cause the point is called the " Suicide's Cliff." It is the highest and most vertical part of the precipice, which extends in a nearly southerly direction for a couple of miles.

The first foreigner to ascend this famous mountain was the late E. Colborne Baber, who visited it in July 1877, and whose incomparable and accurate account of this region has never been equalled.[1] Unfortunately Baber paid little or no attention to the flora, nor did the equally distinguished traveller and writer Hosie,[2] who ascended Omei shan in 1884. It was not until 1887 that any plants were collected on this mountain. In that year it was visited by a Rhenish missionary, who was also an industrious botanical collector—the late Dr. Ernst Faber. During a fortnight's stay this enthusiast made a most interesting collection; which was found on critical examination to contain no fewer than seventy novelties. In 1890 an English naturalist, Mr. A. E. Pratt, visited the mountain and collected a few plants. Since Baber's visit many

[1] *Royal Geographical Society, Supplementary Papers*, vol. i.
[2] Sir Alexander Hosie, K.C.M.G., H.B.M.'s Consular Service in China.

hundreds of foreigners have ascended Mount Omei, but with the exception of those of Faber and Pratt, there is no record of any one having collected plants during their visits. For this reason alone I hope this chapter will find justification. The mountain and its temples have been well described by Baber and others, and I have no desire to attempt to repeat descriptions which have been made by abler pens than mine. With this prelude I append the following record of my visit :—

It was on the morning of 13th October 1903 that I set out from the city of Kiating intent on investigating the flora of this famous mountain. Traversing the highly cultivated plain, which is intersected here and there by low hills, charmingly wooded, the little town of Omei Hsien (alt. 1270 feet) was reached at the close of the day. The next morning, after journeying 10 li across the plain along a road shaded with trees of Alder and Nanmu, we reached the village of Liang-ho-kou, situated at the foot of the sacred mountain. Here the road bifurcates and both paths lead by different routes to the summit. They are paved with blocks of stone throughout, an undertaking that must have entailed a vast expenditure in labour and money, but it would be impossible to traverse certain of the steeper parts unless paving existed. I ascended by one of the routes and returned by the other, so that I saw as much as was possible of the mountain and its rich flora.

Between Omei Hsien and Liang-ho-kou are a number of truly magnificent Banyan trees (*Ficus infectoria*), known locally as Huang-kou-shu. These trees shelter some old temples and are of enormous size. I measured one, which appeared to be the largest specimen ; it was about 80 feet tall, and had a girth of 48 feet at 5 feet from the ground. We also passed some fine trees of Oak (*Quercus serrata*) and Sweet Gum (*Liquidambar formosana*). The sides of the rice fields are studded with thousands of pollarded trees of the Chinese Ash (*Fraxinus chinensis*) on which an insect deposits a valuable white wax. The ditches were gay with the spikes of cream-coloured, fragrant flowers of a species of Hedychium, the golden-flowered *Senecio clivorum*, flowers of many kinds of Impatiens, and other moisture-loving herbs.

On leaving Liang-ho-kou the ascent began, and journeying slowly three days' hard climbing brought us to the " Golden Summit."

For the purpose of grouping the flora it is convenient to divide the mountain into two regions—(1) from the base to 6000 feet, and (2) 6000 feet to the summit (10,800 feet). Thus divided the flora falls into two well-defined altitudinal zones. The lower zone is made up of such plants as enjoy a warm-temperate climate. Evergreen trees and shrubs predominate, and in the shady glens and ravines Selaginellas and Ferns luxuriate. Of these latter I, in one day, collected over sixty species ! The upper zone consists entirely of plants requiring a cool-temperate climate. With the exception of Rhododendron and Silver Fir it is composed almost entirely of deciduous trees and shrubs and herbaceous plants. The belt between 4500 feet and 5500 feet may be termed the Hinterland. Here the struggle for supremacy is most keen and the fusion of the zones most marked. At 6000 feet the boundary line is unusually well defined.

Cultivation extends up to 4000 feet, maize and pulse being the principal crops, with rice relegated to the valleys and bottom-lands. Plantations of Ash trees for the culture of insect-wax extend up to 2600 feet. The foot-hills around the base of the mountain are covered with Pine (*Pinus Massoniana*), Cypress (*Cupressus funebris*), and Oak (*Quercus serrata*). The sides of the streams which meander among these hills are clothed with Alder (*Alnus cremastogyne*), *Pterocarya stenoptera*, and the curious *Camptotheca acuminata*. Around the temples and farmsteads Nanmu and tall-growing Bamboos abound ; on the more exposed hillsides the climbing fern *Gleichenia linearis* forms impenetrable thickets. and *Onychium japonicum*, *Melastoma candida*, *Mussœnda pubescens*, are common road-side plants. At 3000 feet all these plants drop out and give place to others. *Cunninghamia lanceolata*, which occurs sparingly in the valleys, gradually increases in number, and between 2500 and 4500 feet large areas are covered solely with this invaluable Conifer. Apart from the Cunninghamia, the family of *Lauraceœ* forms, between 2000 and 5000 feet, fully 75 per cent. of the arborescent vegetation. This " Laurel zone," as it may be termed, is composed chiefly of evergreen trees and shrubs, the genera Machilus, Lindera, and Litsea being exceptionally rich in species. Within this zone also occur the following interesting monotypic trees : Tapiscia, Carrieria, Itoa, Emmenopterys, and Idesia. The evergreen *Viburnum coriaceum*, with blue-black fruits, and five species of evergreen Barberries are also found here.

In ascending any high mountain, more especially in these latitudes, it is most instructive and interesting to note the aggressiveness of the temperate flora. Mount Omei offers special facilities for studying this phenomenon. Everything around us looks so smiling that all nature seems to be at peace. In these days, however, every one is alive to the fact that a stern and relentless war of conquest is being continually waged on all sides, and that every inch of ground is contested. It is well that plants cannot speak, or the exultations of the victors and the groans of the vanquished would be too much for humanity to bear ! But to note the struggle : The large-leaved Cornel (*Cornus macrophylla*) manages to extend its area nearly to the base of the mountain, being closely attended by several species of Maple, among which *Acer Davidii*, with white-striped bark, is particularly prominent. A Black Birch (*Betula luminifera*), several species of Viburnum, Pyrus, Malus, Rubus, and Prunus are also well to the fore ; but it is in the Hinterland (4500 to 5500 feet) that the main battle between the zones is fought. This narrow belt is extraordinarily rich in woody plants. Of those peculiar to it I may mention *Pterostyrax hispidus, Pterocarya Delavayi, Euptelea pleiosperma, Decaisnea Fargesii*, Horse Chestnut (*Æsculus Wilsonii*), and the monotypic genera Tetracentron, Emmenopterys, and Davidia. At least five species of Maple occur with many fine specimens of each. Several species of Evonymus, Holbœllia, Actinidia, and Holly (*Ilex*) are also common. The bulk of the *Lauraceæ* have given up the struggle, their place being taken by Evergreen Oak and Castanopsis. In this belt monkeys are common, and are fond of the blue pod-like fruit of the Decaisnea, the shining black, flattened seeds of which, however, I noticed they cannot digest.

On clearing a dense thicket and emerging on to a narrow

ridge, 6100 feet above sea-level, a magnificent view presented itself. Above towered gigantic limestone cliffs nearly a mile high ; below spread valleys and plains filled with a dense, fleecy cumulus, through which the peaks of mountains peered like rocky islands from the ocean's bed ; to the westward the mighty snowclad ranges of the Thibetan border, 80 miles distant as the crow flies, presented a magnificent panorama stretching northward and southward as far as the eye could range. The contrast between the floral zones was equally startling and impressive. Below, until lost in the clouds, was a mass of rich, sombre, green vegetation ; above were autumnal tints of every hue, from pale yellow to the richest shades of crimson, relieved by clumps of dark green Silver Fir. The whole scene was bathed in sunlight, a gentle zephyr stirred the air, and gorgeous butterflies flitted here and there seemingly unconscious of winter's near approach. The stillness and quiet was most solemn, and was broken only by the warbling of an occasional songster in some adjacent tree or bush. It was indeed a never-to-be-forgotten scene !

At 6200 feet the Cunninghamia gives up the fight, having struggled nobly until reduced to the dimensions of an insignificant shrub. A Silver Fir (*Abies Delavayi*) next assumes the sway, and right royally does it deserve the sceptre, for no more handsome Conifer exists in all the Far East ; its large, erect, symmetrical cones are violet-black in colour and are usually borne in greatest profusion on the topmost branches. The temples on the higher parts of the mountain are constructed almost entirely of the timber of this tree. It is first met with on Mount Omei, at 6000 feet, at which altitude it is of no great size and unattractive in appearance ; at 6500 feet it is a handsome tree. It is, however, between 8500 and 10,000 feet that this Silver Fir reaches its maximum size. In this belt hundreds of trees 80 to 100 feet tall, with a girth of 10 to 12 feet, are to be found. Hemlock Spruce (*Tsuga yunnanensis*) occurs sparingly, but always in the form of large and shapely trees. An occasional Yew tree (*Taxus cuspidata*, var. *chinensis*) and, on the summit, dwarf Juniper (*J. squamata*) complete the list of Conifers growing on the higher parts of this mountain. The unspeakably magnificent autumnal tints already referred to are principally due to numerous species of Viburnum, Vitis, Malus, Sorbus, Pyrus, and Acer, together with *Enkianthus deflexus*, which surpasses all in the richness of its autumn tints of orange and crimson.

At 6200 feet the ascent becomes increasingly difficult, and having surmounted a formidable flight of steps, 800 feet high, we were glad to rest at the temple of Hsih-hsiang-chüh. All the temples on Mount Omei occupy lovely and romantic situations, but none more so than this, which has one side flush with the edge of a precipice, and the others sheltered by a grove of Silver Fir. The hospitable priests regaled us with tea and sweetmeats and entertained us with much that was curious and amusing. They claimed that it was at this particular place that P'u-hsien Pu'ssa alighted from his elephant to allow the footsore animal to bathe in a near-by pool ; the spot to-day is marked by a cistern.

Immediately on leaving this temple two steep flights of steps, followed by a slight descent, led us to a small wooded plateau which shelves away from a vertical precipice. Hereabouts *Sorbus munda*, with white fruits, was a most conspicuous shrub. A climbing Hydrangea (*H. anomala*) reaches to the top of the tallest trees. Several other species of Hydrangea grow epiphytically on the larger trees and so also do two or three species of Sorbus. Rhododendrons are fairly abundant, more especially near the edge of the precipice. The first few Rhododendron bushes were noted growing at 4800 feet, and altogether I gathered thirteen species on this mountain. But as compared with the region to the westward Mount Omei is poor in Rhododendrons. The same is true of Primulas, of which four species only were met with.

At 9000 feet the most difficult stairway of all occurs, and I was fairly exhausted when the top of it was reached at 10,100 feet. Winter had laid his stern hand heavily here, and most of the woody plants were leafless. At 10,000 feet Bamboo-scrub puts in an appearance and increases as the summit is neared until finally it crowds out nearly everything else and forms an impenetrable jungle about 4 to 6 feet high.

From the top of the last stairway an easy pathway of planking leads to the summit, which we reached just as the sun was setting behind the snowclad ranges of the Thibetan border.

A perfect night succeeded the day, and our hopes were high for the morrow. Alas! a thick fog and a drizzle of rain was what we awoke to find. A terrible precipice in front and a more or less shelving away behind was all we could make out of the lay of the land. To find out what the summit is really like, a long walk was undertaken, but resulted in little beyond a thorough drenching. The mountain-top is somewhat uneven, sloping away from the cliffs by a fairly easy gradient. It is everywhere covered with a dense scrub, composed mainly of dwarf Bamboo, with bushes of Willow, Birch, Sorbus, Barberry, Rhododendron, Spiræa, and *Rosa omeiensis* interspersed. Near the watercourses these shrubs are more particularly abundant. Trailing over the scrub *Clematis montana*, var. *Wilsonii*, is very common. At least five species of Rhododendron grow on the summit, but, judging from the paucity of fruits, they flower but sparingly. In places sheltered from the winds fine groves of Silver Fir remain, but in the more fully exposed sites these trees are very stunted and weather-beaten. The dwarf Juniper, with twisted, gnarled stems, is also plentiful in rocky places.

Around the temples small patches of cabbage, turnips, and Irish potato are cultivated, and several favourite medicines are grown in quantity, such as Rhubarb, "Huang-lien" (*Coptis chinensis*), "Tang-shên," and "Tang-kuei."

Here and there on the mountain we passed hucksters' stalls, on which various local products were exposed for sale. These consist chiefly of medicines, porcupine quills, crystals of felspar, sweet tea, and pilgrim staves. The latter, made from the wood of an Alder (*Alnus cremastogyne*), are carved in representation of fantastic dragons and Buddhas. The sweet tea is a peculiarity of Mount Omei, being prepared from the leaves of *Viburnum theiferum*.

CHAPTER XVIII

THROUGH THE LAOLIN (WILDERNESS)

NARRATIVE OF A JOURNEY FROM KIATING TO MALIE, VIA WA-WU SHAN

LEAVING the city of Kiating on 4th September 1908, we followed the main road to Yachou Fu and stayed for the night at Kiakiang Hsien, a small city, altitude 1200 feet, 70 li from our starting-place. It had rained heavily in the early morning, but cleared just before we set out, and was cool and fine, although dull the whole day. The road is broad, mostly well paved, and leads through a rich and highly cultivated region. Around Kiating the rice had been harvested, much of the land reploughed, and another crop, chiefly buckwheat and turnips, planted. A few miles beyond this city, however, the rice crop was not so forward, and though a portion was being reaped the bulk would not be ripe for some weeks.

Around the margins of rice fields trees for the culture of insect white-wax are abundantly planted. Pollarded Ash (*Fraxinus chinensis*) were chiefly noticeable, but in places trees of Privet (*Ligustrum lucidum*) are used for this industry. Much of the wax had been collected, but in one place we were fortunate enough to witness the process and obtain photographs. (In Vol. II., Chapter X., this interesting industry is fully described.) Sericulture was very much in evidence, and all the alluvial flats are planted with Mulberry trees, but trees of Cudrania are not common. In this region in particular the silkworms are fed on the leaves of both these trees ; the people claim that this mixed diet results in a stronger kind of silk.

The Szechuan Banyan (*Ficus infectoria*) is the most striking tree hereabouts ; its widespreading umbrageous head usually shelters some wayside shrine. Venders of cakes, pea-nuts,

and fruit are also to be found occupying some temporary
stall under these beautiful trees.   The road skirts the sides of
low hills of red sandstone for considerable distances, and is
mainly parallel with, and in full view of, the Ya River.   The
hills are clad with common Pine (*Pinus Massoniana*), Cypress
(*Cupressus funebris*), a jungle-growth of low shrubs, and the
scandent *Gleichenia linearis*.   Small trees of Oak and Sweet
Chestnut and larger ones of Alder are also common.   Groves
of tall-growing Bamboos, of course, are everywhere abundant.
In the sandstone cliffs are very many square-mouthed Mantzu
caves ; the scenery is distinctly pretty and pleasing.

We left Kiakiang at 6.30 a.m. the following day, and
quickly reached a ferry, where we crossed over the Ya River,
a broad, stony, shallow stream.   Quite near this place are
two really fine and very large old temples known as Ping-
ling-ssu and Kuei-ling-ssu.   The first named, in particular,
contains some very fine idols ; both, however, have a very
deserted and neglected appearance, and give the impression of
" glories departed."   The sandstone cliffs at the ferry are
highly sculptured, but are rapidly weathering away, much
of the work being undecipherable and hidden by vegetation.

The li proved very long, and we did not reach Che-ho-kai
until 7 p.m., going steadily the whole day.   The distance is
80 li, and three ferries, which hinder considerably, have to be
crossed.   Near the city of Hungya Hsien, which we sighted
in the late afternoon, large plantations of Ash trees for the
culture of insect white-wax abound.   Rice is everywhere
the great crop ; the yield was heavier than usual, and the
people were busy reaping and threshing it.   Fine Banyan
trees are plentiful, Alder is abundant, and handsome Nanmu
trees are not infrequent around temples and houses.   We
also noted a small tree of the Hog-plum (*Spondias axillaris*)
bearing quantities of its oblong, yellow, edible fruits.   The
vegetation generally is similar to that around Kiating, but
the Chinese Fir (*Cunninghamia lanceolata*) is more common
and Pine and Cypress less so.

Che-ho-kai, alt. 1400 feet, is a large and important
market village, situated on the right bank of the Ya River.
The inn is very fair.   I occupied a large room overlooking

the river, but, as I discovered later, with a piggery and latrine below.

The next day we began our real journey. Instead of following the main route to Yachou Fu by crossing over the river, we ascended the right bank for a couple of li beyond Che-ho-kai, and then crossed a considerable affluent of the main stream. Rafts of good-sized poles of Chinese Fir descend this tributary from Liu ch'ang, a market village, and ordinary bamboo-rafts ascend to this place. After climbing to the tops of some low hills the road zigzags around considerably through fields of rice and wooded knolls, and affords an unusually fine view of the Ya Valley. Passing the tiny market village of Tung-to ch'ang we reached Kuang-yin pu (or ch'ang) at 10.45 a.m., having covered 30 li.

From Kuang-yin pu we engaged in a steep ascent over a well-paved if narrow road, and after four hours' climbing reached the summit of the Fung-hoa-tsze, alt. 4100 feet. This ridge is of red sandstone throughout, and is well timbered with small trees of the Chinese Fir. This conifer abounds on the slopes flanking the roadway to the top of the pass and forms pure woods. Though the timber is of no great size, the area covered with this tree compares most favourably with any other I have seen. Where timber is scarce the jungle growth is very thick, warm-temperate in character, and of little interest.

Descending, at first steadily, through knolls covered with Chinese Fir and the densest fern jungle composed of *Gleichenia linearis* I have ever seen, we soon reached an area under maize. From this point a steep descent led to a cultivated flat, then, after winding through rice fields with tiny wooded hillocks on all sides, we crossed a neck and entered the hamlet of Liang-ch'a Ho, alt. 2350 feet, and 65 long li from our starting-point. We found very decent accommodation, all things considered, but mosquitoes were most unpleasantly numerous and hungry.

It rained very heavily during the early morning of the next day, so we delayed our starting until eleven o'clock. We found all the streams in flood, and to cross one larger than the ordinary we had to engage local assistance. After a

rather steep ascent of 500 feet from Liang-ch'a Ho we crossed
a narrow ridge and descended to the market village of N'gan
ch'ang.   This is a poor place, partly in ruins, situated on
the right bank of the stream which unites with the Ya Ho,
2 li above Che-ho-kai.   On leaving N'gan ch'ang we ascended
the right bank of the stream to Pao-tien-pa, alt. 2600 feet.
This scattered hamlet possesses no inn, but we found quarters
in a schoolhouse devoted to the "New Learning" (*i.e.*
Western Knowledge).   A scholar from this place had recently
gone to Japan to increase his store of knowledge, and the
dominie was very proud of this success.   This hamlet boasts
a ruined pavilion, a temple, and a stone gateway, evident
signs of former prosperity.

During the short journey of 25 li the road led through
fields of rice, bounded by wooded knolls and sandstone
bluffs.   The flora was of little interest ; *Idesia polycarpa* and
Kalopanax ricinifolium are fairly common in places, but the
trees are of small size.   Alongside the ditches and roadway
the handsome *Lycoris aurea* abounds, and the golden-yellow
flowers with recurved, wrinkled, perianth-segments made
a gay display.   Its red-flowered counterpart, *L. radiata*, also
occurs, but is much less frequent.   The local name for this
plant is " Lao-wa-suan," which signifies " Crow's foot Onion,"
a very apt term in so far as the shape of the flower is concerned.

The following day was fine but hot, and more or less
cloudy.   With only 35 li to cover, we journeyed slowly after
making an early morning start.   A moderately steep ascent
of 15 li brought us to the summit of the Tsao shan, alt.
4100 feet.   This ridge is covered with an uninteresting jungle
of coarse grass and scrub, with odd trees of Chinese Fir, but
in the ascent I gathered specimens of a fine new species of
Castanopsis.

From the summit of Tsao shan we obtained our first view
of the Wa-wu shan, an extraordinary-looking massive mountain,
singularly like Wa shan in contour, resembling a huge ark
floating above clouds of mist.   Following an easy path which
led through fine woods of Evergreen Oak, Nanmu, and
Castanopsis we descended to Ma-chiao-kou, where there is an

iron suspension bridge over a wide torrent. This hamlet consists of one large house and a mill, where a specially good and tough bamboo paper is made, which is used at Yachou Fu for wrapping up brick tea. The bamboo is obtained from the surrounding mountains, and is a species with dull green culms about the thickness of a man's thumb, growing 12 to 15 feet tall. On crossing over the bridge, I photographed a fine specimen of *Alniphyllum Fortunei*, one of the rarest of Chinese trees. A short steep ascent, then a rather drawn-out descent, ultimately brought us to the banks of a clear-water stream of considerable size, which we crossed by an iron suspension bridge 50 yards long, and soon reached the market village of Ping-ling-shih, alt. 2900 feet. This is a small and dirty place of about 50 houses, situated on the left bank of a stream which joins the Ya Ho, some 10 li below Yachou Fu. It is in Hung-ya Hsien, in full view of Mount Wa-wu, and the most important place in the Laolin (Wilderness), as this region is denominated.

The flora of the day's journey was rather more interesting than heretofore. Wooded knolls are the rule. Evergreen trees, more especially Oak and Castanopsis, are very general, and of large size. I gathered four species belonging to the latter genus, all handsome umbrageous trees. A fine specimen of the curious Hazel-nut (*Corylus heterophylla*, var. *crista-galli*), 60 feet tall, 5 feet in girth, was one of the most interesting trees noted. The nut in this variety is hidden in a crested cup. The Chinese Fir is most abundant, being the only Conifer met with. The absence of Pine and Cypress since leaving the valley of the Ya River has been a most remarkable feature. The country generally is very broken, the sandstone bluffs bold, and clad with the usual jungle growth wherever trees are sparse.

In order to ascend Mount Wa-wu from Ping-ling-shih it was necessary for us to make a detour from our intended route. The summit was said to be 70 li distant, but, owing to the steep and difficult road, two days are required to cover this. We left behind all our spare gear and arranged what it was necessary to take into light loads. The road on clearing Ping-ling-shih ascends a rock-strewn tributary of the main stream, through a region given over to rice fields and cultivation generally.   At eleven o'clock in the forenoon after traversing 30 li we reached the large temple of Tsung-tung-che, alt. 4000 feet, situated at the foot of the real ascent of Mount Wa-wu.   This temple is built of wood, very old, and in poor repair.   A priest and one attendant were in charge ; the rooms, though dingy and damp, were alive with fleas.   But since there is no other accommodation between this place and the summit it was necessary to make the best of things.   I had my bed arranged in a large hall where three huge images of Buddha looked down benignly upon me.   During the morning occasional showers fell, but in the afternoon a steady downpour set in, which added to the cheerlessness of our roomy but dilapidated quarters.

Just before reaching the temple we passed through the hamlet of Tung-ch'ang Ho, where there is a very large iron foundry employing a considerable number of men.   Iron ore is common in the surrounding mountains, and costs 12,000 to 13,000 cash per 10,000 catties.   Every 10,000 catties of ore yields about 4000 catties of pig iron, which was said to be of good quality, and sells for 2500 to 3000 cash per picul of 100 catties.   The smelting is done in furnaces heated by charcoal, which costs at the foundry 12 to 13 cash per catty.   Most of the smelting is done during the winter, the summer months being given to the collecting of charcoal and iron ore.   Large iron cooking-pans are also made here in considerable quantities.

Copper is also found in the same range as the iron ore, but on the opposite side.   Formerly it was worked and smelted here, the name Tung-ch'ang signifying " copper-shop " or factory.   From what I could learn the industry was abandoned some ten years or more ago when copper mining became a Government monopoly controlled by the officials.   The people told me that they could not produce copper on paying lines under Tls. 35·00 to Tls. 36·00 per picul   The officials would only pay Tls. 28·00, consequently copper smelting was given up and replaced by that of iron.   A hard, smokeless coal occurs in the neighbourhood, but is not much used.   Altogether, this Tung-ch'ang Ho with its iron foundry, coal mines, and abandoned copper workings constitutes an interesting mining centre.

Around the temple are many fine trees of Castanopsis,

and the finest specimen of the interesting monotypic *Tapiscia sinensis* I have seen.   This tree is fully 80 feet tall, with a girth of 12 feet.   Many fine trees of the Kuei-hwa (*Osmanthus fragrans*) are planted in the temple grounds, and were in full flower, scenting the atmosphere all around.   Near streams Alder (*Alnus cremastogyne*) is abundant, and on the hills the Chinese Fir is common.

It rained heavily all night, and a drizzle fell when we set out next morning at 6.30 a.m.   This drizzle developed into a steady downpour as we advanced, and continued with increased violence the whole day.   The road is atrocious from the very beginning.   For the first 2500 feet there is a semblance of a track, some of it being made by laying pieces of split timber crosswise.   The next 2500 feet is a rough scramble upwards through cane-brake and brushwood until the summit is reached.   The ascent is up the north-north-east angle of the mountain, and though never really dangerous is always very difficult.   We dragged ourselves upward by grasping shrubs, and it was a marvel to me how the coolies with their loads managed to overcome the ascent.   The foothold was precarious, and it was often a case of one foot forward and two backward !

On reaching the summit we followed a winding path for 12 li to the temple of Kwanyin-ping, alt. 9100 feet.   The mountain-top is undulating, park-like, and covered with an impenetrable jungle of Bamboo-scrub about 6 feet tall, arising from a floor of Sphagnum moss.   Silver Fir (*Abies Delavayi*), called Lien sha, *i.e.* Cold Fir (signifying that it is only found in cold regions), is scattered through in quantity, but I saw no really handsome trees, all of them showing the effects of wind-storms, age, and decay.   The pathway across the summit is about 2½ feet wide, paved throughout with split timbers, though here and there fallen Silver Fir trees, slightly notched and flattened, have been utilized in making this roadway.   We passed three temples in absolute ruins, but saw no signs of life of any description.   The heavy rain and dense mists obscured all views, and I saw nothing of the country or scenery except what was encompassed in a perspective of 30 yards.   Drenched to the skin but mildly describes the plight in which we reached the temple. Our gear arrived equally wet some two hours afterwards, and we were some time getting things dry and shipshape.

The temple of Kwanyin-ping is very large, with many outhouses, and is built entirely of wood. It contains many scores of idols, but is in a poor state of repair. The main road hither is from Yungching Hsien, distant 120 li. During the Chinese fifth and sixth moons (June, July) some two to three thousand pilgrims visit this temple, but for the rest of the year it has scarcely a visitant. The priests reside at Yungching Hsien except at the pilgrim season, a novice being left in charge. This novice lives all alone, without even a dog for a companion. As a reward he receives 1½ catties of rice per diem as rations and 2000 cash (say, half a crown) per annum salary ! In spite of his lonely life, and he has been in charge for three years, this novice was a very cheery person. He moved around quickly, had a ready smile, and chanted hymns and prayers wherever he went. He speedily made a fire for us to dry ourselves and clothing, and made himself generally useful. His cheery influence made itself felt, and my men soon ceased their grumbling over the vileness of the road and my madness in wanting to visit such a place. The novice told us that the first temple was built on this mountain during the Eastern Han Dynasty (A.D. 25–87). At one time there were as many as 40 temples here, but during Ming times the majority were destroyed, and the temple ornaments melted down. To-day there are only two in any sense habitable, and in one only is a man kept the year round. This same authority vouchsafed the information that the heavy rains were due to the felling of timber ; the country folk holding this view were opposed to further cutting, but the Magistrate at Yungching Hsien pooh-poohed the idea, and insisted on the slaughter being continued, with the result that torrential rains fell every day except in winter, when snow took their place.

The next morning opened dull and threatening, but eventually the sun came out and we enjoyed a fine day. The temple stands in Hungya Hsien, and is situated on the edge of a precipice. The views looking north-east over the Ya Valley and west to the Thibetan alps are very fine ; some almost vertical limestone cliffs near by the temple are covered in a remarkable manner with Silver Fir. The whole surroundings are wildly romantic, and it is small wonder that the place is deemed sacred and holy.

Wa-wu shan or Wa shan, as it is much more frequently but erroneously called, is one of three sacred mountains, forming the three corners of and enclosing a triangular tract of wild, sparsely inhabited country known as the Laolin (Wilderness). On even the most recent maps the term Lolo is written across this region, but as a matter of fact no Lolos live here. The few people found here are Chinese—peasants, charcoal-burners, miners, and medicine-gatherers. The other two mountains, Omei shan and Wa shan, have been described by former travellers, but, with the possible exception of some Roman Catholic priest, my visit was the first undertaken by any foreigner to the summit of Wa-wu shan.

Like its sister mountains, Wa-wu is a gigantic upthrust of hard limestone, but of lesser altitude than they, being only 9200 feet above sea-level. It is a huge oblong mass, composed of a series of vertical cliffs 2000 feet and more sheer, reared on a base of red sandstone rocks. The summit is flat with sand and mudstone shales scattered about, and is said to be 60 li long by 40 li wide, but this is an exaggeration—30 li by 15 li being, probably, nearer the truth. Its appearance from a distance has already been given, and the nearer the approach the more impressive become the perpendicular walls of rock. The similarity in appearance between this mountain and the real Wa shan has also been alluded to, and I strongly suspect that the mountain seen from the summit of Omei shan and called Wa shan is really this Wa-wu shan. Their extraordinary vertical sides and flat summits make these two peaks unique among the mountains of Western China.

From a botanical standpoint Mount Wa-wu proved disappointing. In the first place, its altitude was some 1500 less than I had hoped for. Secondly, all the mixed timber has been felled for making charcoal and other purposes, leaving only a dense shrubbery in which variety is not great. Thirdly, the paucity of *Coniferæ* on the summit other than Silver Fir and the impenetrable thickets of slender Bamboos which render any extended exploration impossible. The flora generally is that common to every mountain in this region of similar altitude, but, of course, it has a certain number of species peculiarly its own in the same way as every other mountain in China has. The outstanding feature is its wealth of Bamboo-scrub ; its speciality, the abundant carpet of Sphagnum moss on the summit. This moss occurs on Wa shan and virtually on all the other mountains of this region, between 8000 and 11,500 feet, but nowhere have I seen it so luxuriantly plentiful as on Wa-wu shan.

The day being fine and clear I obtained good views of everything. The summit is made up of low, wooded hillocks, tiny dales, and glades. Here and there it is a morass, and on one occasion from such a place we flushed a Solitary Snipe. The feathery Bamboo-culms are very beautiful, and the scattered, often sentinel-like, old trees of Silver Fir quite picturesque. A few trees of Hemlock Spruce occur, but their number is infinitesimal. Some of the Silver Fir were 100 feet tall, and 10 to 12 feet in girth, but all such trees contain much dead wood. Here and there saplings are common, but they can scarcely compete with the Bamboo in the struggle for possession. At one time Davidia (both hairy and glabrous-leaved forms), Tetracentron, Magnolia, various species of Acer, Pyrus, Castanopsis, Evergreen Oak, and *Lauraceæ* covered the lesser slopes, but, to-day, these are all represented only by bushes which have sprung up from the felled trees. Rhododendrons are fairly numerous, and I noted about ten species. One of these forms a tree 25 feet tall and 3 to 4 feet in girth. (It proved to be new, and has been named in honour of the Rev. Harry Openshaw, of Yachou Fu.) Various Araliads are plentiful, and were mostly in ripe fruit. The Chinese Fir ascends to 4500 feet altitude, and very few of the evergreens other than Rhododendron extend above 6000 feet. Herbs, of course, occur, but none of any great value or interest.

A local industry of considerable importance at the season of the year my visit occurred, and for six weeks previously, is the collecting and preparing of young bamboo shoots for culinary purposes. The species in request is one having culms the thickness of a man's thumb, and growing 10 feet tall.

The young shoots are culled when 8 to 12 inches above the ground, stripped of their sheaths and apices, leaving only the white, brittle succulent central part. These are boiled in water, then removed, suspended from rafters in a close chamber and dried by means of heat from steady-burning fires fed from locally made briquettes. When thoroughly dry they are packed in bales and carried to Chengtu and other cities, where they are esteemed a great delicacy. We saw fully a score of rude shanties where this industry was in full swing. On the spot the raw shoots are bought for 6 cash per 16-oz. catty, the collecting being done by contract. The prepared article, known as " Tsin-tzu," sells at Ping-ling-shih for 8 to 9 Tls. per 100 catties of 20 oz. each. This region is famed far and wide for its product of dried bamboo shoots, and the industry affords employment for a large number of people.

Many wild animals, including Budorcas, Serow, Goral, Leopard, and Bear were said to occur on Wa-wu, but hunting them would be almost an impossibility. We saw no animals of any kind, but I do not doubt the reports given as to their presence on this jungle-clad mountain.

A day sufficed for our investigations, and leaving the next morning about nine o'clock, a hard day's march brought us back to Ping-ling-shih at 5.45 p.m.

Our object being to traverse this Laolin country through its greatest width to some point in the valley of the Tung River, we readjusted our loads, and the following day continued our march. Crossing the tributary stream by a rickety iron suspension bridge, we soon left Ping-ling-shih behind. The path ascends the right bank of the main stream frequently high above its waters, and at times some little distance removed. As soon as it enters limestone country the river becomes gorged. The li were long, the road rough, and it took us five hours to cover 30 li to Yüeh-ch'a-ping. This place consists of a single house, situated near where the stream bifurcates. One branch and a companion roadway leads off in a south-easterly direction, and by this track it is possible to reach Huang-mu ch'ang. The path we followed ascends the branch which swings round from the south-west, skirting the base of Wa-wu shan. After crossing a cultivated shoulder we plunged into a deep, narrow gorge, traversing a difficult roadway usually high up above the stream. The scenery is very fine—steep cliffs, either bare or clothed with shrubs, on every side. Journeying slowly we reached the solitary house at Chang-ho-pa, alt. 4000 feet, about 5 p.m., having covered 50 li.

During the day's march we saw a number of interesting trees, and obtained specimens and photographs. *Carrieria calycina*, a widespreading flat-topped tree, is very common in rocky places by the stream-side, and was laden with its torpedo-shaped, velvety-grey fruit which was not ripe. The Tapiscia is fairly numerous, but the trees are of no great size. Perhaps the most noteworthy tree of this region is *Meliosma Kirkii*, which has a shapely port, rigid branches, and handsome pinnate leaves, 2 feet long. Evergreen Oak, various *Lauraceæ*, tall-growing Bamboos, and a Fan Palm (*Trachycarpus excelsus*) are abundant, denoting a mild, moist climate. The Chinese Fir is the only Conifer. The quantity of this useful tree and the many fine and shapely specimens were among the leading features of this trip. We had left rice behind at last, and entered a region where only maize is grown. Every available bit of land is under cultivation, but the district is very sparsely populated. A certain amount of tea is grown around Ping-ling-shih, but the industry is of little importance commercially.

The people at Chang-ho-pa informed us that the road before us was much worse than that which we had traversed. For the first 10 li after leaving our lodgings I thought they had dissembled, but afterwards the truth of their statement was only too evident The stream flows through a narrow, wild gorge or succession of gorges ; the road is either some hundreds of feet above the stream, or down by the water's edge. The " ups and downs " repeat themselves with monotonous and irritating frequency. The path is very much overgrown with weeds and brush, always very narrow, the ascents and descents precipitous and difficult. It is misleading and foolish to term it a " road." Goats would make a better pathway, did they travel it frequently !

The scenery is grand, though mists and a drizzle of rain did their best to rob us of its enjoyment. The cliffs are in the main clothed with shrubby vegetation, but alongside the stream large trees are common. The climate is evidently very moist and warm, since broad-leaved evergreens abound. Perhaps the most common shrub or small tree is a Walnut or Chinese Butternut (*Juglans cathayensis*), which has six to twelve fruits arranged in a raceme, and leaves up to a yard in length. The Horse Chestnut (*Æsculus Wilsonii*), Yellow-wood (*Cladrastis sinensis*), Hornbeam, and various Maples are among the more interesting trees hereabouts. Clearings and abandoned cultivated areas are overgrown with the handsome *Anemone vitifolia*, var. *alba*, which was 4 to 5 feet tall, and bore myriads of large attractive flowers. This herb made a wonderful display, and I do not remember having seen it so luxuriant elsewhere in my travels. Beneath cliffs dripping with moisture, Begonias, Impatiens, Ferns, and various *Cyrtandreæ* in masses made pretty effects. The Chinese Fir ceases at 4800 feet altitude, but limestone country is not to its liking, and the trees quickly become scarce on quitting the red sandstone.

Houses and patches of cultivation are few and far between, but it is surprising that any should be found in such a precipitous country. We put up for the night at one of the three small houses which collectively form the hamlet of Peh-sha Ho, altitude 5000 feet, 40 li from Chang-ho-pa. The house is built on a steep bank, overlooking a point where the stream divides, the larger branch flowing from a southerly direction.

On leaving Peh-sha Ho we headed for the source of the lesser of the two streams—a mere mountain torrent. Our difficulty all day was in discerning the track and keeping to it. I lost it early in the morning, and wasted two hours in a jungle of Bamboo ; my Boy had the same misfortune in the afternoon. The collecting of bamboo shoots is an industry here as on the other side of Wa-wu, and the tracks made by men engaged in this are many. The path we endeavoured to follow was frequently less well-defined than these tracks and, moreover, was overgrown with vegetation. It crossed the torrent many times, but the fords were difficult to discover. We passed neither house nor person, and perforce had to explore our own route. It rained heavily the whole day, increasing our difficulties and discomforts.

Our objective for the day was some lead mines, but early in the afternoon it became evident that we could not reach them before night was well advanced.   Darkness overtook us, and we had visions of spending the night in the woods, which bound the torrent ;   suddenly, however, the welcome glare from a charcoal-burner's hut gladdened our hearts.   Scrambling somehow down the steep slope, and across the torrent, we quickly reached this haven of shelter.   It proved a wretched hovel, but the warmth from the charcoal pit was comforting since we, and all our belongings, were wet through.   My bed was fixed up in a shed where prepared charcoal was stored, the men taking possession of the hut, thankful that a refuge of some sort had been found.

Much of the day's journey had consisted in struggling through brush and Bamboo, and by way of variety wading the torrent was thrown in.   Whenever the mists lifted, cliffs and crags, densely covered with vegetation, were to be seen on all sides.   The flora is apparently rich, but it was impossible for us to investigate it.   All the larger trees have been cut down and converted into charcoal.   Davidia, Tetracentron, Cercidiphyllum, and *Cornus sinensis* are common as bushy trees by the wayside ;   Maples are plentiful, and stout climbers, such as Actinidia, Clematoclethra, and Holbœllia are rampant.

Two men were in charge of the charcoal pits.   They told us the place is called Tan-yao-tzu, and that we had only covered 30 li !   All the hardwood trees having been felled they are now forced to use the softwood of Silver Fir and Hemlock Spruce, which, they said, grow in quantity on the higher crags. The charcoal is all used for smelting lead at the mines.

The roof of the shed leaked freely, but an arrangement of oil-sheets kept my bed fairly dry, and I enjoyed a good night's sleep.   Awaking soon after daybreak we found it was still raining.   Leaving the hut (alt. 7250 feet), we crossed two branches of the stream and scrambled up the mountain-side to rejoin the track.   Soon afterwards we entered a narrow scrub-clad valley, at the head of which a precipitous, circuitous ascent brought us to the top of a ridge where the lead mines are situated.   In the ascent, *Rhododendron Hanceanum* and two other species are particularly abundant, forming thickets ;

Lonicera deflexicalyx is also plentiful, and was a wealth of orange-coloured fruit. On humus-clad rocks a pretty little prostrate Gaultheria with snow-white fruits is common. The hovels at the lead mines are miserable structures, but we were glad of their shelter from the rain and cold. The whole mountain appears to be full of lead, the ore (galena) being very rich. Well-shored adits are carried for considerable distances into the mountain-side, and the ore is brought out in baskets fitted on runners. The galena is pounded by hand labour into small particles ; the lead is obtained by levigation and stored in large wooden vats. Subsequently it is melted into large oblong ingots, in which form it is carried to Chengtu and Sui Fu. The freight down to the nearest waterway is very considerable. Lead has been worked in this neighbourhood for many years, and the mines are owned by a man who resides at Kiating. The labourers are paid 1800 cash per month. We were told that the previous year's output was 10,000 catties, but little reliance can be placed on this statement. Such an output is very small, but the primitive methods employed are slow and expensive. For smelting and other purposes the mountain has been denuded of its timber, and is now in its upper parts a grassy, scrub-clad wilderness. I made the altitude of the mines 9400 feet, that is to say, 2000 feet above the charcoal pits whence the fuel necessary to melt down the lead is drawn. The sides of the workings are bare and gravelly, and were covered with rich yellow flowers of a Sedum-like plant, which was new and is unknown to me.

On leaving the lead mines and crossing a slight dip we reached a babbling brook which forms the roadway for the next few li. On deserting this we made a very steep ascent to the top of a grassy ridge, alt. 10,400 feet, only to find that a deep ravine separated us from the watershed proper. After a most precipitous descent of 1600 feet over a rocky and difficult path, we reached the bed of a torrent, which I take to be the stream we noted at Peh-sha Ho flowing from a southerly direction.

On reaching this stream the rain ceased, the mists cleared away rapidly, and the sun showed itself for the first time in four days. The surrounding country is savage, and is made up of a magnificent series of limestone cliffs, their steepest crags clothed with weather-worn trees of Silver Fir. Everywhere else the trees have been cut down.

From the torrent we struggled up a severe ascent of 1000 feet, and reached the summit of the watershed, alt. 10,100 feet. Here we got a very fine view of the country, which is simply a succession of cliffs and crags capped by rugged trees of Silver Fir, and with a dense growth of broad-leaved trees in the more inaccessible pockets.

The rest of the day's journey was all downhill over a vile pathway. We reached the tiny hamlet of Yang-tientsze, alt. 7600 feet, at 6 p.m., having occupied eleven hours in covering 30 li. Two men who carried our food-stuffs arrived just as darkness closed in, and reported the rest of our gear far behind. Our lodgings were poor enough in all conscience, but most acceptable after such a fatiguing tramp. After dinner I tried to sleep on an oil-sheet spread over one of the native beds, but was soon discovered by hungry, tormenting fleas, and, tired as I was, sleep proved impossible. About one o'clock my bed and some other gear arrived. The carriers had been forced to wait after darkness fell until the moon was up in order to see the path. I could not complain; they had done their best over a most heart-breaking road. The rest of our loads turned up soon after daybreak, and we left Yang-tientsze at 7.30 a.m. Descending by a comparatively easy road for 30 li we reached before noon the village of Malie, alt. 5300 feet, a very poor place, situated on the main road between Omei Hsien and Fulin via Wa shan.

Thus had the Laolin been crossed from north-east to south-west, and, personally, I have no desire to repeat the journey. The continued rains increased considerably the difficulties of the bad roads and made what, under the most favourable weather conditions, must always be a fatiguing journey, an exceedingly arduous and miserable one. The rain and dense mists robbed the trip of its greatest charm, namely, the scenery. Except on odd occasions I saw nothing outside a radius of 50 yards. The unpropitious weather also prevented any investigation of the flora other than that alongside the pathway. In so far as it came under my observation this region possesses very little in the way of woody plants beyond what are common to the same altitude everywhere in western Szechuan.   For richness in species it does not compare favourably with Mount Omei or Mount Wa.   However, there are some points of interest.   The region evidently enjoys a warm, wet climate, and the belt of broad-leaved evergreens, especially Oak and *Lauraceæ*, extends to a greater altitude than usual. The abundance of Chinese Fir and such interesting trees as Davidia, Tetracentron, Cladrastis, Magnolia, Æsculus, Cercidi-phyllum, and Chinese Butternut (*Juglans cathayensis*) is perhaps the outstanding feature.   Strong-growing climbers such as Hol-bœllia, Actinidia, and Clematoclethra abound, and I obtained seeds of several species.   Many kinds of Sorbus with white, red, and purple fruits occur, and seeds of these were also secured. Honeysuckles, Brambles, and Rhododendrons are also abundant. The scarcity of Birch, Beech, deciduous Oak, and Sweet Chest-nut, and the entire absence of Pine, Cypress, and Poplar are marked features of the region.   Throughout the higher altitudes Silver Fir and Hemlock Spruce are the only Conifers, although in one place I thought I detected some Spruce trees high up on the cliffs.   I saw no fine trees of either of these Conifers ; all that now remain grow on the crags and other equally inaccessible places, and have suffered much from the winds and weather generally.   The jungle growth of Gleichenia on the sandstone, and the impenetrable Bamboo thickets everywhere between 6000 and 10,000 feet altitude, are the most striking floral characteristics of the entire region.   The mining in-dustries have been the cause of the wholesale felling of the timber.

The entire absence of decent roads, the sparse population, wretchedly poor accommodation, the savage cliffs, and jungle-clad mountain-sides sufficiently entitle this region to be termed " Laolin," *i.e.* a " Wilderness."

CHAPTER XIX

WA SHAN AND ITS FLORA

THE sister mountain to the sacred Omei is Wa shan, situated about long. 103° 14' E., lat. 29° 21' N., six days' journey (roughly 80 miles) from the city of Kiating. The intervening country is very rough, wild, and mountainous. The road is execrable. Baber, the first foreigner to visit and ascend this mountain, as well as Mount Omei, gives its altitude as 10,545 feet above the sea-level, 4560 feet above the neighbouring valleys. My readings were 11,250 feet above the sea, 5150 feet above the surrounding country. Allowing for error in the barometer, I think the mountain cannot be less than 11,000 feet. The flora—always a fair guide as to altitude—proves it to be higher than Mount Omei (10,800 feet) ; and this agrees with the opinion of the natives, who assert that it is the higher of the two mountains.

As seen from the top of Mount Omei it resembles a huge Noah's Ark, broadside on, perched high up amongst the clouds. Viewed from a near distance it is seen to consist of a succession of tiers of vertical limestone cliffs, only seriously broken at one point; with a peculiarly flat summit. From the hamlet of Ta-t'ien-ch'ih (6100 feet), which is situated in a depression at its base, the mountain is remarkably square looking, its four sides being more or less perpendicular. It appears to be no more than 2000 feet above the hamlet, and yet it is really 5000 feet higher. When it was first pointed out to me, 20 miles or so distant, I could not believe it was Wa shan—it looked so like a huge precipice, its massiveness belittling its height.

As already stated, the first foreigner to visit Wa shan was the late E. Colborne Baber, who made the ascent on 5th June 1878. The description of this mountain, given by him, is so accurate and beautiful that I cannot do better than quote it : " The upper storey of this most imposing mountain is a series of twelve or fourteen precipices, rising one above another, each not much less than 200 feet high, and receding very slightly on all four sides from the one next below it. Every individual precipice is regularly continued all round the four sides. Or it may be considered as a flight of thirteen steps, each 180 feet high and 30 feet broad. Or, again, it may be described as thirteen layers of square, or slightly oblong, limestone slabs, each 180 feet thick and about a mile on each side, piled with careful regularity and exact levelling upon a base 8000 feet high. Or, perhaps, it may be compared to a cubic crystal, stuck amid a row of irregular gems. Or, perhaps, it is beyond compare. Some day the tourist will go there and compose ' fine English ' ; he could not choose a better place for a bad purpose ; but if he is wiser than his kind he will look and wonder, say very little, and pass on.''

It was on the afternoon of 30th June 1903 that I arrived at the scattered hamlet of Ta-t'ien-ch'ih, from whence the ascent can be made. This tiny hamlet is situated in an oval depression, locked in by high mountains on all sides. The depression is about a mile long and rather less than half a mile broad at its widest point, a small lake surrounded by a luxuriant greensward occupies the lower end. A species of Delphinium, with lovely blue flowers, is very abundant. The Chinese call it " Wu-tzu," and say that it is poisonous to man and cattle alike. Around the farmhouses, maize, peas, beans, buckwheat, and Irish potato are cultivated. The people here mostly profess Christianity, and a Roman Catholic mission-house is the only decent building in the hamlet.

Having procured a guide, I left the inn at 5.45 a.m. on 1st July, to ascend the mountain. Mists obscured everything as we set out, and it felt very raw and cold. The path is the merest track—very sinuous, steep, and difficult. Rain commenced at 2.30 p.m., and continued during the whole of the descent. We reached our inn at 6.30 p.m., drenched through and through.

At one time a dense forest of Silver Fir covered the mountain, but this has long since been felled, and the majority of the trees still lie rotting where they fell. It is a common sight to see bushes of Rhododendrons, 20 feet or more tall, growing on the rotting trunks. Some of these Firs could not have been less than 150 feet in height and 20 feet in girth. On the summit there are still a number of trees left, but none of great size, and nearly all have their tops broken off, either by the wind or by the snow. This mountain, in common with others I have visited, shows only too plainly the destructive nature of the Chinese. Fifty years more, under the present regime, and there will not be an acre of accessible forest left in all central, southern, and Western China. The making of charcoal alone imposes a very heavy toll on hardwood trees and shrubs. The preparing of potash salts is a common industry on the mountains west, and is another means of clearing away the vegetation in a ruthless manner. It is to the charcoal-burning industry that I attribute the marked absence of Oak, Beech, and Hornbeam.

Besides the Silver Fir (*Abies Delavayi*), the only other Conifers are *Tsuga yunnanensis*, *Juniperus formosana*, and *Picea complanata*. Rhododendrons constitute the conspicuous feature of the vegetation, and their wood is, luckily, not esteemed for making charcoal. They begin at 7500 feet, but are most abundant at 10,000 feet and upwards. In the ascent I collected 16 species. They vary from diminutive plants 4 to 6 inches high, to giants 30 feet or more tall. Their flowers, also, are of all sizes and colours, including pale yellow. It was most interesting to watch the displacement of one species by another as we ascended. One of the commonest species is *R. yanthinum*, which has flowers of various shades of purple.

The ascent of the mountain commences 100 yards or so from the inn ; cultivation ceases at 6200 feet. Above this, for 1000 feet, is a belt, which has at some time been cleared for cultivation, but is now densely clad with coarse weeds. Among these occur quantities of *Rodgersia pinnata*, var. *alba*, *Spiræa Aruncus*, Astilbe, and Pedicularis, with a few bushes of *Deutzia longifolia*, *Philadelphus Wilsonii*, and Poison Ivy (*Rhus orientalis*) interspersed. Above this, for 500 feet, comes a wellnigh impenetrable thicket of Bamboo scrub. The species (*Arundinaria nitida*) is of remarkably dense growth, with thin culms, averaging 6 feet in height. Next above this, till the plateau is reached, is a belt of mixed shrubs and herbs, conspicuous amongst which are *Syringa Sargentiana*, *Hy-*

drangea anomala, *H. villosa*, *Neillia affinis*, *Dipelta ventricosa*, *Ribes longeracemosum*, var. *Davidii*, *Enkianthus deflexus*, *Styrax roseus*, Deutzia (2 spp.), Rubus (5 spp.), Viburnum (4 spp.), Spiræa (4 spp.), Acer spp., Malus spp., Sorbus spp., *Meconopsis chelidonifolia*, *Fragaria filipendula*, *Lilium giganteum*, and the herbs of the lower belt. A few Rhododendrons occur chiefly on the cliffs.

The plateau (8500 feet) is about half a mile across, marshy in places, and densely clad with shrubby vegetation and Bamboo scrub. In addition to those already noted as occurring in the belt below, we here found *Hydrangea xanthoneura*, *Rosa sericea*, and *Aralia chinensis*, also a species of Caltha and a few Conifers. Rhododendrons become more abundant as we advanced. Crossing this plateau we reached the north-west angle of the upper storey, and scrambled upwards by a narrow, rocky, tortuous path through dense thickets of mixed shrubs, which gradually give place to Rhododendrons as the narrow ledge at 10,000 feet is reached. *Rosa sericea*, which was past flowering below, was here a mass of lovely white. Two or three species of Lonicera and various *Labiatæ* occur within this belt, and on shady rocks at least three species of Primula, including *P. ovalifolia*.

From 10,000 feet to the summit of the mountain Rhododendron accounts for fully 99 per cent. of the ligneous vegetation. A few Conifers, Lonicera, *Rosa sericea*, *Clematis montana*, var. *Wilsonii*, Pieris, and Gaultheria make up the remaining one per cent. Of the herbs, Primula is the most noteworthy. Five fresh species of this genus occur, and amongst them, though uncommon, the lovely yellow-flowered *P. Prattii*. A blue-flowered Corydalis, *Cypripedium luteum*, with large yellow flowers ; *Rubus Fockeanus* and another herbaceous species are other pleasing plants. On shady rocks the curious *Berneuxia thibetica* abounds. This interesting plant was first referred to the genus Shortia by Franchet, and was later made the type of a new genus by Decaisne. The flowers are small and insignificant, white or pale pink in colour. On bare rocks I gathered the pretty white-belled *Cassiope selaginoides*.

My attention and interest, however, were chiefly taken up with the Rhododendrons. The gorgeous beauty of their flowers defies description. They were there in thousands and hundreds of thousands. Bushes of all sizes, many fully 30 feet tall and more in diameter, all clad with a wealth of blossoms that almost hid the foliage. Some flowers were crimson, some bright red, some flesh-coloured, some silvery-pink, some yellow, and others pure white. The huge rugged stems, gnarled and twisted into every conceivable shape, are draped with pendant Mosses and Lichens, prominent among the latter being *Usnea longissima*. How the Rhododendrons find roothold on these wild crags and cliffs is a marvel. Many grow on the fallen trunks of the Silver Fir and some are epiphytic. Beneath them Sphagnum moss luxuriates and makes a pretty but treacherous carpet. On bare exposed cliffs I gathered two diminutive species of Rhododendron, each only a few inches tall, one with deep purple and the other with pale yellow flowers.

Dense mists obscured our view, though about ten o'clock the sun broke through and made a temporary rift in the clouds of mist, disclosing a scene which made us hunger for more. In one place we leant over a precipice and could hear the roar of a torrent some 2000 or 3000 feet below. Near the summit three precipices, each 40 or 50 feet in height, have to be ascended by means of wooden ladders. Up these I carried my dog, never thinking of the descent. On returning he got frightened, and though we blindfolded him, he struggled hard, and on one occasion his struggles all but upset my balance. I was heartily thankful when safe ground was reached. It requires all one's nerve to mount a ladder with no balustrade, fixed to a vertical cliff 40 feet high, and on either side a yawning abyss lost in the clouds. It is at 10,700 feet— a narrow ridge not 8 feet broad—that the first ladder is encountered. From here to within a few feet of the summit the path is terribly steep, difficult, and dangerous. On clearing the topmost ladder and the remains of another, we unexpectedly reached the summit by the easiest path imaginable—for all the world like a woodland path at home.

The summit is a slightly undulating plateau, many acres in extent, with thickets of tall Rhododendrons festooned with *Clematis montana*, var. *Wilsonii*, and clumps of Silver Fir, the remnant and offspring of giants which once clothed this magnificent mountain alternating with glades carpeted with Anemones and Primulas and tiny streamlets meandering hither and thither. Baber aptly describes it as " the most charming natural park in the world."

In times past several temples existed on the summit, of which ruins only now remain. At present there is but one temple, which contains an image of P'u-hsien Pu'ssa seated on a plaster elephant. It is built of the timber of the Silver Fir (*Abies Delavayi*) and was in excellent repair. Near the temple a small patch of medicinal Rhubarb, a few cabbages, and Irish potatoes are cultivated.

The partly shrubby *Sambucus adnata* and several herbs, including Pedicularis, Microula, *Fragaria filipendula*, and *F. elatior*, range from base to summit. *Fragaria filipendula* is a new Strawberry worthy of note ; the fruit is red, more or less cylindrical in shape, often an inch in length, and of very good flavour. It is widely distributed in Western China, and at Tachienlu I have enjoyed many a dish of this fruit with cream from yak's milk.

Two days later I ascended a lofty spur (10,000 feet) of this mountain and added several new plants to my collection. Of these I may mention *Pæonia Veitchii*, *Rubus tricolor*, *Clematis Faberii*, *Ribes laurifolium*, *Potentilla Veitchii*, *Pyrola rotundifolia*, *Styrax Perkinsiæ*, *Aristolochia moupinensis*, Acer, Anemone, Pyrus, Sorbus, Berberis, and Primula. High up on the cliff *Leontopodium alpinum* and several species of Anaphalis abound. Amongst the Sphagnum at least three species of Lycopodium occur. On dripping, shady rocks and trunks of the Rhododendrons, a filmy Fern (*Hymenophyllum omeiense*) is abundant.

During the four days I botanized on this mountain I added some 220 odd species to my collection. On each of these days the work was excessively hard, and " drenched to the skin " but mildly describes our condition each evening as we reached our inn. On one occasion, through treading on some loose debris, I was only saved from being precipitated over a steep cliff by the presence of mind of a coolie who happened to be near me at the moment.

Zoölogically, Mount Wa and the surrounding wilderness is particularly interesting as being one of the places where wild cattle (*Budorcas tibetanus*) are found. I saw their footprints only ; they were nearly as large as those of a cow. Ornithologically, it is interesting as being the home of at least five species of Pheasant, including the " Blood " and " Amherst " varieties.

I have climbed and botanized on many mountains in different parts of China, some much higher than this, but none have I found richer in cool-temperate plants, and more especially flowering shrubs. Altogether, with its rich flora, peculiar fauna, its singular geological formation, and its magnificent natural park on the summit, Wa shan has many claims on the attention of the naturalist.

END OF VOLUME I

A NATURALIST IN
WESTERN CHINA

WITH VASCULUM, CAMERA, AND GUN

BEING SOME ACCOUNT OF ELEVEN YEARS' TRAVEL,
EXPLORATION, AND OBSERVATION IN THE MORE
REMOTE PARTS OF THE FLOWERY KINGDOM

BY

ERNEST HENRY WILSON, V.M.H.

WITH AN INTRODUCTION BY

CHARLES SPRAGUE SARGENT, LL.D.

VOL. II

METHUEN & CO. LTD.
36 ESSEX STREET W.C.
LONDON

TO

MY WIFE

First Published   November 6th 1913

CONTENTS

A NATURALIST IN WESTERN CHINA

CHAPTER I

THE FLORA OF WESTERN CHINA

A Brief Account of the Richest Temperate Flora in the World

IN previous chapters the wildly mountainous character of Western China has been emphasized. Such a region, affording, as it does, altitudinal extremes, a great diversity in climate, and a copious rainfall, is naturally expected to support a rich and varied flora. Yet after making every allowance for the favourable conditions that obtain in this region the wealth of flowers which meets the eye of the botanist is astonishing and surpasses the dreams of the most sanguine. Competent authorities estimate the Chinese flora to contain fully 15,000 species, half of which are peculiar to the country. These figures speak for themselves and yet fail to give a truly adequate idea of the profusion of flowers. The remote mountain fastnesses of central and Western China are simply a botanical paradise, with trees, shrubs, and herbs massed together in a confusion that is bewildering. On first arriving in a new and strange country it is difficult to recognize the plants one is familiar with under cultivation, and many months necessarily elapse before one is in any sense familiar with the common plants around him. During the eleven years I travelled in China I collected some 65,000 specimens, comprising about 5000 species, and sent home seeds of over 1500 different plants. Nevertheless, it was only during the latter half of this period that I was able to form an intelligent idea of the flora of China and to properly appreciate its richness and manifold problems.

The Chinese flora is, beyond question, the richest temperate flora in the world. A greater number of different kinds of trees are found in China than in the whole of the other north-temperate regions. Every important genus of broad-leaved trees known from the temperate regions of the Northern Hemisphere is represented in China except the Hickory (*Carya*), Plane (*Platanus*), and False Acacia (*Robinia*). All the coniferous genera of the same regions, except the Redwoods (*Sequoia*), Swamp Cypress (*Taxodium*), Chamaecyparis, Umbrella Pine (*Sciadopitys*), and true Cedars (*Cedrus*), are found there. In North America, excluding Mexico, about 165 genera of broad-leaved trees occur. In China the number exceeds 260. Of the 300 genera of shrubs enumerated in the *Kew Hand-List of Trees and Shrubs* (1902 ed.) fully half are represented in China.

The great interest and value, however, of the Chinese flora lies not so much in its wealth of species as in the ornamental character and suitability of a vast number for the embellishment of parks and outdoor gardens throughout the temperate regions of the world. My work in China has been the means of discovering and introducing numerous new plants to Europe and North America and elsewhere. But previous to this work of mine the value of Chinese plants was well known and appreciated. Evidence of this is afforded by the fact that there is no garden worthy of the name, throughout the length and breadth of the temperate parts of the Northern Hemisphere, that does not contain a few plants of Chinese origin. Our Tea and Rambler Roses, Chrysanthemums, Indian Azaleas, Camellias, Greenhouse Primroses, Moutan Pæonies, and Garden Clematis have all been derived from plants still to be found in a wild state in central and Western China. The same is true of a score of other favourite flowers. China is also the original home of the Orange, Lemon, Citron, Peach, Apricot, and the so-called European Walnut. The horticultural world is deeply indebted to the Far East for many of its choicest treasures, and the debt will increase as the years pass.

Our knowledge of the marvellous richness of the Chinese flora has been very slowly built up. Travellers, missionaries of all denominations, merchants, consuls, Maritime Customs officials, and all sorts and conditions of men have added their quota; but, as in geography and other departments of knowledge relating to the Far East, the Roman Catholic priests have played the prominent part. The exclusive policy of the Chinese has necessarily increased the difficulties of Europeans who sought to acquire an intimate knowledge of the country, and all honour is due to the workers who have exploited this field in the past

On behalf of the Royal Horticultural Society of London and others, Robert Fortune, in the 'Forties and 'Fifties of last century, completed the work of his predecessors and exhausted the gardens of China, to our gardens' benefit; but the difficulties of travel were such that he had practically no opportunity of investigating the natural wild flora. With the exception of perhaps half a dozen plants, everything he sent home came from Chinese gardens. But one of his wildlings—*Rhododendron Fortunei*, to wit—has proved of inestimable value to Rhododendron breeders.

Charles Maries, collecting on behalf of Messrs. Veitch, in 1879, ascended the Yangtsze as far as Ichang. He found the natives there unfriendly, and after staying a week was compelled to return. During his brief stay, however, he secured *Primula obconica*, one of the most valuable decorative plants of to-day. Near Kiukiang he secured *Hamamelis mollis, Loropetalum chinense*, and a few other plants of less value, and then hied himself away to Japan. For some curious reason or other he concluded that his predecessor, Fortune, had exhausted the floral resources of China, and, most extraordinary of all, his conclusions were accepted! When at Ichang, could he but have gone some three days' journey north, south, or west, he would have secured a haul of new plants such as the botanical and horticultural world had never dreamed of. By the irony of Fate it was left for two or three others to discover and obtain what had been almost within his grasp.

The enormous Chinese population, especially in the vicinity

of the Lower Yangtsze, and its vast alluvial delta and plains, no doubt mizzled Maries, as it has done others. So densely is China populated that every bit of suitable land has been developed under agriculture. A Chinese is capable of getting more returns from a given piece of land than the most expert agriculturist of any other country. Dry farming and intensive cultivation, though unknown to the Chinese under these terms, have been practised by them from time immemorial. The land is never idle, but is always undergoing tilling and manuring. Nevertheless, in spite of the almost incredible industry of the Chinese cultivator, much of the land in the wild mountain fastnesses of central and Western China defies agricultural skill, and it is in these regions that a surprisingly varied flora obtains. These regions are very sparsely populated, are difficult of access, and, until comparatively recently, were totally unknown to the outside world.

The botanical collections of the two French Roman Catholic priests, les Abbés David and Delavay, of the Russian traveller, N. M. Przewalski, and of the Imperial Maritime Customs officer, Augustine Henry, gave the first true insight into the extraordinary richness of the flora of central and Western China. Delavay's collection alone amounted to about 3000 species, and Henry's exceeded this number ! Botanists were simply astounded at the wealth of new species and new genera disclosed by these collections. An entirely new light was thrown on many problems, and the headquarters of several genera, such as, for example, Rhododendron, Lilium, Primula, Pyrus, Rubus, Rosa, Vitis, Lonicera, and Acer, heretofore attributed elsewhere, was shown to be China.

This extraordinary wealth of species exists, notwithstanding the fact that every available bit of land is under cultivation. Below 2000 feet altitude the flora is everywhere relegated to the roadsides, the cliffs, and other more or less inaccessible places. It is impossible to conceive the original floral wealth of this country, for obviously many types must have perished as agriculture claimed the land, not to mention the destruction of forests for economic purposes.

In order to summarize the account of this wonderful flora

it is convenient to divide the region into altitudinal zones or belts. The mountainous nature of the country lends itself admirably to such an arrangement, and it is perhaps the only feasible way of dealing with a subject so vast and unwieldy. The chart (p. 7) represents an ideal section of the region and may possibly convey a clearer idea of the subject than the text which follows :—

Division 1.—" The belt of cultivation—2000 feet altitude." The climate of the Yangtsze Valley, up to 2000 feet altitude, is essentially warm-temperate. Rice, cotton, sugar, maize, tobacco, sweet potatoes, and legumes are the principal summer crops ; in winter, pulse, wheat, rape, hemp, Irish potato, and cabbage are generally grown. It is a region of intense cultivation and the flora is neither rich nor varied. The following wild plants are characteristic : Bamboos (*Bambusa arundinacea, Phyllostachys pubescens,* and other species), Fan Palm (*Trachycarpus excelsus*), " Pride of India " (*Melia Azedarach*), Crêpe Myrtle (*Lagerstræmia indica*), Winter Green (*Xylosma racemosum*, var. *pubescens*), Chinese Banyan (*Ficus infectoria*), Gardenia (*Gardenia florida*), Roses (*Rosa lævigata* and *R. microcarpa*), Nanmu (*Machilus nanmu* and other species), Pine (*Pinus Massoniana*), Soap tree (*Gleditsia sinensis*), Alder (*Alnus cremastogyne*), Privet (*Ligustrum lucidum*), *Paulownia Duclouxii*, oranges, peaches, and other fruit trees, ferns, especially *Gleichenia linearis*, weeds of cultivation, miscellaneous shrubs and trees, including *Pterocarya stenoptera*, Celtis spp., *Cæsalpinia sepiaria*, Wood Oil (*Aleurites Fordii*); and Cypress (*Cupressus funebris*) ; the last two occurring particularly in rocky places.

Division 2.—" Rain forests belt—2000 to 5000 feet altitude." Between 2000 and 5000 feet are found rain forests, consisting largely of broad-leaved evergreen trees, mainly Oak, Castanopsis, Holly, and various *Lauraceæ*. The latter family constitutes fully 50 per cent. of the vegetation in this zone. Ferns, evergreen shrubs, Chinese Fir (*Cunninghamia lanceolata*), and Cypress are other prominent components. This belt is interesting also as being the home of nine-tenths of the monotypic genera of trees that are so prominent a feature of the Chinese flora. The more interesting of these are : Eucommia, Itoa, Idesia, Tapiscia, Sinowilsonia, Platycarya, Davidia, Carrieria,

Pteroceltis, and Emmenopterys.   Cultivation is less general in
this region, and the winter crop especially is of less importance.
The crops are similar to those of the belt below except that
maize is the staple and displaces rice.   In Hupeh this zone is
much less extensive and can hardly be said to exist when
comparison with its development in western Szechuan is
made.

Division 3.—" Cool-temperature belt—5000 to 10,000 feet
altitude."   From 5000 to 10,000 feet is the largest and most
important zone of all.   It is composed principally of deciduous
flowering trees and shrubs characteristic of a cool-temperate
flora and belonging to familiar genera.   To these must be
added forests of Conifers and many ornamental tall-growing
herbs.   It is in this zone that is found the astonishing variety
of flowering trees and shrubs so pre-eminent a feature of this
flora : of Clematis 60 species are recorded from China ; of
Lonicera, 60 ; of Rubus, 100 ; of Vitis, 35 ; of Evonymus, 30 ;
of Berberis, 50 ; of Deutzia, 40 ; of Hydrangea, 25; of Acer, 40;
of Viburnum, 70 ; of Ilex, 30 ; of Prunus, 80 ; of Senecio, 110 ;
and the enumeration might be further extended.   Pyrus (including Malus, Sorbus, Micromeles, and Eriolobus) is a prominent family in the belt; and behaves in China in the same
manner as Cratægus does in the United States of America.

Amongst such botanical wealth it is difficult to make
selections, but if any one genus has outstanding claims it is
Rhododendron.   As in the Himalayan region, so in Western
China, the Rhododendrons are a special feature.   The genus is
the largest recorded from China, no fewer than 160 species being
known.   I, myself, have collected about 80 species and have
introduced upwards of 60 into cultivation.   Rhododendrons
commence at sea-level, but do not become really abundant
until 8000 feet is reached.   They extend up to the limits of
ligneous vegetation (15,000 feet, *circa*).   These plants are
gregarious in habit and nearly every species has a well-defined
altitudinal limit.   In size they vary from alpine plants only a
few inches high to trees 40 feet and more tall.   The colour of
their flowers ranges from pure white, through clear yellow to
the deepest and richest shades of scarlet and crimson.   In late
June they are one mass of colour, and no finer sight can possibly

CHART ILLUSTRATING ZONES OF VEGETATION

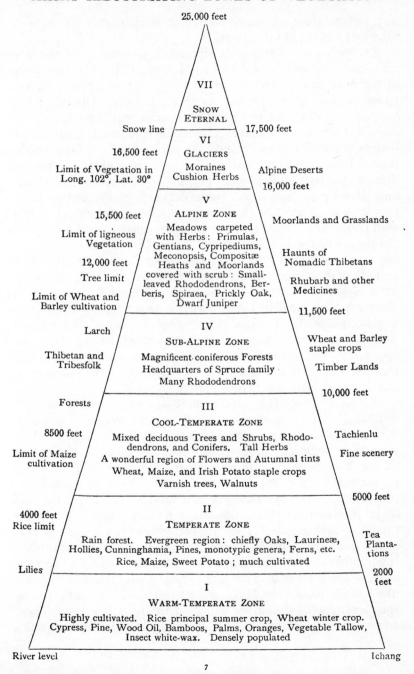

25,000 feet

VII

SNOW
ETERNAL

Snow line   17,500 feet

16,500 feet   **VI**

GLACIERS

Limit of Vegetation in
Long. 102°, Lat. 30°

Moraines
Cushion Herbs   Alpine Deserts

16,000 feet

V

15,500 feet   ALPINE ZONE   Moorlands and Grasslands

Limit of ligneous
Vegetation

Meadows carpeted
with Herbs: Primulas,
Gentians, Cypripediums,
Meconopsis, Compositæ   Haunts of
Nomadic Thibetans

12,000 feet

Tree limit

Heaths and Moorlands
covered with scrub: Small-
leaved Rhododendrons, Ber-   Rhubarb and other
Medicines

Limit of Wheat and
Barley cultivation

beris, Spiraea, Prickly Oak,
Dwarf Juniper

11,500 feet

Larch   **IV**   Wheat and Barley
staple crops

SUB-ALPINE ZONE

Thibetan and
Tribesfolk

Magnificent coniferous Forests
Headquarters of Spruce family
Many Rhododendrons   Timber Lands

10,000 feet

Forests   **III**

COOL-TEMPERATE ZONE

8500 feet   Tachienlu

Mixed deciduous Trees and Shrubs, Rhododendrons, and Conifers. Tall Herbs

Limit of Maize
cultivation   Fine scenery

A wonderful region of Flowers and Autumnal tints
Wheat, Maize, and Irish Potato staple crops
Varnish trees, Walnuts

5000 feet

4000 feet   **II**
Rice limit

TEMPERATE ZONE

Tea
Planta-
tions

Rain forest. Evergreen region: chiefly Oaks, Laurineæ,
Hollies, Cunninghamia, Pines, monotypic genera, Ferns, etc.
Rice, Maize, Sweet Potato; much cultivated

Lilies   2000
feet

I

WARM-TEMPERATE ZONE

Highly cultivated. Rice principal summer crop, Wheat winter crop.
Cypress, Pine, Wood Oil, Bamboos, Palms, Oranges, Vegetable Tallow,
Insect white-wax. Densely populated

River level   Ichang

be imagined than mile upon mile of mountain-side covered with Rhododendrons in full flower.

Division 4.—" Temperate alpine belt—10,000 to 11,500 feet altitude." Above 10,000 feet in Western China the character of the flora undergoes a great change, and the narrow belt between 10,000 and 11,500 feet forms the hinterland between the temperate and alpine zones. This narrow belt is mostly moorland, but where the nature of the country admits, magnificent forests occur. The moorlands are covered with dwarf, small-leaved Rhododendrons and scrub-like shrubs, chiefly Berberis, Spiræa, Caragana, Lonicera, *Potentilla fruticosa, P. Veitchii,* and *Hippophaë salicifolia,* with Willow, prickly Scrub Oak, coarse herbs, grasses, and impenetrable thickets of dwarf Bamboo. The forests are composed almost exclusively of Conifers, chiefly Larch, Spruce, Silver Fir, Hemlock Spruce, and here and there Pine. A few trees of Red and White Birch and Poplar occur, chiefly near streams. Specifically very little is known about the constituents of these forests, but, to illustrate their wealth, I may mention that on my last journey I collected seeds of some 16 different species of Spruce and 5 of Silver Fir. These forests are, unfortunately, fast disappearing, and are only to be found in the more inaccessible regions. The tree-limit varies according to rainfall, and may be put down as between 11,500 and 12,500 feet.

Division 5.—" The alpine belt—11,500 to 16,000 feet altitude." The alpine zone extends from 11,500 to 16,000 feet. The wealth of herbs in this belt is truly astonishing. Their variety is wellnigh infinite, and the intensity of the colour of the flowers is a striking feature. The genus *Pedicularis* (Louseworts), with 100 species, is perhaps the most remarkable constituent. The Louseworts are largely social plants and occur in countless thousands, their flowers being all colours save blue and purple. They are really most fascinating plants, and it is a great pity that their semi-parasitic nature prevents their cultivation. The Ragworts (*Senecio*), with 100 species, have yellow flowers, and the plants vary in size from low cushion-like plants to strong herbs 6 feet tall. Blue is supplied by the Gentians (*Gentiana*), of which there are 90 species. These again are social plants, and on sunny days the ground for miles is often nothing but a carpet of Gentian flowers of the most intense blue. The Fumeworts (*Corydalis*), with 70 species, supplies both yellow and blue flowers and cannot be denied a place. Then there are the wonderful alpine Primroses (*Primula*). This family is represented in China by some 90 species, four-fifths of which occur in the west. These, like Gentians, take unto themselves in season large tracts of country and carpet them with flowers. Sometimes it is a marsh, at other times bare rock or the sides of streams. One of the most beautiful is *Primula sikkimensis*. Along the sides of streamlets and ponds this species is as common as the Cowslip in some English meadows. Associated with it is its purple congener *P. vittata*. Other striking species are *P. Cockburniana*, with orange-scarlet flowers, a colour unique in the genus ; *P. pulverulenta*, a glorified *P. japonica*, with flower-scapes 3 to 4 feet tall, covered with a white meal and flowers of a rich purple colour ; and *P. Veitchii*, which is best described as a hardy *P. obconica*. Other striking herbs are *Incarvillea compacta* and *I. grandiflora*, both with large scarlet flowers, and *Cypripedium tibeticum*, a terrestrial orchid with enormous pouches, dark red in colour. Also we have Meconopsis in half a dozen species, including *M. Henrici*, with violet-coloured flowers ; *M. punicea*, with dark scarlet flowers ; and *M. integrifolia*, with yellow flowers 8 inches or more across —possibly the most gorgeous alpine plant extant.

Division 6.—"High alpine belt." The limit of vegetation is about 16,500 feet ; a few cushion-like plants belonging to *Caryophyllaceæ*, *Rosaceæ*, *Cruciferæ*, and *Compositæ*, with a tiny species of Primula and *Meconopsis racemosa* being the last to give out. Above this altitude are vast moraines and glaciers, culminating in perpetual snow. The snow-line cannot be less than 17,500 feet. Although at first sight remarkable, the high altitude of the snow-line is easily accounted for by the dryness of the Thibetan plateau and the highlands to the immediate west.

Having briefly outlined the different altitudinal zones and instanced some of the more striking plants characteristic of each, it may be of interest to point out the more important absentees. In China there is no Gorse (*Ulex*), Broom (*Cytisus*),

Heather (*Erica*), nor Ling (*Calluna*) ; the Rock-rose family (*Cistus* and *Helianthemum*) is also unrepresented. The place of Gorse and Broom is inadequately taken by Forsythia, Caragana, Berberis, and various Jasmines ; that of Heather by dwarf, tiny-leaved Rhododendrons, of which there are a dozen or more species. The Cistus family has no representative group unless Hypericum be considered its substitute.

There is virtually no pasture-land in central and Western China, but such open country as would compare with commons in England is covered with bushes of Berberis, Spiræa, *Sophora viciifolia*, Caragana, Pyracantha, Cotoneaster, Philadelphus, Holly, and various Roses. The anomalous conditions obtaining in the river-valleys of the west and the peculiar flora found there have been described in Vol. I, Chapter XII.

Another interesting fact, and one that has peculiar reference to the flora of western Hupeh, is the number of plants bearing the specific name *japonica*, which are only Japanese by cultivation and are really Chinese in origin. The following well-known plants are examples : *Iris japonica, Anemone japonica, Lonicera japonica, Kerria japonica, Aucuba japonica, Senecio japonicus*, and *Eriobotrya japonica*. Possibly some of these (and there are many more) may be common to both countries, but I am convinced that when the subject is properly worked out, it will be found that fewer plants are common to both countries than is generally supposed to be the case.

The Chinese flora is largely peculiar to the country itself, the number of endemic genera and species being remarkable even when the size of the country is given due consideration. Yet, in spite of its generally local character, the Chinese flora presents many interesting problems in plant distribution. Not the least interesting is to account for the presence of a species of Libocedrus (*L. macrolepis*), seeing that the other members of this genus are found in California, Chili, and New Zealand. Another noteworthy feature is a species of Osteomeles (*O. Schwerinæ*), which occurs in the far west of China, the other member of this family being found scattered through the islands of the Pacific Ocean. But perhaps the most extraordinary fact in this connexion is the presence on Mount Omei of a species of Nertera (*N. sinensis*), the other members of this family being purely insular and confined to the Southern Hemisphere.

The affinity of the Chinese flora, with contiguous and distant countries, is an interesting theme and one that could be enlarged upon at length. The Himalayan flora is represented by certain species in Western and central China, and there is a considerable affinity between the floras of these regions. This is to be expected, yet it presents problems of exceptional interest, since it is the Sikhim element which comes out strongest. When the flora of Bhutan and of the country between Bhutan and Western China is properly explored it will probably be found that Sikhim represents the most western point of distribution for certain plants rather than their real headquarters. Of Himalayan plants commonly met with in the region, with which this work is intimately concerned, the following examples may be given : *Evonymus grandiflora, Euptelea pleiosperma, Clematis montana, C. grata, C. gouriana, Rosa sericea, R. microphylla, Primula sikkimensis, P. involucrata, Podophyllum Emodi*, and *Amphicome arguta*. In Yunnan there is a decided affinity with the Malay-Indian flora.

The aggressive nature of the Scandinavian (British) flora is evidenced by the following herbs and shrubs which are locally very common : Vervain (*Verbena officinalis*), Agrimony (*Agrimonia Eupatoria*), Buttercups (*Ranunculus acris, R. repens*, and *R. sceleratus*), Silver-weed (*Potentilla anserina*), Great Burnet (*Poterium officinale*), False Tamarisk (*Myricaria germanica*), Ivy (*Hedera Helix*), Bird Cherry (*Prunus Padus*), and Plantain (*Plantago major*).

In the north and throughout the upland valleys and highlands of the west a few Central Asian and Siberian forms occur, such as *Sibiræa lævigata, Spiræa alpina, Cotoneaster multiflora, Thalictrum petaloideum, Delphinium grandiflorum*, and *Lonicera hispida*.

At first sight it would very naturally be supposed that the Chinese flora was most closely allied if not to that of Europe at least to that of the Asiatic continent generally. Yet this is not so. The real affinity is with that of the Atlantic side of the United States of America !

This remarkable fact was first demonstrated by the late

Dr. Asa Gray when investigating the early collections made in Japan. Modern work in China, and especially central China, has given overwhelming evidence and established beyond question Asa Gray's conclusions. There are many instances in which only two species of a genus are known—one in the eastern United States and the other in China. Noteworthy examples are the Tulip tree, Kentucky Coffee tree, the Sassafras, and the Lotus Lily (*Nelumbium*). A considerable number of families are common to both countries, and in most instances China is the dominant partner. Usually the U.S.A. have one and China several species of the same genus, but here and there the opposite obtains. Magnolias afford a good illustration of this affinity. This genus, absent from Europe and western North America, is represented by 7 species on the Atlantic side of the North American continent, and by 19 species in China and Japan.

The following brief list still further illustrates this :—

SOME GENERA COMMON TO CHINA, JAPAN, AND THE ATLANTIC SIDE OF THE UNITED STATES OF AMERICA

CHINA AND JAPAN		UNITED STATES OF AMERICA	
Genus	*No. of Species*	*Genus*	*No. of Species*
Magnolia . .	19	Magnolia . .	7
Schisandra . .	10	Schisandra . .	1
Itea . . .	5	Itea . . .	1
Gordonia . .	3	Gordonia . .	2
Hamamelis . .	2	Hamamelis . .	2
Shortia . . .	3	Shortia . . .	1
Catalpa . .	5	Catalpa . .	2
Negundo (Acer) .	5	Negundo (Acer) .	1
Wisteria . .	4	Wisteria . .	2
Astilbe . . .	10	Astilbe . . .	1
Podophyllum . .	6	Podophyllum . .	1
Illicium . .	6	Illicium . .	2
Stewartia . .	2	Stewartia . .	2
Berchemia . .	8	Berchemia . .	1
Nyssa . . .	1	Nyssa . . .	4

In a few cases the same species is common to both countries. The most extraordinary instance of this is *Diphylleia cymosa* (Umbrella Leaf). This plant occurs in localities separated by 140° of longitude and exhibits absolutely no marked variation.

In the instances mentioned above, the families are absent

from any other region in the world.   In others,—for example, Oak, Hornbeam, Elm, Birch, Ash, Beech, and Sweet Chestnut, —where the families range around the whole temperate zone of both Old and New Worlds, the individual Chinese species are usually more closely akin to those of North America than to those of Europe.

The explanation of this phenomenon is to be found in the glaciation of the Northern Hemisphere in prehistoric times. In those far-off times the land connexion between Asia and North America was far more complete than it is to-day, and the flora extended much farther to the north.   The ice-cap which gradually crept down forced the flora to travel towards the equator.   Later, when the period of great cold was over, and the ice-cap receded, the plants crept back ; but the ice-cap remained at a more southern latitude than before, and consequently rendered much of the land formerly covered with forests too cold to support vegetable life of any sort.   This rearrangement after the Ice Age caused a break between the two hemispheres, and the consequent isolation and cutting off of the floras.   Other agencies and factors played a part, but the above explains briefly and roughly why the floras so much alike should to-day be so widely separated geographically.

That the Chinese flora is an ancient one is evidenced by the number of old types it contains.   For example, in ancient times, *Ginkgo biloba* (Maidenhair tree) was found, not only in Asia, but in Western Europe, Northern California, and Greenland, as the fossil remains found in Jurassic beds of these countries testify.   To-day it exists only in China and Japan as a cultivated tree, being preserved to us by the Buddhist and other religious communities who plant it in the neighbourhood of their temples.   Cycas, Cephalotaxus, Torreya, and Taxus are other old types, but these occur in a wild as well as in a cultivated state in China to-day.   Many of the older ferns, such as Osmunda, Gleichenia, Marattia, and Angiopteris, are common in China and widely spread.   In speaking of the older ferns it may be of interest to note that Augustine Henry discovered in Yunnan an entirely new genus of *Marattiaceæ*, which has been named Archangiopteris.

From the evidence before us it would appear that the Chinese flora suffered less during glacial times than did that of Europe and North America. This may possibly have been due to the greater continuity of land towards the equator which obtains in Asia as compared with that of the continents of Europe and America.

CHAPTER II

THE PRINCIPAL TIMBER TREES

THE forested regions of China are to-day remote from the populous parts of the country, and are only to be found in the more wildly mountainous parts, which are little suited to agriculture, and where the rivers are unnavigable rock-strewn torrents, and roads, as such, can scarcely be said to exist. Such districts are always at considerable elevation and are but sparsely peopled. In all the more accessible regions agriculture has claimed the land, and the trees are only met with around houses, temples, tombs, stream-sides, or crowning cliffs. The scarcity of timber is acutely felt throughout the length and breadth of the land. Dressed logs and poles are carried long distances to navigable waterways and floated either down or up-stream, consequently their cost is high. The ports on the sea-board and lower Yangtsze import timber in quantity for general construction purposes from Puget Sound and British Columbia. A certain amount also comes from Japan. Hardwoods for miscellaneous purposes are imported from various parts of Malaysia, and a certain amount of Jarrah wood for railway work has recently been sent from Australia. The famous blackwood furniture of China is not made of native wood, but of timber imported from Bangkok, Saigon, and other places in Indo-China. Botanically the source of " Chinese blackwood " is unknown. The so-called " Bombay blackwood " is derived from *Dalbergia latifolia*, and possibly the " Chinese " kind is from a closely allied species. Western China is rather better off for timber than other parts of China, and fortunately so, since the importation of timber as a business is utterly impossible. Nevertheless there is a great dearth of wood for building purposes, and timber prices have doubled during the last decade. The massive timbers to be seen in old Chinese temples and houses are now unobtainable from the native trees of China.

Since the scarcity of timber is so great, every kind of tree found in the thickly populated regions furnishes wood of some value, but for the purpose of this chapter it suffices to give a brief account of the more important kinds and those most generally useful.

By far the most important "timber" in China is, of course, the stems of the Bamboo. The Jesuit priest, Trigault, in a work on China, published in 1615, states : " They have a kind of reed called *Bambu* by the Portuguese. It is almost as hard as iron. The largest kind is scarcely encompassed with two hands. It is hollow inside and presents many joints outside. The Chinese use it for pillars, shafts of lances, and for 600 other domestic purposes."

Although three centuries have elapsed since the above quotation was written it applies equally to the conditions of the present day, for the uses to which the Bamboo is put in China are indeed limitless. It supplies many of the multifarious needs of the people with whose everyday life, from birth to death, it is inseparably entwined. From Bamboo stems are fashioned the various household utensils, furniture, the house itself, many agricultural implements, masts and gear for boats, rafts, ropes, bridges, irrigation-wheels, water-pipes, gas-pipes, tubes for raising brine, sedan-chairs, tobacco and opium-pipes, bird-cages, snares for entrapping insects, birds, and animals, umbrellas, raincoats, hats, soles for shoes, under-shirts, sandals, combs, musical instruments, ornamental vases, boxes, and works of art, the pen (brush) to write with, the paper to write upon, everything, in fact, useful and ornamental, from the hats of the highest officials to the pole with which the coolie carries his load. Formerly the records of the race were written on bamboo tablets which were strung together at one end like a fan. Records of this description, dug up in A.D. 281, after having been buried for 600 years, were found to contain the history of Tsin from 784 B.C., and incidentally also that of China for 1500 years before that date.

Bamboo shavings are used in caulking boats and for stuffing pillows and mattresses. The young shoots are a valued vegetable. According to popular belief, in times of scarcity a compassionate Deity causes the Bamboo to flower and yield a harvest of grain to save the people from starvation.

The Bamboo flourishes everywhere in the Far East, and is just as beautiful when sheltering the peasant's cottage or beggar's hut as when ornamenting the courtyards of temples and the mansions of the wealthy. It is the one woody plant that is really abundant throughout all but the coldest parts of the Middle Kingdom. The Occident possesses no tree or shrub which for all-round general usefulness compares with the Bamboo of the Orient.

The Chinese generic name for the Bamboo family is " Chu," the different kinds being distinguished by a prefix. The natives have no difficulty in recognizing the various species, but botanists generally have found Bamboos exceedingly difficult to deal with systematically. In the *Index Floræ Sinensis* 33 species are enumerated, but for the purpose of this chapter only 4 or 5 species are involved.

Throughout the Yangtsze Valley, up to about 2500 feet altitude, the " Pan chu " (*Phyllostachys pubescens*) is one of the commonest species. Its young spear-like stems rear themselves 30 to 40 feet, and finally develop into beautiful arched plumes. The stems are about 3 or 4 inches in diameter, dark shining green, becoming yellow with age. The wood is moderately thick and is used for a great variety of purposes. It is largely employed on the Yangstze, above Ichang, for making tracking lines for the various river craft. A species allied to this, but smaller in every way, never exceeding 20 feet in height, is the Ch'ung chu (*P. heteroclada*). This Bamboo is commonly used in western Hupeh for paper-making.

A very common species in the warmer parts of Szechuan is the " Tz'u chu " (*Bambusa arundinacea*, often called *B. spinosa*), the Spiny Bamboo. This magnificent species produces stems 50 to 75 feet tall and 8 to 10 inches in diameter at base. It does not spread very much, but forms compact clumps, which are impenetrable on account of their density and the presence of innumerable, slender, ferociously spiny stems which develop among and around the larger culms. This Bamboo has a small core and very thick wood. It is used in household carpentry, for furniture, ornamental vases, boxes, and scaffolding, and has a hundred and one other uses.

Another species is the Nan chu (*Dendrocalamus giganteus*), the largest growing of all the Bamboos found in western Szechuan. This is confined to the warmer parts of the province, where it forms wide-spreading groves. The stems grow 60 to 80 feet tall and are 10 or 12 inches thick. The core is very large, the wood thin and light. It is commonly used for constructing the rafts which ply on the shallow but turbulent rivers of western Szechuan. It has also many other uses and is especially prized for making chop-sticks.

Yet another very commonly cultivated species is *Bambusa vulgaris*, sometimes called the Kwanyin chu, which produces pale-coloured stems 30 to 50 feet tall. The wood is thin and is used for a variety of purposes, but is less valuable than any of the foregoing. The young shoots of these large-growing Bamboos are cut just as they appear above the ground, and eaten as a vegetable, the flesh being white, firm and crisp.

Apart from Bamboo the most common timber for all-round use is that derived from the " Sha shu," or " China Fir " (*Cunninghamia lanceolata*). This coniferous tree is widely spread throughout warm-temperate parts of China and is especially partial to red sandstone. It is particularly abundant in the Yachou prefecture and on the mountains bordering the north-west corner of the Chengtu Plain. It grows from 80 to 120 feet tall, and has a straight mast-like stem ; after the trees are cut down this Conifer reproduces itself by sprouts from the old stumps. The bark is commonly employed for roofing purposes. The wood is light, fragrant, and easily worked. For general building purposes, house-fittings, and indoor carpentry it is the most esteemed of all Chinese timbers ; also it is in great request for coffin-making, the fragrant properties of the wood being considered to act as a preservative. For ordinary coffins several logs are dressed and fastened together laterally to form a thick, wide plank called " Ho-pan," four of which, with two end pieces added, make a coffin. All who can afford it have such coffins lacquered a shining jet-black. But the more expensive coffins are those in which each Ho-pan is hewn from a single log of timber, and the most valuable of all are those made from Hsiang Mu (fragrant wood), or Yin-chên Mu (long-buried wood). For such a coffin 400 to 1000 ounces of silver is the usual price. For the most part, Yin-chên Mu comes from the Chiench'ang Valley, where it was probably engulfed as the result of an earthquake in times past. In 1904 I ascended the Tung Valley from Fulin to Moshi-mien, *en route* for Tachienlu, and near the hamlet of Wan-tung came upon a place where natives were engaged in excavating buried timbers. The work was being carried on in a narrow valley. At the head of the valley a torrent had been dammed up and the accumulated waters, released at will from time to time through a sluice, carried much of the overlying debris away. Many of the excavations were fully 50 feet deep. All sorts of timber is found buried in this place, but only the " Hsiang Mu " (fragrant wood) is considered of value. I procured a specimen of this wood, and subsequent microscopic examination has proved it to be that of *C. lanceolata*. The Chinese consider that these trees have been buried for two or three hundred years. The timber is wonderfully preserved and is more compact in texture and more fragrant than that of recently felled trees. Ho-pans made from " Hsiang Mu " average about 30 inches wide and 7 feet in length. In all my travels in Western China I have seen only one living specimen of Cunninghamia approaching to the size of these long-buried giants.

In Chengtu and neighbouring cities, the timber known as " Lien sha," derived from *Abies Delavayi* and allied species, is generally employed for all the larger beams, pillars, and planking in house-building. This handsome Silver Fir (*Abies Delavayi*) is common on all the higher mountains of the west, but that growing in the Yachou prefecture is most accessible, and this district is the main source of the timber-supply. The timber is soft and not very durable, but the large size of the logs render it most serviceable. The Pine (*Sung shu*) is very common, the most widely distributed species being *Pinus Massoniana*. This tree ascends from sea-level to 4000 feet altitude. The timber obtained from the higher altitudes is close-grained, resinous, and durable, but that from low-levels is soft, very open, and of little value.   Other Hard Pines, such as *P. Henryi*, *P. densata*, *P. Wilsonii*, *P. prominens*, are found at higher altitudes (up to 10,000 feet) and yield valuable timber, but unfortunately they occur only in inaccessible places.   The Chinese White Pine (*P. Armandi*) is widely spread in the more mountainous parts. This tree never attains any great size, but the timber is very durable and resinous.   It is esteemed for building purposes and for making torches.

All the Conifers yield useful timber, but unfortunately few are found to-day in accessible regions.   Around Tachienlu the Hung sha (Red Fir), *Larix Potaninii*, is esteemed the most valuable of all timbers.   The Tieh sha (*Tsuga yunnanensis, T. chinensis*) is made into shingles for roofing purposes and is also valued for planking.   In the Lungan prefecture the Mê-tiao sha (*Picea ascendens*) is a most valuable timber for general building purposes.   Many other kinds of Spruce (*Picea*) occur on the mountains, and with Silver Fir (*Abies*) and Larch (*Larix*) form the only remaining Conifer forests in Western China.   A Juniper (Hsiang-peh sha), *Juniperus saltuaria*, is common north of Sungpan, where it is valued for building purposes.   *Cupressus torulosa* (K'an-peh sha) occurs in the arid valleys of the west ; *Taxus cuspidata*, var. *chinensis* (Tuench'u sha), and *Keteleeria Davidiana* (Yu sha or Oil Fir) are found scattered all over Western China between 2000 and 5000 feet altitude, but are nowhere really abundant.

From Ichang westward, up to 3500 feet altitude, the commonest Conifer next to Pine is the Peh sha or White Fir (*Cupressus funebris*), and in the more rocky limestone regions it is the more common tree of the two.   This handsome Cypress, with its pendant branches, is generally planted over tombs and shrines and in temple grounds.   The wood is white, hard, heavy, and exceedingly tough.   It enters largely into the structure of all boats plying on the Upper Yangtsze, forming the sides, bulkheads, and often the cross-beams and decks.   It is also made into chairs, tables, and other furniture.   The superstructure of the boat is usually of Sha Mu (*Cunninghamia*), the bottom and main timbers of Oak and Nanmu.

Oak is widely dispersed from river-level to 8000 feet altitude, but large trees are scarce except in the vicinity of tombs, shrines, and other sacred places. A general name for the family is " Li," and the Chinese distinguish many kinds, such as Peh-fan, Hwa, Hung, Tueh, and Chu li ; botanically about a score of species occur in this region, of which the commonest are *Quercus serrata*, *Q. variabilis*, and *Q. aliena*. All yield close-grained timber, highly valued for a variety of purposes apart from boat-building.

Nanmu (Southernwood) includes a number of species of Machilus and Lindera. All are evergreen and singularly handsome trees. They are largely planted around homesteads and temples in Szechuan, and are a prominent feature of the scenery of parts of the Chengtu Plain and around the base of Mount Omei. They grow to a great size and have clean, straight trunks and wide-spreading, umbrageous heads. The timber is close-grained, fragrant, greenish and brown in colour, easily worked, and very durable. It is highly esteemed for furniture-making, and for pillars in the temples and the houses of the wealthy. As planking it is used for boat bottoms. Nanmu is one of the most valuable of all Chinese timbers, and the tree itself among the handsomest of evergreens. Camphor (Ch'ang shu), *Cinnamomum Camphora*, is found scattered over western Hupeh and Szechuan up to 3500 feet altitude, and its fragrant timber, like that of Nanmu, is made into high-class furniture. The wood furnished by the thick main roots of this tree is known as " Ying Mu " and is valued for cabinet work.

For high-grade cabinet work, picture frames, and the very best furniture the timber most highly esteemed in Szechuan is the " Hung-tou Mu," derived from *Ormosia Hosiei*, a tree allied to the Sophora. In the spring *O. Hosiei* produces large panicles of white and pink pea-shaped flowers, and at all seasons of the year is a striking tree. The wood is heavier than water, of a rich red colour, and beautifully marked. It is the most high-priced of all local timbers, and is now very scarce. In north-central Szechuan it is still fairly common, but on the Chengtu Plain it is only found in temple grounds or over shrines. The native name signifies " Red Bean tree," the seeds being red and contained in bean-like pods. Allied to the foregoing is

Dalbergia hupeana, which yields the valuable " T'an Mu," a wood whitish in colour, very heavy, and exceedingly hard and tough. It is almost exclusively employed in building the wheelbarrows used on the Chengtu Plain; for the handles of carpenters' tools, rammers for oil-presses, blocks and pulleys used on boats, and for every purpose where stress and strain obtain. This tree grows tall (80 feet) but is never of any great thickness ; it is widely spread in the west up to 3000 feet altitude.

Three other members of the Pea family that yield useful woods of greater or less value, are the " Huai shu " (*Sophora japonica*, " Tsao-k'o shu " (*Gleditsia sinensis*), and " Yeh-ho shu " (*Albizzia lebbek*). All three species are common, the first two forming a characteristic feature of the vegetation of the more arid river-valleys of the west. The wood of these trees is used in general carpentry and furniture-making.

One of the commonest trees throughout the hot, rather arid river-valleys, up to 8500 feet altitude (but by no means confined thereto), is *Juglans regia*, the Walnut (Hei-tou shu). It is cultivated for its fruits, which are a valued article of food and a source of oil. The wood has recently become in great demand in the newly established arsenals for making rifle-stocks. The supply is not equal to the demand, and much Nanmu timber is used as a substitute. This latter is lighter and less serviceable for this purpose than that of the Walnut.

The best rudder-posts are made from the wood of the " Huang-lien shu " (*Pistacia chinensis*), a large-growing tree found everywhere up to 5000 feet altitude. A log having a natural " fork " at one end is in general use for the balance-rudder on all the larger boats. The wood of the Loquat (Pi-pa shu), *Eriobotrya japonica*, which is red-coloured, heavy, and of great strength, is also employed for this purpose. The young shoots of the Pistacia, known as " Huang-ni ya-tzu," are cooked and eaten as a vegetable, and so also are the shoots of the " Ch'un-tuen shu " (*Cedrela sinensis*). This last-named tree furnishes a valuable timber, beautifully marked with rich red bands on a yellowish-brown ground. Foreigners call it Chinese Mahogany. It is easily worked, does not warp nor crack, and is esteemed for making window-sashes, door-joists, and furniture. The tree grows 80 feet tall, the trunk is very straight, and but little branched. It is quite common in western Hupeh up to 4500 feet altitude, but much less so in Szechuan.

Tea-chests for all the higher-grade teas are made of wood derived from the Chinese Sweet Gum (Feng-hsiang shu), *Liquidambar formosana*. This is a strikingly handsome tree, growing 80 to 100 feet tall, with a girth of 12 to 15 feet. It occurs scattered all over the west up to 3500 feet altitude ; the leaves turn a rich red-brown in autumn and remain on the trees far into the winter.

The best carrying poles are made from the " Tzu-k'an shu " (*Ehretia acuminata* and *E. macrophylla*), the wood of these trees being light but very tough. Oak and Bamboo are also used for the same purpose and are cheaper. For making the drums used on boats and in temples the wood of the " Tzu-ch'in shu " (*Kalopanax ricinifolium*) is considered best, being easily worked, pliable, and resonant. The two ends of the drum are covered with hide.

The finest Joss-sticks (Chinese incense) are composed of the pounded leaves and branches of various members of the Laurel family (*Lauraceæ*), all of which are rich in fragrant, essential oils. As an adulterant the pulped wood of Cypress and Birch is commonly employed.

On the barren hills around Ichang and elsewhere the Common Pine (Sung shu), *Pinus Massoniana*, has been planted as a source of fuel. Along the stream-sides and canals on the Chengtu Plain, Alder (Ching shu), *Alnus cremastogyne*, is generally planted for the same purpose. The Alder and Pine, together with Bamboo, are the only trees planted for the economic value of their timber. On the mountains, Beech, Ash, Poplar, Sweet Chestnut, Hornbeam, Birch, and many other valuable and useful timber trees occur, but are difficult of access and consequently not in general use.

CHAPTER III

FRUITS, WILD AND CULTIVATED

CHINA is the original home of several fruits which are now cultivated all over the world, as, for example, the orange, lemon, pomelo, peach, and Japanese plum. In the south a number of tropical fruits, such as banana, pineapple, papaw, areca-nut, litchi, longan, and "Olives" (*Canarium*), are grown, but only the last three, and these in very small quantities, are found in the regions with which we are concerned. In the north, more especially around Chefoo, apples and pears, introduced from America, are cultivated and very excellent fruit is produced. In the north, too, very fine grapes are grown, and the fruit generally is of a high order. But, in general, little attention is given to fruit-culture; pruning the trees and thinning the fruit is not attended to, with the result that nearly all Chinese fruit is lacking in quality. Usually it is gathered before it is properly ripe, and this has much to do with the absence of flavour which is unfortunately characteristic. Particularly is this indifference and neglect evident in central and Western China, where a very considerable quantity and variety is grown. The oranges, peaches, and persimmons are equal to those obtainable anywhere, but all the other succulent fruits are of very low-grade quality. It is to be regretted that more attention is not given to the subject, for the region could undoubtedly be made to produce the very best of fruits.

In ascending the Yangtsze River, from where the foothills commence below Ichang, and westward to Sui Fu, Orange-groves are a feature, attaining their greatest luxuriance between Chungking and Lu Chou. In December, when the trees are laden with ripe fruit, these groves are a remarkable sight. The Orange is happiest when growing on the leeside of rocky escarpments, or at their base, where it is protected from the winds. It is very partial to the clayey marls and sandstones of the Red Basin. In western Szechuan the loose-skinned or Mandarin Orange (*Citrus nobilis*) is most generally grown. In season the fruit can be purchased on the spot at the rate of 500 to 1000 for a shilling. Unfortunately this orange does not keep well, but when removed and dried the rind constitutes a favourite medicine known as " Chien-yün-p'i." The fibres and pithy substance surrounding the fleshy carpels within the rind also form a medicine which is called " Chü-lo." In the gorges a tight-skinned or Sweet Orange, " Shan K'an-tzu " (*C. Aurantium*, var.), is more usually met with. The so-called Ichang orange of this type is noted far and wide in China. It has a higher market-value than the " Mandarin " and keeps well. In Chengtu these oranges are kept fresh and good all through the summer, but by what process I failed to discover.

A Lemon (*C. ichangensis*) is also grown in the Ichang Gorge, but is not common. The fruit of this species is broadly oval in shape and of excellent flavour. Pomelos, " Yō-tzu " (*C. decumana*, var.), are met with, but the fruit seldom contains any pulp worthy of the name, consisting usually of little but pith and seeds. The Kumquat (*C. japonica*) is sparingly cultivated for its fruits, which, preserved with sugar, are an esteemed delicacy. A Citron (*C. Medica*, var. *digitata*) is also occasionally grown for its curious-looking fruit which is known as " Fingered Citron," or " Buddha's Hand."

The Orange and allied fruit trees are propagated by notching the shoots which arise from the base of the tree and fixing earth around the cut. A framework of bamboo or a broken earthenware pan is used to keep the soil in place. When many roots have been formed in the heaped-up soil a final severance of the shoot from the parent tree is made, and in due course the new plant is removed to a permanent site. Boring-insects are unfortunately making sad havoc among the Orange-groves in Western China. No attempt at prevention or control is made by the owners, and nothing but the wonderful vitality of the tree saves it from extinction.

The Peach, " Tao-tzu " (*Prunus Persica*), is abundantly

cultivated in Hupeh and Szechuan from river-level to 9000 feet altitude. Freestone and clingstone varieties and oval and flattened kinds occur ; those from the vicinity of Ichang are of delicious flavour and are probably not excelled anywhere in the world. The climate more than anything else is responsible for this, since the trees are little cared for and generally covered with the San José scale-insect. The trees are grown in orchards or in small groups around houses, but sub-spontaneous bushes are met with everywhere by the wayside and on cliffs. An oil is extracted from the kernels in northern China, but not in the western parts of the Empire, as far as my observation goes.

The Peach was introduced into Asia Minor and Europe from Persia somewhere about 300 B.C., but it has been cultivated in China from very remote times and was probably carried to Persia by way of the old trade route via Bokhara. Whilst it is now accepted that China is the original home of this invaluable fruit, it is by no means certain as to what particular plant represents the wild type. A species found in northern China and known as *P. Davidiana* is generally regarded as the source of origin of the cultivated peach. From this view I, however, dissent. My opinion is that the species are distinct, and that the type of the garden peach is no longer to be found in a wild state. The nearest to it is the sub-spontaneous form, plants of which are abundant on the cliffs and by the waysides all over western Hupeh and Szechuan. In this connexion it may be of interest to record that in the neighbourhood of Tachienlu I discovered a new species of Peach which has since been named *P. mira*. This plant is a typical freestone Peach in every respect, but has a small, smooth, ovoid stone. It is now in cultivation, and, coming as it does from a very cold climate, may eventually prove the progenitor of a hardier race of cultivated Peaches.

The Apricot (*P. Armeniaca*) is generally supposed to be a native of Armenia, as its name implies, from whence it was introduced to China, where it has long been cultivated ; but Maximowicz regarded it as spontaneous in the mountains near Peking. The Apricot tree grows to a large size (40 to 50 feet), but the fruit, known as " Hun-tzu," is fibrous and very harsh in flavour. There is room for the improved varieties of apricot in China, as the dried apricots prepared in northern India, which find their way across Thibet to Western China, are highly esteemed by Thibetans and Chinese alike.

Plums, " Ku-li-tzu," are commonly cultivated, the fruits being round in shape and either green, yellow, red, or purple in colour, but all are of indifferent flavour. All these cultivated forms are derived from *P. salicina*, a tree common in the thickets and margins of woods throughout Hupeh and Szechuan. Under the name of Japanese Plum this species has been introduced into California, Europe, and elsewhere, and is now widely cultivated. Authentic specimens of the species from which the plums cultivated in Europe have been derived (*P. communis*) have not been recorded from China, and very probably it does not occur there. The Japanese Apricot (*P. mume*), so widely cultivated in China and Japan, where it is dwarfed and trained into curious shapes and much appreciated for its early flowering propensities, is wild in western Hupeh and Szechuan, being known as " Oo-me." The fruit is round, usually red on one side and yellow on the other, of indifferent flavour, and rendered less palatable by its felted, woolly stone.

The Common Almond is not grown in China, but in 1910, near Sungpan, I discovered an allied species, since named *P. dehiscens*, in which the ripe fruit opens and exposes the stone. The kernel of this fruit is eaten and locally is much esteemed. The plant forms a very dense, spiny bush, 5 to 12 feet tall, and is very abundant in the upper reaches of the Min Valley. The fruit may be described as " dry," since hardly any " flesh " is developed. This species is now in cultivation, and is certainly an interesting addition to the Almonds hitherto grown.

Cherries, "Ying-tao," are abundant in the woods and forests and run riot in species. In *Plantæ Wilsonianæ*, Part II, Koehne describes no fewer than 40 species based on material collected by me alone ! The Cherry is, however, rarely cultivated, and such fruit as is on sale at Ichang and elsewhere is small and lacking in flavour. Its chief merit is in being the first stone-fruit of the season, coming into the market the end of April. The Cherry cultivated around Ichang is *P. involucrata*. The species from which the European cherries have been derived (*P. avium* and *P. Cerasus*) are not found in China.

The Pear, "Li-tzu," is very generally cultivated and is especially abundant throughout the upper reaches of the river-valleys in the west. It is also common in the higher parts of the glens which lead off from the gorges in western Hupeh. Several kinds are grown, and in some instances the fruit attains a very large size. Usually these pears are as hard as rock, and though very useful for cooking purposes are of little value for dessert. Propagation by crown-grafting is commonly practised, but little attention is given to the trees afterwards. All the varieties of Chinese pears have been evolved by long cultivation from native species (probably *Pyrus sinensis*, *P. ussuriensis*, and another species not yet authentically named, but known in China as the " Tang-li "), and have not common origin with those cultivated in the Occident which have been derived from *P. communis*. Around Peking the Chinese cultivate a peculiar kind of Pear under the name of " Peh-li-tzu " (White Pear). The fruit is apple-shaped, about 1¾ inches in diameter, pale yellow in colour, and of most delicious flavour. This pear is probably a superior variety of *Pyrus ussuriensis*.

Apples are much more sparingly cultivated than pears, with which they are grown in association. They are more frequent around Sungpan Ting and Tachienlu than in Hupeh. The fruit is small, green, or greenish-yellow on one side and rosy on the other in the best variety, with an agreeable bitter-sweet flavour. It is uncertain as to what species these apples belong, but possibly to *Malus spectabilis*, *M. prunifolia*

The Quince, " Mu-kua," is commonly cultivated in central China, but less so in the west. The fruits are oiled and kept as ornaments in houses, being appreciated for the fragrant odour. They are also used as medicine. Two species occur— *Chaenomeles sinensis* with nearly round leaves and dark red flowers and *C. cathayensis* with elongated leaves and white flowers, flushed pink. Closely allied to the quince is *Docynia Delavayi*, which is very abundant in Yunnan, where the fresh fruits known as " Tao yi " are used in ripening persimmons. The fruits of each are arranged in alternate layers in large jars and covered with rice-husks, and in ten hours the persimmons are bletted and fit for eating. The Docynia occurs sparingly in western Szechuan, but in that locality the fruit is not utilized.

The Loquat, " P'i-pa " (*Eriobotrya japonica*), both wild and cultivated, occurs in quantity up to 4000 feet altitude, and is most abundant in rocky places. This handsome evergreen forms a tree 30 feet tall, and produces its fragrant white flowers in the early winter, the fruit being ripe in April. The fruit is orange-coloured, of a pleasant sub-acid flavour, but there is very little " flesh " surrounding the large, soft brown seeds, which have an almond-like taste and might be used for flavouring purposes.

In different parts of China various species of Hawthorn, " Shan-li-hung-tzu " or " Shan-cha," are cultivated for their fruits. In Hupeh the species thus favoured is *Cratægus hupehensis*; orchards of this tree occur in the neighbourhood of Hsingshan Hsien. The fruit is scarlet, nearly 1 inch in diameter, but of insipid flavour.

One of the most delicious of all fruits grown in China is the Persimmon, " Tsze-tzu " (*Diospyros kaki*). The Persimmon tree is abundant up to 4000 feet altitude, and usually forms handsome specimens 60 feet or more tall. The fruit may be ovoid or flattened-round, and with or without seeds. It is not really edible until dead ripe, at which stage all the tannic acid is dissipated or changed into sugar. The Chinese have various methods of ripening this fruit to bring out its full flavour. The process, in the main, consists in stratifying and covering them with rice-husks and admitting only a modicum of air. Persimmons are often allowed to remain on the trees long after the leaves have fallen, and the masses of orange-coloured fruits on such trees present a wonderful sight.

In the neighbourhood Lu Chou are cultivated Litchis (*Nephelium Litchi*) and Longans (*N. longana*) as orchard fruits. They thrive very well in this district, and the fruits command high prices in the market. The Chinese Olive (*Canarium album*) is also grown in the same locality. In the arid river valleys of the west the Chinese Date-plum, " T'sao-tzu "

(*Zizyphus vulgaris*), is frequently cultivated, but the quality of the fruit is very poor, and cannot compare in size and flavour with that produced in Shantung and other parts of north-eastern China.   In the warmer parts the Pomegranate, " Tsze-niu " (*Punica Granatum*), is commonly met with, but the fruit is scarcely edible.   In Yunnan very fair pomegranates are grown. Although widely spread and naturalized in parts of China, competent authorities consider the Pomegranate to have been introduced there.

Grapes, " Chia-p'u-tao," are sparingly cultivated in the west, but the quality is very inferior to those grown around Peking.   The only kind I have seen has white fruit.   The varieties commonly' cultivated are all forms of *Vitis vinifera*, which, according to Bretschneider, was introduced into China from Western Asia during the second century B.C.   Around Kiukiang the Spiny Vitus, " P'u-tao-tzu " (*V. Davidii*), is sometimes cultivated.   This vine produces black, globose grapes of good size and appearance, but the flavour is very harsh.   It occurs as a common wild plant in the mountains of the west.

The Walnut, " Hei-tao " (*Juglans regia*), is an exceedingly common tree throughout the regions with which we are concerned, ranging up to 8500 feet altitude.   It is especially abundant in the arid river valleys of west Szechuan, and equally so in the mountains and valleys of Hupeh.   The nuts vary considerably in size, shape, and in the thickness of the shell. The best are of large size and have very thin shells.   They are valued not only as a food but for their sweet-oil, which is expressed and used for culinary purposes.   A Butternut, " Yeh Hei-tao " (*J. cathayensis*), is also common in the woods and thickets.   The kernels are eaten, but the shell is very thick and difficult to crack.

The seed of the Maidenhair tree, " Peh-k'o " (*Ginkgo biloba*), after being roasted is esteemed as a dessert nut.   The seed of the Lotus Lily, " Lien hwa " (*Nelumbium speciosum*), Ground-nut, " Lao-hua-tsen " (*Arachis hypogæa*), are similarly valued. The Water-chestnut, " Ling-chio " (*Trapa natans*), is abundantly cultivated and the fruit is eaten.

In the woods and thickets many kinds of wild fruits are

found which are eaten locally. Brambles (*Rubus*) in great variety occur, over 100 species being recorded from China. The majority yield edible fruit, and in some cases this is superior to any found elsewhere in the world. I have succeeded in introducing about 30 species, and look forward to the day when some one will seriously take up the culture of brambles and by hybridizing them evolve a new race of berries to add to the soft fruits at present in cultivation. The three best of the new introductions, according to my own palate, are *Rubus pileatus*, *R. amabilis*, and *R. corchorifolius*, all vinous-flavoured; raspberry-like fruits. The black fruits of *R. omeiense* and *R. flosculosus* are also good eating, as are the orange or red coloured fruits of *R. biflorus*, var. *quinqueflorus*, *R. innominatus*, and *R. ichangensis*. At Ichang in early spring the raspberry-like fruit of *R. parvifolius* is commonly on sale, being locally known as " Ts'ai-yang-p'ao-tzu." (The term " P'ao-tzu " is comprehensive, covering berries generally.) At Sungpan in August it is possible to secure fruit of the dwarf *R. xanthocarpus* in quantity for a few cash pieces.

In the mountains during June and July wild strawberries are plentiful, and the fruit is of delicious flavour. Two kinds occur—the white-fruited Hautboy, " Ti-p'ao-tzu " (*Fragaria elatior*), and the red-fruited " She-p'ao-tzu " (*F. filipendula*). At Tachienlu, where cream from yak milk is obtainable, I have enjoyed many a dish of strawberries and cream, and also strawberry pie. By the roadsides the Indian Strawberry (*F. indica*), also called " She-p'ao-tzu," is everywhere abundant up to 3000 feet altitude. The brightly-coloured but flavourless fruit of this plant is considered poisonous by the Chinese.

In the woods species of Currant (*Ribes*) with both red and black fruit are common. One species (*R. longeracemosum*) bears large, black fruit of good flavour, on racemes 1½ foot long ! This plant is now in cultivation, and should be utilized as a parent by the hybridist. A Gooseberry (*R. alpestre*, var. *giganteum*) is a common hedge-plant throughout the Chino-Thibetan borderland between 8000 and 11,000 feet altitude. The small, round, green-coloured fruit is, however, extremely harsh in flavour. A Strawberry tree, " Yang-mei," is common in the margins of woods and thickets between 2000

to 6000 feet altitude, throughout Hupeh, and less so in western
Szechuan. The flattened-round red fruit is rough on the exterior, very juicy, and of fair flavour. In the above region the
tree so named is *Cornus kousa*. In Yunnan the vernacular name
is applied to *C. capitata*, an allied species, but in south-eastern
China the " Yang-mei " is *Myrica rubra*, a relative of our
Sweet Gale, and belonging to a widely different family.

A climber called " Yang-tao " in Hupeh and " Mao-erh-tao "
in Szechuan (*Actinidia chinensis*) is very abundant from 2500 to
6000 feet altitude. It produces excellent fruit of a roundish or
oval shape, 1 inch to 2½ inches long, with a thin, brown, often
hairy skin covering a luscious green flesh. This is an excellent
dessert fruit, and makes a fine preserve. In 1900 I had the pleasure of introducing this fruit to the foreign residents of Ichang,
with whom it found immediate favour, and is now known throughout the Yangtsze Valley as the " Ichang Gooseberry." I also
was privileged to introduce it into European cultivation, and it
fruited in England for the first time in 1911. This valuable
climber has, in addition to its edible fruit, ornamental foliage
and shoots, and large, fragrant flowers, white fading to buff-
yellow. It is a good garden plant ; the only drawback is that
the flowers are polygamous, and it is necessary to secure the
hermaphrodite form to ensure fruit. Several other species of
Actinidia yield edible fruits of fair flavour, one of the best
being *A. rubricaulis*, which is now in cultivation.

The Chinese eat the white inner pulp of the pod-like, purple
fruits of several species of *Holbœllia* ; these plants known as
" Pa-yueh-cha " are stout climbers. The teat-like fruits of
several species of *Elæagnus*, known as " Yang-mu-nai-tzu," are
also eaten. These have a rather pleasant acid flavour, but are
usually astringent in character. The fleshy, thickened fruit-
stalks of *Hovenia dulcis*, called " Kuai-tsao," are eaten to annul
the effects of wine.

Sweet Chestnut trees are abundant in the woods up to 7500
feet altitude, and excellent nuts, known as " Pan-li," are produced. Several species occur, one of the most common and
widely diffused being *Castanea mollissima*. As scrub on the
hills up to 3500 feet altitude, the Chinese Chinquapin, " Mao
Pan-li " (*C. Seguinii*), is very abundant. Bushes only 2 feet

tall produce quantities of small, good-flavoured nuts, but the best are from bushes 5 to 8 feet tall. The best eating chestnuts are, however, those of *C. Vilmoriniana*. This species makes a large tree 60 to 80 feet tall, and has glabrous leaves and a single ovoid nut within each spiny fruit. It is very distinct from all the other members of its family. The acorns of several kinds of Oaks and the nuts of different species of Castanopsis are also eaten by the peasants. This is true of different Hazel-nuts, " Shan-peh-k'o " (*Corylus* spp.), and Beech-nuts (*Fagus* spp.).

A Nut Pine (*Pinus Armandi*) is abundant on the mountains from 3500 to 9000 feet, and the seeds are eaten locally. These seeds, however, are not much sought after, and are far from having the economic importance of the Corean Nut Pine (*P. koraiensis*).

The " Wampi " (*Clausena punctata*) is sparingly grown around Lu Chou.

CHAPTER IV

CHINESE MATERIA MEDICA

NATIVE practitioners in China have very crude ideas of human anatomy, and to be able to " read " the pulse is proof positive of medical skill. Certain foreign drugs like quinine are highly esteemed, but on the whole their faith is in native medicines. Inoculation for smallpox has long been practised, so also has acupuncture for rheumatism, and the value of mercury for certain diseases is well known and it is largely employed. The Chinese materia medica is probably the most varied and comprehensive known. It includes all sorts of the most extraordinary things, ranging from tiger bones to bat's dung, and worse. It is principally, however, vegetable, and the majority of plants found in China are considered to possess medicinal properties to a greater or less extent. Of all this vast array only rhubarb and liquorice have any real value in Occidental practice. The majority of Chinese drugs are supposed to possess tonic and aphrodisiac properties, and the higher a drug is estimated in these respects the greater its commercial value, as witness ginseng and deerhorns in velvet.

The " Father of Chinese medicine " is the Emperor Shen-nung, who, according to legend, ruled from 2737–2697 B.C. This same emperor is also the " God of Agriculture." We are told that Shen-nung went very deeply into the study of herbs, in order to find remedies for the diseases of his people. He is said to have been very successful in his investigations. As an example of his energetic pursuit of this study, it is declared that in one day he discovered 70 poisonous plants and as many that were antidotes to them. Tradition is also responsible for the native belief that he had a glass covering to his stomach, in consequence of which he could watch the process of digestion of each herb and mark its influence on the system. A pharmacopœia, said to have been written by him, formed the nucleus of the " Pun-tsao " or *Herbal*, a great work on the Chinese materia medica. In every druggist's shop of repute there is an image of Shen-nung, and he is looked upon as the presiding deity of the business.

The *Herbal* above referred to was published about A.D. 1590, and its compiler, one Li Shi-chin, spent 30 years in collecting the information. He consulted some 800 previous authors, from whose writings he selected 1518 prescriptions, and added 374 new ones, arranging his materials in 52 chapters in a methodical and (for his day) scientific manner. The work, which is usually bound in 40 octavo volumes, was well received, and attracted the notice of the emperor, who ordered several succeeding editions to be published at the expense of the State. It was, in fact, so great an advance on all previous books, that it checked future writers on the subject, and Li is likely now to be the first and last Chinese critical writer on Natural Science in his mother tongue.

Many curious statements naturally occur in this extensive old work. For example : " The heart of a white horse, or that of a hog, cow, or hen, when dried and rasped into spirit, and so taken, cures forgetfulness." " Above the knees the horse has *night-eyes* (warts), which enable him to go in the night ; they are useful in the toothache." Another is : " If a man be restless and hysterical when he wishes to sleep, and it is requisite to put him to rest, let the ashes of a skull be mingled with water and given him, and let him have a skull for a pillow and it will cure him."

Some very extraordinary remedies are practised to-day. For example : Human milk is supposed to give strength to enfeebled old age. It is considered a meritorious filial act for daughters, granddaughters, and others to thus succour their aged relatives. In Chungking in 1908 an extraordinary case came to my knowledge. A native doctor informed a young woman that the only way to save her mother's life was to administer to her a portion of human liver. This daughter took a large knife and deliberately plunged it into her own body and cut away a portion of her liver. Dr. Asmy, a noble, self-sacrificing German doctor, working among the Chinese in Chungking, was informed of the case immediately after it took place, and succeeded in saving the self-mutilated woman's life. Dr. Asmy has the piece of liver preserved in spirit and kept as a memento in his hospital. Among the Chinese soldiers of the old school it was firmly believed that to eat the heart of a brave enemy was a sure way of obtaining the courage he possessed.

These nauseating and nonsensical ideas, however, are not all taken from the Chinese *Herbal*, and much as we may feel disposed to smile at the advice contained in this work, it is well to remember that Western literature on medicine of the same period contains very much the same sort of instruction. In Europe as late as the end of the sixteenth century plants were looked upon from a purely utilitarian point of view, not only by the masses, but also by very many professed scholars. Just as men lived in the firm belief that human destinies depended upon the stars, so they clung to the notion that everything upon the earth was created for the sake of mankind ; and, in particular, that in every plant there were forces lying dormant which, if liberated, would conduce either to the welfare or injury of man. People imagined they discerned magic in many plants, and even believed that they were able to trace in the resemblance of certain leaves, flowers, and fruits to parts of the human body, an indication emanating from supernatural powers, of the manner in which the organ in question was intended to affect the human constitution. The similarity in shape between a particular leaf and the liver did duty for a sign that the leaf was capable of successful application in cases of hepatic disease, and the fact of a blossom being heart-shaped must mean that it would cure cardiac complaints. Thus arose the so-called Doctrine of Signatures, which, brought to its highest development by the Swiss alchemist, Bombastus Paracelsus (1493–1541), played a great part in the sixteenth and seventeenth centuries, and still survives at the present day in the mania for nostrums.

In ancient Greece there was a special guild, the " Rhizo-tomoi," whose members collected and prepared such roots and herbs as were considered to be curative, and either sold them themselves or caused them to be sold by apothecaries. The " Medicine Guild " in China to-day performs much the same work, and its origin is long anterior to the Greek Rhizo-tomoi. If, then, Chinese pharmacology is to-day several centuries behind that of the Occident, there was a time when it was equally far in advance. Marco Polo makes many references to the value of Chinese drugs. For example : " All over the mountains of the province of Tangut, rhubarb is found in great abundance, and thither merchants come to buy it, and carry it thence all over the world."

All parts of the Chinese Empire contribute something to the native pharmacy, but, with the exception of ginseng, cassia-bark, camphor, and areca-nut, nearly all the more highly valued drugs come from the forests and scrub-clad highlands of the west. The famous drug, ginseng, the root of *Aralia quinquefolia*, comes from Corea and Manchuria, and the best quality sells for its weight in gold. To the Chinese this drug is the *radix vitæ*, restoring strength, vitality, and power to old and young. So precious is this " life-giving root " that the best plants are, in theory, reserved entirely for the emperor's use. On the Chinese system this drug unquestionably acts as a strong restorative, tonic, and aphrodisiac, adverse Western opinion notwithstanding. In the forests of the west certain " bastard ginsengs " occur, but are little valued.

Cassia-lignea, the bark, buds, and leaves of *Cinnamomum Cassia*, comes from certain districts (Luk-po, Lo-ting) in Kwang-tung and (Tai-wu) in Kwangsi, provinces in the south, where it is largely cultivated and exported to all parts of the Empire and elsewhere. Cassia-bark, " Kuei-p'i," is valued as a tonic, stimulant, and condiment. Areca-nut, the seed of a palm (*Areca catechu*), occurs in these southern provinces, and also in Yunnan. It is also imported from Cochin-China. Betel-chewing is not in general vogue among the Chinese, who value the nuts more as a medicine, chiefly as an astringent and anthelmintic.

Camphor is in general use all over China. The most valued kind is the Baros Camphor (*Dryobalanops Camphora*), imported from Malaysia (Borneo), the camphor produced in Japan, Formosa, and Fokien from *Cinnamomum Camphora* being less esteemed, and chiefly valued for purposes of export to other parts of the world.   The Chinese value Baros Camphor as a tonic and aphrodisiac.

The Imperial Maritime Customs officials have paid considerable attention to Chinese medicines, and in 1889 a list was published by order of the Inspector-General, the late Sir Robert Hart.   This list was compiled from the Returns of each Treaty port, and an attempt was made therein to identify the plants yielding the drugs and to give their province of origin.   The difficulties besetting such a task were enormous, but much good work was accomplished.   Consul-General Hosie, in his *Report on the Province of Ssuch'uan*, has compiled a list of Szechuan medicines which very accurately represents the present state of our knowledge on this subject.   Not until a complete collection of herbarium material covering flowers and fruits is made, and the whole submitted for identification to some one or other of the great herbaria in Europe, will it be possible to assign correct scientific names to a vast number of these medicines.

Hosie's list comprises 220 different kinds, of which number 189 are of vegetable origin.   The trade importance of drugs is enormous ; the exports passing through the Maritime Customs, at the port of Chungking, in 1910, being valued at over Tls.   1,540,000 ;   those from   Hankow at over Tls.   1,780,000.

I do not propose entering into a detailed account of the Chinese medicines, but will briefly note a few of the more important and their uses, which may not be without interest. Perhaps the most generally useful drug known from China is rhubarb, " Ta-huang."   The Rhubarb plant occurs throughout the highlands of the Chino-Thibetan borderland, but, as in the days of Marco Polo, the best comes from the " Province of Tangut."   This region stretches from Sungpan in a northwesterly direction, and includes part of the modern province of Kansu.   Rhubarb is found growing among scrub and near rocky watercourses between 7500 feet and 12,500 feet altitude. It is also commonly cultivated, but the wildling is esteemed the best drug.   The finest rhubarb is obtained from the plant known botanically as *Rheum palmatum*, var. *tanguticum*, and this is the variety most commonly met with throughout the extreme north-west of China and the contiguous Thibetan regions. From Tachienlu are exported considerable quantities of a second-grade rhubarb, which is mainly derived from *R. officinale*, although the variety *tanguticum* also occurs sparingly in that neighbourhood. Other species of Rheum grow in the west, and are used as adulterants. In north-western Hupeh *R. officinale* occurs in the forests, and is also cultivated by the peasants, but the quality of the drug is very poor. The so-called " Tangut regions " enjoy a dry, sunny climate, and curing the drug is a much easier task than in the other districts mentioned. This also probably affects the quality. In China, rhubarb is valued as a purgative, and is employed in the same way as in the Occident.

The best liquorice, " Kan-tsao " (Sweet-herb), is also a product of the grasslands north-west of Sungpan ; inferior kinds grow elsewhere in China. The source of the Sungpan product has been identified as *Glycyrrhiza uralensis*. It is valued as an emollient, and small quantities enter into nearly every prescription intended for internal application. The drug known in the vernacular as " Ch'ung-tsao " is a caterpillar infested with the mycelium and the projecting fructification of a Fungus (*Cordyceps sinensis*). This is another valued product of the western uplands, where it is found at from 12,000 to 15,000 feet altitude. The body of the caterpillar is yellowish, the fructification of the fungus black, the two together being stick-like in appearance and about 5 inches in length. As a medicine it is esteemed for a variety of purposes—boiled with pork it is employed as an antidote for opium-poisoning and as a cure for opium-eating ; also with pork and chicken it is taken as a tonic and mild stimulant by convalescent persons, and rapidly restores them to health and strength.

The tiny white bulbs of the Fritillary (*Fritillaria Roylei*, and other allied species), known as " Pei-mu " or " Jên Pei-mu," constitute one of the most highly valued medicines from the alpine regions of the west, where the plants grow at from 12,000 to 15,000 feet altitude. Large quantities of this drug are exported from Monkong Ting and Tachienlu. The bulbs are pounded, then boiled with dried orange skin and sugar. The resultant is taken as a cure for tuberculosis and asthma. In Hupeh the pseudo-bulbs of two terrestrial Orchids, *Pleione pogonioides* and *P. Henryi*, are used for the same purpose, and are known as " Ch'uan Pei-mu." These plants grow on moist, humus-clad rocks in the woods between 3000 and 5000 feet altitude.

In clearings in the woods throughout western Hupeh and on Mount Omei plantations of Huang-lien (*Coptis chinensis*) are maintained as a profitable investment. The dried rhizome is an all-round medicine, and particularly valued as a stomachic. An infusion is considered a cure for dyspepsia ; used by women nursing children, it is said to promote the flow of milk ; pounded and mixed with the white of eggs it is applied as a poultice to boils. Personally I can testify that it makes an excellent and appetizing bitters.

The thickened roots of a number of umbelliferous plants are esteemed for their medicinal virtues, as tonics and blood puri-fiers generally. One in general use and commonly cultivated is " Tang-kuei " (*Angelica polymorpha*, var. *sinensis*). An ex-tract obtained by boiling the root-stock of *Platycodon grandi-florum*, a campanulaceous plant known locally as " Chieh-k'eng," is a cure for chill in the stomach. The small pods of *Gleditsia officinalis*, " Ya-tsao," sliced and boiled with " Tang-kuei," forms an infusion which is considered a certain cure for coughs and colds.

For medicinal purposes the Aconite, " Tsao-wu-tu " (*Aconi-tum Wilsonii*), is cultivated, the powdered root being mixed with the white of eggs and applied externally as a remedy for boils. The " Ch'uan-wu-tu " (*A. Hemsleyanum*, and other climbing species) has similar uses to the foregoing. Also after frequent boilings the root is used in minute quantities as a drastic cure for coughs. Another twining herb, " Tang-shên " (*Codonopsis tangshen*), is commonly cultivated in the moun-tains, the thickened root-stock being valued as an all-round tonic.

The barks of many trees are used in medicine, and the identification of these is not so difficult as in the case of the herbs. One of the most esteemed is " Hou-p'o " (*Magnolia officinalis*). The best quality bark is worth 1000 cash per ounce. An extract is taken as a tonic, aphrodisiac, and a certain cure for colds, all in one. The dried flower-buds of this tree called " Yu-p'o " yield an extract by boiling which is taken by women to correct irregularities of menstruation.

The bark of *Eucommia ulmoides*, " Tu-chung " or " Tsze-mien," is pounded and boiled, the extract being taken with wine and pork as a cure for troubles of the kidney, liver, and spleen. It is also supposed to be a diuretic and aphrodisiac, and is a valuable general tonic. The bark of *Picrasma quassioides*, " Ku-lien-tzu," yields, on boiling, an extract which is used in cases of colic and pains in the stomach generally ; also as a febrifuge. The bark of *Phellodendron chinense*, " Huang-po " or " Huang-peh," is a complete materia medica in itself, it being used internally and externally as a general remedy for almost every ailment known to the Chinese, and, being cheap, is a poor man's " cure-all."

These selected examples, although few in number, are perhaps sufficient for the purpose of this chapter. Undoubtedly many of the drugs used by the Chinese possess sound medicinal properties, and their proper investigation is well worth the attention of Occidental pharmaceutists.

CHAPTER V

GARDENS AND GARDENING

Favourite Flowers Cultivated by the Chinese

ORNAMENTAL gardening has been practised in China from time immemorial, and the people are endowed with an innate love for flowers and gardens. Floral calendars are kept in every house above the poorest, and volumes of poems have been written in praise of the Moutan Pæony, Camellia, Plum, Chrysanthemum, Lotus-lily, Bamboo, and other flowers. The appearance of the blooms on the more conspicuous flowering shrubs is eagerly watched for, and excursions into the country are taken to enjoy the sight of the first bursting into blossom of favourite plants. The dwelling of the poorest peasant is usually enlivened by an odd plant or two, and the courtyard of the shopkeeper and innkeeper always boasts a few flowers of one sort or another. The temple grounds are frequently very beautiful, and attached to the houses of the cultured and wealthy are gardens often of great interest. In the neighbourhood of wealthy cities like Soochou, Hanchou, and Canton, are public and private gardens which are famed throughout the length and breadth of the Empire. The finest example I have seen is fittingly associated with the emperor's summer palace, a few miles outside Peking. There Chinese gardening may be seen at its best, and it calls forth admiration from all visitors.

Chinese landscape-gardening is represented at its best in the so-called " Japanese gardens " of to-day. The Japanese have undoubtedly carried the art to a higher state of perfection than the Chinese, but the latter unquestionably originated it. In all these gardens the love of the grotesque predominates, and the landscape effect is essentially artificial ; yet in accordance with their own ideals the Chinese are most skilful and accomplished gardeners. Given a piece of ground, no matter if it be small, and devoid of all natural beauty, or badly situated, they will patiently transform it into a mountain-landscape in miniature. With strange-looking, weather-worn rocks, dwarfed trees, bamboos, herbs, and water, a piece of wild country-side is evolved replete with mountain and stream, forest and field, plateau and lake, grotto and dell. A network of narrow winding paths traverses the garden, and rustic bridges in various designs are thrown across the infantine streams. The whole effect is often encompassed within a comparatively few square yards, though the perspective is one of seemingly many miles. In all the larger gardens, closely associated with and usually in part overhanging a pool where the Lotus-lily is grown, a small pavilion is erected. Here the proprietor and his guests resort to drink tea or wine, chat, and admire the various flowers. When no male guests are present the garden is frequented by the female members of the family; with whom it is ever a favourite sanctum.

The Chinese do not cultivate a very great variety of plants, and the contents of the various gardens are much the same, though necessarily the selection is modified by climate and locality. To all the flowers grown in Chinese gardens some peculiar significance or æsthetic value is attached. An orchid (*Cymbidium ensifolium*), called "Lan hwa," is regarded as the "king of flowers," the modest appearance of the plant. and the delicate odour of its blossoms, representing the very essence of refinement. The "Mei hwa" (*Prunus mume*), owing to the beauty and perfume of its flowers, which are produced in winter when few plants are in blossom, is very highly prized and regarded as a "flower of refinement." Around Peking the same vernacular name and attributes are attached to *P. triloba* and its double-flowered form. The Winter-sweet, "La-mei hwa" (*Meratia præcox*), is similarly esteemed.

The various Bamboos, emblems of grace and culture, and beautiful at all seasons of the year, are indispensable garden plants. "No man can live without a Bamboo tree in the immediate vicinity of his house, but he can live without meat," is a favourite Taouist saying. The Chrysanthemum, "Chu

hwa," and Moutan Pæony are other " flowers of refinement "
almost reverently appreciated for the colour and beautiful
form of their flowers. The Lotus-lily, " Lien hwa " (*Nelumbium
speciosum*), is regarded as an emblem of purity, and the Goddess
of Mercy (Kwanyin) is always represented seated in the centre
of a Lotus flower. The Chinese " Luck Lily " or " Water
Fairy " (*Narcissus tazetta*) is cultivated in vast quantities,
more especially throughout the eastern part of the Empire,
and is in blossom for the New Year festival. It is appreciated
for its odoriferous flowers, and its luxurious growth is considered
prophetic of wealth and prosperity. This Narcissus is not a
Chinese plant, but is a native of the Mediterranean region, from
whence it was long ago introduced into China by Portuguese
traders, and it together with the Pomegranate are virtually
the only exotic flowers in high favour with the Chinese.

The Pearl Orchid, " Chu-lan hwa " (*Chloranthus incon-
spicuus*), is valued for the delicate odour of its flowers, which
are used in the Anhui province in scenting green tea for the
Chinese market. Table grass (*Liriope spicata*) is admired for
its graceful habit, and is placed on a desk or table, to afford
rest to the eyes when reading or studying. Lastly in this
relation may be mentioned the " Hoary Pine," which is
emblematical of revered old age. This name is applied to
several kinds of Conifers other than Pinus proper.

To complete the list of favourite Chinese flowers we may
enumerate Camellia, Heavenly Bamboo, " Tien-ch'u " (*Nandina
domestica*), " Kuei hwa " (*Osmanthus fragrans*), " Tzu-ching "
(*Lagerstrœmia indica*), " Tiao-chung " (*Enkianthus quinqueflorus*), " Chin-yin hwa " (*Lonicera japonica*), numerous
varieties of Azaleas, Roses, Balsams, Cockscombs, double-
flowered Peaches, various Conifers, and Box (*Buxus japonica*). Some or all of the above are to be found in every
Chinese garden of note. Though the cultural skill expended
on many of them is in the direction of dwarfing and training
into grotesque shapes, this treatment in no sense robs the
flowers of the qualities attributed to them in literature and
song. The decoration found on Chinese porcelain well
illustrates the nation's love of beautiful flowers and quaint-
shaped trees.

China is a land of contrariety—a land whereof no general statement or observation holds good. In spite of their love for the grotesque and the artificial landscapes seen in their gardens, the Chinese have a strong appreciation of natural beauty. This is evidenced by the sites chosen for their temples and shrines and for the tombs of the wealthy. Apart from situation, which is usually perfect, such sanctuaries always nestle beneath the shade of magnificent trees, and are approached as a rule through avenues or groves of large trees. Though a few deciduous trees are commonly found, evergreens always have distinctive preference. In the temple grounds around Peking are noble avenues of Arbor-vitæ (*Thuya orientalis*), Juniper (*Juniperus chinensis*), Elm (*Ulmus pumila*), and Sophora (*S. japonica*) ; in the south, centre, and west of the Empire, Pine (*Pinus Massoniana*), China Fir (*Cunninghamia lanceolata*), Cypress (*Cupressus funebris*), Nanmu (*Machilus nanmu*, and allied species), "Yu-la shu" (*Photinia Davidsoniæ*), Wintergreen (*Xylosma racemosum*), Banyan (*Ficus infectoria*), and a few other kinds of trees are always present. Many of these trees are extremely rare, except in the precincts of religious sanctuaries.

The world at large does not realize how deeply it is indebted to religious communities for the preservation of many trees. In Europe, for example, most of the best varieties of Pears originated in the gardens attached to religious establishments in France and Belgium and were introduced into England and other countries after the battle of Waterloo. In China, where every available bit of land is devoted to agriculture, quite a number of trees must long ago have become extinct but for the timely intervention of Buddhist and Taouist priests. The most noteworthy example of this benevolent preservation is the Maidenhair tree (*Ginkgo biloba*). This strikingly beautiful tree is associated with temples, shrines, courtyards of palaces, and mansions of the wealthy throughout the length and breadth of China, and also in parts of Japan. But it is nowhere truly wild, and is a relic of a very ancient flora. Geological evidence shows that it is the last survivor of an ancient family, which flourished during Secondary times, and can even be traced back to the Primary rocks. In Mesozoic

times this genus played an important part in the arborescent
flora of north-temperate regions. Fossil remains, almost
identical with the present existing species, have been found,
not only in this country and North America, but also in
Greenland.

Though to-day Chinese gardens, nurseries, and temple
grounds do not contain anything new in the way of ornamental
or economic plants, it was otherwise up to the middle of the
last century. Our early knowledge of the Chinese flora was
based on plants procured from gardens, notably from those
around Canton. The plants were brought to Europe by trading
vessels, especially those of the East India Company, at the
end of the eighteenth and early in the nineteenth centuries.
Different patrons of horticultural and botanical institutions
in England lent financial assistance, and collectors were dispatched to investigate and send home all that they could
possibly find.

By these means our gardens first secured the early varieties
of Roses, Camellias, Azaleas, greenhouse Primroses, Gardenias,
Moutan Pæonies, Chrysanthemums, Chinese Asters, and such-
like familiar plants. The Chrysanthemum, for instance, has
been cultivated in China and Japan from time immemorial,
and its parent forms (*Chrysanthemum sinense* and *C. indicum*)
are common wild flowers around Ichang and elsewhere in
China. In Europe *C. sinense* was first cultivated in Dutch
gardens as early as 1689, no less than six kinds being then
known. But these were subsequently lost, and when the
plant was again introduced in 1789, through the agency of
Sir Joseph Banks, the plant was unknown to Dutch gardeners.
The famous gardener, Philip Miller, cultivated *C. indicum* in
the Chelsea Physic Gardens in 1764, it having been discovered
in 1751, near Macao, south China, by Osbeck. This species
has, however, had much less to do in the evolution of our
present-day Chrysanthemum than *C. sinense*.

The parent of our Tea Roses is *Rosa indica*, the Chinese
Monthly Rose, long cultivated in China and still to be found
wild in the central and western parts of the Empire. It was
introduced into England through the efforts of Sir Joseph
Banks in 1789. The parent of our greenhouse Primroses

(*Primula sinensis*) was introduced from Canton into the garden of Thomas Palmer, Esq., of Bromley, Kent, by John Reeves about 1820. It is a native of Hupeh, where it occurs in great abundance on the dry, precipitous, limestone cliffs of the Ichang Gorge and its lateral glens. The wildling is a true perennial with flowers of a uniform mauve-pink colour. Another greenhouse Primrose (*P. obconica*) occurs in the same region but in moist loamy situations.

The Indian and Mollis Azaleas and a score of other favourite plants of our gardens all came originally from Chinese gardens through various agencies. It is true we have developed most of these introductions almost beyond recognition, and the Chinese are now acquiring new forms and varieties from us, yet without these early arrivals how much poorer our gardens and conservatories would be to-day! In bygone times, even only about a century ago, that part of the world which we know as China was loosely spoken of as the " Indies," and this geographical blunder is perpetuated in the specific name " indica " which botanists have attached to some of these plants. In the middle of last century many ornamental plants were received from the gardens of Japan, and botanists, assuming that these were natives of the country, gave the specific name " japonica " to certain of them. Subsequent knowledge has, however, conclusively proved that a number of the so-called Japanese plants are only cultivated forms of plants originally natives of China. Thus has the geographer and botanist unwittingly obscured China's right to be termed the " Kingdom of Flowers."

CHAPTER VI

AGRICULTURE

THE PRINCIPAL FOOD-STUFF CROPS

THE Chinese might appropriately be termed a "Nation of Shopkeepers," yet, in spite of their commercial enterprise, the agricultural industry is the backbone of the nation. With a vast population to support, every possible inch of land has been brought under cultivation, and prodigious efforts have been made to obtain the greatest returns from the soil. In spite of it all, millions are ever on the verge of starvation, and almost annually either drought or flood brings famine to some part of the Empire.

Landed property is held in clans or families as much as possible and is not entailed, nor are overgrown estates frequent. The land is all held directly from the Crown, no freehold being acknowledged. The conditions of common tenure are the payment of an annual tax, the fee for alienation, with a money composition for personal service to the Government. The proprietors of land record their names in the district and take out an original deed (called "red deed") which secures them in possession as long as the ground tax is paid. This sum varies very much according to the fertility, location, and nature of the land, but is nowhere heavy or severe. Naturally, good rice-land pays the heaviest tax. The paternal estate, and the property thereon, descends to the eldest son, but his brothers can remain upon it with their families and devise their portion *in perpetuo* to their children, or an amicable composition may be made ; daughters never inherit, nor can an adopted son of another clan succeed. A mortgagee must enter into possession of property and make himself responsible for the payment of taxes levied thereon. The enclosure of recent alluvial deposits cannot be made without the cognizance of the authorities, but the terms in such cases are not onerous. When waste hillsides and poor areas are brought under cultivation ample time is allowed for a return of the capital expended in reclaiming them before assessment is made.

Since the food-supply of the Chinese population has always been supplied from within the Empire, agriculture has rightly been accorded first place among all branches of labour from time immemorial. According to legend, the Emperor Shen-nung (2737–2697 B.C.) established agriculture as a science. He examined the various kinds of soils and gave directions as to what should be cultivated in each. He taught the people how to make ploughs, and instructed them in the best methods of husbandry. Immediate results were seen in the improved conditions of the people, and succeeding generations have amply testified their gratitude to him. Under the title of " Prince of Cereals " he has long since been deified, and is worshipped throughout the length and breadth of the land. In Peking there is an altar dedicated to him, enclosed within a large park. Formerly, at the vernal equinox, the ruling emperor, assisted by various officials, performed an annual commemorative ceremony of ploughing a portion of the park.

The Chinese nation is to a very large extent vegetarian, flesh being eaten only in small quantities except on festival occasions. Pork, chickens, ducks, and fish comprise the meat-diet, and of these the Chinese are excessively fond, but to the great majority they are luxuries, only to be indulged in on rare occasions. Rice is to them what wheat is to us, only more so. So long as the average Chinaman can get rice he is happy ; but this would be scarcely true of ourselves if we could only get bread ! Next to rice the more important food-stuffs are wheat, maize, pulse, and cabbage. The Chinese fry most of their vegetables, and for this purpose a vegetable oil is nearly always used. The oils expressed from the seeds of members of the Cabbage (*Brassica*) family, the Soy Bean (*Glycine hispida*), and Sesamé (*Sesamum indicum*) being most in request.

Whilst the Chinese cultivate a great variety of vegetables the quality of one and all, judged from our standard, is wretchedly inferior. With the exception of maize and sweet potatoes, it is safe to say that not a single Chinese vegetable would command attention in this country.   In this chapter I have attempted a fairly exhaustive account of this subject, in so far as it came under my observation during the eleven years I travelled in China.   These observations were mainly limited to three provinces, namely, Yunnan, Hupeh, and Szechuan. The estimated area of these territories is about 372,500 square miles—more than three times that of the United Kingdom.   Other parts of China have vegetables peculiarly their own.   Again, at the treaty ports, where foreigners have settled, varieties of our own vegetables have been introduced and are cultivated for their use.   These, with rare exceptions, do not come within our province.

In China the fields are all so small that market-gardening rather than farming best describes the agricultural industry. Long experience has taught the people how to obtain the maximum returns without unduly exhausting the soil, indeed, the extraordinary thing about Chinese agriculture is the fact that, although cultivation has been so long in progress, the soil shows practically no sign of exhaustion.   Artificial manures are unknown to the Chinese farmer, and ordinary farmyard manure is scarce and almost a negligible factor.   Constant tillage, aided by as much sewage as can be possibly obtained, are relied upon to produce full crops.   The sewage from cities and villages is carried long distances away in buckets or in tubs to the fields, and nowhere else in the world is human excrement so highly valued or so laboriously collected.   In matters of seed-selection, plant-breeding, and the higher arts of agriculture, the Chinese have everything to learn.   Rotation of crops and the enrich-ment of the soil by leguminous crops they understand and practise as fully as circumstances permit.

Rice (*Oryza sativa*) is, of course, the favourite cereal, but being a tropical plant, requiring an aquatic habitat, its area of cul-tivation is restricted in China, and probably a third of the people never taste this grain save on festival occasions.   In southern China two crops of rice are obtainable annually, but throughout the greater part of the land where this cereal is cultivated only one crop can be grown in a season.   This occupies the ground from May until early in September.

In the cultivation of rice, the patience, ingenuity, and incredible industry of the Chinese are particularly well exemplified. The terraced fields, necessary to ensure a flow of water, whether it be on a seemingly flat plain or on a steep hillside, meet the eye of the traveller on all sides. It is little short of marvellous when one reflects on the skilful way in which the entire rice-belt in China is terraced, and the enormous amount of time and labour involved in the undertaking indicate what a hard task-master necessity has been. In matters of irrigation the Chinese are past masters. They have not yet succeeded in making water run uphill, but with their various contrivances they lift it bodily from streams and ditches and convey it long distances to wherever it is needed. The number of devices for irrigation purposes is almost legion, and though simple in principle and efficacious in results they are intricate in detail. Some are operated by hand, others by the foot, and many are automatically worked by the current of the streams. The large skeleton-like water-wheels depicted in the photographic illustration (p. 52), represent one of the methods commonly in use in central and Western China.

Rice-cultivation presents many tedious details and the layman will probably find it difficult to realize that in China the whole crop is planted by hand. The grain is sown thickly in nursery-beds, and when the seedlings are 5 or 6 inches tall they are transplanted in small clumps equidistant in the flooded, prepared fields. Men and women take part in this work, and it is surprising how rapidly the fields are planted. The rice plants are made firm in the mud by treading around them immediately they are established. The fields are kept free of weeds and the requisite supply of water is maintained until, as the crop ripens, the fields are finally allowed to get dry. The rice crop is reaped by hand, and without being removed from the field the grain is at once beaten off into wooden bins ; afterwards it is dried and stored. The Chinese cultivate three well-marked varieties of rice—namely, ordinary, red, and glutinose. The first two are grown for food only; the red, being the hardiest, is cultivated at higher altitudes than the other, but is by no means confined thereto. This Red Rice, " Hung-mê " (*O. sativa*, var. *præcox*), gets its name from the reddish colour of the pellicle, which adheres tenaciously to parts of the grain after milling. Glutinose Rice (*O. sativa*, var. *glutinosa*) does not take the place of the other two as a food-stuff, being only eaten for a change. It is valued for the weak spirit which is made from it, for the sugar which is extracted from it, and for making into cakes and sweetmeats. It is later in ripening than the other varieties, and always commands a higher price in the market. In Yunnan a variety which will thrive without water is grown. This Upland Rice (*O. sativa*, var. *montana*) yields but a poor crop and is very inferior.

Whilst the Chinese are pre-eminently a rice-eating race, it should be borne in mind that there are millions of Chinese who, save on rare occasions, never eat rice at all. To these people, wheat, maize, and buckwheat are the staple cereals. In the rice-growing districts of China, Wheat (*Triticum sativum*) is a winter crop, occupying the ground from October to early May. In the mountainous districts and in the colder provinces it is a most important summer crop. I have noted no fewer than five very distinct varieties, comprising both " red " and " white " wheats, and both awned and awnless kinds. In late August the mountain-sides and valleys in western Szechuan present a glorious picture of miles and miles of rolling grain fields. In this region 8000 to 10,500 feet represent the wheat-growing belt. The grain is sown by hand in rows, the seeds being dropped in clusters a few inches apart. In the Yangtsze Valley, if the wheat crop is late in ripening, it is ploughed in to make way for rice. In the plains of central China the grain is threshed out the moment it is harvested. On the Thibetan borderland it is tied into sheaves and stacked, ears downwards, on tall hurdle-like arrangements (Kai-kos) until time and weather admit of its being threshed. (These remarks also apply to barley, oats, and other crops.) The grain is ground into flour and made into cakes and vermicelli. Chinese flour is usually gritty and of bad colour.

Barley is sparsely cultivated throughout the Yangtsze Valley, and it is only in the mountainous Thibetan borderland that it is largely grown. The Chinese do not care for the meal, and the grain is chiefly used for making spirit and for feeding pigs and other domestic animals. The Thibetans, on the other hand, highly esteem barley. Roasted and ground into meal and mixed with tea and rancid butter it forms " Tsamba," their national and staple food. Since it is hardier than wheat its culture extends to a greater altitude; the highest point at which I noted it was 12,000 feet. Both Chinese and Thibetans cultivate several varieties, but the six-rowed variety, *Hordeum hexastichon*, is most in favour. Around Sungpan a variety of the above, having purple paleæ, is largely grown, being considered hardier than the type. This variety is apparently peculiar to this region, being quite distinct from the two-ranked chocolate Barley (*H. cœleste*), which is cultivated in parts of the Himalaya. Ordinary Barley (*H. vulgare*) is cultivated in smaller quantities than the preceding kinds by Chinese and Thibetans. In Hupeh and in the river-valleys of western Szechuan I met with occasional patches of *H. hexastichon*, var. *trifurcatum*. This variety is the Mi-mê (Rice-wheat) of the Chinese.

In the mountains Rye (*Secale fragile*) is sparingly grown and the grain eaten.

Oats are not much grown by the Chinese in the parts through which I travelled, but they are cultivated to a considerable extent by the Thibetan and other tribesmen in the highlands. The Chinese prefer *Avena nuda*, which they designate " Yenmê " ; the Thibetans and tribesfolk favour *Avena fatua*. The grain of both these kinds is roasted and ground into oatmeal, or cooked and eaten whole.

Next to rice and wheat, Maize, or " Pao-k'o " (*Zea Mays*), is the most important cereal. This plant is of American origin; but it has been so long cultivated in China that the date of introduction is not ascertainable. In the rice-belt it is relegated to land that for one reason or another is not suitable for rice. It is in the more mountainous parts that maize is the staple crop. It occupies the gullies and slopes of the mountains, and commonly so steep are these that one wonders how the people manage to sow and reap the crop. Wild pigs rob the maize fields, and when the crop is in ear the farmers beat gongs and make as much noise as possible during the night to scare these animals away. In open country tall thatched look outs are erected, where the juvenile and female members of the family sit and watch for thieves during the daylight.

In the Yangtsze Valley maize is always a summer crop, and two crops are frequently harvested. In the mountains its cultivation extends up to 8000 feet, and in exceptionally favourable districts even higher. Green corn is really a delicious vegetable, and ought to be used in this country. The Chinese, however, do not employ it extensively in this form. When ripe the sheaths of the cobs are folded back, exposing the grain. They are then tied in bunches and suspended from the roofs of houses, where they can be kept dry. The grain is ground and made into meal-cakes ; it is also used for making spirit. From the culms sugar is sometimes extracted, but their chief use is for fuel.

False Millet (*Sorghum vulgare*), the " Kao-liang " or " Hsu-tzu " of the Chinese, is largely used for making wine. It is cultivated generally throughout central and Western China, but not so extensively as in the northern parts of China, and notably Manchuria. The largest areas I noted were on the plateaux of Yunnan, the plain of Chengtu, and the fluviatile areas of the Min and Fou Rivers. Its altitudinal limit is about the same as that of maize, and, like this latter, it is always a summer crop. Two distinct varieties are grown, one with purple, the other with yellowish " heads." It is occasionally employed as food, more particularly in mountainous districts, but 90 per cent. of it is used for making wine.

Other Millets met with in cultivation are *Panicum miliaceum*, " Chan-tzu " ; *Setaria italica*, " Hsiu-ku " ; and *Panicum crusgalli*, var. *frumentaceum*, " Lung-tsao-ku," but not in large quantities. The grain is used in making cakes and for feeding bird-pets. The cereal commonly known as Job's Tears, " Tawan-tzu" (*Coix lachryma*), is cultivated in small patches throughout central and Western China. Though occasionally used as food in the form of gruel, " Job's tears " are chiefly valued as medicine. They are supposed to possess tonic and diuretic properties, and are administered in cases of phthisis and dropsy.

Of Buckwheat two species are commonly cultivated, namely, *Fagopyrum esculentum* and *F. tataricum*, the " T'ien-ch'iao-mê " and " K'u-ch'iao-mê " respectively of the Chinese. These constitute a most important crop, especially in the highlands. Under favourable climatic conditions two crops are harvested.

A field of the pink Buckwheat (F. *esculentum*) in flower is one of the prettiest sights imaginable. It is most commonly grown on terraced mountain-sides. The other species grows twice as tall as the above, and bears greenish-white flowers. The altitudinal limit of buckwheat equals and possibly exceeds that of barley. After the seeds are threshed out they are ground up in water, and the husks are removed by a fine sieve. The flour is then made into dough with a little salt, to which lime is added. This dough is made into vermicelli, when it is ready for cooking and eating. Buckwheat constitutes a most important article of food among the Chinese who live in the mountainous districts, and also with the tribesfolk of the borderland. It is a very accommodating crop, for it thrives on the poorest of soils, requires little attention beyond sowing and harvesting, and matures very quickly.

Since the Chinese are to such a large extent a vegetarian people, the various members of the pea and bean family are necessarily most important crops. The Common Pea, " Mê-wan-tzu " (*Pisum sativum*), and Broad Bean (*Vicia Faba*), with the Soy Bean (*Glycine hispida*), are the most important. The two former are winter crops in the valleys and summer crops in the highlands. The soy bean is everywhere a summer crop. Peas and broad beans are eaten both fresh and dried. They are also ground into flour and made into vermicelli. The young shoots of the pea are eaten as a vegetable. The soy bean, " Huang-tou," is of even greater value than the preceding ; it is planted everywhere—in fields by itself, around rice and other fields, and as an undercrop to maize and sorghum. It yields seeds of three colours, namely, yellow, green; and black. The Chinese distinguish three kinds of the yellow and two kinds each of the green and black. These varieties yield a succession of beans, the black being fully a month later than the others. The " Huang-tou " is cooked and eaten as a vegetable, or ground into flour and made into vermicelli ; preserved in salt it makes an excellent pickle. It is also extensively used in the manufacture of soy sauce and soy vinegar. A variety with small yellow seeds is largely employed in making bean-curd. While in central and Western China the soy bean is cultivated exclusively as a food-stuff, in Manchuria it is grown almost solely for the oil which is obtained from the seeds by pressure; and for the residual-cakes that remain after the oil had been expressed. From Newchwang, the port of Manchuria, there is an enormous export trade done in " Bean-cake," which is in great demand as an agricultural fertilizer in all parts of China. The soy bean has recently been exported to Europe in large quantities, and the soy-bean oil is employed in soap-making and for culinary purposes.

Two kinds of Gram, *Phaseolus mungo*, " Lu-tou," and *P. mungo*, var. *radiatus*, " Hung-tou," are grown as summer crops. The seeds of the " Lu-tou " (green bean) are especially valued for their sprouts. To obtain these the beans are put in jars with water and covered over. Under these conditions they quickly develop shoots a couple of inches or more long, which are highly esteemed as a vegetable. Of the " Hung-tou " (red bean) there are two or three varieties. The seeds of these are used as a vegetable or ground into flour and employed for stuffing cakes and sweetmeats.

The Lentil (*Ervum Lens*), " Chin-mê-wan-tzu," is cultivated as a winter crop, being commonly associated with peas and broad beans. It is, however, by no means extensively grown. The seeds are eaten cooked. Oil is occasionally expressed from the seeds and used for lighting purposes. Other pulses are *Dolichos Lablab*, " Pien-tou," of which there are several varieties, *Canavalia ensiformis* (Sword Bean), *Phaseolus vulgaris*, " Yün-tou," *Vigna Catiang*, and *Cajanus indicus*, all commonly and extensively cultivated. Though the seeds of the first four are eaten, it is more for the pods, which are sliced, cooked, and eaten as a vegetable, that these plants are valued. The cylindrical pods of *Vigna Catiang* are from 1½ to 2 feet long, and about the thickness of a lead-pencil. Though the Chinese esteem it, I have found it only a very tasteless vegetable. As a winter crop in parts of the Yangtsze Valley, *Melilotus macrorhiza*, " Yeh-hua-tsen," is sparingly cultivated. The green shoots are sometimes eaten as a vegetable ; the seeds are used medicinally for colds.

Of cabbages the Chinese have their own peculiar varieties, all of them very different from those grown in this country. The favourite variety, " Peh-ts'ai," or Shantung cabbage, as foreigners have styled it, is more like a huge cos lettuce than a cabbage. This kind is grown everywhere, but attains its greatest perfection in the colder parts of China. In the Yangtsze Valley it is best when grown as a winter crop. Another striking variety is the white-ribbed cabbage, " Kin-ta-ts'ai," which is said to be peculiar to Szechuan. In addition to these some half-dozen other varieties are cultivated. Cabbages are eaten fresh or are preserved by salting and drying in the sun. From a European standpoint none is worth growing, being so very inferior in flavour to our own. The Roman Catholic priests have introduced the common European cabbage, but though its culture has spread widely the Chinese much prefer their own varieties. While the Chinese cabbages are all really referable to *Brassica campestris*, it is convenient to group them under *B. chinensis*. As a winter crop green kale, " Kan-kan-ts'ai," and dark-red kale, " Ts'ai-tai " are cultivated through the Yangtsze Valley. The young shoots of *Brassica juncea* and *B. campestris*, var. *oleifera*, are also used in the same way as kale.

The Chinese cultivate a great many gourds for food, the whole cucurbitaceous family being known under the general name of " Kua." Some are eaten raw, and others cooked. The male flowers, too, are eaten by the peasantry. The seeds of the water-melon are esteemed a great delicacy. They are slightly roasted, and are consumed in enormous quantities ; no banquet is complete without them, and over their gossip in tea-shops or restaurants, scholars and coolies alike regale themselves with these delicious morsels. Preserved in sugar, melon-seeds form a favourite sweetmeat. As a summer crop throughout the Yangtsze Valley the following cucurbitaceous plants are commonly cultivated : *Cucurbita Citrullus*, " Hsi-kua " ; *C. Pepo*, " Hsi-hu-lu " ; *C. moschata*, " Huo-kua " ; *C. maxima*, " Nan-kua " ; *C. ovifera*, " Sun-kua " ; *Cucumis Melo*, " Tien-kua " ; *C. sativus*, " Huang-kua " ; *Benincasa cerifera*, " Tung-kua " ; *Lagenaria vulgaris*, var. *clavata*, " Hu-tzu-kua " ; *L. leucantha*, var. *longis*, " Ts'ai-kua." When very young the fruit of *Momordica charantia*, " Ku-kua," is eaten, and when old is used as medicine. *Luffa cylindrica*, " Ssu-kua," is cooked and eaten when young ; when old the fibre is esteemed as medicine. *Lagenaria vulgaris*, " Hu-lu," is cultivated for its hard shells, which are converted into receptacles for holding water, oil, or wine. In addition to the above, several gourds are cultivated for their ornamental fruits, which are used for decorative purposes.

In the valleys and on the plains and low hills bordering them throughout the Yangtsze Valley and Yunnan, the Sweet Potato (*Ipomœa Batatas*) is the most important root crop. The crop is always cultivated on ridges and is grown from both old tubers and cuttings. Tubers are planted out in May, and cuttings from the shoots of these are inserted in July and early August, and produce a fine crop in October and November. The crop from the old roots is ready in August. Sweet potatoes are eaten after being boiled, baked, and dried in chips, and constitute a truly delicious dish. As they deteriorate by keeping, they are cut into slices, scalded, and then dried in the sun. The tubers are also macerated in cold water, and the resultant starch dried and made into vermicelli. In Hupeh the sweet potato is known as the " Hung-shao," in Szechuan as the " Pen-shao."

In the mountainous districts the sweet potato is displaced by the Irish potato, or " Yang-yü " (*Solanum tuberosum*), which, like maize, is another plant of American origin that has become a most important crop. It was introduced by the Roman Catholic priests at the time of a great famine some forty odd years ago. Its culture has spread enormously, and though it is despised by the rice-eating Chinese of the plains it has become a staple article of food with the highland peasantry. In the valleys it is cultivated as a late winter crop, in the mountains as a summer crop. Its culture is unfortunately but little understood ; it is always grown too thickly, and seldom if ever properly earthed up. Both red and white-skinned varieties are grown, but the flavour is usually very poor. The potatoes cultivated by the Buddhist priests on Mount Omei are justly celebrated, but the best I ever ate in China were grown by Sifan tribesfolk around Sungpan.

Two kinds of Yam are commonly cultivated, namely, *Dioscorea alata*, the " Chieh-pan-shao," which has enormously

large, flat, branching tubers, and *D. Batatas*, " Pai-shao " ;
both are cooked and eaten. Around Ichang the tubers
of a third species are eaten. This species is known as *D.
zingiberensis*, the " Huang-chiang," or Yellow Ginger. The
tuber is bitter, and is valued chiefly as a medicine. Chinese
yams do not equal the sweet potato in flavour, and are not so
extensively grown. Around Chengtu *Pachyrhizus angulatus*,
the " Ti-kua," is commonly grown. The white, firm-fleshed,
turnip-like tubers are eaten either raw or cooked.

White turnips, " Lo-po," both the long and round kinds,
are cultivated everywhere, but the flavour is very poor. Also
the so-called red turnip, which really is a Radish (*Raphanus
sativus*). All three are cooked and eaten when fresh, or preserved by being sliced and dried in the sun. *Brassica Napus*,
var. *esculenta*, the " Ta-t'ou-ts'ai," is very generally cultivated,
but I met with it most frequently on the Chengtu Plain. The
whole plant is pickled and eaten with rice. The Szechuanese
also cultivate most excellent Kohl-rabi (*Brassica oleracea*, var.
caulo-rapa).

Two aroids, *Colocasia antiquorum* and its variety *Fontanesii*,
" Kiang-tou," are very extensively cultivated for their tubers,
which are cooked and eaten in various ways. Both are grown
on ridges in flooded ground. The purple-coloured petioles
of the " Kiang-tou " are sliced, pickled, and eaten. The
flavour of the tubers of these plants is similar to that of
the Jerusalem artichoke, but inferior. *Sagittaria sagittifolia*,
" T'zu-ku," is cultivated in Szechuan and Yunnan, and the
tubers are cooked and eaten in the same way as those of the
Colocasia. The tubers of *Scirpus tuberosus*, " P'ei-chi," and the
fruits of the Water Chestnut (*Trapa natans*), " Ling-chio,"
two very common aquatics, are esteemed valuable articles of
food.

The Lotus-lily (*Nelumbium speciosum*), " Lien hwa," is
cultivated both for its seed and its rhizome. These are used
as food, but being expensive are luxuries enjoyed only by the
wealthy. The fibres of the rhizome are used medicinally.
Ginger (*Zingiber officinale*), " Seng-chiang," is very extensively
grown. It is prepared for the table in various ways. From
Canton, ginger preserved in sugar is exported in quantity to

this country. *Amorphophallus konjac*, " Mo-yü," is sparingly cultivated throughout the Yangtsze Valley. The tubers are ground up with water and made into a curd-like compound. On Mount Omei and in north-west Szechuan this plant is more generally cultivated. The bulbs of *Lilium tigrinum*, the " Chia-peh-ho," are highly esteemed, and occur both cultivated and wild. The white bulbs of this lily are more expensive in China than they are in this country. When properly cooked these bulbs are not at all bad eating. They somewhat resemble the parsnip in flavour.

Of the onion family, Garlic, or " Ta-suan " (*Allium sativum*), and the common Onion; or " Ts'ong " (*A. Cepa*); are cultivated extensively. Garlic is highly esteemed. Onions are eaten as " spring onions," large bulbs being absolutely unknown. *A. fistulosum* is the Chinese Leek, " Chiu-ts'ai," and is very widely grown. The leaves are flattened and covered with earth to ensure blanching. The blanched leaves, " Chin-huang," are considered a delicacy. In the mountains *A. odorum*, *A. chinense*; and other species are common. These are culled and eaten by the peasantry. Szechuan, especially the more alluvial areas, produces remarkably fine Carrots (*Daucus Carota*), " Hung Lo-po." They are grown in large quantities and eaten with great relish. The Parsnip (*Peucedanum sativum*), " Uen-shui " are cultivated, but the roots are seldom thicker than a pencil. The whole plant is cooked and eaten.

Although in central and Western China quite a number of plants are grown for their oil, fully 75 per cent. of the oil commonly used is the product of two members of the cabbage family. After a careful investigation of the subject I have satisfied myself that the two plants in question are *Brassica juncea*, var. *oleifera*, and *B. campestris*, var. *oleifera*. The latter is the " Ta-yu-ts'ai " of the Chinese, the former the " Hsao-yu-ts'ai;" or " Ch'ing-yu." Both kinds are loosely designated " rape " by the foreigners resident in China ; but in my wanderings there I never met with the true rape plant. Throughout the entire Yangtsze Valley, during the winter months, enormous areas are given over to the cultivation of these two plants. Though the " Hsao-yu-ts'ai " is the earlier of the two, the other is the more extensively grown.

These plants are in flower in February and March, and the crop is harvested in April. The seeds are crushed and steamed, and the oil obtained by expression. In Szechuan the use of the oil as an illuminant equals its culinary value. It also enters very largely into the composition of Chinese candles.

Oil is also expressed from the seeds of the Ground-nut (*Arachis hypogœa*), the Opium Poppy (*Papaver somniferum*), the Sunflower (*Helianthus annuus*), Cotton seed (*Gossypium herbaceum*), the Soy Bean (*Glycine hispida*), and members of the cabbage family, other than those already mentioned, notably the kales, and in the highlands from Flax seed, " Shan-chih-ma " (*Linum usitatissimum*). These oils are all used for cooking and lighting purposes and for adulterating the more valuable " Ts'ai-yu." With the exception, however, of the ground-nut, they are not extensively employed. In Hupeh and Szechuan, *Sesamum indicum* is cultivated sparingly as a summer crop. In Yunnan its cultivation is more general. The oil from its seeds is very highly esteemed, and commands a high price in the market. It is known as the " Hsiang-yu," or fragrant oil, and is eaten raw, mixed with cooked vegetables. From the seeds of *Perilla ocymoides* an oil, known as " Su-ma," and similar to sesamum oil, is expressed ; it is used in salads. This plant is, however, but very sparingly cultivated.

A large number of miscellaneous vegetables are used as food in various ways. Some are wild, but most are cultivated, and many of them are strange and novel to Europeans. A handsome if tasteless fruit, the Brinjal, " Chuei-tzu " (*Solanum Melongena*), is largely cultivated as a vegetable. The Chinese distinguish at least 5 varieties that differ from each other in colour, shape, and time of maturing. Some of them are truly enormous, often weighing 2½ lbs., and measuring 1 foot in length. They are in the market from June till October. The Tomato (*S. Lycopersicum*) has been introduced by foreigners, and in Yunnan is frequently met with semi-wild as an escape from cultivation. The Chinese, as far as my observations go, do not eat it themselves.

A small-fruited variety of the Chilli-pepper, " Ai-chiao " (*Capsicum frutescens*), is commonly cultivated, and is particularly happy in the dry, hot valleys of the Tung and Min

Rivers, where it is grown as an article of export for other parts of China. Both long and round (heart-shaped) forms of Capsicum (*C. annuum*) are cultivated in the plains, and especially the plain of Chengtu. These chillies and capsicums constitute the most important relish used by the Chinese. In a green state the latter are fried and eaten with rice and cabbage. When ripe they are pounded up in a mortar, and with water added form a sauce. Roasted and ground into meal they are used for seasoning purposes. The ripe chillies and capsicums are also boiled in oil, and impart to it their pungent flavour. Oil so treated will keep for an indefinite period. The true Chinese pepper, known as " Hua-chiao," is the ground-up fruit of *Zanthoxylum Bungei*. This is a thorny shrub cultivated everywhere in small quantities, but it is only in the Min Valley that I have noted it extensively grown for export.

As previously mentioned, bamboo shoots are eaten both fresh, dried, and salted. When cooked as a vegetable or made into a salad, these shoots are very fair eating, but it is ridiculous to compare them with asparagus, as some writers have done. In the warmer parts of China it is the young shoots of *Bambusa arundinacea* and *B. vulgaris* that are employed. They are also an article of export to other parts of China, and can usually be bought in a dried state in most of the large cities. In mountainous districts the young succulent shoots of other species of Bamboo are eaten. In the west, one of the commonest of these is the lovely *Arundinaria nitida*.

Celery (*Apium graveolens*), " Ch'ing-ts'ai," and Lettuce (*Lactuca Scariola*), " U'sen," are commonly cultivated. The celery is never bleached, and it is the stem of the lettuce rather than the leaves that is in request. The leaves and young shoots of the following plants are used as vegetables : *Cedrela sinensis*, " Ch'un-tuen shu "; *Pistacia chinensis*, " Huang-nien-ya"; *Chrysanthemum segetum*, " Tung-hao "; *Malva parviflora*, " Mao-tung-han-ts'ai "; *M. verticillata*, " Tung-han-ts'ai "; *Chenopodium album*, " Hui-t'ien-han "; *Acroglochin chenopodioides*, " Yeh-han-ts'ai "; *Ipomœa aquatica*, " Wêng-ts'ai "; *Anaphalis contorta*, " Tak'ing-ming-ts'ai "; *Coriandrum sativum*, " Yen-ts'ai "; *Taraxacum officinale*, " Ku-ts'ai"; *Beta vulgaris*, " T'ien-ts'ai "; *Lactuca denticulata*, " Wo-sheng-

ts'ai " ; *Spinacia oleracea,* " Po-ts'ai " ; *Crepis japonica,*
" Huang-hua-ts'ai " ; *Basella rubra,* " Juan-chiang-tzu " ;
Celosia argentea, " Chi-kung-hua " ; and *Amaranthus panicu-
latus,* " Ya-ku."

The " Kao-sên " (*Zizania latifolia*) is very generally cultivated.
Its succulent stem and very young inflorescence are cooked and
eaten as a vegetable. From a European standpoint it is really
very good eating. From the rhizome of the Bracken Fern
(*Pteridium aquilinum*) an arrowroot-like substance called
" Chüeh-fen " is prepared. In the mountains the young fronds
of this fern are eaten by the peasantry. From the thick woody
root of *Pueraria Thunbergiana* an " arrowroot " similar to the
above is prepared. It is, however, in very little request, save in
times of scarcity. The starchy roots of *Potentilla discolor* and
P. multifida are also occasionally used for preparing a food-stuff.

The flowers of *Lilium Sargentiæ,* " Yeh-peh-ho," and of
Hemerocallis flava, " Huang-hua-ts'ai," are eaten, as also are
the yellow pea-like flowers of *Caragana chamlagu.* The
mucilaginous seeds of *Plantago major,* " Ch'e-ch'ien-ts'ao,"
enter into the composition of a jelly, " Liang-fen," which is
used in summer. The Chinese are very fond of several species of
Fungi, and distinguish quite a number of edible kinds. Amongst
their favourites are *Hirneola polytricha, Cantharellus cibarius,
Tricholoma gambosa, Lactarius deliciosus,* and *Agaricus campestris,* the Common Mushroom. Seaweed is imported in quantity
from Japan, and is on sale in the shops of all the larger towns
and villages. From this Seaweed (*Porphyra vulgaris*) the
Chinese prepare a very nutritious jelly.

The difficulty of tracing the original types of plants that
have long been in cultivation and of affixing the correct scientific
names to them is a very real one, and one that can be appreciated by all who have studied the history of our common
garden plants. While in the foregoing pages I cannot hope
to have altogether escaped error in this matter, I have used
every means at my command to ensure accuracy.

CHAPTER VII

THE MORE IMPORTANT PLANT PRODUCTS

Wild and Cultivated Trees of Economic Importance

CHINA is remarkably rich in raw economic products of vegetable origin, especially in oil, fat, and saponin-yielding fruits and seeds, lacquer-varnish, tannin, and dye-products, fibres and paper-making material. Some of these products are in increasing demand for export trade with the outside world, and will undoubtedly develop into great industries of the future. In this and the succeeding chapter is given an account of the more important of the products derived from central and Western China. This region is the source whence the majority of the raw articles are obtained that are exported from Hankow, the great trade entrepôt of the Yangtsze Valley.

One of the most important of all Chinese products is wood oil. This is obtained from the seeds of two species of Aleurites, a small genus of low-growing trees belonging to the Spurge family. The two species for the most part occupy distinct geographical areas, but both have been recorded as growing close together in the province of Fokien. In the south of China wood oil is the product of *A. montana*, which bears its flowers on the current season's shoots at the time when the leaves are expanded, and has an egg-shaped fruit, sharply pointed, and unevenly ridged on the outside. This is the " Mu-yu shu "—literally " Wood Oil tree " of the Chinese. In central and Western China it is *A. Fordii*, known as the " T'ung-yu shu "—literally " T'ung Oil tree," which produces this valuable oil. This latter species bears its flowers at the ends of the previous year's shoots before the leaves unfold, and has a flattened-round, apple-like fruit, only slightly pointed, and perfectly smooth on the outside. These two trees have been very much confused by botanists, and it is well to emphasize their distinctive characters. The " T'ung-yu " is the more hardy tree of the two, and is much more widely distributed, furnishing fully nine-tenths of the so-called " wood oil " used in China and exported from thence. Within the last decade " wood oil " has attracted considerable attention in Europe and in the United States of America as a possible substitute for linseed oil, and it is annually imported into these countries in vastly increasing quantities. Chemists have investigated the products of these two trees, and find no appreciable difference in the oils.

The " Mu-yu " (*A. montana*) is common in the regions around Wuchou to the west of Canton, where it is chiefly used, and from whence it is exported to Hongkong and elsewhere. The trade is not large ; in 1910 it was estimated at 52,106 piculs.[1]

The " T'ung-yu " (*A. Fordii*) is abundant throughout the Yangtsze Valley from Ichang westwards to Chungking ; more especially it luxuriates in the region of the gorges and the contiguous hilly country up to 2500 feet altitude. It is essentially a hillside plant, thriving in the most rocky situations, and on the poorest of soils, where there is a minimum rainfall of 29 inches ; it will also withstand drought and a few degrees of frost. It is a quick-growing tree, seldom exceeding 25 feet in height and averaging less, with a much-branched, flat-topped head, 15 to 30 feet or more through, and is highly ornamental in flower and foliage. The flowers, produced in great profusion during April, are white, stained with pink and yellow markings, especially near the base. These are always followed by green, apple-like fruits, which ripen in September and are hidden amongst the large, glossy-green, heart-shaped leaves. Each fruit contains three to five seeds, which somewhat resemble shelled Brazil-nuts, but are much smaller.

The fruits break naturally in three parts when dead ripe, but they are invariably gathered before this period, and collected into heaps which are covered with straw or grass. Fermentation sets in and quickly disposes of the thin fleshy part of the

[1] One picul equals 133⅓ lbs.

fruit, after which the seeds are easily removed. The process of extracting the oil is very simple. The seeds are first crushed in a circular trough beneath a heavy stone wheel revolved by horse or ox-power. The comminuted mass is then partially roasted in shallow pans, after which it is placed in wooden vats, fitted with wicker bottoms, and thoroughly steamed over boiling water. Next, with the aid of an iron ring and straw, it is made into circular cakes about 18 inches in diameter. These cakes are arranged edgeways in a large press and, when full, pressure is exerted by driving in one wedge after another, thereby crushing out the brown, somewhat watery and heavy-smelling oil, which falls into a vat below. This " T'ung oil " is packed in tubs and bamboo baskets, and is ready for export. The yield is about 40 per cent. by weight of the kernels. The refuse cakes are used on the fields as fertilizers.

" T'ung-yu " is the chief paint oil throughout the Chinese Empire, being used for all outside woodwork ; as a " drier " it excels linseed oil. The Chinese do not paint their boats, they oil them, and the myriads of such craft which ply on the Yangtsze and other rivers of China are all coated and the upper works kept waterproof with this oil. The crude oil boiled for an hour becomes a syrupy oil or " P'ei-yu," which is used as a varnish for boats and furniture. Boiled for two hours with the addition of certain mineral substances (" T'u-tzu " and " T'o-shên "), a varnish called " Kuang-yu " is produced which, when applied to silk gauze and pongees, renders them waterproof. " T'ung-yu " is also used as an illuminant and as an ingredient in concrete ; mixed with lime and bamboo shavings it is used for caulking boats. Besides these, and dozens of other legitimate uses, " wood oil " is also employed as an adulterant in lacquer-varnish. Lamp-black produced by burning this oil or the fruit-husks is a most important ingredient in the manufacture of Chinese ink. The trade in " T'ung oil " is very large. From Hankow in 1900 the quantity exported was 330,238 piculs, valued at Tls. 2,559,344. In 1910 the trade had risen to 756,958 piculs, valued at Tls. 6,449,421.

I have given rather full details of this subject on account of its great importance, and because its value is only beginning

to be realized by the Western manufacturer. The U.S.A.
Department of Agriculture has introduced *Aleurites Fordii*
into its experimental stations, and expects to establish an
industry in the production of " T'ung oil " somewhere in the
United States of America.   It is worthy of the serious attention
of countries other than the United States of America.   In
South Africa, Australia, Algeria, Morocco, and other regions,
for instance, this tree would probably thrive, and its experimental culture might with advantage be undertaken by the
various Departments of Agriculture in those British Colonies
and French Protectorates.   Of all the varied economic vegetable products of China, the wood oils are pre-eminently
of a kind to receive attention, with a view of establishing
the industry in Colonial possessions.

Another member of the Spurge family yields the valuable Chinese " vegetable tallow " of commerce.   This tree,
Sapium sebiferum, occurs in all the warmer parts of China, and
is remarkable for the beautiful autumnal tints of its foliage.
This tree is known by several colloquial names—in southern
China it is the " Chiu-tzu shu " ; in central parts the " Mou-tzu
shu " ; in the west the " Ch'uan-tzu shu."   It is a long-lived
tree, growing 40 to 50 feet tall, and having a girth of 5 or 6 feet
at maturity.   In Hupeh, where the industry is well looked
after, the larger branches are kept " headed in " to facilitate
the gathering of the fruits.   The fruits are three-celled,
flattened-ovoid, about 15 mm. in diameter.   When ripe they
are blackish-brown and woody in appearance, and are either
gathered from the trees by hand or knocked off by the aid of
bamboo poles.   After being collected, the fruits are spread
in the sun, where they open, and each liberates three elliptical
seeds, which are covered with a white substance.   This covering
is a fat or tallow, and is removed by steaming and rubbing
through a bamboo sieve having meshes sufficiently small to
retain the black seeds.   The fat is collected and melted ;
afterwards it is moulded into cakes, in which state it is known
as the " Pi-yu " of commerce.   After the fatty covering has
been removed the seeds are crushed, and the powdered mass
undergoes the same processes as are described for extracting
wood oil.   The oil expressed from the seeds is the " Ting-yu "

of commerce. Very often no attempt is made to separate the fat and the oil. The seeds with their white fatty covering are crushed and steamed together and submitted to pressure, the mixed product so obtained being known as " Mou-yu." The yield of fat and oil is about 30 per cent. by weight of the seeds. In China all three products are largely employed in the manufacture of candles. The pure " Pi-yu " has a higher melting point than the " Ting-yu " or the mixture " Mou-yu." All Chinese candles have an exterior coating of insect white wax, but when made from " Pi-yu " only the thinnest possible covering of wax is necessary (one-tenth of an ounce to a pound). All three products of the Vegetable Tallow tree are exported in quantity to Europe; where they are used in the manufacture of soap, being essential constituents of certain particular forms of this article. Chinese vegetable tallow is an increasingly important article of trade. In 1910 some 178,204 piculs, valued at Tls. 1,878,418, were exported from Hankow.

Every one is familiar with some form or other of the lacquer-work of China and Japan, but the varnish employed for lacquering has not yet found a market in Western countries, owing to certain poisonous properties it possesses, and to the want of knowledge as to the correct way of applying it. Lacquer is prepared from a varnish obtained in its crude state from *Rhus verniciflua*, the " Che shu " of the Chinese. This tree grows 25 to 60 feet tall, producing handsome pinnate leaves, 1 to 2½ feet long, and large panicles of small greenish flowers, which are followed by fruits rich in fatty oil. It is wild in the woods and abundantly cultivated along the margins of fields throughout central China, especially in the mountainous areas of western Hupeh and eastern Szechuan, but is much less common west of these regions. Its altitudinal range is from 3000 to 7500 feet, the optimum being 4000 to 5000 feet. This tree, like the art of lacquering, was introduced from China into Japan in very early times, and is commonly cultivated there to-day. It is one of the many plants which first reached Europe from Japan, of which country it was erroneously considered native.

In China, Varnish trees are the property of the ground landlord and not of the tenant who holds the land ; the varnish is also claimed by the former. When the tree has attained a diameter of about 6 inches, tapping for varnish commences, and this operation is continued at intervals until the tree is 50 or 60 years of age. If the tapping is too severe, or the trees too young, injury or death ensues. The tapping operation is begun in late June or early July at a time corresponding with the opening of the flowers, and is continued throughout the summer. Oblique incisions from 4 to 12 inches in length, and about 1 inch in width, are made in the bark of the tree down to the wood, and the sap which exudes is collected in shells, bamboo tubes, and similar receptacles. Wooden pegs are driven into the trunk to facilitate climbing, in order to reach the main branches. The tapping is done early in the morning and the sap gathered from the receptacles into which it has flowed from the incisions each evening. In showery weather it dries rapidly, and often has to be scraped away. The sap continues to exude from the wound for about seven days, and then a fresh, thin slice of bark is removed, which causes another exudation. This is repeated seven times with an interval of about seven days between each operation, so that the work on each tree occupies about fifty days. After being tapped, the tree is allowed a period of from five to seven years to recover ; the old wounds are then reopened and fresh ones made. A arge tree yields from 5 to 7 lbs. of varnish. This, as it exudes, is pure white in appearance, but quickly oxidizes to greyish-white, changing to black. To prevent contact with the air the crude varnish is covered as soon as possible with layers of oil-paper.

Crude varnish furnishes only one colour, namely, black, and when applied to wood floors, or pillars, is the most indestructible varnish known. To obtain brown varnish " P'ei-yu " (*ante*, p. 66) is added, in the proportion of 25 to 50 per cent., to the crude varnish, according to the shade of brown required. The more " P'ei-yu " added, the quicker the varnish will dry. Red varnish is produced by adding cinnabar (mercuric sulphide) to brown varnish in about equal parts. Yellow varnish is obtained by adding to the " brown varnish " orpiment (arsenic sulphide) in slightly less than equal quantity.

Enormous quantities of raw varnish are exported from

central China to other parts of the Empire and to Japan. In 1910 the exports of varnish from Hankow totalled 15,424 piculs, valued at Tls. 1,043,434. This commercial product is frequently adulterated with wood oil. Three tests for adulteration are commonly employed—(1) Smell ; (2) the varnish is held up and allowed to drop, the strand of varnish will remain unbroken if it is pure, but will break if adulterated ; (3) placed on a sheet of soft Chinese paper, the varnish " runs," if it is adulterated, owing to the paper absorbing the oil adulterant. Everywhere in China this varnish is known to resident foreigners as " Ningpo varnish." The genesis of the name is interesting, since the substance itself is not produced in the neighbourhood of Ningpo, but is imported from Hankow and elsewhere. In the early days, when foreigners first settled at Shanghai, most of the carpenters employed to build houses for them were Ningpo men. For all indoor work—floors, pillars, and furniture—they employed this varnish, and foreigners promptly dubbed it " Ningpo varnish."

A peculiarity of " Ningpo varnish," or Chinese lacquer, to use its correct name, is that it hardens only in a moist atmosphere and remains in a tacky condition if exposed to sunlight and heat, the essentials in hardening copal varnish. In China it is applied only during cloudy weather when the atmosphere is surcharged with moisture or when a drizzle of rain is falling. For indoor work its drying is facilitated by hanging about the rooms cloths saturated with water. The kind used on ships contains " P ei-yu " in almost equal parts, and this mixture dries rapidly even in moderately dry, hot weather. How important the knowledge of this peculiarity is may be gathered from the following fact. Many years ago an experimental consignment of " Ningpo varnish " was received in London. It was applied in the same way as ordinary copal varnish, in full sunlight and heat, with the result that it refused to harden, and remained " tacky," and the failure resulted in its being condemned as worthless !

The only change which takes place in the composition of the lacquer in drying at ordinary temperatures is the slow absorption of oxygen, finally amounting to 5.75 per cent. by weight of the original substance. Complete oxidation is found to be due to the action of a ferment, to which the name *laccase* has been applied, which is only active in a certain humidity of the atmosphere. Quite recently, however, the presence of a special ferment has been questioned, and the absorption of oxygen attributed to an obscure chemical reaction depending on the presence of a compound of manganese with a proteid-like substance. Chinese lacquer, in a raw state, unfortunately possesses properties which are poisonous to many people, producing swellings and eruptions of the skin in the same way as does its close ally, the " Poison Ivy " (*Rhus Toxicodendron*). Certain people are immune, but this property will probably always militate against its use in Western lands. Perhaps the chemists will one day discover a means whereby this poisonous property can be neutralized or eliminated.

The fruit of *R. verniciflua* is shining, greyish-yellow, roundish and flattened on two sides, 6 to 10 mm. long. These when crushed and treated in a wedge-press in the same way as wood oil seeds, yield a fatty oil known as " Che-yu," which is used for making candles.

Trees belonging to three different families produce fruits rich in saponin which are in common use for laundry-work and other purposes. The most generally distributed of these " Soap trees " is *Gleditsia sinensis*, a handsome tree known colloquially as " Tsao-k'o shu," abundant throughout the Yangtsze Valley up to 3500 feet altitude. It grows 60 to 100 feet tall, and has a thick trunk, smooth grey bark, a spreading head with massive branches, furnished with small, pinnate leaves and inconspicuous greenish flowers, unisexual or hermaphrodite in character. The latter are followed by pods or " beans " which, when ripe, are black, 6 to 14 inches long and $\frac{3}{4}$ to $1\frac{1}{2}$ inch wide. These pods are broken up and are in general use for ordinary laundry-work, producing a good lather in either cold or hot water. They are also used in the process of tanning hides. The saponaceous fat is contained in the pod itself, which is the only part utilized, the hard, flattened, brown seeds being discarded. It is probable that more than one species is included under the above name, for the Gleditsia family is in need of revision. In Yunnan another species which has much larger (20 inches) and wider pods is employed for the same purposes.

It is known as *G. Delavayi*. Around Peking a third species, designated *G. horrida*, occurs. A much rarer Soap tree, except in the vicinity of Kiukiang, is *Gymnocladus chinensis*, the " Yu-tsao-chio " of the Chinese, which is the Asiatic representative of the " Kentucky Coffee tree " of North America. This tree grows 50 or 60 feet tall, and though occasionally seen with a flat, fairly widespreading head, has usually only short branches ; the bark is smooth and light grey, the leaves much divided, often 2 feet across, pea-green in colour, and very handsome. The flowers, clustered, greyish without, purple within, are followed by flattened, brown pods, 3 or 4 inches long, and 1½ inch broad. These pods or " beans " are immersed for a time in hot water, which causes them to swell and become rounded in outline. Afterwards they are strung on short strips of bamboo and are then marketed. These swollen pods, colloquially " Fei-tsao-tou," are broken up and used in laundry-work, more especially for cleansing choice fabrics. They are also cut up into fine shreds and ground to a paste with sandalwood, cloves, putchuck, musk, camphor, etc., and thoroughly mixed with honey to form a perfumed soap called P'ing-she Fei-tsao (camphor-musk soap). This is a dark-coloured substance of the consistency of soft soap. It is used by women for cleansing their hair, and as a cosmetic for their hands and face ; also by barbers as a salve on the heads of their customers after shaving.

Yet another Soap tree is *Sapindus mukorossi*, colloquially known as the " Hou-erh-tsao." This occurs throughout the Yangtsze Valley up to 3000 feet altitude, growing 60 to 80 feet tall, with a huge trunk, smooth grey bark, and widespreading umbrageous head ; the pinnate leaves are 8 to 12 inches long. The flowers are small, greenish-white, produced in large terminal panicles, and are followed by shining brown, globose fruits about the size of a large marble. The fruits are used for washing white clothes, being considered for this purpose superior to the pods of Gleditsia. Each fruit contains a large, round, black seed. These are strung into rosaries and necklaces, which are much worn during hot weather.

During recent years the demand for vegetable products useful for tanning purposes has become unlimited. For certain purposes Chinese nut-galls furnish the finest tanning material in the world. These "nut-galls" ("Wu-pei-tzu") develop on the leaves of *Rhus javanica*, "Peh-fu-yang shu," as an excrescent growth due to protoplasmic irritation, occasioned by an insect (*Chermes*) which punctures the leaf to deposit its eggs. The tree is of small size, and very abundant in the Yangtsze Valley up to 3500 feet, more especially in rocky places, producing panicles of white flowers in late August and September. The galls are hollow and brittle, and vary considerably in shape and size, being more or less irregular, and 1 to 4 inches long. In China they are used for dyeing blue silk and blue cotton cloth black. The Occidental demand for nut-galls is greater than the supply, and the exports increase annually. In 1900, 24,800 piculs, valued at Tls. 454,584, were exported from Hankow; in 1910 the exports from this port had increased to 53,784 piculs, valued at Tls. 936,234.

Another less common species is *R. Potaninii*, colloquially known as the "Ch'ing-fu-yang," which produces galls known as "Ch'i-pei-tzu." These are used in Chinese medicine. The world is sadly in need of an indelible black ink, and chemists might well turn their attention to Chinese nut-galls in their quest for this treasure, since they possess possibilities worthy of investigation.

In the chapter on fruits reference is made to the cultivated Persimmon (*Diospyros kaki*), but it is necessary here to mention the feral form, known as "Yu-shih-tzu" (literally "Oil Persimmon"). This wildling is abundant in the mountains of central and Western China up to 4000 feet altitude, where it forms a large tree 50 or 60 feet tall. The fruit varies from flattened-round to ovoid, and from ¾ to 2½ inches in diameter. It is always rich golden yellow in colour when ripe, and this colour best distinguishes the smallest fruited forms from its close ally *Diospyros Lotus*, "Kou-shih-tzu," which has flattened-round fruit, dark purplish coloured when dead ripe. To obtain the varnish oil for which this tree is esteemed, the fruit is plucked in July when about the size of a crab-apple, and still green. By means of a wooden mallet the fruits are reduced to pulp, which is placed with cold water in large earthenware jars fitted with covers, and allowed to decompose.

The contents of these jars are stirred occasionally, and at the end of thirty days the residue of the pulp is removed and the resultant liquid, now a nearly colourless varnish, is poured into other jars.   To give the varnish a warm brown tint, the leaves of *Ligustrum lucidum*, " La shu," sometimes erroneously called the " Tung-ching shu," are steeped in the jars for ten days or so, according to depth of tint desired.   This varnish is used for waterproofing purposes generally, its principal use being in the manufacture of umbrellas.   For this purpose it is applied as a gum varnish between the several layers of paper forming the screen of the umbrella, and serves to make them adherent as well as waterproof.   When completed, the umbrella receives a thin outside coating of " Kuang-yu," or lustrous oil (*ante*, p. 66).   Persimmon varnish is widely used, and is in great demand for the above purposes.   It is produced in most parts of China, but scarcely figures as an article of export.

The art of making paper in China dates back to about the commencement of the Christian era.   Previous to this, silk and cloth were employed for writing upon, but the early annals of the race were recorded on tablets of bamboo, and this latter method obtained in the days of Confucius (552-478 B.C.). What materials were first employed by the Chinese in paper-making are not known with certainty, but were probably bamboo or Paper-mulberry, " Kou shu " (*Broussonetia papyrifera*).   A good case in favour of the latter could be made out, since the inner bark of this tree requires less preparation than bamboo culms.   True paper money first originated in the province of Szechuan during the reign of the first emperor of the Sung Dynasty (A.D. 960).   A certain Chang-yung introduced it to take the place of the iron money then in use, which was inconveniently heavy and troublesome.   These notes were called " Chih-tsi " or " Evidences," and were apparently made from the inner bark of the Paper-mulberry.   Marco Polo, speaking of Kublai Khan's mint at Peking, says, " He makes them take of the bark of a certain tree, in fact, of the Mulberry tree, the leaves of which are the food of the silkworms—these trees being so numerous that whole districts are full of them. What they take is a certain fine white bast or skin which lies between the wood of the tree and the thick outer bark, and this they make into something resembling sheets of paper, but black." The famous Venetian's error in calling this the silk-worm Mulberry is pardonable enough, since the trees are very closely allied, and somewhat similar in appearance. Paper money is still made from the paper prepared from the bark of the " Kou shu," and the same paper, " P'i-chih " owing to its toughness, is used for wrapping up silver, for tags on silk goods, and as a lining between the fur or cotton and the outer fabric in fur-lined or wadded garments. The *B. papyrifera* occurs all over China up to 4000 feet altitude, and if left alone forms a much-branched tree 35 to 45 feet tall with a smooth dark grey bark. In a bush form it is abundant by the way-side and on cliffs. Most of the paper (which is called Kou-p'i-chih—literally bark paper) made from this tree and used in Western China comes from the province of Kweichou. In Hupeh the slender branches from young trees and bushes are cut into lengths, steamed in vats to facilitate the removal of the bark, which is converted into string and cordage.

The material from which the original India paper (a Chinese, not an Indian product), which came from Canton, was made is unknown. Possibly it was prepared from Ramie fibre (*Bœhmeria nivea*), but I venture the suggestion that it may have been obtained from the bark of *Broussonetia papyrifera*.

Bamboo supplies the material for the manufacture of all the better class papers used for printing and writing upon, papering windows, and a hundred and one other purposes. Several species are employed for this purpose, one of the commonest being *Phyllostachys heteroclada*. This bamboo is abundant in central and Western China, especially in alluvial areas near streams up to 4000 feet altitude. It grows 12 to 18 feet tall, with fairly slender dark green culms ; commonly it forms extensive groves. The stems are cut into lengths, made into bundles, and immersed in concrete pits, being weighted down and kept under water by heavy stones. After three months they are removed, opened up, and thoroughly washed. Next they are restacked in layers, each layer being well sprinkled with lime and water, holding potash salts in solution. After two months they are well retted. The fibrous mass is then washed to remove the lime, steamed for fifteen days, when it is removed, thoroughly washed, and again placed in concrete tanks. The mass is next reduced to a fine pulp with wooden rakes, and is then ready for conversion into paper. A quantity of the pulp is put into troughs with cold water and mucilage prepared from the roots of *Hibiscus Abelmoschus*. An oblong bamboo frame, the size of the desired sheet of paper, having a fine mesh, is held at the two ends by a workman and drawn down endways and diagonally into the liquid contents, which are kept constantly stirred in the trough. It is then gently raised to the surface, and the film which has collected on the top is deposited as a sheet of moist paper when the frame is turned over. After the surplus water has drained away from the mass of moist sheets of paper the whole is submitted to pressure. It is then dried either in kilns or in the sun, according to quality, the sun-dried being the inferior. Since much water is necessary in the process of paper-making the mills are always erected alongside streams.

The more common paper in daily use is made from rice-straw by a similar but less intricate and quicker process. The stems of a reed (*Imperata arundinacea*, var. *Kœnigii*), known as "Mao-ts'ao," and common in many parts of Western China, are also used locally in the manufacture of paper, being frequently mixed with rice-straw.

Chinese "rice-paper," so called by foreigners, is prepared from the pith of *Tetrapanax papyrifera*, a shrub closely allied to the common Ivy of Europe, and colloquially known as "T'ung-ts'ao." This plant has handsome palmate leaves, and stems filled with a pure white pith. This pith is cut, using a rolling, circular motion, by means of a sharp, heavy knife, into thin sheets. Formerly much of this cutting was done in Chungking, the raw material being imported from the province of Kweichou. Rice-paper is used by Chinese artists for painting upon, and also in the manufacture of artificial flowers.

Sericulture and silk-weaving are among the most important industries of Szechuan. Nearly every part of the province produces silk, but there are certain well-defined areas in which the industry is famous—for example, Kiating Fu, Chengtu Fu, and Paoning Fu.   Hosie[1] estimates the annual production of raw silk at lbs. 5,439,500, valued at Tls. 15,025,230.   This industry has been exhaustively dealt with by Hosie (loc. cit.) and others, and I propose here only to mention briefly certain trees, the leaves of which the silkworms are fed upon.   The overwhelming proportion of Szechuan silk is produced by the " worm " of *Bombyx mori*, the common domesticated species, which is fed principally on the leaves of the White Mulberry (*Morus alba*), known as the " Sang shu."   The Mulberry tree is abundantly cultivated up to 3000 feet altitude, and in the more populous parts of the province a traveller is seldom out of sight of groves of this tree.   The trees are kept low by pollarding to admit of the leaves being easily gathered, but little attention is otherwise given them.   Since the suppression of opium cultivation the officials have turned their attention to improving and extending the sericulture industry. The finest Chinese silk is produced in the neighbourhood of Hanchou in the Chekiang province, where a broad-leaved and particularly fine Mulberry is cultivated (*M. alba*, var. *latifolia*), for the purpose of feeding the silkworms.   The recently established Bureau of Agriculture at Chengtu Fu, and magistrates in charge of certain districts, have introduced the Hanchou Mulberry in the hope of improving the local product. During the last two or three years there has been a considerable increase in the area devoted to sericulture, and there is a possible danger of over-production.   More attention might well be paid to the spinning of the yarn in order to produce a more even thread, which would result in a smoother and finer woven fabric.

Around Kiating Fu the infant silkworms are fed for the first 22 days of their lives on the finely chopped leaves of *Cudrania tricuspidata*, the "Tsa" or "Cha shu," a low-growing tree (very often only a bush), closely allied to the Mulberry, with thorny branches and dark green, tough leaves.   For the succeeding and final 26 days they are fed on the Mulberry. By feeding first on the Cudrania leaves, it is claimed that the

[1] *Report on Province of Ssuch'uan*, p. 61.

worms produce more silk of a tougher and more durable quality. Hosie [1] was the first to discover and make known this interesting fact to the outside world, and subsequent observers have confirmed his statements.

Around Paoning Fu in the north, and Kikiang Hsien in the south, a certain amount of silk is obtained from the worm of *Antheræa pernyi*. This species feeds on the leaves of various scrub oaks, and being bivoltine, produces two crops a year. Several species of Oak are concerned, including *Quercus variabilis*, *Q. serrata*, *Q. Fabri*, and *Q. aliena*, all of which, though they attain to the dimensions of trees, are commonly met with from 2000 to 4000 feet in the form of bushes covering the hillsides. This Oak-feeding silkworm was introduced from the province of Shantung many years ago, and the industry is much more important in Kweichou province than it is in Szechuan. This "Wild-silk," as it is called, differs from ordinary silk in its harder texture and is spun from dry cocoons, whereas ordinary silk is spun from cocoons lying immersed in boiling water.

In 1907, near the hamlet of Lu-yang-ho, alt. 2500 feet, in the north-west corner of Fang Hsien, I chanced upon several plantations of *Ailanthus Vilmoriniana*, grown for feeding the worm of *Attacus cynthia*. The trees were all young saplings. This was the only place in my travels where I saw this particular kind of sericulture practised. In parts of north-eastern China I understand it is more general, the species there employed being the ordinary *Ailanthus glandulosa*, the "Ch'ou-ch'un shu" of the Chinese, and "Tree of Heaven" of foreigners.

[1] *Three Years in Western China*, p. 21.

CHAPTER VIII

THE MORE IMPORTANT PLANT PRODUCTS

Cultivated Shrubs and Herbs of Economic Value

C HINESE agriculture is mainly devoted to the production of food-stuffs for local consumption, the surplus being disposed of by sale and the proceeds invested in the necessities or luxuries of life which cannot be produced locally. Nevertheless, in the more fertile parts of the Empire, certain economic crops other than those for culinary purposes are grown expressly for sale or exchange. This is particularly true of the rich province of Szechuan, where a number of such products are produced, as will be seen from the brief account of the more important which follows.

Had this been written five years previously it would have been necessary to give considerable space to the Opium Poppy, but so vigorously has the edict for the suppression of this crop been promulgated that only a brief notice of it is necessary. When the Imperial Decree, prohibiting the cultivation and consumption of opium throughout the Chinese Empire within a period of ten years, was published on 20th September 1906, I confess to having been one of those who considered it a fatuous effort calculated to accomplish nothing, though well-meaning enough. It seemed impossible that such a gigantic task could be accomplished in such a brief period of time. Public sentiment was obviously in favour of the Decree, but to certain provinces, for example Szechuan and Yunnan, the export of opium represented their principal source of income. That Indian opium could be dispensed with and none be inconvenienced save the wealthy opium-smoking connoisseurs living in the prosperous coast ports, was perfectly clear to any one who had travelled in Western China. In 1908 the area under poppy in Szechuan was far greater than it had ever been before. In 1910 I traversed this province from east to west and north to south, and was amazed to find the whole industry of poppy-growing blotted out of existence. Except in a few out-of-the-way places, where it was grown by stealth, the cultivation had ceased. What has happened since the end of 1910 I do not know, but from what I saw brought to pass in a couple of seasons; together with the undoubted general disfavour in which opium-smoking was viewed by the people, I am constrained to think that the poppy and opium will disappear from China as it has done from Japan. The problem before officials, and more especially those of the western provinces, is to find a source of revenue to take the place of that formerly derived from opium. In 1904 Hosie estimated the production of opium in Szechuan at 250,000 piculs. In 1910 some 28,530 piculs of opium (produced in Szechuan, Yunnan, and Kweichou provinces), valued at about Tls. 29,000,000, passed through the port of Ichang. In 1909, 51,817 piculs passed through this port. Formerly the exports of opium alone from Szechuan nearly sufficed to cover the imports of cotton-yarn and piece-goods, commodities essential to the people of that province.

The literature on Chinese opium and opium-smoking in China is enormous, and with exception of what is written above; I desire to add only three significant facts, which, if known, are not generally appreciated. For the benefit of those who believe, and those who do not believe, that India, abetted by the British Government in times past, is responsible for the opium vice in China, I would mention that (a) opium has been known in China since the T'ang Dynasty (A.D. 618), and was cultivated in Szechuan for medicinal purposes during the closing years of that Dynasty (circa A.D. 900) ; (b) the pipe used for smoking opium in China is of a design peculiar to the country itself ; (c) the races of Poppy cultivated in Western China are allied to the races grown in Persia and quite distinct from those grown in India.

It is known that in early times the peach, orange, and silk travelled from China by the ancient trade route across Central Asia to Persia, from whence they reached Europe. Is it not, therefore, reasonable enough to suppose that the opium poppy may have travelled from Persia to China by this same overland route ?

The poppy is (or was) a winter crop in Szechuan, being garnered in April and May in ample time to prepare for the rice-crop. No other crop even remotely approximating the pecuniary value of opium can take its place.

Several plants yielding fibres valued for textile and cordage purposes are grown in China.   In Szechuan the most important of these is the true Hemp (*Cannabis sativa*), colloquially known as " Hou-ma." This crop is abundantly cultivated around Wênchiang Hsien and P'i Hsien.   It is a spring crop, the seeds being sown in February and the plants harvested the end of May and beginning of June, just as they commence to flower. The stems are allowed to grow thickly together and reach 8 feet in height.   The culms are reaped, stripped of their leaves, and often the fibre is removed there and then.   More commonly, however, the stems are placed in pits filled with water and allowed to ret for a few days ; they are then removed, sun-dried, stacked in hollow cones, surrounded by mats, and bleached by burning sulphur beneath the heaps.   After these processes the fibrous bark is stripped off by hand.   The woody stems that remain after the bark has been removed are burned, and the ashes resulting, mixed with gunpowder, enter into the manufacture of fire-crackers.   Hemp, or " Hou-ma," is the best of the fibres produced in Western China for rope-making and cordage purposes generally.   It is also used locally for making grain-sacks and coarse wearing apparel for the poorer classes. Quantities are used in the city of Paoning Fu for these latter purposes.   It is in great demand on native river-craft and is largely exported down river to other parts of China.   It is this hemp that is principally exported from Szechuan.   True Hemp (*Cannabis*) is an annual and is grown as a summer crop in the mountains for the sake of its oil-containing seeds. Hemp oil is expressed and used as an illuminant and is said not to congeal in the coldest weather.   In Hupeh it is known as " T'ang-ma."

Another annual plant cultivated for its fibre is *Abutilon Avicennæ*, the T'ung or T'uen-ma of Szechuan and Hupeh. This plant is widely cultivated as a summer crop in Western China up to 3000 feet altitude. The fibre is of inferior quality and is used locally for making cordage and in caulking boats, but is less valuable than that of the true Hemp (*Cannabis*) and less important as an article of export from Szechuan. Jute (*Corchorus capsularis*), colloquially known in Szechuan as "Huang-ma;" is very sparingly cultivated on the Chengtu Plain and elsewhere. It is not exported from the province.

The brown fibre from the leaf-bases of a palm, *Trachycarpus excelsus*, known in Hupeh as "Chung-ma," is the "coir-fibre" of the Yangtsze Valley. This "coir" is made into bales and exported down river from Szechuan in quantity. It is used for rope-making, mats and mattresses, brushes, is converted into rude raincapes, and is an all-round useful fibre.

The most important textile plant in China is the much-discussed China-grass, Ramie, or Rhea (*Bœhmeria nivea*). This member of the nettle family is both wild and cultivated in all the warmer parts of the Middle Kingdom up to 4000 feet altitude. It is a herbaceous perennial and grows 3 to 6 feet tall ; the leaves, broadly ovate, abruptly cuneate, or truncated at base, have dentate margins and are silvery on the underside. In Hupeh the wild plant is called "Ch'u-ma," the cultivated plant "Hsien-ma." In Szechuan the cultivated plant is also known as "Hsien-ma" and occasionally as "Yuang-ma." These various colloquial names are most perplexing and are almost hopelessly confused.

In Szechuan small patches of this "China-grass" are to be found around nearly every peasant's home. South-west of Chungking and also north of Lu Chou in several districts, it is cultivated on a very extensive scale. Much of the fibre is woven into "grass-cloth" and used locally. A certain amount is also exported down river. Szechuan "grass-cloth" is rather coarse and very much inferior to that produced in parts of southern China. It is not a prominent export from the west. In 1910 the exports from Hankow amounted to 120,034 piculs, valued at Tls. 183,332. This is classified in the Customs returns as Ramie fibre, and does not include that woven into grass-cloth.

Cotton-cultivation is a comparatively recent industry in China, having been introduced early in the eleventh century A.D., from Khoten. It met with strong opposition from those interested in the production of silk, China-grass, and other fibres, and was not fairly established until some time during the Yuan (Mongol) Dynasty (A.D. 1206–1386), when a public-spirited woman, Lady Hwang, distributed seeds throughout Kiangan, now the great cotton region of China. Chinese cotton has a notoriously short staple, but is strong and durable. It has undoubtedly become exhausted from lack of any attempt at seed-selection and from long cultivation in the same regions. Cotton-cultivation should receive early attention from the new Government, and seeds of standard varieties from India, Egypt, America, and elsewhere might be secured and experimentally grown. There is no question but that China could produce cotton infinitely superior to the present product if new and suitable varieties were obtained and properly cultivated.

Very little cotton, " Mien-hwa," is grown in Western China; and cotton-yarn and cloths are the great import into Szechuan. The value of foreign imports into Chung-king is about Tls. 20,000,000, five-sixths of which is made up of cotton manufactures, the bulk of which comes from India.

Before the importation of mineral-oil from foreign countries became general, the only lamps in use were vessels filled with vegetable-oil and fitted with rush-wicks. These " rush-lights " are still in common use in the west, more especially among the poorer classes. The wick consists of the pith of *Juncus effusus*, known as " Teng-ts'ao," which is widely cultivated for this purpose. The plant grows 3 to 6 feet tall and is also largely employed in the manufacture of matting and mats used under bed-mattresses and on divans. It is expressly cultivated for this purpose in parts of Szechuan, the principal seat of the matting industry being Sui Fu, where both whole and split rushes are used. In Yunnan *Scirpus lacustris*, " Pu-chih-ts'ao," which produces stems 6 to 8 feet tall, cylindrical at base, gradually tapering upwards and becoming obtusely triangular near the summit, is used for mat-making. It is also sparingly employed for the same purpose in Szechuan, where, however, it is chiefly used by the shop-keepers as string.

Rice-straw is largely used for making bed-mattresses and sandals and to a less extent for ropes. Wheat-straw is braided and used for making large, wide-brimmed summer hats. Certain districts like Shuangliu Hsien, near Chengtu, are famed for their straw-braid, but the industry is of local importance only.

Tobacco (*Nicotiana Tabacum*), called " Yen," was probably introduced into China from America, contemporaneously with maize—just when is a matter of dispute, but some sinologues consider it was about A.D. 1530. It is cultivated all over China, and nowhere within the Middle Kingdom are finer tobacco leaves produced than in Szechuan. Within the rice-belt tobacco is a spring crop, the seeds being sown in late October and the crop harvested by mid-June. In the maize-belt it is grown as a summer crop but not extensively. The districts of Chint'ang and P'i Hsien, on the Chengtu Plain, are noted for their tobacco. In these districts one crop only is taken from the plants, but in the warmer parts of the province contiguous to the Yangtsze River, three crops are secured before the plants are ploughed under.

Tobacco leaves are prepared in three ways : (1) the large leaves are dried on screens, kept flat, packed into bales to form " Ta-yen," or large tobacco ; (2) the smaller leaves are dried in the same way to form " Erh-yen," or second tobacco, which, when treated with Chinese rape-oil and red-earth (Tu-hung) is pressed and shaved into fine shreds and used for smoking in water-pipes; being known as " Shui-yen," or water tobacco ; (3) " So-yen," or cord tobacco, prepared by cutting off the leaves with a piece of the stem to form a hook, by means of which the leaves are suspended under the eaves of houses or from rafters indoors and allowed to dry, naturally shrivelling and curling in the process. This " So-yen " is rolled into rough cigars, which are inserted into the bowl of long-stemmed pipes and smoked. It is also exported from Szechuan. In the mountains up to 9000 feet altitude the small-leaved *Nicotiana rustica*, " Lan-hwa-yen," is sparingly cultivated for local use.

This receives no preparation beyond being dried in the sun, and naturally the quality is very inferior.

Undoubtedly the climate and soil of Szechuan are suitable for the growth of tobacco, but, unfortunately, the Chinese methods of curing the leaf are slovenly in the extreme, with the result that the prepared article is of low-grade quality. The Chinese are, unfortunately, fast becoming a nation of inveterate cigarette-smokers. Much of the local Szechuan tobacco could be used in the manufacture of cigarettes were proper factories erected. This has been done at Hankow and elsewhere, where cigarettes are manufactured from tobacco grown in the neighbourhood and in near-by provinces.

Sugar is a very important crop in Western China, and enormous quantities are produced in certain parts of Szechuan, where it is cultivated in the drier regions of the rice-belt up to 2500 feet altitude. Two kinds of Sugar-cane (*Saccharum officinarum*) are grown : (1) red-cane, used for chewing ; (2) white-cane, for the extraction of sugar. The Red-cane (*S. officinarum*, var. *rubricaule*) produces culms 8 feet tall, an inch or more in diameter, and is treated as an annual. The canes are cut as they mature and sold as required ; the canes that remain at the end of the season are taken up by the roots in November, cleaned and stored in earth-burrows until required for sale. About the end of March portions of these canes are laid lengthwise under the soil, and young growths that develop from each joint in due season constitute sugar-canes. These culms are dark red-purple outside, yellowish within, very firm, and rich in sugar.

The White-cane (*S. officinarum*, var. *sinense*) is treated as a perennial, producing two or three crops before being renewed. It grows 10 to 15 feet tall, with " long-jointed " stems nearly an inch in diameter. This is much more extensively grown than the " red " variety, and supplies nearly all the sugar used locally or exported from the province. Chinese methods of crushing the cane are very imperfect, and their refining processes are most primitive. The canes contain a high percentage of saccharine, and the industry, if perfected, could become of vast importance.

Sugar has been cultivated in China from time immemorial.

It is everywhere called " T'ang," and generally supposed to commemorate the T'ang Dynasty (A.D. 618–907), one of the most famous in Chinese history.   Sugar, however, was known to the Chinese at least as early as the second century B.C., and is mentioned in a poem which was written sometime between A.D. 78 and 139.

Formerly the Chinese used only vegetable dyes for their silk and other fabrics, and it is much to be regretted that in China, as elsewhere in the world, these are being rapidly displaced by aniline dyes derived from coal-tar.   The latter are more convenient to handle, but unfortunately the colours are not " fast."   The coal-tar product is on sale in every town and market village in Western China, made up in small bottles and imported from Germany.

The only dye-plant at all extensively grown in Szechuan to-day is *Strobilanthes flaccidifolius*, " T'ien-hwa," which produces an " indigo."   In certain parts of the Chengtu Plain this is grown in quantity, and the same is true of the district of Mien Chou and elsewhere, but its cultivation is on the decline.   It is planted on ridges which are kept flooded between.   When the plants are about 3 feet tall they are cut down and the leafy shoots placed in concrete pits full of cold water.   After steeping for about five days the stems are removed, leaving a green-coloured water.   Slaked lime is placed in the water to precipitate the indigo.   The water is allowed to drain off, and the dye is found deposited at the bottom of the pit.

Around Shasi, in Hupeh, *Polygonum tinctorium* is cultivated as the source of an " indigo " which is there used for dyeing cotton cloth.

As a red dye Safflower (*Carthamus tinctorius*), " Hung-hwa," was formerly very extensively grown, but it is only occasionally met with to-day, though still esteemed for dyeing the more costly silk fabrics.   The flowers of the Balsam (*Impatiens Balsamina*), colloquially " Chih-chia-ts'ao," are similarly used and valued.

Yellow dyes are obtained from turmeric, the root of *Curcuma longa*, still extensively grown in Chienwei Hsien on the Lower Min River, and from the flowers of the Huai shu (*Sophora japonica*), a common and widely dispersed tree. Another, but much more rare tree (*Kœlreuteria apiculata*), is known by the same colloquial name, and the flowers are used for the same purpose as those of the Sophora. The fruit of *Gardenia florida*, " Chih-tzu-hwa," is used for dyeing certain woods yellow, and also as a yellow colour in paint.

Green dyes were formerly obtained from the leaves of *Rhamnus davuricus*, known as the " Tung-lu," a very common Chinese species of Buckthorn, extremely variable in the size and shape of its leaves and abundant as a thorny bush by the wayside everywhere up to 4000 feet altitude. Another species (*Rhamnus tinctorius*), " Chiao-lu-tsze," was also employed for the same purpose. These have been almost totally displaced by aniline dyes.

As mentioned on page 73, the gall-nuts (Wu-pei-tzu) produced on the leaves of *Rhus javanica* are extensively employed for dyeing fabrics—more especially silk—black. With this dye it is essential that the material be first dyed blue. The burr-like cupules of two very common species of Oak (*Quercus serrata, Q. variabilis*), known as the " Hwa-li" and " Hwa-k'o-li" respectively, are also commonly employed as black dye for silk-yarn and fabrics. In this case it is immaterial what the original colour may be. The curious cone-like fruits of *Platycarya strobilacea*, colloquially known as the " Huan-hsiang shu," are in general use as a black dye for cotton-yarn and cotton goods generally. Pine soot, obtained by burning the branches of the Common Pine (*Pinus Massoniana*), is also employed as a black dye for cotton goods.

As a dark brown dye and tanning agent the tubers of a yam are commonly used in Yunnan and are exported in quantity to Tonking and elsewhere. It is probably *Dioscorea rhipogonioides*, a species common in Formosa, where it is called " Shu-lang " and much used for dyeing and tanning fish-nets. In western Hupeh the root-bark of *Rosa Banksiæ*, called " Hu-p'i," is used for this purpose.

Both sesamum and soy bean are cultivated extensively in Western China, but for local consumption only. The large exports of these products that pass through Hankow are brought down by the Peking-Hankow railway. Szechuan is capable of growing enormous quantities of these valuable plants, but cheaper and better facilities for transport are necessary before the products can become articles of external trade. When the much-discussed Hankow-Szechuan railway is *fait accompli* the raw products of the west will be available as articles of export, and a much-needed stimulus given to the agricultural industries of the regions concerned.

CHAPTER IX

TEA AND " TEA-YIELDING " PLANTS

THE TEA INDUSTRY FOR THE THIBETAN MARKETS

THE most widely known product of China is, of course, Tea, "Ch'a," which to-day is very extensively cultivated in India, Ceylon, and Java, and also experimentally in several other countries. In China the value of this plant has been appreciated from very early times. It is known to have been cultivated in Szechuan during the early Han Dynasty (202 B.C.–A.D. 25). However, it was not in general use among all classes before the sixth and seventh centuries A.D. Very early in the seventeenth century tea first became known in Europe, having been brought from China by Dutch traders.

The Tea plant (*Thea sinensis*) is considered to be a native of Assam, whence it was long ago introduced and cultivated in China. Augustine Henry, in 1896, received through a Chinese collector whom he had trained specimens of undoubted *Wild Tea*. Henry writes :[1] "Hitherto the Tea plant has been found wild only in Assam, the cases of its spontaneity recorded from China being very doubtful. In all my trips in Szechuan and Hupeh I never met with it. The present specimens are above suspicion, coming from virginal forest (in the extreme south-south-east corner of Yunnan) and at an immense distance from any tea-cultivation, the nearest being P'uêrh, 200 miles west. Bretschneider, in his *Botanicon Sinicum*, Part II, p. 130, has some remarks on the antiquity of tea in China. It is probable that it was found wild in these southern provinces which did not form a part of the ancient Chinese Empire, and I dare say it will be found wild in these mountains from Mengtse to Szemao. *It is not probable at all that tea came from so far away*

[1] *Kew Bulletin*, 1897, p. 100.

as Assam." I have italicized Henry's concluding statement, with which I most emphatically agree. As recorded in Vol. I, Chapter VIII, I discovered specimens of the Tea plant in north-central Szechuan growing in situations which left no good reason for regarding them as other than spontaneous. However, in view of the long-cultivated character of this shrub I prefer to regard them as " probably wild plants." It is worthy of note that growing in the same locality I found wild plants of the Tea Rose (*Rosa indica*) in some quantity. The Tea plant is an evergreen, belonging to the rain-forest area of the temperate zone in China. This represents the rice-belt throughout the Yangtsze Valley, which has long since been cleared in all but the most precipitous places to make way for cultivation. This fact would account for the present absence of the Tea plant in a wild state in these regions.

The great tea-growing districts for export trade with the Occident and for consumption within China itself are in the middle-eastern parts of the Empire. The export trade in this commodity has declined enormously during the last quarter of a century. Some 60 years ago the tea industry was introduced as a business into India and Ceylon, with the result that to-day these countries supply the greater portion of the world's demand. Antiquated methods of cultivation and preparation, absence of co-operation amongst the growers, and heavy taxation, are responsible for the decline of the Chinese product. It is true that Chinese tea is in quality and delicacy of flavour far ahead of Indian and Ceylon teas, but tea-drinkers generally have acquired a taste for the rougher, dark-coloured teas, and China's conservative methods are killing what was once her greatest export industry. Hankow is to-day the great tea-mart of China, the trade being largely in the hands of Russians. Large factories have been established expressly for the purpose of preparing teas for the Russian market, Indian and Ceylon teas being imported for blending purposes. In 1910 the exports of tea from Hankow were valued at Tls. 18,423,474.

With the ordinary tea industry of eastern China we are not further concerned, but in the west a specialized form of this obtains which merits a detailed description. Tea is grown all over Szechuan for provincial consumption, but in the western parts it assumes much greater magnitude, being there grown and specially prepared for the Thibetan market. The one great export from China to Thibet is tea, either in the form of compressed " bricks " or " bales." The subsidy given by the Chinese Government to the Thibetan authorities at Lhassa and elsewhere in Thibet is also paid in tea.

To the Thibetans tea is an absolute necessity of life, and deprived of this astringent they suffer in various ways. That astringency is one of the properties most desired is evidenced by the fact that the bark of Oak trees is ofttimes used when tea cannot be obtained. The ordinary everyday meal of these people consists of tea mixed with a little butter and salt. To this mixture roasted barley-meal is added, and the whole is kneaded to the consistency of dough, in which condition it is eaten. Buttered tea is also their national beverage. To the European palate this concoction as prepared by the Thibetans bears only the remotest possible resemblance to " tea." I have tried it often but never succeeded in persuading myself to like it.

Much has been written on the possibility of Indian tea-planters having a share in this tea trade with Thibet. From the close proximity of Assam to Lhassa and south-eastern Thibet generally, one would suppose that the difficulties would not be very great, yet the trade has made little progress. The opposition of the Lamas and the obstinate conservatism of the people are very real difficulties in the way. There is also another and equally important factor which should not be lost sight of, namely, the nature and quality of the tea that is in demand. Now it is safe to say that the veriest sweepings from the Indian tea factories would make better tea than that partaken of by the average Thibetan ; but this is not the important point. To secure a share of this trade Indian planters must be prepared to supply the Thibetans with the kind of article to which they are accustomed, and not with something different, even though it be of a superior quality. The trade is very considerable and worth striving after; further-more, there is no reason why it should not be increased. I was travelling on the Chino-Thibetan frontier during the time of the British Expedition to Lhassa, and discussed with Chinese merchants interested in the Thibetan tea trade the possibility of India taking a share in the trade.   It was very evident that they greatly feared Indian competition, and were keenly alive to the possibilities of it.   From Darjeeling to Lhassa is only about 30 stages (350 miles approx.), whilst from Tachienlu the journey occupies over three months.   The physical difficulties of the route are greater on the Chinese than on the Indian side, yet the people of Lhassa still draw their tea-supply from China. And further, Chinese tea, apart from that taken in exchange for musk, skins, wool, gold, and medicines, was, until very recently, paid for by the Thibetans in Indian rupees.

The brick-tea prepared for Thibet is a totally different article from that prepared in Hankow for the Russian market. It is also so totally different from ordinary Chinese tea that some have supposed it to be the product of a distinct plant. My wanderings in Western China led me through the tea-producing areas and the markets which supply the commodity to the Thibetans, my observations, therefore, may be of interest and value.

The two great trade-marts for China and Thibet are Tachien-lu, in the west of Szechuan, and Sungpan, in the extreme north-west corner of that province.   The official route to Lhassa passes through Tachienlu, and this town is the mart for southern and central Thibet, including Lhassa, Chamdo, and Derge. The mart for the Amdo and Kokonor regions generally is Sungpan.   At this latter town the trade is purely one of barter, tea being taken in exchange for furs, wool, musk, and medicines.   The tea for the two markets is prepared very differently, grown in distinct localities, and is best discussed separately.

The tea for the Tachienlu market is practically all grown within the prefecture of Yachou Fu, more especially in the mountainous districts to the north-west and south of the town. The manufacturing business is controlled by the Government and provincial authorities, who issue a definite number of licences to establishments in the towns of Yachou, Mingshan, Yungching, and T'ienchüan—all within the Yachou prefecture. The independent department of Kiung Chou, a little to the north-east of Yachou, also has a share in this trade, but there the licences are all issued by the Imperial Government and are not connected with the provincial authorities at Chengtu. The industry is a very ancient one, the plant itself having been grown in this vicinity since the dawn of the Christian era.

To supply the licensed establishments the peasants and farmers cultivate the tea plant. The culture extends up to 4000 feet altitude, the bushes being planted round the sides of the terraced fields on the mountain-sides. Very little attention is given them and they are usually allowed to grow smothered in coarse weeds to a height of from 3 to 6 feet. Less frequently are the bushes kept free of weeds. During the summer months the leaves and young twigs are plucked off and placed, handfuls at a time, in heated pans for a few minutes, and then spread out in the sun to dry. They are then collected into large sacks or into loose bales and carried down to the towns and villages, where they are purchased by agents of the tea establishments. Occasionally the bushes, when they have become old, are cut down, the branches dried in the sun, and afterwards tied into bundles and carried down for sale. The very young leaves and tips of the shoots are commonly gathered by the growers and prepared into tea for home consumption and local trade, the old coarse leaves and branches being considered good enough for the Thibetans.

I visited a brick-tea factory in Yachou, where I observed the following processes of manufacture : The sacks of leaves and bundles of leafy sticks, after they had fermented for a few days, were taken in hand by women and children who picked off the leaves and shoots, sorting them into four grades, each grade being determined by the size and age of the leaves. The sticks, often 1 to 2 inches in circumference, after the leaves have been removed, were chopped small by means of a large knife fixed in a block of wood. Mixed with coarse leaves and sweepings these chopped-up sticks constitute the fourth grade. A small packet of the very worst of this grade is inserted in the ends of each bamboo-cylinder as a gratuity to the repackers and muleteers at Tachienlu.

A certain British consul has likened this brick-tea to " crows' nests pressed into cakes." This aptly describes the product so far as the fourth quality is concerned, but the first quality, prepared at Yachou, is really very good tea.   I was surprised at the care and attention bestowed on its manufacture, the processes being as follows : After the leaves had been sorted and graded they were steamed in a cloth suspended over a boiler.   The steamed mass was then put into collapsible moulds, together with a little of the dust from smashed sticks and leaves which had been treated with glutinous rice-water to make it cohere, and then the whole was submitted to great pressure.   When the mould was removed the tea was in the form of bricks (Chuan), each measuring 11 inches by 4 inches and weighing 6 English pounds.   After being dried for three days, these bricks are wrapped in paper on which the maker's trade-mark is stamped, a patch of gold-leaf of minute proportions or a plain piece of red paper to denote the quality being also enclosed.   Four of the bricks are then placed end to end in a plaited bamboo-cylinder, and after this has been fastened at the ends the tea is ready for transit.   These bamboo-cylinders, when filled with tea, are called " Pao " ; they weigh 25 lbs. and measure about 4 feet in length.   They are carried on the backs of coolies to the town of Tachienlu, where they pass into the hands of Thibetans.   The bricks of the finer quality teas and those intended for the interior of Thibet and distant Lhassa, are removed from the bamboo-cylinders and repacked, 12 together, in raw yak-hides, with the hair inside and the free edges neatly sewn together.   The inferior quality teas are largely consumed in eastern Thibet and are not repacked.   From Tachienlu the packages are carried on the backs of yak and mules to their destination.

The " Pao " packed in Yachou city always weigh 18 catties [1] (24 lbs. English), but in other places they vary according to quality, being either 12, 13, 14, 15, or 16 catties, each town having its own particular weight for the different qualities. Tea from Yachou city and Yungching Hsien follow the main road ;   that from Mingshan and T'iench'uan a by-road. Both routes converge at the town of Luting chiao, and there pay toll on crossing the river.   Either route is terribly difficult, and one marvels how such loads can be carried by men over

[1] Catty =1⅓ English pounds.

such fearfully mountainous roads.   The average load consists of 10 pao of 18 catties each.   But loads of 12 and 13 pao are very common, and on several occasions I have seen men carrying 20 pao.   These, however, only weighed 14 catties each, but even then the total weight of the load was 370 English pounds !

The distance between Yachou and Tachienlu is about 140 miles (probably less), and the journey for coolies laden with tea occupies 20 days.   Although the work is so inhuman, thousands of men and boys are engaged in this traffic.   With their huge loads they are forced to rest every hundred yards or so, and as it would be impossible for the carrier to raise his burden if it were once deposited on the ground he carries a short crutch, with which he supports it when resting, without releasing himself from the slings.

For each pao carried from Yachou to Tachienlu the carrier receives 400 cash (about a shilling in English money).   Out of this he has to keep himself and pay for his lodgings.   Nevertheless, the pay is really good for the country, and it is this extra remuneration that tempts so many to engage in this work.

It is very difficult to obtain accurate information as to the extent of this transfrontier tea-trade, but statistics culled from various, more or less reliable, sources, show that at the lowest estimate some 5400 tons of brick tea worth approximately £150,000 enter Tachienlu annually.

Tea for the Sungpan market is grown in two distinct localities, in the west and north-north-west of the Chengtu Plain respectively.   Each district has its own peculiar mode of packing the product.   In the west it is grown in the mountains bordering the banks of the Min River in the district of Kuan Hsien.   A centre of the industry is the market village of Shui-mo-kou, some 90 li beyond the city of Kuan Hsien itself.   This tea is not pressed into bricks after the manner of that for the Tachienlu market, but is made into rectangular bales some $2\frac{1}{2}$ feet by $2\frac{1}{2}$ feet by 1 foot each, weighing 120 catties (160 English pounds), and covered with bamboo-matting.   A considerable quantity of this tea finds a market among the Chiarung tribes, the distributing centres being Monking Ting and Lifan Ting. The mountainous regions of An Hsien and Shihch'uan Hsien constitute the north-western tea district, the principal centre being the market village of Lei-ku-ping within the district of An Hsien. The prepared product, however, all passes through Shihch'uan Hsien, and is controlled by specially appointed officials. The tea prepared in this region is packed in oval bales, each weighing 65 to 70 catties (about 90 English pounds), encased in the usual bamboo-matting.

The routes by which Kuan Hsien and Shihch'uan Hsien teas travel converge at Mao Chou, an important town situated on the left bank of the Upper Min River, six days' journey south of Sungpan Ting. To Mao Chou the tea is mostly carried by men, two small or one large bale being the usual load. From Mao Chou to Sungpan mules and ponies are largely employed for transporting it, their loads being twice the weight of those carried by men. Both women and men, however, are also engaged in the carriage of tea from Mao Chou northward, and the merchants constantly complain of insufficient means of transport.

The preparatory processes undergone by the tea destined for the Sungpan market are less intricate than those described for brick tea. The leaves and young branches are gathered, panned, and dried in the sun. The panning process is sometimes omitted, and very commonly the bushes and their overgrowth of coarse weeds are cut together, dried in the sun, and tied into bundles. The leaves are collected into sacks or bales, and with the bundles of leafy sticks carried down to the market villages and sold to tea establishments. The manufacturers allow the leaves to ferment in heaps for a few days, and afterwards submit them to a rough sorting. The sticks are chopped up with the coarse leaves and steamed over a large pan of boiling water. The moist, heated mass is then firmly pressed into bales, covered with matting, and allowed to dry.

The tea is practically all of one quality, and very little superior to the most inferior kind entering Tachienlu. Cheapness is the main consideration, a bale of 120 catties being valued in Sungpan at Tls. 8. This trade is a monopoly in the hands of five establishments, which pay to the provincial government at Chengtu a fixed tax of about 1 cent. per catty. Payment is done by purchasing permits called " Yin piao," which bear the official stamp. Each permit covers a bale of 120 catties or two smaller ones, and costs Tls. 1·20.

Whereas at Tachienlu the tea passes directly into the hands of Thibetans, at Sungpan it remains in the hands of the five tea establishments. These are owned by Mohammedan Chinese, who, in addition to carrying on a considerable local trade, have trusted agents travelling all over north-eastern Thibet bartering tea for furs, wool, musk, medicines, and other Thibetan commodities.

The tea-trade of Sungpan is an improving one, but it is practically impossible to obtain reliable figures of its volume. There are, of course, Chinese Official Returns stating the number of " Yin piao " sold annually, but where official peculation is so general such returns are notoriously untrustworthy. Piecing together information gathered during my three visits to Sungpan, I suggest that the tea-trade averages about £75,000 annually.

From all sources the total annual value of the tea exported from China to Thibet is about a quarter of a million sterling. On paper this may not appear very great, but if the sparse population of Thibet and the difficult means of intercommunication be duly considered, it will be seen that the trade is really a very considerable one. Indian teas cannot compete with the Chinese product in central and northern Thibet, but around Lhassa and in southern Thibet generally, they ought to command a market.

In all the larger medicine shops in Szechuan and, incidentally, elsewhere in the Empire, a product known as " P'uêrh tea " is on sale. It is packed in circular cakes, flat at top and bottom, about 8 inches across, and covered with bamboo leaves fastened by strips of palm leaves. This tea is grown in the Shan states, largely in the district of I'bang, and is the product of a variety of the true Tea plant (*Thea sinensis*, var. *assamica*). It takes its name from P'uêrh Fu, a prefecture in southern Yunnan, and the trade entrepôt of that region. The leaves, after the necessary preliminary processes, are steamed and pressed into the cakes, in which form they are easily transported. P'uêrh tea has a bitter flavour, and is famous as a medicine all over China, being esteemed as a digestive and nervous stimulant. It also finds its way into the wealthy lamaseries of Thibet, where its medicinal properties are highly appreciated.

Although a beverage known as tea is partaken of throughout the length and breadth of the Middle Kingdom, it is by no means all infused from the leaves of the genuine tea plant. In the mountainous parts of central and Western China many substitutes are employed by the peasants, who seldom taste the real article. In western Hupeh the leaves of several kinds of Wild Pear and Apple, grouped under the colloquial name of " T'ang-li-tzu," are used as a source of tea and exported to Shasi for the same purpose. The infusion prepared from these leaves is of a rich brown colour, very palatable and thirst-quenching. It is called Hung-ch'a (red tea), and is in general use among the poorer classes in the west.

The leaves of *Pyracantha crenulata*, the Chinese " Buisson ardent," are also in common use as a source of tea. This ever-green is everywhere abundant up to 4500 feet altitude, and is known as the " Ch'a kuo-tzu," literally, " Tea shrub." Like its European relative it produces a wealth of scarlet fruit in autumn. The leaves of several species of Spiræa (*S. Henryi, S. Blumei, S. chinensis,* and *S. hirsuta*) are less commonly used as tea, being known as " Tsui-lan ch'a." The leaves of the Weeping Willow (*Salix babylonica*) are occasionally employed as tea, and in the Upper Min Valley chips of willow-wood are likewise used. I have drunk all these various " teas," but that infused from these willow-chips was the worst, being de-cidedly weak and nasty !

In the chapter on Mount Omei mention is made of the sweet tea prepared from the leaves of *Viburnum theiferum.* The leaves of the common White Mulberry, steamed, mixed with cabbage-oil, and pressed into cakes, constitute " Ku-ting-ch'a " (bitter tea). The infusion prepared from this is drunk in hot weather and esteemed as a cooling beverage.

The product known as tea-oil is not produced by the tea plant, but is expressed from the seeds of *Thea Sasanqua,* known as the " Ch'a-yu kuo-tzu," a relative of the true tea plant, from which it may be readily distinguished by its hairy shoots.   It is a shrub, common as a wild plant in the sandstone ravines of north-central Szechuan.   In parts of eastern China it is abundantly cultivated for the sake of its oil, but in the west I only met with plantations in the district of An Hsien. It is, however, reported as being cultivated in the department of Kiung Chou and elsewhere.   The oil is used to adulterate cabbage-oil, and by Chinese ladies as a dressing for their hair. The refuse cake is valued as a fertilizer, and when applied to rice fields is said to destroy the earth-worms which often attack the young rice plants.

CHAPTER X

INSECT WHITE-WAX

NEXT to sericulture the most important industry in the prefecture of Kiating is that concerned with the production of insect white-wax or "Peh-la." This product has attracted the attention of many travellers, and has been often discussed before. It possesses several peculiarly interesting features, and cannot be omitted from any account of the economic products of western Szechuan. It is produced by a scale-insect (*Coccus pela*), and is deposited on the branches of an Ash (*Fraxinus chinensis*) and a Privet (*Ligustrum lucidum*); the scale-insects are bred in one district and transported to another for the production of the wax. All this sounds very simple, yet it has taken nearly five centuries to establish these facts. According to Chinese historians insect white-wax first became known to the Chinese about the middle of the thirteenth century. Nicolas Trigault, a Jesuit missionary, wrote some account of the industry in parts of Eastern China in the year 1615. During succeeding centuries several accounts of it were published, but it was not until 1853, when Mr. William Lockhart, of Shanghai, sent specimens of crude wax to England, that the wax-producing insect became scientifically known in England. In the crude wax a number of dried, full-grown bodies of the female insect were discovered, and were identified by Westwood as a new species of Coccus. Robert Fortune, in his travels around Ningpo in 1853, had noted the industry, and stated that " the tree on which the wax is deposited is undoubtedly a species of Ash." In 1872 the illustrious Baron Richthofen wrote of the production of insect white-wax in Western China, a fact not previously known to the people of the Occident.

In 1879 Mr. E. C. Baber made a lengthy report on the

white-wax industry of Western China from observations near Fulin. Unfortunately, this talented observer possessed no botanical knowledge, and, being misled by vernacular names, he increased if anything the mystery which shrouded the botanical aspect of the subject.

In 1884 Mr. (now Sir Alexander) Hosie, then Consular Agent at Chungking, undertook, at the instigation of the Kew authorities, the thorough investigation of the subject. He travelled through the principal wax-producing districts of Szechuan, collected specimens of the two host-plants and of the wax itself, noted the mode of culture and the preparation of the commercial white-wax. The two host-plants were identified by the Kew authorities as *Ligustrum lucidum* and *Fraxinus chinensis*, the first named being the tree on which the insects breed and the latter the tree on which the wax is deposited. There can be little doubt that the Ligustrum is the natural host of the wax-insect, and much of the difficulty in elucidating the subject was due to the fact that this tree has two or three different vernacular names. In central and Western China it is usually designated the " La shu " (Wax tree) or " Ch'ung shu " (Insect tree), but it is occasionally, and particularly in the eastern provinces, called the " Tung-ching shu." This last name simply means " Winter-green tree," and is usually applied to *Xylosma racemosum*, var. *pubescens*, a tree commonly planted around shrines and tombs. Many wild guesses were made as to the identity of this " Tung-ching shu," and with each guess the subject became further involved.

The districts of Omei Hsien and Hungya Hsien, both within the prefecture of Kiating, are the headquarters of the wax-producing industry, but the insects are bred in the Chiench'ang Valley, in the prefecture of Ningyuan Fu, nearly 200 miles distant. A few insects are bred near the town of Chienwei Hsien, a day's journey to the south of Kiating, but these are said not to produce so much wax or of such good quality as those from the Chiench'ang Valley.

The insects develop during the winter months, and the cone-like scale or " gall " is ready for removal about the end of April, being then full of the minute eggs of the insect. So far as my observations go, they indicate that it is always on the Privet that the insect breeds, but Baber asserts that either tree will serve, and this is probably true.

Several of these cone-like scales, full of eggs, are wrapped together in thin paper bags, which are arranged in airy crates and carried by porters with all possible speed to the city of Hungya, where they are disposed of to the farmers. During the month of May hundreds of coolies are engaged in this traffic. The larvæ hatch out quickly, more especially if the season is hot and early, in which case the travelling is mostly done at night by the aid of lanterns. The journey of nearly 200 miles over difficult mountain roads is accomplished in six days. Aided by relays, the porters who carry these insects cover 30 to 40 miles per day ; in ordinary circumstances 20 miles a day is a high average for porters in the west.

For the production of the wax it is immaterial whether the Ligustrum or Fraxinus is used. Some districts favour the latter, others the former ; very frequently the two trees are grown side by side. The trees are planted round the edges of the fields, and are polled some 5 or 6 feet from the ground. The lateral shoots, which develop from the polled heads, are always one or more years old ere the insects are placed on them. The propagation of these trees is effected by taking thick branches, slicing off a portion of the bark and a little of the wood, and surrounding the incised area with a ball of mud and straw. Roots form in the ball of mud, and the branch is then severed from the parent tree, and is planted at the side of a field, where it quickly develops into a tree.

In the wax-producing area of the Kiating prefecture myriads of these pollarded trees are cultivated by the farmers and peasants. Previous to the arrival of the insects in May, the branches on which it is intended to place insects are denuded of their laterals along the basal half of their length. The cultivator, having purchased his insects, wraps loosely a few cones in a broad leaf and suspends these tiny " bags " among the branches of either Fraxinus or Ligustrum trees, or of both. The larvæ quickly hatch out and crawl up into the tree and ascend to the leaves, where they remain for fourteen days until " their mouths and limbs are strong." During this period they are said to " moult," casting off " a hairy garment which forms in the earliest larval stage." After this period the insects descend to the naked branches, on the underside of which they attach themselves and commence at once to deposit wax. During this early stage heavy rains and wind are much dreaded, since they dislodge the insects, and consequently ruin the business for the season. The deposit of wax, which at first looks very like hoar-frost on the branches, continues up to the latter end of August. (The Chinese reckon 100 days from the time of suspending the insects in the trees.) The deposit is always heaviest on the underside of the branch, and seldom extends equally all round it.

About the end of August the white coating is scraped from the branches (very often the branches are cut off) and thrown into boiling water. The wax is dissolved and floats on the surface of the water. It is collected by being skimmed off, and whilst in a plastic state is moulded into thick saucer-shaped cakes. The insects sink to the bottom of the vessel containing the boiling water, and are collected and thoroughly crushed to express every particle of wax before being finally flung to the pigs.

The wax excretion has been attributed to disease, but in the light of present knowledge it seems feasible to regard it merely as a device on the part of Nature to protect the insect from its enemies. The Chinese idea is that the insects live on dew, and the wax perspires from their bodies !

The natural enemy of the wax-insect is a species of " Lady-bird," which breeds with them and preys on the larvæ. The Chinese designate this enemy " Wax-dog " (La-gho). After the larvæ have hatched out, the farmer visits his trees in the heat of the day, and belabours their stumps with a club for the purpose of dislodging this foe.

The co-operation which obtains in this industry between two separate and distinct districts has led to much confusion. The explanation seems to be that owing to peculiar climatic conditions the insect breeds freely in Chiench'ang Valley, and for similar reasons deposits wax freely in the Kiating pre-fecture. At any rate, it is obvious that one cannot have wax and insects too, since to obtain the former it is necessary to kill the latter by immersion in boiling water. I am convinced that the co-operation or mutual dependency is simply one of self-interest on the part of both districts.

Insect white-wax bears a close resemblance to spermaceti, but is much harder. It is colourless and inodorous, or nearly so, tasteless, brittle, and readily pulverisable at 60° F. It is slightly soluble in alcohol, and dissolves with great facility in naphtha, out of which fluid it may be crystallized. It melts at about 180° F., floats in water, and is said to harden by long immersion in cold water.

The wax is largely used in the manufacture of Chinese candles, a little being mixed with the fats and oils employed in their manufacture ; a thin coating is also applied to the outside of the candles. The best candles contain 2½ ounces to the lb., inferior ones not more than 1 ounce. Since the ordinary fats and oils melt at about 100° F., the advantage of an outer coating of white-wax with its high melting-point is obvious. In paper-shops insect white-wax is largely employed to impart a gloss to the higher grades of paper. In medicine-shops it is universally used as a coating for pills, and is itself supposed to possess medicinal properties. It is also employed as a polish on jade and soap-stone ware and on the more delicate articles of furniture, to give lustre to cloth, and is made into ornaments of Buddha ; but its primary uses are in the manufacture of candles and in paper-glazing.

The annual output varies considerably, the industry being almost entirely dependent upon suitable climatic conditions. In poor seasons 50,000 piculs is an average crop, whereas in very favourable years it is more than double this quantity. Formerly the prefecture of Paoning produced a fair amount of white-wax, but the industry has there become neglected of recent years. To-day virtually the whole supply of Western China is produced in the Kiating prefecture.

In spite of the increased consumption of foreign candles and kerosene oil, the demand for insect white-wax remains steady, and the industry concerned with its production shows very little sign of decline. In Western China, owing chiefly to difficulties and dangers of navigation on the Yangtsze, and the consequent heavy freights, foreign goods are an expensive luxury enjoyed only by the wealthy. With the advent of railways vast changes will certainly take place, and this interesting insect-wax industry may at some future date become extinct.

CHAPTER XI

SPORT IN WESTERN CHINA

Pheasants and other Game Birds

A TRAVELLER in Western China who is fond of the sport will, in season and from time to time, have opportunity of enjoying some good rough shooting. During my travels in that land I have had with dog and gun some splendid days—days which afford keen pleasure to look back upon. My aspirations in the matter of shooting never extended beyond the Pheasants, though at odd times I have shot a few River Deer, Muntjac, and, of course, Hares. But my extensive and prolonged journeys in the more mountainous parts of China have afforded me great opportunities of gaining a knowledge of the game-fauna of Western China.

During the years 1907–09, the expedition under my charge paid particular attention to the fauna, and amassed a collection of some 3135 birds, skins of 370 mammals, and specimens of various reptiles and fishes. My associate on this particular expedition, Mr. Walter R. Zappey, had especial charge of the collecting work in this department, and it speaks volumes for his enthusiasm, untiring energy, and skill that in so short a time he succeeded in making such a magnificent collection. The specimens he obtained are, through the munificence of John E. Thayer, Esq., Lancaster, Mass., U.S.A., preserved in the Museum of Comparative Zoölogy at Harvard College. The entire collection has been worked up by various specialists, and the results published in the *Memoirs* (vol. xl. No. 4, August 1912) of that Museum.

This expedition gave me facilities for acquiring an intimate acquaintance with the fauna of Western China, and enables me to submit to readers much first-hand information relative to this subject.

Mr. Oliver G. Ready in his *Life and Sport in China*, and Mr. H. T. Wade in his *With Boat and Gun in the Yangtsze Valley*, with other writers, have given accounts of the game-fauna found in the more accessible parts of eastern China, but I am unacquainted with any work giving a general, descriptive account of the game animals and birds of the mountainous parts of central and Western China. In *The Middle Kingdom*, by S. Wells Williams, a brief notice of the fauna of China is given, but this was written long ago, and is based largely upon Chinese evidence and hearsay, and in consequence cannot be regarded as either complete or accurate. Unfortunately in the new edition of this work, published in 1900, very little revision of the chapter dealing with the fauna was attempted, and not much new matter was added.

Since the subject under discussion is a large and comprehensive one, it is simplest, perhaps, to divide it into two distinct parts, one dealing with the birds and the other with the mammals.

BIRDS

There is a great variety of game birds and wild-fowl found all over China ; moreover, this land is the headquarters of the Pheasant family. This latter fact is alone sufficient to make China of particular interest to all sportsmen, even had she no other attraction to offer. A Chinese Pheasant, commonly called the " Chinese Ring-neck " (*Phasianus torquatus* in the widest sense), was, as the world of sport well knows, long ago introduced into Europe and crossed with the native bird. To-day practically all the Pheasants bred in England for purposes of sport have more or less of this Chinese blood in them. The Mongolian Pheasant (*P. mongolicus*), a hardier bird, with lighter plumage in the female and young birds, is now being commonly bred for shooting purposes. In the United States of America the same obtains, but to a much more limited extent. Other Chinese Pheasants such as the " Reeves," " Golden," " Amherst," " Tragopan," etc., have been introduced, but have not been so readily acclimatized, and are comparatively seldom seen outside the aviary.

The country of western Hupeh, of which the city of Ichang may be regarded as the " Gate," constitutes a natural boundary for members of the animal and vegetable kingdoms.   The flora and fauna found east of this region are, generally speaking, totally different to that found to the westward.   The explanation is to be found in the character of the country.   At Ichang commence the series of mountain ranges which, rising higher westward, finally culminate in the mighty snowclad ranges of the Chino-Thibetan borderland.   Enclosed within this mountain-system is the Red Basin of Szechuan which is described in Vol. I, Chapter VI.   This highly cultivated Basin again constitutes a barrier, and very few of the game birds or animals are common to both its eastern and western boundaries. East of Ichang for 1000 miles to the coast lay the vast alluvial plains and flats of the Yangtsze Valley.   Here and there mountain ranges crop out like islands in the ocean, and so long have these elevations been isolated that they support in the main a peculiar flora and fauna.   The surprisingly restricted range of the component species is one of the most interesting facts in Chinese natural history.

Of true Pheasants (*Phasianus*) some six species occur in the region with which this work is concerned.   Each of these species occupies its own particular geographical area.   But it must be admitted that the modern tendency of systematic ornithologists to split up species into subspecies and varieties based on very slight variations renders the subject complicated and difficult.   Indeed to such an extent is subdivision carried that one is sometimes inclined to think the actual differences exist on paper only.

The low foot-hills, which commence some 30 miles east of Ichang, constitute the western limit of the common Ring-neck Pheasant of middle eastern China and the Yangtsze Valley in particular (*P. torquatus*, var. *kiangsuensis*).   It is likewise the eastern boundary of a Pheasant in which the ring is usually quite absent (*P. holdereri*).   The " Ring-neck " is essentially a bird of the plains, whilst the other is a mountain bird, adapted to more austere conditions of life.

The bird of the plains is almost semi-aquatic in its habits, breeding in swamps and places more generally associated with waterfowl than pheasants. In the reed-bed region bordering the Tungting Lake I have, on several occasions, enjoyed good shooting, and it was always in the wet marshy places that the birds were most plentiful. Winter Snipe are common in this same region, and a right and left Pheasant and Snipe is commonly obtainable. On my first shooting trip in the reed-bed region I was ignorant of the aquatic habits of this Pheasant, and a friend and I worked all the dry, likely-looking places for the best part of a day with most discouraging results, until we accidentally plunged into a swampy region and found the birds. Water, food, and cover are everywhere the three essentials for pheasants of all kinds, but this bird of the plains seems to have a stronger predilection for the first-named than does any other species. The probable explanation is that in the marshes it enjoys greater protection from enemies, both two and four footed, than in the dry, open, and highly cultivated plains.

In times past some extraordinary bags of this Pheasant have been made, and records of such are given in Mr. Wade's book. The bird is still quite common in the Yangtsze Valley, but natives, shooting for the market supply of the various treaty-ports, and especially that of Shanghai, have cleared many of the best districts known to foreigners. Phenomenal bags are no longer obtainable, and each year the foreign sportsman has to go farther afield if he wishes to enjoy good shooting.

The cunning of the " Ring-neck " is proverbial, and the bird is so well known that description is unnecessary. The white ring round the neck and the white eyebrows are constant features that distinguish this bird from other species. The average measurement of the male is 32 to 34 inches tip to tip.

The common Pheasant of the mountains of central China (*P. holdereri*) is about the same size as the " Ring-neck." The head and neck black with bluish and green reflections, occasionally with a more or less complete white neck-ring ; breast purplish, abdomen black ; sides dull yellow, each feather having a black spot near the tip ; upper back dull yellowish, feathers notched and margined narrowly with black ; lower back bluish-slate, tail broadly barred, sides of upper tail-coverts light chestnut ; length about 32 to 34 inches tip to tip. The more broadly-barred tail-feathers, absence of white eyebrows, and the usual absence of the white neck-ring distinguish this bird from the common " Ring-neck."

If the Pheasant of the plains is notoriously cunning, his confrère of the mountains is equally so, and the nature of his haunts aids him considerably in escaping his enemies. A common habit when hunted is for him to work his way quickly to the top of a steep hill and take wing on the crest. A study of his habits is necessary before much success attends one's efforts at shooting this Pheasant. The haunt of this mountain bird is the woods, copses, and scrub-clad mountain-sides, but he is seldom found in quantity other than in close proximity to cultivation. Just how far west this bird ranges I do not know, but he has not yet been authentically recorded west of the eastern limits of the Red Basin. His headquarters is undoubtedly western Hupeh and southern Shensi. His altitudinal range in this region is only limited by cultivation. In the mountains a favourite food of this bird is the fruit of many Rosaceous shrubs, particularly that of Cotoneaster. Scrub Oak retaining its warm brown foliage through the winter is general throughout this region, and is in winter a favourite haunt of this bird. In heavy snow he seeks the forest, especially that composed of evergreen trees.

This Pheasant is strong on the wing and capable of carrying away a lot of shot. Much of the shooting in mountainous country is snap-shooting, and one's powder should " hit hard " or the bird is round the corner out of sight, and probably lost. Shooting this mountain bird is much finer sport than that afforded by the plains species. Every bird secured in the mountains is earned, and this combined with the bracing air gives additional zest and pleasure to the sport. I have spent some very pleasant days after this bird, and though I have never made a big bag I have enjoyed some enviable sport.

Around Ichang, where this Pheasant occurs in sparse and ever-decreasing numbers, the hills are covered with a " Spear grass " (*Heteropogon contortus*), called " Hung-tsao " by the Chinese. The seeds of this annoying grass are barbed, and they drill their way through clothing deep into the flesh, from whence they are not readily extracted. Their power of penetration is truly marvellous. Ordinary cloth, such as serge, flannel, and khaki, is useless against them—they will even penetrate through the leather tongue of a shooting boot ! Stout duck and drill, starched and glazed, are the only kinds of woven material that will resist them, and then only as long as the material remains dry. In this spear-grass country only smooth-haired dogs are useful and capable of facing the cover. In the more mountainous country, three or four days removed from the river, the most useful kind of dog to cover the country is probably the Spaniel.

In the mountains of south-western Szechuan west of the Min River Valley and as far north as lat. 31° N. the common Pheasant is Anderson's (*Phasianus elegans*). This lovely bird differs from Holderer's Pheasant in having a dark green instead of purple breast and terra-cotta instead of dull yellow sides ; the rump more pronounced slaty-grey with green reflections ; the tail is shorter, and the bird, which averages 29 to 30 inches tip to tip, is smaller in all its parts. The average weight of full-grown cocks is 2½ lbs. An imaginary line connecting Kuan Hsien and Tachienlu roughly marks its northern range ; southwards it extends through western Yunnan to the borders of Burmah. Its altitudinal range is from 2500 feet up to 10,000 feet, or even higher where cultivation obtains. Around Tachienlu, at alt. 8000 to 9500 feet, this Pheasant is quite common, and I have here seen in mid-July little chicks only a few days old. Around Wa shan this bird is fairly common, but from all accounts it is much more abundant in Yunnan. The habitat of this Pheasant is similar to that of Holderer's kind, and it affords similar sport.

Around Sungpan, in the north-west corner of Szechuan, occurs in quantity a Pheasant which closely resembles Anderson's, but is even smaller and rather different in colour. It may be a local form of this species. The predominant colour is a rich dark coppery bronze with dark green chest and breast, some feathers of the wing and rump are slate coloured ; head and neck very dark purplish-green, shading to black on the throat ; length, 28 to 30 inches, tip to tip ; average weight, 2½ lbs.

This Pheasant ranges up to the limits of cultivation (*circa* 11,500 feet), and is partial to brush-clad mountain-slopes bordering the fields of wheat and barley, the staple crops in this region. He descends the Upper Min Valley to about 6000 feet altitude, but is essentially a bird of high elevations.

At Sungpan I have shot this bird inside the city walls, and so abundant are they there that the Chinese declare that in winter they can be walked up to and killed with a stick ! Though this is probably an exaggeration the bird is undoubtedly very common, and the broad valleys and fairly easy slopes render the sport enjoyed after this Pheasant less fatiguing than that after any other of the mountain species. In the brushwood haunts of this bird, however, the Sallowthorn (*Hippophaë salicifolia*) abounds, and one's shins and knees need good protection against the stout thorns which beset this shrub. The true *Phasianus elegans* and this variety (or species, as the case may be) are hardy birds, and their introduction into the west is much to be desired. In North America in particular they would probably prove of greater value than the varieties of the more tender *P. torquatus*. They are as strong on the wing as any kind of Pheasant, lie close and afford the finest of shooting.

On the mountains bordering the Red Basin from Wênch'uan Hsien northward to the borders of Kansu, from 4000 to 9000 feet elevation, the Pheasant commonly met with is *P. berezovskyi*. In this bird the crown of the head is purplish ; neck, dark lustrous green; chest and breast, rich coppery-bronze, with the breast-feathers narrowly margined with black ; flanks, dark ; rump, slaty-blue ; total length about 36 to 38 inches.

On one occasion, in 1908, two companions and myself enjoyed some excellent sport after this bird in the mountains to the immediate east of Mao Chou. Had we been out for a bag we could easily have secured a hundred brace in the four days we spent in this region. One of the cocks shot measured over 40 inches, tip to tip. Scrub-clad mountain-slopes near cultivation is the home of this handsome Pheasant.

Some confusion has arisen in the matter of identification of the Ringless Pheasant (*P. decollatus*) through l'Abbé David and others referring the Ringless Pheasants found in Shensi

and western Szechuan to this species. As far as I can determine this Pheasant is restricted to the low hilly country
bordering the Yangtsze River from Wan Hsien westward to
Sui Fu. It is also found in the valley of the Min River around
Kiating Fu, which district may be regarded as its northern
limits. It ranges from the river-level up to about 3000 feet
altitude, and possibly to 1000 feet higher south of Chungking,
which is about the regional optimum of the species. Scrub-
clad hillsides and thin woods bordering cultivation in the
Yangtsze region of the Red Basin is the home of this Pheasant.

The species was founded by Swinhoe (*Proceedings, Zoölogical
Society, London,* 1870, p. 135), on a bird purchased by his Boy
in the market at Chungking on 13th May 1869; a Pheasant
without a ring was a surprising novelty to Swinhoe, and he
could scarcely credit the story of a Ring-neck bird being unknown around Chungking.

This Pheasant is characterized by having the crown deep
brown, with the feathers margined with bronzed reflections;
no white superciliary markings and no indication of white
neck-ring; bare red patch on face very small; entire neck
duck-green with purple reflections; feathers of upper back
have the centres black with a narrow, medium, yellowish streak
and broad chestnut cross mark; breast, chestnut-brown, with
broad black margins reflecting green; flanks, buff; tail,
broadly barred with black; total length, 36 to 39 inches.

It is distinguished from *P. holdereri* by its differently coloured
breast, longer tail, and different markings on the feathers of
the upper back. Its closest ally is *P. berezovskyi* (*ante*, p. 112).
P. decollatus and its allied species form a well-marked group,
in which the greenish colour of the neck-feathers stops abruptly
at apex of the breast, forming a sharp line of demarcation in
colour. In *P. elegans* and allied species, which constitute
another well-marked group, no such line of demarcation is
found, the colour of the lower neck and chest merging gradually
into that of the breast.

Strauch's Pheasant (*Phasianus strauchi*) occurs in Kansu
province and on the mountains bordering the Amdo region,
frequenting woody places up to 10,000 feet altitude, and may
possibly extend into north-western Szechuan. It is described

as near *P. decollatus*, and is distinguished by the chest- and breast-feathers being narrowly margined with black ; flanks, darker ; mantle, fiery orange with narrow wedge-like apical streaks of blackish green, broad scapulars margined with dark maroon-red ; tail, more rufous-grey. The chest- and breast-feathers are bright, fiery chestnut-red, edged with purplish green ; flanks, bright chestnut-red, tipped with purplish green ; middle of breast and sides of belly dark green.

It is possible that the Pheasant found in the neighbourhood of Sungpan Ting should be referred to this species. Unfortunately my notes, made in 1904, are too incomplete to hazard an opinion either way. My impression, however, is that this Sungpan bird belongs to the *elegans* rather than the *decollatus* group.

Apart from species of the genus *Phasianus*, a large number of birds commonly spoken of as Pheasants in the broad sense of the term are found in the country with which we are concerned, and I now propose to deal with them in detail.

In the wooded country north and south of Ichang, between 2000 and 5000 feet altitude, the Reeves Pheasant (*Syrmaticus reevesi*) is abundant. This region is the real home of this magnificent bird. Westward he ranges as far as Lu Chou, but I never saw or heard of one west of the Min River ; northwards his range extends into southern Shensi. Every year numbers of badly prepared skins are brought into Ichang for sale. In Chungking dead birds are frequently to be seen on sale in the market. The flesh is very white and firm, but scarcely equal in flavour to that of a common Pheasant.

Marco Polo makes mention of this remarkable bird, and specimens were secured by Mr. Thomas Beale in Canton during 1808. Mr. John Reeves sent specimens to England in 1832. Nevertheless, it is only comparatively recently that its habitat has become known, and very few have seen the bird truly wild, and fewer still have shot it. Though I have seen many hundreds in their native woods, I have not shot more than a dozen. My largest specimen measured 6 feet and $\frac{1}{2}$ an inch. A bird shot by my associate, Mr. Zappey, in January 1909, and now in the Museum of Comparative Zoölogy, Harvard College, measures 6 feet $9\frac{3}{4}$ inches, tip to tip. The largest specimen I ever saw was shot near Nanto, at the head of the Ichang Gorge; it measured 7 feet 2 inches, tip to tip!

The Reeves Pheasant is now so well known in aviaries that the following description is scarcely necessary: Crown and throat, white; upper-parts, dull yellow; feathers, narrowly margined with black, giving a scaly appearance; breast, spotted and barred with black, white, and chestnut, on the sides the chestnut colouring shading into deep rufous-red; abdomen, black; tail, grey, barred with black to tip. The female averages about 32 inches, tip to tip, and is a very pretty bird; the entire plumage is mottled, black, white, and brown, with the outer tail-feathers barred deep rufous-red.

Rocky, well-wooded country, where the undergrowth is not dense and in the neighbourhood of cultivation throughout the altitudes mentioned above, is the haunt of this bird. He has a partiality for oak woods and is very fond of acorns; the pulpy fruit of various Rosaceous plants, especially of Côton-easter, is another favourite food.

The Reeves Pheasant is a wary bird and a great runner, quickly zigzagging to the mountain-top, from whence he prefers to take wing. He is very quick on the wing, shooting up through the trees at a sharp angle and then sailing from one ridge across to another. It is a fine sight to see this bird on a sunny day sailing across from ridge to ridge; the great length detracts from the spread of the wings and he resembles some strange Chinese kite floating high up across the valleys. A strong bird, he flies with little apparent effort, and always puts at least one ridge between himself and the foe that caused his flight, and usually alights on a tree. The female when startled behaves similar to the male in running to the mountain-top. She then takes flight, making a curious chickering noise, and quickly dodges behind a tree-trunk. A common practice with the female bird is to alight on the upper branches of some convenient tree before essaying a long flight. The curious, weak, twittering call is more like that of some small animal than that of a bird.

The Chinese name for the Reeves Pheasant is "Ch'u che" (Arrow Chicken). The tail-feathers are largely used in Chinese theatricals. L'Abbé David suggests that this bird may be the original of the mythical Chinese Fung Hwang (Phœnix bird). To my mind this is extremely probable, but Williams in *The Middle Kingdom* considers the Argus Pheasant, found in Tonking and southern Yunnan, the origin of this fabulous bird.

THE GOLDEN PHEASANT

This well-known bird (*Chrysolophus pictus*) is abundant on the mountains of western Hupeh and eastern Szechuan, where it has much the same geographical range as the "Reeves." West of the Red Basin its place is taken by its congener, the Amherst Pheasant. Though so common, and in spring and early summer heard calling on all sides, the Golden Pheasant is rarely seen. Large numbers are entrapped alive by the Chinese and sold as pets. Few foreigners have had the luck to shoot this bird on his native heath. I had one chance only in my travels and that a very easy one, which I missed with both barrels. This bird frequents dense woods, where Evergreen Oak, Holly, Rhododendron, and other broad-leaved evergreen trees occur ; woods of Pine and Oak scrub are also a favourite haunt, and a strong partiality to rocky ground is shown. It ranges from 2000 to 8000 feet altitude, but is commonest between altitudes of 3000 to 5000 feet. This Pheasant feeds largely on berries, but is not averse to small acorns. He is a timid and crafty bird and seldom strays far from thick cover. He is also a great runner, only taking wing when hard pressed ; the flight is always low, fairly straight, and of short duration into the nearest thicket.

In the adult male the crest and rump are golden yellow ; feathers forming the cape, deep orange margined with black ; breast, flanks, and upper tail coverts tipped with scarlet ; tail, dark brown, barred with black ; average length about 42 inches, tip to tip. The young males resemble the females more than the adult males, having the head and rump rufous-chestnut ; rest of the body brownish and barred. The female is considerably smaller than the male, measuring 24 to 26 inches, tip to tip ; the colour of the plumage is uniform buff-brown, barred.

The Chinese designate this bird "Chin che" (literally,

Golden Chicken). To write it savours of vandalism, but this bird is really excellent eating, though there is little of him. Two or three guns properly posted, with some trained beaters or Sussex spaniels, might enjoy good sport after Golden Pheasants in the regions given above, but the work would involve plenty of hard climbing.

LADY AMHERST'S PHEASANT

West of the Red Basin this Pheasant (*Chrysolophus amherstiæ*) takes the place of the Golden Pheasant. The exact boundary line between the two species is difficult to determine, but I have not seen or heard of them being found in the same region. On Wa shan and Mount Omei and the jungle-clad regions west of these high mountains, the Amherst is abundant. North of Kuan Hsien he crosses the Min River, but the eastern limit everywhere is the western edge of the Red Basin ; north of lat. 32° he quickly disappears.

The habits and haunts of this bird are similar to those of the Golden Pheasant ; the altitudinal range is from 3000 feet to about 10,000 feet in the south-west, and 8000 feet in the north-west of Szechuan. In these regions dwarf-growing Bamboos are a feature of the vegetation, forming absolutely impenetrable jungle. Such is the natural home of this bird, and though in season he is heard calling on all sides he is seldom actually seen. The Amherst is a very noisy bird, with a call very like the Golden. In the dense thickets it is of course impossible to shoot this bird, but in the early morning and late afternoon he is to be found in cultivated areas bordering the thickets, and occasionally a lucky snap-shot rewards the sportsman. The flight is similar to that of the Golden, and the natives entrap him in the same way. In the mountains bordering the Chiench'ang Valley in south-west Szechuan this bird must be very abundant, for the tail-feathers and cape are common articles of export from this region. They are used in Chinese theatricals in the same way as the tail-feathers of the Reeves Pheasant. The cape is also used in west Szechuan to adorn the caps of favourite male children.

In the adult male the crown, upper back, and breast are

resplendent dark green ; rump, ochre-yellow with scarlet feathers in the upper coverts and on the lower rump ; from the back of the crown projects a crest composed of a few long crimson feathers ; the cape is white, margined with black, with outer feathers deep brown, barred with black ; tail white, speckled and barred with black ; length about 44 inches, tip to tip. The female is considerably smaller than the male and shows no sign of the cape ; the crown and hind neck plumage is washed with greyish ; back, buff-brown, barred ; chest, buff, with under-parts lighter.

The Amherst has long been known in Occidental aviaries, and some interesting crosses between it and the Golden have been made. To my mind this bird is the most beautiful of all the Pheasants found in Western China. A colloquial name around Wa shan for it is " Kwong-kwong che." The shooting of this Pheasant, save by chance, is very difficult, but there are places where, by adopting the methods advocated for securing the Golden Pheasant, a few birds at any rate would reward an ardent sportsman. As a table-bird the Amherst is scarcely worthy of consideration ; the flesh is coarse and without flavour.

BLOOD PHEASANTS

A common bird in the upland thickets between 8000 to 12,000 feet elevation throughout western Szechuan is *Ithagenes geoffroyi*. Around Tachienlu it is abundant, especially in thickets of Evergreen Oak and Juniper. This bird lies very close and is usually found in small coveys. When pressed by the dog it flies up into the taller bushes, making at the same time considerable noise, half fear, half scold in tone.

In the male the crest is dark grey ; feathers of the back and chest lance-shaped, grey, each with a fine longitudinal white stripe ; breast and sides, light green ; under tail-coverts and few of upper coverts, crimson ; tail-feathers, light grey, edged with crimson ; spurs, 1 to 4 on each leg ; length, about 18 inches, tip to tip. Female very similar to male ; length, 16½ inches, tip to tip.

On Wa shan Mr. Zappey shot specimens of what proved

to be a species new to science, and Messrs. Thayer and Bangs have done me the honour of naming it *I. wilsoni*. This new Blood Pheasant differs in its smaller size, measuring only 14½ inches, tip to tip. The wing is very much shorter, and the whole bird is only about two-thirds the size of *I. geoffroyi*. The colour of the plumage is similar in both species.

In a region considerably to the west of Tachienlu (Yerkalo, on the Upper Mekong River), the Himalayan species (*I. cruentus*) has been reported, but I have no personal knowledge of this bird.

The colloquial name throughout west Szechuan for the Blood Pheasants is " Song che," which may be interpreted " Chicken of the thickets." This bird feeds on Juniper berries and buds of Larch amongst other things, and the whole flesh is permeated with a decided flavour of resin, rendering it unfit for the table.

PUCRAS PHEASANTS

Three distinct species of Pucrasia are now known from China, two of them occurring in the regions with which we are concerned. In western Szechuan, ranging (at least) from Wa shan in the south to Tachienlu in the west, and northwards to Kansu, *Pucrasia xanthospila* is met with. This is essentially a woodland bird, frequenting the forests of Spruce and Silver Fir between 8000 feet and the tree-limit (11,000 to 13,000 feet, *circa*), where the undergrowth is mostly composed of Rhododendrons. It is particularly partial to places where fir needles cover the outcropping rocks. In such places in the forests these birds are frequently to be seen walking silently about with the dignified deliberateness of a barnyard fowl. They are silent (almost uncannily so) in their movements ; they skulk about amongst the timber, and refuse to take wing unless very hard pressed by a dog, when they fly up into the branches of the nearest tree. The males measure 22 to 23 inches, tip to tip ; ground colour of sides and flanks, grey; nape, rufous-yellow; basal parts of outertail-feathers, grey. The common name of this pheasant is " Sung che," literally, " Pine Chicken." (*Sung*, strictly speaking, denotes the genus Pinus only, but in Western China the term has a wider application, and includes Spruce, Silver Fir, and Larch, as well as Pines proper.) This species of Pucras Pheasant has a very wide distribution, extending through the mountain ranges of northern China to eastern Manchuria. It is everywhere esteemed as a table-bird, the flesh having a particularly delicate flavour.

A variety of this species was obtained in the Shensi province by l'Abbé David and named *P. xanthospila*, var. *ruficollis*. This is distinguished in having the side of the neck very deep red ; lateral white spot little developed and surrounded on all sides by the metallic black ; median chestnut band less extended on the belly than in the type ; black tints more developed on the back and wings. Very probably this should rank as a distinct species, but more material is wanted to determine this point.

In western Hupeh a new species has recently been reported and named *Pucrasia styani*. This bird measures about 18 inches, tip to tip ; the middle of the chest, breast, and underparts are streaked like the sides, and there is no trace of the uniform chestnut band down the middle of the under-parts, which is characteristic of all the other species. The female is alike in all the species of Pucrasia, being similar in size and appearance to a common hen pheasant with a short tail and red legs. Styan's Pucrasia occurs in the vicinity of the Yangtsze River from near Kui Chou in Hupeh, westward (at least) as far as Yunyang Hsien, in eastern Szechuan. I flushed a small covey near Kui Chou in February 1901 and secured a female. The birds rose after the manner of ordinary hen pheasants, but scattered in several directions. Near Yunyang Hsien I saw several others in more open rocky ground. Stony, brush, and Pine-clad hillsides of no great altitude appear to be the home of this rare and interesting bird. As to how far it ranges to the north and south of the Yangstze River is not known.

TEMMINCK'S TRAGOPAN

This strikingly handsome bird (*Tragopan temmincki*) is fairly common in parts of western Hupeh and western Szechuan between 4000 and 9000 feet altitude, frequenting woods and shrub-clad country. It prefers steep mountain-slopes, covered with arborescent vegetation, and in summer, when the foliage is on the trees, is most difficult to find. In winter it may occasionally be surprised, early in the morning and evening, near the margins of cultivation and close to thick cover. Like all the woodland pheasants these birds will only take wing when hard pressed and usually afford only a chance snap-shot. A heavy bird, the Tragopan flies at almost the speed of an ordinary pheasant, and always makes straight for dense brush or timber. The Chinese entrap them alive in the same way as they do the Golden and Amherst Pheasants. They are esteemed highly as pets and they sell for 3 to 5 ounces of silver each—a high price in these regions. The markings on the wattle are supposed to resemble the Chinese character for longevity, hence the common name, " T'so che." They are regarded as birds of good omen, bringing good-luck and long life to their fortunate owners. Every year numbers are brought down to Ichang for sale, where they find ready purchasers. In the mountains they apparently adapt themselves to captivity, but in the Yangtsze Valley proper the climate is too hot for them.

In the male the plumage of the upper-parts of the body generally is dark brownish-crimson, spotted with small whitish spots ; breast, indian-red, blotched with grey ; crown, rufous-crimson ; ears and lower eye-patch, indigo blue ; wattle, indigo blue with flesh-coloured markings ; tail, short and broad ; total length, 24 to 26 inches. The female has no wattle and the general colour of the plumage is brownish-buff, barred and spotted with darker colours"; total length, 18 to 20 inches.

The short tail and heavy body make the birds appear heavy in flight, and shooting them would be moderately easy did one but get fair chances. The Tragopan is a good table-bird, but to shoot them for this purpose alone would be gross vandalism. They feed on grain and berries, and are especially fond of the fruits of Cotoneaster and allied shrubs and of maize. South of Ichang this bird is much rarer than in the mountains north-west of this town and in western Szechuan.

The other species of Tragopan (*T. caboti*) found in China is confined to the eastern part of the country, being found in the provinces of Fokien and Kiangsu.

EARED PHEASANTS

Of the three species of these birds (*Crossoptilun*) known from China two are found in the far west. The only one I have seen and shot is the " White " or " Thibetan " species (*C. tibetanum*), which is abundant in the neighbourhood of Tachienlu. This bird frequents the upper timber-belt between 9500 and 13,000 feet, being commonly met with in large flocks, more especially in autumn, when it is probable that several coveys join forces. West of Tachienlu on the highway to Batang it is frequently to be seen strolling about in open grassy places and across the roadway. The walk is suggestive of a fine farmyard rooster, and with its broad, slightly raised, arching, plume-like tail the bird looks very stately. It is a great runner and always makes straight up the mountain-side into thick cover. When flushed it takes wing with the speed of a bullet, and with its heavy body makes a great noise on rising. The flight is of short duration and only attempted as a last resource ; generally the bird alights on trees.

The male has the crown black ; wing primaries, blue-black ; secondaries, blue-black shading into ashy-grey ; upper wing-coverts, grey ; middle tail-feathers, ashy-grey shading to iridescent blue-black with green reflections ; rump and abdomen clear white, rest of the plumage creamy white ; feet, coral-red, and the legs armed with long murderous-looking spurs ; total length, 38 to 40 inches. The female is similar to the male, with a total length of 34 to 35 inches.

Hunting this strong-legged, handsome bird is most " winding " and fatiguing sport. A favourite food is wild onions, and the strong flavour of this esculent permeates the flesh, which is dark-coloured and coarse and of little value for the table. The average weight of adult male is about 8 to 9 lbs.

This Crossoptilun ranges throughout the sub-alpine regions, bordering the timber-line from south-west of Tachienlu to the neighbourhood of Sungpan Ting and is one of the commonest birds found in this region. The vernacular Chinese name for this bird is " Ma che " ; a Thibetan name is " Shar har." How far to the south and west of the regions indicated this bird ranges I have no knowledge.

The eggs are described by Pratt as being " light olive-dun colour." [1] Brooding commences about beginning of June and possibly earlier. By the end of July the " chicks " are of good size and strong on the wing.

According to l'Abbé David,[2] the " Blue-Eared Pheasant " (*Crossoptilun auritum*) occurs in the north-west of Szechuan and extends northwards to the Kokonor region, but is everywhere rare. He also says it is called " Ma che " (Ma ky), a name cited above as applied to the Thibetan-Eared Pheasant. I have no personal knowledge of this Blue Crossoptilun, but in the neighbourhood of Sungpan I was informed that " Ma che " occur, but are rare. I had presumed the white kind was meant, since the vernacular name was the same, but very probably I was mistaken.

In size and shape the Blue Crossoptilun is described as being similar to the Thibetan species ; the ear-tufts are longer; body, slate-blue ; tail-coverts passing from slate-blue to metallic black, lateral tail-coverts pure white in basal half; under-throat, white; eye-patch, blood-red ; feet, coral-red. Female similar in plumage to male, but slightly smaller in size.

The specimens David sent to Europe he secured in Peking and I can find no record of any specimens having been shot in north-west Szechuan by a foreigner. Future travellers will do well to investigate this bird more fully, for there is a possibility of the species being distinct.

MONAL PHEASANT

Scattered through the same region as the White Crossoptilun, only at greater altitudes, occurs the magnificent " Monal Pheasant" (*Lophophorus lhuysi*), at once the most gorgeous and rarest of all game-birds found in these regions. Both David and Pratt comment on the rarity of this bird, and my experience is in accord with theirs. The King of Chiala detailed hunters specially for the purpose of securing specimens for Zappey, but no birds could be found. I was informed this bird was comparatively common east-north-east of Sungpan Ting,

[1] *The Snows of Thibet*, p. 202.
[2] *Les Oiseaux de la Chine*, i. p. 406.

in rocky places between 13,500 and 14,500 feet altitude, but I never met with one in that region.   The only specimen that came under my observation was strolling about the margin of rocky scrub immediately above a wood of alpine Larch on the Ta-p'ao shan (between Romi Chango and Tachienlu), alt. 12,000 feet.   In this particular locality I was told the Monal was fairly plentiful, but I doubt it.   Hunters are ever on the look out to shoot and trap this bird, and the species is undoubtedly threatened with extinction.

In the adult male the top and side of head is metallic green with violet reflections ;   eye-patch naked, very bright blue ; occipital tuft of long feathers, purple with metallic reflections ; back of neck and upper part of back intense golden-copper colour ;   upper side of wings with bright blue and green reflections, washed with golden green on the shoulders ; lower part of back and rump white, with some angular blue spots on side of upper tail-feathers, the longest of which are steel-blue ;   underparts of body black, glossed with green ;   tail rather broad and rounded ;   coverts, black and green with white spots ;   legs feathered to the spur, which is stout ; below spur the legs and also the feet are greenish-brown ; total length, 36 to 40 inches.   The females are brown, mixed with blackish and grey.   The males assume adult plumage the second year ; in their first year's plumage they are similar to the female birds.

The magnificent bird has several local names.   Around Tachienlu it is commonly called " Hwa-t'an che " (" Oak Charcoal Chicken "), or " Hoa-t'an che " (" Burning Charcoal Chicken "), both names having reference to the colour of the upper-part of the back and neck, which resembles the intense glow of a charcoal fire in full blast.   A Thibetan name, which is used around Tachienlu and Sungpan Ting, is " Koā-loŏng." This name has reference to, and indeed simulates, the call of these birds, which is clear and distinctly quadrisyllabic.   This call is usually heard in the early morning, but in wet weather it may be heard at any time of the day.

A favourite food of this bird is said to be the bulbs of various species of Fritillaria.   The bulbs, known as " Pei-mu," are highly valued as medicine by the Chinese, and many men earn their livelihood collecting these and other medicinal herbs in the alpine regions of Western China. According to l'Abbé David, a local name for the Monal is " Pei-mu che " (Paé-mou ky), in consequence of its feeding on these bulbs. Around Tachienlu this name is applied to a Pheasant Grouse described below, but it is highly probable that both birds are sometimes known by the same vernacular name. Mr. A. E. Pratt (loc. cit. p. 203) reports that he succeeded in introducing a single specimen of the magnificent Monal to England and handing it over to the Zoölogical Society, together with several *Crossoptilun tibetanum*.

In the province of Kweichou the mountains do not approach the snow-line, and in consequence it seems highly probably that l'Abbé David (loc. cit. p. 404) was wrongly informed as to this bird being found there.

PHEASANT GROUSE

This fine bird (*Tetraophasis szechenyi*), commonly called " Pei-mu che " by hunters around Tachienlu, is a denizen of the alpine woodlands between 12,500 to 14,000 feet elevation. West of Tachienlu, towards Litang, and more especially on the slopes of the Rama-lal Pass, it is fairly common, but always in open timber near the upper limits of the forests. It takes wing with the characteristic grouse whirr and swings through the glades at a great speed. The plumage of the adult male is : wings brownish, feathers margined with whitish buff ; throat, chin, and forepart of the neck pale fawn colour ; breast, slate with triangular black spots ; rump, light grey ; tail, greyish-brown, tipped with broad band of white ; wattle side of head, orange-scarlet ; total length, 18½ to 19 inches. Female similar to male, but about half an inch shorter. This is a very heavy bird for its size and most excellent eating. Mr. Zappey, who shot quite a number, considers this the finest for the table of all gallinaceous birds found in Western China.

In Mupin, a small principality a little to the east-north-east of Tachienlu, l'Abbé David secured the type of this genus, *Tetraophasis obscurus*. This species is distinguished from that described above in having the chin, throat, and forepart of the neck dark chestnut colour. In size the two species are very similar. David says the local name is " Yang-ko che,"

which may be translated the " Chicken of the Western kingdoms," signifying that it is peculiar to the Chino-Thibetan
borderland.

THIBETAN HAZEL-HEN

This interesting bird (*Tetrastes severtzovi*) is fairly common
throughout the Chino-Thibetan borderland, where it frequents
the upper timber-belt, bordering the brush-clad moorlands.
Alpine woods of Larch, such as occur on the Ta-p'ao shan,
north of Tachienlu, is a favourite haunt of this bird. It is a
plump, rather small bird, fairly easy to shoot, and of excellent
flavour. In the male the upper-parts are brown, mottled
with black ; throat, black ; under-parts, whitish-grey ; chest,
mottled ; total length about $14\frac{1}{2}$ inches. Female similarly
coloured to the male, but without any black on the throat ;
total length, $12\frac{1}{2}$ inches. The dark, rich-brown general
colouring, darker and more distinct markings on the breast
and abdomen readily distinguish this bird from its near ally
the " Hazel-hen " of northern Europe.

SNOW-COCK

This denizen of upper alpine moorlands is rather rare and
very difficult to shoot, too difficult for me, in fact, and
though I have seen several I never succeeded in bagging a
specimen. At 14,000 to 16,000 one has very little breath to
spare, and a strong bird which prefers running and hiding
among rocks to flight has considerably the best of the contest.
As known to me, this bird (*Tetraogallus henrici*) is solitary
or in pairs, with a penchant for hiding amongst the boulders
of old moraines. The plumage of the back is grey, finely
vermiculated with pale buff; wing-coverts with large buff
and pale chestnut spots ; crown, ashy-grey with chestnut and
white markings on side of head ; throat, white ; chest, grey ;
abdomen, dark grey, striped chestnut on the sides ; total length,
20 to 22 inches. This bird is very solid, with a heavy, almost
vulture-like, beak.

The only place I have seen this bird in is the neighbourhood of Tachienlu, and it was here that Prince Henri d'Orleans secured the type-specimen. As far as I know no specimen of Snow-cock other than Prince Henri's has been collected in this region and sent to Western museums. L'Abbé David and others have stated that the Himalayan species (*T. tibetanus*) occurs in this same region, but no specimens have been taken. It is improbable that two species so closely allied inhabit the same locality. The principal difference is the grey chest of *T. henrici*, and white chest, divided from breast by a grey band, in *T. tibetanus*. Personally, I am of the opinion that the only Snow-cock found in the neighbourhood of Tachienlu and Mupin is *T. henrici*.

SNOW-PARTRIDGE

Colloquially known as the Hsueh che (literally, " Snow Chicken "), this bird (*Lerwa lerwa*) is not uncommon in the alpine moorlands of the Chino-Thibetan borderland. I have met with it around Sungpan Ting and on the Pan-lan shan, between Kuan Hsien and Monking Ting, at elevations of 11,500 to 14,000 feet. Hereabouts it is found on open moorlands amongst herbs and dwarf brush, always in small coveys of six to ten birds. They lie very close, and when they do take wing scatter in all directions. If flushed on the slopes of the mountains the birds fly down and round at great speed and are difficult to shoot. They make considerable noise when rising and never fly any great distance. Good sport can be enjoyed behind a well-trained dog, and the bird is very good eating. The plumage of the back is barred black with yellowish-grey and buff ; under-parts, chestnut with a few pale stripes ; beak and legs, coral-red ; total length about 14 inches.

SIFAN-PARTRIDGE

This dainty bird (*Perdix hodgsoniæ sifanica*), which is about the size of the European Partridge, is common on scrub-clad mountains from Tachienlu to Sungpan Ting at elevations between 9000 and 14,000 feet. It is generally found two or four together, and in late August and September in

small coveys of ten or twelve birds.   They lie close, and when
flushed scatter and fly low and straight down and around
the mountain-sides at great speed.   The plumage is brownish
and barred all over, with a distinguishing chestnut collar :
total length (male) about 11½ inches ; (female) about 10½ inches.
This bird affords similar sport to the Snow-partridge, and is
also excellent eating.

BAMBOO-PARTRIDGE

This bird (*Bambusicola thoracica*) is very common in
western Szechuan up to 2000 feet elevation, but I never met
with it in the eastern part of the province nor in Hupeh.   It
is commonly found in clumps of Bamboo around houses, more
rarely in dense scrub and margins of copses.   A ditch overgrown with rank weeds and shrubs is its favourite haunt.   It
is usual to find coveys of ten to twelve birds ; they lie very close,
and will not take wing until hard pressed by the dog.   They
skulk and run, and, when forced, rise in a " bunch " with much
noise, and scatter in all directions.   They do not travel far on
the wing, and usually two or three merely fly up into the nearest
bush ; it is seldom, too, that the whole covey takes flight, one
or two stragglers generally skulk behind.   The bird is swift
on the wing, flying low and straight to the nearest Bamboo
clump or thicket.   In consequence of this and the fact of
their usually being found near houses, the shooting is highly
dangerous.   It is always snap-shooting, and people are everywhere around, so that the sport is tantalizing at best.

This bird is a rather gross feeder, and might almost be
termed a scavenger.   The flesh is white, but often strong
flavoured.   When found some distance removed from houses
where they have fattened on sweet potato, pulse, and grass
seeds, they are really good eating.   Around Kiating this bird
is very common.   The throat and breast is bright chestnut
with a grey crescent across the chest ; crown, grey ; back,
greyish-olive with chestnut markings ; wings with pale
greyish marking ; belly, buff ; sides spotted with very dark
chestnut ; tail, dull chestnut with pale vermiculations ; total
length, 11 to 12 inches.   Female similar to male.

Though a quiet-coloured bird, the Bamboo-partridge is really very handsome, and the colours of its plumage harmonize together splendidly. The males are great fighters. The Chinese commonly keep them in cages as pets, and derive much amusement from their pugnacious habits. The common name of these birds is " Chu che " (Bamboo Chicken).

Between the Ichang Gorge and the Niukan Gorge on the Yangtsze River Bamboo groves are a special feature. In these groves I have several times flushed an odd covey of Bamboo-partridge. This kind is smaller than the one described above, and is either a new species or *B. fytchi*, a species known to occur in western Yunnan. Unfortunately, our expedition did not secure any specimens, and I have no precise data.

WOODCOCK

The common Woodcock (*Scolopax rusticula*) is found scattered all over Western China. Anywhere and everywhere it may be found, but never in any great quantity. From October to the end of April, Woodcock are " in," and an odd bird is almost sure to be sighted in a walk after Pheasant or Bamboo-partridge. I have met with this bird from river-level (Ichang 120 feet altitude) up to 7000 feet altitude in western Szechuan in a variety of places. A favourite haunt is the side of a ditch, where there is a little cover. In spring, Woodcock are commonly to be found in the beanfields (Broad Bean, *Vicia Faba*), especially if there are a few trees near by to afford greater shade. Near Ichang in April 1907 I shot five within an hour, in a patch of beans beneath Plum and Pear trees, with houses not 50 yards away. When found in these moist shady beanfields the birds are usually very fat. One of the five birds alluded to above turned the scale at 15 ounces, and was a male at that ! It is commonly supposed that the female is larger than the male, but after measuring and weighing many birds I can find no decided difference. When the feeding is good the sexes attain about equal weight. The largest bird I have shot was a male.

As all who have given any attention to the matter know, Woodcock are to be found in the same spots year after year.

This is equally true in China as elsewhere.   Though found with greater frequency in the vicinity of habitations where cultivation obtains and food in consequence more abundant, Woodcock are commonly met with on the mountains where little cultivation is carried on.   When shooting east of Mao Chou in October 1908 at about 6000 feet elevation Woodcock were fairly abundant.   I have also enjoyed good sport immediately outside of the city wall of Kiating Fu.   The usual flight of a Woodcock is slow, rather erratic and owl-like, but when fairly roused there are few birds that fly at greater speed. All its movements in rising and flighting are silent, almost uncannily so.

PAINTED-SNIPE

This bird (*Rostratula capensis*) is more a Woodcock than a real Snipe, and is easily recognized by its curved bill.   In plumage there is a vast difference between the young and adult birds.   This difference is commonly attributed to sex, the better coloured birds being regarded as females.   This is wrong. The adult birds are alike in both sexes.   The primary quills of the wing are marked with buff-coloured, eye-like spots ; neck, deep chestnut shading to black on the breast ; outermost of the inner secondaries, white, forming a conspicuous stripe ; tail, olive-grey with four or five buff spots on both webs of the feathers, all of which are tipped with buff ; lower breast, white, this area passing on to the shoulder forming a stripe on the scapular region.   The young birds have a much lighter plumage all over, and look very different, but a series will show every gradation up to the adult plumage.

The Painted-snipe has an exceedingly wide range, but I have only met with it in the neighbourhood of Ichang, where it arrives in September and remains to about the end of October. Some years it is more plentiful than others, but it is a rare bird at any time in this region, and I never saw it in western Szechuan.   It is said to breed in the Yangtsze Valley, and I assume this refers to the alluvial reed-clad marshlands of the Yangtsze delta.   At Ichang it is simply a visitant.

The favourite haunt of this bird is wet, weedy places,

including Lotus and other ponds where the Rush and False Rice (*Zizania*) are cultivated. The flight is low, similar to that of a Woodcock, affording easy shooting. Painted-snipe measure about 10 inches, and though very beautiful are of inferior flavour, and not worth shooting for the table.

SNIPES

Central and Western China has little to offer in the way of good snipe-shooting, and the phenomenal bags annually made in the Yangtsze Valley from Shasi eastward are not obtainable farther west. The high barrier mountains (Tsing-ling and Kiutiao ranges) running eastward from the Thibetan frontier and disappearing about long. 112° 30′ E. have probably more to do with this than anything else, the migratory flight of the main body of the birds being east of these ranges. In Szechuan there is plenty of good snipe-ground but very few birds. Snipe are not partial to the red sandstone soil, which predominates in Szechuan, presumably because it does not afford the best feeding ground. But most of the rice belt in this province has been so long under cultivation that the soil has been changed to black mud. Particularly true is this of the Chengtu Plain, which I have been told Snipe never frequent. This is not correct. Snipe can occasionally be purchased during the season in Chengtu city. I have shot them in several places on the Chengtu Plain, and in one instance found the birds fairly common around Mei Chou. I have also shot them around Kiating Fu and Hungya Hsien. In a marsh around the base of Wa shan during November 1904 I enjoyed some excellent snipe-shooting. These few facts show that Snipe are scattered over western Szechuan generally though sparingly.

Around Ichang quite a number of Snipe are shot annually, but the advent of the railway has destroyed the best ground. This strip of country, only some 2 miles long, was very dear to the heart of every foreigner interested in shooting who sojourned in Ichang. Now this much-loved spot is given over to railway-sidings, workshops, etc., and no longer affords any sport to the would-be shooting man.

In the regions we write of the three species common to the greater part of China occur, namely, Winter Snipe, Pin-tailed and Swinhoe's Snipe.

The Winter or Common Snipe (*Gallinago gallinago*) begin to arrive early in October, and some at any rate remain throughout the winter, migrating northward early in April. It is essentially a marsh and mud-loving bird, and is generally to be found in wet rice-fields, more especially those recently ploughed up; in muddy ponds amongst the Lotus (*Nelumbium speciosum*); in wet grass-clad marshes, sides of ditches, etc. When in good condition it weighs 4 to 4½ ounces, but when it first arrives it is usually very thin and weighs no more than 3 ounces. Compared with the two following species the Winter Snipe is rather lighter coloured, more slightly built bird with rather longer legs and bill; tail composed of 14 normal feathers all of the same size.

The "Pin-tailed" or "Lesser Spring Snipe" (*Gallinago stenura*) arrives from the north earlier and passes northwards again later than does the Winter Snipe, and it does not winter in the Yangtsze Valley. Around Ichang the Pin-tailed begins to arrive from the north about 20th August, and by the 1st of October has passed southwards. In spring it begins to arrive from the south about 1st April, and by 20th May has passed northwards. How this bird (and the same remarks apply to Swinhoe's Snipe) gets through the whole business of breeding and maturing the plumage on the young in so short a time (three months at most) is a mystery. I have never shot (nor heard of others shooting) a Pin-tailed in immature plumage or one which was obviously a young bird. That the birds should be hatched and reach adult size and plumage in such a brief period of time is one of the many wonders associated with migratory bird-life. Every one has of course shot birds varying considerably in weight, but this is merely a condition due to abundance or scarcity of food. When the birds arrive first from the north they are usually in poor condition.

The Lesser Spring Snipe frequents much drier ground than does the Winter Snipe. In spring it is partial to fields of wheat, pulse, and poppy, and grassy places either dry or rather wet. In autumn the favourite haunt is the fields of cotton and the margins of fields of maize and millet. In short, this bird favours cultivated crop-clad areas which the Winter Snipe, on the contrary, avoids. The Pin-tailed is readily recognized by its tail, which normally consists of 26 feathers; the 10 central feathers are ordinary in appearance, and these are flanked on either side by 8 short, narrow, stiff feathers, from the presence of which the bird derives its name. The plumage generally is slightly darker and the bird rather stouter built than the Winter Snipe, though the scales show very little difference between them.

Around Ichang "Swinhoe's" or the "Greater Spring Snipe" (*G. megala*) is about as numerous in season as the Pin-tailed. It frequents the same haunts and arrives and leaves about the same time. In 1907 our first bird of the spring migration was shot on 27th March; of the autumn migration on 26th August. These dates indicate pretty closely its earliest arrival in the two seasons.

Swinhoe's Snipe is much the largest and finest flavoured of the three common snipe. Its flight is slower, and it is easily recognized by its size, rather shorter bill, and normally 20 tail-feathers, of which the central 8 are ordinary with 6 narrow, stiff feathers of nearly equal length on each side. The colour of the plumage is similar to that of the Pin-tailed; length, 11 to 12 inches; weight, 6 to 8 ounces. When in good condition no finer table bird exists than Swinhoe's Snipe. I never met with this bird in western Szechuan.

The Solitary Snipe (*G. solitaria*) is to be met with on rare occasions throughout central and Western China. It is essentially a mountain bird, being partial to long grass and thin shrubberies bordering the sides of mountain streams. In the winter of 1900–1 I shot one bird immediately behind the town of Ichang, but this is the only one I have seen in the immediate vicinity of the Yangtsze River. On the mountains several days' journey south of Ichang at 4000 feet altitude, and again at 6000 feet altitude, I have shot solitary specimens; also in north-western Hupeh at 5500 feet altitude I have secured this bird. In western Szechuan, around Wa shan, 5600 feet altitude, and around Mao Chou, at 5000 to 6000 feet altitude, I have been fortunate enough to shoot this bird.

It is, however, everywhere rare as far as my knowledge goes.

When in good condition this bird weighs 8 to 10 ounces, and is most delicious eating. It is the largest of the Snipes, measuring 12 to 13 inches. In the upper parts the plumage is uniformly dark brown ; under-parts, lighter brown, with the feathers narrowly edged with white ; tail of 16 to 24 feathers, the central feathers are normal, and are flanked by 4 to 6 narrow, stiff feathers on either side.

Latham's Snipe (*G. australis*) and the Jack Snipe (*Limnocryptes gallinula*) have been reported from eastern China, but I have never met with either in central and Western China.

QUAIL

This dainty little bird (*Coturnix japonica*) is found scattered all over central and Western China from river-level up to 7000 feet altitude, but is nowhere really common in these regions. Throughout eastern China it is abundant. Probably those found in the central and western regions breed there, whereas in the eastern parts of China they are largely migrants. These birds frequent dry grassy places, and are partial to the edges of maize and bean fields amongst the grass and weeds ; they are also commonly to be found amongst the dry stubble in rice fields before they are flooded and ploughed. They fly low and straight, and afford pretty and easy shooting when the crops are all cut. But when the maize is standing, the sport is very dangerous. Quail make straight for the standing crop, and as often as not Chinese will be found working hidden or half-hidden amongst the culms.

The densely populated nature of all the agricultural parts of China detracts considerably from the pleasure of shooting thereabouts. The danger of lodging pellets in some unfortunate native is ever present in the mind of the sportsman when after low-flying birds like Quail and Bamboo-partridge. Accidents happen to the most careful of shots, and the sport afforded by these birds in such places is not worth the risk. In parts of eastern China it is said (and there is no reason to question the statement) that the natives deliberately place themselves in dangerous places for the purpose of obtaining money if stung by pellets. Further, they are said not to be above malingering in this matter if there is a possible chance of money being forthcoming. In the west they are less sophisticated, and I never heard of such a thing happening.

The little Bustard Quail (*Turnix blandfordi*) is also fairly common around Ichang. It is easily recognized by the absence of the hind-toe, its rather long slender bill, and bright rufous-yellow chest. It measures 6 to 7 inches tip to tip, being about the same size as the Common Quail, and its haunts and habits are similar.

Grilled with a rasher of bacon and served on toast, Quail forms a tit-bit, worthy of any table. They are not so easily spoilt in the cooking as Snipe and Woodcock.

Quail are pugnacious birds, and are frequently kept as pets by Chinese on this account. Quail-fighting is a pastime much enjoyed in certain parts of China.

DOVES AND PIGEONS

It remains now only to say a brief word about the various Doves and Pigeons of this region. Up to about 4000 feet altitude in the Bamboo clumps and trees surrounding villages and homesteads the Common Turtle Dove (*Turtur chinensis*) is everywhere abundant. This pretty bird is inferior eating, and unless one is hard up for meat there is no excuse for shooting it. In the thin woodlands, and ranging up to about 6000 feet or even higher in well-cultivated regions, the Greater Turtle Dove (*T. orientalis*) occurs, but is much less plentiful than the Common Turtle Dove. This is a very good table bird, perhaps the best of its family. The Pallid Turtle Dove (*T. decaocta*) is also found scattered through north-western Hupeh and eastern Szechuan, but is nowhere common. Around Ichang and westwards into eastern Szechuan the small Turtle Dove (*T. humilis*) [1] occurs as a late spring visitant, and breeds

---

[1] Ornithologists now put the Doves in several different genera, and the species referred to above are spoken of respectively as *Spilopelia chinensis, Turtur orientalis, Streptopelia decaocta, Onopopelia humilis.*

there. This small bird has a very distinct, hoarse croaking note, and is partial to the tallest trees around houses and cultivation.

Of Pigeons proper at least 6 species occur, but 2 only are really abundant. The Rock Pigeon (*Columba rupestris*) is found in quantity throughout the valleys of the Upper Min River from near Wênch'uan Hsien (alt. 3900 feet) to beyond Sungpan (up to 11,000 feet altitude), where steep cliffs abut on cultivated areas. It is equally common around Monkong Ting, in the valley of the Little Gold River (Hsaochin Ho), and around Romi Chango, situated on the Upper Tung River. It descends the valley of the Tung River to near Luting chiao, but is not plentiful in that neighbourhood. This bird is also common north and west of Tachienlu and in the valley of the Yalung River. Indeed, it is generally distributed throughout the whole Chino-Thibetan borderland from 4000 feet altitude to the limits of cultivation (*circa* 11,000 to 13,000 feet). Large flocks are to be seen on all sides perched on the cliffs, in the fields feeding, or circling around. This Pigeon breeds in the holes in the cliffs, and excellent shooting can be had wherever these birds occur. For the table, however, it is inferior to the Greater Turtle Dove. In the Upper Min Valley all the villages are walled, and ruined forts and guard-houses are met with on all sides. Associated with these places, and breeding therein, and also high up in the cliffs, occurs a species of Pigeon which I assume to be *C. intermedia*,[1] a species very closely allied to the Rock Pigeon of Europe (*C. livia*). This Pigeon is easily domesticated, and under the eaves of their houses the villagers and peasants fix crude bamboo baskets for this bird to nest in. It is regarded as a bird of good omen, and is reputed to shun the haunts of evil-doers ! In the Min Valley this Pigeon is in a state of more or less semi-domestication, and the birds exhibit very considerable variation in plumage, many being indistinguishable from ordinary tame pigeons. It may be that the Rock Pigeon (*C. rupestris*) mentioned above enters somewhat into the production of this semi-domesticated race. Both races occupy much the same territory, and both are met with in flocks of from 20 to 100 or more birds.

[1] This species is possibly the one from which the Chinese domesticated races of Pigeon have been evolved.

In alpine regions, from 10,000 to 14,000 feet elevation, in proximity to snowclad peaks, there is a species of Pigeon which may be termed the " Snow Pigeon." This bird (*C. leuconota*) is larger than either of the foregoing species, with much lighter-coloured plumage. I first noted this Pigeon on the slopes of the Ta-p'ao shan north of Tachienlu. It also occurs on the Cheto shan and other places west of Tachienlu. It is met with in flocks, but does not appear to be common.

A Green Pigeon, possibly *Sphenocercus apicicauda*, is occasionally met with in the Chino-Thibetan borderland, but is rare, and probably only a summer visitant. The long tail and beautiful plumage render this a strikingly handsome bird. I met with it once only, and that was around the hamlet of Mao-niu, situated about midway between Romi Chango and Tachienlu. This little village is surrounded on all sides by large forests, and a small flock of Green Pigeons was circling around high up out of gun range. L'Abbé David mentions the Green-winged Ground Dove (*Chalcophaps indica*) as occurring around Mupin. The same authority says that two other Himalayan pigeons—the Spotted Pigeon (*Columba hodgsoni*) and the Long-tailed Pigeon (*Macropygia tusalia*)—are also occasionally met with around Mupin. I have no knowledge of either of these birds.

In north-western Hupeh Mr. Zappey and I saw on one occasion a couple of pigeons that looked distinctly green in colour, but we were unable to obtain specimens. Probably these birds were *Crocopus phœnicopterus*.

The Chinese name for Pigeons and Doves alike is " Panchu." My followers gave the name " Lu (green) Pan-chu " to the *Sphenocercus*, but this is the only kind to which I ever heard a special vernacular name applied.

Pigeons are everywhere domestic pets with the Chinese, and pigeons' eggs enter very largely into a much-esteemed Chinese soup. Like many other of their favourite foods and medicines, pigeons' eggs are supposed to possess aphrodisiac properties. A common practice in Western China is to fix on the top of the pigeon's tail at its base a small, round, hollow piece of wood having a slit on one side, which produces a humming, whistling noise as the birds circle around in flight.

CHAPTER XII

SPORT IN WESTERN CHINA

Wild-Fowl: Shooting on the Ya River

WILD-FOWL in great variety abound all over China, and the West has its share, though a lesser one, it is true. In that great alluvial plain and swamp bordering the Tungting Lake in central China they occur in myriads during the winter season. The same is true of the Lower Yangtsze delta. Throughout the region of the Gorges wild-fowl are comparatively rare, for the simple reason that steep cliffs and deep water are not to their liking. Above Kuichou Fu they are more common, but not nearly as much so as farther west. On the lower reaches of the Min River, and its tributary the Ya, which unites with the Tung at Kiating Fu, they are very plentiful. Sandbars difficult of access and stony places near the rapids and races of the more shallow parts of the rivers are favourite daytime haunts. At night the farmers' wheat and pulse fields near the rivers are freely visited. The wild-fowl which frequent Western China in the winter season probably breed in the Kokonor region, whereas those which visit the eastern parts of China breed in the tundras of Eastern Siberia. The mountains of western Hupeh, eastern Szechuan, and Shensi constitute barrier-ranges demarking the lines of migratory flight. Apropos of this boundary it is worthy of note that Geese have never been shot, neither have they been observed resting, west of Ichang as far as records and my own observations go. Yet to the east of this point they are probably more abundant than any other family of wild-fowl.

In the more eastern parts of the Empire, Chinese wildfowlers find a lucrative business in supplying the markets of Shanghai and other large Treaty ports. They frequently employ methods peculiarly their own, and the following account, by a Chinese sportsman, is taken from that interesting book by H. T. Wade, *With Boat and Gun in the Yangtsze Valley*, pp. 139–41 :—

"*Catching Wild Ducks.*—At the close of a cold December, some 7 miles from the walled city of Kintang, near a large pond, I saw a man beckoning to me, and as I approached he asked me not to shoot the ducks in the pond. He explained that his friend was in the water ; so I waited to see what would happen. After some time his friend landed, wearing a large bamboo collar or cangue, and carrying a basket containing a few wild and three tame ducks secured together by a string. He was dressed in goat-skin, with the wool inside ; his stockings were stitched to the clothing, and so oiled as to be nearly waterproof. Thus accoutred, he immersed his body, using the cangue as a float. On his hat were placed bunches of grass, and on the cangue two or three decoy-ducks. He slowly approached the wild-fowl, and when near enough dexterously caught the unsuspecting duck by the leg, and dragged it under water. I watched him until he had gathered nearly the whole lot."

"*Shooting Wild Ducks.*—Probably no man in the world but the Chinese fowler would enter the water up to his neck, in the coldest weather, to shoot ducks. His *modus operandi* is like this : a light wooden frame or a small punt supports his gingal. The fowler lets the frame with its freight float in front of him, while he, following, is concealed from view by bunches of grass and weeds stuck into his hat. As soon as within range, which is invariably a very short one, he fires into ' the brown ' a heavy charge of iron shot. He never fires at two or three fowls, as his shot costs money. He bides his time, and then fires into the *brown*."

"*Catching Geese.*—A common method is to lay down a long line, to which is attached a number of thin bamboo slips, bent double, and the two ends of the bamboo inserted in a bean. This bait is laid on a regular feeding ground, and the hungry goose swallows it greedily, with the result that the act of swallowing liberates the bent bamboo, which, resuming its original shape, chokes the bird."

The annual slaughter of wild-fowl in China is enormous, but the birds are as wary as their kind is anywhere else in the world. On bright sunny days they are more easily caught " napping," but the man with a twelve-bore earns all the wild-fowl he bags in a season. At least, such is my experience. I have no intention of entering deeply into this subject, since the sport differs in no particular from that of the same nature elsewhere in the world. There is, however, a novel form of duck-shooting obtainable on the Ya River, in western Szechuan, which affords both excitement and good sport, and should not be missed by anyone to whom an opportunity offers.

The Ya, which unites with the Tung River a mile or so beyond the west gate of the city of Kiating, is a swift-running stream thickly bestrewn with boulders, shingle, and sandbanks. Boats are in use at the various ferries, but the river generally is unsuited to navigation, and merchandise is conveyed up and down on rafts. These latter are specially built for shallow rivers, and ply principally between Yachou Fu and Chong-peh-sha via the Ya River to Kiating Fu, thence on the Min to Sui Fu, and from there on the Yangtsze to Chong-peh-sha. With the exception of Lu Chou, Chong-peh-sha is the largest town between Chungking and Sui Fu, although it has no official status. It is a great and famous wine-mart, and rafts are very largely employed in carrying wine in large jars from this town to the inland markets situated on the shallow rivers farther west.

Although fragile-looking affairs, these rafts are quite unsinkable, and the best of their kind in existence. They are built entirely of the culms of a giant Bamboo, known as " Nan chu " (*Dendrocalamus giganteus*). Each raft is about 66 feet in length and 11 feet wide. The canes are laid side by side in one plane and securely lashed to numerous cross-beams, not a single nail being used in the whole construction. Several unequal lengths of bamboo are used so that the end-to-end joints occur at irregular intervals. The stern of the raft is square, the prow bent upwards to serve as a fender against rocks and shoals. The outer silicious " skin " of the canes is removed and the nodes hardened over a hot fire. The bending of the canes to form the upturned prow is done by heating and weighting with heavy stones. A narrow wicker-staging is carried down the centre of the raft, and is raised about a foot above the floor ; on this the merchandise is placed to keep it dry, or, in the case of wine-jars, they are lashed to the staging.

These rafts are capable of yielding both transversely and laterally, and can thus pass over any slightly submerged obstruction. Fully loaded, one raft will carry a freight of about 30,000 lbs. weight, and then draw only about 6 inches of water, owing to the great buoyancy of the hollow cylinders of bamboo. Down-stream a crew of four men manipulates each craft, which is propelled by an oar on either side and steered by a scull aft and another forward, but the latter is only used in the more difficult places. The sculls and oars are fitted to Alder stumps, which serve as rowlocks. The rafts are hauled up-stream by men attached to bamboo lines, and several usually travel in company, in order that the crews may assist one another over the more difficult rapids.

The Ya when not in flood is a clear-water stream, and from the raft the stony river-bottom is plainly visible ; often the boulders look so dangerously near the bottom of the raft that the passenger expects a bump every few minutes. A curious hissing and crackling noise accompanies the raft's progress over the more shallow places. This noise is due to the movement of the boulders and stones in the bed of the stream, the hollow bamboo tubes acting as sounding boards. There are many angry and dangerous rapids and whirlpools on the Ya, and the current is very swift : shooting these places is most exciting work. There is really very little possibility of an accident unless the raft is overladen, but as every rock and stone is visible in the clear water the uninitiated feel the presence of danger in a rather alarming fashion.

In the winter season this stony river is the haunt of thousands of Wild Duck, which congregate in the daytime in the vicinity of rapids, races, and boulder-strewn shoals. Excellent and highly exhilarating sport may be obtained by engaging a raft at Yachou and shooting wild-fowl from it as the stream is descended. A little noise will scare the birds on the approach of the raft, and whilst the latter successfully shoots the rapid or race it is up to the man with the gun to bring down the ducks. The size of the bag depends largely upon the steadiness of nerve, but it takes a few cartridges before one can fairly well judge just how much to "lead" a bird when pulling the trigger. The movement of the craft, both forward and sideways, considerably increases the difficulties of aim. Two guns are best, one forward and the other aft. The dead birds are easily retrieved at the foot of the rapids; the wounded ones are carried over by the force of the current, and can then be finished off. Those falling on land are difficult to mark down and retrieve. After a little practice a steady shot can make a good bag of duck from these rafts.

Early in December 1908 my companion, Mr. Zappey, accompanied me on a journey by raft from Yachou to Kiating, which occupied a couple of days. The weather was boisterous and wet, and wild-fowl comparatively scarce. We shot and retrieved 53 ducks, and probably killed in addition about a third of that number. Although the bag was not large the excitement and fun was immense. To anyone in search of exhilarating sport, Duck-shooting from a raft journeying down the Ya River can be confidently recommended.

The common wild ducks found in the west are Mallard, Wax-bill, and ordinary Teal. Others occurring there in lesser numbers are Falcate Teal, Spectacled Teal, Golden-eye, Pin-tail, Goosander, Smew, Pochard, Shoveller, Lesser Grebe, and Ruddy Sheldrake (Brahminy) (apropos of the latter it may be of interest to mention that I once found a couple breeding in the margin of an alpine lake near Tachienlu, at 15,500 feet altitude). Three species of Gull—two large grey kinds and a kittiwake—ascend to this region, 2000 miles inland from the coast. Widgeon I never saw in the west, and the same remark applies to the Mandarin Duck, Swan, and Geese. At Kiating the harsh cry of a very large kind of Crane may be heard any night during November, and on dull wet days small flocks may be seen flighting southward. Very seldom, however, do they alight in this neighbourhood, and still more rarely are they to be seen resting during the daytime. These birds winter around the lakes in Yunnan, and apparently make a post-haste thousand-mile flight thither from their breeding grounds in the Kokonor region.

The Goosander, Smew, Pochard, and one or two others are diving, fish-eating ducks, but if skinned they lose their fishy flavour and become palatable, but even then they are inferior eating in comparison with Mallard, Wax-bill, and the Common Teal.

CHAPTER XIII

SPORT IN WESTERN CHINA

RUMINANT AND OTHER GAME ANIMALS

IN the matter of large game animals Western China is of special interest, since the country being so little known there is a possibility of new and undescribed species or varieties rewarding the energetic sportsman-explorer. The difficulties in the way of any systematic exploration of the Chino-Thibetan borderland are to-day very great, and many years will elapse before the world is thoroughly informed on this fascinating region. My friend, Captain Malcolm M'Neill, of Oban, Scotland, visited this region in 1908, and in a brief season secured a nice collection of different trophies. These included the Takin and new varieties of a Bear and Stag, which Mr. R. Lydekker has named in his honour. Mr. Zappey whose primary object was the collecting of birds, found opportunity to shoot quite a number of animals, including the Takin ; the last-named, by the way, he was the first white man to secure by actually shooting the beast.

Quite a number of different kinds of game animals are now known from Western China, but only odd specimens of each have reached the Occident, and there is much yet to be learnt regarding every one of them. More especially is information needed on the habits, colour-variation, and geographical range of the different species and varieties. The affinity of the fauna is with that of Upper Burmah and the Himalayas as far as the animals of the forests are concerned, but in every instance peculiar species or subspecies obtain. The animals of the higher altitudes above the tree-line are mostly common to the whole of the Thibetan highlands. Indeed, the uplands of the Chino-Thibetan borderland constitute the eastern limit of the Central Asian fauna.

Personally I have hunted none of the larger animals, but I have been associated in the field with those who have. I have at different times seen in a living or dead state nearly all the animals described below, and in many ways have enjoyed exceptional opportunities for acquiring information. The following pages, compiled mainly from notes collected during my travels in this region, make no pretence of being exhaustive, but they may perhaps add something to the present scant store of knowledge.

BLUE SHEEP (BHARAL)

Bharal or Pan-(often pronounced Pai)-yang (*Ovis nahura*), as they are locally called, are common throughout the Chino-Thibetan borderland on the higher ranges above the timber-line. During the summer-time they frequent the alpine regions between 13,000 and 17,000 feet elevation. At Tachienlu (alt. 8400 feet) they have been shot in June on the cliffs that overlook the town itself. Around Sungpan Ting they are common, and in the uplands everywhere between the above points they are to be found roaming about in flocks, often of considerable size. In the winter they descend to 8000 or 10,000 feet altitude. When fired upon, the " Pan-yang " has a characteristic habit of running a short distance, then halting and looking round at the enemy.

The adult animal stands about a yard tall at the withers and has a long, narrow head, short ears, no mane or beard, and a thick, close coat of hair. The general colour of the upper-parts is brownish-grey tinged with slaty-blue, darker in summer than in winter ; under-parts white ; lower part of tail black. In adult rams the face and chest are black, with a black band along the flanks, white knee-patches, and a black stripe down the front of all four legs. The horns are blackish-olive with an S-like curvature, rounded and nearly smooth save for the annual rings of growth. The horns of the ewes are short, drawn together at the base, curving upwards and outwards in a somewhat scimitar-like fashion.

The "Pan-yang" is a rather heavily built animal, strong and active, and very much at home amongst steep, difficult cliff-country. It is fairly easy to stalk, though the nature of the country and the rarefied atmosphere render the work tiring and arduous. A full-grown animal weighs between 125 and 140 lbs.; the mutton is of good flavour, without any suspicion of "goaty" odour. The colloquial name, "Pan-yang," is very descriptive, signifying "half-sheep, half-goat," thereby denoting the somewhat intermediate appearance and character of this animal. Shooting on the Hsueh-lung shan range west of the Min River in the territory of Wassu on 13th June 1908 Captain Malcolm M'Neill secured two heads, which he informs me have horns measuring as follows :—

	Length	Circumference at base	Tip-to-tip
No. 1 . .	26¼ inches	12 inches	27 inches
No. 2 . .	25⅝ inches	12 inches	30 inches

N.B.—Extreme tip of the last head stripped, otherwise it would probably have spanned more.

The Bharal of this region apparently differs in no particular from that found in the western parts of the Thibetan plateaux. Quite a number of these animals are annually shot by hunters, and I have seen many skins on sale in the streets of Chengtu city. The skins are not much valued, being used for lining the cheap winter garments worn by the lower middle class of that region.

Another Sheep, probably Hodgson's (*O. ammon hodgsoni*), occurs immediately to the west and north of Tachienlu, but is very rare. It has been seen in the neighbourhood of Litang by at least two travellers, but there is no record of one being shot. This Sheep frequents the alpine regions above 13,000 feet. Zappey saw three near the Rama-lal Pass, but failed to get within comfortable range. He says they were larger than Bharal, as they should be if they are Hodgson's variety.

SEROW, "YEH LAU-TSZE"

There are two distinct-looking kinds of Serow in Western China, but the colouring in these animals is variable, age having much to do with it. Zoölogists are not yet agreed upon the systematic rank of these two varieties, but Mr. R. Lydekker (*Proceedings of the Zoölogical Society of London*, published April 1909), summing up all the evidence before him, considers them two distinct species. This arrangement seems logical, and is certainly more convenient than that of regarding them as forms of the Sumatran Serow (*Capricornis sumatrensis*), as some authorities do.

Throughout Western China this animal is common, and is everywhere known as " Yeh Lau-tsze " (Wild Donkey) or " Ai (Ngai) Lau-tsze " (Cliff Donkey), the long ears being responsible for the vernacular name. Between 5000 and 10,000 feet elevation in west Szechuan, Serow is probably the commonest wild animal. Around Wa shan, Tachienlu, Lungan Fu, and throughout the Upper Min Valley it occurs. I have seen specimens killed in all these places, and elsewhere also. The flat skins are commonly used as bed mattresses throughout these regions. Mr. Zappey shot two near Wa shan, and Captain M'Neill secured three specimens near Tachienlu. The lamented Mr. J. W. Brooke and his companion, Mr. C. H. Mears, shot a couple (at least) in the Upper Min Valley, below Wên-ch'uan Hsien. The above were all killed in 1908. But previous to this Messrs. Brown and Wilden, respectively of the British and French Consular services in China, had shot examples of this animal in the Upper Min Valley. In 1893–4 Mr. M. M. Berezovski secured specimens in the mountains north-west of Lungan Fu. The earliest known examples of these Serow were taken by l'Abbé David in the principality of Mupin in 1869. These animals are always found in wild, precipitous, brush-clad country, and, in consequence, are difficult to hunt. In the Upper Min Valley the mountains are mainly composed of mud shales, and landslips are frequent, rendering the hunting of these animals highly dangerous work. When startled, Serow plunge into the thickest cover on the cliffs, and are difficult to drive out into a position affording a decent shot. The natives snare them, hunt them with dogs, and shoot them, and occasionally capture them in dead-falls. The native dog is extremely useful in hunting Serow, commonly hounding them into positions where they cannot escape, save by rushing their tormentors. Though naturally timid, dogs madden them into making wild rushes, and they are fierce and dangerous when at bay. They have been known to kill the dog hunting them and badly wound the hunters themselves. In steep, difficult country an animal driven to charge by fear is extremely dangerous owing to the precarious foothold obtainable.

Around Wa shan the White-maned Serow (*Capricornis argyrochætes*) is the common species; around Tachienlu Milne-Edwards' Serow (*C. milne-edwardsi*) is the common animal found. In the Upper Min Valley and around Lungan Fu both species occupy the same regions, and this is probably true for western Szechuan generally with one or other species more common in certain districts.

A female of the White-maned Serow shot in May 1908 near Wa shan by Mr. Zappey gave the following measurements : length, $66\frac{1}{16}$ inches; tail, $4\frac{3}{5}$ inches ; height at shoulder, $35\frac{1}{2}$ inches. Colour : mane, light brownish; body and legs darker and brighter than in Milne-Edwards' species (*infra*).

Zappey's experience was that the male and female kept together. He shot a female in the later afternoon ; the dogs remaining at the foot of the cliff all night kept the male in a place from whence it could not escape, and Zappey returned at daylight and shot it.

A male of Milne-Edwards' Serow, which Zappey secured near Tachienlu, measured as follows : length, $66\frac{1}{4}$ inches ; tail, $4\frac{4}{5}$ inches ; height at shoulder, 39 inches ; horns, $8\frac{1}{4}$ inches long. Colour : mane, whitish, 10 inches long ; back of rump, fore-legs to just above the knee, and hind-legs to half-way up the thigh, chestnut ; back and sides, dark iron-grey ; belly, dark grey.

The flesh of the Serow is dark coloured, tough, of poor flavour, and the least desirable meat I have tasted.

On the high mountains of north-western Hupeh, forming the Han-Yangtsze water-shed, a Serow occurs sparingly, and is called " Ming-tsen Yang." The characters denoting this name were interpreted by a Chinese gentleman as meaning " Clear-maned Goat." This is a very appropriate name for the White-maned Serow (*C. argyrochætes*), though it is possibly a distinct animal. Neither Zappey nor myself succeeded in obtaining one of these animals, though we came upon fresh tracks and dung in quantity. As a result of some ten days' hunting, Zappey only once sighted this Serow. A loud, angry snort in the brush, a momentary glance, and all was over. The animal covered 15 to 20 feet at a bound, and was through the thicket and over the ridge in less time than it takes to tell. As the country is everywhere difficult, and the animal scarce, there is very little chance of securing a trophy. On the high mountains south-west of Ichang this same Serow occurs, but is even more rare there than in the north-west of the province.

We secured fragments of a flat skin and several pairs of horns, but these are insufficient to show what the species is. A pair of these horns I obtained in exchange for a couple of empty bottles measure : length, 10¾ inches ; circumference at base, 5 inches ; tip interval, 4¼ inches.

The horns of all the Chinese Serow are very similar, being jet-black in colour, ringed, and tapering to a point ; the position is erect and curving backwards. The hair is coarse, long, and shaggy, with a short woolly underfur, and neither in the colour of the pelt nor in the size of the horns is there any marked difference between the sexes, age having more to do in these matters than anything else.

GORAL, " YEH YANG-TSZE "

Three species of Goral have been recognized in Western China, two in west Szechuan and one in west Hupeh. Quite recently they have been lumped under one species, but this is scarcely a satisfactory method of classifying them. The Goral found in Hupeh and Szechuan are readily distinguished by their colour, and it is convenient at any rate to keep them under separate names. These animals make their home amidst limestone crags and precipices, and though quite common are rarely seen, and not easily hunted. They are not so difficult to shoot as to retrieve afterwards, consequent upon the precipitous nature of their haunts. During sunny weather they lay up during the daytime on scrub-clad ledges of rock or in the mouths of caves that are so common in limestone regions. They feed in the early morning and in the evening, except during misty, rainy weather, when they are not particular.

The limestone crags and cliffs of the Yangtsze Gorges and the glens leading therefrom are favourite haunts of the Hupeh species. In the Ichang Gorge itself this animal is quite common, and anywhere in the limestone regions in western Hupeh up to 4000 feet altitude it is to be found.

The natives assert that Goral are found even up to 7000 feet altitude. There is a precipitous range near the tiny hamlet of Kuan-pao in Changyang Hsien, four days' journey south-west of Ichang, where they may be found. This range reaches 7000 feet altitude in its higher parts, and a variety of game occurs there. Quite a number of foreigners have enjoyed good sport after Goral in the glens around Ichang. Probably the first to shoot one hereabouts was Dr. Aldridge in the early 'eighties of last century. The late Père Heude named this animal *Kemas aldridgeanus* [1] in his *Les Mémoires concernant l'Histoire Naturelle de l'Empire Chinois* (pub. 1880–1901). This naturalist made a great study of Eastern Asian mammals, and his specimens went chiefly to the Museum at Sicawei, just outside Shanghai. Unfortunately these specimens have been sadly neglected. The author above quoted was not sufficiently careful in the matter of defining his species, in publishing good descriptions, and in preserving his types. The consequence is, that much animal life has been wasted and the nomenclature of Chinese mammals rendered exceedingly difficult to later systematic zoölogists. Anyone who has seen the collections at Sicawei must regret that the types were not sent to Paris or some other western centre where they would have been properly looked after, and accessible for comparative study.

The Chinese who hunt Goral usually study their runs and snare them, or occasionally they shoot them. The method of hunting them for shooting is as follows : The man with his rifle (matchlock in case of natives) is posted on one side of a

[1] In accordance with modern nomenclature this name becomes *Næmorhedus aldridgeanus*. The specific name, *henryanus*, had been earlier applied by Sclater to this same animal. Milne-Edward's specific name, *griseus*, was published in 1871, and has priority over the above names if it be accepted that the Ichang and Mupin Goral represent the same species.

glen or ravine, high up at a point of vantage where a clear view may be had. The " beaters " then traverse the opposite side, hurling down rocks and making a great noise. This startles the animal, which then skulks along the ledges, through the brush until driven out on to bare cliff. If there is any possible ledge it will descend almost vertical cliffs, dropping easily 18 or 20 feet from ledge to ledge. Excellent rifle-shooting is afforded by this beast if only the beaters can be kept sufficiently out of the way of danger.

My companion, Mr. Zappey, enjoyed good sport after these Goral, and secured several specimens. The illustration (p. 152) shows an adult male and female and a young male shot by him in the western end of the Ichang Gorge during January 1908.

This same Goral is common to all the gorges, and in the long, gloomy, and forbidding Wushan Gorge it occurs in plenty. As an example of luck and good shooting I give the following experience :—

On our journey up river to west Szechuan in late March 1908 we were sailing up through the Wushan Gorge enjoying a moderately strong, fair wind, and were just off the hamlet of Nanmu-yuan. My companion, Mr. Zappey, was seated on the prow of the boat, and with his field-glasses scanning the cliffs from time to time. " This looks ideal country for Goral," he said to me, standing near him ; " has anyone ever seen them hereabouts? " " I don't know, but there is no record of anyone having shot one," I replied. Scarcely had the words left my mouth when Zappey quietly said, " There's one ! " He rushed into the cabin and secured his rifle ; meanwhile the crew shortened sail. The animal stood under the lee of a cliff some 500 feet above the river ; it was about 4.30 in the afternoon. There was considerable weigh on the boat, and Zappey's first shot struck a little above and in front of the Goral, and the beast scarcely heeded it. The second shot was again a little high, and immediately in front, and the animal swung round, ran a few yards, and then stopped, half facing us. The third shot found its mark ; the soft-nosed bullet passed anglewise through the jugular vein far into the body, and the Goral sank stone dead in his tracks. It was a pretty shot, and, from the motion of the boat, not an easy one. But the good fortune did not end here. This Gorge is some 30 miles long, and throughout its entire length there are scarcely half a dozen places where it is possible to scale the cliffs to any height above high-water mark. This was one of the few places! Willing feet rushed up the cliffside, and in about twenty minutes the Goral was landed on deck. It proved to be a fine male. Our crew were delighted, and the incident afforded them conversation for days. They did not allow the result of my companion's prowess to remain at one trophy. By the time we reached Chungking, rumour, having fleet wings, had reported a bag of five! The fact will probably form the basis for a legend in these parts, in which at least a score of Goral will be substituted for this solitary trophy.

The "Ichang Goral" (*Næmorhedus henryanus*), as it may be styled, has the sides of the body dark greyish; whole of the tail, front part of upper fore-leg, and line down centre of back, blackish; fore and hind legs from knee and hock to hoof, light chestnut; and throat-patch, pale buff. The largest male shot by Zappey gave the following measurements: length, $46\frac{4}{5}$ inches; tail, $4\frac{3}{5}$ inches; height at shoulder, $24\frac{1}{8}$ inches.

Returning from Tachienlu on 30th September 1908 Mr. Zappey secured two of the "Grey Thibetan Goral" (*N. griseus*). Here is his account from a letter he wrote me immediately afterwards: "At Liuyang, some 10 miles below Tachienlu, I got two Goral on the cliffs across the torrent with one shot. The bullet passed through the neck of one and through the body of the other. I only saw one when I fired; both dropped stone dead. It was a hard and difficult job retrieving them, taking us nearly two hours climbing and circumventing cliffs. This Goral differs from those secured in the Gorges in being much lighter in colour all over—the legs are light creamy buff instead of light chestnut; the head is dull grey with a black line from top of eye to the horns; the throat is very light coloured." The largest, a female, gave the following measurements:—total length, $51\frac{1}{16}$ inches; tail, $4\frac{3}{5}$ inches; height at shoulder, $25\frac{1}{16}$ inches. The animal is rather larger than the Ichang Goral, but the tail is the same length.

On the cliffs bordering the Tung River near the base of Wa

shan Zappey shot, in June 1908, a Goral which he thought looked different from either of the above. Unfortunately it fell on a ledge and could not be retrieved. Possibly this was referable to the Ashy Thibetan Goral (*N. cinereus*), which is distinguished from the foregoing species by its nearly uniform, distinctly ashy colour ; the whitish patches on the throat and feet smaller ; tail longer and more bushy.

Though of quiet colour, Goral are pretty little beasts, and their heads make neat trophies. In a general way they look like small Serow, having similar but smaller horns, and a rather coarse shaggy hair, with a wool-like under-fur, but they have no mane, though the hair along the back of the neck is somewhat crested. They make a curious, rather penetrating, hissing noise when alarmed, and in early April, at any rate, this noise is commonly heard when traversing their haunts. Unlike their near allies, the Serow, they are comparatively social animals, and several are usually found together. The native name is " Yeh Yang-tsze " (Wild Goat) or " Ai (Ngai) Yang-tsze " (Cliff Goat). The flesh is dark coloured and moderately good eating, far superior to that of the Serow or Takin.

The " Grey Goral " ranges up to 8000 feet altitude in the summer, but comes lower down in winter. The haunts are always scrub-clad cliff-country, and it does not appear to frequent timber. The geographical range is considerable, being apparently limited only by the nature of the country up to the altitude given. To my knowledge this animal extends from Lungan Fu in the north to Tachienlu in the west and Wa shan in the south. Goral also occur in western Yunnan, and extend down to Burmah, where the species is different. The probability is that Goral are common to all the precipitous country between 1000 and 8000 feet from western Hupeh, through western Szechuan and southward to Burmah.

TAKIN, " YEH NIU " (WILD CATTLE)

Few animals have attracted more attention during recent years than this strange and interesting ruminant. The existence of this animal in Western China has been known these many years, but it was not until 1908 that specimens were

authentically shot by a foreigner.   L'Abbé David secured the
first examples of this race through native hunters in 1869, from
the quasi-independent principality of Mupin.[1]   In 1893–4 a
Russian traveller, M. M. Berezovski, secured specimens from
the Kansu-Szechuan border.   I have no precise information as
to just how this traveller obtained them, but I was told, when
travelling through this region, that natives shot them and sold
them to him.   But this is all quite modern.   Marco Polo heard
of these animals during his travels in this region and speaks
of them as " very wild and fierce animals " under the name
of " Beyamini," probably having in mind the wild cattle of
Bohemia.

In the *Field* newspaper of 15th July 1905 appeared an
article under my signature drawing attention to the game
animals of Western China, and the Takin in particular.   This
article attracted attention, and two or three sportsmen visited
that country in quest of this animal.   Ill-health caused one of
them to abandon the enterprise when nearly on the ground.
A second was boycotted by Chinese officials at Tachienlu, and
his expedition rendered abortive thereby.   In 1908 I was again
in Western China, and I invited my friend, Captain Malcolm
M'Neill, to join me and try and secure this animal.   He came,
and success crowned his efforts.

In 1908 there were three distinct parties after this Chinese
Takin, and each party secured trophies.   The first specimen
authentically shot and killed by a foreigner fell to the rifle of
Mr. Walter R. Zappey on 27th May 1908.   Mr. C. H. Mears,
the companion of the ill-fated Mr. J. W. Brooke, followed closely
on Mr. Zappey's heels, securing his trophy on or about 30th
May.[2]   In August, Captain M'Neill, shooting in the petty state
of Yutung with hunters supplied by the Chiala chieftain,
happened upon a herd in open country, and killed several.   In

---

[1] Much confusion has arisen through wrongly calling this country Eastern
Thibet.   Politically the region belongs to China proper, forming part of
Szechuan province.   Since the boundary generally is ill-defined on all maps,
and the country peopled largely by non-Chinese races, the term Chino-
Thibetan borderland (see *ante*, Vol. I, Chap. XII) may be employed for the
entire region.   But it should be remembered that, so far, every specimen
of the Takin has been taken in China and none in Thibet proper.

[2] See *Life of John Weston Brooke*, by W. N. Ferguson, p. 136.

September, Mr. Zappey, shooting south-west of Tachienlu, secured a fine female, and most unfortunately lost a large bull, which he had knocked over and left for dead.

Since fictitious claims to shooting and many other erroneous statements have been made in regard to the Chinese Takin, I have thought it well to place on record here the names of the sportsmen who shot the first specimens of this interesting animal. Up to Christmas 1910 no other specimens had been shot and retrieved by a foreigner.

This Takin has a wide range in Western China. To my knowledge it is to be found from south of Tachienlu north to the Kansu border, and from this point east into Shensi province, where it occurs on the Tsin-ling range. In certain places, like the wild country between Lungan Fu and Sungpan, the Pan-lan range, and in the petty state of Yutung, it may be said to be common. Anywhere in these regions where there are " salt-licks " this animal is to be found. In western Szechuan its eastern limits are the high ranges forming the western boundary of the Red Basin. As to how far southward this animal occurs we are without precise information, and it is possible that it traverses the whole mountain-system down to Assam. However, since it has not been reported from Yunnan, it may well be that the southern limit is marked by the Upper Yangtsze, where it makes its great bend to the east.

It frequents difficult country between 8000 and 14,000 feet altitude, making its home in the dense Rhododendron and Bamboo thickets in fairly open forests near the upper limits of the tree-line. It took Mears, as he himself told me in Chengtu city soon afterwards, three weeks' hard hunting in the fiercest and roughest of country to secure his trophy. Mr. Mears said that he shot big game in many lands, but the quest of the Takin proved the hardest and most difficult he had ever experienced. M'Neill, on the other hand, happened on a herd in open country where one would expect to find sheep, but thick cover was not very far off.

A powerful animal, the Takin has no difficulty in forcing its way through dense thickets, tramping out well-defined paths which are regularly used in the passage to and from grazing grounds and salt-licks. Advantage of this habit is taken by native hunters to spear this animal. Two trees growing side by side are selected, and a large, heavy log-beam is attached to a pivot resting in the fork of convenient branches. This beam measures about 8 feet in length, and in the extremity a stout stake about 15 inches long and shod with a barbed spear some 8 inches long is fixed. From the end nearest the pivot a bamboo rope is suspended. The beam is poised by pulling down this rope and attaching it to a cunningly arranged contrivance some 14 inches above the ground (see illus. p. 170). To the stout fixed parts are arranged two collapsible rods, to one of which a trip-rope is attached. This trip-rope is stretched across the " run " and lashed to a tree on the opposite side, the height above the ground being about the same as the animal's knee-height. The whole trap is a rough and strong yet a delicate and devilish contrivance. An animal coming down the run touches the trip-rope with its forelegs, and is immediately impaled by the spear. The cross-beam, to which the spear is attached, is so heavy that the spear is driven almost through the animal's body behind the shoulder, inflicting a mortal wound. Death may often be slow, but it is always sure, and very seldom can a wounded beast break away. The " run " is only roughly trampled out, and the bamboo stems and other brush effectually hide the trip-rope. These traps are in common use, and are a source of considerable danger to anyone traversing these runs. A Chinese youth employed by Zappey accidentally released the trip-rope of one of these traps, and the iron spear-head passed right through the thick of his thigh, luckily missing the arteries and bones. The spear-head (see figure, p. 170) was cut off on the inside of the thigh, and the shaft tugged out on the opposite side. The youth recovered, but suffered a very bad wound for many weeks.

Dead-falls are also employed by the natives in trapping many animals, but these are scarcely sufficient to kill a large adult Takin. These dead-falls are fitted with a treadle arrangement, and the animal stepping upon this causes the whole mass to fall, crushing him to death.

Around Wa shan the Takin is killed by an arrow shot from a cross-bow fixed by hunters alongside the run or by an ingenious gun device. It is also captured by cunningly arranged foot-snares.

The Takin retires during the daytime into thickets, and feeds during the early morning and late evening in the open country above. On misty, foggy days they may feed in the open all day long. During August and early September, at any rate, cows and young bulls are found severally together in the more open country high up, where there is good pasturage in close proximity to thick cover. Old bulls are solitary and wander considerably. The rutting season is around the end of July, and the calves are born in the March following.

The natives regard this animal with considerable awe and dread, affirming it is both fierce and revengeful. Near where Zappey shot his cow a hunter had been killed only a few weeks previously. Doubtless this animal, when wounded, is a nasty customer at close quarters, especially to anyone armed with nothing more effective than a native gun and spear. A foreigner armed with a modern rifle of high velocity, and exercising a moderate amount of caution, has nothing to fear. Accompanied by a native hunter, Zappey shot and killed two calves, and the mother immediately made off through the bamboo jungle, and did not attempt to attack the hunters. These calves were secured in the neighbourhood of Wa shan on 27th May, and according to the natives were about two months old. The legs were soot-black; ridge down centre of back, black; sides, brown; under-parts, black with long whitish hairs interspersed; pelage, woolly. Both were male and, in size, nearly equal, measuring: length, $38\frac{5}{8}$ inches; tail, 3 inches; height at shoulder, $22\frac{1}{2}$ inches; no vestige of horns was discernible.

The adult Takin is a rather awkward-looking, clumsily built animal, strong and powerful, weighing 5 to 6 cwt., or more. None of the animals shot by the sportsmen mentioned above was weighed. The cow killed by Zappey fell in a bad place, and six men could not turn her over, but only roll the carcase from side to side. The skinning under the difficulties took six hours. This animal gave the following measurements: total length, $80\frac{1}{2}$ inches; tail, $6\frac{3}{8}$ inches; heel, $16\frac{1}{8}$ inches; height at shoulder, $42\frac{1}{8}$ inches; height at hip, $39\frac{3}{4}$ inches. The nose, chin, and face half-way up to eyes, area around eyes, tip to tail, hock and legs almost up to knees, black ; ears, greyish ; rest of body light creamy-white ; fore-part of body clearer and lighter than hind-part, which is mixed with greyish hairs. This animal was killed on 17th September 1908, and contained a fœtus about the size of an ordinary squirrel. The adult males are more orange-yellow in colour, particularly on the neck and shoulders, with a dark stripe extending from nape of neck to withers. The bulls run rather larger than the cows. The horns are alike in both sexes, though rather smaller in the female. These horns somewhat resemble those of the Blue Wildebeeste, and are jet-black. They grow downwards and outwards for a short distance, then take a sharp curve upwards and backwards. A pair of horns purchased near Wa shan, and in my possession, measure : length, $20\frac{3}{4}$ inches and 20 inches ; circumference at base, $11\frac{1}{2}$ inches ; tip interval, $11\frac{3}{8}$ inches ; widest spread, $16\frac{3}{8}$ inches. This is the largest pair I have seen in Western China.

Zoölogists attach considerable taxonomic importance to colour, but in the Chinese Takin they must be prepared to grant a wide range of variation. I have seen probably 100 flat skins in addition to the specimens killed by the sportsmen mentioned above. Nearly all showed some distinct coloration, and hardly two were alike, whilst the extreme forms look very dissimilar. The general colour of the bulls may be put down as tawny-grey and black, with shoulders and neck bright golden-brown ; the mane is grey. The cows are much lighter grey, and the older ones are almost white in their upper-parts.

The curved nose, short, almost square ears, and minute stump-like tail give this animal a strange and most distinct appearance. The limbs are very short, thick, and muscular, and the lateral pairs of hoofs are very large. The flesh is dark coloured, and in inferiority of flavour surpassed only by that of the Serow. The animal is hunted for its meat, which is esteemed by the natives, my poor opinion notwithstanding. Flat skins are commonly used in bed-mattresses, and also frequently made into leather. The horns are used as powder-flasks by hunters.

This Chinese Takin was originally described as *Budorcas*

taxicolor, var. *tibetanus*, by the late Prof. A. Milne-Edwards
.(*Recherches pour servir à l'Histoire naturelle des Mammifères*,
1874, p. 367, plates lxxiv. and lxxix.). Since then two other
names have been applied to this same animal. In the *Proceedings of the Zoölogical Society* (pp. 795–802, with plate),
published April 1909, Mr. R. Lydekker considers it a
species distinct from the Mishmi Takin, and named it *B.
tibetanus*. This seems the most expedient thing to do, but it is
unfortunate that the laws of priority necessitate the keeping
up of the name "*tibetanus*," which is a misnomer, in preference
to the name "*sinensis*," which is both accurate and descriptive
from a geographical standpoint. The natives everywhere in
Western China designate this animal " Yeh Niu " ; this may be
translated " Wild Cattle," though " Wild Cow " or " Wild
Ox " is an equally correct rendering. Old, solitary bulls
are occasionally spoken of as " Ta Yeh Niu," " Large (Great)
Wild Ox." Baber (*Royal Geographical Society, Supplementary
Papers*, vol. i. p. 39) calls it " Ngai Niu," " Hill (Cliff) Cattle,"
but has evidently confused it with the Serow, his account
unconsciously covering both animals. The people around
Wa shan (where Baber collected his information) seem to
confuse these animals strangely. In 1904 they insisted to
me that the Takin was called "Pan-(or Pngai)-yang " (see
article in *Field*, loc. cit.), a name which properly belongs to the
Bharal, an animal not found anywhere around that immediate
neighbourhood. Experience teaches one to be very cautious
in accepting vernacular names, most of them at best are purely
local in application, and the natives will readily invent a name
to satisfy an inquisitive foreigner.

I have written at length partly on account of the great
interest which attaches itself to this remarkable animal and
partly in the endeavour to correct certain erroneous statements and misrepresentations which have appeared in reference to the Chinese Takin.

GOA (THIBETAN GAZELLE)

The Thibetan Gazelle (*Gazella picticaudata*) gets as far east
as Tachienlu. Indeed, its eastern limit may be put down as the

snowclad barrier ranges which, running almost due north and south, are a feature of the Chino-Thibetan borderland. In early summer Goa are found in small herds at elevations of between 14,000 and 17,000 feet, in open moorland country backed by perpetual snows. Later in the season the bucks separate into parties of two to five head. Goa are wary animals, difficult to detect when stationary, since their coloration harmonizes closely with their surroundings. When fired upon they generally run a short distance, then halt, and commence to feed again.

The summer colour of the head and back is grey (in winter light fawn with a grizzly tinge) ; under-parts, white ; on the buttocks the white area forms a large, conspicuous patch ; tip of tail, black. The male has black horns, nearly erect for a short distance, then curving sharply backwards, the extreme points deflected upwards, with transverse ridges closely crowded together. Horns 13 inches long are good specimens, and above the average. These horns are commonly used by muleteers to fasten the bit through in bridles for ponies and mules. A full-grown Goa stands about 24 inches high at shoulder ; the flesh is said to be good eating.

CHIRU (THIBETAN ANTELOPE)

This animal (*Pantholops hodgsoni*) scarcely enters the region with which we are concerned. It is said to occur north of Litang and in the Thibetan province of Derge, on the alpine regions bordering the limits of vegetation. The horns of the male are extremely handsome, being erect, slightly curved, sub-lyrate, jet-black, 20 to 26 inches long, with very fine grain and a number of bold, transverse ridges in front, smooth behind. These horns are occasionally to be seen on sale in Tachienlu. They are used to form the resting-fork on guns of first-class workmanship, and every Thibetan of wealth and property possesses one or more such guns.

It is generally assumed (and with very good reason) that this animal gave rise to the legend of the Unicorn. Among the tribesfolk inhabiting the little-known region south of Tachienlu down to Yunnan, the belief in the existence of the

Unicorn is general ; they declare that it frequents the country immediately to the west. A friend of mine who accompanied the Younghusband Expedition to Lhassa saw a number of Chiru, and he assured me that when seen in profile nearly every animal appeared to have but a solitary horn. The Unicorn figures prominently in Chinese mythology, where, under the name of " Ki-ling," it is placed at the head of all hairy animals. Its influence is always benevolent, and it appears at the birth of men destined to become great sages and wise beings. Its last advent was at the time of Confucius's birth (552 B.C.) !

DEER

Of Cervus proper three species at least are found in the forested regions of the Chino-Thibetan borderland, distinguished by the natives as " black," " white," and " red " respectively. These Deer are sadly persecuted for their horns when in velvet. Fortunately, it is the males only that are so keenly sought after, otherwise they must have become extinct ere this. The full extent of this dreadful trade it is impossible to determine, but the following figures will give some glimmering of its enormity. In his *Report on a Journey to the Eastern Frontier of Thibet* (presented to both Houses of Parliament, August 1905), speaking of the trade of Tachienlu (p. 80), Sir Alexander Hosie says : " Deer horns in velvet, to the value of Tls. 30,000, are exported annually." Earlier (p. 38) he gives the value of these Deer horns as 2 to 20 rupees per catty (1 catty = 1⅓ lb. English ; Rs. 1 = Tls. 0·3 approx.).

In his " Journey to Sungpan " (*Journal China Branch, Royal Asiatic Society*, 1905, vol. xxxvi. p. 38), Mr. W. C. Haines-Watson gives 1500 catties of Deer horns in velvet, valued at Tls. 30,000, as the annual export from Kuan Hsien. Again, on page 41, he puts the annual export of Deer horns in velvet from Sungpan at Tls. 15,000. There are other places like Chungpa, Kiung Chou, and Sui Fu where a large annual export of Deer horns in velvet obtains, but no figures are obtainable. However, the above is sufficient to indicate how great a slaughter of stags there must be annually in these regions. At the lowest estimate at least a thousand stags are killed every year for their horns in velvet.

The Chinese consider these horns, called " Lu-jung," an extraordinarily valuable medicine, possessing wonderful tonic and aphrodisiac properties. This is evidenced by the almost fabulous prices they will pay for them. In the Imperial Maritime Customs returns for 1910, under Hankow, is the item : " 93 pairs of young Deer Horns ; value, Tls. 8090." (Tl. 1 =2s. 9d. approx.) Western pharmacologists may say there is no virtue or medicinal value in these horns, but John Chinaman believes otherwise, and is willing to pay the price, high and extortionate as it may be.

The leg sinews of these Deer are also of considerable medicinal value and are exported in quantity from the far west. Shed horns are valued for making medicinal glue, used in mixing pills, etc. There is a large trade in these, the annual exports from Tachienlu alone being estimated at 30,000 catties, valued at Tls. 8500.

In every medicine shop of note, in every village and town throughout the length and breadth of China, Deer horns are in evidence. In Szechuan and other wealthy regions they are abundantly so. If one inquires in the east and central parts of China where they come from, the answer received is invariably Chungking and Yunnan. At Chungking it is always Yunnan and Thibet. West of the Min River one begins to close up to the question pretty quickly. Coolies laden with Deer horns are frequently met with on all the roads leading from the far west of Szechuan. Tachienlu, Sungpan, and other towns mentioned on page 161 are all trade entrepôts, and are fed from the surrounding country.

The highlands of Thibet proper probably contribute to this trade, but the headquarters is the wild, almost unknown, region lying between the Upper Min River, the Chiench'ang Valley, and the frontier of eastern Thibet. This is a region of high mountain ranges where virgin forests of great size still remain. The upper limits of these forests are the home of these Deer. These haunts are very difficult of access, and very few foreigners have had opportunity of shooting these Deer, consequently information is most meagre.

The Black Deer, " Hei Lu-tsze," is the Szechuan Sambar (*Cervus unicolor dejeani*).[1] I believe I am correct in stating that this animal is known only from its horns, no skull or skin having yet been received by Western scientists. The horns of this Sambar can be seen in any large medicine shop in Chungking, Sui Fu, and other cities, and are said to come from Yunnan. But this is only partly correct. This Sambar occurs west of Tachienlu around Litang, and northward at least as far as the high mountains west of Lifan Ting. Unlike the type, this race frequents cold regions, and is in all probability a distinct species. Captain M'Neill saw, west of Tachienlu, a hind and one calf. He describes the hind as looking very black, so much so that in thick scrub for a moment he mistook it for a bear. This Sambar is undoubtedly rare in these regions, but it is remarkable that a race should be found so far north.

WAPITI (RED DEER)

This is the " Hung Lu-tsze " (Red Deer) of the Chinese, the " Ghwar " of the Thibetans around Tachienlu, and is perhaps the commonest of the three species found in these regions. It ranges from the Yunnan border northward to south-western Kansu and possibly beyond. The local chief of Chiala, residing at Tachienlu, keeps several in captivity at his summer palace (so-called) a few miles outside the town. These animals are about the size of a large donkey, and the stags carry fine horns, as witness the illustration (p. 164). The winter coat is light grey, and the summer coat rufous-brown, with a light rump-patch. There is no record of any foreign sportsman having shot this Wapiti, and its identity is uncertain. Possibly it is a local race of the Thian shan Wapiti (*C. songaricus*). Captain M'Neill, when shooting west of Tachienlu, saw a few hinds but no stag, and suggests it may be the Asiatic Wapiti (*C. asiaticus*). In 1904, in open forested country three

---

[1] Named after Père Dejean, a Roman Catholic priest formerly stationed at Tachienlu. He first arrived in that neighbourhood about 1870, and never left it, dying there in 1906. He trained natives to collect Butterflies, Moths, etc., and he sent to Paris very large collections. In many ways the late Père Dejean was a remarkable man, kindly, courteous, and noble in character. It is most fitting that this fine Sambar commemorate his name.

days west of Tachienlu, I got a fleeting view of two or three of these Deer, but being taken by surprise I noted nothing beyond their size and general colour. The antlers here figured I purchased in Sungpan in 1903. They weighed 11½ catties, and were fresh from an animal killed a few days previously only a few miles west of that town. Unfortunately, I lost them, with other trophies, through a fire in 1909.

WHITE DEER, " PEH LU-TSZE "

The first specimen of this Deer was shot by Captain M'Neill west of Tachienlu, in 1908, and it proved to be a new race. It is described and figured under the name of *C. cashmirianus macneilli*, by Mr. R. Lydekker, in *Proceedings of the Zoölogical Society of London*, published October 1909. M'Neill kindly informs me that in height and size this animal approximates to the American Wapiti. The colour is creamy whitish-grey, but some are darker than others. He shot two hinds, but was unable to get a stag. He saw some, however, but none with horns more than 18 to 20 inches in length.

Mr. Lydekker (loc. cit.) describes this Deer as " allied to *C. cashmirianus*, but much paler and more profusely speckled, the general colour being grey-fawn, becoming whitish-fawn on the throat and limbs, and the speckling as fully marked on the neck and flanks as on the back. No white on the chin ; but the whole of the under-parts dirty-white, instead of merely the abdomen. Dark dorsal line stopping short about the midde of the back." In the absence of male specimens Lydekker regards the systematic position of this animal as tentative. Geographically this new race is very far removed from the most eastern known haunt of the " Kashmir Stag," and time will probably prove it to be a distinct species.

When examining, near Mao Chou, some loads of shed antlers, M'Neill pointed out to me several which he thought were those of Thorold's Deer. I strongly suspect they belonged to the race which now bears his name. Under its native name of Peh Lu-tsze I have heard this animal spoken of as far north as Sungpan, and very likely it ranges throughout the whole Chino-Thibetan borderland. The type-specimen of this new

Deer can be seen in the Natural History Museum, South Kensington, S.W.

" CRYING MUNTJAC "

This animal (*Muntiacus lacrymans*), known locally as " Hung Chee-tsze," or simply " Chee-tsze," derives its specific name from the presence of a large gland below the eye. This Muntjac occurs in the immediate neighbourhood of Ichang, but is more common some distance removed from this town, ranging from river-level to 5000 feet altitude. In certain places in Patung and Hsingshan Hsiens it is abundant. Quite a number have been shot above the village of Nanto, situated on the left bank of the Yangtsze River at the head of the Ichang Gorge. This Muntjac frequents brush-clad rocky places and thin woods of Pine and Oak where a plentiful undergrowth obtains. Scrub-clad narrow ravines and gullies are a favourite " lying-up " place during the daytime, and it at all times prefers steep slopes to the more level country.

One method of hunting this animal is to have men hurl rocks down the steep scrub-clad slopes, with a " gun " placed top and bottom walking a few yards ahead of the men. But the general method employed is to use native dogs, and this is one of the few things that these dogs are really of any use, for, from a foreigner's point of view. These dogs give tongue loudly, and hound and bewilder the beast until finally he is caught by them or shot by the hunter. Stationed at the bottom of some gulley or point of vantage, the dogs being put in at the top, the sportsman gets his chance as the Muntjac attempts to make his escape. But the trouble is that the dogs are seldom well trained, and knowing no discipline go off at a tangent anywhere, scaring everything for miles around. A point to be remembered in shooting a Muntjac under these circumstances, is to run and pick it up immediately. If the dogs arrive first, woe betide the trophy ; they eat and mangle the carcass in double-quick time. At best these dogs are very exasperating, and as often as not cause needless annoyance and yield no returns. Occasionally one happens on a pack owned by a keen and able hunter, and then one's efforts are usually rewarded with some tangible result.

Muntjac are solitary animals, though several may be found within the same square mile. In their haunts they have well-defined tracts which they usually make for when roused. In running they carry the head and neck low and have a rather ungainly motion. They are not fast, though at a pinch they can get through cover at a good speed, wriggling through and attempting to slink out at the bottom in the least-expected place.

The Crying Muntjac stands 18 to 20 inches at shoulder, and the total length is 38 to 40 inches. The body is reddish-brown ; top of tail bright chestnut, under-side white ; belly and inside of hind-legs white, front and outside of fore-legs brownish, inside buff ; the head and neck is yellowish-brown, with blackish lines down face ; the whole pelt is smooth and glossy. The horns of the bucks are 5 to 6 inches long, erect, curving slightly outwards, with the apex sharply curved inwards ; in adult males a small basal tine is developed. The antlers are shed annually, though in old animals they are occasionally retained over two seasons. The upper canine teeth in the males are protruded downwards, forming two sharp tusks about 2 inches long. The does are of the same colour as the bucks, slightly smaller, with no tusks or antlers. The young are spotted with white. Muntjac-hunting is quite good sport, and the flesh is most excellent eating. A 12-bore, using large shot (A.A. or B.B.), is the best weapon to use after these and other small Deer, it being safer than a rifle.

Muntjac are found scattered through the hilly country all over the province of Szechuan, and are quite common in regions bordering the western limit of the Red Basin up to 7000 feet elevation. Being almost nocturnal in habit they are seldom seen in the daytime, but on wet, foggy days they are occasionally met with. How far south they range I have no knowledge, but I have seen them to the south-east of Tachienlu and around Fulin.

Mupin is the type-locality for *M. lacrymans*, but our specimens all came from western Hupeh, and the town of Ichang may be put down as roughly marking the eastern limits of this species.

The late F. W. Styan, in Wade's *With Boat and Gun in the Yangtsze Valley*, p. 126, reports the killing of *M. lacrymans* around Kiukiang and also as far east as Ningpo, but regards them as strays rather than residents. This Muntjac is in all probability Sclater's variety (*M. sclateri*), the type-locality for which is Hanchou, a prefecture near Ningpo. This Muntjac is the eastern representative of *M. lacrymans* and is distinguished by its light yellow face and black outer surface of the lower fore-legs. The two species are very closely allied and very possibly be only geographical forms of one species. Sclater's Muntjac has also been reported from Anhui province.

In the Chekiang province, in eastern China, a smaller and paler-coloured Muntjac (*M. reevesi*) occurs. A race of this animal has been described from Ping-hsiang, a coal district on the borders of Hunan and Kiangsi provinces, under the name of *M. reevesi pingshiangicus*, but more material is needed. Indeed, this latter remark is applicable to every animal reported from interior China. Nearly every foreigner, resident or travelling in interior China, carries a gun for pot-hunting purposes, if nothing else, and I am sure each and all would willingly assist science did they but know in what particular they could be useful. From personal experience I know the need for some accurate account of the different game-birds and animals of interior China to assist those who are quite willing to help scientists in these matters to the best of their ability and power. To do something towards supplying this want is the object I have at heart.

Another species, the "Hairy-fronted Muntjac" (*M. crinifrons*), occurs in eastern China, and shows a distinct approach to the Tufted Deer (*Elaphodus*). It is described as larger than the foregoing species, "plum-coloured, distinguished by a crest of long coarse hairs on the crown of the head, almost completely concealing the pedicles of the antlers." [1]

TUFTED DEER (BLACK MUNTJAC)

These animals are placed in a distinct genus (*Elaphodus*), but are closely allied to the Muntjac, from which they may be distinguished "by the pedicles supporting the very minute antlers of the males converging above, and not being con-

[1] R. Lydekker, *Game Animals of India*, p. 264.

tinued as ridges in front of the eyes. There are also marked differences in the form of the skull. These Deer derive their name from the tuft of long hairs crowning the head—a character possessed also by some of the Muntjacs. In the males the upper tusks are very large, and in both sexes the hair is remarkably coarse." [1] Tufted Deer, " Hei Chee-tsze " (Black Muntjac), of the Chinese, are rare animals. Of the three species described from China I have personal knowledge of one only, namely, that found in western Hupeh. This species was first shot by Mr. A. E. Leatham, south of Ichang, in February 1904, and described by R. Lydekker as a new species under the name of *E. ichangensis*.

This animal is sparingly scattered through western Hupeh between 3000 and 8000 feet altitude, frequenting similar country to that favoured by the ordinary Muntjac, but not descending to the river-level. In early April 1907, when hunting ordinary Muntjac, I was fortunate enough to shoot a Tufted Deer. It was driven by dogs along a mountain spur towards me, and I shot it with No. 4's as it tried to descend into a low ravine. The locality was near the hamlet of Putze in Patung Hsien, some three days' journey south-west of Ichang, and very near the spot where the type-specimen was shot by Leatham. Some six weeks later, in the mountains of Hsingshan Hsien, in company with Mr. Zappey, I saw two of these animals together, but they disappeared before we had a chance to shoot. During our subsequent travels in these regions we often heard of this animal, but we saw no others. The animal shot near Putze was a female and carried a young, about the size of a small cat, and black in colour. The adult measured 28¼ inches at shoulder ; total length, 67¼ inches. The body and top of tail was brownish-black, stern and under-tail white, fore-legs brownish-black. Being a female it had neither horns nor tusks.

In Mupin, western Szechuan, *E. cephalophus*, the type of the genus, occurs. This species differs from the foregoing in being rather less uniform in colour, and from measurements recorded is apparently a rather smaller animal. But the species are evidently very closely allied. Around Ningpo, in eastern

[1] British Museum, *Guide to Great Game Animals*, 1907, p. 56.

China, a third species (*E. michianus*) occurs. This is a much lighter-coloured animal than either of the above, being deep brown all over except white belly, white tip to ears, and pale line over the eye.

The ears in all three species are relatively large, broad, and rounded. The lateral hoofs are almost rudimentary in character, and the sabre-like tusks in the upper jaw of the males are not turned outwards as in the Muntjac. They have the same " hunched-up " appearance and gait when running, and do not travel fast. The flesh is very good eating.

MUSK DEER, " CHANG-TSZE "

This pretty little animal (*Moschus sifanicus*) is still fairly common throughout the length and breadth of the Chino-Thibetan borderland, but is everywhere sorely hunted for its musk. This highly valued product is secreted during the rutting season by a skin-gland situated on the genital organ of the male. The whole gland is removed and constitutes the " Musk-pod " (Chinese, Hsiang-p'i) of commerce. This Musk (Shê-hsiang) is by far the most important export passing through the border towns of western Szechuan. Hosie (*ibid.* p. 38) says that some 60,000 pods of musk, worth from 20 to 50 rupees each, according to size and quality, are annually sent through the district of Litang to Tachienlu, where they are trimmed and prepared for the Chinese and foreign market. An ordinary pod in a raw state weighs about an ounce, and with its fringe of skin and hair is about an inch across. Adulteration is commonly practised, but Chinese dealers are experts in detecting this. They have many ingenious tests : If the smell is unsatisfactory, or any doubts exist as to its genuineness, a few grains are extracted from the pod and placed in water. If these remain granular the musk is genuine ; if they melt it is false. Another test is to place a few grains on a live piece of charcoal. If they melt and bubble on the red surface the musk is pure ; if they at once harden and become cinder it is adulterated. The product exported through Tachienlu is esteemed more valuable than that from Sungpan and other border towns.

Hosie (*ibid.* p. 81) puts the annual exports of musk from Tachienlu at over 24,500 ounces, valued at Tls. 300,000. Watson (*ibid.* p. 38) gives the export of musk through Kuan Hsien as 16,000 ounces, valued at Tls. 216,000 ; from Sungpan (p. 41) to the value of Tls. 60,000. Through the Imperial Maritime Customs at Chungking between 40,000 and 50,000 ounces of musk pass annually. For the ten years ending 1901, some 483,174 ounces of musk were exported through the Imperial Maritime Customs at Chungking. But these figures represent only a part of the export, since they do not cover what passed through the Native Customs. In addition to this export large quantities are consumed in the wealthy cities west of Chungking. In the last Decennial Report (pub. 1904) the Commissioner of Customs, Chungking, writes : " The destruction of these animals must be enormous and must lead to their extinction if the present slaughter continues." The figures given above amply justify the commissioner's views.

This much-persecuted little animal frequents the upper wooded country between 8000 feet altitude and the tree-limit (11,500 to 14,000 feet, according to climate), where forests composed of Spruce, Silver Fir, and Larch, with a thin undergrowth and plenty of rocks, obtain. It occurs solitary or in pairs, though in a small area several may be found. It is a very agile little beast, and a favourite retiring-place during the daytime is the upper part of some half-fallen, sloping tree-trunk. Such trees it ascends with ease, and hunters closely examine every one of these trees for the marks made by the sharp hoofs of this animal. It lies close to the trunk and is not readily detected. Among rocks in the forests is another favourite haunt. A 12-bore with S.S.G. or A.A. shot is the best weapon for hunting these animals. The natives trap, snare, and more rarely shoot them. A male shot west of Tachienlu by Mr. Zappey measured : total length, 34 inches ; height at shoulder, 21¾ inches ; tail, 1⅝ inches. Legs, grey ; body, dark brown (back, reddish-brown), speckled with greyish and tawny yellow ; head, grey ; front of neck, light grey ; belly, yellowish-brown ; ears, dark grey, except outside edge, which is light brownish-yellow ; upper canine teeth sabre-like, 1½ inches long.

Neither sex has horns, and the long tusks and musk-gland distinguish the male from the female.   The hair is hollow, very coarse and loose, and readily pulls away.   The flesh is excellent eating (equal to the best Muntjac), and the heads make pretty trophies.   The Chiala chieftain keeps some of these animals in an enclosure at Tachienlu.   They appeared, when Zappey and I saw them, to be very happy and contented, and we were informed that they bred under captivity.   Certainly they make most charming pets with their shapely face and head.

For a small animal, Musk Deer is of stout and rather heavy build ; the hind-limbs are longer than the front ones, raising the rump above the level of the fore-quarters, giving the animal a hunched-up appearance.

The type-locality of *M. sifanicus* is the province of Kansu, and quite likely the Musk Deer found west of Tachienlu represent a local race.   Perhaps it should be identified with the Himalayan *M. moschiferus.*

RIVER DEER, " CHEE-TSZE "

It is customary to write disparagingly of this interesting little animal (*Hydrelaphus inermis*), both as to the sport it affords and its value for the table.   This attitude may be attributed to " familiarity breeding contempt."   For the table there are kinds of venison which are certainly superior, but it is wholesome, palatable, and very much superior to the beef obtainable in most of the riverine ports of China.   Properly kept and properly cooked, there are many worse things than a cutlet of this much-abused River Deer.

Formerly this animal was extraordinarily abundant throughout the fluviatile regions of the Lower Yangtsze basin, and it is still very common in many places.   It is hunted mercilessly by the Chinese, and several thousands are sold annually in the markets from Shasi down river to Shanghai and elsewhere.   The low hills which commence some 30 miles east of Ichang mark the western boundary of this animal as they do of the Ring-neck Pheasant.   Its home is the great alluvial plain of the Yangtsze, which extends from the point mentioned above, eastwards 1000 miles to the sea.   Any cover is sufficient to hold River Deer, and though it is not averse to water and swamps it prefers the drier land afforded by any rising ground. In winter an ideal spot in which to find this animal is long grass on rising ground near to reed-clad marshes. When the cover is mostly cut (mid-winter) it will be found in open fields lying in the furrows and hollows.

Small shot is usually recommended as sufficient to kill this deer, and so it is at 15 to 20 yards. A charge of No. 8 shot will kill almost any thin-skinned animal a few yards from the muzzle of the gun if it happens to strike a vital spot. A famous big-game shot (the late Mr. H. C. Syers) once killed a Black Panther with a charge of No. 9's when returning at dusk from snipe-shooting. It was a snap-shot at something which crossed the path and entered the brush immediately in front of him. The next day, when he discovered what animal he had shot, he realized the foolishness of his action and the terrible danger it might have involved him in. But this by the way. No danger is to be apprehended from a River Deer, wounded or otherwise, though it is courageous in its own way. I have seen one beat off and wound a Pointer dog almost its own size. There is certainly no sport in killing deer at 15 to 25 yards. Beyond this distance no true sports-man would fire using small shot on the offchance of bringing the animal down. The sportsman is out to kill mercifully and not to maim game.

The only time I have really hunted River Deer was during the winter of 1907–8. Mr. Zappey wanted specimens, and we made a trip down river below Shasi in quest of them. In this flat country a rifle is out of the question, otherwise some excellent sport could be enjoyed. Using B.B. shot we had good sport, bagging every deer but one we fired at. We had men to beat the likely places and to drive the deer across. Most of the bag were killed at about 40 yards, but several fell at over 55 yards and one at 74 yards. Two or three of them shot square through the heart ran 50 to 100 yards before they dropped dead in their tracks.

We limited ourselves to 20, but could have killed many more had we been so minded ; our best day was 9. A couple of heads mounted and in my possession form a pretty trophy, and are a pleasant memento of days spent in the Chinese wilds. Though so abundant, this River Deer is quite rare in museums, and it was the knowledge of this fact that induced us to kill so many.

River Deer stand about 20 to 22 inches at shoulder ; total length, 40 inches ; tail, 3 inches ; heel, 11 inches. The body is tawny grey ; legs and belly, buff ; top of shoulders and rump somewhat chestnut in old males. The hair is coarse and bristle-like and easily pulls out. No horns are developed. In the males the upper canine teeth are protruded downwards, forming scimitar-shaped tusks 2 to 2½ inches long. These tusks are said to develop in old females, but I never met with this phenomenon. The tusks are brittle and easily broken, at least after the animal is dead. The legs are lightly but muscularly built, and the animal can cover the ground at good speed, running great distances and taking to water like a duck. They are prolific breeders, dropping 4 to 6 fawns annually in May. The average weight is 20 to 24 lbs. ; the flesh is dark coloured. Swinhoe, who described this animal, gave it the generic name of *Hydropotes*, signifying " Water-drinker."

This concludes the list of Deer found in the regions coming within the purview of this work as far as is at present known. In the eastern and northern parts of the Empire there are, of course, others. One of these is particularly worthy of mention, namely, Kopsch's Deer (*Cervus kopschi*), found in the province of Anhui, up country from Tatung on the Lower Yangtsze River. Very few foreigners have seen this deer wild, and only one or two have shot it. Captain Malcolm M'Neill made an abortive attempt to secure specimens of this animal, and writes me as follows : " *Cervus kopschi* are very hard to get and extremely shy, being much hunted by the Chinese for their horns when in velvet. They inhabit rough, stony, and brush-clad hills about 4000 feet high, and lie up in the scrub and long grass during the day. Size slightly larger than a Scottish Red Deer, and the mature animals very much darker in colour as a rule. Horns pretty much the same as the Scottish Red Deer—possibly a little longer."

WILD PIG, " YEH CH'U "

These animals are very common through western Szechuan and scarcely less so in western Hupeh, doing great damage to the crops of Irish potato and maize.   Repeatedly have peasants almost begged of me to go with them and hunt Pig, but I never felt that a 12-bore and S.S.G.'s (my largest shot) were good enough for a possible encounter with Mr. Pig.   When the crops are ripening, the peasants, on the approach of dusk and for several hours afterwards, beat gongs and make all the noise possible in order to scare these animals away.   On moonlight nights the din is maintained incessantly the whole night through, and every traveller in Western China must have heard the weird noises emanating from the crop-clad mountain-sides after dark. The natives hunt these animals most assiduously and many are killed annually.   The flesh is esteemed and the killing of a Wild Pig is an event for twofold rejoicing.

These animals are nocturnal in their habits, lying up during the daytime in brush and under ledges of rock.   They often build large mounds of dry, long grass and sleep under them during the daytime.   One day, whilst botanizing over an elevated sloping plateau in Patung Hsien, I chanced on one of these " houses " and was considerably startled by a loud, angry grunt, and just got a glimpse of the black rump of a Pig as it rushed out and plunged out of sight through some bushes. Signs of Wild Pig are everywhere abundant is the mountains, and in any day's march acres of ground can be seen which have been rooted over by these animals searching for succulent starchy rhizomes and roots.   Wa shan is a great place for Pig. Hereabouts in 1908 Zappey witnessed the killing of one by three Wild Dogs.   He reached the carcass some five minutes afterwards, but it had been disembowelled and rendered decidedly nasty to look upon.

I have repeatedly been told that the flesh of Wild Pig is good eating.   I have tried it several times, but consider it decidedly strong and inferior flavoured.   Maybe the young are all right.   The only young one I ever saw looked reddish-brown from a distance and was too far off to tell if the animal was striped or uniformly coloured.

I assume that the Pig found in Hupeh is *Sus leucomystix*, the species occurring all over eastern China and distinguished by a pale streak on either side of the face. This animal was formerly very abundant in the Lower Yangtsze delta and is found there still in decreasing numbers. Examples have been shot weighing over 400 lbs., but the average weight is between 240 and 300 lbs. In western Hupeh this species or local race, as it very possibly is, ranges up to 9000 feet altitude.

The species found in western Szechuan is *S. moupinensis*, which has short ears and is said to be closely allied to the Wild Pig of Europe and southern Asia (*S. scrofula*). This animal was first secured by l'Abbé David in 1869, from Mupin. It ranges up to 9000 feet altitude and even more, and is abundant from Lungan Fu in the north to Wa shan in the south and Tachienlu in the west. In towns, Mao Chou for example, the flesh is often on sale in the shops. The Chinese are a pork-loving people and esteem the flesh of Wild Pig above that of any other of their wild animals.

HARES

Hares are fairly common in the neighbourhood of cultivation through the whole region coming within our purview, but no Rabbits are found. Around Ichang Hares are fairly plentiful, though they are getting shot out. They keep close to cultivation, and I never met with one in the sparsely populated mountains of western Hupeh above 5000 feet altitude. Around Tachienlu, Sungpan, and other places throughout the Chino-Thibetan borderland a species occurs in situations ranging from 8000 to 13,000 feet elevation. For our purpose, the terms " upland " and " lowland " may be conveniently used to distinguish these Hares.

The upland or " Szechuan " Hare (*Lepus sechuenensis*), as it is called, has the body brown (winter light grey) ; belly, white ; ears, large, brown and grey ; a white ring around the eyes. Weight about 6 lbs. A specimen shot by Mr. Zappey measured : total length, 20 inches ; tail, 2¾ inches ; heel, 4¾ inches. This Hare looks much bigger than it really is, possibly the long ears give this appearance. The measurements given above are those of a Hare shot west of Tachienlu; possibly that found around Sungpan is a different species. They look the same in colour, but my memory of the Sungpan animal pictures a Hare approximating to the Blue Hare of Europe (*L. timidus*) in size. However, I may have been mizzled by the long ears.

The city wall of Sungpan Ting (alt. 9200 feet) encloses a mountain-side, the summit of which is 1000 feet above the level of the town proper. The mountain-side is largely given over to terraced fields of wheat, barley, and peas. In these fields I have on several different occasions put up these Hares, and the animal is common throughout the moorlands bordering the wheat-field area of north-western Szechuan. It is very good eating and much superior in flavour to the lowland species.

The lowland Hares are sadly confused, and it is not easy to quote names with any degree of certainty. All those we collected around Ichang, both north and south of the river, have been determined as a variety of Swinhoe's Hare (*L. swinhoei filchneri*). The colour of the body is tawny above; belly, white; throat, buff; upper part of tail, black; lower part, white. A large male measured: total length, 20 inches; tail, 3¼ inches; heel, 4½ inches. The ears are short and the ends are black, tipped with white; average weight, 4½ to 5 lbs. The measurements show an animal equal in size with the Szechuan Hare, but it looks very much smaller when running. In the reed-bed region, where River Deer and Ring-neck Pheasant occur, the small Chinese Hare (*L. sinensis*) is common. This animal is about the size of a common English Wild Rabbit, weighing 3½ to 4 lbs. The general colour is reddish-brown with a rufous patch at the base of neck; ears and upper part of the tail same colour as back. This Hare is said to be restricted to the south bank of the river, but in the region mentioned above it is equally common on the north bank.

It is possible that other species of Hare occur in these regions and more especially in central Szechuan (Red Basin). Sportsmen should closely examine any they may happen to kill. The colour and length of tail and ears are good distinguishing characters.

The foregoing are all the grazing game animals yet recorded from central and Western China as far as my knowledge goes. In shops in the town of Wênch'uan Hsien, two days' journey up the Min Valley from Kuan Hsien, and in Tachienlu, I have seen a few horns of a Roe Deer (*Capreolus*), but could obtain no satisfactory evidence as to their origin. However, it is highly probable that some day a race of Roe Deer will be discovered in this little-known Chino-Thibetan borderland. The nature of the country is unsuitable for Yak and other wild-game of the Thibetan plateaux proper.

CHAPTER XIV

SPORT IN WESTERN CHINA

Carnivorous and other Animals, including Monkeys

QUITE a variety of Carnivora occurs in central and Western China, but none is really common, although, in certain places, Leopard and Black Bear have some claims to be considered so. In western Hupeh a few Tiger (Lao Hu) are to be found, and odd skins are brought into the towns for sale at frequent intervals. Nearly every year tales of man- and cattle-eating tigers reach Ichang, and several times foreigners have made futile expeditions after "Mr. Stripes." The rocky, precipitous regions of Changyang and Patung are favourite haunts of this beast. In 1907, when travelling through these districts, I saw some fragmentary remains of clothing belonging to an old woman who had been attacked and killed by one of these animals. A tigress with two cubs had been located in a cave a few miles away, and my companion and self were invited to take part in their death-hunt. To capture the lordly tiger the Chinese collect together to the number of a hundred or more and make a tremendous noise by shouting and beating gongs. When satisfied that the beast is ensconced within a cave they build a large bonfire at the entrance in order to smoke the animal out. All the hunters are armed with guns, spears, knives, clubs, etc., and when the stupefied tiger attempts to escape they make a concerted and bold attack upon him. As often as not he gets away and frequently some of the people get badly mauled. Tigers are also taken in heavily constructed log-traps, partitioned, baited with a live goat, and fitted with a trigger-released door. Another method is by poisoning the "kill."

The Tiger found in Hupeh is a rather small animal, but is

generally broadly and evenly striped, and the fur, though short, is a rich and glossy chestnut-red. The skin of a young male in my possession, which was killed in Changyang Hsien, in the early summer of 1907, measures only 82 inches, total length; height at shoulder about 22 inches; yet a more perfectly marked specimen could scarcely be found.

In western Szechuan this animal is very rare, but is occasiona. y found in the jungle-clad wilderness around Wa shan, In the Chiench'ang Valley and southward through the Yunnan province it is more common and attains to a larger size. From its geographical range this Tiger would appear to constitute a local race which does not ascend to any great altitude, but is thinly scattered through the warmer parts of central and Western China.

Tiger-bones (Hu-ku) are a highly prized Chinese medicine, and are supposed to transmit vitality, strength, and valour to those who partake of them. In the Imperial Maritime Customs Trade Returns of Hankow for 1910 is the following item : " Tiger-bones, 77 piculs ; value, Tls. 6522."

LEOPARD

Two distinct races of Leopard (Lao Pa-tsze) are found in western Hupeh, namely, a lowland variety (*Felis pardus variegata*), distinguished by its darker, more red colour and less bushy tail, which extends inland from the coast to the neighbourhood of Ichang, where it is rare ; and an upland variety, (*Felis pardus fontanieri*) which differs in its smaller size, paler colouring, and more bushy tail. This latter animal ranges westward from Ichang to the Chino-Thibetan borderland, in places being fairly common. The two varieties are found in brush-clad, rocky country, the upland kind ranging to 11,000 feet altitude or more. In western Szechuan, Leopard is scarce north of Mao Chou, but from Mount Omei southward into Yunnan it is prevalent.

This animal is usually taken by the natives in log-traps, as described above for the Tiger ; but occasionally it is noosed in bamboo snares in the same way as Goral. When after the latter animal, near the head of the Ichang Gorge, Mr. Zappey came upon fresh tracks of a Leopard, but lost them again.   In the afternoon of the same day he met two hunters who had captured this animal in a bamboo noose and purchased from them the skin and skull.

The Sifan and other tribesfolk are very fond of leopard skins, making them into girdles and robes.   On one occasion, when descending the valley of the Upper Min River, I met three men laden with over a hundred of these skins.   The men had come from Sui Fu, and were bound to Sungpan.   The skins they were carrying came from Yunnan and Kweichou provinces, where the animal is comparatively abundant.

THE SNOW LEOPARD OR OUNCE

The beautiful skin of this animal (*Felis uncia*), known as Hsueh Pao-tsze, can frequently be purchased in Chengtu and Chungking, where it is said to come from Thibet.   At Tachienlu and Monkong Ting this skin is more frequently on sale, being brought there from Derge.   This prosperous and famous Thibetan state is surrounded on three sides by lofty snow-clad ranges, and these mountains are the haunt of Snow Leopard, which prey on Goa, Chiru, Bharal, and other animals fairly abundant in those regions.

A skin of the Hsueh Pao-tsze in my possession which I purchased at Tachienlu for Tls. 8, measures 94 inches, tip to tip, the tail itself being 44 inches long and extremely bushy. I have seen better-marked skins than this, but never one quite so large.   The fur is very soft, long, and thick, of a white ground colour, covered with irregularly shaped black spots, each with a light centre ; on the head the spots are all black. The stomach is pure white and the rings on the part lower of the tail are broad and well defined.   Unfortunately, the head was badly skinned and the ears cut away.   The Thibetans hunt and trap this animal for its pelt.

The Clouded Leopard (*Felis nebulosa*) is found in Yunnan and Kweichou, and skins are commonly on sale in Chungking and Sui Fu. In size this animal is nearly as large as the Common Chinese Leopard, with a longer tail.   The ground colour is pale fulvous grey, heavily covered with large, irregular-shaped, nearly black blotches. The skins are remarkably handsome and rich in appearance.

Lynx skins, locally known as " She-li p'i," are brought in from the Thibetan regions to the north and west, to Sungpan, where they find a ready market among the wealthy Chinese. The pelt is rather dark grey, very thick and soft, and when tanned weighs only a few ounces. They sell in Sungpan for 5 to 7 taels each, according to quality and the supply forthcoming. Possibly this Lynx is a local race of the ordinary Thibetan kind (*Felis lynx isabellina*).

A number of different kinds of Cats occur in Western China, and their skins are commonly on sale in the shops at Chungking, Sui Fu, and Chengtu. The identification of these animals is by no means easy, but the following have been recognized : Chinese Marbled-cat (*Felis scripta*) ; Chinese Jungle-cat (*F. pallida*) ; Fontanier's Cat or Asiatic Ocelot (*F. tristis*) ; Leopard-cat (*F. bengalensis*), and a local race of the Golden or Bay-cat (*F. temmincki mitchelli*). In the mountains of western Hupeh *F. ingrami* occurs. This latter is a rather small tabby-coloured cat ; the head and body measures 19¼ inches ; the tail, 8 inches. It is a particularly vicious animal.

Civet-cats are common all over the warmer parts of central and Western China. Several species occur, but exactly how many is not at present known. The largest and most handsome closely resembles the Indian Civet (*Viverra zibetha*) and may be this species or a local race. It has the same general colouring and alternate white and black rings on the tail, these being usually about nine in number. The other species are smaller and less attractively marked. A dark grey Palm Civet or Toddy-cat (*Paradoxurus* sp.) is also fairly common, and is sometimes kept as a pet.

Residents in Western China interested in natural history would do well to collect skins and skulls of all the smaller Cats, Civets, etc., for our knowledge of the species found in this region is most inadequate. Such a collection would be a boon to systematic zoölogists, and new species and races would undoubtedly be found.

THE PANDA

This richly coloured animal is rare in Szechuan, but more common in Yunnan.   In the former province it occurs in the south-west corner beyond the Chiench'ang Valley, frequenting the forested and brush-clad country between 5000 and 10,000 feet altitude.   In Chungking, Sui Fu, Chengtu, and other cities the skin is often on sale.

In the shape of its head, short, broad face, and short ears this animal is very catlike ; the claws too are partially retractile. The limbs are short and stout ; the soles of the feet furry ; the tail is 16 to 18 inches long ; stout, cylindrical, and ringed at intervals like a civet-cat.   The fur is long, soft, rich, dark, ferruginous on back, shoulders, and flanks ; under-parts, black ; claws, white ; soles of feet, greyish ; forehead, chestnut with rufous stripe running down from the eye to near the snout ; face, lips, edges, and inner surface of ears, white ; outer surface of ears, dark red.

The Chinese Panda ranges from 38 to 44 inches, tip to tip, and weighs 9 to 10 lbs.   It is darker and rather larger than the typical Himalayan species, and has been recognized as a distinct race under the name of *Ailurus fulgens styani*.   Its colloquial name is " Chu-chieh-liang," which refers to the nine rings on the tail.

THE PARTI-COLOURED BEAR OR GIANT PANDA

This unique animal (*Ailuropus melanoleucus*) is perhaps the most interesting beast found in Western China.   Originally discovered by l'Abbé David in Mupin (1869), it was again met with by M. M. Berezovski in the Kansu-Szechuan frontier during 1892–94, but so far there is no record of a foreigner having killed a specimen ; those obtained by the above collectors were taken by natives.   Several skins, more or less imperfect, have reached Europe within recent years, but no foreigner has so far seen a living example.   The natives of the Chino-Thibetan borderland know this animal well and call it the " Peh Hsiung " (White Bear).   In Chinese literature it is referred to as the " Pi."   Skins are, on rare occasions, on sale in Chengtu, where they command high prices.   In that city I have seen in the possession of Europeans several fine examples in use as floor-rugs, but I was never able to secure a specimen myself.

The ears, shoulders, and legs of this animal are black, and black rings surround the eyes; the rest of the body is rich creamy white. It has a distinct if short tail, and the soles of the feet are hairy. The fur on the pelt is long, glossy, rather soft, and very handsome in appearance. " Parti-coloured " well describes this beast, though from the preponderance of white the native name " White Bear " is very applicable, especially in contradistinction to the Black and Brown Bears of the same region.

The Parti-coloured Bear ranges from the vicinity of Wa shan westwards to the forests beyond Tachienlu, northwards to Sungpan, and thence eastwards through the high mountains to the vicinity of Lungan Fu. It is essentially a denizen of the Bamboo jungles between 6000 and 11,000 feet, feeding on the young shoots of these plants. The natives declare that it eats nothing else, but this assertion is probably too sweeping. Throughout the large area encompassed within the above boundaries, Bamboo jungles are a characteristic feature, forming well-marked zones. In the sparsely timbered belts and in open Silver Fir forests, Bamboo forms absolutely impenetrable thickets. The culms are slender and grow some 10 to 12 feet tall. These plants are impatient of shade from above and grow so thickly together as to starve out all undergrowth and rival shrubs. The young shoots which continue to spring up from June to end of September, according to altitude and species, are white within and excellent eating. The Giant Panda shows good taste in confining his diet mainly to this excellent vegetable !

This animal is not common, and the savage nature of the country it frequents renders the possibility of capture remote. It is occasionally shot by native hunters when after Budorcas and Serow, but is not regularly hunted. It is also sometimes captured in dead-fall traps.

According to the natives, the Peh Hsiung hibernates for the six or seven months in hollow trees, dry, rocky hollows, and caves. Both Mr. Zappey and myself saw evident signs of

this animal around Wa-wu shan and south-west of Tachienlu
and have every reason to believe that the accounts given by
natives are substantially correct.   It is a solitary animal, and
makes beaten tracks through the forest, frequenting the same
haunts for long periods, as is evident from the large heaps of
its dung which are often met with in the Bamboo jungle.   An
adult specimen is said to measure 4 to 5 feet and to weigh
about 200 lbs.   The furry soles probably form a protection
against the splintery stumps of the dead Bamboo culms.

In general appearance this animal is distinctly bearlike,
but the skull is much broader than in the Bears proper, and in
the teeth and general skeleton it approximates more closely
to true Panda.   It is the sportsman's prize above all others
worth working hard for in Western China.

BEARS

Of Bears proper one species only is common in western
China.   This is a Black Bear which the Chinese term " Gho
Hsiung " (Dog Bear).   This animal gets east as far as north-
western Hupeh, where, however, it is rare.   In the forested
regions of the Chino-Thibetan borderland it is fairly abundant,
ranging as far north at least as Sungpan.   Between this town
and Lungan Fu, several days' journey to the eastward, it is
prevalent.   Around Wa shan in the south and westwards to
Litang it is also common.   Its altitudinal range depends largely
upon the agricultural possibilities of the country, for although
this Bear is essentially a lover of rocky forested regions it
keeps in the vicinity of cultivation.   It is fond of maize cobs
and is often surprised and captured whilst feeding on this crop.
The limit of maize-cultivation varies from 7500 to 9000 feet,
according to climatic conditions.   The Dog Bear ranges 1000
feet or so above these limits, and descends to 5000 feet altitude,
and even lower in sparsely peopled districts.   Starchy roots
and the various fruits of the forests constitute the principal
food.   It hibernates during the winter in dry, rocky caves and
in hollow tree-trunks.   Cubs are frequently to be seen in June—
pretty little black fuzzy fellows, having all the playfulness
characteristic of the family.   They become ugly with age,

however, and treacherous even towards the hand that feeds and pets them. Herr Weiss, German Consul at Chengtu, had a couple which he kept in the Consulate garden for nearly three years, finally presenting them to the Chinese authorities for transmission to the Zoo in Peking. I saw these animals on many occasions and it was amusing to watch them enjoying a bath and frolicking together. Their presence was known to every one in Chengtu, and the local Chinese were much afraid of them and gave their quarters a wide berth. But hunters do not fear them, and the beast is often surrounded by a group of men and killed at close quarters. An adult averages about 6 feet in length, and weighs about 250 lbs. when fat. The fur is jet-black, with a clear white V-shaped mark on the chest and a white spot on the lower jaw ; the muzzle is dark brown, claws dark horn colour ; the hair is long and soft. A specimen secured in western Hupeh by our expedition measured 73 inches from nose to tip of tail ; 40 inches across skin at widest part ; height at shoulder, 38 inches ; hind-paw, 9 inches long, $3\frac{1}{2}$ inches wide ; fore-paw, $7\frac{3}{8}$ inches long, $4\frac{3}{8}$ inches wide ; claws, $3\frac{1}{2}$ inches long.

Some confusion exists as to the specific identity of this Bear. Captain Malcolm M'Neill shot two specimens near Tachienlu in 1908. A skin and skull of one of these was submitted to Mr. R. Lydekker for determination. In the *Proceedings of the Zoölogical Society of London*, pp. 607–10, with figures (pub. October 1909), Mr. Lydekker discusses this animal and considers it a distinct race of the Himalayan Black Bear,[1] naming it in honour of its discoverer, *Ursus*

---

[1] The oldest name for the Himalayan Black Bear is *Ursus thibetanus*, F. Cuvier, and the reason given by Dr. Blandford (p. 198, *Fauna of British India* ; Mammalia) in rejecting this name in favour of *Ursus torquatus*, " because the animal is unknown from Thibet," is scarcely adequate. It is perfectly true that no specimen, not excepting M'Neill's, Berezovski's, and Mitchell's, has been reported from Thibet proper, and consequently the name " thibetanus " is a misnomer. But if this argument was generally accepted in scientific literature it would be necessary to change a very large number of specific names. For example, the names of *Crossoptilun tibetanum* and *Budorcas tibetanus* would have to be altered, since neither occurs in Thibet proper. Following the laws of priority, therefore, the Szechuan Black Bear becomes *Ursus thibetanus macneilli*. (See Allen in *Mem. Mus. Comp. Zoöl. Harvard*, 1912, xl. No. 4, p. 239.)

torquatus macneilli. He describes it as differing from the type in the " greater length and softness of the hair, much smaller size of the cheek-teeth, rather broader skull, and distinctly vaulted palate which is nearly flat in the typical Himalayan race." The Szechuan race is founded on a male, and the skull is in the British Museum, Natural History Branch. This museum, Lydekker states, " is in possession of a skull of a female collected by Berezovski," which he also refers to his new race.[1]

All this is clear and would be amply sufficient to settle the identity of this animal, but for the fact of the same author having, at an earlier date, referred a Black Bear from Szechuan to the Malay Bruang, as a distinct race under the name of *Ursus malayanus wardi,* in compliment to Rowland Ward, from whom he received the skull. This latter (communicated, I believe, by Mr. Mason Mitchell, erstwhile American Consul at Chungking) came " from the Thibetan area," and " belonged to a fully adult Bear of the *Ursus malayanus* type, as is evident from its width and relative shortness " (Lydekker, *Game Animals of India,* p. 388).

In 1905 Rowland Ward had received a skull and skin of a Bear, " reputed to come from either eastern Thibet or the north-western provinces of China." The skull "was clearly that of a Bruang," but the skin had " much larger black hair than the ordinary Malay Bear, with long fringes to the ears, and the usual whitish gorget on the throat." " The entire specimen was mounted and sold to the Bergen Museum as *Ursus torquatus* " (Lydekker, loc. cit.). And on p. 389 : " The skin of the Bergen specimen is stated to be more like that of a Himalayan Black Bear than a Malay Bruang."

From the above it would appear that there are two races of Black Bear in Szechuan belonging to distinct species. Without in the least doubting Mr. Lydekker's correct identity of the skulls in question, there are good grounds for being sceptical about the occurrence of these two kinds of bears in

---

[1] M. M. Berezovski made his greatest and last collection of animals in the region of the Kansu-Szechuan border, a little to the north-west of Lungan Fu, from 1892–94, and in all probability this Bear was obtained there, since it is common in that neighbourhood.

Szechuan or in the nondescript regions bordering this province and Thibet proper. I have seen in these regions several Dog Bears in the flesh, and a great number of skins, and all were uniform in appearance. Every person I have met in Western China, having personal knowledge of this bear, considered it as the Himalayan Black Bear. Captain M'Neill, who knows the Himalayan animal well, considered the two bears he shot near Tachienlu as identical with the Himalayan race. Mr. Lydekker's examination of M'Neill's specimen confirms this statement in so far as the specific affinity is concerned.

The skull of the specimen secured in western Hupeh and referred to above is in the Museum of Comparative Zoölogy at Harvard College, and agrees exactly with Lydekker's figures of the race *macneilli*. Mr. A. E. Pratt (*Snows of Tibet*, p. 233) says that he secured two bear cubs near Tachienlu : " One reached England alive and was sent to the Zoo." It would be interesting to learn what became of this animal.

The Gho Hsiung is well known locally to natives and foreigners alike as the Common Black Bear of Western China, and it seems scarcely possible that two kinds could be confused under one vernacular name. In the medicine and skin shops of Sui Fu, Chungking, and other large cities in the west, all sorts of curious specimens brought from long distances, and notably from Yunnan, are on sale. There is no reason why the Malay Bruang, or a local race of this animal, should not occur in the warmer parts of southern and south-western Yunnan, and the skulls (like those of other animals occasionally used by fortune-tellers) find their way into the larger cities of Szechuan, after the manner of other products of those regions. I venture the suggestion that the skulls referred by Mr. Lydekker to a race of the Malay Bruang may possibly have had such an origin, and that the skin of the Bergen specimen is that of the Szechuan race of the Himalayan Black Bear. If the specimens were purchased from Chinese sources such a confusion could very easily arise. Whilst I incline to the belief that the race *macneilli* represents the only Black Bear found in western Szechuan, it is obvious that more information in the shape of authentic skins and skulls is needed before the point can be finally settled.

Another Bear is commonly spoken of by the natives of the Chino-Thibetan borderland under the name of " Ma Hsiung " (Brown Bear). This animal is said to be larger and more savage than the Common Black Bear and to frequent the upper limits of the timber-belt bordering the grasslands of eastern Thibet. A gentleman in Chengtu had a reputed skin of this Ma Hsiung, which he used as a floor-rug. Unfortunately I was prevented from seeing this pelt. It was described to me as " dark chestnut-brown, with hair long and coarse."

The skins of the Black Bear are not much valued but are commonly used by muleteers as rough garments and cover-alls, and by peasants and others as bed-mattresses.

Bears' gall (Hsiung tan) constitutes a medicine in considerable repute among the Chinese.

MISCELLANEOUS ANIMALS

Wolves are not unknown in central China, but are very rare, and the same is true in the west also. On the confines of Thibet they are more numerous, and in the grasslands they are common. Quantities of the pelts are imported into Western China by way of Tachienlu, Monkong Ting, and Sungpan Ting. These skins, known as Lang p'i, sell for Tls. 1·75 to 2·50 each, according to supply and quality. The colour varies very considerably, but all that I have seen were, relatively, very pale grey, with the hair on the back tipped with black. The pelage is long, thick, and woolly below. In size these skins vary greatly ; of the several in my possession the largest measures 70 inches total length. This came from Tachienlu. Two species of Wolf (*Lupus filchneri* and *L. karanorensis*) have recently been described from north-eastern Thibet and may range southward to the vicinity of Tachienlu.

Around Ichang and other places in that vicinity an animal spoken of as the " Dog-headed Fox " (Gho-tou Hu) occasionally puts in an appearance, and is much dreaded by the people on account of its partiality for carrying off small children and goats. Some have supposed this animal to be a Jackal, but skins of two specimens that had been killed near Ichang and brought to us represented nothing other than two old and mangy wolves.

Wild Dogs (Tsai Gho) haunt parts of western Szechuan and quickly drive or kill out all game animals. One afternoon, in 1908, when after pheasants, I saw eight or ten of these beasts within a mile of the hamlet of Tatienchih, situated at the foot of Wa shan. There were three or four together and very brazen, allowing me to approach within 100 yards of them before they slowly moved off. Wild pigs are common in this neighbourhood, and on one occasion Mr. Zappey saw a pig attacked and partly devoured in a few minutes by three of these Wild Dogs. This animal is rather larger than a Fox and decidedly lanky in appearance. The general colour is rufous-grey, the front part of the lower legs being black. The hair is long, and the animal probably represents a local race. Unfortunately, our expedition failed to secure a specimen.

Foxes are more or less common all over central and Western China, and enormous numbers of skins are imported into China from Thibet. The ordinary kind met with in central China has rather short fur, reddish-chestnut in colour, and is of fair size. The Thibetan animal is more fulvous in colour and has longer fur. The skins known as Hu-li p'i are much esteemed by the Chinese for lining silk garments, and are worth Tls. 1·40 to 1·75, according to quality. In Hupeh this animal is colloquially known as " Mao Gho," and this particular species may be *Vulpes lineiventer*, which is common in eastern China.

Three or four species of Fox (*Vulpes filchneri*, *V. ladacensis*, *V. aurantioluteus*, *V. waddelli*) have been reported amongst the trade-skins which enter China from Thibet.

Raccoon Dogs (Gho Wan-tsze) are rather common at low altitudes in central and Western China. Their burrows are frequently met with, and they levy a severe toll on pheasants in particular. On one occasion in Hupeh I killed and marked down a hen pheasant, and on going to retrieve it a few minutes later, found that the bird had fallen opposite the mouth of one of these burrows and had been drawn inside by a Raccoon Dog. The animal found in Hupeh is about the size of a large tom-cat, dark brown in colour, with a short, bushy, ringed tail. I do not know what particular species this kind is referable to, possibly it is *Nyctereutes procyonides*. In western Szechuan a species, pale buff in colour, with the centre of the back and upper part of the tail black, occurs. This has been named *Nyctereutes stegmanni*.

Badgers are not uncommon, and at Ichang Otters are used for catching Fish.

It is not easy to draw the line between game and verminous animals, but several of the above obviously belong to the latter class.

Above the tree-limit in open grassland areas the Himalayan Marmot, or " Hsueh Chu-tsze " (Snow-pig) (*Marmota himalayanus*), is abundant, especially around Sungpan and west of Tachienlu between 10,000 and 15,000 feet altitude. This animal lives in colonies and has a habit of standing on its hind legs at the mouth of its burrow and uttering a shrill noise, half squeal, half whistle. It can be easily shot, but is with difficulty retrieved, for unless killed outright it disappears into the inner recesses of its warren. The male animal is ochre-grey in colour ; the female nearly cream-buff. Adults measure about 28 to 30 inches in length, including the tail, which latter measures about 5½ inches. The fur is coarse and thick, and the skins are an article of commerce in Sungpan, Monkong, and Tachienlu, from whence they are exported to various parts of Western China. These skins, known as Ma-sha p'i, are valued at about 45 tael cents each.

Many kinds of fur-bearing animals of small size occur in central and Western China. These include the Mouse-hare (*Ochotona*), Bamboo-rat (*Rhizomys*), Martin (*Martes*), Flying Squirrel (*Pteromys*), and many species of Squirrel proper. Of these latter I do not remember seeing one frequenting a tree in central China. All of them were rock-loving squirrels. The Bamboo-rat (*Rhizomys vestitus*) is an interesting animal, about 16 to 18 inches long, grey with a white streak down the chest, and has sharp vicious front teeth and powerful jaws. It is common in the jungles up to 8000 feet altitude from Sungpan southwards to Wa shan.

Travellers through the Ichang gorges are commonly regaled with stories of Monkeys roaming in troupes over the cliffs and occasionally throwing stones at passing boats. The stone-throwing proclivities of these animals were once solemnly

SPORT IN WESTERN CHINA   191

advanced by local Chinese officials as a reason why foreign
steamships should not be allowed to ply between Ichang and
Chungking !   I have been through these gorges many times, but
have never seen a Monkey.   However, it is probable that they
do occur in this region.   The Chinese are very fond of Monkeys
as pets, and have many curious legends concerning them.

A number of species are known to occur in China, especially
in the west, where is found the Snub-nose Monkey, or Chinese
Langur (*Rhinopithecus*), of which three species are now known.
The members of this curious family all have ridiculously
upturned noses, tails of great length, and remarkably long
and silky hair.   The oldest-described species is *R. roxellanæ*,
which is fairly common in the forests of the Chino-Thibetan
borderland, from the neighbourhood of the Kansu frontier
southwards, but more especially in the Chiarung states of Wassu
and Mupin and the region lying between Romi Chango and
Tachienlu, where it occurs in troupes in the coniferous forests
between 8000 and 12,000 feet altitude.   In the males the
cheeks, throat, sides of the head and neck are bright rusty red,
with light patches over the eyes ;   crown of head and nape,
rich red-brown ;   back, grey ;   inner sides of the limbs, under-
parts, upper sides of the hands and feet, rich orange or bright
golden-red ;   tail, grey, tipped creamy white ;   the bare parts
of the face and nose, blue.   The female is rather smaller and
lighter-coloured in general, with the forehead uniformly coloured
bright orange.   The male measures about 30 inches head and
body, and has a tail about 28½ inches long.   The skin of this
animal, especially that of the under-parts with the long golden
tresses of hair, is used as a lining for garments and worn by
the Chinese as a cure for, and preventive of, rheumatism.

In the upper reaches of the Mekong River a second species
(*R. bieti*) occurs.   The head and body of the male measures
about 33 inches and the tail 28½ inches ;   the throat, chest,
sides of the rump, and flanks are white, the rest of the body
is more or less slaty or bluish-grey ;   the bare parts of the face
bluish-green.   The female is smaller, more greyish on the
throat and stomach.   The very young animals are pale grey,
or almost white.   The male of this species has a remarkably
fine and thick tail.

Quite recently a third species has been described from north-eastern Kweichou under the name of *R. brelichi.* This is apparently the finest of its family, and is one of the largest Monkeys known apart from the anthropoid Apes. It is only known from a flat skin of a female animal, in which the head and body measures about 29 inches and the tail nearly 39 inches. In colour the back is slaty-grey, with a white patch between the shoulders; crown suffused with yellowish hairs, having black tips; ears, white; front of shoulders and inner sides of forearms, deep yellow; tail, dark with white tip, and longer than in any other known species. The type-specimen is said to have come from "Van Gin shan, about lat. 29° N., long. 108° E." If this is correct the region is several days' journey to the south-south-east of Chungking. Sportsmen-naturalists sojourning at this port would do well to interest themselves in this remarkable animal, for, since only a flat skin is known, it is obvious that specimens (skulls and skins) are much needed.

It is probable that this species is the famous Hai-tuh of Chinese literature of which the following account is given: " Its nose is turned upward, and the tail very long and forked at the end; whenever it rains, the animal thrusts the forks into its nose. It goes in herds and lives in friendship; when one dies the rest accompany it to burial. Its activity is so great that it runs its head against the trees; its fur is soft and grey and the face black."

Several species of short-tailed Baboons (*Macacus*) are found in Western China. L'Abbé David secured in Mupin specimens of *M. tibetanus,* and this is probably the same Monkey common on the middle slopes of Mount Omei and in the region of Wa shan. In the valley of the Upper Yangtsze, near Batang, *M. vestitus* was discovered by M. Bonvalot and Prince Henri d'Orléans. In the valley of the Yalung River, near Hokou (Na-chu-ka), between 9000 and 11,000 feet altitude, *M. lasiotis* is quite common. A female specimen, secured by my companion Mr. Zappey, measured 20½ inches, the tail being 6¼ inches long. The fur is soft and silky, of an olivaceous tint on the head, brightening to nearly clear pale orange-ochraceous on the hips; feet and fore-limbs greyish.

Monkeys are of course outside the pale of game animals, and many sportsmen strongly object to shooting them. They are, however, of peculiar interest to all, and since more specimens are badly needed, I have thought it advisable to allude to them here. It is not easy to draw the line between game animals and vermin, but those interested should bear in mind that the animals of central and Western China are far from being well known, and that all are rare in museums. Anything and everything of this nature, therefore, is of interest and value, even trade-skins. Sportsmen-naturalists sojourning or travelling in these regions may confer a boon to the science of systematic zoölogy by collecting skins and skulls of all mammals they meet with.

CHAPTER XV

WESTERN CHINA

Minerals and Mineral Wealth

MINING has been carried on in China for some thousands of years and, in spite of crude methods and the superstition of Fung Shui against which the industry has had to contend, an enormous quantity of mineral wealth has been won from the earth. During the Han Dynasty (206 B.C. to A.D. 25) coal was used as fuel in certain districts, and taxes were levied on iron and salt. Iron mines have been worked in China from very remote times, and this industry, like that of coal-digging, has always been fairly free from official interference. But mining for other minerals and metals has ever been more or less a Government monopoly, and especially is this true of gold, copper, tin, and salt. Intermittently during past centuries, the industry has been vigorously pursued in restricted localities, yet, paradoxically enough, mining in China is in its infancy, for the science of the subject has not been understood or developed, even though the products of the industry have been fully appreciated and generally applied. During the past quarter of a century there has been a real awakening on the part of the Chinese to the importance of developing the mining industry, and it is safe to say that the next fifty years will see the mineral and metalliferous resources of the country tapped and worked on all sides, and mining will assume an importance colossal in comparison with its position in the past.

The mineral wealth of China has attracted very considerable attention from Occidentals during the last decade or two, and concession-hunters have been busy acquiring mining rights and grants from the Central Government at Peking.

These favours have usually been strongly opposed by the provincial authorities, backed by the local gentry, and have involved all parties in endless trouble and difficulty. With one or two noteworthy exceptions these concessions have never been seriously taken up. Vexatious restrictions, official double-dealing, and the opposition of the local gentry have generally proved too much for the foreign concessionaire, and after a time the rights have been allowed to lapse. Western China being so remotely situated from the coast has naturally received less attention in these matters from foreigners, and I am only familiar with one such concession which has been developed by foreign capital. This is a coal mine, located a few miles to the north of Chungking, with which the late Archibald Little was concerned. This notable pioneer eventually disposed of his rights to a Syndicate, which almost immediately, and through no fault of its own, became involved in difficulties with the local gentry. Ultimately realizing the absolute impossibility of developing the purchase satisfactorily, the Syndicate sold it back to the Chinese, which was exactly what the gentry had determined should come to pass.

In Vol. I Chapter VI mention is made of the mineral wealth of the Red Basin, and it is unnecessary to enter more deeply into the subject in so far as this particular region is concerned. Although coal, iron, and salt abound throughout the Red Basin the province of Szechuan is not otherwise rich in mineral wealth. In the south-west corner of the province is found an extension or, perhaps more correctly, a terminative outcropping of the rich metalliferous strata which is so important a feature of Kweichou and Yunnan provinces to the south. These regions supply Szechuan with copper and other metals. Although quantity may be lacking, unquestionably a considerable variety of metals and minerals do occur in western Szechuan, and, whatever wealth in this direction there may be, it is practically as intact to-day as it was a thousand years ago. Chinese antipathy to mine-development is well known, but it is probable that official rapacity and peculation has had more to do with the non-development of this industry than has mere prejudice to disturbing the fabled dragon which slumbers beneath the earth's crust. In Vol. I Chapter XVIII it is told how official exactions had resulted in the closing down of certain copper-workings ; the same story could be told of silver and gold mining in various places throughout the Chino-Thibetan borderland. In several instances Chinese capital has been invested in mines and work commenced, but after a few months the whole thing has been abandoned for reasons usually connected with peculation official and otherwise.

The districts supposed to be rich in precious metals are zealously guarded by official eyes, and foreigners are less welcome guests in such places than elsewhere in China. My business had nothing to do with mines or mining, and it was politic to keep away from any gold or silver workings. I never exhibited any curiosity in this direction, although both in Yunnan and Szechuan I have passed within close range of several mines reported rich in one or other of these metals. But without being obtrusive it is possible to gather information of all sorts, yet this short chapter is written with great reluctance, and only because of its necessity in order to complete the account of these little-known regions.

In earlier chapters mention is made of the rude placer-mining carried on by the unemployed peasantry on the fore-shores of all the larger streams throughout Szechuan. The returns are most insignificant, and the industry would never be attempted in lands less overpopulated than China. In the district of An Hsien and in the prefecture of Lungan Fu, both situated in the north-west of the province, gold-bearing quartz occurs and is worked and crushed, but the industry is only on a small scale. In the district of Mienning Hsien, in the Chiench'ang Valley, there is a Government gold mine fitted out with foreign machinery. This Moha mine, as it is named, a few years ago received a development grant of 100,000 taels from the provincial treasury, and intermittent attempts at working it have been made without, however, any substantial returns.

Most of the gold used in, and exported from, Szechuan comes from the western limits of the Chino-Thibetan border-land and from Thibet proper. The district of Litang is one of the principal sources of supply, and there, as elsewhere, it is obtained by placer-mining. In the Chiarung state of Badi-

Bawang there is much gold, but it is jealously guarded from Chinese hands. This small State comprises a narrow strip of country on both sides of the upper reaches of the Tung River, thereabouts known as the Tachin Ho (Great Gold River). From time immemorial this and the surrounding regions have been famous for their precious metals.

The aggregate of gold won from these various places must be very great. Practically all has been obtained by placer or pocket mining, and the metalliferous lodes appear never to have been found *in situ*. Possibly these exist in regions more remote and nearer the sources of the Tachin, Yalung, and Dre Rivers. Certain it is that the nearer the head-waters are approached the richer in gold become the sands and shingle-beds of these great streams. The gold is melted and made into small bars weighing 10 or 12 Chinese ounces. A surplus is exported down river either in the form of bars or converted into gold-leaf. The trade in gold is in the hands of Shensi men, as is also the trade in silver. These Shensi men are also largely concerned in the cash shops, native banks, and banking.

Silver-ores occur throughout the Chino-Thibetan border-land from Sungpan in the north to the borders of Yunnan in the south, but though mines are, or have been, worked in many places the region is really poor in silver. The provincial mint at Chengtu is mainly supplied by imports from down river. A certain amount of silver also enters the province from Kweichou.

Copper-ores are much more abundant than silver, and occur from Pêng Hsien southward to Yunnan. In the south-west corner of the province, especially in the department of Huili Chou, copper mining and smelting are considerable industries. The mines are worked by private companies holding licences which compel them to sell the metal at a fixed price to persons duly authorized by the Government. Both the Provincial and Imperial Governments appear to have a controlling hand in this industry, and the companies frequently complain that they cannot work the mines with anything like commensurate profit. Enormous quantities of copper are used in Szechuan for a variety of purposes apart from that of minting cash pieces of various denominations.   Tribute-copper from Yunnan is sent down river by way of Chungking to Ichang in native craft, and at the latter port is placed on board steamers for its intended destination.

The department of Huili Chou also yields white copper (Peh-tung) in considerable quantities.   This alloy is produced directly from the ores, in which the composing metals appear to be always present in little varying proportions.   The coppersmiths receive it in round cakes about 7 inches in diameter.   They remelt and alloy it with copper, zinc, tin, and lead in varying proportions to suit different purposes. White copper is used for an infinity of purposes, of which the making of water-pipes is one of the most extensive.

Spelter or zinc (Peh-yuen) is found from the prefecture of Yachou southward to the boundaries of the province.   Lead-ores occur from Sungpan Ting southward to Yunnan, but are perhaps more abundant in the district of Chingchi Hsien than elsewhere.   Sulphur is found in the district of Kuangyuan Hsien in the north, the department of Mao Chou in the west, and the prefecture of Nanch'uan in the south.   This latter region supplies the greater part of the province.   The industry is carried on under Government surveillance, and the retail price is regulated by the provincial authorities.   Iron-ores are found all over the mountainous regions of the west, but except in the prefecture of Yachou are less worked than in the region of the Red Basin.

Coal is scarcely found west of the limits of the Red Basin, and antimony, which has recently figured as a large export from the Hunan province,[1] has so far only been recorded from one district in Szechuan, and that in the extreme south-east corner of the province.   A very inferior kind of jade occurs in the district of Wênch'uan Hsien, where it is mined and exported to Kuan Hsien and Chengtu Fu, at which places it

[1] This antimony is exported through Hankow.   The Imperial Maritime Customs Returns of that port for 1910 give the following figures relative to this trade :—

			Piculs		Taels
Crude antimony .	.	.	157,486	value	900,377
Ore .	.	.	21,909	,,	58,004
Refuse .	.	.	41,568	,,	13,871

is made into bracelets, rings, and other ornaments, and sold at a very low price.

Asbestos in small quantities is found in the prefecture of Kuichou, and also in the Chiench'ang Valley, but the supply is apparently insignificant. Tin has not yet been discovered in Szechuan, and I never heard of any precious stones being found there either. However, the country bounding the Liu-sha River from a little south of Chingchi Hsien to Fulin certainly looks as if it might contain the latter.

From the foregoing brief and scrappy résumé it will be evident to those interested that before any accurate and comprehensive account of the mineral and metalliferous wealth of this region can be written a mineralogical survey must be undertaken by competent persons. It may be that the wild mountain fastnesses of the west contain mineral wealth of great value, yet the probability is to the contrary. That the south-western corner of the province is rich in metalliferous lodes is as far as our present knowledge goes. All the more accessible and populous parts of Szechuan are well supplied with coal, iron, and lime of good quality. The Red Basin is extraordinarily rich in brine deposits, and salt, which is a Government monopoly, is the only mineral at present exported from Szechuan.

The most fascinating subject connected with the mineral deposits of Szechuan is that of the famous "Fire-wells" of Tzu-liu-ching, the gas from which is employed locally in salt evaporation. There is good reason to believe that this gas emanates from petroleum beds which have not as yet been reached. The late Baron Richthofen estimated the coal-bearing ground in Szechuan to exceed in size the total area of every other province of China, though, at the same time, he pointed out that the bulk was too deeply buried to be ever of practical value. Possibly the untapped mineral-oil deposits of Tzu-liu-ching will some day become available and exceed in value that of all other mineral deposits found in the vast province of Szechuan.

CHAPTER XVI

CONCLUSION

Some General Remarks on the Rebellion, the Causes which have produced it; the People and Future Possibilities

DURING the past two years events in China have followed so rapidly on one another that it is scarcely wise to attempt to discuss any phase of the situation other than that presented at the moment. Much history has been made in a very short period, and he would be a bold man who ventured to predict, other than in a general way, the possibilities or probabilities of the near future. Such conflicting accounts of the progress of events have been published that it is next to impossible for the man in the street to obtain anything like an accurate idea of the situation. According to a certain section of the foreign Press the Chinese in dethroning the Manchu Dynasty emancipated themselves from a veritable Kingdom of Belial, and in its stead have established a promising Utopia. The more reliable section of this Press, however, takes a rather different view. That there has been a tremendous upheaval is perfectly obvious, but what the permanent result will be is undeniably obscure. The progress of the revolution has been amazingly rapid, and the results to date have been achieved with a minimum loss of life. Much privation and suffering has been wrought among all classes, but on the whole the dynastic dethronement has been more peaceably brought about than changes of a similar character in the past.

It cannot be said that the revolution came as an unexpected event to those intimately acquainted with China. On the contrary, the surprise was that it had been so long deferred.

Many students of things Chinese fully expected that an up-heaval would follow immediately upon the death of their Majesties, the late Empress Dowager and Emperor Kwang Hsü. During the period of nearly three years of grace which followed their demise, the Central Government became more and more inept, puerile, and rotten; the provincial gentry and the student class more openly rebellious. The sanctioning of a foreign loan by the Central Government, which, among other purposes, provided for the construction of the Hankow-Szechuan Railway and the employment of foreign engineers, was merely the last straw. It is difficult to see how anything could have saved the late Dynasty short of a complete renovation of its system of government and the installation of a totally new class of officials capable of honestly conducting the necessary reforms. Such a change was an impossibility, but the Dynasty's life was prolonged a few months by a succession of fair promises which, if made in good faith, it had not the strength to carry into effect.

The late Manchu Dynasty has been equal to any of the long line of Dynasties that have ruled China. But it outlived itself and became an effete anachronism. In accordance with natural law it had to disappear and make way for another more in accord with the times. This Dynasty reached its zenith during the reign of the Emperor Kien-lung (A.D. 1736–96), and on his death it commenced to wane and wane rapidly. But for foreign intervention it would probably have disappeared during the great Tai-ping rebellion (A.D. 1850–64). With the merits or demerits of this foreign intervention we are not concerned. The fact remains that the time was only postponed. It gave the Dynasty a lease of life, but all to no purpose, as the recent disasters amply prove. There is, after all, nothing fundamentally new in the present unfortunate condition of affairs. During her long history China has been through it all before, and many times. But the forces which have induced the present rebellion are novel, since in her past rebellions she has not felt the power of Western civilization in the sense that she is feeling it now. The oldest of existing nations, China is attempting to attune herself anew in order to maintain her position as a nation, and to successfully compete with the modern and more aggressive civilization of the West. This latter, which came faintly knocking at her door a hundred odd years ago, has proved an irresistible power, and in spite of the, metaphorically speaking, heavily bolted and barred gates has made entrance, and is to-day well within the citadel. By riots, massacres, and several wars, China has tried her utmost to thrust back this forceful alien, but all to no purpose. The Boxer Rising in 1900 was the final effort. This failed utterly and miserably, and China gave up the contest.

Long previous to this last effort, the most upright and far-seeing of China's statesmen had realized the hopelessness of the struggle, and had begun to urge upon the nation the importance of learning from the Occident all that was useful and helpful in order to renovate their country's condition, and render China strong and able to withstand foreign aggression. The progress and enlightenment on Western lines since 1900 has been nothing short of marvellous. But, unfortunately, the ultra-progressives wanted to run before they could walk, and the ultra-conservatives were scarcely willing to move at all. For the time being the ultra-progressives are foremost, but this can only be a transient phase. Those adhering to the broad, happy medium of holding fast to all that is good of the old and building on it the best of the new must come into their own eventually. The earlier this happens the shorter will be the bitter period of travail. China's essential need to-day is what it has been for a century—a strong central government. Until this is vouchsafed there can be no lasting peace within her borders.

Parliaments have been spoken of as a panacea for all evils of government. If one looks around, very pertinent questions concerning the universal fitness of this system present themselves. In discussing the East it should ever be remembered that the Oriental mind is far from being in complete accord with the Occidental mind. Parliaments are of the West, and the Western model will have to be very considerably altered and modified before it can be successfully employed in the East. A republic, theoretically the highest and best form of government, has not altogether proved to be so in practice, judging by world-wide examples of to-day. When every republican citizen realizes fully the enormous responsibility resting upon him, and acts accordingly, the theory will become accomplished fact. The peoples of the most advanced Western nations are scarcely yet equal to this ; how then can such a form of government succeed in the Far East ? A strong, just man is appreciated the world over. In the East he ranks as a demi-god, and his authority quickly becomes undisputed. China's salvation will not yet be found in any advanced Western system of government, but in a wise, liberal despotism. Granted this, peace would speedily spread throughout the length and breadth of the empire, bringing with it prosperity and content to the industrious, patient, peace-loving millions.

But lest the noise of the revolution, the effeteness of the late Dynasty, and the question of the stability of the present system of government obscure the real China, it may be well to pause for a moment to consider the country itself and the people inhabiting it. The eighteen provinces which make up China proper have a total area of, roughly, 1,500,000 square miles, and form a nearly square tract of country some 23° long. by 20° lat. The size is about fifteen times that of the United Kingdom, or seven times the size of France, or nearly half as large as the continent of Europe. Compared with the United States of America, it is equal in area to all the region east of the Mississippi River with Texas, Arkansas, Missouri, and Iowa added. It is broken up into mountain, valley, and vast alluvial plains, and is drained by a magnificent network of navigable streams. The climate is continental in character and temperate over the greater part of the country. The south is within the tropics, but in the north the winters are almost arctic in severity. Three-fourths of the entire area is well adapted to agriculture, for which purpose it compares advantageously with any similar region in the world. The potential wealth represented in its mineral and metalliferous deposits is beyond computation. Such is the country of China proper without reference to the wealth of Manchuria or the vast area of the Outer Dominions.

The Chinese are a homogeneous race, estimated at not less than 400,000,000 of people, and are without caste pre-judices. They have unquestionably great brain-power, and possess many solid virtues as well as peculiar national defects. They are also an extraordinarily virile and fertile people. So virile are they that as a nation they have absorbed their conquerors as readily as they have done the nations which they have conquered. It is astounding the influence they wield in this direction. As an example, take the late Manchu Dynasty. So completely have the Chinese absorbed the Manchus that to-day they are more "Chinese" than the Chinese themselves. Yet no other nation can absorb the Chinese, and though they are found the world over their nationality is everywhere unmistakable. This virility is likewise exemplified in many other ways. For example, they are apparently indifferent to climate, and are to be found as workers from the arctic regions to the tropics. The Chinese are everywhere the one coloured race which can work and will work. Wherever they are found they are industrious and capable. They wax wealthy where whites would starve, and no nation in matters of labour can compete with the Chinese on equal terms. They can copy anything and everything, and under foreign supervision have already turned out such complex machines as railway engines and steamships.

Malthusian principles have never been listened to, much less practised in China. Large families are everywhere gloried in, and children abound throughout the land. Since a son is necessary to carry out the rites of ancestor-worship, boys are more generally in favour than girls, yet it is a mistake to think that the latter are despised or ignored. Even if preference be shown to sons, the daughters have a share of the family's affection. Infanticide, save in times of famine and dire distress, is not practised, all the stories written about it notwithstanding. Anent ancestor-worship we have nothing to say, except to remark that the respect and esteem for parents and old age, so characteristic of the Far East, is a wholesome example to the Occident.

A keynote to the Chinese character is pride. They are an intensely proud people, and it must be confessed that their pride is justified. Look on their history, their conquests, their inventions, their arts, and crafts. In the history of the world few nations have equal claims to honour and greatness with the Chinese. They have also grave national faults, and this pride and its concomitant conservatism is largely the cause of their present position. Considering themselves the " whole earth," they have persistently and most superciliously ignored the " outer barbarian," as they termed the rest of the world, until disaster upon disaster has shaken the very foundations of their empire. That the scales are falling from their eyes is evident, but as a nation they have yet to grasp the fact that Western knowledge, even though it be of comparative " mushroom growth," cannot be acquired by the study of a few months, and neither can Western institutions be transplanted bodily and in adult form into China. I have met in China hundreds of students intent on acquiring Western knowledge, but scarcely one who in any sense realized the immensity of the task before him. These students persistently refuse instruction in the elementary branches of this knowledge, and are ever clamouring for their instructors to pass at once to the advanced and honours stages. The national defect, pride, is at the bottom of this attitude, and they have yet to appreciate that they must crawl first, then walk before they can safely run.

The merchant class in China is as honourable as that of any country in the world, and foreign relationship with this body has always been satisfactory and mutually advantageous. The artisan, peasants; and farmers are unsophisticated, and every traveller has a good word for them. They are peace-loving, law-abiding, and very easily governed. It is somewhat otherwise with the gentry, students, and officials, who, as a class, have in the main always been more or less opposed to foreign intercourse, and have been the direct cause of many difficulties. For generations China went in for competitive examinations to supply all official posts, and had, as a result, a body of truly incapable officials. The principles associated with Tammany in the West were rampant in this class. Offices were sought and held for personal profit without any regard for public good. But individuals were less to blame than the system which time and pernicious methods had produced. The salaries attached to the various posts were ridiculously inadequate, and the holders had to peculate in order to exist, if for nothing else. Had the Government provided for its officials a " living wage " it could then have expected and demanded an honest, civil, and military service. Instead of this, offices were commonly sold by the Government for large sums, and the purchasers allowed to farm them to their own advantage.

It has been a rule in China that no important office could be held by an official in his native province. Theoretically, like much else in the Chinese system of government, this was an excellent rule, but in practice it had decided drawbacks. All officials, in consequence, were in the nature of aliens coming as they did from other provinces. At best they were strangers and, according to their strength of character, usually became subservient to, or at variance with, the local gentry. In wealthy provinces like Szechuan and Hunan, for example, these local gentry wield enormous power and are, in fact, the real rulers of the province. Local patriotism and self-interest are combined in this class, which commands a large following. The policy and actions of the late Government at Peking were very often antagonistic to the views of these gentry. Especially was this so in the matter of mining-concessions, open ports, and foreign loans. The Provincial Governments were frequently in a quandary in their efforts to harmonize the diametrically opposed views of both authorities. As the Central Government weakened, the provinces became more and more under the power of the gentry. The climax as the world now knows was reached in the early autumn of 1911, when the local gentry of Chengtu Fu induced open rebellion which, spreading with marvellous rapidity, very soon brought about the dethronement of the Dynasty.

The Provincial and National Assemblies which the late Government was virtually forced to call into existence were mainly composed of gentry. The student class, both of the old and new schools of learning, in the main is made up of the sons of this same body. These students are far from being seekers after knowledge for knowledge's sake. In Chengtu they were several times openly mutinous, setting the Viceroy's authority at naught, and compelling him to grant their desires. In many parts of the country the authorities were almost openly afraid of these headstrong students, and totally unable to check their follies or curb their rebellious ardour.

It is impossible to estimate how much the famous work called the *Chuen Hioh Pien*,[1] written by the late Chang Chih Tung, when Viceroy of Liang Hu (Hupeh and Hunan provinces), has influenced recent events in China. Since 1900 many of the things advocated in this book have been put into practice, especially the matter of schools for Western learning, army reform, and newspapers. But the moral teachings the Viceroy enunciated so earnestly have been set at naught, and republicanism, which he so emphatically denounced, has been brought into being. China for the Chinese was the patriotic vision of this grand old man of China, but perhaps the fates were kind in removing him from this sphere before he had time to see his vision so passionately taken up as a slogan and pressed so hastily forward.

It was fortunate for China that at least one practical statesman remained to take up the reins of government in the hour of need. Yuan Shih Kai is very human, but he has best right to be acclaimed the saviour of China. If his health and strength remain he may, in a few years, weld the country into a solid nation. If loyally supported by those who seek their country's good he can utilize all that is useful and worthy in the schemes of the more visionary ultra-progressive reformers, and render it of practical value. That his hands will be forced at times is certain, but granted time Yuan Shih Kai will succeed in bringing order out of chaos and place the Government of China on a sound basis. At present his position may be likened to that of a skilled driver who has had the reins of a runaway team thrust into his hands from those of an incompetent person. In time he will get his countrymen down to a common-sense trot, and then all danger will be past. If allowed by the passionate rush of events to exercise the rights of his office Yuan Shih Kai will be able to surround himself with advisers Chinese and Foreign, whose interests will be none other than the welfare of China.

The pressing need of the moment is, of course, funds to carry

[1] Translated into English, under the title *Learn*, by the Rev. S. I. Woodbridge.

on the Government and to disband the soldiery. This difficulty involves the vexed question of foreign loans, which has
significance far beyond that current in Occidental newspapers.
It is the reef on which the young republic may wreck its
ship of State. To the narrow view-point of the local gentry
and their following these loans will doubtless continue to
appear unessential, and if their interests, real or supposed, are
affected by the security demanded, their antagonism will be
as bitter as formerly. Another difficult class, which if more
evident under the old régime has not yet had time to disappear
completely, consists of officials who desire to handle loans for
the benefits they personally can derive from them. The
competent body of officials who know and appreciate the
absolute necessity of maintaining the country's credit by
meeting all obligations, and also the importance of developing
the resources of the empire, will most certainly have a difficulty
in disposing of the opposition of one party and the mercenary
desires of the other.

That there are financiers willing to lend money on question-
able security and a gullible public willing to subscribe to such
loans is everyday history. Money is absolutely necessary
to carry on this new republic of China, but it is trite to say
that she must beware how and in what manner it is obtained.
The integrity of China is the one thing above all others which
the Government must maintain, and promiscuous borrowing,
even if it tides over present difficulties, may lead to even
greater danger in the near future. The one foreign-supervised
service which the late Dynasty grudgingly became reconciled
to, namely, the Imperial Maritime Customs, has proved the
strongest security possessed by the Central Government.
Further, the international character of its personnel has been
a tremendous factor in maintaining the integrity of the empire.
The present Government will surely be well advised to ponder
this thoughtfully. Until China has evolved a thoroughly competent civil service the example of her plucky and illustrious
neighbour, Japan, is worthy of deep consideration. However
galling it may be to the pride of the Chinese, it would appear
absolutely essential in the best interests of China herself and the
integrity of the empire that all foreign loans should be obtained

through highly accredited international agencies. And, further, that foreign supervision of these loans, their application and disbursement, should be allowed, consistent with the maintenance of the dignity and prestige of the Chinese Empire.

For many years past the Occident has been urging the Chinese to " wake up ! " Towards the end of the last century the clamours in this direction became most vociferous. The present upheaval is China waking up—nothing else. The outcome is fraught with colossal possibilities. China needs roads, railways, rolling-stock, machinery to develop her agriculture, mineral resources, and potential wealth generally. All these and very much more she stands in need of. Will the Occident merely furnish the samples and patterns for the Chinese to imitate, and ultimately supply ? Or—and who knows ? Granted a staple Government, the Chinese people can accomplish much. I do not believe in a " Yellow Peril " in the nature of a possible military conquest of the West. It would be necessary to fundamentally alter the Chinese character in order to make it militantly aggressive. But in their virility and industry they are unconquerable people, quite the equals of the West in these qualities. If they thoroughly " awaken," what is to prevent them becoming in commerce and industry the great competitors of the white race ? Time solves and adjusts all problems, and it will this, the real Yellow Peril, if such a thing be within the realm of possibility.

To the people of the Occident in general all forms of civilization other than their own appear effete and retrograde. This is, perhaps, very natural, but will the Western ideal always dominate and remain the criterion, and must all the other peoples of the earth conform to it or become nonentities in the world's future history ? The people of the Middle Kingdom will undoubtedly accept from the West and utilize all the material advantages and mechanical appliances that have resulted from the discovery of steam and electricity and may yet retain their own ideals of life. On the tenets of their older civilization these people can wisely build and maybe they will evolve a state of existence intrinsically higher, more restful, and better suited to their nature and needs than that contained in the Western ideal.

China is a continent rather than a country, and everything is so entirely different from and opposite to Western ideas and practice. Hundreds of books have been written on China and the Chinese, yet little more than the fringe of the subject has been really broached. There is, indeed, no finality, and in any one book it is impossible to do more than itemize an occasional fact or two. Nearly eleven years of my life have been spent wandering up and down the by-ways of interior China. I was there through the Boxer crisis and the Russo-Japanese War, and also through certain local riots and disturbances. My experiences in China, though varied, have on the whole been very pleasant. To speak as we find and courageously is the only just stand to take. With all their peculiarities, conservatism, and faults, the Chinese are a great people. Phœnix-like, China has arisen time and again from the ashes of decadent dynasties, and there is every reason to believe she will accomplish this again. Her peace-loving, industrious millions can never be utterly smothered or nationally effaced. Sooner or later they must come into their own, and side by side with the people of the Occident help forward the destiny of the world.

INDEX

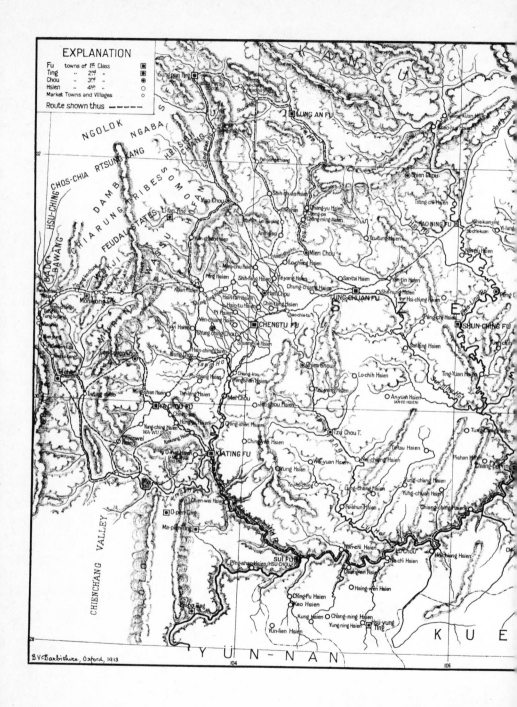

EXPLANATION

Fu   towns of 1st Class   ■
"   Ting   "   2nd   "   ▣
"   Chou   "   3rd   "   ◉
"   Hsien   "   4th   "   ○
Market Towns and Villages   ○
Route shown thus ─ ─ ─ ─ ─

B V. Darbishire, Oxford, 1913